Inger & Wendell

A New Star-Rating System & Other Exciting News from Frommer's!

In our continuing effort to publish the savviest, most up-to-date, and most appealing travel guides available, we've added some great new features.

Frommer's guides now include a new **star-rating system.** Every hotel, restaurant, and attraction is rated from 0 to 3 stars to help you set priorities and organize your time.

We've also added **seven brand-new features** that point you to the great deals, in-the-know advice, and unique experiences that separate travelers from tourists. Throughout the guide, look for:

Finds	Special finds—those places only insiders know about
Fun Fact	Fun facts—details that make travelers more informed and their trips more fun
Kids	Best bets for kids—advice for the whole family
Moments	Special moments—those experiences that memories are made of
Overrated	Places or experiences not worth your time or money
Tips	Insider tips—some great ways to save time and money
Value	Great values—where to get the best deals

We've also added a **"What's New"** section in every guide—a timely crash course in what's hot and what's not in every destination we cover.

W9-APH-009

Here's what the critics say about Frommer's:

"Amazingly easy to use. Very portable, very complete."

—*Booklist*

"Detailed, accurate, and easy-to-read information for all price ranges."
—*Glamour Magazine*

"Hotel information is close to encyclopedic."

—*Des Moines Sunday Register*

"Frommer's Guides have a way of giving you a real feel for a place."
—*Knight Ridder Newspapers*

Other Great Guides for Your Trip:

Frommer's Scandinavia
Frommer's Denmark
Frommer's Sweden
Frommer's Europe

Frommer's®

Norway

1st Edition

by Darwin Porter & Danforth Prince

WILEY

Wiley Publishing, Inc.

About the Author

Co-authors **Darwin Porter** and **Danforth Prince** have written numerous best-selling Frommer's guides, notably to England, France, the Caribbean, Italy, and Germany. Porter was a bureau chief for the *Miami Herald* when he was 21, and Prince was formerly with the Paris bureau of the *New York Times.* They are also the authors of Frommer's guides to Scandinavia, Sweden, and, Denmark.

Published by:

Wiley Publishing, Inc.

909 Third Ave.
New York, NY 10022

ISBN 0-7645-2467-4
ISSN 1541-650X

Editor: Lisa Torrance Duffy
Production Editor: Heather Wilcox
Cartographer: Dorit Kreisler, Roberta Stockwell
Photo Editor: Richard Fox
Production by Wiley Indianapolis Composition Services

For information on our other products and services or to obtain technical support, please contact our Customer Care Department within the U.S. at 800-762-2974, outside the U.S. at 317-572-3993 or fax 317-572-4002.

Wiley also publishes its books in a variety of electronic formats. Some content that appears in print may not be available in electronic formats.

Manufactured in the United States of America

5   4   3   2

Solvorn

Contents

Appendix: Norway in Depth   401

Index   412

List of Maps

An Invitation to the Reader

In researching this book, we discovered many wonderful places—hotels, restaurants, shops, and more. We're sure you'll find others. Please tell us about them, so we can share the information with your fellow travelers in upcoming editions. If you were disappointed with a recommendation, we'd love to know that, too. Please write to:

Frommer's Norway, 1st Edition
Wiley Publishing, Inc. • 909 Third Ave. • New York, NY 10022

An Additional Note

Please be advised that travel information is subject to change at any time—and this is especially true of prices. We therefore suggest that you write or call ahead for confirmation when making your travel plans. The authors, editors, and publisher cannot be held responsible for the experiences of readers while traveling. Your safety is important to us, however, so we encourage you to stay alert and be aware of your surroundings. Keep a close eye on cameras, purses, and wallets, all favorite targets of thieves and pickpockets.

New! Frommer's Star Ratings & Icons

Every hotel, restaurant, and attraction listing in this guide has been ranked for quality, value, service, amenities, and special features using a star-rating scale. In country, state, and regional guides, we also rate towns and regions to help you narrow down your choices and budget your time accordingly. Hotels and restaurants are rated on a scale of zero (recommended) to 3 stars (exceptional). Attractions, towns, and regions are rated according to the following scale: zero stars (recommended), one star (highly recommended), two stars (very highly recommended), and three stars (must-see).

In addition to the rating system, we also use seven icons to highlight insider information, useful tips, special bargains, hidden gems, memorable experiences, kid-friendly venues, places to avoid, and other useful information:

Finds   *Fun Fact*   *Kids*   *Moments*   *Overrated*   *Tips*   *Value*

The following abbreviations are used for credit cards:

AE American Express	DISC Discover	V Visa
DC Diners Club	MC MasterCard	

FROMMERS.COM

Now that you have the guidebook to a great trip, visit our website at **www.frommers.com** for travel information on nearly 2,500 destinations. With features updated regularly, we give you instant access to the most current trip-planning information available. At Frommers.com, you'll also find the best prices on airfares, accommodations, and car rentals—and you can even book travel online through our travel booking partners. At Frommers.com, you'll also find the following:

- Online updates to our most popular guidebooks
- Vacation sweepstakes and contest giveaways
- Newsletter highlighting the hottest travel trends
- Online travel message boards with featured travel discussions

The Best of Norway

The "Land of the Midnight Sun" offers a special experience. Norwegians view their scrub-covered islands, snow-crested peaks, and glacier-born fjords as symbols of a wilderness culture. The majestic scenery inspired the symphonies of Grieg, the plays of Ibsen, and the paintings of Munch. The landscape has also shaped the Norwegians' view of themselves as pastoral dwellers in one of the world's most splendid countrysides.

The name Norway (in Norwegian, *Norge* or *Noreg*) is derived from *Norvegr,* meaning "the way to the north." The Vikings used the term more than 1,000 years ago to describe the shipping route along the west coast of Norway. Norwegians have been seafarers since the dawn of history, so it seems natural for the country to have a nautical name.

To the ancients, Norway was a mythical land. A journey held unspeakable perils. Writers called the mythical land "Ultima Thule," and feared that strange, barbaric, even fabulous creatures inhabited it. In the 4th century B.C., the Greek writer Pytheas thought the laws of nature did not apply there, and said that everything—water and earth included—floated in midair. In what may have been an attempt to describe a snowstorm, Herodotus claimed that in Norway feathers covered everything and constantly blew into one's face.

Norway is a land of tradition, exemplified by its rustic stave churches and its folk dances. But Norway is also modern. This technologically advanced nation is rich in petroleum and hydroelectric energy. Norwegians also enjoy a well-developed national social insurance system that provides pensions, health insurance, unemployment insurance, and rehabilitation assistance. The system is financed by contributions from the insured, which makes Norway one of the most heavily taxed nations on earth.

One of the last great natural frontiers of the world, Norway invites exploration, with its steep and jagged fjords, salmon-filled rivers, glaciers, mountains, and meadows. In the winter, the shimmering aurora borealis (northern lights) are the lure, before giving way to the midnight sun of summer.

So you won't have to exhaust yourself making difficult decisions, we've compiled the best deals and once-in-a-lifetime experiences in this chapter. What follows is the best of the best.

1 The Best Travel Experiences

- **Enjoying Nature:** Norway is one of the last major countries of the world where you can experience nature on an exceptional level. The country extends 1,770km (1,100 miles) from south to north (approximately the distance from New York to Miami). Norway, which means "the way to the North," is riddled with 20,000km (12,400 miles) of fjords, narrows, and straits. It's a land of contrasts, with soaring mountains, panoramic fjords, ice-blue glaciers, deep-green forests, fertile valleys, and rich pastures. The glowing red midnight sun reflects off snow-covered mountains, and the northern lights have fired the imagination of artists and craftspeople for centuries.

- **Experiencing "Norway in a Nutshell":** One of Europe's great train rides, this 12-hour excursion is Norway's most exciting. The route encompasses two arms of the Sognefjord, and the section from Myrdal to Flåm—a drop of 600m (2,000 ft.)—takes you past seemingly endless waterfalls. Tours leave from the Bergen train station. If you have limited time but want to see the country's most dramatic scenery, take this spectacular train trip. See "Flåm: Stopover on Europe's Most Scenic Train Ride" in chapter 11.

- **Visiting the North Cape:** For many, a trip to one of the northernmost inhabited areas of the world will be the journey of a lifetime. Accessible by ship, car, or air, the North Cape holds a fascination for travelers that outweighs its bleakness. Ship tours started in 1879 and, except in wartime, have gone to the Cape ever since. Hammerfest, the world's northernmost town of significant size, is an important port of call for North Cape steamers. See chapter 14.

- **Exploring the Fjord Country:** Norway's fjords are stunningly serene and majestic, some of the world's most awe-inspiring sights. The fjords are reason enough for a trip to Norway. Bergen can be your gateway; two of the country's most famous fjords, the Hardangerfjord and the Sognefjord, can easily be explored from there. You can go on your own or take an organized tour, which will probably include the dramatic Folgefonn Glacier. Norway's longest fjord, the Sognefjord, can be crossed by express steamer to Gudvangen. See chapter 11.

- **Seeing the Midnight Sun at the Arctic Circle:** This is one of the major reasons visitors flock to Norway. The Arctic Circle marks the boundary of the midnight sun of the Arctic summer and the sunless winters of the north. The midnight sun can be seen from the middle of May until the end of July. The Arctic Circle cuts across Norway south of Bodø. Bus excursions from that city visit the circle. The adventurous few who arrive in the winter miss the midnight sun, but are treated to a spectacular display of the aurora borealis, the flaming spectacle of the Arctic winter sky. In ancient times, when the aurora could be seen farther south, people thought it was an omen of disaster. See chapter 14.

2 The Best Scenic Towns & Villages

- **Fredrikstad:** Founded in 1567 at the mouth of the River Glomma, Fredrikstad preserved its Old Town, which had become a fortress by 1667. Today Fredrikstad (97km/60 miles south of Oslo) offers a glimpse of what a Norwegian town looked like several hundred years ago. The old buildings in the historic district have been converted into studios for craftspeople and artisans, while maintaining their architectural integrity. After a visit here, you can drive along Oldtidsveien (the "highway of the ancients"), the most concentrated collection of archaeological monuments in Norway. See "Fredrikstad: Norway's Oldest Fortified Town" in chapter 6.

- **Tønsberg:** On the western bank of the Oslofjord, this is Norway's oldest town. It was founded in A.D. 872, a year before King Harald Fairhair united parts of Norway. This Viking town became a royal coronation site. Its hill fortress is sometimes called "the Acropolis of Norway." Its ancient district, Nordbyen, is filled with well-preserved houses, and the folk museum houses a treasure trove of Viking-era artifacts. See "Tønsberg: The First Settlement" in chapter 6.

- **Bergen:** The gateway to Norway's fjord country, this town is even more scenic than the capital, Oslo. It was the capital of Norway for 6 centuries, and a major outpost of the medieval Hanseatic merchants. The town's biggest tourist event is the Bergen International Music Festival, but there are also many year-round attractions. Many visitors come to explore Bergen's museums (including Edvard Grieg's former home) as well as its varied environs—fjords galore, mountains, and waterfalls. See chapter 10.

- **Trondheim:** Norway's third-largest city traces its history from 997, when the Vikings flourished. Norway's kings are crowned at the ancient cathedral, Nidaros Cathedral; Scandinavia's largest medieval building, the cathedral was erected over the grave of St. Olaf (also spelled Olav), the Viking king. Trondheim is the popular stopover for travelers from Oslo to destinations north of the Arctic Circle. See chapter 12.

- **Bodø:** Lying 1,305km (811 miles) north of Oslo, this far northern seaport, the terminus of the Nordland railway, is the gateway to the Arctic Circle, which lies just south of this breezy town. Another excellent place to observe the midnight sun from June 1 to July 13, Bodø is the capital of Nordland. From the center, you can also explore the environs, filled with glaciers and "bird islands." Bodø is also a gateway to the remote Lofoten Islands. See "Bodø: Gateway to the North" in chapter 14.

3 The Best Active Vacations

- **Fishing:** The cold, clear waters of Norway's freshwater streams are renowned for their salmon and trout, and the storm-tossed seas off the coast have traditionally provided enough cod and mackerel to satisfy most of the nation's population. Serious anglers sometimes end up losing themselves in the majesty of the scenery. Tips on fishing in and around the Norwegian fjords are provided by the **Bergen Angling Association,** Fosswinckelsgate 37, Bergen (© **55-32-11-64**), and the tourist information offices in Oslo and Bergen. Rural hotels throughout the nation can also give pointers to likely spots. For a truly unusual fishing experience, **Borton Overseas** (© **800/843-0602**) can arrange treks and accommodations in old-fashioned fishermen's cottages in the isolated Lofoten Islands. The rustic-looking, fully renovated cottages are adjacent to the sea. Rentals are for 3 days, and include bed linens, maid service, boat rentals, and fishing equipment. The most popular seasons are March, when cod abounds, and June through August, when the scenery and weather are particularly appealing.

- **Hiking:** The woods *(Marka)* around Oslo are ideal for jogging or walking. There are thousands of kilometers of trails, hundreds of which are lit. If you don't want to leave the city, Frogner Park also has many paths. Any Norwegian regional tourist bureau can advise you about hiking and jogging. In Bergen, for example, you can take a funicular to Fløyen, and within minutes you'll be in a natural forest filled with trails. Longer, guided hikes (from 5–8 days) may be arranged through the **Norwegian Mountain Touring Association,** Stortingsgata 3, N-0125 Oslo 1 (© 22-82-28-05; www.dntoa.no).

- **Skiing:** This is the undisputed top winter sport in Norway, attracting top-notch skiers and neophytes from around the world. Norway is a pioneer in promoting skiing as a sport for persons with disabilities. Modern facilities comparable to those in Europe's alpine regions

dot the landscape. If you're a serious skier, consider the best winter resorts, in Voss, Geilo, and Lillehammer (site of the 1994 Winter Olympics). See "Lillehammer of Olympic Glory" in chapter 7 and "Voss" and "Geilo" in chapter 11.

- **Mountain Climbing:** Local tourist offices can offer advice. What we like best are guided hikes to the archaeological digs of the 8,000-year-old Stone Age settlements near the Hardangerjøkulen (Hardanger Glacier). The digs are about an hour's drive north of the mountain resort of Geilo. For information, contact the **Geilo Tourist Office** (© 32-09-59-00). See "Geilo" in chapter 11.

4 The Best Festivals & Special Events

For more details on these events, see "Norway Calendar of Events," in chapter 4.

- **Bergen International Festival:** This European cultural highlight, which takes place in late May and early June, ranks in importance with the Edinburgh and Salzburg festivals. Major artists from all over the world descend on the small city to perform music, drama, opera, ballet, folkloric presentations, and more. The works of Bergen native Edvard Grieg dominate the festival, and daily concerts are held at his former home, Troldhaugen. Contemporary plays are also performed, but the major focus is on the works of Ibsen. See chapter 10.

- **Molde International Jazz Festival:** In this "city of roses," Norway's oldest jazz festival is held every summer, usually around

mid-July. Some of the best jazz artists in the world wing in for this event. People stay up most of the night listening to music and drinking beer. Sometimes the best concerts are the impromptu jam sessions in smoky little clubs. See "Molde: City of Roses" in chapter 11.

- **Nobel Peace Prize Ceremony:** The most prestigious event on the Oslo cultural calendar, the ceremony takes place at Oslo City Hall on December 10. The invitation-only event is broadcast around the world.

- **Holmenkollen Ski Festival:** This large ski festival takes place in February at the Holmenkollen Ski Jump, on the outskirts of Oslo. The agenda is packed with everything from international ski-jumping competitions to Norway's largest cross-country race for amateurs.

5 The Best Hotels

- **Grand Hotel** (Oslo; © 800/ 223-5652 in the U.S., or 23-21-20-00): This is Norway's

premier hotel, the last of Oslo's classic old-world palaces. It opened in 1874 and is still going strong. Ibsen and Munch were regular visitors. Constant renovations keep the hotel up-to-date and in great shape. The opulent suites house the Nobel Peace Prize winner every year. See p. 67.

- **Hotel Bristol** (Oslo; ℂ **22-82-60-00**): Inspired by Edwardian-era British taste, the interior design is the most lavish and ornate in Oslo. You enter a world of rich paneling, leather chairs, glittering chandeliers, and carved pillars. The most inviting area is the bar off the lobby, decorated in a library motif. The guest rooms boast painted classic furnishings and rich fabrics. See p. 70.

- **Skagen Brygge Hotell** (Stavanger; ℂ **51-85-00-00**): Southwestern Norway's most architecturally impressive hotel at the harbor front duplicates the look of a string of antique warehouses that used to stand here. Some of the preferred bedrooms are in the original 19th-century core. It's superb in comfort. See p. 210.

- **Radisson SAS Hotel Norge** (Bergen; ℂ **800/333-3333** in the U.S., or 55-57-30-00): This grand hotel on Norway's west coast is sleek, modern, and cosmopolitan. The center of Bergen's major social events, the hotel is both traditional and handsomely up-to-date. It's also equipped with all the amenities guests expect in a deluxe hotel. The service is highly professional. See p. 233.

- **Solstrand Fjord Hotel** (Os, outside Bergen; ℂ **56-57-11-00**): This is the finest hotel in the fjord district around the city of Bergen. With its history going back to 1896, the hotel evokes the nostalgia of the Belle Epoque era, and you're coddled in comfort in cheerfully decorated bedrooms. Come here for a vacation retreat instead of an overnight stopover. See p. 240.

- **Dr. Holms Hotel** (Geilo; ℂ **32-09-57-00**): One of Norway's most famous resort hotels, this establishment was opened by Dr. Holms in 1909. It still stands for elegance, comfort, and tradition, all of which are especially evident during the winter ski season. After its face-lift in 1989, the hotel offers beautifully furnished rooms with classic styling, and two new wings with a swimming complex. Famed musical artists often perform here. See p. 287.

- **Clarion Grand Olav Hotel** (Trondheim; ℂ **73-80-80-80**): This is the most stylish hotel in Norway's medieval capital, a tasteful enclave of comfort and good living. Located next to the city's concert house, the property is modern, filled with amenities, and imaginatively decorated. See p. 317.

- **Rica Ishavshotel** (Tromsø; ℂ **77-66-64-00**): Although chain-owned and -run, this is the best hotel in the chilly north of Norway. From its dramatic perch, the hotel provides views in all directions. Looking like a space-age yacht, it nicely houses guests near the pier where the coastal steamers stop. See p. 349.

6 The Best Restaurants

- **Annen Etage** (Oslo; ℂ **22-82-40-70**): In the Hotel Continental, and in spite of a certain stuffiness, this is one of the grand dining rooms of Norway. There is a certain charm and fragrance to every dish, and some of the platters are nothing short of sensational, with the finest of market-fresh ingredients available in Oslo. See p. 78.

- **Oro** (Oslo; ℂ **23-01-02-40**): A hyper-stylish restaurant, Oro is as good as it gets in Norway's capital, ranking right up there with anything Norway has to offer. The Continental cuisine at this first-class dining citadel evokes the best of the restaurants of Paris. See p. 78.

- **Statholdergaarden** (Oslo; ℂ **22-41-88-00**): Gourmets from all over Norway have flocked here to sample chef Bent Stiansen's interpretation of modern Norwegian cooking. Stiansen is almost fanatically tuned to what's best in any season, and he serves some of the capital's finest dishes. He uses great imagination and widely varied ingredients—everything from Arctic char to a rare vanilla bean imported from Thailand. See p. 86.

- **Restaurant Julius Fritzner** (Oslo; ℂ **23-21-20-00**): One of the most impressive dining establishments to make its debut in Norway in the mid-1990s, this restaurant in the Grand Hotel is still getting rave reviews. The chef uses only the finest Scandinavian ingredients in contemporary and traditional dishes; the emphasis is on enhancing and balancing flavors rather than creating surprises. See p. 79.

- **Elizabeth Restaurant** (Stavanger; ℂ **51-53-33-00**): A fine international and Spanish cuisine lures the oil barons of this rich city to this converted 1860 building. A product of a combined Norwegian and Basque partnership, the downstairs is an informal bodega, like a tavern in the Pyrenees, and upstairs is the more formal dining venue, featuring a cuisine that is both amusing and savory. See p. 215.

- **Finnegaardstuene** (Bergen; ℂ **55-55-03-00**): In a converted Hanseatic League warehouse, this Norwegian-French restaurant is one of the finest in western Norway. The cuisine revolves around only the freshest ingredients, especially fish. The kitchen uses classical French preparation methods to create such delectable items as lime-marinated turbot in caviar sauce or breast of duck in lime and fig sauce. See p. 241.

- **Bryggen** (Trondheim; ℂ **73-52-02-30**): This restaurant's excellent cuisine is a harmonious blend of Norwegian and French dishes. Menus change seasonally so that only the best and freshest ingredients are used. Ever had reindeer filet salad with a cranberry vinaigrette? Here's your chance. Norwegian duck, when it appears on the menu, is a rare treat. See p. 323.

- **Emma's Drømmekjøkken** (Tromsø; ℂ **77-63-77-30**): Anna Brit, called "Emma," operates this dream kitchen, and is the best-known culinary personality in the north of Norway. Although she uses mainly ingredients from the north, often fish from Arctic waters, she wanders the globe for her flavors that might include everything from chile to wasabi. See p. 352.

7 The Best Museums

- **Viking Ship Museum** (Oslo): Three stunning burial vessels from the Viking era were excavated on the shores of the Oslofjord and are now displayed in Bygdøy, Oslo's "museum island." The most spectacular is the *Oseberg,* from the 9th century, a 20m (64 ft.) dragon ship with a wealth of ornaments. See p. 104.

- **Edvard Munch Museum** (Oslo): Here you'll find the most significant collection of the work of Edvard Munch (1863–1944), Scandinavia's most noted artist. The museum, his gift to the city, contains a staggering treasure trove: 1,100 paintings, 4,500 drawings, and about 18,000 prints. See p. 107.
- **Norwegian Folk Museum** (Oslo): Some 140 original buildings from all over Norway were shipped here and reassembled on 14 hectares (35 acres) at Bygdøy. Although Scandinavia is known for such open-air museums, this one is the best. The buildings range from a rare stave church constructed around 1200 to one of the oldest wooden buildings still standing in Norway. Old-time Norwegian life is captured here as nowhere else. See p. 103.
- **Vigelandsparken** (Oslo): This stunning park in western Oslo displays the lifetime work of Gustav Vigeland, the country's greatest sculptor. In 30-hectare (75-acre) Frogner Park, you can see more than 200 sculptures in granite, bronze, and iron. Including the "Angry Boy," his most celebrated work, and the most recognizable. See p. 102.
- **Det Hanseatiske Museum** (Bergen): Depicting commercial life on the wharf in the early 18th century, this museum is housed in one of the city's best-preserved wooden buildings. German Hanseatic merchants lived in similar medieval houses near the harbor. See p. 249.

8 The Best Buys

Most of the products mentioned below are available at better shops in Oslo and Bergen; see "Shopping" in chapters 4 and 10.

- **Ceramics:** In the 1960s and 1970s, Norway earned a reputation among potters and stoneware enthusiasts for its chunky, utilitarian pottery. The trend today is to emulate the fragile, more decorative designs popular in France, England, and Germany, so Norwegian ceramists are producing thinner, more delicate, and more ornate forms.
- **Costumes:** Norway boasts more than 450 regional costumes, especially in the coastal communities. The original fishermen's sweater was knit of naturally colored wool (beige, brown, black, or off-white) in a deliberately large size, and then washed in hot water so that it shrank. The tightly woven sweater could then resist water. Modern versions of these sweaters are known for their nubbly texture, sophisticated patterns, and varying shades of single colors.
- **Crystal:** In Norway you can buy flawless crystal that's as clear as a Nordic iceberg. Norwegian tastes lean toward the clean, uncluttered look, stressing line, form, and harmony.
- **Knitwear:** Many visitors eagerly seek Norwegian knitwear. Among the best buys are hand-knit or "half-handmade" garments. The latter, knit on electric looms, are so personalized and made in such small quantities that only an expert can tell that they aren't completely handmade. The tradition of women hand-knitting sweaters while rocking a cradle or tending a fire thrives in rural Norway, especially during the long winter.

9 The Best Websites

- **Norwegian Tourist Board, www. visitnorway.com**: This is the official travel guide to Norway, welcoming you to this far northern outpost with lots of tips on attractions and special interests, accommodations, dining, and entertainment, along with maps and notes on the weather.

- **Norway.Com, www.norway.com**: This is a good website for Norway, covering all the major cities, not just Oslo and Bergen, but Ålesund, Tønsberg, Hamar, Kristiansand S, and Lillehammer, among others. Travel planning data is highlighted, as are the best travel deals.

- **Official Internet Site for Trondheim, www.trondheim.com/engelsk**: The first capital of Norway, today a modern university city, is explored in this databank, with pictures, useful information, a city map, and details about accommodations and attractions.

- **Explore Fjord Norway, www. fjordnorway.com**: This site focuses on one of Scandinavia's most visited attractions, the fjord country of western Norway. It provides information on fjord trips and cruises, with details for the active vacationer on climbing, walking, and cycling, plus information about fjord culture.

- **Bergen Guide, www.bergenguide.com**: Norway's second city is explored in some detail on this site, with a comprehensive database on maps, restaurants, shops, sports, sightseeing, transportation, accommodations, and other useful information.

- **Cruise Norway, www.cruisenorway.com**: This site previews the best itineraries for those who'd like to cruise the fjords of Norway or take various Scandinavian cruises in general. Independent vacation packages are highlighted.

- **Visit Flåm, www.visitflam.com**: This site offers information about charming Flåm in the heart of the Sognefjord district. It's a major stop on the Flåm Railway, the world's most spectacular and panoramic line.

- **Skiing Norway and Lillehammer, www.lillehammerturist.no/english/start.htm**: This site is loaded with details about Norway's oldest sports resort and a venue for the winter Olympics in 1994. The skiing terrain is previewed, along with tips on activities, accommodations, and attractions.

- **Official Site Oslo Tourist Office, www.oslopro.no**: This site promises "everything else you need to know about Oslo." That is a bit of an exaggeration, but the site explores the city in detail, with tips on attractions, restaurants, activities, accommodations, and shopping.

- **European Travel & Tourism Bureau, www.alltravelnorway. com/Norway/Destination_Guides/cities/Stavanger.htm**: This site explores Norway's oil capital of Stavanger, with tips on accommodations, attractions, bars, cafes, sights, and restaurants.

- **European Travel & Tourism Bureau, www.alltravelnorway. com/Norway/Destination_Guides/Cities/Tromso.htm**: Like the site on Stavanger (see above), this site takes you to Norway's small but spirited capital of the far north: the city of Tromsø.

2

Planning Your Trip to Norway

In the pages that follow, we've compiled everything you need to know about the practical details of planning your trip—airlines, a calendar of events, details on currency, and more.

1 The Regions in Brief

WESTERN NORWAY Western Norway is fabled for its fjords, saltwater arms of the sea that stretch inland. Many date from the end of the last Ice Age. Some fjords cut into mountain ranges as high as 1,006m (3,300 ft.). The longest fjord in western Norway is the Sognefjord, north of Bergen, which penetrates 177km (110 miles) inland. Other major fjords in the district are the Nordfjord, Geirangerfjord, and Hardangerfjord. The capital of the fjord district is **Bergen,** the largest city on the west coast. **Lofthus,** a collection of farms extending along the slopes of Sørfjorden, offers panoramic views of the fjord and the **Folgefonn Glacier.** Hiking is the primary activity in this region. The area north of the **Hardangerfjord** is a haven for hikers. Here you'll find Hardangervidda National Park, on Europe's largest high-mountain plateau, home to Norway's largest herd of wild reindeer. The town of **Voss,** birthplace of the American football great Knute Rockne, is surrounded by glaciers, fjords, rivers, and lakes.

CENTRAL NORWAY Fjords are also common in central Norway; the two largest are the Trondheimsfjord and Narnsfjord. It's not unusual for roads to pass waterfalls that cascade straight down into fjords. Many thick forests and snowcapped peaks fill central Norway. The town of **Geilo,** halfway between Bergen and Oslo, is one of Norway's most popular ski resorts. It boasts more than 129km (80 miles) of cross-country trails. **Trondheim,** central Norway's largest city, is home to Nidaros Domen, the 11th-century cathedral that was once the burial place for kings. **Røros** is a well-preserved 18th-century mining town. The medieval city of **Molde,** Norway's capital during the Second World War, plays host to one of Europe's largest jazz festivals. **Geiranger,** site of the Seven Sisters waterfall, is one of Norway's most popular resorts.

EASTERN NORWAY On the border with Sweden, eastern Norway is characterized by clear blue lakes, rolling hills, and green valleys. In some ways it's the most traditional part of the country. Because of its many fertile valleys, it was one of the earliest areas to be settled. Some of the biggest valleys are Valdres, Østerdal, Hallingdall, Numedal, and Gudbrandsdalen. Campers and hikers enjoy the great forests of the Hedmark region, site of Norway's longest river, the Glomma (Gløma), which flows about 580km (360 miles). The area has many ski resorts, notably **Lillehammer,** site of the 1994 Winter Olympics. Norway's most visited destination is the capital, **Oslo,** which rises from the shores of the Oslofjord.

The city of **Frederikstad,** at the mouth of the Glomma, was once the marketplace for goods entering the country. Its 17th-century Kongsten Fort was designed to defend Norway from Sweden. **Tønsberg,** Norway's oldest town, dates to the 9th century. This area is also the site of the **Peer Gynt Road,** of Ibsen fame, and the mountainous region is home to numerous ski resorts.

SOUTHERN NORWAY Southern Norway is sometimes referred to as "the Riviera" because of its unspoiled and uncrowded—but chilly—beaches. It's also a favorite port of call for the yachting crowd. **Stavanger,** the oil capital of Norway, is the largest southern city and also quite popular. There is much to explore in this Telemark region, which is filled with lakes and canals popular for summer canoeing and boating. **Skien,** birthplace of the playwright Henrik Ibsen (1828–1906), is primarily an industrial town. In Skien, you can board a lake steamer to travel through a series of canals. The southern part of **Kristiansand** links Norway with continental Europe. Close by is 10km (6-mile) **Hamresanden Beach,** one of the longest uninterrupted beaches in Europe. Along the western half of the district are more fjords, notably the Lysefjord, Sandefjord, and Vindefjord.

NORTHERN NORWAY The "Land of the Midnight Sun" is a region of craggy cliffs that descend to the sea and of deep, fertile valleys along the deserted moors. It has islands with few, if any, inhabitants,

where life has remained relatively unchanged for generations. The capital of the Nordland region is **Bodø,** which lies just north of the Arctic Circle; it's a base for Arctic fishing trips and visits to the wild Glomfjord. Norway's second-largest glacier, **Svartisen,** is also in this region, as is the city of **Narvik,** a major Arctic port and the gateway to the **Lofoten Islands.** The islands, which have many fishing villages, make up one of the most beautiful areas of Norway. Visitors come here from all over the world for sport fishing and bird-watching.

TROMSØ The main city in this region is **Tromsø,** from which polar explorations launch. A key attraction is the world's northernmost planetarium. Tromsø contains one of Norway's most impressive mountain ranges, the Lyngs Alps, which attract winter skiers and summer hikers. **Alta,** site of the Altafjord, is reputed to have the best salmon-fishing waters in the world.

FINNMARK At the top of Norway is the Finnmark region, home of the Lapps (or Samis). Settlements here include **Kautokeino** (the Lapp town) and **Hammerfest,** the world's northernmost town. Most tourists come to Finnmark to see the **North Cape,** Europe's northernmost point and an ideal midnight sun viewing spot. **Vardø** is the only Norwegian mainland town in the Arctic climate zone. In the 17th century Vardø was the site of more than 80 witch burnings. The town of **Kirkenes** lies 274km (170 miles) north of the Arctic Circle, close to the Russian border.

2 Visitor Information

In the **United States,** contact the **Norwegian Tourist Board,** 655 Third Ave., Suite 1810, New York, NY 10017 (© **212/885-9700**), at least 3 months in advance for maps, sightseeing

pointers, ferry schedules, and other information.

In the **United Kingdom,** contact the **Norwegian Tourist Board,** a division of the Scandinavian Tourist Board, Charles House, 5 Lower Regent St.,

Norway

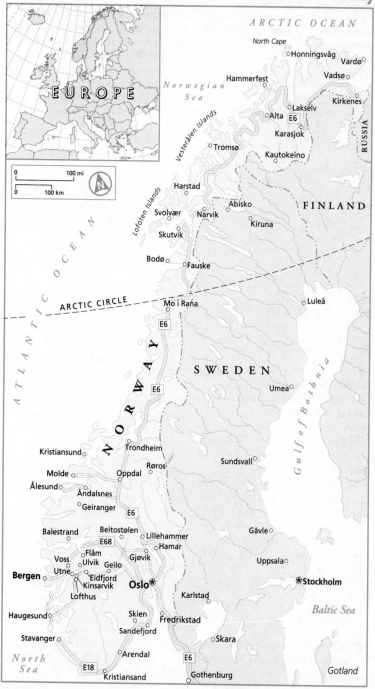

London SW1Y 4LR (© **0906/302-2003,** cost 500p per min.).

You might also try the tourist board's official website: **www.visit norway.com.**

If you get in touch with a **travel agent,** make sure the agent is a member of the American Society of Travel Agents (ASTA). If a problem arises, you can complain to the Consumer Affairs Department of the society at 1101 King St., Alexandria, VA 22314 (© **703/706-0387;** www.astanet.com).

3 Entry Requirements & Customs

ENTRY REQUIREMENTS

Citizens of the United States, Canada, Ireland, Australia, and New Zealand, and British subjects, need a valid **passport** to enter Norway. You need to apply for a visa only if you want to stay more than 3 months.

A British Visitor's Passport is also valid for holidays and some business trips of less than 3 months. The passport can include your spouse, and it's valid for 1 year. Apply in person at a main post office in the British Isles, and the passport will be issued that day.

Your current domestic **driver's license** is acceptable in Norway. An international driver's license is not required.

CUSTOMS
WHAT YOU CAN BRING INTO NORWAY

With certain food exceptions, personal effects intended for your own use can be brought into Norway. If you take them with you when you leave, you can bring in cameras, binoculars, radios, portable TVs, and the like, as well as fishing and camping equipment. Visitors of all nationalities can bring in 400 cigarettes, or 500 grams of tobacco, and 200 sheets of cigarette paper, or 50 cigars, and 1 liter of spirits or 1 liter of wine. Upon leaving, you can take with you up to 25,000NOK ($3,325) in Norwegian currency.

WHAT YOU CAN TAKE HOME

Returning **U.S. citizens** who have been away for at least 48 hours are allowed to bring back, once every 30 days, $800 worth of merchandise duty-free. You'll be charged a flat rate of 4% duty on the next $1,000 worth of purchases. Be sure to have your receipts handy. On mailed gifts, the duty-free limit is $200. You cannot bring fresh foodstuffs into the United States; tinned foods, however, are allowed. For more information, contact the **U.S. Customs Service,** 1300 Pennsylvania Ave., NW, Washington, DC 20229 (© **877/287-8867**), and request the free pamphlet *Know Before You Go.* It's also available on the Web at www.customs.gov. (Click on "Traveler Information" then "Know Before You Go.")

For a clear summary of **Canadian** rules, write for the booklet *I Declare,* issued by the **Canada Customs and Revenue Agency** (© **800/461-9999** in Canada, or 204/983-3500; www. ccra-adrc.gc.ca). Canada allows its citizens a C$750 exemption, and you're allowed to bring back duty-free one carton of cigarettes, 1 can of tobacco, 40 imperial ounces of liquor, and 50 cigars. In addition, you're allowed to mail gifts to Canada valued at less than C$60 a day, provided they're unsolicited and don't contain alcohol or tobacco (write on the package "Unsolicited gift, under $60 value"). All valuables should be declared on the Y-38 form before departure from Canada, including serial numbers of valuables you already own, such as expensive foreign cameras. *Note:* The $750 exemption can only be used once a year and only after an absence of 7 days.

U.K. citizens returning from a non-EU country have a customs allowance of 200 cigarettes; 50 cigars; 250g of smoking tobacco; 2 liters of still table wine; 1 liter of spirits or strong liqueurs (over 22% volume); 2 liters of fortified wine, sparkling wine or other liqueurs; 60cc (ml) perfume; 250cc (ml) of toilet water; and £145 worth of all other goods, including gifts and souvenirs. People under 17 cannot have the tobacco or alcohol allowance. For more information, contact **HM Customs & Excise,** Passenger Enquiry Point, 2nd Floor Wayfarer House, Great South West Road, Feltham, Middlesex, TW14 8NP (✆ **0181/910-3744,** or 44/181-910-3744 from outside the U.K.), or consult their website at www.open.gov.uk.

The duty-free allowance in **Australia** is A$400 or, for those under 18, A$200. Upon returning to Australia, citizens can bring in 250 cigarettes or 250 grams of loose tobacco and 1,125ml of alcohol. If you're returning with valuable goods you already own, such as foreign-made cameras, you should file form B263. For more information, contact **Australian Customs Services,** GPO Box 8, Sydney NSW 2001 (✆ **02/6275-6666** in Australia, or 202/797-3189 in the U.S.), or go to www.customs.gov.au.

The duty-free allowance for **New Zealand** is NZ$700. Citizens over 17 can bring in 200 cigarettes, or 50 cigars, or 250 grams of tobacco (or a mixture of all three if their combined weight doesn't exceed 250g); plus 4.5 liters of wine and beer, or 1.125 liters of liquor. New Zealand currency does not carry import or export restrictions. Fill out a certificate of export, listing the valuables you are taking out of the country; that way, you can bring them back without paying duty. Most questions are answered in a free pamphlet available at New Zealand consulates and Customs offices: *New Zealand Customs Guide for Travellers, Notice no. 4.* For more information, contact **New Zealand Customs,** 50 Anzac Ave., P.O. Box 29, Auckland (✆ **09/359-6655**).

4 Money

NORWEGIAN KRONER The Norwegian currency is the **krone** (plural: **kroner**), written as "NOK." There are 100 **øre** in 1 krone. Bank notes are issued in denominations of 50, 100, 200, 500, and 1,000 kroner. Coins are issued in denominations of 50 øre, 1 krone, and 5, 10, and 20 kroner.

ATMS PLUS, Cirrus, and other networks connecting automated-teller machines operate throughout Norway. If your credit card has a PIN (Personal Identification Number), you can probably use your card at Norwegian ATMs to withdraw money as a cash advance on your card. Always determine the frequency limits for withdrawals, and check to see if your PIN code must be reprogrammed for use abroad. Discover cards are accepted in the United States only. For **Cirrus** locations abroad, call ✆ **800/424-7787.** For **PLUS** usage abroad, check www.visa.com or call ✆ **800/843-7587.**

CREDIT CARDS These are useful throughout Norway. American Express, Diners Club, and Visa are widely recognized. If you see a Eurocard or Access sign, it means the establishment accepts MasterCard. With an American Express, MasterCard, or Visa card, you can also withdraw currency from cash machines (ATMs). Always check with your credit- or charge-card company about this before leaving home.

CURRENCY EXCHANGE Many hotels in Norway simply do not accept a dollar- or pound-denominated personal check; those that do will certainly charge for making the conversion. In

Emergency Cash—The Fastest Way

If you need emergency cash over the weekend when all banks and American Express offices are closed, you can have money wired to you from **Western Union** (② 800/325-6000; www.westernunion.com). You must present valid ID to pick up the cash at the Western Union office. However, in most countries, you can pick up a money transfer even if you don't have valid identification, as long as you can answer a test question provided by the sender. Be sure to let the sender know in advance that you don't have ID. If you need to use a test question instead of ID, the sender must take cash to his or her local Western Union office, rather than transferring the money over the phone or online.

some cases a hotel may accept countersigned traveler's checks or a credit or charge card.

If you're making a deposit on a hotel reservation, it's cheaper and easier to pay with a check drawn on a Norwegian bank. This can be arranged by a large commercial bank or by a specialist like **Ruesch International,** 700 11th St. NW, 4th floor, Washington, DC 20001 (② **800/424-2923** or 202/408-1200; www.ruesch.com). It performs a wide variety of conversion-related tasks, usually for about $15 per transaction.

If you need a check payable in a Norwegian currency, call Ruesch's toll-free number, describe what you need, and write down the transaction number. Mail your dollar-denominated personal check (payable to Ruesch International) to the Washington, D.C., office. When it's received, the company will mail you a check denominated in the requested currency for the specified amount, minus the $3 charge. The company can also help you with wire transfers, as well as the conversion of VAT (value-added tax) refund checks. Information is mailed upon request.

In England, contact Ruesch International Ltd., Marble Arch Tower, 14th Floor, 55-Bryanston St., London W1H 7AA (② **0207/563-3300;** fax 0207/563-3390).

TRAVELER'S CHECKS   Traveler's checks are a bit outdated in the wake of ATMs, but some visitors still prefer this old-fashioned means of carrying money. Most banks give you a better exchange rate for traveler's checks than for cash. Checks denominated in U.S. dollars or British pounds are accepted virtually anywhere; sometimes you can also get checks in a local currency.

The agencies listed below will replace checks if they're lost or stolen, provided you produce documentation. When purchasing checks, ask about refund hot lines. American Express has the most offices around the world.

Issuers sometimes have agreements with groups to sell traveler's checks without a commission. For example, American Automobile Association (AAA) clubs sell commission-free American Express checks in several currencies.

American Express (② **800/721-9768** in the U.S. and Canada; www.americanexpress.com) is one of the largest and most recognizable issuers of traveler's checks. Holders of certain types of American Express cards pay no commission. For questions or problems arising outside the United States or Canada, contact any of the company's many regional representatives. We list locations throughout this guide.

The Norwegian Krone

For American Readers   At this writing, $1 = approximately 7.5 kroner (or 1 krone = approximately 13 US¢); this was the rate of exchange used to calculate the dollar values given throughout this edition. Bear in mind that throughout the context of this book, dollar amounts less than $10 are rounded to the nearest nickel, and dollar amounts greater than $10 are rounded to the nearest dollar.

For British Readers   At this writing, £1 = approximately 11.5 kronor (or 1 krone = approximately 8.7p). This was the rate of exchange used to calculate the pound values in the table below.

Regarding the Euro   At the time of this writing, the U.S. dollar and the Euro traded almost on par (i.e., $1 approximately equals 1€). But that relationship can and probably will change during the lifetime of this edition. For more exact ratios between these and other currencies, check an up-to-date source at the time of your arrival in Norway.

NOK	US$	UK£	Euro€	NOK	US$	UK£	Euro€
1.00	0.13	0.09	0.13	75.00	9.98	6.53	9.98
2.00	0.27	0.17	0.27	100.00	13.30	8.70	13.30
3.00	0.40	0.26	0.40	125.00	16.63	10.88	16.63
4.00	0.53	0.35	0.53	150.00	19.95	13.05	19.95
5.00	0.67	0.44	0.67	175.00	23.28	15.23	23.28
6.00	0.80	0.52	0.80	200.00	26.60	17.40	26.60
7.00	0.93	0.61	0.93	225.00	29.93	19.58	29.93
8.00	1.06	0.70	1.06	250.00	33.25	21.75	33.25
9.00	1.20	0.78	1.20	275.00	36.58	23.93	36.58
10.00	1.33	0.87	1.33	300.00	39.90	26.10	39.90
15.00	2.00	1.31	2.00	350.00	46.55	30.45	46.55
20.00	2.66	1.74	2.66	400.00	53.20	34.80	53.20
25.00	3.33	2.18	3.33	500.00	66.50	43.50	66.50
50.00	6.65	4.35	6.65	1000.00	133.00	87.00	133.00

Citicorp (© 800/645-6556 from all over the world; www.citibank.com) issues checks in several currencies.

Thomas Cook (© 800/223-7373 from all over the world; www.thomas cook.com) issues MasterCard traveler's checks denominated in several currencies; not all currencies are available at every outlet.

Visa Travelers Checks (© 800/732-1322 in the U.S. and Canada, or 212/858-8500 collect from most other parts of the world; www.visa.com) sells Visa checks denominated in several major currencies.

5 When to Go

CLIMATE

In the summer, the average temperature in Norway ranges from 57°F to 65°F (13°C–18°C). In January, it hovers around 27°F (2°C), ideal for winter sports. The Gulf Stream warms

What Things Cost in Oslo	U.S.$
Taxi from Gardermoen Airport to the city center	67.00
Bus from Gardermoen Airport to the city center	15.00
Local telephone call	.65
Double room at the Grand Hotel (very expensive)	257.00
Double room at the Tulip Inn Rainbow Cecil (moderate)	182.00
Double room at the Cochs Pensjonat (inexpensive)	80.00
Lunch for one at the Primo Restaurant Ciaou-Ciaou (moderate)	34.00
Lunch for one at Mamma Rosa (inexpensive)	26.00
Dinner for one, without wine, at Babette's Gjestehus (expensive)	66.00
Dinner for one, without wine, at Lipp (moderate)	40.00
Dinner for one, without wine, at Friskport Vegeta Vertshus (inexpensive)	19.00
Pint of beer (draft Pilsner)	6.00
Coca-Cola (in a restaurant)	3.20
Cup of coffee	2.95
Admission to Viking Ship Museum	5.30
Movie ticket	10.00
Theater ticket (at National Theater)	20.00–29.00

the west coast, where winters tend to be temperate. Rainfall, however, is heavy.

Above the Arctic Circle, the sun shines night and day from mid-May until late July. For about 2 months every winter, the North Cape is plunged into darkness.

May to Mid-June is when the scenery in Norway is at its most spectacular with fruit trees in blossom, snow in the mountains, and meltwater swelling the waterfalls. There are several public holidays in May, and the Norwegians make full use of them to celebrate springtime after a long winter. In particular, the National Day on May 17 is marked by parties, music, and street parades with many people dressed in beautiful national costumes. Low-season rates apply during this period.

Late June to early August is the high season in Norway when the weather is warmest and the schools are on holidays. The most popular tourist places can be busy, but finding peace and quiet, if you wish, is easy. All the

man-made tourist attractions are open, and public transport services are more frequent.

From **mid-August to October,** there is little change in the weather in the second half of August. Accommodation and ferries are at mid- or low-season rates. There is so little traffic that you may feel as if you have the whole country to yourself. The temperature drops slowly through September when you can enjoy the simple pleasures of picking wild berries and mushrooms in the forests. The glorious colors of autumn are at their best in October.

Norway's **summer** weather is variable and unpredictable, with a number of surprising features. The Atlantic Gulf Stream keeps the western fjord area and the coast up into the Arctic North much warmer than you might expect. The west coast receives the most rain, but the area farther east is drier. The sea temperature can reach 64°F (18°C) or higher on the south coast,

---

Fun Fact **Land of the Midnight Sun**

In these locations, you can see the whole disk of the sun on the given dates.

Place	From	To
Nordkapp	May 13	July 29
Hammerfest	May 16	July 26
Vardo	May 17	July 25
Tromsø	May 20	July 22
Harstad	May 24	July 18
Svolvær	May 28	July 14
Bodø	June 3	July 8

---

where swimming is a popular pastime. Surprisingly, the water is often calm as most of the inhabited places in Norway are sheltered from the prevailing wind by mountains and forest.

The warmest and most stable weather occurs on the eastern side of the southern mountains, including the south coast between Mandal and Oslo. Even in the north, summer temperatures are pleasantly warm; however, as nearly all of this area is near the west coast, the weather can be wet and changeable. If you should be unlucky with the weather, remember a wise Norwegian saying, "There is no such thing as bad weather, only bad clothing." Take waterproof clothing.

In **winter** much of Norway is transformed into a snow-clad paradise from November to April. The best way to enjoy it is undoubtedly on skis, but there are many other things to do as well. Just sitting by the fire in a warm and cozy log cabin is a pleasure for some, as is the friendly, relaxed atmosphere of the hotel bar. Children of all ages (and many grown-ups) never get tired of just playing in the snow. Active types can go tobogganing, skating, ice fishing, ice climbing, dogsledding, and more.

Norway's Average Daytime Temperatures (°F/°C)

Months	Jan	Feb	Mar	Apr	May	June	July	Aug	Sept	Oct	Nov	Dec
OSLO												
Temp. (°F)	25	26	32	41	51	60	64	61	53	42	33	27
Temp. (°C)	–3.9	–3.3	0	5.0	11	16	18	16	12	5.5	–0.6	–2.8
BERGEN/STAVANGER												
Temp. (°F)	35	35	38	41	40	55	59	58	54	47	42	38
Temp. (°C)	1.7	1.7	3.3	5.0	4.4	13	15	14	12	8.3	5.5	3.3
TRONDHEIM												
Temp. (°F)	27	27	31	38	47	53	58	57	50	42	35	31
Temp. (°C)	–2.8	–2.8	–0.6	3.3	8.3	12	14	14	10	5.5	1.7	–0.6

THE MIDNIGHT SUN In the summer, the sun never fully sets in northern Norway, and even in the south, the sun may set around 11pm and rise at 3am. Keep in mind that although the sun shines at midnight, it's not as strong as at midday. Bring a warm jacket or sweater.

HOLIDAYS

Norway celebrates the following public holidays: New Year's Day (Jan 1), Maundy Thursday, Good Friday, Easter, Labor Day (May 1), Ascension

Day (mid-May), Independence Day (May 17), Whitmonday (late May), Christmas (Dec 25), and Boxing Day (Dec 26).

NORWAY CALENDAR OF EVENTS

Specific dates are for 2003; others are approximate. Check with the local tourist office before making plans to attend a specific event, especially in 2004.

January

Northern Lights Festival, Tromsø. Classical and contemporary music performances by musicians from Norway and abroad. www.nordlys festivalen.no. Late January.

February

Kristiansund Opera Festival. Featuring Kristiansund Opera's productions of opera and ballet, plus art exhibitions, concerts, and other events. www.oik.no. Early February.

March

Holmenkollen Ski Festival, Oslo. One of Europe's largest ski festivals, with World Cup Nordic skiing and biathlons, international ski-jumping competitions, and Norway's largest cross-country race for amateurs. Held at Holmenkollen Ski Jump on the outskirts of Oslo. To participate, attend, or request more information, contact Skiforeningen, Kongeveien 5, Holmenkollen, N-0390 Oslo 3 (© 22-92-32-00). www.skiforenin gen.no. March 6 to 9.

Narvik Winter Festival. Sports events, carnivals, concerts, and opera performances highlight this festival dedicated to those who built the railway across northern Norway and Sweden. www.vinterfestuka.no. Second week of March to mid-April.

Birkebeiner Race, Rena to Lillehammer. This historic international ski race, with thousands of participants, crosses the mountains between Rena and Lillehammer,

site of the 1994 Olympics. It's a 53km (33-mile) cross-country trek. © 61-27-58-00; www.birke beiner.no. March 21.

April

Vossa Jazz Festival. Three days of jazz and folk music performances by European and American artists. www.vossajazz.no. First week of April.

May

The Grete Waitz Run, Oslo. A women's run through the streets of Oslo, with participation by the famous marathoner Grete Waitz. © 23-21-55-00; www.gwl.no. May 2.

The Viking Run, Sognefjord. An international half-marathon is staged in the Sognefjord. Some participants extend their stay to participate in other sports, such as summer skiing, glacier climbing, biking, boating, or mountain climbing. Late May.

Bergen International Festival (Bergen Festspill). A world-class music event, featuring artists from Norway and around the world. This is one of the largest annual musical events in Scandinavia. Held at various venues in Bergen. For information, contact the Bergen International Festival, Slottsgaten 1, 4055, Dregen N-5835 Bergen (© 55-21-06-30). May 21 to June 1.

June

Faerder Sailing Race. Some 1,000 sailboats participate in this race, which ends in Borre, by the Oslofjord. First week of June.

North Cape March. This trek from Honningsvåg to the North Cape is one of the world's toughest. The round-trip march is 68km (42 miles). Mid-June.

Emigration Festival, Stavanger. Commemoration of Norwegian immigration to North America,

Tracing Your Norwegian Roots

If you're of Norwegian ancestry, you can get information on how to trace your family history from the nearest Norwegian consulate. In Norway, contact the **Norwegian Emigration Center,** Strandkaien 31, N-4005 Stavanger (℃ **51-53-88-60;** www.emigrationcenter.com), for a catalog of information about Norwegian families who emigrated to the United States.

In the United States, the **Family History Library of the Church of Jesus Christ of Latter-day Saints,** 35 N. West Temple, Salt Lake City, UT 84150 (℃ **801/240-2331**), has extensive records of Norwegian families that emigrated to the United States and Canada. The library is open to the public without charge for genealogical research. Mormon churches in other cities have listings of materials available in Salt Lake City; for a small fee you can request pertinent microfilms, which you can view at a local church.

with exhibitions, concerts, theater, and folklore. Mid-June.

Midsummer Night, nationwide. Celebrations and bonfires all over Norway. June 23.

Emigration Festival, Kvinesdal. Commemorates the Norwegian immigration to the United States. Late June to early July.

July

Kongsberg International Jazz Festival. International artists participate in one of the most important jazz festivals in Scandinavia, with open-air concerts. ℃ **32-73-31-66;** www.kongsberg-jazzfestival.no. July 1 to 4.

Midnight Sun Marathon, Tromsø. The marathon in northern Norway starts at midnight. ℃ **77-69-61-24;** www.msm.no. July 4.

Exxon Mobil Bislett Games, Oslo. International athletic competitions are staged in Oslo, with professional participants from all over the world. ℃ **22-59-17-59;** www.bislettgames.com. July 15.

Molde International Jazz Festival. The "City of Roses" is the site of Norway's oldest jazz festival. It attracts international stars from both sides of the Atlantic every year. Held at venues in Molde for 6 days. For details, contact the Molde Jazz Festival, Box 271, N-6401 Molde (℃ **71-21-60-00**). www.moldejazz.no. Mid-July.

Norway Cup International Youth Soccer Tournament, Oslo. The world's largest youth soccer tournament attracts 1,000 teams from around the world to Oslo. ℃ **22-28-90-57;** www.Norway-cup.no. Last week of July.

August

International Folk Music Festival, Bø. An international festival of folk music and folk dance takes place in the home of many famous fiddlers, dancers, and singers. July 30 to August 2.

Peer Gynt Festival, Vinstra. Art exhibitions, evenings of music and song, parades in national costumes, and other events honor Ibsen's fictional character. ℃ **61-29-47-70;** www.peergynt.no. July 31 to August 8.

Oslo Jazz Festival. This annual festival features music from the earliest years of jazz (1920–25), as well as classical concerts, opera, and ballet. ☎ **22-42-91-20;** www.oslojazz.no. First week of August.

Chamber Music Festival, Oslo. Norwegian and foreign musicians perform at Oslo's Akershus Castle and Fortress, which dates from A.D. 1300. ☎ **23-10-07-30;** www.oslo kammermusikkfestival.no. Second week of August.

World Cup Summer Ski Jumping, Marikollen. Takes place in Marikollen, Raelingen, just outside the center of Oslo. Mid-August.

September

International Salmon Fishing Festival, Suldal. Participants come from Norway and abroad to the Suldalslagen River outside Stavanger in western Norway. www.vestkysten.no. Dates vary.

Oslo Marathon. This annual event draws some of Norway's best long-distance runners. Mid-September.

December

Nobel Peace Prize Ceremony, Oslo. A major event on the Oslo calendar, attracting world attention. Held at Oslo City Hall on December 10. Attendance is by invitation only. For information, contact the Nobel Institute, Drammensveien 19, N-0255 Oslo 2 (☎ **22-44-36-80;** www.nobel.se).

6 Health & Insurance

TRAVEL INSURANCE AT A GLANCE

Since Norway for most of us is far from home, and a number of things could go wrong—lost luggage, trip cancellation, a medical emergency—consider the following types of insurance.

Check your existing insurance policies before you buy travel insurance to cover trip cancellation, lost luggage, medical expenses, or car rental insurance. You're likely to have partial or complete coverage. But if you need some, ask your travel agent about a comprehensive package. The cost of travel insurance varies widely, depending on the cost and length of your trip, your age and overall health, and the type of trip you're taking. Insurance for extreme sports or adventure travel, for example, will cost more than coverage for a European cruise. Some insurers provide packages for specialty vacations, such as skiing or backpacking. More dangerous activities may be excluded from basic policies.

For information, contact one of the following popular insurers:

- **Access America** (☎ 866/807-3982; www.accessamerica.com)
- **Travel Guard International** (☎ 800/826-4919; www.travel guard.com)
- **Travel Insured International** (☎ 800/243-3174; www.travel insured.com)
- **Travelex Insurance Services** (☎ 888/457-4602; www.travelex-insurance.com)

TRIP-CANCELLATION INSURANCE (TCI)

There are three major types of trip-cancellation insurance—one, in the event that you prepay a cruise or tour that gets cancelled, and you can't get your money back; a second when you or someone in your family gets sick or dies, and you can't travel (but beware that you may not be covered for a pre-existing condition); and a third, when bad weather makes travel impossible. Some insurers provide coverage for events like jury duty; natural disasters close to home, like floods or fire; even the loss of a job. A few have added

> **Tips Quick ID**
>
> Tie a colorful ribbon or piece of yarn around your luggage handle, or slap a distinctive sticker on the side of your bag. This makes it less likely that someone will mistakenly appropriate it. And if your luggage gets lost, it will be easier to find.

provisions for cancellations because of terrorist activities. Always check the fine print before signing on, and don't buy trip-cancellation insurance from the tour operator that may be responsible for the cancellation; buy it only from a reputable travel insurance agency. Don't overbuy. You won't be reimbursed for more than the cost of your trip.

MEDICAL INSURANCE

Most health insurance policies cover you if you get sick away from home—but check, particularly if you're insured by an HMO. With the exception of certain HMOs and Medicare/Medicaid, your medical insurance should cover medical treatment—even hospital care—overseas. However, most out-of-country hospitals make you pay your bills up front, and send you a refund after you've returned home and filed the necessary paperwork. Members of **Blue Cross/Blue Shield** can now use their cards at select hospitals in most major cities worldwide (© **800/810-BLUE** or www.blue cares.com for a list of hospitals).

Some credit cards (American Express and certain gold and platinum Visa and MasterCards, for example) offer automatic flight insurance against death or dismemberment in case of an airplane crash if you charged the cost of your ticket.

If you require additional insurance, try one of the following companies:

- **MEDEX International,** 9515 Deereco Rd., Timonium, MD 21093-5375 (© **888/MEDEX-00** or 410/453-6300; fax 410/453-6301; www.medexassist.com)

- **Travel Assistance International** (© **800/821-2828;** www.travel assistance.com), 9200 Keystone Crossing, Suite 300, Indianapolis, IN 46240 (for general information on services, call the company's Worldwide Assistance Services, Inc., at © **800/777-8710**)

The cost of travel medical insurance varies widely. Check your existing policies before you buy additional coverage. Also, check to see if your medical insurance covers you for emergency medical evacuation. If you have to buy a one-way same-day ticket home and forfeit your nonrefundable round-trip ticket, you may be out big money.

LOST-LUGGAGE INSURANCE

On International flights (including U.S. portions of international trips), baggage is limited to approximately $9.05 per pound, up to approximately $635 per checked bag. If you plan to check items more valuable than the standard liability, you may purchase "excess valuation" coverage from the airline, up to $5,000. Be sure to take any valuables or irreplaceable items with you in your carry-on luggage. If you file a lost luggage claim, be prepared to answer detailed questions about the contents of your baggage, and be sure to file a claim immediately, as most airlines enforce a 21-day deadline. Before you leave home, compile an inventory of all packed items and a rough estimate of the total value to ensure you're properly compensated if your luggage is lost. You will only be reimbursed for what you lost, no more. Once you've filed a complaint, persist in securing your reimbursement; there are no laws governing the length of time it takes for a carrier to reimburse you. If you arrive at a destination without your bags, ask the airline to forward them to your hotel or to your next destination; they will usually comply. If your bag is delayed or lost, the airline may reimburse you for reasonable expenses, such as a toothbrush or a set of clothes, but the airline is under no legal obligation to do so.

Lost luggage may also be covered by your homeowner's or renter's policy. Many platinum and gold credit cards cover you as well. If you choose to purchase additional lost-luggage insurance, be sure not to buy more than you need. Buy in advance from the insurer or a trusted agent (prices will be much higher at the airport).

THE HEALTHY TRAVELER

All of Norway is viewed as a "safe" destination, although problems, of course, can and do occur anywhere. You don't need to get shots, most foodstuff is safe, and the water in cities and towns potable. If you're concerned, order bottled water. It is easy to get a prescription filled in towns and cities, and nearly all hospitals have English-speaking doctors and well-trained medical staffs.

WHAT TO DO IF YOU GET SICK AWAY FROM HOME

If you get sick, consider asking your hotel concierge to recommend a local doctor—even his or her own. You can also try the emergency room at a local hospital; many have walk-in clinics for emergency cases that are not life threatening.

If you worry about getting sick away from home, consider purchasing **medical travel insurance** and carry your ID card in your purse or wallet. In most cases, your existing health plan will provide the coverage you need. See the section on insurance earlier in this chapter for more information.

If you suffer from a chronic illness, consult your doctor before your departure. For conditions like epilepsy, diabetes, or heart problems, wear a **Medic Alert Identification Tag** (© 800/825-3785; www.medicalert.org), which will immediately alert doctors to your condition and give them access to your records through Medic Alert's 24-hour hot line.

Pack **prescription medications** in your carry-on luggage, and carry prescription medications in their original containers. Also bring along copies of your prescriptions in case you lose your pills or run out. Carry the generic name of prescription medicines, in case a local pharmacist is unfamiliar with the brand name.

7 Tips for Travelers with Special Needs

FOR TRAVELERS WITH DISABILITIES

Norway has been in the vanguard of providing services for people with disabilities. In general, trains, airlines, ferries, and department stores and malls are accessible. For information about wheelchair access, ferry and air travel, parking, and other matters, contact the Norwegian Tourist Board (see "Visitor Information," earlier in this chapter).

The **Norwegian Association of the Disabled,** Schweigaardsgt #12, 9217 Grænland, 0312 Oslo (© 22-17-02-55; www.nhf.no), provides useful information.

If you're flying around Norway or Europe in general, the airline and ground staff can help you on and off planes and reserve seats with enough legroom, but you must arrange for this assistance *in advance* through the airline.

AGENCIES/OPERATORS

- **Flying Wheels Travel** (© 507/451-5005; www.flyingwheels travel.com) offers escorted tours and cruises that emphasize sports and private tours in minivans with lifts.
- **Access Adventures** (© 716/889-9096), a Rochester, New York–based agency, offers customized itineraries for a variety of travelers with disabilities.
- **Accessible Journeys** (© 800/TINGLES or 610/521-0339; www.disabilitytravel.com) caters specifically to slow walkers and wheelchair travelers and their families and friends.

ORGANIZATIONS

- **The Moss Rehab Hospital** (© 215/456-5882; www.moss resourcenet.org) provides helpful phone assistance through its **Travel Information Service.**
- **The Society for Accessible Travel and Hospitality** (© 212/447-7284; fax 212/725-8253; www. sath.org) offers a wealth of travel resources for all types of disabilities and informed recommendations on destinations, access guides, travel agents, tour operators, vehicle rentals, and companion services. Annual membership costs $45 for adults; $30 for seniors and students.
- **The American Foundation for the Blind** (© 800/232-5463; www.afb.org) provides information on traveling with Seeing Eye dogs.

PUBLICATIONS

- **Mobility International USA** (© 541/343-1284; www.miusa. org) publishes *A World of Options*, a 658-page book of resources, covering everything from biking trips to scuba outfitters, and a biannual newsletter, *Over the Rainbow.* Annual membership is $35.
- **Twin Peaks Press** (© 360/694-2462) publishes travel-related books for travelers with special needs.
- *Open World for Disability and Mature Travel* magazine, published by the Society for Accessible Travel and Hospitality (see above), is full of good resources and information. A year's subscription is $14 ($21 outside the U.S.).

FOR BRITISH TRAVELERS

The **Royal Association for Disability and Rehabilitation (RADAR),** Unit 12, City Forum, 250 City Rd., London EC1V 8AF (© 020/7250-3222; www.radar.org.uk), publishes three holiday "fact packs" for £2 each or £5 for all three. The first provides general information, including tips for planning and booking a holiday, obtaining insurance, and handling finances; the second outlines transportation available when going abroad and equipment for rent; the third deals with specialized accommodations.

FOR GAY & LESBIAN TRAVELERS

As one of the most sophisticated countries on the planet, Norway is one of the most gay-friendly countries in the world. Most Norwegians are tolerant of the lifestyles of others, and that spills over into sexual preference. Obviously an urban center such as Oslo will have a more openly gay life than rural areas.

In Norway, gays and lesbians have the same legal status as heterosexuals, with the exception of adoption rights. Legislation passed in 1981 protects gays and lesbians from discrimination. In 1993, a law was passed recognizing the "partnerships" of homosexual couples—in essence, a recognition of same-sex marriages. The age of consent for both men and women in Norway is 16 years of age.

For more information, call **Gay/Lesbian Visitor Information,** St.

Olavs Plass 2, N-0165 Oslo (✆ 22-11-05-09). An English-speaking representative will give you up-to-date information on gay and lesbian life in Oslo and let you know which clubs are currently in vogue.

The International Gay & Lesbian Travel Association (IGLTA; ✆ 800/448-8550 or 954/776-2626; fax 954/776-3303; www.iglta.org) links travelers with gay-friendly hoteliers, tour operators, and airlines. It offers monthly newsletters, marketing mailings, and a membership directory that's updated once a year. Membership is $200 yearly, plus a $100 administration fee for new members.

AGENCIES/OPERATORS

- **Above and Beyond Tours** (✆ 800/397-2681; www.above beyondtours.com) offers gay and lesbian tours worldwide and is the exclusive gay and lesbian tour operator for United Airlines.
- **Now, Voyager** (✆ 800/255-6951; www.nowvoyager.com) is a San Francisco–based gay-owned and -operated travel service.
- **Olivia Cruises & Resorts** (✆ 800/631-6277 or 510/655-0364; http://olivia.com) charters entire resorts and ships for exclusive lesbian vacations all over the world.

PUBLICATIONS

- *Frommer's Gay & Lesbian Europe* is an excellent travel resource.
- *Out and About* (✆ 800/929-2268 or 415/644-8044; www.out andabout.com) offers guidebooks and a newsletter 10 times a year ($49) packed with solid information on the global gay and lesbian scene.
- *Spartacus International Gay Guide* and *Odysseus* are good English-language guidebooks focused on gay men, with some information for lesbians. You can

get them from most gay and lesbian bookstores, or order them from **Giovanni's Room** bookstore, 1145 Pine St., Philadelphia, PA 19107 (✆ 215/923-2960; www.giovannisroom.com).

- *Gay Travel A to Z: The World of Gay & Lesbian Travel Options at Your Fingertips,* by Marianne Ferrari (Ferrari Publications), is a very good gay and lesbian guidebook series.

SENIOR TRAVEL

Mention the fact that you're a senior citizen when you first make your travel reservations. All major airlines and many Norwegian hotels offer discounts for seniors.

In Norway, people over age 67 are entitled to 50% off the price of first- and second-class train tickets. Ask for the discount at the ticket office.

Members of **AARP** (formerly known as the American Association of Retired Persons), 601 E St. NW, Washington, DC 20049 (✆ 800/424-3410 or 202/434-2277; www. aarp.org), gets discounts on hotels, airfares, and car rentals, worldwide. AARP offers members a wide range of benefits, including *Modern Maturity* magazine and a monthly newsletter. Anyone over 50 can join.

Alliance for Retired Americans, 888 16th St. NW, Washington, DC 20006 (✆ 888/373-6497 or 202/974-8256; www.retiredamericans. org), offers a newsletter six times a year and discounts on hotel and auto rentals; annual dues are $10 per person or couple. *Note:* Members of the former National Council of Senior Citizens receive automatic membership in the Alliance.

AGENCIES/OPERATORS

- **Grand Circle Travel** (✆ 800/221-2610 or 617/350-7500; www. gct.com) offers package deals for the 50-plus market, mostly of the tour-bus variety, with free trips

People to People: Reaching Out

Established in 1971, **Friends Overseas** matches American visitors and Norwegians with similar interests and backgrounds. Names and addresses are given to each applicant, and letters must be written before the visitors depart. For more information, write to Friends Overseas, 68–04 Dartmouth St., Forest Hills, NY 11375 (℗ 718/544-5660 after 5pm Eastern Standard Time; www.nordbalt.com). Send a self-addressed, stamped, business-size envelope, and include your age, occupation or occupational goals, approximate dates of your visit, and names of your traveling companions. The fee is $25.

thrown in for those who organize groups of 10 or more.

- **SAGA Holidays** (℗ **800/343-0273;** www.sagaholidays.com) offers inclusive tours and cruises for those 50 and older. SAGA also offers a number of single-traveler tours. Order a free brochure from the website.

- **Elderhostel** (℗ **877/426-8056;** www.elderhostel.org) arranges study programs for those aged 55 and over (and a spouse or companion of any age) around the world, including Scandinavia. Most courses last 5 to 7 days in the U.S. (2–4 weeks abroad), and many include airfare, accommodations in university dormitories or modest inns, meals, and tuition.

- **Interhostel** (℗ **800/733-9753;** www.learn.unh.edu), organized by the University of New Hampshire, also offers educational travel for senior citizens. On these escorted tours, the days are packed with seminars, lectures, and field trips, with sightseeing led by academic experts. Interhostel takes travelers 50 and over (with companions over 40), and offers 1- and 2-week trips, mostly international.

PUBLICATIONS

- *The Book of Deals* is a collection of more than 1,000 senior discounts on airlines, lodging, tours, and attractions around the country; it's available for $9.95 by calling ℗ **800/460-6676.**

- *101 Tips for the Mature Traveler* is available from Grand Circle Travel (℗ **800/221-2610** or 617/350-7500; fax 617/346-6700).

- *Unbelievably Good Deals and Great Adventures That You Absolutely Can't Get Unless You're Over 50* (Contemporary Publishing Co.).

STUDENT TRAVEL

If you're planning to travel outside the U.S., you'd be wise to arm yourself with an **international student ID card,** which offers substantial savings on rail passes, plane tickets, and entrance fees. It also provides you with basic health and life insurance and a 24-hour help line. The card is available for $22 from the **Council on International Educational Exchange,** or CIEE (www.ciee.org). **STA Travel** (℗ **800/781-4040;** www.statravel.com) is a travel agency catering especially to young travelers, although their bargain-basement prices are available to people of all ages.

In Canada, **Travel Cuts** (℗ **800/667-2887** or 905/361-2022; www.travelcuts.com), offers similar services. In London, **Usit Campus** (℗ **0870/240-1010;** www.usiworld.com), opposite Victoria Station, is

Britain's leading specialist in student and youth travel.

FAMILY TRAVEL

The family vacation is a rite of passage for many households, one that in a split second can devolve into a *National Lampoon* farce. But as any veteran family vacationer will assure you, a family trip can be among the most pleasurable and rewarding times of your life.

Most Norwegian hoteliers will let children 12 and under stay in a room with their parents for free; others do not. Sometimes this requires a little negotiation at the reception desk.

At attractions, and even if it isn't specifically posted, inquire if a kids' discount is available.

Throughout this guide, look for the kid-friendly icons that point out those businesses that are particularly welcoming to families.

AGENCIES/OPERATORS

Familyhostel (© **800/733-9753;** www.learn.unh.edu) takes the whole family on moderately priced domestic and international learning vacations. All trip details are handled by the program staff, and lectures, field trips, and sightseeing are guided by a team of academics. For kids ages 8 to 15 accompanied by their parents and/or grandparents.

PUBLICATIONS

- *How to Take Great Trips with Your Kids* (The Harvard Common Press) is full of good general advice that can apply to travel anywhere, including Norway.

WEBSITES

- **Family Travel Network** (www. familytravelnetwork.com) offers travel tips and reviews of family-friendly destinations, vacation deals, and thoughtful features such as "What to Do When Your Kids Are Afraid to Travel."
- **Travel with Your Children** (www. travelwithyourkids.com) is a comprehensive site offering sound advice for traveling with children.

Tips   What You Can Carry On—And What You Can't

The **Transportation Security Administration (TSA)**, the government agency that now handles all aspects of airport security, has devised new restrictions for carry-on baggage, not only to expedite the screening process but to prevent potential weapons from passing through airport security. Passengers are now limited to bringing just one carry-on bag and one personal item onto the aircraft (previous regulations allowed two carry-on bags and one personal item, like a briefcase or a purse). For more information, go to the TSA's website, www.tsa.gov. The agency has released an updated list of items passengers are not allowed to carry onto an aircraft:

Not permitted: knives and box cutters, corkscrews, straight razors, metal scissors, golf clubs, baseball bats, pool cues, hockey sticks, ski poles, ice picks.

Permitted: nail clippers, nail files, tweezers, eyelash curlers, safety razors (including disposable razors), syringes (with documented proof of medical need), walking canes and umbrellas (must be inspected first).

The airline you fly may have **additional restrictions** on items you can and cannot carry on board. Call ahead to avoid problems.

Tips **All About E-Ticketing**

Only yesterday **electronic tickets (E-tickets)** were the fast and easy ticket-free alternative to paper tickets. E-tickets allowed passengers to avoid long lines at airport check-in, all the while saving the airlines money on postage and labor. With the increased security measures in airports, however, an E-ticket no longer guarantees an accelerated check-in. You often can't go straight to the boarding gate, even if you have no bags to check. You'll probably need to show your printed E-ticket receipt or confirmation of purchase, as well as a photo ID, and sometimes even the credit card with which you purchased your E-ticket. That said, buying an E-ticket is still a fast, convenient way to book a flight; instead of having to wait for a paper ticket to come through the mail, you can book your fare by phone or on the computer, and the airline will immediately confirm by fax or e-mail. In addition, airlines often offer frequent flier miles as incentive for electronic bookings.

- **The Busy Person's Guide to Travel with Children** (http://wz.com/travel/TravelingWith Children.html) offers a "45-second newsletter" where experts weigh in on the best websites and resources for tips for traveling with children.

8 Getting There

BY PLANE

All transatlantic flights from North America land at Oslo's Fornebu Airport. **SAS** (☏ **800/221-2350** in the U.S.; www.scandinavia.net) flies nonstop daily from Newark to Oslo. The trip takes about 7½ hours. Most other SAS flights from North America go through Copenhagen. Flying time from Chicago is 10¾ hours; from Seattle, 11¾ hours, not including the layover in Copenhagen.

Transatlantic passengers on SAS are occasionally allowed to transfer to a Norwegian domestic flight from Oslo to Bergen for no additional charge.

If you fly to Norway on another airline, you'll be routed through a gateway city in Europe, and sometimes continue on a different airline. **British Airways** (☏ **800/AIRWAYS** in the U.S.), for example, has dozens of daily flights from many North American cities to London, and you can continue to Oslo. **Icelandair** (☏ **800/223-5500** in the U.S.; www.icelandair.com) can be an excellent choice, with connections through Reykjavik. **KLM** (☏ **800/347-7747** in the U.S.; www.nwa.com) serves Oslo through Amsterdam.

For passengers from the U.K., **British Airways** (☏ **08457/733-377** in London) operates at least four daily nonstops to Oslo from London. **SAS** (☏ **020/8990-7159** in London) runs four daily flights from Heathrow to Oslo. Flying time from London to Oslo on any airline is around 2 hours.

Summer (generally June–Sept) is the peak season and the most expensive. Norway's off-season is winter (about Nov 1–Mar 21). Shoulder season (spring and fall) is in between. In any season, midweek fares (Mon–Thurs) are lowest.

REGULAR AIRFARES & APEX FARES

Regular airfares include, in order of increasing price, economy, business class, and first class. These tickets carry no restrictions. In economy you pay for drinks, and the seats are not spacious; in business, the drinks are free, and the seats are wider; in first class, amenities and services are the best.

Currently the most popular discount fare is the **APEX** (advance-purchase excursion), which usually carries restrictions—advance-purchase requirements, minimum or maximum stays—and cancellation or change-of-date penalties.

In addition, airlines often offer **promotional discount fares.** Always check the travel sections of your local newspapers for such advertisements.

NEW AIR TRAVEL SECURITY MEASURES

In the wake of the terrorist attacks of September 11, 2001, the airline industry began implementing sweeping security measures in airports. Expect a lengthy check-in process and extensive delays. Although regulations vary from airline to airline, you can expedite the process by taking the following steps:

- **Arrive early.** Arrive at the airport at least 2 hours before your scheduled flight.
- **Try not to drive your car to the airport.** Parking and curbside access to the terminal may be limited. Call ahead and check.
- **Don't count on curbside check-in.** Some airlines and airports have stopped curbside check-in altogether, whereas others offer it on a limited basis. For up-to-date information on specific regulations and implementations, check with the individual airline.
- **Be sure to carry plenty of documentation.** A government-issued photo ID (federal, state, or local) is now required. You may need to show this at various checkpoints. With an E-ticket, you may be required to have with you printed confirmation of purchase, and perhaps even the credit card with which you bought your ticket (see "All About E-Ticketing," above). This varies from airline to airline, so call ahead to make sure you have the proper documentation. And be sure that your ID is **up-to-date;** an expired driver's license, for example, may keep you from boarding the plane altogether.
- **Know what you can carry on— and what you can't.** Travelers in the United States are now limited to one carry-on bag, plus one personal bag (such as a purse or a briefcase). The Transportation Security Administration has also issued a list of newly restricted carry-on items; see the box "What You Can Carry On—And What You Can't."
- **Prepare to be searched.** Expect spot-checks. Electronic items, such as a laptop or cellphone, should be readied for additional screening. Limit the metal items you wear on your person.
- **It's no joke.** When a check-in agent asks if someone other than you packed your bag, don't decide that this is the time to be funny. The agents will not hesitate to call an alarm.
- **No ticket, no gate access.** Only ticketed passengers will be allowed beyond the screener checkpoints, except for those people with specific medical or parental needs.

FLYING FOR LESS: TIPS FOR GETTING THE BEST AIRFARE

Passengers within the same airplane cabin are rarely paying the same fare. Business travelers who need to purchase tickets at the last minute, change their itinerary at a moment's notice, or

---

> ## Tips Canceled Plans
>
> If your flight is canceled, don't book a new fare at the ticket counter. Find the nearest phone and call the airline directly to reschedule. You'll be relaxing while other passengers are still standing in line.

---

get home for the weekend pay the premium rate. Passengers who can book their ticket long in advance, who can stay over Saturday night, or who are willing to travel on a Tuesday, Wednesday, or Thursday after 7pm, will pay a fraction of the full fare. Here are a few other easy ways to save.

- **Take advantage of APEX fares.** Advance-purchase booking, or APEX, fares are often the key to getting the lowest fare. You generally must be willing to make your plans and buy your tickets as far ahead as possible: The **21-day APEX** is seconded only by the **14-day APEX,** with a stay in Norway of 7 to 30 days. Because the number of seats allocated to APEX fares is sometimes less than 25% of plane capacity, the early bird gets the low-cost seat. There's often a surcharge for flying on a weekend, and cancellation and refund policies can be strict.

- **Watch for sales.** You'll almost never see sales during July and August or the Thanksgiving or Christmas seasons, but at other times you can get great deals. If you already hold a ticket when a sale breaks, it might pay to exchange it, even if you incur a $50 to $75 penalty charge. Note, however, that the lowest-priced fares are often nonrefundable, require advance purchase of 1 to 3 weeks and a certain length of stay, and carry penalties for changing dates of travel. Make sure you know exactly what the restrictions are before you commit.

- If your schedule is flexible, ask if you can secure a cheaper fare by staying an extra day or by flying midweek. (Many airlines won't volunteer this information.)

- **Consolidators,** also known as bucket shops, are a good place to find low fares, often below even the airlines' discounted rates. Basically, they're just big travel agents who get discounts for buying in bulk and pass some of the savings on to you. Before you pay, however, be aware that consolidator tickets are usually nonrefundable or come with stiff cancellation penalties.

  STA Travel (✆ 800/781-4040; www.statravel.com) caters especially to young travelers, but their bargain-basement prices are available to people of all ages. Other reliable consolidators include **FlyCheap.com** (✆ 800/FLY-CHEAP;** www.1800flycheap.com) and **TFI Tours International** (✆ 800/745-8000 or 212/736-1140; www.lowestairprice.com).

- Join a travel club such as **Moment's Notice** (✆ 718/234-6295; www. moments-notice.com) or **Sears Discount Travel Club** (✆ 800/433-9383,** or 800/255-1487 to join; www.travelersadvantage.com), which supply unsold tickets at discounted prices. You pay an annual membership fee to get the club's hot line number. Of course, you're limited to what's available, so you have to be flexible.

- Join **frequent-flier clubs.** It's best to accrue miles on one program, so you can rack up free flights and achieve elite status faster. But it makes sense to open as many accounts as possible, no matter how seldom you fly a particular airline.

- Search the **Internet** for cheap fares—though it's still best to compare your findings with the research of a dedicated travel agent, if you're lucky enough to have one, especially when you're booking more than just a flight. Among the better-respected virtual travel agents are **Frommers. com, Travelocity.com, Expedia. com,** and **Orbitz.com.** See "Planning Your Trip Online," later in this chapter, for more details.

A NOTE FOR BRITISH TRAVELERS

Because regular airfares from the U.K. to Norway tend to be high, savvy Brits usually call a travel agent for a "deal"—a charter flight or special promotion. These so-called deals are often available because of Norway's popularity as a tourist destination. If you can't get a deal, the next-best choice is an APEX ticket. Although these tickets must be reserved in advance, they offer a discount without the usual booking restrictions. You could also inquire about a "Eurobudget ticket," which carries restrictions or length-of-stay requirements.

British newspapers typically carry lots of classified advertisements touting "slashed" fares from London to other parts of the world. One good source is *Time Out,* a magazine published in London. London's *Evening Standard* has a daily travel section, and the Sunday editions of almost all British newspapers run ads. Although competition is fierce, one well-recommended company that consolidates bulk ticket purchases and passes the savings on to its customers is **Trailfinders** (© 020/ 7937-5400 in London; www.trail finder.com). It offers tickets on such carriers as SAS, British Airways, and KLM. You can fly from London's Heathrow or Gatwick airport to Oslo.

In London, many bucket shops around Victoria Station and Earl's Court offer low fares. Make sure the company you deal with is a member of the IATA, ABTA, or ATOL. These umbrella organizations will help you if anything goes wrong.

CEEFAX, a television information service carried on many home and hotel TVs, runs details of package holidays and flights to Europe and beyond. On your CEEFAX channel, you'll find a menu of listings that includes travel information.

BY CAR

If you're driving from the Continent, you must go through Sweden. From **Copenhagen,** take the E47/55 express highway north to Helsingør and catch the car ferry to Helsingborg, Sweden. From there, E6 runs to Oslo. From **Stockholm,** drive across Sweden on E18 to Oslo.

BY TRAIN

Copenhagen is the main rail hub for service between Scandinavia and the rest of Europe. There are three daily trains from Copenhagen to Oslo. All connect with the Danish ferries operating either to Norway through Helsingør or Hirtshals.

Most rail traffic from Sweden into Norway follows the main corridors between Stockholm and Oslo and between Gothenburg and Oslo.

If you plan to travel a great deal on Norwegian railroads, it's worth securing a copy of the *Thomas Cook European Timetable of European Passenger Railroads.* It's available exclusively in North America from **Forsyth Travel Library,** 44 S. Broadway, White Plains, NY 10601 (© **800/FORSYTH**), for $28, plus shipping.

Thousands of trains run from Britain to the Continent, and at least some of them go directly across or under the Channel, through France or Belgium and Germany into Denmark where connections can be made to Norway. For example, a train leaves London's Victoria Station daily at 9am and arrives in Copenhagen the next day at 8:25am. Another train leaves London's Victoria Station at 8:45pm and arrives in Copenhagen the next day at 8:20pm. Both go through Dover-Ostende, or with a connection at Brussels. Once you're in Copenhagen, you can make rail connections to Oslo. Because of the time and distances involved, many passengers rent a couchette (sleeping berth), which costs around £18 per person. Designed like padded benches stacked bunk-style, they're usually clustered six to a compartment.

RAIL PASSES FOR NORTH AMERICAN TRAVELERS

EURAILPASS If you plan to travel extensively in Norway, the **Eurailpass** may be a good bet. It's valid for first-class rail travel in 17 European countries. With one ticket, you travel whenever and wherever you please; more than 100,000 rail miles are at your disposal. Here's how it works: The pass is sold only in North America. A Eurailpass good for 15 days costs $588, a pass for 21 days is $762, a 1-month pass costs $946, a 2-month pass is $1,338, and a 3-month pass goes for $1,654. Children under 4 travel free if they don't occupy a seat; all children under 12 who take up a seat are charged half price. If you're under 26, you can buy a **Eurail Youthpass,** which entitles you to unlimited second-class travel for 15 days ($414), 21 days ($534), 1 month ($664), 2 months ($938) or 3 months ($1,160). Travelers considering buying a 15-day or 1-month pass should estimate rail distance before deciding whether a pass is worthwhile. To take full advantage of the tickets for 15 days or a month, you'd have to spend a great deal of time on the train. Eurailpass holders are entitled to substantial discounts on certain buses and ferries as well. Travel agents in all towns and railway agents in such major cities as New York, Montréal, and Los Angeles, sell all of these tickets. For information on Eurailpasses, and other European train data, call RailEurope at © **800/ 438-7245,** or visit them on the Web at **www.raileurope.com**.

Eurail Saverpass offers 15% discounts to groups of three or more people traveling together between April and September, or two people traveling together between October and March. The price of a Saverpass, valid all over Europe for first class only, is $498 for 15 days, $648 for 21 days, $804 for 1 month, $1,138 for 2 months, and $1,408 for 3 months. Even more freedom is offered by the **Saver Flexipass,** which is similar to the Eurail Saverpass, except that you are not confined to consecutive-day travel. For travel over any 10 days within 2 months, the fare is $592; any 15 days over 2 months, the fare is $778.

Eurail Flexipass allows even greater flexibility. It's valid in first class and offers the same privileges as the Eurailpass. However, it provides a number of individual travel days over a much longer period of consecutive days. Using this pass makes it possible to stay longer in one city and not lose a single day of travel. There are two Flexipasses: 10 days of travel within 2 months for $694, and 15 days of travel within 2 months for $914.

With many of the same qualifications and restrictions as the Eurail Flexipass, the **Eurail Youth Flexipass** is sold only to travelers under age 25. It allows 10 days of travel within 2 months for $488 and 15 days of travel within 2 months for $642.

SCANRAIL PASS If your visit to Europe will be primarily in Norway, the Scanrail pass may be better and cheaper than the Eurailpass. This pass allows its owner a designated number of days of free rail travel within a larger time block. (Presumably, this allows for days devoted to sightseeing scattered among days of rail transfers between cities or sites of interest.) You can choose a total of any 5 days of unlimited rail travel during a 15-day period, 10 days of rail travel within a 1-month period, or 1 month of unlimited rail travel. The pass, which is valid on all lines of the state railways of Denmark, Finland, Norway, and Sweden, offers discounts or free travel on some (but not all) of the region's ferry lines as well. The pass can be purchased only in North America. It's available from any office of **RailEurope** (© **800/848-7245** in the U.S., or 800/361-RAIL in Canada) or **ScanAm World Tours,** 108 N. Main St., Cranbury, NJ 08512 (© **800/ 545-2204;** www.scandinaviantravel. com).

Depending on whether you choose first- or second-class rail transport, 5 days out of 2 months ranges from $214 to $290, 10 days out of 2 months ranges from $288 to $388, and 21 consecutive days of unlimited travel ranges from $332 to $448. Seniors get an 11% discount; students a 25% discount.

RAIL PASSES FOR BRITISH TRAVELERS

If you plan to do a lot of exploring, you may prefer one of the three rail passes designed for unlimited train travel within a designated region during a predetermined number of days. These passes are sold in Britain and several other European countries.

An **InterRail Pass** is available to passengers of any nationality, with some restrictions—they must be under age 26 and able to prove residency in a European or North African country (Morocco, Algeria, and Tunisia) for at least 6 months before buying the pass. It allows unlimited travel through Europe, except Albania and the republics of the former Soviet Union. Prices are complicated and

vary depending on the countries you want to include. For pricing purposes, Europe is divided into eight zones; the cost depends on the number of zones you include. The most expensive option (£249) allows 1 month of unlimited travel in all eight zones and is known to BritRail staff as a "global." The least expensive option (£119) allows 12 days of travel within only one zone.

Passengers age 25 and older can buy an **InterRail 26-Plus Pass,** which, unfortunately, is severely limited geographically. Many countries—including France, Belgium, Switzerland, Spain, Portugal, and Italy—do not honor this pass. It is, however, accepted for travel throughout Norway. Second-class travel with the pass costs £169 for 12 days or £209 for 22 days. Passengers must meet the same residency requirements that apply to the InterRail Pass (described above).

For information on buying individual rail tickets or any of the just-mentioned passes, contact **National Rail Inquiries,** Victoria Station, London (© **08705/848-848** or 0845/748-4950). Tickets and passes also are available at any of the larger railway stations as well as selected travel agencies throughout Britain and the rest of Europe.

BY SHIP & FERRY

FROM DENMARK The trip from Frederikshavn at the northern port of Jutland in Denmark to Oslo takes 11 hours. **Stena Line** (© **08705/ 707070**) for general reservations 24 hours operates the service.

FROM SWEDEN From Strømstad, Sweden, in the summer, the daily crossing to Sandefjord, Norway, takes 2½ hours. Bookings can be made through **Color Scandi Line,** Tollbugata 5, N-3210 Sandefjord (© **33-42-10-00**).

FROM ENGLAND The **Norwegian Coastal Voyages/Bergen Line,**

405 Fifth Ave., New York, NY 10022 (© **800/323-7436** in the U.S., or 212/319-1300; www.coastalvoyage. com), operates from Newcastle, England, to Stavanger and Bergen on the west coast of Norway.

BY CRUISE SHIP

Norway's fjords and mountain vistas are among the most spectacular panorama in the world. Many ship owners and cruise lines offer excursions along the Norwegian coast.

One of the most prominent lines is **Cunard** (© **800/528-6273** in the U.S. and Canada; www.cunard.com).

Readers using this guide in 2004 will be able to sail on 14-day cruises on the new Cunard flagship, *Queen Mary 2.* This new vessel re-creates the grandeur of those old queen liners, *Queen Mary* and *Queen Elizabeth,* but overall is more modern and larger. The 150,000-ton ship carries a total of 2,620 passengers.

Departing from Southampton, England, the ship calls at Oslo, Bergen, Trondheim, the offshore island of Spitzbergen, Stavanger, and the North Cape; en route it also stops at the most frequently visited fjords. Prices for the 5-day cruise include round-trip airfare to London on British Airways from 79 gateway cities throughout the world.

Cunard also maintains about half a dozen smaller ships; one of the most luxurious specializes in cruises through the Baltic Sea and along the coast of Norway. The 677-passenger *Caronia* offers cruises throughout the summer from Southampton, England, that travel as far north as Norway's North Cape and as far east as St. Petersburg, Russia. Cruises last 13 to 21 days and include round-trip airfare on British Airways from most cities along the eastern seaboard of North America. Transportation from the West Coast can be arranged for a reasonable supplement. Hotel or theater

packages in London or side trips to almost anywhere else in Europe can be arranged through Cunard and British Airways at favorable discounts.

The Bergen Line offers much less expensive cruises aboard steamer ships that also carry mail and supplies to fjord communities. For more information, see "By Coastal Steamer" in section 10, "Getting Around," below.

PACKAGE TOURS

For travelers who feel more comfortable if everything is prearranged—hotels, transportation, sightseeing excursions, luggage handling, tips, taxes, and even meals—a package tour is the obvious choice, and it may even help save money.

FROM THE U.S.   One of the best tour operators to Norway is **Bennett Tours,** 342 Madison Ave., New York, NY 10073 (© **800/221-2420** in the U.S., or 212/697-1092), which offers land packages with experienced guides and a wide range of prices.

Other reliable tour operators include **Olson Travelworld,** 1145 Clark St., Stevens Point, WI 54481 (© **800/826-4026**), and **Scantours, Inc.,** 3439 Wade St., Los Angeles, CA 90006 (© **800/223-7226** or 310/636-4656; www.scantours.com).

For a vast array of other tours of Norway, many of them appealing to the active vacationer and special-interest traveler, refer to chapter 3, "The Active Vacation Planner."

FROM THE U.K.   The oldest travel agency in Britain, **Cox & Kings,** Gordon House 10, Greencoat Place, London SW1P 1PH (© **020/7873-5000**; www.coxandkings.co.uk), was established in 1758. Today the company specializes in unusual, if pricey, holidays. Its offerings in Norway include cruises through the spectacular fjords and waterways, bus and rail tours through sites of historic and aesthetic interest, and visits to the region's best-known handcraft centers, Viking burial sites, and historic churches. The company's staff is noted for its focus on tours of ecological and environmental interest.

9 Planning Your Trip Online

Researching and booking your trip online can save time and money. Then again, it may not. It is simply not true that you always get the best deal online. Most booking engines do not include schedules and prices for budget airlines, and from time to time you'll get a better last-minute price by calling the airline directly, so it's best to call the airline to see if you can do better before booking online.

On the plus side, Internet users today can tap into the same travel-planning databases that were once accessible only to travel agents—and do it at the same speed. Sites such as **From mers.com, Travelocity.com, Expedia. com,** and **Orbitz.com** allow consumers to comparison shop for airfares, access special bargains, book flights, and reserve hotel rooms and rental cars.

But don't fire your travel agent just yet. Though online booking sites offer tips and hard data to help you bargain shop, they cannot endow you with the hard-earned experience that makes a seasoned, reliable travel agent an invaluable resource, even in the Internet age. And for consumers with a complex itinerary, a trusty travel agent is still the best way to arrange the most direct flights to and from the best airports.

Some sites, such as Expedia.com, will send you **e-mail notification** when a cheap fare becomes available to your favorite destination. Some will also tell you when fares to a particular destination are lowest.

TRAVEL-PLANNING & BOOKING SITES

Keep in mind that because several airlines are no longer willing to pay commissions on tickets sold by online travel agencies, these agencies may either add a $10 surcharge to your bill if you book on that carrier—or neglect to offer those carriers' schedules.

The list of sites below is selective, not comprehensive. Some sites will have evolved or disappeared by the time you read this.

Travelocity (www.travelocity.com or www.frommers.travelocity.com) and **Expedia** (www.expedia.com) are among the most popular, offering an excellent range of options. Travelers search by destination, dates and cost.

Qixo (www.qixo.com) is another search engine that allows you to search for flights and accommodations from some 20 airline and travel-planning sites (such as Travelocity) at once. Qixo sorts results by price.

SMART E-SHOPPING

The savvy traveler is one armed with good information. Here are a few tips to help you navigate the Internet successfully and safely.

- **Know when sales start.** Last-minute deals may vanish in minutes. If you have a favorite booking site or airline, find out when last-minute deals are released to the public. (For example, Southwest's specials are posted every Tues at 12:01am Central Standard Time).
- **Shop around.** Compare results from different sites and airlines— and against a travel agent's best fare. If possible, try a range of times and alternate airports before making a purchase.
- **Follow the rules of the trade.** Book in advance, and choose an off-peak time and date if possible. Some sites will tell you when fares to a particular destination tend to be cheapest.

- **Stay secure.** Book only through secure sites (some airline sites are not secure). Look for a key icon (Netscape) or a padlock (Internet Explorer) at the bottom of your Web browser before you enter credit-card information or other personal data.
- **Avoid online auctions.** Sites that auction airline tickets and frequent-flier miles are the number-one perpetrators of Internet fraud, according to the National Consumers League.
- **Maintain a paper trail.** If you book an E-ticket, print out a confirmation or write down your confirmation number, and keep it safe and accessible—or your trip could be a virtual one!

ONLINE TRAVELER'S TOOLBOX

Veteran travelers usually carry some essential items to make their trips easier. Following is a selection of online tools to bookmark and use.

- **Visa ATM Locator** (www.visa.com) or **MasterCard ATM Locator** (www.mastercard.com). Find ATMs in hundreds of cities in the U.S. and around the world.
- **Foreign Languages for Travelers** (www.travlang.com). Learn basic terms in more than 70 languages and click on any underlined phrase to hear what it sounds like. *Note:* Free audio software and speakers required.
- **Intellicast** (www.intellicast.com). Weather forecasts for all 50 states and cities around the world. *Note:* Temperatures are in Celsius for many international destinations.
- **Mapquest** (www.mapquest.com). The best of the mapping sites, Mapquest lets you choose a specific address or destination, and in seconds, it returns a map and detailed directions.
- **Cybercafes.com** (www.cybercafes.com) or **Net Café Guide** (www.netcafeguide.com). Locate Internet cafes at locations around the globe. Catch up on your e-mail and log onto the Web for a few dollars per hour.
- **Universal Currency Converter** (www.xe.com). See what your dollar or pound is worth in more than 100 other countries.
- **U.S. State Department Travel Warnings** (www.travel.state.gov). Reports on places where health concerns or unrest may threaten U.S. travelers and lists the locations of U.S. embassies around the world.

10 Getting Around

BY PLANE

The best way to get around Norway is to take advantage of air passes that apply to the whole region. If you're traveling extensively, special European passes are available.

SAS'S VISIT SCANDINAVIA FARE

The vast distances encourage air travel between Norway's far-flung points. One of the most worthwhile promotions is SAS's **Visit Scandinavia Pass.** Available only to travelers who fly SAS across the Atlantic, it includes up to six coupons, each of which is valid for any SAS flight within or between Denmark, Norway, and Sweden. Each coupon costs $75, a price that's especially appealing when you consider that an economy-class ticket between Stockholm and Copenhagen can cost as much as $250 each way. The pass is especially valuable if you plan to travel to the far northern frontiers of Sweden or Norway; in that case, the savings over the price of a regular economy-class ticket can be substantial. For information on buying the pass, call **SAS** (✆ **800/221-2350**).

WITHIN NORWAY Norway has excellent air service. In addition to SAS, two independent airways, Braathens and Wideroe Flyveselskap, provide quick and convenient ways to get around a large country with many hard-to-reach areas. All three airlines offer reduced rates available when booked outside Norway, known as "minifares."

BRAATHENS In a new partnership with **SAS,** Braathens (© **67-12-20-70** in Oslo, or 55-23-55-23 in Bergen; www.braathens.no) carries more passengers on domestic routes than any other airline in Norway. It has regularly scheduled flights inside Norway, linking major cities as well as more remote places not covered by other airlines. Its air routes directly link Oslo with all major Norwegian cities; it also offers frequent flights along the coast, from Oslo to Tromsø and to Longyearbyen on the island of Spitsbergen.

You might also inquire about the **Northern Light Pass,** which provides discounts and is valid for 1 month between May and September. There are two sets of fares. Flights between airports in north Norway are short journeys, and the one-way fare for pass-holders is $84. Flights from south Norway to north Norway or vice versa count as long journeys, and the one-way fare is $155. The Visit Norway Pass is sold by airlines that have agreements with Braathens airlines. To buy one, call **Passage Tours of Scandinavia** (© **800/548-5960** in the U.S.) or **SAS** (© **800/221-2350** in the U.S.).

SAS Regularly scheduled domestic flights on SAS (© **800/221-2350** in the U.S., or 81-00-33-00 in Oslo) crisscross Norway. They connect Bergen, Oslo, Trondheim, and Bodø. SAS also flies to the Arctic gateway of Tromsø; to Alta in Finnmark, the heart of Lapland; and to Kirkenes, near the Russian border. Transatlantic SAS passengers might also consider SAS's Visit Scandinavia Fare (see above).

OTHER AIRLINES Linked to the SAS reservations network, **Wideroe** specializes in STOL (short takeoff and landing) aircraft. It services rarely visited fishing communities on offshore islands, isolated fjord communities, and destinations north of the Arctic Circle. For more information or tickets, contact SAS or local travel agents in Norway.

BY TRAIN

Norway's network of electric and diesel-electric trains runs as far as Bodø, 100km (62 miles) north of the Arctic Circle. (Beyond that, visitors must take a coastal steamer, plane, or bus to Tromsø and the North Cape.) Recently upgraded express trains (the fastest in the country) crisscross the mountainous terrain between Oslo, Stavanger, Bergen, and Trondheim.

The most popular, and the most scenic, run covers the 483km (300 miles) between Oslo and Bergen. Visitors with limited time often choose this route for its fabled mountains, gorges, white-water rivers, and fjords. The trains often stop for passengers to enjoy breathtaking views.

Second-class travel on Norwegian trains is recommended. In fact, second class in Norway is as good as or better than first-class travel anywhere else in Europe, with reclining seats and lots of unexpected comforts. The one-way second-class fare from Oslo to Bergen is 633NOK ($84), plus a mandatory seat reservation of 20NOK ($2.65). Another popular run, from Oslo to Trondheim, costs 707NOK ($94) one-way in second class.

One of the country's obviously scenic trips, from Bergen to Bodø, is not possible by train because of the terrain. Trains to Bodø leave from Oslo. Express trains are called *Expresstog,* and you have to read the fine print of a railway schedule to figure out whether an Expresstog is much faster than a conventional train.

On express and other major trains, you must reserve seats at the train's starting station. Sleepers are priced according to the number of berths in each compartment. Children 4 to 15 years of age and senior citizens pay 50% of the regular adult fare. Group and midweek tickets are also available.

There are special compartments for persons with disabilities on most medium- and long-distance trains. People in wheelchairs and others with physical handicaps, and their companions, may use the compartments. Some long-distance trains offer special playrooms ("Kiddie-Wagons") for children, complete with toys and educational items.

NORWAY RAIL PASS A restricted rail pass applicable only to the state railway lines, the Norway Rail Pass is available for 7 or 14 consecutive days of unlimited rail travel in 1 month, or any 3 days of travel within 1 month. It's suitable for anyone who wants to cover the long distances that separate Norwegian cities. The pass is available in North America through Rail Europe (✆ **800/848-7245** in the U.S., or 800/361-RAIL in Canada; www.rail europe.com). The costs are $190 for adults in first class or $146 in second class for any 3 days in 1 month; $236 in first class or $182 in second class for any 4 days in 1 month; and $264 in first class or $202 in second class for any 5 days in 1 month. Children 4 to 15 years of age pay half the adult fare. Those under 4 ride free.

OTHER SPECIAL TICKETS & DISCOUNTS With a **Miniprice Ticket** you can travel in second class for 360NOK ($48) one-way, but only on routes that take you more than 150km (93 miles) from your point of origin. No stopovers are allowed except for a change of trains. Tickets are valid only on selected trains, for boarding that begins during designated off-peak hours. You can buy Miniprice Tickets at any railway station in Norway.

Travelers over age 67 are entitled to a 50% discount, called an **Honnorrabatt,** on Norwegian train trips of more than 50km (31 miles). Regardless of age, the spouse of someone over 67 can also receive the 50% discount.

BY BUS

Where the train or coastal steamer stops, passengers can usually continue on a scenic bus ride. Norway's bus system is excellent, linking remote villages along the fjords. Numerous all-inclusive motor-coach tours, often combined with steamer travel, leave from Bergen and Oslo in the summer. The train ends in Bodø; from there you can get a bus to Fauske (63km/39 miles east). From Fauske, the Polar Express bus spans the entire distance along the Arctic Highway, through Finnmark (Lapland) to Kirkenes near the Russian border and back. The segment from Alta to Kirkenes is open only from June to October, but there's year-round service from Fauske to Alta. Passengers are guaranteed hotel accommodations along the way.

Buses have air-conditioning, toilets, adjustable seats, reading lights, and a telephone. Reservations are not accepted on most buses, and payment is made to the driver on board. Fares depend on the distance traveled. Children under 4 travel free, and children 4 to 16 and senior citizens pay half-price. For the Oslo-Sweden-Hammerfest "Express 2000," a 30-hour trip, reservations must be made in advance.

For more information about bus travel in Norway, contact **Norway Buss Ekspress AS,** Karl Johans Gate (✆ **81-54-44-44;** www.nor-way.no) in Oslo, or **Passage Tours of Scandinavia** (✆ **800/548-5960** in the U.S.).

If you plan extensive travels, the best bet is a **Norway Bus Pass** issued year-round by Norway Bus Ekspress

> ### Tips   Winter Motoring in Norway
>
> If you are going to drive in Norway in winter you must be prepared for the conditions. Most of the main roads are kept open by snowplows year-round, but the road surface will often be hard packed snow and ice. Journey times will be much longer than in summer, 50km (31 miles) per hour is a typical average, and in bad weather there can be long delays over mountain passes. Most Norwegians use winter tires with metal studs, which cope well in most conditions and any rented car will be equipped with these. Temperatures as low as 25°F (–3°C) are common. A good ice scraper and snow brush are essential, and diesel vehicles should use winter-grade fuel available in Norway.

on national routes. It's good for 7 or 14 days of consecutive travel, priced from 1,222NOK to 1,958NOK ($176–$282), respectively. Children 3 and under travel free, and ages 4 to 16 pay 75% of the adult price.

BY CAR & FERRY

Dazzling scenery awaits you at nearly every turn. Some roads are less than perfect (often dirt or gravel), but passable. Most mountain roads are open by May 1; the so-called motoring season lasts from mid-May to the end of September. In western Norway hairpin curves are common, but if you're willing to settle for doing less than 240km (about 150 miles) a day, you needn't worry. The easiest and most convenient touring territory is in and around Oslo and south to Stavanger. However, you can drive to the North Cape.

Bringing a car into Norway is relatively uncomplicated. If you own the car you're driving, you must present your national driver's license, car registration, and proof that the car is insured. (This proof usually takes the form of a document known as a "Green Card," which customs agents will refer to specifically.) If you've rented a car in another country and want to drive it into Norway, be sure to verify at the time of rental that the registration and insurance documents are in order—they probably will be. Regardless of whether you own or rent

the car you're about to drive into Norway, don't assume that your private North American insurance policy will automatically apply. Chances are good that it will, but in the event of an accident, you may have to cope with a burdensome amount of paperwork.

If you're driving through any of Norway's coastal areas, you'll probably have to traverse one or many of the country's famous fjords. Although more and more bridges are being built, Norway's network of privately run ferries is essential for transporting cars across hundreds of fjords and estuaries. Motorists should ask the tourist bureau for the free map "Norway by Car" and a timetable outlining the country's dozens of car ferry services. The cost for cars and passengers is low.

RENTALS   Avis, Budget, and Hertz offer well-serviced, well-maintained fleets of rental cars in Norway. Prices and terms tend to be more favorable for those who reserve vehicles in North America before their departure and who present evidence of membership in such organizations as AAA or AARP. The major competitors' prices tend to be roughly equivalent, except for promotional deals scheduled from time to time.

The prices quoted here include the 23% government tax. At **Budget** (© **800/472-3325** in the U.S. and Canada), the cheapest car is a cramped but peppy Volkswagen Polo that rents for $569 a week with unlimited mileage. **Hertz** (© **800/654-3001** in the U.S.) charges $584 a week, with unlimited mileage, for its VW Polo. **Avis** (© **800/331-1084** in the U.S.) charges around $594 for its cheapest car, a Nissan Micra. Despite pressure from the telephone sales representative, it pays to ask questions before you commit to a prepaid reservation. Each company maintains an office at the Oslo airport, in the center of Oslo, and at airports and city centers elsewhere around the country.

Note: Remember that prices and the relative merits of each company can and will change during the lifetime of this edition, depending on promotions and other factors.

An alternative to the big three companies is a small but reliable outfit called **Kemwel** (© **800/678-0678** in the U.S.). As part of a special promotion, Kemwel sometimes offers discounts to some SAS passengers.

INSURANCE Rates include nominal insurance coverage, which is probably enough for most drivers and most accidents. However, if you did not buy additional insurance and you have a mishap, your responsibility depends on the car-rental firm. At some companies, without additional insurance you might be held responsible for the car's full value. Obviously, you need to learn what your liability would be in case of an accident. To avoid this responsibility, you might want to get an additional insurance policy (a collision-damage waiver) for about $20 a day. We usually find that buying additional insurance is well worth the expense, considering the unfamiliar driving conditions.

Note that when certain credit or charge cards are used to pay for a car rental, no additional insurance purchases are necessary. Although many readers have taken advantage of this cost-saving approach, the fine print of these insurance options must be individually verified directly with the card issuer.

No matter what type of insurance you choose, remember that driving after having consumed even a small amount of alcohol is punishable by heavy fines, imprisonment, or both.

BY COASTAL STEAMER

The fjords of western Norway are among the most beautiful sights in Europe. For a seagoing view, nothing beats the indomitable steamer ships that carry mail, supplies, and passengers. If you have the time and enjoy an offbeat adventure, you can book a 12-day, all-inclusive round-trip steamer trip from Bergen to Kirkenes (one of the northernmost ports). It covers some 4,023km (2,500 miles) of jagged, scenic coastline.

Because of the long distances, steamers are equipped with cabins similar to those on a transatlantic liner. Depending on the accommodations and the time of year, cabins cost $981 to $1,340 per person, double occupancy, for the 12-day round-trip excursion. Because sailings in June, July, and August are the most expensive, many visitors choose a spring or autumn trip. All meals are included in the price. Children under 12 receive a 25% discount on round-trip voyages. During special periods, travelers over age 67 may be eligible for discounts. Steamers make scheduled stops in hamlets and cities along the way, ranging from half an hour to half a day. Passengers who prefer to spend more time in selected cities usually choose port-to-port tickets, for which children under 12 receive a special rate. Be warned, however, that booking cabins on a port-to-port basis from May to August is often extremely difficult because of the popularity of these cruises. Cruises are available even in winter—the Norwegian coast is famous for remaining ice-free all year.

For reservations and information, contact the **Norwegian Coastal Voyages/Bergen Line,** 405 Park Ave., New York, NY 10022 (© **800/323-7436** in the U.S., or 212/319-1300; www.coastalvoyage.com).

SUGGESTED ITINERARIES

If You Have 1 Week

Day 1 Fly to Oslo, check into your hotel, and relax. Few can fight jet lag on their first day in the Norwegian capital.

Day 2 After breakfast in Oslo, take the ferry to the Bygdøy peninsula to visit the *Kon-Tiki* Museum, the polar ship *Fram,* the Viking ships, and the Norwegian Folk Museum.

Day 3 In Oslo, visit Frogner Park to see the Vigeland sculptures and Edvard Munch paintings. You should have enough time to see the Henie-Onstad Foundation art center 11km (7 miles) from Oslo. Return in time to go to the Lookout Tower and ski jump at Holmenkollen, where you can dine and enjoy a panoramic view of Oslo.

Day 4 Head south for a day trip to some of the major towns along the Oslofjord. In the morning, drive to Fredrikstad on the Glomma River, and visit its Old Town as well as Norway Silver Designs, its handicraft center. Drive back to Moss and take a ferry across the fjord. From Horten on the west bank, drive south to Tønsberg, Norway's oldest town, and visit the Vestfold Folk Museum. Drive back to Oslo for dinner.

Day 5 Head west to Bergen by train on a 483km (300-mile) all-day trip. You go across the "rooftop of Norway," past the ski resorts of Geilo and Voss, before reaching Bergen.

Day 6 Explore Bergen's many attractions, such as Troldhaugen

(Trolls' Hill), the summer villa of composer Edvard Grieg.

Day 7 Visit Ulvik, on the Hardangerfjord in the western fjord district, reached by public transportation from Bergen. Spend the night in the beautiful town, which typifies the fjord towns in this district.

If You Have 2 Weeks

Week 1 See "If You Have 1 Week," above.

Day 8 In Ulvik (see "Day 7," above), continue exploring the fjord district.

Day 9 Return to Bergen, and then fly to Trondheim.

Day 10 If it's summer, take a 13-hour train ride from Trondheim to Bodø on the *Midnight Sun Special.* Spend the night in Bodø, north of the Arctic Circle.

Day 11 From Bodø, fly to Tromsø, 402km (250 miles) north of the Arctic Circle (it doesn't have rail service). Stay overnight in Tromsø and see its limited, but interesting, attractions.

Day 12 Rent a car in Tromsø and head north for the last leg of the trip: a 450km (280-mile) run over the Arctic Highway. Spend the night in Alta. Travel is slow, because the road wraps around inlets and fjords.

Day 13 Continue driving north to Hammerfest, the world's northernmost town of any significant size. Stay overnight.

Day 14 From Hammerfest, take an excursion boat directly to the North Cape. Those with more time can drive to Honningsvåg, the world's northernmost village and the gateway to the North Cape. Buses leave its marketplace daily for the cape, a 35km (22-mile) run.

Return to Tromsø, where air connections can be made to Oslo and your return flight to North America or elsewhere.

If You Have 3 Weeks

Day 1–4 Spend the first 4 days as described in "If You Have 1 Week," above.

Day 5 Explore Oslo in greater depth visiting Akershus Castle, with its Norwegian Resistance Museum, and the National Gallery. Take one of the walking tours mapped out for Oslo in chapter 5—two if you have the time and the stamina.

Day 6 Drive north from Oslo along the E6 to the ski resort of Lillehammer, site of the 1994 Winter Olympics. Stop for lunch at Gjøvik, "the white town on Lake Mjøsa," arriving in Lillehammer in time to view the Sandvig Collections. Either overnight in Lillehammer or return to Oslo.

Day 7 Leave either Oslo or Lillehammer by train, depending on where you spent the night, heading west for Bergen across the rooftop of Europe.

Day 8 Spend the day sightseeing Bergen, visiting Trolls' Hill (the summer villa of composer Edvard Grieg).

Day 9 Take a trip to the Hardangerfjord and the Folgefonn glacier. Bus trips depart from Bergen for this full-day tour.

Day 10 Board an express steamer from Bergen to Gudvangen to see the Sognefjord, the longest fjord in Norway. From Gudvangen, go by bus to Voss, a famous ski resort.

Day 11 Spend another day in Voss taking excursions and exploring the area.

Day 12 Return to Bergen for an overnight stay. Relax.

Day 13 From Bergen, go to Ålesund at the top of the fjord country and explore the town.

Day 14 While still in Ålesund, take a sightseeing tour for the day to Geiranger, one of the most famous resorts in the fjord country. Waterfalls are in and around the area. Return to Ålesund for the night.

Day 15 From Ålesund, make air connections to Trondheim, the third-largest city of Norway and a historic capital. Explore some of its attractions.

Day 16 Explore Trondheim fully and spend the night.

Day 17–21 Follow the schedule outlined for Days 10 to 14 listed in "If You Have 2 Weeks," above.

11 Tips on Accommodations

Hotel passes (see below) can save you big money. In addition, there are several imaginative lodging possibilities, other than hotels, that are not only workable but a lot of fun and a change of pace.

BOOKING A HOTEL The Norwegian Tourist Board does not provide a hotel booking service. Your local travel agency will be able to do this for you, or ask one of the tour operators. Alternatively, you can book accommodations directly by post, fax, or telephone. Practically everyone in Norway speaks English, and you will rarely encounter any difficulty. If traveling in the high season (mid-June to mid-Aug), it is advisable to book in advance. Information offices in Norway often have a reservation service. You can also make bookings at the website, www.visitnorway.com.

HOTEL PASSES In Norway you will find several passes, discount schemes, and check systems in operation that are valid at hotels and offer reduced prices. For further information contact your local travel agency or the following addresses:

Best Western euro Guestcheque, Best Western Hotels Norway (© 800/780-7234 in U.S. and Canada; www.bestwestern.no); **Norway Fjord Pass,** Fjord Tours AS, P.O. Box 1752 Nordnes, NO-5816 Bergen (© 55-55-76-60; fax 55-55-16-40; www.fjordpass.no); **Scan + Hotel Pass,** Norlandia Hotellene, P.O. box 6615 St. Olavs pl., NO-0129 Oslo (© 23-08-02-80; www.norlandia.no); **Scandic Club Card,** Scandic Booking Services (© 51-75-17-00; www.scandichotels.com); **Rica Hotellferie Pass,** Rica Hotels, Slependv. 108, NO-1375 Billingstad (© 66-85-45-60; www.rica.no); **Nordic Hotel Pass,** Choice Hotels ASA, P.O. Box 2454 Solli, NO-0201 Oslo (© 22-40-13-00; www.choice.no).

CHALET HOLIDAYS Norway offers one of the least expensive vacation bargains in all of Europe. Ideal for outdoors-loving families or groups, log-cabin chalets are available throughout the country, on the side of a mountain or by the sea, in a protected valley or woodland, or by a freshwater lake. Some lie in what is known as chalet colonies; others are set on remote and lofty peaks. At night, by paraffin lamplight or the glow of a log fire, you can enjoy aquavit or an early supper, as many Norwegians do. Some cabins are fully equipped with hot and cold running water, showers, and electricity; others are more primitive, evoking pioneer living. Naturally, the price of the rental varies according to the amenities, as well as the size (some with as many as three bedrooms, most with tiered bunks). The price range is 2,000NOK to 10,000NOK ($266–$1,330) weekly, the latter price for completely modern structures. There are chalets in most parts of the country—in the mountains, near lakes,

along the coast, and in the fjord country. For a catalog with prices, locations, and other data, write to **Novasol,** Postboks 309, Sentrum, N-0103 Oslo (© 81-54-42-70; www.novasol.com).

FISHERMEN'S CABINS In the Lofoten islands in Northern Norway, you can rent a traditional former fisherman's cabin, called a *rorbu.* The fishermen used to come to Lofoten from other parts of the coast for the winter cod-fishing season for January to April, and would make these cabins their temporary homes for the duration. Most have been modernized, and a number of them have their own shower and toilet. Nowadays you also find newly built fishermen's cabins too. Although most *rorbus* are in the Lofoten islands, you can rent these cabins all along the coast of Norway from north to south. The cabin is by the seashore with excellent fishing. Prices range between 400NOK and 1,500NOK ($53–$200) per night. Local regional tourist boards will supply you with further information. Additionally see websites at www.lofoten-rorbuferie.no or www.lofoten-info.no.

THE B&B WAY British-style bed-and-breakfasts are developing in Norway—all of a high standard. These are generally booked through the local tourist office upon arrival. You may find accommodation signs displayed along roads or directly outside houses, reading *Rom* or *Husrom.*

In larger towns private rooms are priced from 400NOK to 600NOK ($53–$80) for a double, breakfast included. A B&B guidebook for Norway titled *Bed & Breakfast Norway* has full details; copies are available in Norway at general bookshops. For more information contact **B&B Norway AS,** Østerdalsgt. 1 J, NO-0658 Oslo (© 22-67-30-80; fax 22-19-83-17; www.bbnorway.com).

FARM HOLIDAYS Farm holidays in Norway are many and varied. Farms all over the country offer accommodation, ranging from the western farms in the mountains, sometimes with impressive fjord views, to those in northern Norway facing the open sea. Guests usually stay in their own comfortable cabin or house, complete with kitchen facilities, in or near the farmyard. Some farms also provide breakfast. Many offer the opportunity to participate in various activities and aspects of daily life on a farm. The standards, activities, and prices vary a great deal. Farm holidays provide an excellent base for activities and experiences in an area. Contact the local tourist information office. More information is available on the Internet at www.visitnorway.com.

CAMPING Norway has more than 12,000 campsites, so you are sure to find somewhere to stay in the area you want to visit. The sites are classified one to five stars, depending on the standards, facilities, and activities available. There is no standard price and rates vary. Normally, the fixed charge per site for two to three stars is 80NOK to 160NOK ($11–$21), four to five stars is 120NOK to 300NOK ($16–$40), with additional charges per person.

Many campsites have cabins that can be booked in advance. Most cabins have electricity and heating, but note that you may need to bring bedding. Check when making your booking. Cabins are classified one to five stars depending on size and standard. Prices range from 250NOK to 750NOK ($33–$100).

The **Camping Card** (Norsk Campingkort) entitles you to a faster checking-in service along with special deals. The Camping Card can be ordered before traveling, from Norwegian Hospitality Association (Reiselivsbedriftenes Landsforening or RBL),

P.O. Box 5465, Majorstua, N-0305 Oslo (✆ **23-08-86-20;** fax 23-08-86-21; www.camping.no). The 1-year stamp can be purchased from participating campsites for 90NOK ($12). RBL also provides a camping guide with extensive information.

HOME STAYS **Friendship Force,** 34 Peachtree St. NW, Suite 900, Atlanta, GA 30303 (✆ **404/522-9490;** www.friendshipforce.org), is a nonprofit organization that encourages friendship among people worldwide. Dozens of branch offices throughout North American arrange visits, usually once a year. Because of group bookings, the airfare to the host country is usually less than the cost of individual APEX tickets. Each participant spends 2 weeks in the host country, one as a guest in the home of a family and the second traveling in the host country.

Servas, 11 St. John St., Suite 505, New York, NY 10038 (✆ **212/267-0252;** www.usservas.org), is an international nonprofit, nongovernmental, interfaith network of travelers and hosts whose goal is to help promote world peace, goodwill, and understanding. (Its name means "to serve" in Esperanto.) Servas hosts offer travelers hospitality for 2 days. Travelers pay a $65 annual fee and a $25 list deposit after filling out an application and being approved by an interviewer (interviewers are located across the U.S.). They then receive Servas directories listing the names and addresses of Servas hosts.

HOME EXCHANGES One of the most exciting breakthroughs in modern tourism is the home exchange. Sometimes the family automobile is included. Of course, you must be comfortable with the idea of having strangers in your home, and you must be content to spend your vacation in one place.

Home exchanges cut costs. You don't pay hotel bills, and you can also save money by shopping in markets and eating in. One potential problem, though, is that you may not get a home in the area you request.

Intervac, U.S., 30 Corte San Fernando, Tuburon, CA 94159 (*©* **800/ 756-HOME** or 415/435-3497; www. intervacus.com), is part of the largest worldwide exchange network. It publishes four catalogs a year, containing more than 10,000 homes in more than 36 countries. Members contact each other directly. The cost is $65 plus postage, which includes the purchase of three of the company's catalogs (which will be mailed to you), plus the inclusion of your own listing in whichever one of the three catalogs you select. If you want to publish a

photograph of your home, there is an additional charge of $11. Depending on your type of membership, fees begin at $87, going up to $148.

The Invented City, 41 Sutter St., Suite 1090, San Francisco, CA 94104 (*©* **800/788-CITY** or 415/252-1141; www.invented-city.com), publishes home-exchange listings three times a year. For the $75 membership fee, you can list your home with your own written descriptive summary.

Home Link, P.O. Box 47747, Tampa, FL 33647 (*©* **800/638-3841** or 813/975-9825; www.homelink. org), will send you five directories a year—in one of which you're listed— for $98.

12 Recommended Books

HISTORY & MYTHOLOGY *The Vikings,* by Johannes Brøndsted (Penguin), is one of the most enjoyable and best-written documents of the Age of the Vikings.

Quisling: A Study in Treason, by Oddvar K. Hoidal (Oxford University Press), studies the world's most famous traitor, Quisling, who was executed by the Norwegians for running the Nazi puppet government there.

Viking fans will not put down *The Vinland Sagas: The Norse Discovery of America,* translated by Magnus Magnusson and Hermann Palsson (Penguin), an incredible saga, detailing how Viking Norwegians sailed in their long ships to the eastern coast of "Vinland" (America) as early as the 10th century.

The Norwegians, by Arthur Spencer (David & Charles), is the best book on the market today for understanding the Norwegian people and their advanced society.

ADVENTURE *The Kon-Tiki Expedition,* by Thor Heyerdahl (Washington Square Press), made into a film,

details the saga of a modern Norwegian "Viking," who set out on a raft with five comrades and sailed 6,920km (4,300 miles) in 1947—all the way from Peru to Polynesia. *Kon-Tiki Man: An Illustrated Biography of Thor Heyerdahl,* by Thor Heyerdahl with Christopher Ralling (Chronicle), highlights Heyerdahl's attempt to document his idea that Polynesia was settled by people migrating west by water from South America rather than from Asia.

LITERATURE & THEATER *The Governor's Daughter,* by Camilla Collett (several editions), published in 1854, is called the first modern Norwegian novel.

Ibsen Plays: One to Six, by Henrik Ibsen (Heinemann Educational), presents the works of Norway's greatest playwright, including *A Doll's House* and *Hedda Gabler.*

The Ferry Crossing, by Edvard Hoem (Garland), a success in 1989, depicts a tiny Norwegian coastal village in an unorthodox story form.

 FAST FACTS: Norway

Area Code The international country code for Norway is **47**. If you're calling from outside the country, the city code is **2** for Oslo and **5** for Bergen. Inside Norway, no area or city codes are needed. Phone numbers have eight digits.

Business Hours Most **banks** are open Monday to Friday from 8:15am to 3:30pm (on Thurs to 5pm), and are closed Saturday and Sunday. The bank at Fornebu Airport is open daily from 7am to 10:30pm, and there's another bank at Gardermoen Airport, open Monday to Saturday from 6:30 am to 8pm, and Sunday from 7am to 8pm. Most **businesses** are open Monday to Friday from 9am to 4pm. **Stores** are generally open Monday to Friday from 9am to 5pm (many stay open on Thurs until 6 or 7pm) and Saturday 9am to 1 or 2pm. Sunday closings are observed.

Dentists For emergency dental services, ask your hotel or host for the nearest dentist. Most Norwegian dentists speak English.

Doctors If you become ill or injured while in Norway, your hotel can refer you to a local doctor, nearly all of whom speak English. If you don't stay at a hotel, call ✆ **113**, the national 24-hour emergency medical number.

Drugstores Drugstores, called *apotek,* are open during normal business hours.

Electricity Norway uses 220 volts, 30 to 50 cycles, AC, and standard continental two-pin plugs. Transformers and adapters will be needed with Canadian and American equipment. Always inquire at your hotel before plugging in any electrical equipment.

Embassies & Consulates In case you lose your passport or have some other emergency, contact your embassy in Oslo. The Embassy of the **United States** is at Drammensveien 18, N-0244 Oslo (✆ **22-44-85-50**); **United Kingdom,** Thomas Heftyes Gate 8, N-0244 Oslo (✆ **23-13-27-00**); and **Canada,** Wergelandsveien 7, N-0244 Oslo (✆ **22-99-53-00**). The **Irish Embassy** is at Haakon VII's gate 1, N-0161 Oslo (✆ **22-20-43-70**); the **Australian Embassy** at Jernbanetorget N-0244 Oslo (✆ **22-47-91-70**), and the **New Zealand Embassy,** Drammensveien 230, N-0212 (✆ **22-50-90-50**). There is a British consulate in Bergen at Carl Konowsgate 34 (✆ **55-94-47-05**).

Emergencies Throughout Norway, call ✆ **112** for the **police,** ✆ **110** to report a **fire,** or ✆ **113** to request an **ambulance.**

Laundry & Dry Cleaning Most hotels provide these services. There are coin-operated launderettes and dry cleaners in most Norwegian cities.

Liquor Laws Most restaurants, pubs, and bars in Norway are licensed to serve liquor, wine, and beer. The drinking age is 18 for beer and wine and 20 for liquor.

Mail Airmail letters or postcards to the United States and Canada cost 7NOK (95¢) for up to 20 grams (⁷⁄₁₀ oz.). Airmail letters take 7 to 10 days to reach North America. The principal post office in Norway is Oslo Central Post Office, Dronningensgate 15, N-0101 Oslo. Mailboxes are vibrant red, embossed with the trumpet symbol of the postal service. They're found on walls, at chest level, throughout cities and towns. Stamps can be bought at the post office, at magazine kiosks, or at some stores.

Only the post office can weigh, evaluate, and inform you of the options for delivery time and regulations for sending parcels. Shipments to places outside Norway require a declaration on a printed form stating the contents and value of the package.

Maps   Many tourist offices supply free maps of their district. You can also contact the Norwegian Automobile Club, Storgata 2, N-0155 Oslo 1 (© 22-34-14-00), which offers free or inexpensive road maps. Most visitors find it quicker and more convenient to buy a detailed road map; this is the best approach for anyone who plans to tour extensively outside the major cities. Some of Norway's most reliable maps are published by Cappelen.

Police   Dial © 112 nationwide.

Radio & TV   Radio and television broadcasts are in Norwegian. However, Norwegian National Radio (NRK) has news summaries in English several times weekly.

Restrooms   All terminals, big city squares, and the like have public lavatories. In small towns and villages, head for the marketplace. Hygiene standards are usually adequate. If you patronize the toilets in a privately run establishment (such as a cafe), it's polite to buy at least a small pastry or coffee.

Taxes   Norway imposes a 19.4% value-added tax (VAT) on most goods and services, which is figured into your final bill. If you buy goods in any store bearing the tax-free sign, you're entitled to a cash refund of up to 18.5% on purchases costing over 310NOK ($41). Ask the shop assistant for a tax-free shopping check, and show your passport to indicate that you're not a resident of Scandinavia. You may not use the articles purchased before leaving Norway, and they must be taken out of the country within 3 months of purchase. Complete the information requested on the back of the check you're given at the store; at your point of departure, report to an area marked by the tax-free sign, not at customs. Your refund check will be exchanged there in kroner for the amount due you. Refunds are available at airports, ferry and cruise-ship terminals, borders, and train stations.

Telephone & Telegrams   Direct-dial long-distance calls can be made to the United States and Canada from most phones in Norway by dialing © 00 (double zero), then the country code (1 for the U.S. and Canada), followed by the area code and phone number. Check at your hotel's front desk before you place a call. Norwegian coins of 1NOK (15¢), 5NOK (65¢), and 10NOK ($1.35) are used in pay phones.

Telegrams can be sent from private or public phones by dialing © 0138.

Time   Norway operates on Central European Time—1 hour ahead of Greenwich Mean Time and 6 hours ahead of Eastern Standard Time. (For example: at noon Eastern Standard Time—say, in New York City—it's 6pm in Norway.) Norway goes on summer time—1 hour earlier—from the end of March until around the end of September.

Tipping Hotels add a 10% to 15% service charge to your bill, which is sufficient unless someone has performed a special service. Most bellhops get at least 10NOK ($1.35) per suitcase. Nearly all restaurants add a service charge of up to 15% to your bill. Barbers and hairdressers usually aren't tipped, but toilet attendants and hatcheck people expect at least 3NOK (40¢). Don't tip theater ushers. Taxi drivers don't expect tips unless they handle heavy luggage.

Water Tap water is generally safe to drink throughout Norway. Never drink from a mountain stream, fjord, or river, regardless of how clean it might appear.

3

The Active Vacation Planner

Nearly half of the four million people of Norway are members of the Norwegian Sports Federation, and three out of four Norwegian children take part in sporting activities. Norway is the most sports-oriented country in Europe. From sled-dog racing to canoeing, from curling, speed-skating, and skiing, the sports agenda is a full one.

Winter sports are dominated by skiing, of course, along with ice hockey and curling. In the too short summer, virtually all Norwegians head for the outdoors while the sun shines. They sail, swim, canoe, beach it, or whatever. Trails fill with hikers or mountain bikers.

1 Skiing

Norway is the birthplace of skiing, predating the sport in Switzerland or Austria. There are 30,000km (18,750 miles) of marked ski trails.

From November until the last of May, both cross-country and downhill skiing are available, but don't expect the brilliant sun of the Alps. The days get long just before Easter when skiing is best. Lights illuminate many of the tracks for winter skiers, especially helpful in January and February.

From December to April, daylight is limited, but it's still possible to have a full day's skiing if you start early. The bigger resorts have at least one floodlit downhill slope, and many towns and villages have a floodlit cross-country track (lysløype). The days lengthen rapidly through January and February. Mid-February is the most popular period and accommodation prices are higher then. Early March offers a combination of good skiing conditions, daylight, and low prices. Easter and the week before are popular with Norwegians, and accommodation prices are very high. However, from Easter Monday low season rates apply again. Skiing in the higher elevations is possible until May, and you can even ski all summer in a few places (see the last paragraph in this section).

The bigger resorts in Norway have plenty to interest beginners and intermediate skiers for a week or more, and there are many black runs for the more experienced. The snowboard facilities are excellent. Families find free lift passes and helmets for the under 7s, plus plenty of nursery slopes and day-care centers. Lift passes are relatively inexpensive, rental equipment is often cheaper than in other countries, queues are usually short, and the slopes uncrowded. Generally snow conditions are more reliable over a longer period than in southern Europe.

Norway is best known for its cross-country skiing, which is superb almost everywhere. An endless network of marked trails (skiløyper) crosses rolling hills, forests, frozen lakes, and mountains. Numerous small ski centers offer inexpensive ski rental and tuition. All the downhill resorts also have extensive trail networks.

Norwegian ski resorts are known for their informality, which is evident in the schools and the atmosphere. The emphasis is on simple pleasures, not the

---

(*Fun Fact* **The Cradle of Skiing**

A 4,000-year-old rock carving from Nordland shows that Norwegians were already using skis then. Telemark county is regarded as the "cradle of skiing" because Sondre Nordheim from Morgedal created an interest for the sport there in the 1870s and '80s. He devised a binding that made it possible to turn and jump without losing the skis, and also designed a ski with inwardly curved edges—the Telemark ski—that became the prototype of all subsequent skis.

---

sophistication often found at alpine resorts. (Incidentally, the word *ski* is an Old Norse word, as is *slalom*.)

Geilo and **Hemsedal** are the best-known downhill resorts. We recommend either area for keen downhill skiers. Geilo has the most extensive lift system, but Hemsedal has steeper runs and more spectacular scenery. There is also good cross-country skiing near both resorts. The huge mountain area of **Golsfjellet,** between Hemsedal, Gol and Valdres is excellent for cross-country skiers with some experience. The main railway between Oslo and Bergen serves Geilo directly and Hemsedal via a connecting bus service from Gol (3–4 hr.).

Trysil in eastern Norway is less well known than Geilo and Hemsedal, yet it offers equally good downhill skiing. There is a particularly good choice of self-catering chalets and apartments here with skiable access to the lifts. Trysil is easy to reach by a direct express bus service from Oslo airport (3 hr.).

The **Valdres** area between Hemsedal and Lillehammer is famous for its scenery of rolling forested hills with high mountains in the distance. The Aurdal ski center has the unbeatable combination of superb cross-country terrain and good downhill facilities. A good base for both is one of the excellent chalets at the top of the downhill slopes. Direct bus service connects Valdres to central Oslo (3 hr.).

Lillehammer is very well known since the Winter Olympics in 1994 and the competitive facilities are world class. The main downhill slopes are at **Hafjell,** 15km (9⅓ miles) north of Lillehammer. The cross-country skiing through the gentle hills, scattered forests, and lakes of the Sjusjøen area is endless and particularly good for beginners. Lillehammer itself is more cosmopolitan than the other ski towns and has a wide range of shops and places to eat and drink.

North of Lillehammer is the Gudbrandsdal valley surrounded by extensive cross-country areas linked by two long-distance trails, "Troll løype" to the east and "Peer Gynt løype" to the west. Skiers of all abilities enjoy this area, and downhillers find several good ski centers. This region, including **Gålå** and **Fefor,** is especially well served by mountain hotels.

For those traveling with their own car the **Telemark** area is easily accessible from Haugesund or Kristiansand (3–5 hr.). **Gaustablikk,** near the town of Rjukan, is the best all-around center with several lifts and downhill runs of all standards, plus many kilometers of cross-country trails to suit all abilities.

Voss is well known and easily reached from Bergen in about 90 minutes by car or train, but the location near the west coast suffers from unreliable weather, particularly early and late in the season. It is well worth considering for a short break though, or if you want to combine skiing with a winter visit to the fjord area.

> **Impressions**
>
> *"Skiing is the most Norwegian of all our sports, and a glorious sport it is;*
> *if any merits being called the sport of sports, this is surely the one."*
> —Explorer Fridtjof Nansen after crossing
> the interior of Greenland on skis in 1880

Skiing in the summer months is also possible. For information about summer skiing, get in touch with **Stryn Sommerskisenter** (© 57-87-40-40; www.stryn-sommerski.no). The largest mainland glacier in Europe is at Jostedalsbreen, near Stryn.

2 Fishing

With a quarter of Norway's coastline at your disposal, nearly 14,000km (8,699 miles), you obviously have plenty of opportunities for sea fishing.

Norway has long been famous for its salmon and trout fishing. The country boasts more than 100 salmon rivers flowing into fjords. The best months for salmon are June and July, and the season extends into August. Sea trout fishing takes place from June to September, and is best in August. The brown trout season varies with altitude.

Fishing in the ocean is free. To fish in lakes, rivers, or streams, anyone over 16 must have a fishing license. The cost of a license to fish in a lake begins at 90NOK ($12), or 180NOK ($24) to fish in a river. National fishing licenses can be purchased at local post offices. For more information, contact the **Bergen Angling Association,** Fosswinckelsgata 37, Bergen (© **55-32-11-64**).

One company that arranges fishing tours in Norway is **Passage Tours of Scandinavia,** 239 Commercial Blvd., Fort Lauderdale, FL 33308 (© **800/548-5960** in the U.S., or 954/776-7070; www.passagetours.com).

A U.S.-based company that can arrange fishing (as well as hunting) excursions anywhere within Norway and the rest of Scandinavia is **Five Stars of Scandinavia,** 13104 Thomas Rd., KPN, Gig Harbor, WA 98329 (© **800/722-4126;** www.5stars-of-scandinavia.com). For a truly unusual fishing experience, consider renting one of their old-fashioned fishermen's cottages in the isolated Lofoten Islands. The rustic-looking, fully renovated cottages each lie adjacent to the sea, and evoke 19th-century isolation in a way that's wondrous or terrifying, depending on your point of view. Five Stars will rent you a cottage for as short a period as 1 night, although we recommend a minimum stay of 3 nights to best appreciate this offbeat adventure.

One of the most qualified fishing outfitters in Bergen spends part of its time delivering food, tools, and spare parts to the thousands of fishermen who make their living in boats and isolated fjords along the western coast of Norway. **Camperlan,** P.O. Box 11, Strandkaien 2, N-5083 Bergen (© **55-32-34-72;** www.camperlan.no), and its president and founder, Captain Dag Varlo, will take between two and four passengers on deep-sea fishing excursions in the teeming seas off the country's western coast. Although his boats go out in all seasons, midsummer is the most appealing, because of the extended daylight hours. Most avidly pursued are codfish, valued as a "good-eating" fish, and a local species known as saet, prized for its fighting properties as a game fish. (They range anywhere from 3–22 lb. each.) A full-day's fishing excursion, with all equipment included, for up to six passengers, costs 6,000NOK ($798). In midsummer, full-day excursions depart from Bergen's harbor, and are usually scheduled from 9am to around 5pm.

The best salmon-fishing tours take place in central Norway, especially along the Guala River, one of the country's best-known salmon-fishing rivers. **Ursus Major** (© **99-22-49-60**; www.ursus-major.no) offers weeklong fishing tours in Trondheim, which cost from 15,730NOK to 22,750NOK ($2,092–$3,026) per person, including meals and accommodations.

The River Gudbrandsdalslågen, running through a beautiful valley and Hafjell Hunderfossen, is one of the best fishing rivers of Europe, set against a backdrop of the Øyer mountains, with its many fishing lakes and rivers. The main types of fish caught are burbot, trout, char, and grayling. Many lakes in the mountains have rowing boats for free use, and permits are easily obtainable at gas stations, grocery stores, hotels, or inns. For more information, contact Øyer Tourist Office at © **61-27-70-00.**

3 Biking, Hiking & Other Summer Pursuits

BIKING   For the serious cyclist, there are two great routes in Norway: the North Sea Cycleway and the Old Navvy Road. The coastal route is much easier, whereas the Old Navvy Road runs across open mountains, passing through pastures and meadows en route down to the nearest fjord. In Norway you can pick up detailed maps of these routes and how to reach them.

Since the Old Navvy Road follows the Bergen-Oslo train tracks for most of the way, the usual starting point is Haugastøl, known for its herring and jazz.

The North Sea Cycleway stretches for 296km (183 miles) and is mostly rural, with woodland, moors, and crags, passing many a meadow. It runs through such ports as Flekkefjord and Egersund, passing such larger towns as Sandnes and Stavanger.

The Old Navvy Road, called Rallarvegen in Norwegian, was built from 1895 to 1902, starting in the tree-lined east and climbing into the open mountains, with panoramic views of snow-covered slopes; high altitude, incredibly blue lakes; and the Hardangerjøkulen Glacier. The most dramatic point along the route is from Vatnahalsen where the road descends the 21 hairpin bends of Myrdalskleiva, continuing down the Flamsdal Valley to Flåm. The road has been a cycle track since the 1970s.

Bikes can be rented in just about every town in Norway. Inquire at your hotel or the local tourist office. The Norwegian Mountain Touring Association (see "Hiking," below) provides inexpensive lodging for those who take overnight bike trips. For suggestions on tours, maps, and brochures, contact **Den Rustne Eike,** Vestbaneplassen 2, N-0458 Oslo (© **22-83-52-08**). The only large bike-rental firm in Oslo, it can arrange guided tours in the Oslo area and elsewhere in Norway. Tours last from 3 hours to 14 days.

In July and August, 7-day bike trips run through the Lofoten Islands. They offer moderately rolling terrain, dramatic scenery, traditional *rorbuer* (fishing cottage) lodging, and hearty regional cuisine. Prices begin at $2,000. Tours are offered by **Backroads** (© **800/GO-ACTIVE;** www.backroads.com).

To cycle through the splendors of Norway, you can join Britain's oldest and largest association of bicycle riders, the **Cyclists' Touring Club,** Cotterell House, 69 Meadow, Godalming, Surrey GU7 3HS (© **01483/417-217;** www.ctc.org.uk). Founded in 1878, it charges £10 a year for membership, which includes information, maps, a subscription to a newsletter packed with practical information and morale boosters, plus recommended cycling routes

Frommer's Favorite Offbeat Adventures

- **Dogsledding:** Traveling over the frozen tundra or through snow-laced forests at the speed of a dog can be one of the great experiences of the Nordic world. You can be a passenger, bundled aboard a sled, or a driver urging on a team of huskies. A Norway-based outfitter that specializes in the experience, usually as part of midwinter camping trips under a canopy of stars, is **Canyon Huskies,** Stengelsen, N-9518 Alta, Norway (© 78-43-33-06; www.canyonhuskies.no). Tours, conducted by owner Roger Dahl, last from 1 to 10 days between December and May, and involve overnight stays in mountain cabins, which usually contain five to six bunk beds each. Negotiate with these folks directly, or contact U.S.-based outfitter **Borton Overseas** (© 800/843-0602; www.bortonoverseas.com).

- **Observing Musk Oxen:** A remnant of the last Ice Age, the musk ox had become nearly extinct by the 1930s. Between 1932 and 1953, musk oxen were shipped from Greenland to the Dovrefjell (a national park that's about an hour's train ride south of Trondheim), where about 60 still roam. On a safari, you can observe this thriving herd—take along some binoculars—as well as Norway's purest herd of original mountain reindeer. The park, another remnant of the last Ice Age, is Europe's most bountiful wildflower mountain. Accommodations in or near the park can be arranged through **Borton Overseas** (© 800/843-0602; www.bortonoverseas.com). Hotel staff members can direct you to where you're most likely to see the herds.

- **Rafting:** Norway's abundant snow and rainfall and its steep topography feed dozens of roaring whitewater streams. Experience these torrents firsthand as part of white-water treks downriver. One of Norway's most respected river outfitters is **Norwegian Wildlife and Rafting AS,** Randswerk, N-2680 Vågå (© 61-23-87-27; www.nwr.no). Based in central Norway, about a 90-minute drive north of Lillehammer, the company has a flotilla of devices suitable for helping you float, meander, or shoot down the whitewater streams. Whatever conveyance you can imagine (paddle boards, kayaks, canoes, or inflatable rafts), this company can provide it. Trips last from 1 to 8 days.

through virtually every country in Europe. The organization's information bank on scenic routes through Scandinavia is especially comprehensive. Membership can be arranged over the phone with a credit card (such as MasterCard, Visa, Access, or Barclaycard).

One of the best bets for mountain biking is the Setesdal region, with its many small roads and forest trails. **Setesdal Rafting Centre** (© 37-93-11-77), 7km (4⅓ miles) north from Evje on the main road (Rte. 9), are experts in the area, offering both guided trips and bikes for rent with helmets from mid-April to late October.

The Øyer mountains are also excellent for cycling, as the scenery is splendid, the countryside undulating. Mountain roads suitable for cycling shoot out in all directions. For more information, including suggested cycle tours in the Øyer

- **Trekking the Fjords:** Two respected U.S.-based outfitters, **Borton Overseas** (✆ 800/843-0602; www.bortonoverseas.com) and **Five Stars of Scandinavia** (✆ 800/722-4126; www.5stars-of-scandinavia.com), offer 7- and 8-day treks through Norway designed to acquaint you with the country's heritage and its thousands of scenic wonders. Amid the cliffs and waterfalls of the fjords, you can participate in point-to-point guided treks that average around 24km (15 miles) per day. En route, you'll visit wooden churches, mountain hamlets, and, in some cases, snow fields and slow-moving glaciers. Depending on your budget and your tastes, overnight accommodations range from first-class hotels to simple mountain huts favored by rock climbers and many trekkers.

- **Bicycling in the Lofoten Islands:** Some of the weirdest and most isolated tundra and lichen-covered rock formations in Norway lie within the Lofoten archipelago, north of the Arctic Circle. Ecologists claim that one of the best and least invasive ways to experience the wildlife here is on a bicycle.

  Berkeley, California–based **Backroads Travel** (✆ 800/GO-ACTIVE; www.backroads.com) conducts 6-day hiking and biking (they refer to them as "multi-sport") tours of the isolated archipelago at least twice a year, during July and August, with an emphasis on ecology and natural beauty. Washington state–based **Five Stars of Scandinavia** (✆ 800/722-4126; www.5stars-of-scandinavia.com) offers comparable tours and tends to be cheaper than Backroads. Both operators house their participants in simple mountain huts and lodges.

- **Going on a Moose Safari:** Norway's largest animal, the moose, can weigh up to 600 kilograms (1,323 lb.). These forest-dwellers are shy of people and best spotted at night. If you'd like to go on a moose safari, contact **Daesbekken Villmarksenter** in Finneskogen (✆ 62-95-48-57), east of Oslo, near the Swedish border. Individual visitors can arrange tours only in July; otherwise it's strictly group bookings.

mountains, consult the Øyer Tourist Office (✆ 61-27-70-00), and rent bikes from **Hafjellsporten Sports** (✆ 61-27-70-93).

GOLFING   Norway has more than two dozen 18-hole golf courses, and the **Norwegian Golf Federation** (✆ 22-73-66-20; golfforbundet@nif.idrett.no) can provide information.

Many golf clubs are open to foreign guests. Greens fees tend to be moderate. Clubs include the 18-hole **Oslo Golf Klubb**, at Bogstad, Oslo (✆ 22-50-44-02), and the 18-hole **Meland Golf Club**, Meland/Frekhaug (✆ 56-17-46-00), 36km (22 miles) north of Bergen.

HIKING   The mountains and wildernesses of Norway, among the most spectacular in the world, are reason enough to visit the country. If you're a serious hiker, put yourself in the hands of the **Norwegian Mountain Touring**

Association (DNT; see below), terrific experts and trailblazers through Norway since 1868. They maintain affiliations with all the hiking associations of Norway, and provide maps and advice. These local associations mark the routes and operate a network of cabins for hikers to share.

The **Norwegian Mountain Touring Association,** Storgata 3, N-0101 Oslo (© **22-82-28-22;** www.dntoa.no), offers guided hikes that last from 5 to 8 days. They cost from 3113NOK to 3900NOK ($415–$520), including meals and lodging.

Blue Marble Travel, 222A Race St., Philadelphia, PA 19106 (© **800/ 258-8689** or 215/923-3788; www.bluemarble.org), features reasonably priced biking and hiking trips in Norway.

European Walking Tours, 1401 Regency Drive East, Savoy, IL 61874 (© **800/231-8448** or 217/398-0058; www.walkingtours.com), sponsors walking tours for the mature traveler in Norway. The operator, Jacqueline Tofté, is a native of the Swiss Alps, and has charted routes across meadows, remote valleys, and over mountain passes or alongside serene lakes. The search is for wild flowers, birds, and mountain animals, with lessons in local architecture, traditions, and history thrown in as well.

> **Twenty-three Hours of Daylight**
>
> The Norwegian summer has magnificent, long sunny days. Temperatures often reach 86°F (30°C). Daylight on the longest days can last 23 hours, warming the lakes and fjords for all watersports.

HORSEBACK RIDING   Throughout Norway you'll find riding schools with horses for rent. Many country hotels in Norway also keep a few horses for the use of guests. Many organizations offer horseback tours of Norway's wilderness, enabling visitors to see some of the more spectacular scenery. Tours can range from a few hours to a full week. Luggage is transported by car. One tour organizer is **Borton Overseas,** 5412 Lyndale Ave., Minneapolis, MN 55419 (© **800/843-0602** or 612/882-4640; www.bortonoverseas.com).

Some of the best mountain riding is offered by **Stølsheimen Fjellridning & Engjaland Farm** outside the resort of Voss (© **56-51-91-65;** www.engjaland. no). In Panoramic fjord and mountain scenery, you're taken on day or weekend rides, where everything is arranged for you, including accommodations and meals.

4 Canoeing, Sailing & Scuba Diving

CANOEING & KAYAKING   Canoeing and kayaking, two sports increasing in popularity, allow visitors to reach places that are otherwise almost inaccessible. Paddling at sea, on a river, or on a lake are three completely different experiences, but all of them bring you closer to nature, providing you with a unique opportunity of observing animals and birds without frightening them with the sound of an engine.

Crossing Latitudes, 420 W. Koch St., Bozeman, MT 59715 (© **800/572-8747** or 406/585-5356; www.crossinglatitudes.com), offers sea kayaking and backpacking expeditions.

Some of our best experiences out on a canoe have been with the **Setesdal Rafting Center** (© **37-93-11-77**), 7km (4⅓ miles) north from Evje on the main road, Route 9. The region of Setesdal, known for its mountains, rivers, and varied wildlife, contains a stunning stretch of the River Otra—ideal for canoeing—extending from the rafting center south to the village of Evje. En route you'll pass several Osprey nests and beaver lodges. The center is also the best place in southern Norway for white-water rafting from mid-April to late October. From late June until September, water temperatures can reach 68°F (20°C), which makes the River Otra the warmest in Norway. Both half-day and full-day trips can be arranged.

If you'd like to go rafting on the Sjoa River, "the wildest in Norway," you can obtain full information from the **Våga Tourist office,** Vågavegen 37, N-2680 in Våga (© **61-23-78-80**), which also provides information about horseback riding, mountain or glacier climbing, mountain biking, and canoeing.

The rivers around the resort of Voss, in Norway's fjord country, have some of the finest river rafting. **Voss Rafting Center** (© **56-51-05-25**), offers rafting and other watersports such as river-boarding and canyoning. Overnight stays in the wild along with meals can be arranged.

SAILING   Norway's long coast can be a challenge to any yachting enthusiast. The most tranquil havens are along the southern coast. To arrange rafting trips or boat trips, along with boat rentals and evening parasailing, contact **SeaAction** (© **90-58-43-00** or 33-33-69-93; www.seaaction.com).

SCUBA DIVING   Some parts of the Norwegian coast are famous for their underwater environment. Because of the Gulf Stream, the coast is relatively mild, and scuba diving is possible year-round, but we recommend it only in the summer months.

Excellent diving centers provide scuba-diving trips and instruction. Divers who enjoy harpooning can catch their own dinners, with many kinds of fish to choose from. The conditions for submarine photography are generally good, with underwater visibility of 9m to 30m (30 ft.–100 ft.). There are a number of shipwrecks along Norway's extensive coastline and fjords. Diving information is available from **Dykkernett** (© **22-54-78-02;** www.dykkernett.no).

5 Adventure Sightseeing

BIRD-WATCHING   Some of Europe's noteworthy bird sanctuaries are on islands off the Norwegian coast or on the mainland. Rocky and isolated, the sanctuaries offer ideal nesting places for millions of sea birds that vastly outnumber the local human population during certain seasons. Foremost among the sanctuaries are the **Lofoten Islands**—particularly two of the outermost islands, Vaerøy and Røst—and the island of Runde. An almost .5km (¼-mile) bridge (one of the longest in Norway) connects **Runde** to the coastline, a 2½-hour drive from Ålesund. Runde's year-round human population is about 150, and the colonies of puffins, cormorants, razor-billed auks, guillemots, gulls, and eider ducks number in the millions. Another noteworthy bird sanctuary is at **Fokstumyra,** a national park near Dombås.

The isolated island of **Lovund** is a 2-hour ferry ride from the town of Sandnesjøen, south of Bødo. Lovund ("the island of puffins") has a human population of fewer than 270 and a bird population in the hundreds of thousands. You can visit Lovund and the other famous Norwegian bird-watching sites on your own, or sign up for one of the organized tours sponsored by **Borton Overseas,** 5412 Lyndale Ave., Minneapolis, MN 55419 (© **800/843-0602** or 612/882-4640; www.bortonoverseas.com).

Brochures and pamphlets are available from the tourist board **Destination Lofoten** (© **76-07-30-00**).

WHALE-WATCHING   In Norway you can catch a glimpse of 20m (65-ft.), 40,000-kilogram (88,000-lb.) sperm whales, the largest toothed whales in the world. You can also see killer whales, harbor porpoises, minke whales, and white-beaked dolphins. Whale researchers conduct 6-hour whale-watching tours in the Arctic Ocean.

For information and bookings, contact **Passage Tours of Scandinavia,** 239 Commercial Blvd., Fort Lauderdale, FL 33308 (© **800/548-5960** or 954/776-7070). Whale-watching in the Lofoten Islands can be arranged by **Borton Overseas,** 5412 Lyndale Ave., Minneapolis, MN 55419 (© **800/843-0602** or 612/882-4640; www.bortonoverseas.com).

6 Learning Vacations

An international series of programs for persons over 50 who are interested in combining travel and learning is offered by **Interhostel,** developed by the University of New Hampshire. Each program lasts 2 weeks, is led by a university faculty or staff member, and is arranged in conjunction with a host college, university, or cultural institution. Participants may stay longer if they want. Interhostel offers programs consisting of cultural and intellectual activities, with field trips to museums and other centers of interest. For information, contact the University of New Hampshire, Division of Continuing Education, 6 Garrison Ave., Durham, NH 03824 (© **800/733-9753** or 603/862-1147; www.learn.unh.edu).

Another good source of information about courses in Norway is the **American Institute for Foreign Study (AIFS),** River Plaza, 9 West Broad St., Stamford, CT 06902 (© **800/727-2437** or 203/399-5000; www.aifs.org). This organization can set up transportation and arrange for summer courses, with bed and board included.

The biggest organization dealing with higher education in Europe is the **Institute of International Education (IIE),** 809 United Nations Plaza, New York, NY 10017 (© **800/445-0443** or 212/883-8200; www.iie.org). A few of its booklets are free; for $47, plus $6 for postage, you can buy the definitive *Vacation Study Abroad.* The Information Center in New York is open to the public Tuesday through Thursday from 11am to 4pm. The institute is closed on major holidays.

One well-recommended clearinghouse for academic programs throughout the world is the **National Registration Center for Study Abroad (NRCSA),** 823 N. 2nd St., P.O. Box 1393, Milwaukee, WI 53203 (© **414/278-0631;** www.nrcsa.com). The organization maintains language study programs throughout Europe.

4

Settling into Oslo

One of the oldest Scandinavian capitals, Oslo has never been on the mainstream European tourist circuit. Many have the impression that it's lean on historic and cultural sights. In fact, Oslo offers enough sights and activities to fill at least 3 or 4 busy days. It's also the starting point for many easy excursions along the Oslofjord or to nearby towns and villages.

In the '90s Oslo grew—from what even the Scandinavians considered a backwater—to one of the glittering cities of Europe. Restaurants, nightclubs, cafes, and shopping complexes have opened. A Nordic *joie de vivre* permeates the city. The only problem is that Oslo is one of the most expensive cities in Europe. Proceed with caution if you're on a strict budget.

Oslo was founded in the mid-11th century by a Viking king, and became the capital around 1300 under Haakon V. In the course of its history, the city burned down several times; fire destroyed it in 1824. The master builder, Christian IV, king of Denmark and Norway, ordered the town rebuilt near the Akershus Castle. He named the new town Christiania (after himself), its official name until 1924, when the city reverted to its former name.

In 1814 Norway separated from Denmark and united with Sweden, a union that lasted until 1905. During that period the Royal Palace, the House of Parliament, the old university, the National Theater, and the National Gallery were built.

After World War II, Oslo grew to 282 sq. km (175 sq. miles). Today it's one of the 10 largest world capitals in the area. Oslo is also one of the most heavily forested cities, with fewer than half a million inhabitants.

One final point: Oslovians love nature. They devote much time to pursuits in the forests and on the fjords. It takes only half an hour by tram to go from the Royal Palace to the 119m (390 ft.) Tryvann Observation Tower, where you can enjoy a view over Oslo Marka, the giant forest. The Krogskogen forest was the setting for many Norwegian folk tales about princesses, kings, penniless heroes, and the inevitable forest trolls. From this observation tower in the summer, you can look down on hundreds of sailboats, motorboats, and windsurfers among the numerous islands of the Oslo archipelago.

1 Orientation

ARRIVING

BY PLANE   Since the recent closing of a small-scale, relatively outmoded airport named Fornebu, Oslo has coped with all of its air traffic being funneled into the **Oslo International Airport** in Gardemoen (© **81-55-02-50**), about 50km (31 miles) east of downtown Oslo, a 45-minute drive from the center. Through this much-upgraded airport arrive all domestic and international flights coming into Oslo, including aircraft belonging to SAS, British Airways, and Icelandair.

Tips High-Speed Link from Stockholm

The first high-speed train between Stockholm and Oslo has reduced travel time to 4 hours and 50 minutes between these Scandinavian capitals. Depending on the day, there are two to three trains daily in each direction. This high-speed train now competes directly with air travel.

There's frequent bus service, departing at intervals of between 15 and 30 minutes throughout the day, into downtown Oslo. It's maintained by both SAS (whose buses deliver passengers to the Central Railway station and to most of the SAS hotels within Oslo) and the **Norwegian Bus Express** (© 81-54-44-44), whose buses head for the main railway station. Both companies charge 110NOK ($15) per person, each way. There's also a high-speed railway service between Gardemoen and Oslo's main railway station, requiring transit time of only 20 minutes, priced at 180NOK ($24) per person each way. If you want to take a taxi, be prepared for a lethally high charge of around 500NOK ($67) for up to four passengers plus their luggage. If you need a "maxi-taxi," a minivan that's suitable for between 5 and 15 passengers, plus their luggage, you'll be assessed 800NOK ($106).

BY TRAIN   Trains from the Continent, Sweden, and Denmark arrive at **Oslo Sentralstasjon,** Jernbanetorget 1 (© **81-50-08-88** for train information), located at the beginning of Karl Johans Gate, in the center of the city. The station is open daily from 7am to 11pm. From the Central Station, trains leave for Bergen, Stavanger, Trondheim, Bodø, and all other rail links in Norway. You can also take trams to all major parts of Oslo. Lockers and a luggage office are available at the station, where you can also exchange money.

BY CAR   If you're driving from mainland Europe, the fastest way to reach Oslo is to take the car ferry from Frederikshavn, Denmark. From Frederikshavn, car ferries run to several towns near Oslo, and to Gothenburg, Sweden. You can also take a car ferry from Copenhagen to several points in western Sweden, or from Helsingør, Denmark, to Helsingborg, Sweden. Highway E6 runs the length of Sweden's western coast from Malmö through Helsingborg and Gothenburg, right up to Oslo. If you're driving from Stockholm to Oslo, take E3 west to Örebro, where it connects with E18 to Oslo. Once you near the outskirts of Oslo from any direction, follow the signs into the Sentrum.

BY FERRY   Ferries from Europe arrive at the Oslo port, a 15-minute walk (or a short taxi ride) from the center. From Denmark, Scandinavia's link with the Continent, ferries depart for Oslo from Copenhagen, Hirtshals, and Frederikshavn.

From Strømstad, Sweden, in the summer, the daily crossing to Sandefjord, Norway, takes 2½ hours; from Sandefjord, it's an easy drive or train ride north to Oslo.

VISITOR INFORMATION

Assistance and information for visitors are available at the **Tourist Information Office,** Vestbaneplassen 1, N-0250 Oslo (© **22-83-00-50**). Free maps, brochures, sightseeing tickets, and guide services are available. The office is open from June to August daily 9am to 7pm; May and September Monday to Saturday 9am to 4pm; and October to April Monday to Friday 9am to 4pm.

The information office at the **Oslo Sentralstasjon (Central Station),** Jernbanetorget 1, is open daily from 8am to 11pm. There's no phone.

CITY LAYOUT

MAIN ARTERIES & STREETS   Oslo is at the mouth of the Oslofjord, 97km (60 miles) in length. Opening onto the harbor is **Rådhusplassen (City Hall Square),** dominated by the modern City Hall, a major attraction. Guided bus tours leave from this point, and the launches that cruise the fjords depart from the pier facing the municipal building. You can catch Bygdøy-bound ferries from the quay at Rådhusplassen. On a promontory to the east is **Akershus Castle.**

Karl Johans Gate, Oslo's main street (especially for shopping and strolling), is north of City Hall Square. This boulevard begins at Oslo Sentralstasjon (Central Station) and stretches all the way to the 19th-century Royal Palace at the western end.

A short walk from the palace is the famed **Studenter Lunden (Students' Grove),** where seemingly everybody gathers on summer days to socialize. The University of Oslo is nearby. Dominating this center is the National Theater, guarded by statues of Ibsen and Bjørnson, the two greatest names in Norwegian theater. South of the theater, near the harbor, is **Stortingsgaten,** another shop-filled street.

The main city square is **Stortorvet,** although it's no longer the center of city life, which has shifted to Karl Johans Gate.

At a subway stop near the National Theater, you can catch an electric train to **Tryvannstårnet,** the loftiest lookout in Scandinavia, and to the **Holmenkollen Ski Jump.**

FINDING AN ADDRESS   Street numbers begin on the southern end of streets running north-south and on the eastern end of streets running east-west. Odd numbers are on one side of the street, and even numbers on the other. Where large buildings hold several establishments, different addresses are designated with A, B, and C.

STREET MAPS   Maps of Oslo are distributed free at the tourist office (see above). For extensive exploring, especially of some back streets, you may need a more detailed map. Opt for a pocket-sized map with a street index that can be opened and folded like a wallet. Such maps are sold at most newsstands in the central city. If you can't find a map, go to the city's most central bookstore, **Tanum Karl Johan,** Karl Johans Gate 43 (© **22-41-11-00**).

NEIGHBORHOODS IN BRIEF

Oslo is made for walking—in fact, you can walk from the Central Station all the way to the Royal Palace (Slottet) in a straight line. Except for excursions to the museum-loaded Bygdøy peninsula and the Holmenkollen Ski Jump, most attractions can be covered on foot.

Oslo is not neatly divided into separate neighborhoods or districts. It consists mainly of **central Oslo,** with the Central Station to the east of the city center and the Royal Palace to the west. Karl Johans Gate, the principal street, connects these two points. Central Oslo is the heart of the city—the most crowded and traffic congested, but also the most convenient place to stay. It's not a real neighborhood, but the core of the city, as Piccadilly Circus is to London. Most Oslo hotels and restaurants are here, as are almost 50 museums and galleries—enough to fill many a rainy day. The most interesting include Akershus Castle, the Historical Museum, and the National Gallery.

The streets Drammensveien and Frognerveien lead northwest to Frogner Park (Frognerparken), whose main entrance is on Kirkeveien. This historical area is the site of the Vigeland Sculpture Park, which displays some masterpieces of Gustav Vigeland (1869–1943).

The **Old Town** (or Gamlebyen) lies south of the Parliament Building (the Stortinget) and Karl Johans Gate. This section contains some of the city's old-fashioned restaurants, along with the Norwegian Resistance Museum and the Old Town Hall.

Aker Brygge is Oslo's newest neighborhood, an excellent place for dining and diversions, but not for hotels. It emerged near the mouth of the Oslofjord in the old wharf area formerly used for ship-building yards. Fueled by oil wealth, steel-and-glass buildings now rise from what had been a relatively dilapidated section. Some of the best shops, theaters, restaurants, and cultural attractions are here, along with apartments for such well-heeled owners as Diana Ross.

The main attractions in **eastern Oslo** are the Botanisk Hage (Botanic Garden), the Zoological Museum, and the Munch Museum in Tøyen—little more is worth seeing here.

The **West End** is a chic residential area graced with some of the city's finest hotels and restaurants. It's a more tranquil setting than the center, which we prefer, and only 15 minutes away by public transportation.

Farther west—6km (about 4 miles) by car but better reached by car ferry—is the **Bygdøy** peninsula. Here you'll find such attractions as the Norwegian Folk Museum, the Viking ships, the polar ship *Fram,* and the *Kon-Tiki* Museum. Break up your sightseeing venture with a meal here but plan to stay elsewhere.

The suburb of **Frogner** begins a half-mile west of Oslo center and stretches for a mile or so. There's a good hotel and restaurant here.

Lying behind the S-station, the main rail station for Oslo, is the **Grønland district** where many Oslovians go for ethnic dining. There is little of sightseeing interest in this ghettolike area. Many refugees from Pakistan and India, among other countries, fill the area; however, the town's best Indian and Pakistani restaurants lie within more upscale neighborhoods.

At last, once-staid Oslo has grown big and diverse enough to have its own trendy, counterculture district. Lying in East Oslo is trendy **Grünerløkka,** which most of its inhabitants refer to affectionately as "Løkka." This once-rundown sector of Oslo traditionally was known as the worker's district. Today many professional Oslovians are moving in to restore apartments, and the district is the site of several fashionable cafes and restaurants.

Many Oslo neighborhoods lie along the **Oslofjord,** which stretches more than 97km (60 miles) north from the Skagerrak to Oslo. Basins dotted with islands fill the fjord. (There are 40 islands in the immediate Oslo archipelago.)

Nearly all visitors want to see **Holmenkollen,** a wooded range of hills northwest of the city rising to about 226m (1,740 ft.). You can reach it in 35 minutes by electric train from the city center.

Marka, Oslo's forest, is a sprawling recreation area with hiking, bicycle riding, skiing, fishing, wild berry picking, jogging trails, and more. It contains 343 lakes, 500km (310 miles) of ski trails, 623km (387 miles) of trails and roads, 11 sports chalets, and 24 ski jumps and alpine slopes.

2 Getting Around

BY PUBLIC TRANSPORTATION

Oslo has an efficient citywide network of buses, trams (streetcars), and subways. Buses and electric trains take passengers to the suburbs; from mid-April to October, ferries to Bygdøy depart from the harbor in front of the Oslo Rådhuset (City Hall).

DISCOUNT PASSES   The **Oslo Card (Oslo-Kortet)** can help you become acquainted with the city at a fraction of the usual price. It allows free travel on public transportation, free admission to museums and other top sights, discounts on sight-seeing buses and boats, a rebate on your car rental, and special treats in restaurants. You can purchase the card at hotels, fine stores, and tourist information offices, from travel agents, and in the branches of Sparebanken Oslo Akershus. Adults pay 180NOK ($24) for a 1-day card, 270NOK ($36) for 2 days, and 410NOK ($55) for 3 days. Children's cards cost 60NOK ($8), 80NOK ($11), and 110NOK ($15).

The 24-hour **Tourist Ticket (Turistkort)** lets you travel anywhere in Oslo by bus, tram, subway, local railway, or boat, including the Bygdøy ferries in the summer. The Tourist Ticket costs 40NOK ($5.30) for adults, half price for children 4 to 15; children under 4 travel free. The ticket will be stamped when it's used for the first time and is good for the next 24 hours.

BY BUS, TRAM & SUBWAY   Jernbanetorget is Oslo's major **bus and tram** terminal stop. Most buses and trams passing through the heart of town stop at Wessels Plass, next to the Parliament, or at Stortorget, the main marketplace. Many also stop at the National Theater or University Square on Karl Johans Gate, as well as Oslo's suburbs.

The **subway (T-banen)** has four branch lines to the east. The Western Suburban route (including Holmenkollen) has four lines to the residential sections and recreation grounds west and north of the city. Subways and trains leave from near the National Theater on Karl Johans Gate.

For schedule and fare information, call **Trafikanten** (© **22-05-70-37**). Automated machines cancel tickets. Drivers sell single-trip tickets for 22NOK ($2.95); children travel for half-fare. An eight-coupon Maxi card costs 135NOK ($18), half-price for children. Maxi cards can be used for unlimited transfers for 1 hour from the time the ticket is stamped.

BY TAXI

If you need a taxi, call © **22-38-80-90,** 24 hours a day. Reserve at least an hour in advance.

The approximate fare from Oslo International Airport to the center of Oslo is 500NOK ($67). All taxis have meters, and Norwegian cab drivers are generally honest. When a cab is available, a roof light goes on. Taxis can be hailed on the street, provided they're more than 100 yards from a taxi rank. The most difficult time to hail a taxi is Monday to Friday from 8:30 to 10am and 3 to 5pm, and Saturday 8:30 to 10am.

BY CAR

Driving is not a practical way to get around Oslo because parking is limited. The efficient public transportation system makes a private car unnecessary. You can reach even the most isolated areas by public transportation.

Among the multistory parking lots in the city center the best is **Vestre Vika Bilpark,** Dronning Mauds Gate (© **22-83-35-35**). The cost of parking a car in

Oslo Public Transportation

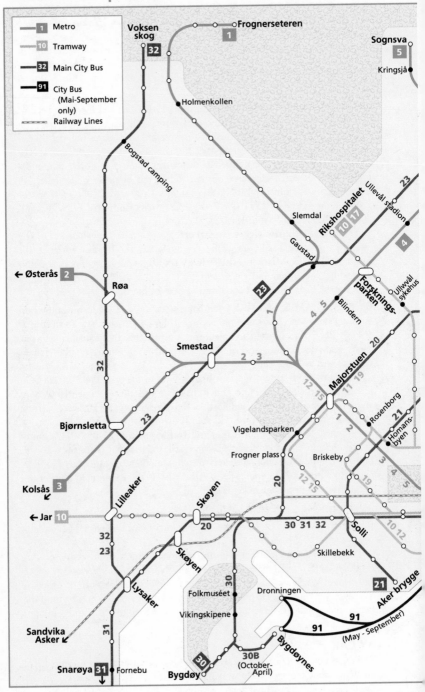

Legend:
- Metro `1`
- Tramway `10`
- Main City Bus `32`
- City Bus (Mai-September only) `91`
- Railway Lines

Voksen skog `32`

Frognerseteren `1`

Sognsva `5`

Kringsjå

Holmenkollen

Bogstad camping

Slemdal

Rikshospitalet `10` `17`

Ullevål stadion `23`

Gaustad

Forsknings-parken

Ullevål sykehus `4`

← Østerås `2`

Røa

Blindern

Smestad

Majorstuen

Rosenborg `21`

Homans-byen

Bjørnsletta `23`

Vigelandsparken

Briskeby

Frogner plass

Kolsås `3`

← Jar `10`

Lilleaker

Skøyen

Solli

Skillebekk

Skøyen

Lysaker

Folkmuséet

Dronningen

Aker brygge `21`

Sandvika Asker ↙

Vikingskipene

Snarøya `31` • Fornebu

Bygdøy `30`

30B (October-April)

Bygdøynes

91

91 (May - September)

62

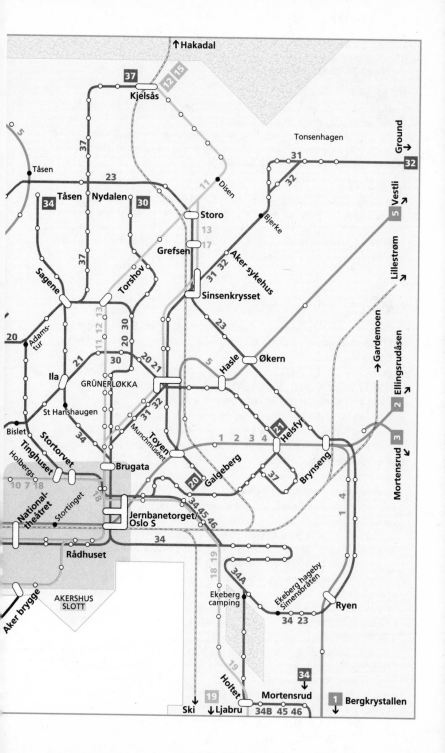

a public garage is 40NOK ($5.30) per hour or 175NOK ($23) for 24 hours. Illegally parked cars are towed away. For car problems, call the **NAF Alarm Center** (© **22-34-16-00**), 24 hours a day.

BY FERRY

Beginning in mid-April, ferries depart for Bygdøy from Pier 3 in front of the Oslo Rådhuset. For schedules, call **Båtservice** (© **23-35-68-90**). The ferry or bus to Bygdøy is a good choice, because parking there is limited. Other ferries leave for various parts of the Oslofjord. Inquire at the **Tourist Information Office,** Vestbaneplassen 1 (© **22-83-00-50**).

BY BICYCLE

Den Rustne Eike, Vestbaneplassen 2 (© **22-83-52-08**), rents bikes at moderate rates, complete with free maps of interesting routes in Oslo and its environs. The cost is 265NOK ($35) per day or 800NOK ($106) per week, with a 1,000NOK ($133) deposit required. It's open May to October, daily from 10am to 6:30pm; in the off-season, Monday to Friday from 10am to 6pm.

 FAST FACTS: **Oslo**

American Express American Express Reisebyrå, Karl Johans Gate 33 (© **22-98-37-00**), is open Monday to Friday from 9am to 6pm, Saturday from 10am to 3pm.

Area Code The country code for Norway is **47.** If you're calling from outside the country, the city code for Oslo is **2.** Inside Norway, no area or city codes are needed. Telephone numbers have eight digits.

Babysitters Hotels can often enlist the help of a housekeeper for "childminding." Give at least a day's notice, two if you can. You can also contact the tourist office (see "Visitor Information," earlier in this chapter), which keeps a list of available sitters on file.

Bookstores Oslo has many bookstores. The most central and one of the best stocked is **Tanum Karl Johan,** Karl Johans Gate 43 (© **22-41-11-00**).

Currency Exchange **Banks** will exchange most foreign currencies or cash traveler's checks. Bring your passport for identification. If banks are closed, try automated machines at the Oslo Sentralstasjon to exchange currency. You can also exchange currency at the **Bureau de Change** at the main Oslo post office, Dronningensgatan 15 (© **22-97-60-00**).

Dentists In an emergency, contact the **Tøyen Senter,** Kolstadgate 16 (© **22-67-78-00**), which is open daily from 11am to 2pm and 7 to 10pm. If you can wait, volume 1B of the telephone directory lists private dentists under *Tannleger* (literally "tooth doctors"). There's rarely a language barrier.

Doctors Some larger hotels have arrangements with doctors in case a guest becomes ill, or try the 24-hour **Oslo Kommunale Legevakten,** Storgata 40 (© **22-93-22-93**). A privately funded alternative is **Oslo Akutten,** Nedre Vollgate 8 (© **22-00-81-60**). For more routine medical assistance, you can contact the biggest hospital in Oslo, **Ullaval,** Kirkeveien 166 (© **22-11-80-80**). To consult a private doctor (nearly all of whom speak English), check the telephone directory or ask at your hotel for a recommendation.

Drugstores A 24-hour pharmacy is **Jernbanetorvets Apotek,** Jernbanetorget 4A (✆ **22-41-24-82**).

Embassies & Consulates See "Fast Facts: Norway," in chapter 2.

Emergencies Dial the Oslo **police** at ✆ **112;** report a **fire** to ✆ **110;** call an **ambulance** at ✆ **113.**

Eyeglass Repair **Ulf Jacobsen Optiker,** Karl Johans Gate 20 (✆ **22-42-85-14**), is a big supplier. Most contact lenses are in stock, too. Unusual prescriptions take about 2 days. Hours are Monday and Wednesday to Friday from 9am to 5pm, Tuesday 9am to 6pm, Saturday 10am to 2pm.

Internet Access You can tap in free at the Rådhuset, the City Hall on Rådhusplassen (✆ **22-46-16-00**). There is also free service at the library (see below, in this section) where you must sign up for slots.

Laundry & Dry Cleaning Washing and drying can usually be completed in an hour. You must have your coins ready to put in the machines. Dry cleaning is extremely expensive in Oslo, and many establishments take more than a week to return clothing. Try **Oslo American Rens,** Griniveien 1 (✆ **22-50-57-41**), which promises 24-hour service.

Libraries The Oslo municipal library, **Diechmann Library,** Henrik Ibsens Gate 1 (✆ **22-43-29-00**), is the largest in Norway. It has many English-language volumes, a children's department, and a music department. Hours are Monday to Friday from 10am to 8pm (to 6pm in summer), Saturday 9am to 2pm.

Lost Property The **Lost and Found Office,** Hittegodskontoret, Grølandsleiret 44 (✆ **22-66-98-65**), is open May 15 to September 15, Monday to Friday from 8:15am to 4:30pm; September 16 to May 14, Monday to Friday 8:15am to 3pm.

Luggage Storage & Lockers Facilities for luggage storage are available at the **Oslo Sentralstasjon,** Jernbanetorget 1 (✆ **81-50-08-88**). It's open daily from 7am to 11pm. Lockers cost 25NOK to 45NOK ($3.35–$6) per day, depending on size.

Newspapers & Magazines English-language newspapers and magazines are sold—at least in the summer months—at newsstands (kiosks) throughout Oslo. International editions, including the *International Herald Tribune* and *USA Today* are always available, as are the European editions of *Time* and *Newsweek.*

Photographic Needs Try **Preeus Photo,** Karl Johans Gate 33 (✆ **22-42-98-04**), for supplies, including black-and-white and color film. Film can be developed in 1 hour. It's open Monday to Friday from 9am to 5pm, Saturday 10am to 3pm.

Police Dial ✆ **112.**

Post Office The **Oslo General Post Office** is at Dronningensgatan 15 (✆ **23-14-90-00** for information). Enter at the corner of Prinsensgate. It's open Monday to Friday from 8am to 5pm, Saturday 9am to 2pm; closed Sunday and public holidays. You can arrange for mail to be sent to the main post office c/o General Delivery. The address is Poste Restante, P.O.

Box 1181-Sentrum, Dronningensgatan 15, N-0101 Oslo, Norway. You must show your passport to collect it.

Radio & TV The most important broadcaster is the Norwegian government, which owns and controls programming on the NRK station. Oslo receives many broadcasts from other countries, including BBC programs from London. Radio Norway International broadcasts on MHz frequency.

Restrooms Clean public toilets can be found throughout the city center, in parks, and at all bus, rail, and air terminals. For a detailed list, contact the Tourist Information Office.

Safety Of the four Scandinavian capitals, Oslo is widely considered the safest. However, don't be lulled into a false sense of security. Oslovians no longer leave their doors unlocked. Be careful, and don't carry your wallet visibly exposed or sling your purse over your shoulder.

Taxes Oslo has no special city taxes. You pay the same value-added tax throughout the country (see "Fast Facts: Norway," in chapter 2).

Taxis See "Getting Around," earlier in this chapter.

Transit Information For information about tram and bus travel, call **Trafikanten** (© **22-05-70-37**), located in front of the Central Station. For information about train travel, go to the Central Station or call © **23-15-00-00**.

Weather See the temperature chart in section 5, "When to Go," in chapter 2.

3 Where to Stay

By the standards of many U.S. and Canadian cities, hotels in Oslo are very expensive. If the prices make you want to cancel your trip, read on. Oslovian hotels lose most of their business travelers, and their main revenue source, during the peak tourist months in midsummer. Even though visitors fill the city, many hotels slash their prices. July is always a month for discounts. Some hotels' discounts begin June 21. Regular pricing usually resumes in mid-August. For exact dates of discounts, which often change from year to year, check with the hotel.

Hotels also slash prices on weekends—usually Friday and Saturday, and sometimes Sunday. Again, hotels often change their policies, so it's best to check when you make your reservations. Don't always expect a discount—a quickly arranged conference could lead hotels to increase their prices.

The most economy-minded tourists can cut costs by staying at one of the old-fashioned hotels that offer a number of rooms without private bathrooms. Sometimes a room has a shower but no toilet. In most cases, corridor toilets and bathrooms are plentiful. Even the rooms without bathrooms usually have a sink with hot and cold running water.

HOTEL RESERVATIONS The worst months for finding a place to stay in Oslo are May, June, September, and October, when many business conferences are held. July and August are better, even though that's the peak time of the summer tourist invasion.

If you happen to arrive in Oslo without a reservation, head for the Oslo Tourist Information Office (see earlier in this chapter), which can find you a room in your price category. The minimum stay is 2 days. Don't try to phone—the service is strictly for walk-ins who need a room on the night of their arrival.

Note: Rates quoted below include the service charge and tax. Breakfast—usually a generous Norwegian buffet—is almost always included. Unless otherwise indicated, all our recommended accommodations come with bathrooms.

CENTRAL OSLO
VERY EXPENSIVE

Grand Hotel ★★★ *(Kids)*   Norway's leading hostelry is on the wide boulevard that leads to the Royal Palace. The stone-walled hotel with its mansard gables and copper tower has been an integral part of Oslo life since 1874. Famous guests have included Arctic explorer Roald Amundsen, Edvard Munch, Gen. Dwight Eisenhower, Charlie Chaplin, Henry Ford, and Henrik Ibsen, who was especially fond of the place. More recent guests include recipients of the Nobel Peace Price, and such celebrities as Elton John and Michael Jackson.

Renovated in 1996, the guest rooms are in the 19th-century core or in one of the tasteful modern additions. Newer rooms contain plush facilities and electronic extras, and the older ones have been completely modernized. Most of the old-fashioned bathrooms are done in marble or tile and have shower-tub combinations. An eight-story extension contains larger, brighter doubles, but many guests prefer the old-fashioned accommodations in the older section.

The hotel has several restaurants that serve international and Scandinavian food. The Palmen, the Julius Fritzner, and the Grand Café offer live entertainment. The Grand Café is the most famous in Oslo. Frankly, although still the grand dame of Norway hotels, we feel the Grand has lost its cutting edge. Both the Hotels Bristol and Hotel Continental aren't as stuffy.

Karl Johans Gate 31, N-0101 Oslo. (*C*) 800/223-5652 in the U.S., or 23-21-20-00. Fax 23-21-21-00. www.grand-hotel.no. 289 units. Summer 1,200NOK ($160) double; 2,160NOK–22,000NOK ($287–$2,926) suite. Fall, winter, spring 1,935NOK ($257) double; 2,740NOK–22,000NOK ($364–$2,926) suite. Rates include buffet breakfast. AE, DC, MC, V. Parking 240NOK ($32). T-banen: Stortinget. **Amenities:** 3 restaurants; 2 bars; nightclub; indoor heated pool; health club; sauna; shopping arcade; limited room service; massage; laundry service; dry cleaning. *In room:* A/C, TV, minibar, hair dryer.

Hotel Continental ★★★   This is a major, immensely prestigious hotel alluring members of Norway's business community. It opened in 1900 as a rival to the also-recommended Grand Hotel. Since then, at least two (Annen Etage and Theatercafeen) of its five dining and drinking outlets have become enduring and successful staples on the city's restaurant scene. The only Norwegian member of Leading Hotels of the World, and the only major hotel in Oslo that's still mostly owned by an individual family (as headed by Elizabeth Brockmann), it's cozy, a bit inbred, and thoroughly conservative in its approach to virtually everything. Expect lots of personalized touches, such as a masterful collection of framed original lithographs and woodcuts by Edvard Munch in a salon near the reception area. Bedrooms are plush and intensely well decorated, often with wallpaper and an unerring upper-crust touch, sometimes evoking comfortable bedrooms in private homes. Bathrooms are tiled or clad in marble, each with a shower and tub combination.

Stortingsgaten 24-26, Oslo N-0117. (*C*) 22-82-40-00. Fax 22-42-96-89. www.hotel-continental.no. 154 units. Sun–Thurs 2,330NOK ($310) double, 3,500NOK ($466) suite; Fri–Sat 1,320NOK ($176) double, 2,650NOK ($352) suite. Rates include breakfast. AE, DC, MC, V. Parking 180NOK ($24). T-banen: National theatret. **Amenities:** 3 restaurants; 2 bars; 2 cafes; limited room service; babysitting; laundry service; dry cleaning. *In room:* A/C (in some), TV, minibar, hair dryer, safe.

EXPENSIVE

Clarion Hotel Royal Christiania ★★   This is the second-largest hotel in Norway, a soaring 14-story tower built to house athletes and administrators

Oslo Accommodations

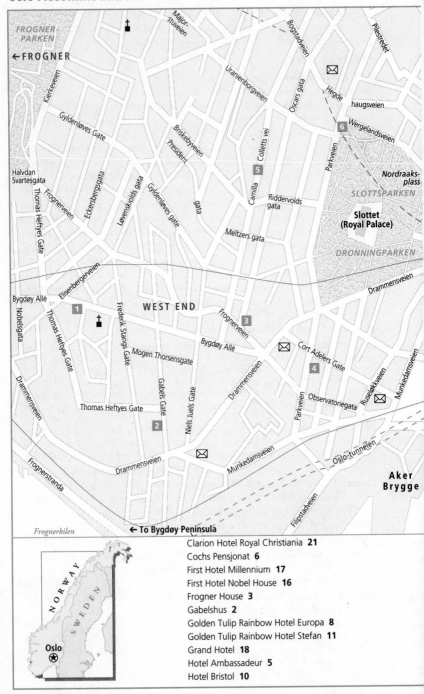

Clarion Hotel Royal Christiania **21**
Cochs Pensjonat **6**
First Hotel Millennium **17**
First Hotel Nobel House **16**
Frogner House **3**
Gabelshus **2**
Golden Tulip Rainbow Hotel Europa **8**
Golden Tulip Rainbow Hotel Stefan **11**
Grand Hotel **18**
Hotel Ambassadeur **5**
Hotel Bristol **10**

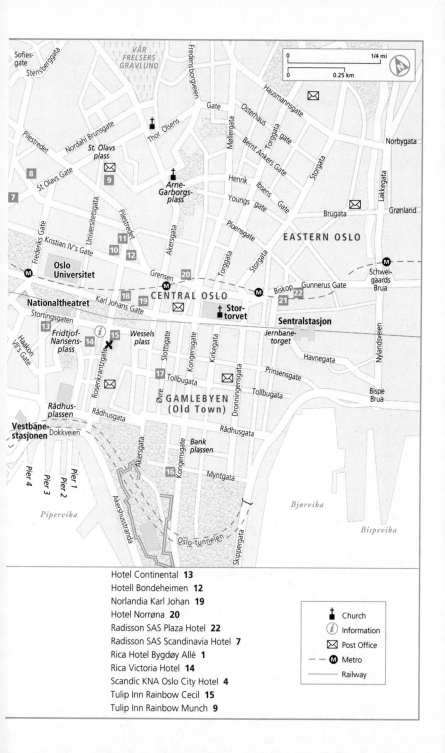

Hotel Continental **13**
Hotell Bondeheimen **12**
Norlandia Karl Johan **19**
Hotel Norrøna **20**
Radisson SAS Plaza Hotel **22**
Radisson SAS Scandinavia Hotel **7**
Rica Hotel Bygdøy Allé **1**
Rica Victoria Hotel **14**
Scandic KNA Oslo City Hotel **4**
Tulip Inn Rainbow Cecil **15**
Tulip Inn Rainbow Munch **9**

✝ Church
ⓘ Information
✉ Post Office
– ⓜ Metro
— Railway

⟮Kids⟯ Family-Friendly Hotels

Grand Hotel (p. 67)   The Grand's indoor pool provides an outlet for your child's energy. The "solve-everything" concierge can recommend babysitting services and diversions for children.

Hotel Bristol (below)   One of the most elegant and comfortable hotels in Oslo welcomes children and lets those under 15 stay free in their parents' room. The chef will even put a "junior steak" on the grill.

Hotel Norrøna (p. 74)   This reliable choice attracts the economy-minded family trade. There's a moderately priced cafe on the premises.

Rica Hotel Oslo Airport (p. 77)   At this spot near the airport, the staff sponsors children's programs and can arrange family outings, such as a trip on a paddle steamer.

---

during the 1952 Winter Olympics. It was extensively upgraded in 1990, with the addition of two nine-story wings, and it was enlarged again in 1999. Today it's a luxury hotel that is often favorably compared to the nearby Radisson SAS Plaza Hotel. This modern hotel and the surrounding high-traffic neighborhood don't evoke old-fashioned Norway, but you will find comfort, efficiency, good design, and a hardworking staff. Guest rooms are quiet, conservatively decorated, and blandly tasteful. The well-maintained bathrooms have shower-tub combinations and heated towel racks.

Biskop Gunnerus Gate 3, N-0106 Oslo. ☎ **23-10-80-00.** Fax 23-10-80-80. www.choicehotels.no/hotels/no036. 503 units. Sun–Thurs 1,995NOK ($265) double, 2,295NOK ($305) suite; Fri–Sat and June 15–Aug 1, 1,095NOK ($146) double, 1,395NOK ($186) suite. Rates include breakfast. AE, DC, MC, V. Parking 195NOK ($26). Bus: 30, 31, or 41. **Amenities:** Restaurant; 2 bars; pool; fitness center; sauna; limited room service; massage; babysitting; laundry service; dry cleaning. *In room:* TV, minibar, hair dryer.

Hotel Bristol ★★★ *Kids*   Loaded with character and anecdotes, this 1920s-era hotel competes aggressively and gracefully with two other historic properties, the Grand and the Continental. Of the three, the Bristol consistently emerges as the hippest and the most accessible. Set in the commercial core of Oslo, 1 block north of Karl Johans Gate, the Bristol is warm, rich with tradition, and comfortable. It also isn't as formal or oppressive as either the Grand or the Continental. To an increasing degree, it's becoming the preferred hotel of the media, arts, and show-biz communities, with a sense of playfulness and fun that's unmatched by either of its rivals.

In 2001, the hotel almost doubled its room count, thanks to the annexation and conversion of an office building next door. Bedrooms are comfortable and dignified, but not as plush or as intensely "decorated" as the rooms in either of its grander competitors. Each accommodation comes with a tiled or marble bathroom with a tub and shower combination. Lavish public areas still evoke the Moorish-inspired Art Deco heyday in which they were built. There's enormous life and energy in this hotel—thanks to active restaurants, piano bars, and a sense of elegant yet unpretentious conviviality.

Kristian IV's Gate 7, N-0164 Oslo 1. ☎ **22-82-60-00.** Fax 22-82-60-01. www.bristol.no. 252 units. Mon–Thurs late Aug to early June 1,350NOK–1,960NOK ($180–$261) double; Fri–Sun year-round and daily late June to early Aug 1,195NOK ($159) double, 4,000NOK–8,000NOK ($532–$1,064) suite. AE, DC, MC, V. Tram: 10, 11, 17, 18. **Amenities:** 3 restaurants; 3 bars; live pianist in the lobby; nightclub/dance bar; small-scale exercise room and health club; limited room service; babysitting; laundry service; dry cleaning. *In room:* A/C, TV, minibar, hair dryer, trouser press.

Radisson SAS Plaza Hotel ★

With an exterior sheathed in blue-tinted glass, and a needle-nosed summit that soars high above everything else in Oslo, this is the tallest building in Norway, and the largest hotel in northern Europe. When the Resa hotel chain built it in 1980, the hotel provoked screams of outrage from traditionalists, some of whom resented the transformation of the Oslo skyline into something that evoked a lesser version of sky-scraping New York or Chicago. Today, after a wrenching shake-up in ownership and many changes to its marketing approach, the hotel is a conservative and somewhat anonymous member of the Radisson SAS chain. The hotel struggles to permeate its vast, impersonal interior with a sense of intimacy and individuality. Many of its clients come as part of corporate conventions; to a lesser degree, as part of organized tours of Scandinavia. Regardless, guests do a lot of high-velocity elevator riding, and stay in hermetically sealed heated or air-conditioned rooms high above the city's commercial core, almost immediately next to the city's bus and railway stations. The high-altitude views are sublime, and the comfortable, well-decorated rooms have flair and original works of art. Each unit comes with an immaculate bathroom with tub-and-shower combination. The bar on the 34th floor has a panoramic view (Mon–Sat 4pm–1am).

Sonja Henies Plass 3. N-0134 Oslo. ☏ 22-05-80-10. Fax 22-05-80-10. www.radissonsas.com. 673 units. Mon–Thurs 1,800NOK–2,100NOK ($239–$279) double, Fri–Sun and daily June–Aug 980NOK–1,280NOK ($130–$170). Rates include breakfast. AE, DC, MC, V. T-banen: Jernbanetorget. **Amenities:** 2 restaurants; 2 bars; 24-hr. room service. *In room:* A/C, TV, minibar, TV, safe.

Radisson SAS Scandinavia Hotel ★

This black, angular building in the International style was built in 1975 as the Norwegian flagship of the hotel group now known as Radisson SAS. Thanks to aggressive, seasonal price adjustments and an appealing setting, this "grandfather" of Oslo's modern hotels boasts an average occupancy rate of 73%, as opposed to the Norwegian national average of only 54%. With 22 floors, this is Oslo's third biggest hotel (after the Radisson SAS Plaza Hotel and the Clarion Hotel Royal Christiana), the second-tallest building, and the first hotel that most Oslovians think of when they hear the name "SAS Hotel." It also has a wider range of amenities than much of its younger competition. (For more on this, see "Amenities" immediately below.) Bedrooms are relatively large, very comfortable, and come in about a dozen different styles, including Scandinavian, Japanese, ersatz "rococo," Art Deco, and (newest of all), a nautical style inspired by the maritime traditions of Norway. The stylish lobby was radically renovated in 2002.

Holbergsgate 30. N-0166 Oslo. ☏ 23-29-30-00. Fax 23-29-30-01. www.radissonsas.com. 488 units. Mon–Thurs 1,800NOK–2,100NOK ($239–$279) double; Fri–Sun and mid-June to Aug 980NOK–1,280NOK ($130–$170) double, 3,500NOK–5,000NOK ($466–$665) suite. AE, DC, MC, V. T-banen: Nationaltheatret. Parking: 195NOK ($26). **Amenities:** 3 restaurants; 2 bars (1 of which has a panoramic view from the 21st floor); indoor pool; health club/fitness center; sauna; concierge; an underground shopping arcade with 8 large boutiques; babysitting; laundry service; dry cleaning. *In room:* A/C, TV, minibar.

Rica Victoria Hotel ★

One of the most appealing modern hotels in its neighborhood, this hotel enjoys an enviable position midway between the Aker Brygge restaurant and office complex and the Norwegian Parliament. Originally built in 1991, the hotel was enlarged in 1994 when the uppermost three stories were added in anticipation of that year's winter Olympics. Often fully booked, the hotel has one of the highest occupancy rates in downtown Oslo. Some of the most charming rooms are on the ninth (uppermost) floor, where the sloping walls of the Mansard-style roof add a general coziness. Regardless of their location within the hotel, rooms have wood flooring and tile-covered bathrooms, about half of which have shower-tub combinations. (The remaining rooms have showers only.) Rooms are conservative, dignified, and comfortable, with an appealingly non-standardized format that includes a number of windows, rounded corners, and color schemes of golds, dark blues, and russets.

Rosenkrantzgate 13, N-0121 Oslo. ✆ **24-14-70-00.** Fax 24-14-70-01. www.rica.no. 199 units. Sun–Thurs 1,480NOK ($190) double; 2,450NOK–2,700NOK ($326–$359) suite. Fri–Sun and mid-June to July 940NOK ($125) double; 1,600NOK–1,850NOK ($213–$246) suite. Rates include breakfast. Parking 175NOK ($23) per night. AE, DC, MC, V. Tram: 10, 11, 17, or 18. **Amenities:** Restaurant (the Victoria Havn); bar; babysitting; laundry service; dry cleaning. *In room:* TV, minibar.

MODERATE

First Hotel Millennium ★ *Finds*   One of Oslo's newest large-scale hotels opened late in 1998 within what was originally a 1930s Art Deco office building. It's within walking distance of virtually everything in central Oslo, including the Akershus fortress and the shops of the Karl Johans Gate. Rising nine floors behind a pale pink facade, it's noted for a stylish kind of minimalism, which in the bedrooms translates into ocher-colored walls with dark wood trim, streamlined wooden furniture, and lots of comfort. This is one of the "personality" hotels of Oslo, known for its atmosphere and character. The accommodations are among the most spacious in town, with many Art Deco touches in the furnishings and designs. Each unit has a large bathroom equipped with a tub-shower combination. Some of the accommodations are suitable for persons with disabilities. The hotel is completely nonsmoking; no cigarettes are allowed anywhere inside.

Tollbugate 25, N-0157 Oslo. ✆ **21-02-28-00.** Fax 21-02-28-30. www.firsthotels.com. 112 units. Mon–Thurs 1,103NOK–1,510NOK ($147–$201) double; Fri–Sun 703NOK–853NOK ($94–$113) double. AE, DC, MC, V. Tram: 30, 42. **Amenities:** Restaurant; bar; limited room service; babysitting; laundry service; dry cleaning. *In room:* TV, minibar, hair dryer.

First Hotel Nobel House ★ *Finds*   This elegant boutique hotel, whose lobby has a seven-story glassed-in atrium with Oriental carpets, columns, and a fireplace, has a personalized feel. A member of a Sweden-based hotel chain, the hotel has a polite staff and a lot of idiosyncratic style. Oddly, this is one of the few hotels anywhere where we prefer the regular rooms to the oddly laid-out, curiously spartan suites, where lots of room might be devoted, say, to an interior hallway. Each of the suites is theme-based on the life of a famous Scandinavian, usually with photographic tributes. Rooms and suites are accessible via a labyrinthine path of stairs and many, angled hallways, and are sometimes a bit hard to find unless you're being escorted by a staff member. Each unit has a minikitchen, some kind of original art, and in many cases, exposed brick. Each unit comes with a neatly tiled bathroom with tub and shower.

Kongensgaten 5, N-0153 Oslo. ✆ **23-10-72-01.** Fax 23-10-72-10. 69 units. Mon–Thurs 1,602NOK ($213) double, 2,149NOK–2,999NOK ($286–$399) suite. Fri–Sun 1,420NOK ($189) double, 1,789NOK–2,499NOK ($238–$332) suite. Rates include breakfast. AE, DC, MC, V. Parking 150NOK ($20) per night. T-banen: Stortinget. **Amenities:** Restaurant; bar; laundry service; dry cleaning. *In room:* A/C, TV, minibar, iron/ironing board.

Golden Tulip Rainbow Hotel Europa   Few other hotels enjoy a position as quiet yet as convenient to Karl Johans Gate as this red-brick member of Holland's Golden Tulip chain. The building faces a large patch of greenery, and the front entrances of two of Oslo's museums, the Tekniska Musuet (Technical Museum) and the Nasjionell Galleriet (National Gallery). The hotel was originally built as a complex of private apartments, before being transformed in the 1970s into this efficient and well-managed hotel. Bedrooms are compact but comfortable, with burl-grained walnut veneers and writing desks, each with a small, shower-only bathtub. In keeping with its name, a large and decorative map of Europe is displayed behind the front desk.

St. Olavs Gate 31, N-0166 Oslo. ℂ 23-25-63-00. Fax 23-25-63-63. www.rainbow-hotels.no/europa. 167 units. Sun–Thurs 1,470NOK ($196) double; Fri–Sat and mid-June to mid-Aug 850NOK ($113) double; year-round daily 1,795NOK–2,195NOK ($239–$292) suite. AE, DC, MC, V. T-banen: Stortinget. **Amenities:** Restaurant; bar. *In room:* A/C, TV, minibar, hair dryer on request, safe.

Golden Tulip Rainbow Hotel Stefan   In an excellent location in the center of the city, this hotel is comfortable and unpretentious. Built in 1952, it has been modernized and much improved, with a partial renovation in 1996. The color-coordinated guest rooms are traditional in style and well furnished and maintained, with small but adequate bathrooms containing shower-tub combinations. Two guest rooms offer facilities for people with disabilities. From May until September 1, weekend rates are granted only to those who make reservations less than 48 hours before arrival.

Rosenkrantzgate 1, N-0159 Oslo 1. ℂ 23-31-55-00. Fax 23-31-55-55. www.rainbow-hotels.no. 139 units. Mon–Thurs 1,015NOK ($135) double; Fri–Sat 735NOK ($98) double. Rates include breakfast. AE, DC, MC, V. Parking 180NOK ($24). Tram: 10, 11, 17, or 18. **Amenities:** Restaurant; bar; limited room service; babysitting; laundry service; dry cleaning. *In room:* TV, minibar, hair dryer, safe.

Hotell Bondeheimen   In the city center, a short block from the Students' Grove at Karl Johans Gate, the Bondeheimen was built in 1913. A cooperative of farmers and students established this hotel to provide inexpensive accommodations when they visited Oslo from the countryside. Although small, the compact rooms are comfortably furnished, often with Norwegian pine pieces; accommodations for nonsmokers are offered. The hotel was renovated in 1995. The beds are good, and the bathrooms, although small and mostly without tubs, contain shower units and heated floors.

Rosenkrantzgate 8 (entrance on Kristian IV's Gate), N-0159 Oslo 1. ℂ 800/528-1234 in the U.S., or 22-21-41-00. Fax 22-41-94-37. www.bondeheimen.com. 81 units. Mon–Thurs 2,105NOK ($280) double; Fri–Sun 834NOK ($111) double. Rates include breakfast. AE, DC, MC, V. Parking 180NOK ($24). Tram: 7 or 11. **Amenities:** Restaurant; bar; boutique; limited room service; laundry service; dry cleaning. *In room:* TV, minibar, hair dryer.

Norlandia Karl Johan ✦   For the past century or so, an old-fashioned aura hung about this gray stone hotel, the former Karl Johan. Now, a recent renovation has made it brighter, more inviting, and a lot less dim compared to its neighbor across the street, the prestigious (yet still far better) Grand Hotel. Filled with Norwegian folk art, the Norlandia welcomes you to a reception area filled with mirrors and marble, along with rugs from Asia and antiques (or reproductions at least). The medium-size bedrooms have a classic decor with excellent fabrics, good beds, double glazing on the windows to cut down on the noise outside, and tiny but marble-clad bathrooms with shower-tub combinations. The best units open onto the front, and contain French windows with a panorama of the central city. About 50% of the accommodations are reserved for nonsmokers.

Karl Johans Gate 33, N-0162 Oslo. ℂ 23-16-17-00. Fax 22-42-05-19. www.norlandia.no. 111 units. Mon–Thurs 1,570NOK ($209) double, 1,890NOK ($251) suite; Fri–Sun 990NOK ($132) double, 2,300NOK ($306) suite. Rates include breakfast. AE, DC, MC, V. Parking 187NOK ($25) in nearby public garage. T-banen: Stortinget. **Amenities:** Restaurant; bar; limited room service; laundry service; dry cleaning. *In room:* TV, minibar, hair dryer.

Tulip Inn Rainbow Cecil   Following a fire in the mid-1980s, when an older building on this centrally located site was destroyed, this contemporary hotel was built. Thanks to the eccentrically shaped site, only four rooms on each of the eight floors overlook the street (the sometimes rowdy, at least late at night, Rosenkrantzgate). The others look out over a quiet inner courtyard. Expect relatively simple styling with none of the trappings of more expensive nearby competitors—there's no health club, sauna, or full-fledged room service. The well-maintained rooms are cozy and contain neatly kept bathrooms with shower-tub combinations.

Stortingsgate 8 (entrance on Rosenkrantzgate), N-0130 Oslo. © **23-31-48-00.** Fax 23-31-48-50. www. rainbow-hotels.no. 112 units. Mon–Thurs 1,370NOK ($182) double; Fri–Sat 830NOK ($110) double. AE, DC, MC, V. Parking 165NOK ($22). T-banen: Stortinget. **Amenities:** Lounge; laundry service; dry cleaning. *In room:* A/C, TV, minibar, hair dryer.

INEXPENSIVE

Cochs Pensjonat *Value* This is a clean, well-conceived, inexpensive hotel that represents excellent value. Built more than a century ago, the building has an ornate facade that curves around a bend in a boulevard that banks the northern edge of the Royal Palace. In 2002, major renovations added a postmodern gloss to many of the bedrooms, with the remainder scheduled for overhauls sometime between 2003 and 2004. The result is a comfortable but simple lodging whose newer rooms are high ceilinged, spartan but pleasant, and outfitted with birch wood furniture. Older rooms evoke touches of the slightly dowdy, slightly battered 1970s, but are still very comfortable. You'll climb a flight of antique steps from the ground floor to reach the second-floor lobby. Rooms—including a communal TV lounge that's sometimes packed with residents—rise for two additional floors above that. Expect very few, if any, amenities and services at this hotel—rooms are without TV or telephone. However, thanks to in-room kitchens and a nearby restaurant that offers hotel guests a 25% discount on meals, no one really seems to mind that the hotel doesn't have food service.

Parkveien 25, N-0350 Oslo. © **23-33-24-00.** Fax 23-33-24-10. booking@cochs.no. 88 units (78 with bathroom and kitchenette). Rooms with bathroom and kitchenette 600NOK–660NOK ($80–$88) double, 735NOK–795NOK ($98–$106) triple, 860NOK ($114) quad. Rooms without kitchenette and without private bathroom 500NOK ($67) double, 615NOK ($82) triple, 740NOK ($98) quad. AE, DC, MC, V. Tram: 11 or 12. *In room:* Kitchen, no phone.

Hotel Norrøna *Kids* Occupying the upper floors of a modernized building, this hotel is ideal for families. Convenient to both sightseeing and shopping, it offers well-equipped rooms, with good beds, furnished in Scandinavian modern style. A few rooms have private balconies. Many rooms are large enough for families of three or four, although bathrooms have only minimal space, but do contain shower-tub combinations.

Grensen 19, N-0159 Oslo 1. © **23-31-80-00.** Fax 23-31-80-01. www.rainbow-hotels.no. 93 units. 850NOK–1,310NOK ($113–$174) double. Rates include breakfast. AE, DC, MC, V. Parking 140NOK ($19). T-banen: Stortinget. Tram: 1 or 7. Bus: 17. **Amenities:** Restaurant; lounge; laundry service; dry cleaning. *In room:* A/C, TV.

Scandic KNA Oslo City Hotel This hotel looks deceptively new, thanks to a futuristic-looking mirrored facade that was added in the 1970s to an older core that was originally built in the 1940s by the Norwegian Auto Club. Room rates rise steeply in winter, but if you come in summer, it's a real bargain. Inside, you'll find a cozy lobby-level bar and restaurant serving Norwegian food, a deeply entrenched kind of informality, and a reception staff that's a bit inexperienced. Bedrooms are simple, clean, and a bit spartan-looking. The small bathrooms are shower-only. A renovation last occurred in the early 1990s. The low summer prices and a neighborhood that's calm, quiet, and close to the Royal Palace, make up for the shortcomings. If you're a self-motivated kind of traveler with a clear idea of what you want to see and where you want to go in Oslo, without much need for attention or advice from the staff, this might be an appropriate choice.

Parkveien 68, N-0254 Oslo. © **23-15-57-00.** Fax 23-15-57-11. www.scandic-hotels.com. 189 units. Sept–Apr 1,645NOK–1,925NOK ($219–$256) double; May–Aug 796NOK–996NOK ($106–$132) double. No discounts on weekends. AE, DC, MC, V. Tram: 12, 15. **Amenities:** Restaurant; bar; health club; sauna; 24-hr. room service. *In room:* TV, minibar, trouser press.

Tulip Inn Rainbow Munch   This hotel, somewhat like a bed-and-breakfast, is just 5 minutes north of Karl Johans Gate. Built in 1983, the solid, nine-floor hotel offers comfortably furnished, well-maintained guest rooms, decorated with reproductions of Edvard Munch's paintings. Although not overly large, the rooms are cozy and comfortable. The bathrooms are tiny but come equipped with shower-tub combinations. If you don't plan to spend a lot of time in your room, this is an adequate choice, charging a fair price for what it offers.

Munchsgaten 5, N-0130 Oslo 1. © **23-21-96-00.** Fax 23-21-96-01. www.rainbow-hotels.no. 180 units. Mon–Thurs 1,145NOK ($152) double, Fri–Sun 720NOK ($96) double. Rates include breakfast. AE, DC, MC, V. Parking 140NOK ($19). T-banen: Stortinget. Tram: 7 or 11. Bus: 37. **Amenities:** Lounge; laundry service; dry cleaning. *In room:* TV, minibar, hair dryer, safe.

WEST END
EXPENSIVE

Frogner House ★   In 1992, a turn-of-the-20th-century red-brick apartment house was transformed into this stylish, upscale hotel. In the affluent Oslo suburb of Frogner, about a half-mile west of the city's commercial core, it's outfitted in conservative but cozy English style, with lots of lace curtains, a scattering of antiques, and soft cheerful colors. This hotel has built its reputation by catering to international business travelers, many involved in shipping and real estate. This is an upscale bed-and-breakfast, loaded with attentive service and comforts, but most luxuries must be arranged through outside suppliers by the reception staff. Each room is well maintained and equipped with well-kept bathrooms with shower-tub combinations.

Skovveien 8, Frogner, N-0257 Oslo. © **22-56-00-56.** Fax 22-56-05-00. www.frognerhouse.com. 60 units. Sun–Thurs 1,515NOK ($202) double, Fri–Sat 1,025NOK ($136) double. AE, DC, MC, V. Tram: 12. **Amenities:** Lounge; limited room service. *In room:* TV, minibar, hair dryer.

Hotel Ambassadeur ★   One of the most consistently reliable hotels in Oslo, the Hotel Ambassadeur was built around 1890 as an apartment house. Near the Royal Palace, in an upscale residential neighborhood, it boasts a well-upholstered salon with tapestries and antiques. The theme-decorated guest rooms were renovated between 1994 and 1998. They have double-glazed windows, good beds, and trouser presses. The small, tiled bathrooms have shower-tub combinations and heated towel racks. Suites are more elaborate.

Camilla Colletts Vei 15, N-0258 Oslo. © **23-27-23-00.** Fax 22-44-47-91. www.bestwestern.com/no/ ambassadeur. 41 units. Mon–Thurs 1,375NOK ($183) double, 1,750NOK ($233) suite; Fri–Sun 910NOK ($121) double, 1,350NOK ($180) suite. Rates include breakfast. AE, DC, MC, V. Free parking. Bus: 21. **Amenities:** Restaurant; bar; fitness room; sauna; laundry service; dry cleaning. *In room:* TV, minibar, hair dryer.

MODERATE

Gabelshus ★ *Finds*   On a quiet, tree-lined street, this 1912 building has been a small hotel since 1945. Discreetly conservative, it looks like an English manor house, laced with climbing ivy. The public rooms are filled with antiques, art, burnished copper, and working fireplaces. Guest rooms are decorated with tasteful colors and textiles, and some have terraces. You have a choice of

Scandinavian modern furniture or traditional styling. The accommodations are well maintained and equipped with double-glazed windows and good beds. Bathrooms are small but immaculate, with shower-tub combinations. The location is a brisk 15-minute walk from the city center.

Gabels Gate 16, N-0272 Oslo 2. ✆ **23-27-65-00.** Fax 23-27-65-60. www.gabelshus.no. 43 units. July and Fri–Sun year-round 950NOK ($126) double; rest of year 1,495NOK ($199) double, 1,790NOK ($238) suite. Rates include breakfast. AE, DC, MC, V. Free parking. Tram: 10. **Amenities:** Breakfast room; lounge; laundry service; dry cleaning. *In room:* TV, hair dryer.

Rica Hotel Bygdøy Allé ★ *(Finds* This intimate, charming hotel, the smallest in the Rica chain, has the air of an artsy boutique hotel. Its designers shoehorned it into the framework of a late 19th-century Flemish-revival brick structure in Oslo's well-heeled West End. Each of the bedrooms is different in its layout, corresponding to the already-existing towers and gables of the older structure. Rooms 206, 214, 406, and 414 are among the most sought-after rooms because of their Victorian-era curved walls and bay windows. Other than that, decors are conservative and predictably upscale, and a bit bland, usually in tones of pale blue. Each unit comes with a small bathroom with shower. There's no restaurant on-site, per se, but the hotel maintains a cooperative relationship with one of Oslo's most vogue-ish restaurants, Magma, which occupies most of its ground floor, and whose outdoor tables (during the warm weather months) flank its front entrance. As such, clients of this hotel walk just a few steps for meals (including breakfast) within one of the capital's most appealing restaurants.

Bygdøy Allé 53, N-0265 Oslo. ✆ **23-08-58-00.** Fax 23-08-58-08. www.rica.no. 57 units. Sun–Thurs 1,220NOK–1,595NOK ($162–$212) double; Fri–Sat 920NOK–1,195NOK ($122–$159) double. Rates include breakfast. AE, DC, MC, V. Tram 10 or bus 30, 31, 32, 33. **Amenities:** Direct access to the dining and drinking facilities of the Magma; laundry service; dry cleaning. *In room:* A/C, TV, minibar.

HOLMENKOLLEN
EXPENSIVE

Holmenkollen Park Hotel Rica Oslo ★ On a panoramic hillside crowning Oslo, this hotel sits on forested land that's devoted to recreation, cross-country skiing, and hiking. Come here for an escape from the commercial core of Oslo, but know in advance that its location outside the center, a short walk from the Holmenkollen ski jump, at the terminus of Tram line #1, seems far removed from the rest of the city and its attractions and diversions. The hotel was built in 1894, rebuilt after a fire in 1904, reconstructed again in 1948 after a 4-year occupation by the Nazis during World War II, and then massively enlarged with four new wings in 1982, when it was taken over by the Rica hotel chain. Today, the oldest part of the hotel (a richly detailed log and timbered building designed in the Viking Revival "dragon" style) is used for check-ins and for convention facilities; the remainder contains modern, comfortable, and cozy bedrooms and all the facilities you'd expect in a modern resort hotel. Bedrooms are cozy, with lots of exposed wood, hints of chalet styling, and in many cases, punctuated with historic photos from the lives of important Norwegians. The well-maintained bathrooms come with tub-and-shower combination. In vivid contrast to the glowing paneling of the oldest sections of the hotel, the convention facilities are extremely modern—the poshest in Oslo.

Kongeveien 26, N-0390 Oslo. ✆ **22-92-20-00.** Fax 22-14-61-92. www.holmenkollenparkhotel.no. 192 units. Mon–Thurs 1,695NOK–1,995NOK ($225–$265) double; Fri–Sun 1,095NOK–1,995NOK ($146–$265) double; daily 2,750–14,000NOK ($366–$1862) suite. Rates include breakfast. AE, DC, MC, V. Tram: 1. **Amenities:** 3 restaurants; bar; health club with indoor pool, sauna, and Jacuzzi; free shuttle service from hotel to Oslo city center and the railway station; babysitting; laundry service; dry cleaning; marked jogging and cross-country ski trails in the vicinity; extensive convention facilities. *In room:* A/C, TV, minibar, hair dryer, safe.

AT THE AIRPORT
EXPENSIVE

Radisson SAS Airport Hotel ✦   This is the kind of airport hotel that you fall into with gratitude, before or after your flight. To travel between the arrivals terminal and the hotel, designed as an integral part of the Gardemoen airport, wheel your luggage, on the free carts distributed at the hotel and throughout the airport, along a series of sloping cement ramps and across a busy access road (cars will stop and wait for you if you cross on any of the clearly designated crosswalks). The architecture is as futuristic and well conceived as you might expect, and rapid checkout (via your TV screen) in the morning eliminates a lot of the fuss and bother that's otherwise associated with getting to the airport on time. Bedrooms have lavishly carved headboards in a style that's vaguely Thai or Indonesian, glistening white-tiled bathrooms, and writing tables, plus bathrooms with tub-and-shower combinations. Like any airport hotel, this one is somewhat impersonal, and trammeled over by hordes of travelers en route to somewhere else, and the restaurants are far from personalized. But here, the mixture of personalities, races, and agendas make people-watching genuinely interesting. Other complaints about this place include an awkwardly designed bar that's a lot less comfortable and accommodating than we might have hoped for, and a health club whose hours simply don't take into account the stress-related tension of guests arriving long after it's already locked its doors for the day and night.

Hotellvegen, Box 163, N-2061 Gardemoen. ✆ **63-93-30-00.** Fax 63-93-30-30. www.radissonsas.com. 350 units. 1,595NOK–1,895NOK ($212–$252) double, 3,900NOK–4,900NOK ($519–$652) suite. AE, DC, MC, V. **Amenities:** 2 restaurants (1 of which is opened only when the hotel is nearly full); bar; health club with sauna; 24-hr. room service; massage; meeting rooms. *In room:* A/C, TV, minibar.

Rica Hotel Oslo Airport ✦ *Kids*   The "other" Gardemoen airport hotel is not as glossy or stylish as the Radisson SAS (see above), but it's well run and an alternative choice if the more popular hotel is full as it often is. Alas, it's not directly at the airport, but only a 5-minute shuttle-hop away. Motorists can easily access the hotel via Route E6. It's a check-in, check-out kind of place housing weary passengers coming and going to Norway from all over the world. The four-story property offers streamlined and rather small bedrooms that are immaculately maintained and comfortable, each with a tiled bathroom with shower. The clients are mostly business travelers or families traveling with kids in tow. The staff sponsors special children's programs. A shuttle service runs back and forth between the hotel and airport. If you want to work off jet lag, the staff will point out jogging trails, arrange golf, or book excursions on a paddle steamer traversing the lake.

Gardemoen Naeringspark, N-2065 Gardemoen. ✆ **63-92-66-00.** Fax 63-92-67-00. www.rica.no. 346 units. 1,095NOK–1,570NOK ($146–$209) double. AE, DC, MC, V. Free parking. **Amenities:** Restaurant; bar; massage; laundry service; dry cleaning. *In room:* A/C, TV, minibar, hair dryer.

4 Where to Dine

You can now "dine around the world" without leaving the city of Oslo. The biggest concentration of restaurants is at Aker Brygge. This former shipbuilding yard on the harbor front is now the smartest dining and shopping complex in Norway.

Not all restaurants in Oslo are new. Some have long been associated with artists and writers—the Grand Café, for example, was the stomping ground of Henrik Ibsen and Edvard Munch.

The influx of foreigners in recent years has led to the growth of Mexican, Turkish, Moroccan, Chinese, Greek, and other international restaurants. Among European cuisines, French and Italian are the most popular. Many restaurants offer American-style food.

At nearly all restaurants recommended below, a 15% service charge and the 20% value-added tax are included in the bill. No further tipping is required, although it's customary to leave some small change if the service has been satisfactory.

Wine and beer can be lethal to your final bill, so be careful.

CENTRAL OSLO
VERY EXPENSIVE

Annen Etage ★★★ CONTINENTAL   This impeccable grande dame of social propriety with vast amounts of bourgeois conservatism and, frankly, not a lot of humor, has long been a staple of Oslo's dining scene. It caters to business dinners, extended Norwegian families celebrating rites of passage, and anyone looking for superb food in a setting that's about as solid as the National Bank of Norway. (True, both Elton John and Gérard Depardieu have been spotted here, but the usual client is a lot less flashy.) The high-ceilinged dining room is one floor above the lobby of the Hotel Continental—thus its name (*Annen Etage* translates as "1st floor").

Annen Etage is one of the great restaurants of Norway. The cuisine makes up for a certain stuffiness—only Oro does it better. Our most recent repast of sautéed scallops with chicken liver purée, suckling pig with an apple compote, and passion fruit soufflé was among the finest we've had in the country. We've also taken delight in the terrine of foie gras served here with Sauternes jelly. The pan-fried bay scallops with a saffron vanilla sauce don't get much better in Norway, nor does the grilled turbot with a vichyssoise of poached oysters. Our table rejoiced when it came time for dessert, and we were served a memorable lemon tart, a white chocolate mousse, and mango-ginger sorbet.

In the Hotel Continental, Stortingsgaten 24–26. ✆ **22-82-40-70.** Reservations recommended. Fixed-price menus 570NOK–890NOK ($76–$118) for 3–7 courses. AE, DC, MC, V. Dinner only Mon–Sat 6–11pm. Closed July. T-banen: Nationaltheatret.

Oro ★★★ CONTINENTAL   Gallons of ink have been used in the Norwegian press to describe this new, hyperstylish restaurant, winner of the American Express service award two years in a row. Norwegian-born chef Terje Ness directs the kitchen of a three-faceted establishment that includes a European gourmet restaurant, a separate but still very glamorous tapas bar, and a boutique-style deli (open Mon–Sat 9am–5pm) for fans of the place who want to haul some of its raw ingredients back home. The restaurant and the tapas bar are curvaceous, slick-looking testimonials to the appeal of stainless steel and warm-toned hardwoods. We recommend the fixed-price menus, although be warned that each of them will be prepared only for every member of the table at the same time. The 925NOK ($123) menu includes 10 different courses, each of them composed differently every day, according to the availability of the ingredients and the whim of the chef. Other options include a seven-course fish and shellfish menu, priced at 825NOK ($110), and a three-course vegetarian menu at 425NOK ($57). Representative dishes, each one delectable, include lobster ravioli, glazed scallops with Serrano ham, a platter that combines three different versions of foie gras (grilled, *en terrine,* and *en brioche*); and spit-roasted pigeon stuffed with foie gras.

Tordenskioldsgate 6A (entrance on Kjeld Stubs Gate). ℂ **23-01-02-40.** Reservations required. Main courses 315NOK–345NOK ($42–$46). Fixed-price menus 425NOK–925NOK ($57–$123). AE, DC, MC, V. Dinner Mon–Sat 6–10pm. Closed 2 weeks in Nov. T-banen: Stortinget.

Restaurant Julius Fritzner ★★★ NORWEGIAN/CONTINENTAL This is one of the best and most impressive restaurants in Oslo. It opened in 1995 to rave reviews and the accolades keep coming. It's one floor above street level in Norway's most prestigious hotel. The venue is appropriately conservative, with a battalion of impeccably trained waiters who maintain their humor and personal touch despite the sophisticated setting. The dishes, all made with the finest Scandinavian ingredients, change with the season and the chef's inspiration. Examples include pan-fried turbot, lobster and caviar sauce, crispy fried cod with sautéed vegetables, poached halibut with vermouth sauce, fillet of veal with crispy fried sweetbreads, and roast saddle of lamb with rosemary. Desserts, which are delicious and occasionally theatrical, include a terrine of chocolate with a compote of peaches and sorbet flavored with basil and cinnamon. The restaurant, incidentally, is named after the controversial entrepreneur who established the Grand Hotel in 1874.

In the Grand Hotel, Karl Johans Gate 31. ℂ **23-21-20-00.** Reservations recommended. Main courses 220NOK–300NOK ($29–$40); 3-course fixed-price menu 470NOK ($63), 4-course fixed-price menu 550NOK ($73), 6-course fixed-price menu 640NOK ($85). AE, DC, MC, V. Mon–Sat 5–10:30pm. Closed July–Aug 5. T-banen: Stortinget.

EXPENSIVE

Babette's Gjestehus ★ *Finds* SCANDINAVIAN Named for the heroine of the film *Babette's Feast*—which almost every Scandinavian has seen at least once—this restaurant is decorated in the style of a turn-of-the-20th-century Norwegian home. Walls are blue, antiques are genuine, curtains are lace, and there's a scattering of old paintings. Menu items are authentic as well, with such time-tested favorites as fillets of reindeer (not Santa's) with lingonberries, steamed brill with mustard sauce and stewed tomatoes, breast of pheasant with mushroom sauce, and pan-fried breast of duck with creamed cabbage. The masterful chefs use seasonal products to produce reliable, good-tasting food all year.

Rådhuspassasjen, Roald Amundsensgate 6. ℂ **22-41-64-64.** Reservations recommended. Main courses 249NOK–265NOK ($33–$35). AE, DC, MC, V. Mon–Sat 5–11pm. T-banen: Centrum.

House of Norway ★ *Finds* NORWEGIAN In the 17th century this was the mayor's residence. Today it is a special discovery devoted to the serving of a quality Norwegian cuisine. Recipes might be more than a century old but are given a modern interpretation. The restaurant has a dark, rustic look. In the cellar patrons sit at tables listening to piano music. Upstairs is a bar in autumnal colors where you can drink and order lunch. From the kitchen emerges such tempting platters as deep pan-fried cod with a rich butter sauce, served with a side order of saffron-flavored risotto. A real Norwegian dish is the elk baked and served with a cauliflower cream sauce, with such sides as cranberry sauce and boiled potatoes. Swordfish is served with potatoes and flavored with wasabi mayonnaise.

Prinsensgate 18. ℂ **22-41-12-10.** Reservations required. Main courses 275NOK–330NOK ($37–$44). AE, DC, MC, V. Tues–Sat 11am–11:30pm. Closed Dec 23–Jan 6 and July. T-banen: Stortinget.

MODERATE

Bristol Grill ★★ CONTINENTAL This is the premier dining room of one of Oslo's most prestigious hotels. You'll find old-world courtliness, formal

Oslo Dining

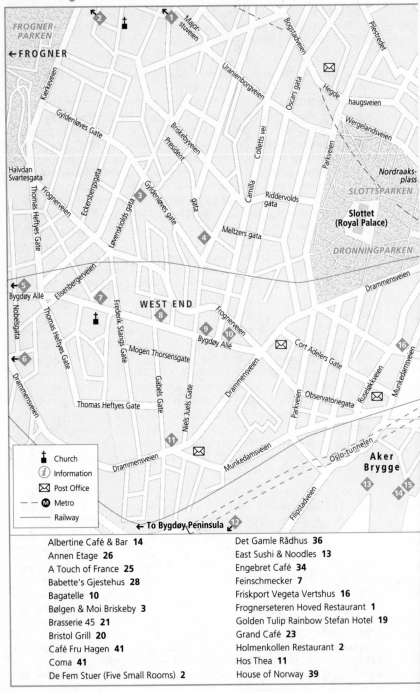

Albertine Café & Bar **14**

Annen Etage **26**

A Touch of France **25**

Babette's Gjestehus **28**

Bagatelle **10**

Bølgen & Moi Briskeby **3**

Brasserie 45 **21**

Bristol Grill **20**

Café Fru Hagen **41**

Coma **41**

De Fem Stuer (Five Small Rooms) **2**

Det Gamle Rådhus **36**

East Sushi & Noodles **13**

Engebret Café **34**

Feinschmecker **7**

Friskport Vegeta Vertshus **16**

Frognerseteren Hoved Restaurant **1**

Golden Tulip Rainbow Stefan Hotel **19**

Grand Café **23**

Holmenkollen Restaurant **2**

Hos Thea **11**

House of Norway **39**

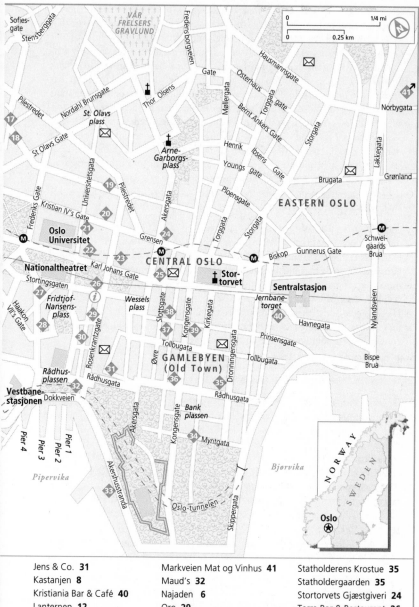

service without a lot of flash or frenzy, and elegant decor that evokes a baronial hunting lodge, from around 1924, the year the restaurant was founded. At that time, it was an all-male smoking, drinking, and dining club. A few years later, it evolved into the dining venue you'll see today, with an allure that eventually welcomed such entertainers as Sonja Henie, Josephine Baker, Eartha Kitt, Frank Sinatra, and Sophia Loren. You'll pass through a cozy, woodsy-looking piano bar to reach the restaurant. In 2002, the menus and culinary focus of this restaurant were radically upgraded, and are now among the finest in the Norwegian capital. There's a spectacular version of bouillabaisse, prepared with Nordic (not Mediterranean) fish and seasoned with saffron, which can be ordered as either a starter or a main course. We followed this with one of the chef's most successful specialties: medallions of venison sautéed with vanilla and bacon, served on a bed of mushrooms with a terrine of potatoes.

In the Hotel Bristol, Kristian IV's Gate 7. ℂ **22-82-60-00.** Reservations recommended. Main courses 210NOK–285NOK ($28–$38). AE, DC, MC, V. Daily 5–11pm. Tram: 10, 11, 17, 18.

Golden Tulip Rainbow Hotel Stefan ✔ᵥₐₗᵤₑ NORWEGIAN This bustling, unpretentious restaurant is better known than the hotel it's in. At lunchtime, local businesspeople come for the city's best smorgasbord, laden with traditional Norwegian foods, that includes cucumber salad, fish and meat salads, sausages, meatballs, potato salad, smoked fish, assorted cheeses, and breads. During the evening, when the buffet is closed, you can order from a rich a la carte menu. Highlights include "Stefan's special platter"—an old-fashioned but flavorful dish that incorporates slices of reindeer, moose meat, and ox tongue, with lingonberries and potatoes, on the same heaping plate.

In the Stefan Hotel, Rosenkrantzgate 1. ℂ **23-31-55-00.** Reservations recommended. Main courses 180NOK–200NOK ($24–$27); lunch smorgasbord 195NOK ($26). AE, DC, MC, V. Smorgasbord Mon–Sat 11:30am–2pm. Dinner (a la carte) Mon–Sat 4:30–9:30pm. Tram: 7 or 11.

Grand Café ★★ NORWEGIAN This traditional cafe is an Oslo legend. A large mural on one wall depicts Ibsen (a fan of whale steaks), Edvard Munch, and many other patrons. A postcard sold at the reception desk identifies the mural's subjects.

You can order everything from a napoleon with coffee to a full meal with fried stingray or reindeer steaks. Sandwiches are available for 80NOK ($11) and up. The atmosphere and tradition here are sometimes more compelling than the cuisine. The menu, nonetheless, relies on Norwegian country traditions (after all, how many places still serve elk stew?). If you like solid, honest flavors, this is the place to eat.

In the Grand Hotel, Karl Johans Gate 31. ℂ **24-14-53-00.** Reservations recommended. Main courses 145NOK–280NOK ($19–$37). AE, DC, MC, V. Mon–Sat 11am–11pm; Sun noon–11pm. T-banen: Stortinget.

La Sangria ★ 𝐹𝑖𝑛𝑑𝑠 SPANISH Established in 1992 in a location across the street from the SAS Scandinavia Hotel, within a dining room sheathed with roughly textured stucco and hand-painted Iberian porcelain, this is one of the best Spanish restaurants in Oslo. It was established by two hardworking brothers (Fernando and Juan-Carlos) from Madrid, whose appreciation for both bullfighting and soccer, especially the Real Madrid team, is obvious. In July 2002, this restaurant hosted the "under 19" Spanish national soccer team after its victory against Germany in the nearby stadium. The arrival at that dinner of the sports minister of Spain made lots of copy in the local newspapers. Menu items here evoke the flavors of Iberia, and include at least two versions of paella;

prawns with garlic; Serrano ham with Manchego cheese and chorizo sausage; gazpacho, and *bacalhau* (cod) alla Vizcaina.

Holbergsgate 19. © **22-11-63-15.** Reservations recommended. Main courses 175NOK–205NOK ($23–$27). AE, DC, MC, V. Mon–Sat 3–11pm, Sun 3–10pm. Closed Dec 23–Jan 2. Tram: 11, 19.

Lipp INTERNATIONAL   Stylish and lighthearted, this restored brasserie is the Oslovian version of Paris in the 1920s. Painted a canary yellow, it employs a staff traditionally dressed, bistro style, in black vests. Each day a special dish is offered of which the chef is justly proud. On our last visit it was roasted grouse served with a wild mushroom pie with crisp bacon. The menu, adjusted seasonally, changes about every 5 weeks and uses the finest of produce from land and field, not to mention river and lake. You might face a delectable salmon in a white wine sauce, or reindeer in a mushroom sauce. Lighter fare is also offered for those watching their weight—perhaps an array of freshly made salads or grilled fish dishes. Succulent pastas are regularly featured.

In the Hotel Continental, Stortingsgaten 24. © **22-82-40-60.** Reservations recommended. Main courses 172NOK–255NOK ($23–$34). AE, DC, MC, V. Daily 4–11:30p.m. T-banen: Nationaltheatret.

Restaurant Holberg ⭐ CONTINENTAL   This is the showcase restaurant within the premier SAS Hotel in Oslo, and as such, it's usually lavished with care, time, and attention from the chain. Set on the hotel's lobby level, it's a large, angular, high-ceilinged space that represents the best of contemporary Scandinavian design, with an open-to-view kitchen where an assembly line of uniformed chefs work under relentless, albeit discreet, pressure. Paintings that line the walls are copies of works by Danish painter Winblad, an early-20th-century artist who illustrated the tales of the restaurant's namesake, Danish-Norwegian author Holberg. The well-prepared meals are beautifully presented. The deftly handled fish dishes are always a favorite. Try the halibut baked with Savoy cabbage and served in a well-flavored rosemary sauce with almond potatoes, or else the herb-sautéed filet of monkfish with vegetables julienne. We also heartily recommend the sole, which is sautéed and served with a rich red wine sauce. The chefs are also skilled at turning out meat dishes, especially rack of lamb seasoned with rosemary and served in a red wine and garlic sauce. A real he-man specialty is the mustard-glazed filet of wild boar with bourbon sauce and lentil purée. A temptation of starters range from a carpaccio of beef with rocket salad to green asparagus with a sweet basil vinaigrette served with a poached quail egg.

In the Radisson SAS Hotel Scandinavia, Holbergsgate 30. © **23-29-30-00.** Reservations recommended. Main courses 186NOK–255NOK ($25–$34). AE, DC, MC, V. Dinner only Mon–Sat 5–11:30pm. T-banen: Nationaltheatret.

Terra Bar & Restaurant MEDITERRANEAN   We come here for the wine list as much as for the food, which is excellent. Against the backdrop of a minimalist decor, this restaurant and bar attracts many Norwegian politicians at lunch, thanks to its location across the street from the Parliament building. During the evening, a younger crowd predominates. Nearly 300 different wines are on the menu. You can eat and drink entirely in the bar area, or enjoy more formal seating in the dining room.

Nearly 50% of the menu is devoted to seafood, and it's always fresh and well prepared. Try, for example, the lemon-baked halibut with a pumpkin and honey chutney accompanied by a bouillabaisse sauce. Meats are also excellent, especially the grilled tenderloin of beef, which comes with baked potato and Jerusalem artichokes. The grilled breast of chicken is served with fresh linguini in a mussel sauce. The pastry chef is justifiably proud of the house dessert

Dining Secrets of Oslo

One of Oslovians' favorite pastimes is visiting **Aker Brygge.** Formerly a dilapidated shipbuilding yard, the futuristic complex now combines more shopping, entertainment, and dining diversions in one area than anywhere else in Norway. Many people, some with children, come here to check out the restaurants and cafes, watch the people, and listen to music in the bars. Part of the fun is strolling through the complex and picking a restaurant. Norwegian food is served along with a representative selection of foreign food offerings, including American. In the summer, visitors and locals fill the outdoor tables overlooking the harbor. There are also many nightlife options (see "Oslo After Dark," in chapter 5). To reach Aker Brygge, take bus no. 27 or walk down from the center west of the Rådhus.

A local favorite here is the **Albertine Café & Bar,** Stranden 3, Aker Brygge (✆ 22-83-00-60), an informal place on the wharf's edge, offering a panoramic view over the harbor and Akershus fortress. Consistently, this place serves some of the freshest and tastiest oysters in Oslo. You can drop in for just a hamburger or a full Norwegian seafood dinner. It's an easy place for meeting singles.

A good choice for the makings of a picnic is **Von Angels Delikatesse,** Karl Johans Gate 41B (✆ 23-13-95-02). It's open Monday to Friday from 10am to 8pm, Saturday 10am to 5pm.

In front of the Rådhuset, you can join Oslovians for a special picnic treat. From 7 to 8am, **shrimp fishermen** pull their boats into the harbor after having caught and cooked a fresh batch of shrimp during their night at sea. You can order shrimp in a bag (it comes in two sizes). Seafood fanciers take their shrimp to the dock's edge, remove the shells, and feast. The fishermen usually stick around until they've sold the last batch, saving just enough for their families.

special, which is homemade vanilla ice cream in a hot brandy sauce laced with espresso flavoring.

Stortingsgaten 2. ✆ 22-40-55-20. Reservations required. Main courses 235NOK–285NOK ($31–$38). AE, DC, MC, V. Mon–Wed 11am–12:30pm; Thurs–Fri 11am–10pm; Sat noon–1am; Sun 5pm–midnight. Closed for lunch in July and on Sun in summer. T-banen: Stortinget.

Theatercafeen ✦ INTERNATIONAL The last of the grand Viennese cafes in the north of Europe, this long-standing favorite was founded a century ago to rival the Grand Café. Each has its devotees, although we like this one better because of its Viennese *schmaltz*. Serenaded by piano and a duet of violins, the style might have pleased the Habsburg emperor Franz-Josef had he ever ventured this far north. It attracts present-day *boulevardiers* and businesspeople. With soft lighting, antique bronzes, cut-glass lighting fixtures, and Art Nouveau mirrors, it's the type of place that encourages lingering. Menu items are well prepared and traditional, and are adjusted accordingly to get the best flavors out of each season. That might mean fresh asparagus and spring lamb, or in the autumn, breast of wild goose and other game dishes. The fish dishes, including a recently sampled casserole of mussels, are particularly good. You can also enjoy such traditional Norwegian fare as reindeer with wild mushrooms or Norwegian fjord salmon.

In the Hotel Continental, Stortingsgaten 24. ℭ **22-82-40-50.** Reservations recommended. Main courses 195NOK–365NOK ($26–$49). 3-course menu 635NOK ($84). Open-faced sandwiches 85NOK–95NOK ($11–$13) at lunch. AE, DC, MC, V. Mon–Sat 11am–midnight; Sun 3–10pm. T-banen: Stortinget.

A Touch of France ☆ FRENCH   This aptly named place is one of Oslo's best French bistros. In summer tables spill out onto the sidewalk. When residents dine here, it puts them in a mood to travel to the real thing, France itself. The decor is that of a typical French brasserie, the kind you find alongside the road in Alsace. Touch of France is known for serving the freshest oysters in town. On our most recent visit, we opted for the traditional salt-baked leg of duck, which was served in a beautifully made garlic sauce. On other occasions we've enjoyed a classic calf's liver with mushrooms, spinach, and bacon. Bouillabaisse is a specialty, but that grand dish loses something in translation this far north. After your main course, a dessert cart is wheeled around, loaded with such temptations as crème brûlée or a delectable chocolate and almond cake.

Øvre Slottsgate 16. ℭ **23-10-01-60.** Reservations recommended. Main courses 185NOK–285NOK ($25–$38). AE, DC, MC, V. Mon–Sat noon–11:30pm. Bus: 27, 29, 30, 41, or 61.

INEXPENSIVE

Brasserie 45 CONTINENTAL   Airy and stylish, this second-story bistro overlooks the biggest fountain along downtown Oslo's showplace promenade. The uniformed staff bears steaming platters of ambitious, imaginative cuisine, including especially flavorful versions of fried catfish with lemon-garlic sauce; fried chicken in spicy, tomato-based sweet-and-sour sauce; pork schnitzels with béarnaise sauce and shrimp; and tartare of salmon with dill-enriched boiled potatoes. For dessert, try chocolate terrine with cloudberry sorbet.

Karl Johans Gate 45. ℭ **22-41-34-00.** Reservations recommended. Main courses 89NOK–189NOK ($12–$25). AE, DC, MC, V. Mon–Thurs noon–midnight; Fri–Sat noon–1am; Sun 2:30–11pm. T-banen: Centrum.

Kristiania Bar & Café   Set within the oldest part of Oslo's railway (the Østbanehallen, or East Wing) this late-19th-century cafe has one of the grandest decors of any cafe in Oslo. You'll dine and drink beneath a soaring ceiling dotted with cavorting cherubs and elaborate plaster reliefs, at a dark-stained Victorian-era bar that's an antique in its own right. Even the toilets of this place (a staff member will tell you the numeric combinations to punch onto a keypad to gain entrance) are historically important, and consequently, ferociously protected against architectural changes. Surprisingly for such a lavish setting, the food is relatively simple, and much less expensive than, say, at equally historic cafes such as the Grand Café in the Grand Hotel. Menu items focus on burgers, salads, club sandwiches, pastas, milkshakes, and specials of the day. We urge you, if the weather is fine, to opt for a table on this cafe's very large outdoor terrace. It's sunnier and brighter than that of more expensive cafes nearby on narrower, darker streets, and it enjoys a close-up view over one of Oslo's most stunning and monumental fountains.

Østbanehallen, Jernbanetorget 1. ℭ **22-17-50-30.** Reservations not needed. Main courses 89NOK–125NOK ($12–$17). MC, V. Mon–Thurs 11am–midnight; Fri–Sat 11am–3am; Sun 2–11pm. T-banen: Jernbanetorget.

Santino's Spaghetteria 〽alue PIZZA/PASTA   This is a relatively unheralded, but relatively inexpensive, Italian restaurant smack in the center of one of the most expensive neighborhoods in Europe. The decor is postmodern and whimsical—a hallucinogenic, rainbow-hued interpretation of a carnival setting in Venice, with warm-colored tones of polished stone, a big circular bar, and a tutti-frutti color scheme of ice cream colors run amok. Its menu sports prices that attract clients who don't want to spend a fortune on dinner. It lists mainly pastas and pizzas. Launch yourself with an antipasti, perhaps the mussels steamed in white wine laced with garlic or else melon and Parma ham, always a winner. A fresh minestrone is made daily. The pastas are among Oslo's best with a wide range of tagliatelle, spaghetti, lasagna, penne, and tortellini, along with fusilli and ravioli. We recently were delighted with our penne with prawns, salmon, and a cream sauce. The pizzas emerge piping hot from the oven topped with virtually anything. A special treat is the alla Romana pizza with tomato sauce, mozzarella, smoked baby pork, and arugula. For dessert, tiramisu and zabaglione are the clear winners.

Tordensskioldsgate 8-10. ⓒ **22-41-16-22.** Reservations not required. Main course pizza and pasta 96NOK–146NOK ($13–$19). Mon–Fri 11am–11:30pm; Sat 1–11:30pm; Sun 3–10:30pm. T-banen: Stortinget.

OLD TOWN (GAMLEBYEN/KVADRATUREN)
VERY EXPENSIVE

Statholderens Krostue ✪ SWEDISH/DANISH   This relatively uncompli-cated cellar-level bistro is associated with Statholdergaarden, one of Oslo's most prestigious restaurants (see below). Unlike its more sophisticated sibling, it's open for lunch as well as dinner, and features relatively uncomplicated food that's mostly based on traditional Swedish and Danish recipes. The cuisine provides many orig-inal and, most of the time, happy combinations of ingredients. Beneath the vaulted Renaissance-era ceiling, you can order *frikadeller* (meatballs), minced veal patties in creamy dill sauce, steak with fried onions, fried eel with potato and herb dumplings, and grilled salmon with saffron-flavored noodles. Lunch specialties include platters piled high with Danish or Norwegian ham, herring, boiled eggs, and vegetables, and a selection of *smørrebrød* (Danish open-faced sandwiches).

Rådhusgata 11. ⓒ **22-41-88-00.** Main courses 245NOK–330NOK ($33–$44); fixed-price menu 400NOK ($53). AE, DC, MC, V. Tues–Sat 11:30am–10pm. Tram: 11, 15, 18.

Statholdergaarden ✪✪✪ NOUVELLE NORWEGIAN   One of Oslo's most historic restaurant settings (the building dates from 1640) has one of its most successful chefs, Bent Stiansen, whose unique interpretation of Norwegian nouvelle cuisine has attracted the admiration of gastronomes throughout the country. At this century-old restaurant (ca. 1901), menu items change fre-quently, according to what's in season. Examples include grilled crayfish served with scallop and salmon tartare, and thyme-infused cod with crabmeat mousse and two sauces (a simple white wine sauce and another based on a rare vanilla bean imported from Thailand). One of our all-time favorite dishes is lightly fried Arctic char with sautéed Savoy cabbage and lime beurre blanc (white but-ter). Also appealing are roasted rack of lamb with sage sauce, platters of French cheeses, and cloudberry crepes. Don't confuse this upscale and prestigious site with the less expensive bistro Statholderens Krostue (see above), which occupies the building's vaulted cellar.

Rådhusgata 11. ⓒ **22-41-88-00.** Reservations recommended. Main courses 290NOK–350NOK ($39–$47); 4-course fixed-price menu 725NOK ($96); 6-course fixed-price menu 875NOK ($116). AE, DC, MC, V. Mon–Sat 6pm–midnight. Tram: 11, 15, or 18.

EXPENSIVE

Det Gamle Rådhus (Old Town Hall) ✪ NORWEGIAN   One of the oldest restaurants in Oslo, Det Gamle Rådhus is in Oslo's former Town Hall (1641). This is strictly for nostalgia buffs, as the restaurant is not at all hipsterish or

---

Kids **Family-Friendly Restaurants**

Mamma Rosa (p. 89)   The best place to fill up on pasta dishes or 15 kinds of pizzas, each a meal in itself.

Najaden (p. 93)   As if being in the Norwegian Maritime Museum weren't enough for kids, those under 12 can also enjoy an elaborate summer lunch buffet for half price.

---

cutting edge. It's there for those wanting to see Oslo the way it used to be, but the innovative fires died a long time ago. You'll dine within a network of baronial or manorial-inspired rooms with dark wooden panels and Flemish, 16th-century-styled wooden chairs. In the spacious dining room, a full array of open-faced sandwiches is served on weekdays only. A la carte dinner selections can be made from a varied menu that includes fresh fish, game, and Norwegian specialties. Although it sounds like a culinary turnoff, the house specialty, lutefisk, is quite delectable. This Scandinavian dish is made from dried fish that has been soaked in lye, and then poached in broth. If you want to sample a dish that Ibsen might have enjoyed, check this one out. More to your liking might be smoked salmon (it's smoked right on the premises), a parfait of chicken livers, freshwater pike-perch from nearby streams sautéed in a lime sauce, or filet of reindeer with lingonberry sauce. Norwegian lamb is coated with herbs and baked with a glaze.

Nedre Slottsgate 1. © **22-42-01-07.** Reservations recommended. Main courses 200NOK–275NOK ($27–$37); open-faced sandwiches 85NOK–115NOK ($11–$15); 3-course set dinner 398NOK ($53). AE, DC, MC, V. Mon–Fri 11am–3pm; Mon–Sat 4–11pm. Kroen Bar Mon–Sat 4pm–midnight. Closed last 3 weeks in July. Bus: 27, 29, 30, 41, or 61.

Maud's ★ *Finds* NORWEGIAN   This is a warm, cozy, well-managed restaurant that celebrates old-fashioned Norwegian decors and cuisines. It was named after one of Norway's most potent symbols of independence, the much-revered Queen Maud (1905–38), wife of King Hakon V and the country's first modern-day queen. The restaurant contains a trio of mostly green dining rooms (one of which, reserved for smokers, lies upstairs), and walls that are lined with photographs of several generations of Norway's royal family. Menu items are mostly composed using Norwegian ingredients, whenever possible, including a creamy white version of fish soup; reindeer filet with mushrooms, root vegetables, artichoke hearts, and black currant/Madeira wine gravy; many different varieties of steamed and grilled fish; and seasonal desserts that celebrate, to every degree possible, the availability of fresh berries from the tundra, valleys, and bogs of Norway.

Brynjulf Bulls Plass. © **22-83-72-28.** Reservations recommended. Main courses 220NOK–300NOK ($29–$40). Fixed-price menus 360NOK–410NOK ($48–$55). AE, DC, MC, V. Oct–Apr Mon–Fri 3pm–midnight; Sat noon–midnight; May–Sept Mon–Sat noon–midnight. Bus: 30, 31, 45, or 81.

MODERATE

Stortorvets Gjæstgiveri ★ NORWEGIAN   This is the oldest restaurant in Oslo, and one of only three buildings to have escaped complete destruction during the many fires that roared through the city during the late 19th century. The present restaurant is composed of a trio of wood-framed buildings, the oldest dating from the 1700s. Originally an inn stood on this spot with stables out back. The inn's upstairs bedchambers with their wood-burning stoves are virtually unchanged since their original construction, although they're now used as private dining rooms. This revered vestige of Oslo's past is one of the principal performance sites during the annual midsummer jazz festival.

This restaurant changes radically throughout the course of an Oslovian day: Expect a cafe near the entrance; an old-fashioned, charming, and usually packed restaurant in back; and a hard-drinking, highly convivial nightclub venue every Thursday through Saturday from 8 to 11pm, when nondiners must pay a 60NOK ($8) cover charge. Menu items are traditional, well prepared, and flavorful, and include grilled halibut with beurre blanc sauce; veal with smoked ham and sausage; chicken breast stuffed with spinach and creamed porcini mushrooms; filet of reindeer with a compote of onions and apples; and freshwater trout with arugula and balsamic vinegar. One of the trademark offerings is lutefisk, a cod dish so complicated (and with such a high possibility of spoilage) that many lesser restaurants don't even try to prepare it. Here, thanks to automated high-tech kitchen equipment, they sell thousands of portions of it a year, mostly in autumn, when it's at its aromatic best.

Grensen 1. ⓒ **23-35-63-60.** Small platters and snacks 92NOK–160NOK ($12–$21). Main courses 170NOK–260NOK ($23–$35). AE, DC, MC, V. Cafe daily 11am–8pm; restaurant daily 3–11pm. Tram: 12, 17, 21.

3 Brødre ⭐ NORWEGIAN   "Three Brothers" is named after the glove manufacturers who once occupied this building. This is a longtime favorite drawing more locals than visitors. Habitués know of its fresh food, which is well prepared with hearty portions and reasonable prices. You might begin with Norwegian salmon tartare or snails, followed by an almond-and-garlic gratinée. The most popular appetizer is a selection of fresh mussels poached with leeks, parsley, garlic, and cream. For a main course, try the fried catfish with prawns, mussels, red peppers, and capers, or beefsteak with béarnaise sauce. The entire street level houses the bustling bar. Upstairs is a piano bar. A large beer costs 56NOK ($7.45). Lighter meals, such as snacks and sandwiches ranging in price from 75NOK to 98NOK ($10–$13), are available on the outside dining terrace in the summer.

Øvre Slottsgate 14. ⓒ **23-10-06-70.** Main courses 138NOK–222NOK ($18–$30). AE, DC, MC, V. Kaelleren Mon–Sat 4pm–1am; street-level bar Mon–Sat 11pm–2:30am; piano bar Mon–Sat 5pm–2:30am. Bus: 27, 29, or 30.

INEXPENSIVE

Engebret Café NORWEGIAN   A favorite since 1857, this restaurant is directly north of Akershus Castle in two landmark buildings. It has an old-fashioned atmosphere and good food, served in a former bohemian literati haunt. During lunch, a tempting selection of open-faced sandwiches is available. The evening menu is more elaborate; you might begin with a terrine of game with blackberry port-wine sauce, or Engebret's fish soup. Main dishes include red wild boar with whortleberry sauce, Norwegian reindeer, salmon Christiania, or Engebret's big fish pot. For dessert, try the cloudberry parfait.

Bankplassen 1. ⓒ **22-33-66-94.** Reservations recommended. Main courses 265NOK–590NOK ($35–$78). AE, DC, MC, V. Mon–Sat 11am–11pm. Bus: 27, 29, or 30.

Friskport Vegeta Vertshus VEGETARIAN   Since 1938 this basement cafeteria near the Rådhus has been Oslo's major vegetarian restaurant. It's a stronghold of social activism and news of countercultural activities. At street level is a cafe with a buffet of 25 salad dishes and many hot dishes, along with bread, butter, cheese, and coffee. A new, smoke-free bar downstairs serves a special student buffet for 112NOK ($15) Tuesday to Saturday. The kitchen is also proud of its pizza. You can order juices, mineral water, soft drinks, or nonalcoholic wine. To go to the buffet once, a small plate costs 85NOK ($11), a large plate, 95NOK ($13).

Munkedamsveien 3B. ☎ 22-83-42-32. Soups and salads 60NOK ($8); buffet 140NOK ($19). AE, DC, MC, V. Daily noon–10pm. Bus: 27.

Jens & Co. NORWEGIAN   Breezy, airy, and lighthearted, and set immediately adjacent to the more formal (and more serious) Den Gamle Rådhus, this place draws a busy lunch crowd throughout the afternoon, and a very active bar crowd after 6pm. In wintertime, its woodsy, hip-looking interior is jammed, and as soon as the weather turns clement, the entire venue moves outside to a big terrace overlooking a cobble-covered plaza. A half-liter of beer costs 48NOK ($6.40); lunchtime platters include focaccia-style sandwiches, salads, omelets, and American-style brownies. An enduringly popular cocktail is a strawberry daiquiri, priced at 88NOK ($12), but lots of people just drink beer.

Rådhusgate 30. ☎ 22-42-11-62. Reservations not necessary. Lunch platters 59NOK–118NOK ($7.85–$16). AE, DC, MC, V. Food daily 11am–6pm. Bar Sun–Mon 11am–midnight and Tues–Sat 11am–3am. Bus: 27, 29, 30, 41, or 61.

Mamma Rosa *Kids* ITALIAN   Established by two Tuscan brothers, this trattoria enjoys popularity that's a good indication of Norwegians' changing tastes. The second-floor dining room is decorated in "reproduction rococo." You can order 15 kinds of pizza, fried scampi and squid, rigatoni, pasta Mamma Rosa (three kinds of pasta with three sauces), grilled steaks, and gelato. Frankly, some of the dishes have lost a bit of flavor on the trip this far north, but Mamma Rosa is nonetheless a marvelous change of taste and texture.

Øvre Slottsgate 12. ☎ 22-42-01-30. Main courses 91NOK–210NOK ($12–$28); pizzas from 97NOK ($13). DC, MC, V. Mon–Sat noon–11:30pm; Sun 3–10:30pm. T-banen: Stortinget.

AKER BRYGGE
EXPENSIVE
Lofoten Fiskerestaurant ✦ SEAFOOD   Near one of the most distant corners of the Aker Brygge dining complex, on the ground floor with views over the harbor, this is one of the city's most appealing seafood restaurants. The interior sports nautical accessories that might remind you of an upscale yacht. In good weather, tables are set up on an outdoor terrace lined with flowering plants. Menu items change according to the available catch, with few choices for meat-eaters. The fish is plentiful, served in generous portions, and very fresh. Examples include filet of trout poached in white wine and served with tomato-enriched beurre blanc sauce; grilled halibut with assorted shellfish and coconut-flavored risotto; and grilled filet of tuna with garlicky potato cakes, Parmesan cheese, and red-pepper cream sauce. Look for culinary inspirations from Italy and France, and ample use of such Mediterranean preparations as pesto.

Stranden 75, Aker Brygge. ☎ 22-83-08-08. Reservations recommended. Lunch main courses 138NOK–258NOK ($18–$34). Main courses 165NOK–320NOK ($22–$43). AE, DC, MC, V. Mon–Sat 11am–11pm; Sun noon–11pm. Bus: 27.

Solsiden ✦ *Finds* NORWEGIAN/SEAFOOD   The degree to which this restaurant is known throughout Oslo seems way out of proportion to its size and season—it's open for 3 months during midsummer. Part of its fame involves its location within an ugly, cement-sided warehouse opening onto a pier that's directly across the harbor from the bigger, glossier restaurants of the Aker Brygge complex, directly below the imposing bulk of Akershus castle. It's especially appealing on sunny midsummer evenings when sunlight streams onto the pier, while many of the restaurants of Aker Brygge lie in the shadows. The venue features an open kitchen, wide views of Oslo's harbor, the setting sun, and a hardworking staff. Menu items include only fish and shellfish, with no meat of any kind on the menu. The highly theatrical house specialty is a platter of shellfish, prepared for a minimum of two diners at a time, artfully draped with seaweed. Monkfish might be served with honey-glazed chiles and a potato-mushroom purée and oven-baked vegetables with soya sauce. Norwegian salmon with herb-flavored oil and potato purée is a perennial favorite.

Søndre Akershus Kai 34. ℂ **23-33-36-30.** Reservations required. Main courses 200NOK–250NOK ($27–$33). Fixed-price menu 385NOK ($51). May–Aug Mon–Sat 5–10pm; Sun 5–9pm. Closed: Sept–Apr. Tram: 10, 15.

INEXPENSIVE

East Sushi & Noodles ASIAN Finding a relatively inexpensive dining option in high-priced Aker Brygge can be lethal, but this member of a chain that extends throughout Norway sometimes provides what you might be looking for. Within a sparsely decorated dining room sheathed with varnished planks, you'll order pieces of sushi, priced at 30NOK to 50NOK ($4–$6.65) for two pieces. Noodle dishes are very popular too.

Bryggetorget 7, in Aker Brygge. ℂ **22-83-63-51.** Reservations not necessary. Main courses 100NOK–195NOK ($13–$26). 3-course fixed-price dinners (available only during happy hour, 4–7pm) 99NOK–145NOK ($13–$19). Daily 1pm–10:45pm. Tram: 10, 15.

Tex-Mex Cactus *Value* TEX-MEX This is the only American-style Tex-Mex restaurant in Oslo, and a relatively inexpensive dining option within Aker Brygge. It features five smallish dining rooms, each with virtually indestructible, thick-planked tables and photographs and paintings of the panoramic U.S. Southwest. Look for a menu roster of dishes that includes those standard favorites, such as fajitas, burritos, nachos, and quesadillas, each available stuffed with either chicken or beef, or, in some cases, vegetables. Nothing is particularly fancy, and the venue is low on the list of Oslovian style-setters, but the food is good and the prices, once again, are among the most affordable within this extremely expensive neighborhood.

Stranden 3, Aker Brygge. ℂ **22-83-06-48.** Reservations not necessary. Main courses 144NOK–215NOK ($19–$29). AE, DC, MC, V. Sun–Mon 4–9pm; Tues–Thurs 4–10:30pm; Fri–Sat 4–11:30pm. Tram: 10, 15.

WEST END
VERY EXPENSIVE

Bagatelle ✿✿ FRENCH This contemporary, informal restaurant is widely regarded as one of Oslo's premier dining choices. Owner-chef Eyvind Hellstrøm serves light, modern cuisine, using market-fresh ingredients. Seafood is the star here, and the menu changes daily. You can begin with a selection of warm or cold appetizers including carpaccio of scallops in oyster sauce. Fish entrees include smoked catch of the day, steamed halibut with caviar cream sauce, and sole steamed in seaweed. Other main dishes are saddle of reindeer with pears and pepper sauce, loin of veal with sage, and herb-roasted Norwegian rack of lamb.

Bygdøy Allé 3. ℂ **22-44-63-97.** Reservations required. Main courses 280NOK–380NOK ($37–$51); 3-course fixed-price menu 650NOK ($86); 5-course fish menu 950NOK ($126); 7-course fixed-price menu 1,150NOK ($153). AE, DC, MC, V. Mon–Sat 6–10:30pm. Bus: 30, 31, 45, 72, or 73.

Bølgen & Moi Briskeby ✿✿ CONTINENTAL This is a showcase branch of a chain that's now scattered throughout the urban centers of Norway. Backed by the creative zest of two Norway-born chefs and entrepreneurs (Mr. Bølgen and Mr. Moi), the chain is known for being creative and stylish, and as a haven for the discreetly rich and the sometimes famous of Norway. It's set in the Oslovian suburb of Briskeby, within a redesigned industrial building whose premises are lined with the original paintings and photographs by avant-garde artists, most of them Norwegian. The fussiest, most prestigious, and most experimental venue here is the gourmet restaurant, one floor above street level, where only about seven tables accommodate diners for elaborate, drawn-out meals. Frankly, we prefer the street-level brasserie, that's a wee bit less self-consciously grand, and the food is good enough to satisfy all but the most jaded palates. Well-flavored examples include a version of bouillabaisse made with Nordic sea fish; oven-baked free-range chicken with lemon-flavored couscous; *pot-au-feu* of breast of veal; and breast of duck with wild mushroom-covered bruschetta.

Løvenskioldsgate 26, Briskeby. ℂ **24-11-53-53.** Reservations recommended, especially for the gourmet restaurant upstairs. Brasserie main courses 195NOK–265NOK ($26–$35), fixed-price menu 445NOK ($59). Gourmet restaurant fixed-price menus 640NOK–980NOK ($85–$130). AE, DC, MC, V. Mon–Fri 7:30am– 12:30am; Sat 9am–12:30am; Sun 9am–6:30pm. Brasserie closed 3 weeks in July; gourmet restaurant closed July to mid-Aug. Tram: 11.

EXPENSIVE

Feinschmecker ✪ SCANDINAVIAN   One of the most prestigious restaurants in Oslo will entertain you with the same style and verve it produced for King Harald and his queen, Sonya, during their recent visit. The dining room's antique furniture and small-paned windows evoke old-time style despite the building's modernity. Menu items change frequently; the roster of staples includes grilled scallops with crispy potatoes; sautéed ocean crayfish tails with apple cider, wild rice, and sun-dried tomatoes; and grilled monkfish with sautéed mushrooms and morel-enriched cream sauce. A particularly sought-after main course is rack of Norwegian lamb. For dessert, try the gratin of raspberries, which has been preeminent here since the place opened in the 1980s. One of our local friends, a savvy food critic, has proclaimed this the best restaurant in Oslo. We're not prepared to go that far, but it ranks at the top.

Balchensgate 5. ℂ **22-44-17-77.** Reservations recommended. Main courses 265NOK–345NOK ($35–$46); fixed-price menu 625NOK ($83). AE, DC, MC, V. Mon–Sat 4:30–10:30pm. Closed 3 weeks in July. Tram: 12 or 19 to Ilesberg.

Magma ✪✪✪ MEDITERRANEAN/CONTINENTAL   This is one of the genuinely hot restaurants of Oslo. Established in 2000 on a busy boulevard within the city's quietly prosperous West End, on the street level of the Rica Hotel Bygdøy (with which it is not directly associated), it's outfitted in a postmodern, punk-conscious style that might have been inspired by a hip-hop club in London or New York's SoHo. Expect lots of space, a postindustrial decor of vinyl/Leatherette sofas and banquettes, pillbox-shaped stools, splashy pop art, and the superb cuisine of Norway's chef-of-the-minute, Ms. Sonja Lee. Born of Korean and Norwegian parents and one of the most successful culinary entrepreneurs in Norway, she studied in Paris, Monaco, and southern France. Even better, she has assembled a team of hip, young assistants (including the brilliant Philip Womersley) who seem to work beautifully together in the hypermodern kitchens, which, incidentally, are available for visits from any diner who's interested in a tour. Ingredients that go into these dishes are pure and perfect, and usually based on flavors of the faraway Mediterranean. Try the braised rabbit with tomatoes and olives; homemade ravioli studded with ricotta and Norwegian wild mushrooms; and (direct from the Ducasse kitchens) spit-roasted veal with a gratin of macaroni and veal jus, a real masterpiece.

Bygdøy Allé 53. ℭ **23-08-58-10.** Reservations recommended. Main courses 180NOK–230NOK ($24–$31); 9-course fixed-price menu 650NOK ($86). AE, DC, MC, V. Daily 11am–2pm and 5:30–10:30pm. Tram: 10, 12, or 15.

MODERATE

Hos Thea SCANDINAVIAN   This stylish, well-managed restaurant attracts a loyal crowd of people active in the media and the arts. The waitstaff and chefs share duties, so the person who prepares your meal is likely to carry it to your table as well. Depending on the staff's mood and the season, the superbly prepared menu items might include medallions of veal served with beurre blanc and carrots, breast of duck with red wine sauce, whitefish fillets with saffron sauce, and venison with a sauce of mixed Nordic berries. The century-old building, once a private home, is in a West End neighborhood 3km (about 2 miles) south of Oslo's commercial center.

Gabelsgate 11 (entrance on Drammensveien). ℭ **22-44-68-74.** Reservations recommended. Main courses 100NOK–250NOK ($13–$33). AE, DC, MC, V. Daily 4:30–10:30pm. Tram: 10 or 13.

Kastanjen NORWEGIAN   Named for the chestnut trees that line the street, this restaurant is in a residential area, near several embassies. The decor, illuminated by candlelight, is modern and unpretentious. The menu changes monthly, and fixed-price menus change daily. Six or seven dishes every night may be ordered as appetizers or main courses; a good choice is salmon with crayfish. There are one or two luxurious main-dish selections, but most are moderately priced. Monkfish is sautéed and served with a crayfish sauce, or you might order reindeer, which is sautéed, baked, and served with reindeer gravy and red currants.

Bygdøy Allé 18. ℭ **22-43-44-67.** Reservations required. Main courses 178NOK–195NOK ($24–$26). AE, DC, MC, V. Mon–Sat 6–11pm. Closed July. Tram: 30.

Village Tandoori ✦ INDIAN   We spent a lot of time admiring the weavings, paintings, chastened brass, and woodcarvings that adorn the walls of this restaurant, a network of dark rooms that evoke an antique house in the Punjab or Rajahstan regions of India. Food is flavorful, exotic, and extremely good, with a wide choice that includes lamb tikki marinated in yogurt and spices; marinated prawns with paprika or garlic; a Village mixed grill (with prawns, chicken, and lamb); Lahore-style lamb marinated in chile; and spicy Punjabi chicken.

Bygdøy Allee. ℭ **22-56-10-25.** Reservations recommended only Fri and Sat nights. Main courses 165NOK–235NOK ($22–$31). June–Aug daily 5–11pm; Sept–May daily 3–11pm. Tram: 10, 12, or 15.

BYGDØY
EXPENSIVE

Lanternen ✦ CONTINENTAL   Set close to the arrivals point for the Bygdøy ferry from the quays near Town Hall, within a low-slung white-painted clapboard-covered house from the 19th century, this restaurant is charming, welcoming, and sophisticated. From the windows of its woodsy, modern interior, you'll see about 1,000 privately owned sailboats and motor craft bobbing in the nearby marina, giving the entire venue a distinct nautical appeal.

Both appetizers and main courses are wisely limited but well chosen and intriguing to the taste buds. On our most recent visit, we launched our repast with a homemade fish soup, our companions delighting in the chile-flavored steamed mussels flavored with fresh garlic and white wine. Fresh, seasonal, and high-quality ingredients characterize the main courses, which range from poached sole with lobster sauce and shrimp to an herb-marinated filet of lamb.

The baked chicken breast is enlivened with the additions of cured ham and mozzarella, bound with a Madeira-laced sauce.

Huk Aveny 2. ⓒ **22-43-78-38**. Reservations recommended. Main courses 245NOK–275NOK ($33–$37). AE, DC, MC, V. Daily 11am–10pm. Closed Nov. Bus: 30 or the Bygdøy ferry from the quays near Town Hall.

MODERATE

Najaden *Kids* NORWEGIAN   In the Norwegian Maritime Museum, this restaurant (the name translates as "mermaid") overlooks a room of sculptures removed from 19th-century clipper ships. The popular summer lunch buffet offers an elaborate array of freshly prepared fish and meat dishes; the rest of the year, lunch is a la carte. You don't get a lot of culinary excitement, but the food is fresh and served in generous portions—and the location is unbeatable when you're sightseeing on Bygdøy.

Bygdøynesveien 37. ⓒ **22-43-81-80**. Reservations recommended. Main courses 193NOK–225NOK ($26–$30); lunch buffet (summer only 11am–3pm) 185NOK ($25), half-price for children under 12. AE, DC, MC, V. May 16–Oct 14 daily 11am–7pm; Oct 15–May 15 Mon–Wed and Sat 11am–4pm, Thurs–Fri 11am–7pm. Bus: 30. Ferry: Bygdøy.

FROGNER
VERY EXPENSIVE

Restaurant Le Canard ★ FRENCH/CONTINENTAL   The mansion that contains this prestigious restaurant is almost as interesting as the cuisine. Designed in the 1880s by a noted Jewish architect named Lowzow, it contains many religious symbols. Look for the Star of David in some of the stained-glass windows, and representations of the Lion of Judah here and there throughout. Everyone from the queen of Norway to British comedian John Cleese has dined on the first-class cuisine here. A meal might include grilled lobster with sautéed chanterelles and watercress sauce, carpaccio of smoked scallops, or baked artichokes with creamy mussel and lobster sauce. One enduringly popular meat dish is roasted duck with fig and foie gras sauce. Guinea fowl is stuffed with foie gras and served with a sauce of Banyuls (a sweet French red wine). The food is always impeccable. The restaurant is in the suburb of Frogner, just over a kilometer (about ¾ mile) west of the center of Oslo.

President Harbitzgate 4. ⓒ **22-54-34-00**. Reservations recommended. Main courses 270NOK–380NOK ($36–$51); 3-course fixed-price menu 545NOK ($72); 5-course fixed-price menu 765NOK ($102); 7-course fixed-price menu 925NOK ($123). AE, DC, DISC, MC, V. Mon–Thurs 5–10:30pm; Fri–Sat 6–10pm. T-banen: Frognerseteren.

HOLMENKOLLEN
EXPENSIVE

De Fem Stuer (Five Small Rooms) ★★ NORWEGIAN/CONTINENTAL Its turn-of-the-20th-century "national romantic" architecture has firmly established this restaurant as something of a historic monument for the diners who trek, ski, or ride uphill on tram no. 1 from Oslo to reach it. On the lobby level of one of our recommended hotels, the restaurant is in a section that retains its original Viking-Revival (or "dragon style") construction. You'll find faded country-Norwegian colors, carved timbers and logs, and a general sense of 19th-century rusticity. As its name implies, the restaurant contains five separate dining areas, four of them small and cozy to the point of being cramped and intimate, the other being high-ceilinged and stately looking. This is the kind of dining venue that a Norwegian family might pick as a celebration of an important birthday, anniversary, or rite of passage. For starters, the chefs make an excellent marinated whale meat in a saffron and chile sauce. You might also try the guinea hen with foie gras or else the pesto-griddled ocean crayfish with tiny peas. Expect such delightful main dishes as a ginger- and chicken-stuffed quail with morels and shiitake mushrooms in a Port wine sauce, or else filet of reindeer with parsnips, perhaps a crispy fried breast of duck with a vegetable spring roll.

In the Holmenkollen Park Hotel Rica Oslo, Kongeveien 26. ☎ **22-92-20-00.** Reservations recommended. Main courses 240NOK–315NOK ($32–$42). AE, DC, MC, V. Mon–Sat noon–2:30pm and 6:30–10:30pm. Take tram 1 to its terminus.

Frognerseteren Hoved Restaurant ✦ NORWEGIAN   Set within a short hike (or cross-country ski trek) from the end of Oslo's tram no. 1. The setting is a century-old mountain lodge in the Viking-Revival style. (Richly embellished with dragon and Viking-ship symbolism, the building helped define the Viking-Revival style that became the architectural symbol of the recently independent Norway.) There's a self-service section and a more formal sit-down area within several small, cozy dining rooms. Throughout, the place has the aura of an antique ski lodge, and for many Oslovians, it's as much a cultural icon as a restaurant. It's also the centerpiece of several kilometers of cross-country ski trails, and a departure point (and destination) for hikers and their families. The chef specializes in succulent game dishes, including pheasant paté with Cumberland sauce, medallions of reindeer, and filet of elk sautéed in honey and nuts. You can also order poached, marinated, or smoked Norwegian salmon. The chef's specialty dessert is a scrumptious apple cake.

Holmenkollveien 200. ☎ **22-92-40-40.** Reservations recommended. Cafe platters 75NOK–110NOK ($10–$15). Restaurant main courses 265NOK–275NOK ($35–$37), fixed-price menus 455NOK–625NOK ($61–$83). DC, MC, V. Restaurant Tues–Fri noon–3pm, Sat–Mon 5–10pm, Sun 1–8pm; cafe daily 11am–10pm. Tram: 1.

MODERATE

Holmenkollen Restaurant   Partially built from logs and local stone, perched near the summit of a hill outside Oslo, close to the city's world-renowned ski jump, this restaurant evokes a mountain chalet. Built in the 1930s, and a frequent target for bus tours whose participants are hauled up to admire the high-altitude view over Oslo, it contains an upscale-looking self-service restaurant on its street level and a richly paneled trio of more formal dining rooms on its upper floor. Frankly, the place would be more appealing without the constant crush of diners, many of whom arrive en masse aboard buses, an oft-repeated phenomenon that drives the staff into near-frenzies of distraction. But when it isn't too crowded, usually at nighttime, with fires blazing softly in the massive stone fireplaces, it's a great deal more charming. Main courses in the self-service restaurant include rib-sticking fare that's substantial and unpretentious, such as platters of roast meats or fish, but also salads and pastas. Meals in the upstairs dining room might begin with a Caesar salad with herb-roasted chicken and a Parmesan crust or else a chilled gazpacho served with pan-fried shrimp. On our most recent visit, our party took delight in the pan-fried trout served with spring-fresh asparagus and a chive sauce and the roasted filet of veal with baby summer vegetables in a wine sauce. Steamed halibut was another delectable treat, with leeks, fresh dill, and a butter sauce.

Holmenkollveien 119. ☎ **22-13-92-00.** Reservations recommended. Main courses in restaurant 198NOK–278NOK ($26–$37). Platters in the self-service restaurant 60NOK–150NOK ($8–$20). AE, DC, MC, V. Cafeteria daily 10:30am–9pm; restaurant daily 11:30am–10pm. Tram: 1.

GRÜNERLØKKA
MODERATE

Coma NORWEGIAN/HAITIAN/FRENCH   Proudly aware of its role as a counterculture gathering point for the slightly crazed, slightly disorganized intelligentsia of Oslo, this is the most upscale of the bars and restaurants in the Grünerløkka district. Its design is postmodern and glossy. You'll get hints of Los Angeles–inspired laid-back-ness, mingled with just a hint of Edvard Munch. A quick dialogue with a staff member will help adjust you to this restaurant's unusual blend of Norwegian New-Age thinking. Lunch dishes might include tortillas with chili-fried vegetables, salsa, guacamole, and melted cheese. Dinners are more elaborate, featuring duck breast with shiitake mushrooms, sweet and sour black bean sauce, kumquats, and hash-brown potatoes. You can, of course, visit just for a drink to absorb the atmosphere. The bar is long and wide, and lots of locals park here for hours after the crush of the evening meal is over.

Helgesensgate 16. ℭ **22-35-32-22.** Reservations recommended. Lunch main courses 82NOK–98NOK ($11–$13); dinner main courses 198NOK–214NOK ($26–$28). AE, DC, MC, V. Mon–Thurs 10am–midnight; Fri–Sat 10am–1am; Sun noon–midnight. Tram: 11, 12, 30, or 56.

Markveien Mat og Vinhus ⟨ℛ⟩ *Finds* NORWEGIAN/FRENCH   In the heart of the increasingly trendy Grünerløkka area, this restaurant evokes a French bistro and the Oslovian version of the Left Bank bohemian life. The walls are covered with the art of a local painter, Jo Stang, and the waiters welcome you— in their terms—as "we would in our own home." This is an amusing choice for dining on a well-prepared cuisine. Many of its patrons are restoring nearby apartments and moving to the district. The menu is rather ambitious. We recently descended with a group to sample such delights as roast suckling pig with a mushroom risotto and baked tomato, everything flavored with a sauce made of fresh herbs. Those herbs appeared again to flavor monkfish with boiled new potatoes and a saffron risotto. For something truly Norwegian, try the reindeer in a green peppercorn sauce, with bacon and Brussels sprouts.

Torvbakkgate 12. ℭ **22-37-22-97.** Reservations recommended. Main courses 210NOK–265NOK ($28–$35). AE, DC, MC, V. Closed July 15–Aug 7. T-banen: Schaus.

INEXPENSIVE

Café Fru Hagen CONTINENTAL   Convivial and hip, with an aura that resembles a coffeehouse more than a full-fledged restaurant, this cafe and restaurant expands onto the sidewalks of the not-so-busy main boulevard of the Grünerløkka district. Inside, you'll find a cozy interior lined with antique sofas and wooden chairs, a chattering group of clients who seem to know one another, and a disc jockey who spins records every Wednesday to Saturday beginning at 10pm. The inner room is for smokers; the outer room (near the entrance) is for non-smokers; regardless of where you sit, the conversational babble will rise like Surround Sound to greet you. The food is competent and filling, although most cafe patrons flock here for the good times and the atmosphere. The establishment's name, incidentally, translates as "Miss Garden" or "Maiden of the Garden."

Torvald Meyergate 40. ℭ **22-35-67-87.** Reservations not required. Burgers, salads, and sandwiches 85NOK–100NOK ($11–$13); platters 160NOK–170NOK ($21–$23). MC, V. Sun–Thurs 11am–2am; Fri–Sat 11am–3am. Tram: 11, 12.

Exploring Oslo

Some would be happy to come to Oslo just for the views of the harborfront city and the Oslofjord. Panoramas are a major attraction, especially the one from Tryvannstårnet, a 117m (390 ft.) observation tower atop 570m (1,900 ft.) Tryvann Hill in the outlying area. Many other attractions are worthy of your time and exploration, too. The beautiful surroundings make these sights even more appealing.

If at all possible, try to allocate 2 or 3 days—a lot more if you can afford it—to exploring Norway's capital.

After a visit here, most visitors head west to Bergen and the fjord district or else continue east by train or plane to Stockholm, the capital of Sweden.

If you arrive in summer, expect the midnight sun to light your late-night revelry. Since they are starved for sunlight, many Oslovians virtually stay up around the clock. If you come in winter, expect short days, with darkness descending around 3pm. The blue light of winter may make you feel you've wandered into an Edvard Munch painting.

SUGGESTED ITINERARIES

If You Have 1 Day

Arm yourself with a bag of freshly cooked shrimp (see the sidebar "Dining Secrets of Oslo," in chapter 4) and take a ferry to the Bygdøy peninsula. Explore the Viking ships, the polar ship *Fram*, the Kon-Tiki Museum, the Norwegian Maritime Museum, and the Norwegian Folk Museum. In the late afternoon, go to Frogner Park to admire the Vigeland sculptures.

If You Have 2 Days

On your first day, follow the itinerary above. On your second day, take a walking tour (you'll find two options later in this chapter), have lunch in a Norwegian restaurant, and explore the Edvard Munch Museum in the afternoon. In the summer, visit the Students' Grove, near the National Theater, for some beer and fresh air.

If You Have 3 Days

For your first 2 days, follow the suggestions above. On Day 3, take another walking tour, eating lunch along the way. Explore Akershus Castle and the adjoining Norwegian Resistance Museum in the afternoon. By late afternoon, visit the lofty lookout tower at Tryvannstårnet and see the Skimuseet at Holmenkollen, taking in a panoramic view of the area. Have dinner at Holmenkollen.

If You Have 4 or 5 Days

For the first 3 days, follow the itinerary above. On Day 4, head south on an excursion to the Oslofjord country, with stopovers at the Old Town at Fredrikstad; Tønsberg, Norway's oldest town; and Sandefjord, an old whaling town. Head back to Oslo for the night.

On Day 5, see the rest of Oslo's major sights, such as the National Gallery, the Historical Museum, and the Henie-Onstad Art Center (11km/7 miles from Oslo), a major museum of modern art.

Oslo's Must-See Attractions

If your time in Oslo is limited, you may have time to see only the top attractions. Here they are:

Edvard Munch Museum (p. 107)   This is a showcase of Edvard Munch (1863–1944), who painted *The Scream* and other works, and became the greatest artist in Scandinavia. The world-famous *Scream*, however, is in the Nasjonalgalleriet (see below).

Frammuseet (p. 103)   Come here to see the polar ship *Fram*, built in 1892 and used by three of Norway's most famous explorers, including Nansaen, who sailed across the Arctic.

Henie-Onstad Kunstsenter (p. 104)   Lying on the beautiful Oslo Fjord, this is the largest collection of modern art in Norway.

Kon-Tiki Museum (p. 103)   The highlight here is the world-famous balsa-log raft that Thor Heyerdahl used in 1947 on his sail from Peru to Polynesia.

Nasjonalgalleriet (p. 109)   The national gallery of Norway contains the largest collection of Norwegian and international art in the country.

Norwegian Folk Museum (p. 103)   This outdoor museum consists of 140 original buildings reassembled on 14 hectares (35 acres) of the Bygdøy peninsula.

Skimuseet (p. 104)   At Holmenkollen, this is the most famous ski area in the world with Norway's greatest panorama.

Vigelandsparken (p. 102)   This park showcases 200 sculptures by Gustav Vigeland (1869–1943), who also designed the layout of the park.

Vikingskiphuset (p. 104)   This Viking ship museum shelters the world's two best-preserved wooden Viking ships dating from the 9th century.

1 The Top Attractions

IN & AROUND CENTRAL OSLO
MUSEUMS

See section 3, "Of Artistic Interest," for Oslo's many art museums.

Forsvarsmuseet (Armed Forces Museum)   This museum documents Norwegian military history from the dawn of the Viking Age to the 1950s. Guns, tanks, bombs, and planes are all here, from fighter planes to German tanks left over from the Second World War. The weapons and modern artillery are housed in a 19th-century military arsenal. The museum has a cafeteria.

Akershus Fortress, Bygning 62. ☎ 23-09-35-82. Free admission. June–Aug Mon–Fri 10am–6pm, Sat–Sun 11am–4pm; Sept–May Mon–Fri 10am–3pm, Sat–Sun 11am–4pm. Tram: 1, 2, or 10.

Historisk Museum (University Museum of Cultural Heritage)   Devoted to ethnography, antiquities, and numismatics, this museum, operated by the University of Oslo, houses an interesting collection of prehistoric objects on the ground floor. Viking artifacts and a display of gold and silver from the 2nd

Oslo Attractions

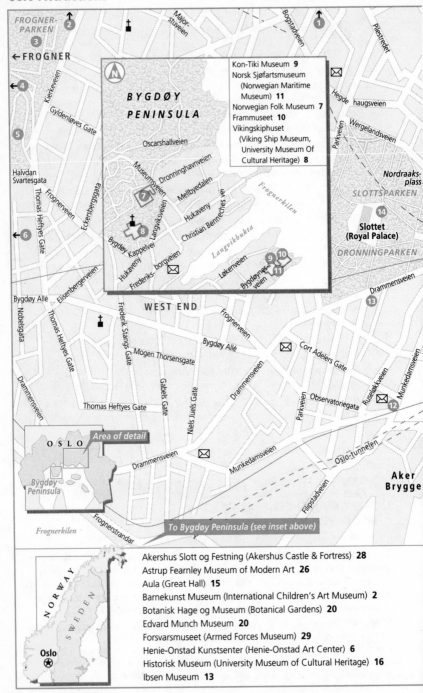

BYGDØY PENINSULA

Kon-Tiki Museum **9**
Norsk Sjøfartsmuseum
(Norwegian Maritime
Museum) **11**
Norwegian Folk Museum **7**
Frammuseet **10**
Vikingskiphuset
(Viking Ship Museum,
University Museum Of
Cultural Heritage) **8**

FROGNER-
PARKEN **2**
3
← FROGNER

4
5
Halvdan
Svartesgata
6

Kjerkeveien
Gyldenløves Gate
Thomas Heftyes Gate
Frognerveien
Eckersberggata

Oscarshallveien
Museumsveien **7**
Dronninghavnveien
Mellbyedalen
Langvikveien
Hukaveny
8
Bygdøy Kappelvei
Hukaveny
Frederiks-borgveien
Løkenveien
Christian Benneches vei

Frognerkilen
Langvikbukta

9 **10**
11
Bygdøynes-
veien

Hegde haugsveien
Parkveien
Wergelandsveien
Nordraaks-
plass
SLOTTSPARKEN
14
Slottet
(Royal Palace)
DRONNINGPARKEN

Pilestredet

Bygdøy Allé
Nobelsgata
Thomas Heftyes Gate
Drammensveien
Thomas Heftyes Gate
Elisenbergerveien
Frederik Stangs Gate
Mogen Thorsensgate
Gabels Gate
Niels Juels Gate

WEST END
Frognerveien
Bygdøy Allé
Drammensveien
Cort Adelers Gate
Observatoriegata
Parkveien
Munkedamsveien
Drammensveien

Rusaløkkveien
Munkedamsveien
12
Oslo-tunnelen
13
Drammensveien

Aker
Brygge

OSLO
Area of detail
Bygdøy
Peninsula
Frognerkilen

Frognerstrandar
Filipstadveien
To Bygdøy Peninsula (see inset above)

NORWAY
SWEDEN
Oslo ✪

Akershus Slott og Festning (Akershus Castle & Fortress) **28**
Astrup Fearnley Museum of Modern Art **26**
Aula (Great Hall) **15**
Barnekunst Museum (International Children's Art Museum) **2**
Botanisk Hage og Museum (Botanical Gardens) **20**
Edvard Munch Museum **20**
Forsvarsmuseet (Armed Forces Museum) **29**
Henie-Onstad Kunstsenter (Henie-Onstad Art Center) **6**
Historisk Museum (University Museum of Cultural Heritage) **16**
Ibsen Museum **13**

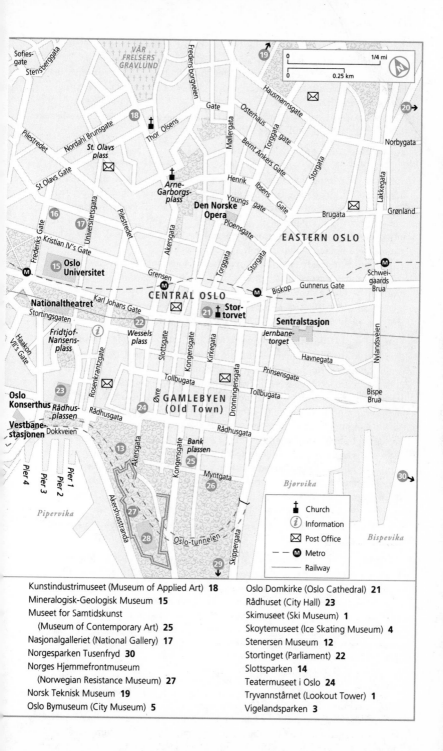

Kunstindustrimuseet (Museum of Applied Art) **18**
Mineralogisk-Geologisk Museum **15**
Museet for Samtidskunst
  (Museum of Contemporary Art) **25**
Nasjonalgalleriet (National Gallery) **17**
Norgesparken Tusenfryd **30**
Norges Hjemmefrontmuseum
  (Norwegian Resistance Museum) **27**
Norsk Teknisk Museum **19**
Oslo Bymuseum (City Museum) **5**

Oslo Domkirke (Oslo Cathedral) **21**
Rådhuset (City Hall) **23**
Skimuseet (Ski Museum) **1**
Skoytemuseet (Ice Skating Museum) **4**
Stenersen Museum **12**
Stortinget (Parliament) **22**
Slottsparken **14**
Teatermuseet i Oslo **24**
Tryvannstårnet (Lookout Tower) **1**
Vigelandsparken **3**

through the 13th century are in the Treasure House. In the medieval hall, look for the reddish Ringerike Alstad Stone, which was carved in relief, and the Dynna Stone, an 11th-century runic stone honoring the handiest maiden in Hadeland. There's also a rich collection of ecclesiastical art in a series of portals from stave churches.

Frederiksgate 2 (near Karl Johans Gate). (C) **22-85-99-12.** Free admission. May 15–Sept 14 Tues–Sun 10am–4pm; Sept 15–May 14 Tues–Sun 11am–4pm. Tram: 7, 8, 11, or 17.

Kunstindustrimuseet (Museum of Applied Art) ✦ Founded in 1876, this is one of the oldest museums in Norway and among the oldest applied-arts museums in Europe. Extensive collections embrace Norwegian and international applied art, design, and fashion. Highlights include the 13th-century Baldishol tapestry and the fashion collection in the Royal Norwegian gallery. The museum displays pieces of 18th-century silver and glass, as well as an impressive selection of contemporary Scandinavian furniture and crafts. The ground floor houses temporary craft and design exhibits.

The museum schedules lectures, guided tours, and concerts. Café Solliløkken and the museum shop on the ground floor are in rooms from the 1830s that originally were in a small country house.

St. Olavs Gate 1. (C) **22-03-65-40.** Admission 65NOK ($8.65) adults, free for children under 12. Tues–Fri 11am–3pm; Sat–Sun noon–4pm. T-banen: Stortinget. Bus: 37.

Mineralogisk-Geologisk Museum (Mineral and Geological Museum) Attached to the University of Oslo, this museum opened in 1920, tracing the geology of the world but of Norway in particular. It's visited by all Oslo school children, but is of interest to the casual visitor as well. You can, for example, learn about the working of a volcano and see how mountains are formed. Norway's more modern role as an oil-producing nation is also explored in rather fascinating detail. One section uses various rock formations to present the geological history of the country. On the second floor is an exhibition of minerals and gemstones from around the globe. There's even a "piece of the moon" on display. In the paleontological section are the skeletons of dinosaurs, along with imagined drawings of what they looked like. You can still see the 9m (30 ft.) skeleton of an Iguanodon, with its nest of half a dozen dinosaur eggs. You can also pay your respects to a million-year-old bradypodidae.

Sars Gate 1. (C) **22-85-17-00.** Admission varies with the changing exhibitions. Tues–Sun 11am–4pm; Wed 11am–8pm. Tram: 15, 17.

Norges Hjemmefrontmuseum (Norwegian Resistance Museum) From underground printing presses to radio transmitters, from the German attack in 1940 to the liberation in 1945, this museum documents Norway's World War II resistance activities. Outside is a monument dedicated to Norwegian patriots, many of whom were executed by the Nazis at this spot.

Akershus Fortress. (C) **23-09-31-38.** Admission 25NOK ($3.35) adults, 10NOK ($1.35) children. Apr 15–June 14 and Sept Mon–Sat 10am–4pm, Sun 11am–4pm; June 15–Aug Mon–Sat 10am–5pm, Sun 11am–5pm; Oct–Apr 14 Mon–Sat 10am–3pm, Sun 11am–4pm. Tram: 10, 12, 15, or 19.

Teatermuseet i Oslo (Oslo Theater Museum) In the hometown of Bjørnson and Ibsen, theater buffs flock to this museum with its theatrical memorabilia. A century and a half of Oslovian theatrical history unfolds here, going through the golden years of the Christiania Theater where many of Ibsen's plays were performed for the first time. The mementoes include pictures and costumes, and exhibitions relive the era of the circus, vaudeville, and the marionette

Frommer's Favorite Oslo Experiences

Enjoying Fresh Shrimp off the Boats   In the morning, head for the harbor in front of the Rådhuset and buy a bag of freshly caught and cooked shrimp from a fisherman. Although this may not be everyone's idea of a good breakfast—sales begin around 7 or 8am and may end in late morning—shrimp fans will love it.

Experiencing Life on the Fjords   In the summer, head for the harbor, where boats wait to take you sightseeing, fishing, or to the beach.

Hanging Out in the Students' Grove   Summer is short in Oslo, and it's savored. Late-night drinkers sit in open-air beer gardens, enjoying the endless nights.

Listening to Street Musicians   Hundreds of musicians flock to Oslo in the summer. You can enjoy their music along Karl Johans Gate and at the marketplace Stortorget.

Taking the Ferry to Bygdøy   The Bygdøy peninsula offers a treasure trove of attractions including Viking ships, Thor Heyerdahl's *Kon-Tiki*, seafood buffets, a sailboat harbor, and bathing beaches. At the folk museum are old farmsteads, houses, and, often, folk dancing.

theater. There is also a rich collection of ballet costumes and the portraits of actors, most of whom are long forgotten.

Christiania Torv 1. ✆ **22-42-65-09.** Admission 25NOK ($3.35) adults, 15NOK ($2) students and children. Sun noon–4pm; Wed 11am–3pm; Thurs noon–6pm. Tram: 10, 12.

HISTORIC BUILDINGS

Akershus Slott og Festning (Akershus Castle & Fortress) ★★ *Kids*   One of the oldest historical monuments in Oslo, Akershus Castle was built in 1300 by Haakon V Magnusson. It was a fortress and a royal residence for several centuries. A fire in 1527 devastated the northern wing, and the castle was rebuilt and transformed into a royal Renaissance palace under the Danish-Norwegian king, Christian IV. Now the government uses it for state occasions. A fortress or *Festning* with thick earth-and-stone walls is constructed around the castle, with protruding bastions designed to resist artillery bombardment. English-speaking guided tours are offered Monday to Saturday at 11am, 1pm, and 3pm, and on Sunday at 1 and 3pm.

Festnings-Plassen. ✆ **22-41-25-21.** Admission 30NOK ($4) adults, 10NOK ($1.35) children, family ticket 70NOK ($9.30). May–Sept 15 Mon–Sat 10am–4pm, Sun 12:30–4pm. Closed Sept 16–Apr. Tram: 10 or 12. Bus: 60.

Oslo Domkirke (Oslo Cathedral) ★   Oslo's 17th-century cathedral at Stortorvet (the marketplace) was restored in 1950, when Hugo Louis Mohr completed its modern, tempera ceiling decorations.

The cathedral contains works by 20th-century Norwegian artists, including bronze doors by Dagfin Werenskiold. Try to view the pulpit and altar, which date from the cathedral's earliest days. There are stained-glass windows by Emanuel Vigeland (not to be confused with the sculptor, Gustav) in the choir and Borgar Hauglid in the transepts. The organ is five stories tall. A bilingual service (in Norwegian and English) is conducted on Wednesday at noon, and an organ recital is presented on summer Saturdays at noon.

Stortorvet 1. ℂ **23-31-46-10.** Free admission. Daily 10am–4pm. T-banen: Stortinget. Bus: 17.

Rådhuset (City Hall)   The modern City Hall, inaugurated in 1950, must be seen to be judged. It has been called everything from "aggressively ugly" to "the pride of Norway." Its simple brick exterior with double towers houses, among other things, the stunning 25m-by-13m (85 ft.-by-43 ft.) wall painted by Henrik Sørensen, and the mural *Life* by Edvard Munch. Tapestries, frescoes, sculpture, and woodcarvings by Dagfin Werenskiold are also on display. Guided tours in English are available. In the courtyard you can see the astronomical clock and Dyre Vaa's swan fountain.

Rådhusplassen. ℂ **23-46-16-00.** 40NOK ($5.30) adults, free for children. May–Sept Mon–Sat 9am–5pm, Sun noon–5pm; Oct–Apr Mon–Sat 9am–4pm, Sun noon–4pm. Guided tours Mon–Fri at 10am, noon, and 2pm. Bus: 30, 31, 32, 45, or 81.

Stortinget (Parliament)   Constructed from 1861 to 1866, the Parliament, in the center of the city, was richly decorated by contemporary Norwegian artists. The style is neo-Romanesque. The public is admitted only on guided tours.

Karl Johans Gate 22. ℂ **23-31-35-96.** Free admission. Guided tours in English July 1–Aug 15 Mon–Fri 10am, 11:30am, and 1pm; Sept 15–June 15 Sat 10am, 11:30am, and 1pm; closed Aug 16–Sept 14 and June 16–30. T-banen: Stortinget. Tram: 13, 15, or 19.

IN FROGNER

Skoytemuseet (Ice Skating Museum)   In the land of skaters and skiers, it seems appropriate to have a museum devoted to ice-skating. This museum tells the story of many fascinating "duels" on ice as well as thrilling competitions on ice. You'll learn about the heroes of the speed-skating world, including Axel Paulsen (1855–1938) and Oscar Mathisen (1888–1954), along with their participation in world championships. You'll also see the first skates ever made in Norway—bone was used—to the most advanced high-tech skates of today. Opening in 1914, this museum displays artifacts illustrating "major moments" in speed and figure skating.

At the Frogner Stadium, Middelthunsgate 26. ℂ **22-43-49-20.** Admission 20NOK ($2.65) adults, 10NOK ($1.35) children. Tues and Thurs 10am–2pm; Sun 11am–2pm. Tram: 11, 19.

Vigelandsparken ★★   The lifetime work of Gustav Vigeland, Norway's greatest sculptor, is on display in the 30-hectare (75-acre) Frogner Park. More than 200 sculptures in granite, bronze, and iron are here. Notice his four granite columns, symbolizing the fight between humanity and evil (a dragon, the embodiment of evil, embraces a woman). The angry boy is the most photographed statue in the park. The most celebrated work is the 16m (52 ft.) monolith composed of 121 colossal figures, all carved into one piece of stone.

Nearby, the **Vigeland Museum,** Nobelsgate 32 (ℂ **22-54-25-30**), is the sculptor's former studio. It contains more of his works, sketches, and woodcuts.

Frogner Park, Nobelsgate 32. ℂ **22-54-25-30.** Free admission to park; museum 40NOK ($5.30) adults, 30NOK ($4) children. Park daily 24 hr. Museum May–Sept Tues–Sat 10am–6pm, Sun noon–7pm; Oct–Apr Tues–Sun noon–4pm. Tram: 12 or 15. Bus: 20, 45, or 81.

ON BYGDØY

Located south of the city, the peninsula is reached by commuter ferry (summer only) leaving from Pier 3, facing the Rådhuset (Town Hall). Departures during the day are every 40 minutes, and a one-way fare costs 22NOK ($2.95). The no. 30 bus from the National Theater also runs to Bygdøy. The museums lie only a short walk from the bus stops on Bygdøy.

Frammuseet ★ *Kids*   This museum contains the sturdy polar exploration ship *Fram*, which Fridtjof Nansen sailed across the Arctic (1893–96). The vessel was later used by the famed Norwegian explorer Roald Amundsen, the first man to reach the South Pole (1911).

Bygdøynesveien. ℂ 23-28-29-50. Admission 30NOK ($4) adults, 15NOK ($2) children. Mar–Apr daily 11am–3:45pm; May 1–15 and Sept daily 10am–4:45pm; May 16–Aug daily 9am–5:45pm; Oct–Nov Mon–Fri 11am–2:45pm, Sat–Sun 11am–3:45pm; Dec–Feb Sat–Sun 11am–3:45pm. Ferry: From Pier 3 facing the Rådhuset (summer only). Bus: 30 from the National Theater.

Kon-Tiki Museum ★ *Kids*   *Kon-Tiki* is a world-famous balsa-log raft. In 1947, the young Norwegian scientist Thor Heyerdahl and five comrades sailed it from Callao, Peru, to Raroia, Polynesia (6,880km/4,300 miles). Besides the raft, there are other exhibits from Heyerdahl's subsequent visits to Easter Island. They include casts of stone giants and small originals, a facsimile of the whale shark, and an Easter Island family cave, with a collection of sacred lava figurines hoarded in secret underground passages by the island's inhabitants. The museum also houses the original papyrus *Ra II*, in which Heyerdahl crossed the Atlantic in 1970.

Bygdøynesveien 36. ℂ 23-08-67-67. www.museumsnett.no/kon-tiki. Admission 35NOK ($4.65) adults, 20NOK ($2.65) children, family ticket 90NOK ($12). Apr–May and Sept daily 10:30am–5pm; June–Aug daily 9:30am–5:45pm; Oct–Mar daily 10:30am–4pm. Ferry: From Pier 3 facing the Rådhuset (summer only). Bus: 30 from the National Theater.

Norsk Sjøfartsmuseum (Norwegian Maritime Museum) ★ *Kids*   This museum chronicles the maritime history and culture of Norway, complete with a ship's deck with helm and chart house. There's also a three-deck section of the passenger steamer *Sandnaes*. The Boat Hall features a fine collection of original small craft. The fully restored polar vessel *Gjoa*, used by Roald Amundsen in his search for the Northwest Passage, is also on display. The three-masted schooner *Svanen* (Swan) is moored at the museum. Built in Svendborg, Denmark, in 1916, *Svanen* sailed under the Norwegian and Swedish flags. The ship now belongs to the museum and is used as a training vessel and school ship for young people.

Bygdøynesveien 37. ℂ 22-43-82-40. Admission to museum and boat hall 40NOK ($5.30) adults, 20NOK ($2.65) children. May–Sept daily 10am–6pm; Oct–Apr Mon and Fri–Sat 10:30am–4pm, Tues–Thurs 10:30am–6pm. Ferry: From Pier 3 facing the Rådhuset (summer only). Bus: 30 from the National Theater.

Norwegian Folk Museum ★★ *Kids*   From all over Norway, 140 original buildings have been transported and reassembled on 14 hectares (35 acres) on the Bygdøy peninsula. This open-air folk museum, one of the oldest of its kind, includes a number of medieval buildings. The Raulandstua is one of the oldest wooden dwellings still standing in Norway, and a stave church dates from about 1200. The rural buildings are grouped together by region of origin, and the urban houses are laid out in the form of an old town.

Inside, the museum's 225,000 exhibits capture every imaginable facet of Norwegian life, past and present. Furniture, household utensils, clothing, woven fabrics, and tapestries are on display, along with fine examples of rose painting and woodcarving. Farming implements and logging gear pay tribute to the development of agriculture and forestry. Also look for the outstanding exhibit on Norway's Lapp population.

Museumsveien 10. ℂ 22-12-37-00. Admission 70NOK ($9.30) adults, 20NOK ($2.65) children under 17. Jan 1–May 14 and Sept 15–Dec 31 Fri–Sat 11am–3pm, Sun 11am–4pm; May 15–June 14 and Sept 1–14 daily

10am–5pm; June 15–Aug 31 daily 10am–6pm. Ferry: From Pier 3 facing the Rådhuset (summer only). Bus: 30 from the National Theater.

Vikingskiphuset (Viking Ship Museum, University Museum of Cultural Heritage) ★★★ *Kids* Displayed here are three Viking burial vessels that were excavated on the shores of the Oslofjord. The most spectacular find is the 9th-century *Oseberg*, discovered near Norway's oldest town. This richly ornamented 19m (64 ft.) dragon ship is the burial chamber of a Viking queen and her slave. The *Gokstad* is an outstanding example of Viking vessels because it's so well preserved. The smaller *Tune* ship was never restored. Look for the *Oseberg*'s animal-head post and four-wheeled cart, and the elegantly carved sleigh used by Viking royalty.

Huk Aveny 35, Bygdøy. (C) 22-43-83-79. Admission 40NOK ($5.30) adults, 20NOK ($2.65) children. Apr daily 11am–4pm; May–Aug daily 9am–6pm; Sept daily 11am–5pm; Oct daily 11am–6pm; Nov–Mar daily 11am–3pm. Ferry: From Pier 3 facing the Rådhuset (summer only). Bus: 30 from the National Theater.

NEAR OSLO

Henie-Onstad Kunstsenter (Henie-Onstad Art Center) ★★★ Former skating champion and movie star Sonja Henie and her husband, shipping tycoon Niels Onstad, opened this museum to display their art collection. On a handsome site beside the Oslofjord, 11km (7 miles) west of Oslo, the museum holds an especially good 20th-century collection. There are some 1,800 works by Munch, Picasso, Matisse, Léger, Bonnard, and Miró. Henie's contributions can be seen in her Trophy Room. She won three Olympic gold medals—she was the star at the 1936 competition—and 10 world championships. In all, she garnered 600 trophies and medals.

Besides the permanent collection, there are plays, concerts, films, and special exhibits. An open-air theater-in-the-round is used in the summer for folklore programs, jazz concerts, and song recitals. On the premises is a top-notch, partly self-service, grill restaurant, the Piruetten.

Høkvikodden, Baerum. (C) 67-80-48-80. Admission 75NOK ($10) adults, 45NOK ($6) visitors ages 15–25, free for children under 15. June–Aug Mon 11am–6pm, Tues–Fri 10am–9pm, Sat–Sun 11am–6pm; Sept–May Tues 10am–9pm, Sat–Mon 11am–5pm. Bus: 151, 152, 251, or 261.

Norsk Teknisk Museum (Norwegian Technological Museum) This museum showcases Norway's prime exhibits in industry, technology, transport, medicine, and science. On the outskirts of the city, it opens onto the banks of the Akerselva River. The museum also hosts the Norwegian Telecom Museum, in which you learn such tidbits that in the age of the Vikings Norsemen communicated with each other through torches. The museum offers a wide array of exhibits that provide fascinating information about energy, gas, oil, electricity, plastic, the wood and metal industries, along with clocks, watches, calculating machines, and computers.

Kjelsåsvn 143. (C) 22-79-60-00. Admission 60NOK ($8) adults, 30NOK ($4) students and children. Daily 10am–6pm. Bus: 22, 25, 37.

Skimuseet (Ski Museum) ★ *Kids* At Holmenkollen, an elevator takes visitors up the jump tower for a **panoramic view** ★★★ of Oslo and the fjord, the greatest such vista you are likely to experience in Norway. At the base of the ski jump, the Ski Museum (Skimuseet) displays a wide range of exhibits. They include a 4,000-year-old pictograph from Rødøy in Nordland, which documents skiing's thousand-year history. The oldest ski in the museum dates from around A.D. 600. The museum has exhibits on Nansen's and Amundsen's polar

Who the Heck Was Sonja Henie?

Even young Norwegians know of one of their most legendary public figures, Sonja Henie (1912–69). In America only an older generation of devotees of late-night television might be able to identify this former figure skater and movie actress who won gold medals for figure skating at the 1928, 1932, and 1936 Winter Olympics. She was the youngest Olympic skating champion—15 years old when she won her first 1928 gold medal.

She was born in Oslo, the daughter of a furrier. Having learned skating and dancing as a child, she became a professional in 1936 on her tour of the United States, performing in ice shows as late as the 1950s. The bright-eyed, bubbly blonde managed to parlay her championships into an effervescent but short motion picture career. She was hardly an actress, but she had a smile that was enchanting, and as long as her pictures featured ice-skating, she was relatively harmless in front of the camera.

Naturally 20th Century Fox ordered writers to tailor film properties for her, to keep the comedy and romance light, and to get her on those skates as much as possible.

Often she was teamed with top-rate stars such as Ray Milland and Robert Cummings in *Everything Happens at Night* in 1939, or Don Ameche, Ethel Merman, and Cesar Romero in the 1938 *Happy Landing*. The year 1939 also saw her teamed opposite Rudy Valee and Tyrone Power in *Second Fiddle*. In 1939 only Shirley Temple and Clark Gable outranked her at the box office.

Although she would continue skating, her movie career had faded by the mid-1940s. She also lost popularity when a photograph of her was published showing her shaking hands with Hitler. Published in 1940, her autobiography was called *Wings on My Feet*.

In 1960 Henie retired to Norway with her third husband, Niels Onstad, a wealthy Norwegian businessman and art patron. Together they founded the Henie-Onstad Kunstsenter (Henie-Onstad Art Center) near Oslo in 1968, which visitors flock to today. The next year, at the relatively early age of 57, Norway's most famous daughter died. She was aboard an aircraft carrying her from Paris to Oslo for medical treatment. At the time of her death she was one of the 10 wealthiest women on earth.

expeditions, plus skis and historical items from various parts of Norway, including the first "modern" skis, from about 1870.

Kongeveien 5, Holmenkollen. © 22-92-32-00. Admission (museum and ski jump) 60NOK ($8) adults, 30NOK ($4) children. May and Sept daily 10am–5pm; June daily 9am–8pm; July–Aug daily 9am–10pm; Oct–Apr daily 10am–4pm. T-banen: Holmenkollen SST Line 15 from near the National Theater to Voksenkollen (30-min. ride), then an uphill 15-min. walk.

Tryvannstårnet (Lookout Tower) *(Kids)*   The loftiest lookout tower in Scandinavia offers a view of the Oslofjord with Sweden to the east. The gallery is approximately 570m (1,900 ft.) above sea level.

A walk down the hill returns you to Frognerseteren. Another 20-minute walk down the hill takes you to the Holmenkollen Ski Jump, where the 1952 Olympic competitions took place. It's also the site of Norway's winter sports highlight, the Holmenkollen Ski Festival.

Voksenkollen. ⓒ **22-14-67-11.** Admission 40NOK ($5.30) adults, 20NOK ($2.65) children. May and Sept daily 10am–5pm; June daily 10am–7pm; July–Aug daily 9am–8pm; Oct–Apr Mon–Sun 10am–4pm. T-banen: Frognerseteren SST Line 1 from near the National Theater to Voksenkollen (30-min. ride), then an uphill 15-min. walk.

2 Parks & Gardens

Marka, the thick forest that surrounds Oslo, is a giant pleasure park, and there are others. You can take a tram marked "Holmenkollen" from the city center to Oslomarka, a forested pleasure and recreational area. Locals go here for summer hikes in the forest and for skiing in winter. The area is dotted with about two dozen *hytter* (mountain huts) where you can seek refuge from the weather if needed. **Norske Turistforening,** Storgate 3 (ⓒ **22-82-28-22**), sells maps with the hiking paths and roads of the Oslomarka clearly delineated. Open Monday to Friday 10am to 4pm, Saturday 10am to 2pm.

Botanisk Hage og Museum (Botanical Gardens) At Tøyen, near the Munch Museum, this is an oasis in the heart of Oslo. It's home to many exotic plants, including cacti, orchids, and palms. More than 1,000 mountain plants can be viewed in the rock garden, which has waterfalls. There's also a museum in the park, with a botanical art exhibit.

Sars Gate 1. ⓒ **22-85-17-00.** Free admission. Apr–Sept Mon–Fri 7am–8pm, Sat–Sun 10am–8pm; Oct–Mar Mon–Fri 7am–5pm (Wed until 8pm), Sat–Sun 10am–5pm. Bus: 20.

Slottsparken The park surrounding the Royal Palace (Slottet) is open to the public year-round. The changing of the guard takes place daily at 1:30pm. When the king is in residence, the Royal Guard band plays Monday through Friday during the changing of the guard.

The palace was constructed from 1825 to 1848. Some first-time visitors are surprised at how open and relatively unguarded it is, without walls or rails. You can walk through the grounds, but can't go inside unless you have an invitation from the king. The statue at the front of the castle (at the end of Karl Johans Gate) is of Karl XIV Johan himself, who ruled Norway and Sweden. He ordered the construction of this palace, but died before it was finished.

Drammensveien 1. Free admission. Daily dawn–dusk. T-banen: Nationaltheateret.

3 Of Artistic Interest

See also listings for **Vigelandsparken** in Frogner and the **Henie-Onstad Kunstsenter (Henie-Onstad Art Center)** near Oslo, both earlier in this chapter.

Astrup Fearnley Museum of Modern Art ⭐ A 5- to 10-minute walk from the Oslo City Hall, this museum was created by some of Norway's leading architects and designers and showcases post–World War II art. The changing exhibits are often drawn from the museum's permanent collection. Here, you might see works by Francis Bacon, Lucian Freud, Gerhard Richter, or less familiar Norwegians, including Arne Ekeland, Knut Rose, or Bjørn Carlsen.

Dronningensgatan 4. ⓒ **22-93-60-60.** Admission 50NOK ($6.65) adults, 25NOK ($3.35) children, students, and seniors. Tues–Wed and Fri 11am–5pm; Thurs noon–7pm; Sat–Sun noon–5pm. T-banen: Stortinget. Tram: 10, 12, 13, 15, or 19. Bus: 60.

A Royal Pair: The Un–Fairy Tale Romance

Prince Haakon of Norway may be a direct descendant of Queen Victoria, but he shares little in common with this staunch monarch. Instead of going to Balliol College in Oxford, as did his father, King Garald V, Haakon was a fun-loving young man on campus at the University of California at Berkeley.

When it came to taking a bride, as he did in Oslo on August 25, 2001, he shocked conservative Norway, challenging one of the world's most tolerant and enlightened societies. Crown Prince Haakon married Mette-Marit Tjessem Hoiby (whom he called, "the love of my life"), an unconventional royal pairing. The prince had never been married before, but the princess and future queen of Norway was a divorcée and mother. The couple lived together before marriage in the palace with her 3-year-old son by a previous marriage to a convicted cocaine supplier.

Before marrying the prince, Mette-Marit, as the Oslo press so delicately phrased it, had a "well-known past in Oslo's dance-and-drugs house-party scene." It was rumored that pressure was brought on the young prince by conservative elements to give up a claim to the throne, eerily evocative of Edward VII's decision to marry the twice-divorced Wallis Warfield Simpson. It is said that Haakon considered renouncing the throne, but decided to maintain his status as the heir apparent. "I think this is where I'm supposed to be," he finally said to the press, ending months of speculation.

King Harald was supportive of his son's decision. The future king himself spent a decade trying to persuade his own father, Olav V, to sanction his marriage to his commoner childhood sweetheart. (The present Queen Sonja was born a shopkeeper's daughter.) Olav himself had also intervened when his daughter, Princess Martha Louise, was cited as a correspondent in a divorce proceeding in London.

The wedding has come and gone, and there is no talk of revolution at this "scandal." Ine Marie Eriksen, a law student from Tromsø, said, "Why should Prince Haakon and Mette-Marit live by rules of the 18th century? That would take away the very thing that the Norwegian people like about our monarchy."

Aula (Great Hall)   Admirers of the work of Edvard Munch will want to see the Great Hall of the university, where Scandinavia's greatest artist painted murals. Until it moved to larger headquarters at the City Hall, this used to be the site of the Nobel Prize award ceremony.

University of Oslo, Karl Johans Gate 47. ✆ **22-85-95-55.** Free admission. June 20–Aug 20 daily 24 hr. T-banen: Stortinget.

Edvard Munch Museum ★★★   Devoted exclusively to the works of Edvard Munch (1863–1944), Scandinavia's leading painter, this collection was his gift to the city. It traces his work from early realism to latter-day expressionism. Munch's art is Norway's only major contribution to the history of world art. The

The Man Behind *The Scream*

Scandinavia's greatest artist, Edvard Munch (1863–1944), was a pioneer in the expressionist movement. *The Scream,* painted in 1893, is his best-known painting. He grew up in Oslo (then called Christiania) and was often ill. Early memories of illness, death, and grief in his family had a tremendous impact on his later works. His father's death may have contributed to the loneliness and melancholy of one of his most famous works, *Night* (1890).

By the early 1890s, Munch had achieved fame (though slight in comparison with his renown today). He was at the center of a *succés de scandale* in Munich in 1892, when his art was interpreted as "anarchistic provocation." A major exhibit was closed in protest.

Munch went to Berlin, entering a world of literati, artists, and intellectuals. He met August Strindberg, and they discussed the philosophy of Nietzsche, symbolism, psychology, and occultism. The discussions clearly influenced his work. His growing outlook was revealed to the world in an 1893 show in Berlin, where several paintings had death as their theme. *Death in a Sickroom* created quite a stir.

In 1896 Munch moved to Paris, where he made exquisite color lithographs and his first woodcuts. By the turn of the century he was painting in a larger format and incorporating some of the Art Nouveau aesthetics of the time. *Red Virginia Creeper and Melancholy* reflects the new influences.

A nervous disorder sent him to a sanitarium, and he had a turbulent love affair with a wealthy bohemian nicknamed "Tulla." The affair ended in 1902 when a revolver permanently injured a finger on Munch's left hand. He became obsessed with the shooting incident, and poured out his contempt for Tulla in such works as *Death of Murat* (1907).

Prominent people asked Munch to paint their portraits, and he obliged. The group portrait of Dr. Linde's sons (1904) is a masterpiece of modern portraiture. Munch became increasingly alcoholic, and in 1906 painted *Self-Portrait with a Bottle of Wine.*

From 1909 until his death, Munch lived in Norway. In his later years he retreated into isolation, surrounded only by his paintings, which he called "my children." The older Munch placed more emphasis on the monumental and the picturesque, as in landscapes or people in harmony with nature.

In 1940 he decided to leave his huge collection of paintings to the city of Oslo upon his death. Today the Edvard Munch Museum provides the best introduction to this strange and enigmatic artist.

collection comprises 1,100 paintings, some 4,500 drawings, around 18,000 prints, numerous graphic plates, six sculptures, and important documentary material. The exhibits change periodically.

Tøyengate 53. *C* **23-24-14-00.** Admission 60NOK ($8) adults, 30NOK ($4) children. June to mid-Sept daily 10am–6pm; mid-Sept to May Tues–Wed and Fri–Sat 10am–4pm, Thurs and Sun 10am–6pm. T-banen: Tøyen. Bus: 20.

Museet for Samtidskunst (Museum of Contemporary Art)   Opened in 1990, this collection of works acquired by the state after World War II presents an array of international and Norwegian contemporary art. Previously grouped together in the National Gallery, the works have more room to "breathe" in their new home. Exhibits change frequently.

Bankplassen 4. ✆ **22-86-22-10.** 40NOK ($5.30) adults, free for children. Tues–Wed and Fri 10am–5pm; Thurs 10am–8pm; Sat–Sun 11am–4pm. Tram: 10, 12, 13, 15, or 19. Bus: 60.

Nasjonalgalleriet (National Gallery) ★★   This state museum, a short walk from the Students' Grove, is recommended chiefly for its paintings by Norwegians but also has an intriguing collection of works by world-famous artists, including Cézanne and Matisse. The leading Norwegian Romantic landscape painter Johan Christian Dahl (1788–1857) is well represented as are three outstanding Norwegian Realists. Harriet Backer, a leading painter in the 1880s, was famous for interior portraits of Norwegian life; Christian Krohg painted subjects from seafarers to prostitutes; and Erik Werenskiold is noted for *Peasant Funeral.* On the main staircase is a display of Norwegian sculpture from 1910 to 1945. Note especially the works of Gustav Vigeland and the two rooms devoted to Edvard Munch. His much-reproduced work *The Scream* was painted in 1893. It was stolen in 1994 and subsequently recovered.

Universitetsgata 13. ✆ **22-20-04-04.** Free admission. Mon, Wed, and Fri 10am–6pm; Thurs 10am–8pm; Sat 10am–4pm; Sun 11am–4pm. Tram: 7 or 11.

Stenersen Museum ★   Part of the City of Oslo Art Collections, this museum is the venue for a series of the most avant-garde temporary exhibitions in the capital. Opened in 1994, it's named for Rolf E. Stenersen, the international art collector. The nucleus of the collection focuses on Stenersen's personally acquired art, including paintings by Edvard Munch. In its permanent collection is a representative collection of Norwegian art beginning in 1850 and going up to 1970. Another part of the permanent collection is devoted to works acquired by other leading artists, Ludvig O. Ravensberg and Amaldus Nilesen.

Munkedamsveien 15. ✆ **23-49-36-00.** Admission 40NOK ($5.30) adults, 20NOK ($2.65) students and children. Tues and Thurs 11am–5pm; Wed, Fri, and Sat–Sun 11am–5pm. Tram: 10, 12.

4 Literary Landmarks

See also "Walking Tour 2: In the Footsteps of Ibsen & Munch," below.

Ibsen Museum   In 1994 Oslo opened a museum to honor its most famous writer. Ibsen lived in an apartment within walking distance of the National Theater from 1895 until his death in 1906. Here he wrote two of his most famous plays, *John Gabriel Borkman* and *When We Dead Awaken.* The museum curators have tried to re-create the apartment (a longtime exhibit at the Norwegian Folk Museum) as authentically as possible. The study, for example, has Ibsen's original furniture, and the entire apartment is decorated as though Ibsen still lived in it. The attraction has been called "a living museum," and regularly scheduled talks on play writing and the theater, recitations, and theatrical performances take place.

Arbinsgate 1. ✆ **22-55-20-09.** Admission 50NOK ($6.65) adults, 20NOK ($2.65) children. Tues–Sun noon–3pm; guided tour in English at noon, 1pm, and 2pm. T-banen: Nationaltheatret.

Oslo Bymuseum (City Museum)   Housed in the 1790 Frogner Manor at Frogner Park, site of the Vigeland sculptures (see the listing for Vigelandsparken, earlier in this chapter), this museum surveys the history of Oslo. It also contains mementos of Henrik Ibsen, such as the chair and marble-topped table where he sat at the Grand Café. Four glasses from which he drank are engraved with his name.

Frognerveien 67. ✆ **23-28-41-70.** Admission 40NOK ($5.30) adults, 20NOK ($2.65) children. June–Aug Tues–Fri 10am–6pm, Sat–Sun 11am–5pm; Sept–May Tues–Fri 10am–4pm, Sat–Sun 11am–4pm. Bus: 20, 45, or 81. Tram: 12 or 15.

5 Especially for Kids

Oslo offers numerous attractions suitable for both children and grown-ups. The top thrill of a trip to the fjord is seeing the excavated Viking burial ships at the **Vikingskiphuset** (p. 104) and the Boat Hall at the **Norwegian Maritime Museum** (p. 103), both on the Bygdøy peninsula.

Other sights of special interest to children include the polar exploration ship *Fram* at the **Frammuseet** (p. 103); the balsa-log raft *Kon-Tiki* at the **Kon-Tiki Museum** (p. 103); the **Ski Museum** (p. 104), **Lookout Tower** (p. 105) and ski jump at Holmenkollen; the **Norwegian Folk Museum** (p. 103), depicting life in Norway since the Middle Ages; and the ancient **Akershus Castle & Fortress** (p. 101) on the Oslofjord.

Barnekunst Museum (International Children's Art Museum)   The collection in this unique museum consists of children's drawings, paintings, ceramics, sculpture, tapestries, and handicrafts from more than 30 countries, some of which would have pleased Picasso. There's also a children's workshop devoted to painting, drawing, music, and dance.

Lille Frøens vei 4. ✆ **22-46-85-73.** Admission 50NOK ($6.65) adults, 30NOK ($4) children. Jan 20–June 25 and Sept 10–Dec 15 Tues–Thurs 9:30am–2pm, Sun 11am–4pm; June 26–Aug 15 Tues–Thurs and Sun 11am–4pm. Closed Dec 16–Jan 19 and Aug 16–Sept 9. T-banen: Frøen.

Norgesparken Tusenfryd   This is the largest amusement park in Norway, conceived as a smaller version of Copenhagen's Tivoli. It includes a number of simple restaurants, a roller coaster with a loop and corkscrew, an amphitheater with all-day entertainment by performers such as musicians and clowns, and many games of skill or chance. The park is 19km (12 miles) south of the Central Station.

Vinterbro by E6/E18/Mossevelen. ✆ **64-97-66-99.** All-day ticket 210NOK ($28) adults, 110NOK ($15) children. June–Sept 19 daily 10:30am–7pm. Closed Sept 20–May. Bus: Shuttle service from Oslo's Central Station daily 10am–1pm (every 30 min.), 3, 4, and 5pm; final return shortly after park closes. Fare 30NOK ($4) adults, 20NOK ($2.65) children.

6 Oslo on Foot: Walking Tours

WALKING TOUR 1   **HISTORIC OSLO**

Start:	Aker Brygge.
Finish:	Royal Palace.
Time:	2½ hours.
Best Time:	Any day when it's not raining.
Worst Times:	Rush hours (weekdays 7–9am and 5–7pm).

Legend:
- ✝ Church
- 🌀 "Take a break" stop
- – – – Tunnel

| 0 | 1/5 mile |
| 0 | 200 meters |

1 Aker Brygge
2 Rådhuset
3 Statue of Franklin D. Roosevelt
4 Christiania Torv
5 Norwegian Resistance Museum
6 Akershus Castle & Fortress
7 Execution Site
8 National Monument to the
   German Occupation

9 Grev Wedels Plass
10 Bankplassen
11 Oslo Sentralstasjon
12 Karl Johans Gate
13 Basarhallene
14 Oslo Domkirke
15 Norwegian Parliament
   (Stortinget)
16 Royal Palace (Slottet)

Start at the harbor to the west of the Rådhuset at:

❶ Aker Brygge

This steel-and-glass complex is a rebuilt district of shops and restaurants that was developed from Oslo's old shipbuilding grounds. It has a fine view of Akershus Castle.

Head east along Rådhusplassen, looking to your left at the:

❷ Rådhuset

The Oslo City Hall, built in 1950, is decorated with artwork by Norwegian artists.

Climb the steps at the east end of the square and a small hill to see the:

❸ Statue of Franklin D. Roosevelt

Eleanor Roosevelt flew to Oslo to dedicate this statue.

This area is the heart of the 17th-century Renaissance city. Take Rådhusgata east to the traffic hub of:

❹ Christiania Torv

The yellow house on your left, the Young Artists Association, was once the home of the dreaded executioner. His fee depended on the type of execution performed.

TAKE A BREAK
To the right of the Young Artists Association is **Kafé Celsius**, Rådhusgatan 19 (☎ **22-42-45-39**), Oslo's oldest residential house. Today it's a charming arts-oriented cafe that serves tasty food. Sandwich prices start at 79NOK ($11). You can also order pasta salads and such dishes as ratatouille or tortellini. On cold days there's a fire in the fireplace. It's open Sunday, Tuesday, and Wednesday from 11:30am to 12:30am, Thursday to Saturday 11:30am to 1:30am.

Continue along Rådhusgata, turning right onto Nedre Slottsgate. Walk to the end of the street. At Myntgata, turn right and pass through a gate. You are now on the greater grounds of Akershus Castle. The first building on the right is the:

❺ Norwegian Resistance Museum

The museum has displays on events related to the Nazi occupation of Norway from 1940 to 1945.

Also at the site is:

❻ Akershus Castle & Fortress

The structure dates from 1300 but was rebuilt in the 17th century. Take a guided tour and walk the ramparts.

In front of the Norwegian Resistance Museum, pause on the grounds to look at the:

❼ Execution Site

Here the Nazis shot prisoners, often Norwegian freedom fighters. There's a memorial to the resistance movement, and you'll have a good view of the harbor in the distance.

Cross the drawbridge to the east, right before Kongens Gate, and continue through the castle grounds to the:

❽ National Monument to the German Occupation

This commemorates Norway's suffering at the hands of the Nazis.

After seeing the monument, turn left (north) into:

❾ Grev Wedels Plass

This is the site of Den Gamle Logen (Freemason's Lodge). In 1850, Ibsen wrote poems here. At no. 9 and Dronningensgatan 4 is the Astrup Fearnley Museum of Modern Art, with changing exhibits of Norwegian and foreign art from the postwar period.

Head north along Kirkegata until you reach:

❿ Bankplassen

This former site of the old Bank of Norway is now the Museum of Contemporary Art (Bankplassen 4), with the state collection of international and Norwegian modern art acquired since World War II. This square was once Oslo's social center. Ibsen staged his first play here in 1851 (at a theater that burned down in 1877).

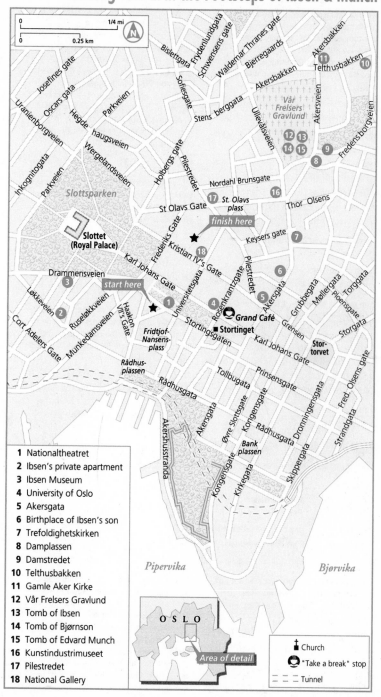

1 Nationaltheatret
2 Ibsen's private apartment
3 Ibsen Museum
4 University of Oslo
5 Akersgata
6 Birthplace of Ibsen's son
7 Trefoldighetskirken
8 Damplassen
9 Damstredet
10 Telthusbakken
11 Gamle Aker Kirke
12 Vår Frelsers Gravlund
13 Tomb of Ibsen
14 Tomb of Bjørnson
15 Tomb of Edvard Munch
16 Kunstindustrimuseet
17 Pilestredet
18 National Gallery

✝ Church
🌀 "Take a break" stop
‒ ‒ ‒ Tunnel

From Bankplassen, turn right onto Revier-stredet and left onto Dronningensgatan. At one time the waterfront came up to this point. Go right at the Central Post Office onto Tollbugata. At the intersection with Fred Olsens Gate, turn left and walk to the:

⑪ Oslo Sentralstasjon

Trains arrive at Oslo's rail hub from the Continent and depart for all points linked by train in Norway.

Turn left onto the main pedestrian-only street:

⑫ Karl Johans Gate

The street stretches from the Central Station in the east to the Royal Palace in the west end.

On your right you'll pass the:

⑬ Basarhallene

Boutiques and shops fill this huge complex.

Turn right at Kirkegata, heading for the:

⑭ Oslo Domkirke

This 17th-century cathedral resides at Stortorvet, Oslo's old marketplace. Like the City Hall, the cathedral is decorated with outstanding works by Norwegian artists.

> **TAKE A BREAK**
> Old Oslo atmosphere lives on at the **Stortorvets Gjaest-giveri**, Grensen 1 (✆ 23-35-63-60), on a busy commercial street. This drinking and dining emporium, dating from the 1600s, is often filled with spirited beer drinkers. A beer costs 49NOK ($6.50). It's open Monday to Saturday from 11am to 9pm, Sunday (from Nov–Apr only) 3 to 9pm.

From Stortorvet, walk west on Grensen until you reach Lille Grensen. Cut left onto this street, returning to Karl Johans Gate. On your left at Karl Johans Gate 22 will be the:

⑮ Norwegian Parliament (Stortinget)

Constructed from 1861 to 1866, it's richly decorated with works by contemporary Norwegian artists.

Continue west along Karl Johans Gate, passing many of the monuments covered on "Walking Tour 2: In the Footsteps of Ibsen & Munch" (see below). Eventually you'll reach Drammensveien 1:

⑯ Royal Palace (Slottet)

This is the residence of the king of Norway and his family. The public is permitted access only to the park.

WALKING TOUR 2	IN THE FOOTSTEPS OF IBSEN & MUNCH

Start:	National Theater.
Finish:	National Gallery.
Time:	2 hours.
Best Time:	Any day when it's not raining.
Worst Times:	Rush hours (weekdays 7–9am and 5–7pm).

The tour begins at Stortingsgaten 15, just off Karl Johans Gate near the Students' Grove in Oslo's center, site of the:

❶ Nationaltheatret

Study your map in front of the Henrik Ibsen statue at the theater, where many of his plays were first performed and are still presented. The Norwegian National Theater (✆ 22-00-14-00), inaugurated in 1899, is one of the most beautiful in Europe.

Facing the statue of Ibsen, continue up Stortingsgaten toward the Royal Palace (Slottet). Cut left at the next intersection and walk along Ruselokkveien. On the right, the Vika Shopping Terraces, an unattractive row of modern storefronts tacked onto an elegant 1880 Victorian terrace, used to be among Oslo's grandest apartments. During the Second World War it was the Nazi headquarters.

Continue along this complex to the end, turning right onto Dronnings Mauds Gate, which quickly becomes Lokkeveien. At the first building on the right, you come to:

2 Ibsen's private apartment

Look for the blue plaque marking the building. The playwright lived here from 1891 to 1895. When his wife complained that she didn't like the address, even though it was one of Oslo's most elegant, they moved. Ibsen wrote two plays while living here.

Turn right onto Arbinsgate and walk to the end of the street until you reach Drammensveien. At Arbinsgate 1 is the:

3 Ibsen Museum

In the first building on the left, at the corner of Arbinsgate and Drammensveien, you'll see an Omega store, but look for the blue plaque on the building. Ibsen lived here from 1895 until his death in 1906. He often sat in the window, with a light casting a glow over his white hair. People lined up in the street below to look at him. The great Italian actress Eleanora Duse came here to bid him a final *adieu*, but he was too ill to see her. She stood outside in the snow and blew him kisses.

The king of Norway used to give Ibsen a key to enter the private gardens surrounding the Royal Palace. Everybody has that privilege today.

Turn right on Drammensveien and continue back to the National Theater. Take Karl Johans Gate, on the left side of the theater, and walk east. On your left at Karl Johans Gate 47, you'll pass the:

4 University of Oslo

Aula, the Great Hall of the university, is decorated with murals by Edvard Munch. The hall is open to the public only from June 15 to August 15, daily from noon to 2pm. For information, call ℭ **22-85-98-55**.

Twice a day Ibsen followed this route to the Grand Café. Admirers often threw rose petals in his path, but he pretended not to see. He was called

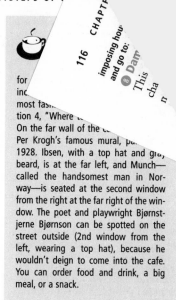

CHAPTER

116

imposing hou
and go to:

8 Dam

This cha
n

for
inc
most fas.
tion 4, "Where
On the far wall of the
Per Krogh's famous mural, p.
1928. Ibsen, with a top hat and gra,
beard, is at the far left, and Munch—called the handsomest man in Norway—is seated at the second window from the right at the far right of the window. The poet and playwright Bjørnstjerne Bjørnson can be spotted on the street outside (2nd window from the left, wearing a top hat), because he wouldn't deign to come into the cafe. You can order food and drink, a big meal, or a snack.

"the Sphinx," because he wouldn't talk to anybody.

Returning to the street, note the Norwegian Parliament building (Stortinget) on your right. Proceed left and turn left onto Lille Grensen. Cross the major boulevard, Grensen, and walk straight to:

5 Akersgata

This street was used for Ibsen's funeral procession. Services were conducted at the Holy Trinity Church on June 1, 1906.

Veer left to see the:

6 Birthplace of Ibsen's son

On your left, at the corner of Teatergata and Akersgata, is the site of the famous Strømberg Theater, which burned down in 1835. It was also a residence, and Ibsen's son was born here in 1859.

Also on Akersgata is:

7 Trefoldighetskirken (Holy Trinity Church)

This church was the site of Ibsen's funeral.

A little farther along Akersgata is St. Olav's Church. Turn on the right side of this

...e of worship onto Akersveien

...lassen

...mall square—one of the most ...ning in Oslo—doesn't appear on ...ost maps. Norway's greatest poet, ...Henrik Wergeland, lived in the pink house on the square from 1839 to 1841.

Take a right at the square and head down:

⑨ Damstredet

The antique, wooden houses along this typical old Oslo street are mainly occupied by artists.

Damstredet winds downhill to Fredens-borgveien. Here, a left turn and a short walk will take you to Maridalsveien, a busy but dull thoroughfare. As you walk north along this street, on the west side look for a large unmarked gateway with wide stone steps inside. Climb to the top, follow a little path-way, and go past gardens and flower beds. Pass a set of brick apartment buildings on the left, and proceed to:

⑩ Telthusbakken

Along this little street, you'll see a whole row of early Oslo wooden houses. Look right in the far distance at the green building where Munch used to live.

Telthusbakken leads to Akersveien. On your left you can see the:

⑪ Gamle Aker Kirke (Old Aker Church)

Enter at Akersbakken, where Akers-veien and Akersbakken intersect. Built in 1100, this is the oldest stone parish church in Scandinavia that's still in use. It stands on a green hill surrounded by an old graveyard and a stone wall.

A short block from the church along Akers-bakken (veer left outside the front of the church and go around a corner), you'll come to the north entrance of the city's expansive burial ground:

⑫ Vår Frelsers Gravlund (Our Savior's Cemetery)

In a section designated as the "Ground of Honor" are the graves of famous Norwegians, including Munch, Ibsen, and Bjørnson.

Signs don't point the way, but it's easy to see a tall obelisk. This is the:

⑬ Tomb of Ibsen

His wife, Susanna, whom he called "the cat," is buried to the playwright's left. She died in 1914. The hammer on the obelisk symbolizes his work *The Miner,* indicating how he "dug deep" into the soul of Norway.

To the right of Ibsen's tomb is the:

⑭ Tomb of Bjørnson

The literary figure Bjørnstjerne Bjørn-son (1832–1910) once raised money to send Ibsen to Italy. Before the birth of their children, Ibsen and Bjørnson agreed that one would have a son and the other a daughter, and that they would marry each other. Miraculously, Ibsen had a son, Bjørnson a daughter, and they did just that. Bjørnson wrote the national anthem, and his tomb is draped in a stone representation of a Norwegian flag.

To the far right of Bjørnson's tomb is the:

⑮ Tomb of Edvard Munch

Scandinavia's greatest painter has an unadorned tomb. If you're visiting on a snowy day, it will be buried, because the marker lies close to the ground. Munch died during the darkest days of the Nazi occupation. His sister turned down a request from the German command to give Munch a state funeral, feeling that it would be inappropriate.

On the west side of the cemetery you'll come to Ullevålsveien. Turn left on this busy street and head south toward the center of Oslo. You'll soon see St. Olav's Church, this time on your left. Stay on the right (west) side of the street. At St. Olavs Gate 1, where Ullevålsveien intersects with St. Olavs Gate, is the:

⑯ Kunstindustrimuseet (Museum of Applied Art)

Even if you don't have time to visit the museum, you may want to go inside to the cafe.

After visiting the museum, continue along St. Olavs Gate to:

⑰ Pilestredet

Look to the immediate right at no. 30. A wall plaque on the decaying building commemorates the fact that Munch lived here from 1868 to 1875. In this building he painted, among other masterpieces, *The Sick Child.* He moved here when he was 5, and many of his "memory paintings" were of the interior. When demolition teams started to raze the building in the early 1990s, a counterculture group of activists known as "The Blitz Group" illegally took over the premises to prevent its destruction. On its brick wall side, his masterpiece *The Scream* was re-created in spray paint. The protesters are still in control of the city-owned building, and they are viewed as squatters on very valuable land. It's suspected that if a more conservative government comes into power, officials will toss out the case, throw out the activists, and demolish the building. For the moment, however, they remain in control.

At Pilestredet, turn left. One block later, turn right onto Universitetsgata, heading south toward Karl Johans Gate. You'll pass a number of architecturally interesting buildings, and will eventually arrive at Universitetsgata 13, the:

⑱ National Gallery

The state museum has a large collection of Norwegian and foreign art. Two rooms are devoted to masterpieces by Munch.

7 Organized Tours

CRUISES AROUND THE FJORD Båtservice Sightseeing, Rådhusbrygge 3, Rådhusplassen (℃ 23-35-68-90), offers a 50-minute boat tour. You'll see the harbor and the city, including the ancient fortress of Akershus and the islands in the inner part of the Oslofjord. Cruises depart from Pier 3 in front of the Oslo Rådhuset (City Hall). They run from mid-May to late August, daily on the hour from 11am to 8pm during the high season, less frequently at the beginning and end of the season. Tickets are 90NOK ($12) for adults, 40NOK ($5.30) for children.

If you have more time, take a 2-hour cruise through the maze of islands and narrow sounds in the Oslofjord. From May to September, they leave daily at 10:30am and 1, 3:30, and 5:45pm; the cost is 165NOK ($22) for adults, 80NOK ($11) for children. Refreshments are available on board. The 2-hour fjord cruise with lunch runs from May to mid-September. It leaves daily at 10:30am and costs 295NOK ($39) for adults, 155NOK ($21) for children. Lunch is served at Lanternen Restaurant after the cruise.

The 2-hour evening fjord cruise includes a seafood buffet, also at the Lanternen. It's offered from late June to August, daily at 3:30 and 5:45pm. Prices are 295NOK ($39) for adults, 155NOK ($21) for children.

CITY TOURS H. M. Kristiansens Automobilbyrå, Hegdehaugsveien 4 (℃ 22-20-82-06), has been showing visitors around Oslo for more than a century. Both of their bus tours are offered daily year-round. The 3-hour "Oslo Highlights" tour is offered at 10am and 1:30pm. It costs 250NOK ($33) for adults, 130NOK ($17) for children. The 2-hour "Oslo Panorama" tour costs 170NOK ($23) for adults, 90NOK ($12) for children. It departs at 10am and 5:30pm. The starting point is the Norway information center, Vestbaneplassen 1; arrive 15 minutes before departure. Tours are conducted in English by trained guides.

Moments   Summer Evenings on the Oslofjord

Summer evenings aboard a boat on the Oslofjord can be restful and exhilarating, but if you happen not to have a private yacht of your own, there are several outfitters who can solve your problem. The best of these is **Båtservice Sightseeing AS** ⭐, Rådhusbrygge 3 (City Hall Pier no. 3; ✆ **23-35-68-90**; www.boatsightseeing.com), which operates from a low-slung concrete building directly atop one of the piers adjacent to Oslo's City Hall. Between late June and the end of August, weather permitting, they operate nightly cruises that showcase, better than any other means of transportation, the intricate cays, skerries, sandbars, and rocks of the Oslofjord.

You'll travel aboard one of three historic sloops, each of which retains its pinewood masts and complicated 19th-century rigging. During the course of these excursions, you'll be moving by diesel-powered engines, not by wind power. The oldest, and most oft-used, of the three ships is the *Johanna,* a wood-sided sloop originally built in 1892. Passengers sit at plank-built tables on an open deck, retreating to a glassed-in cabin, or even below decks, if the weather turns foul.

Included in the price are heaping buckets of Norwegian shrimp, served buffet-style from a central table on deck, which you'll peel yourself, and which taste marvelous with the bread, butter, and mayonnaise provided by the cruise director. Beverages come from a cash bar (beer only), and entertainment derives from the vistas and panoramas that unfold on all sides. They include views of the hundreds of private summer homes, often inhabitable only four months a year, built alongside the Oslofjord. Departures are nightly at 7pm (late June to the end of Aug only) with a return scheduled for 10pm. The price is 295NOK ($39) per person. Significantly, most of the participants aboard these cruises are likely to be Norwegians, some of them from Oslo, who appreciate the chance for a firsthand view of the midsummer sea and its banks.

8 Active Sports

From spring to fall, the Oslofjord is a center of swimming, sailing, windsurfing, and angling. Daily excursions are arranged by motor launch at the harbor. Suburban forest areas await hikers, bicyclists, and anglers in the summer. In the winter, the area is ideal for cross-country skiing (on marked trails that are illuminated at night), downhill or slalom skiing, tobogganing, skating, and more. Safaris by Land Rover are arranged year-round.

BATHS   The most central municipal bath is **Vestkantbadet,** Sommerrogate 1 (✆ **22-56-05-66**), which offers a Finnish sauna and Roman baths. Admission is 100NOK ($13). The baths are reserved for men on Monday, Wednesday, and Friday from noon to 4pm, and for women on Tuesday and Thursday from noon to 9pm and Saturday 9:30am to 3pm. Prices for massages start at 300NOK ($40) for 30 minutes. If you book a massage, you can use the baths free. This

Booked seat 6A, open return.

Rented red 4-wheel drive.

Reserved cabin, no running water.

Discovered space.

With over 700 airlines, 50,000 hotels, 50 rental car companies and 5,000 cruise and vacation packages, you can create the perfect getaway for you. Choose the car, the room, even the ground you walk on.

Travelocity.com
A Sabre Company
Go Virtually Anywhere.

© 2002 Yahoo! Inc.

Book your air, hotel, and transportation all in one place.

Hotel or hostel? Cruise or canoe? Car?
Plane? Camel? Wherever you're going,
visit Yahoo! Travel and get total control
over your arrangements. Even choose
your seat assignment. So. One hump
or two? travel.yahoo.com

powered by
COMPAQ

YAHOO!
Travel

Do You
YAHOO!
?

municipal bath is near the American Embassy, just over a kilometer north from Oslo's center. It's primarily a winter destination, and closed in July.

Frognerbadet, Middelthunsgate 28 (*©* **22-44-74-29**), in Frogner Park, is an open-air pool near the Vigeland sculptures. The entrance fee is 44NOK ($5.85) for adults, 22NOK ($2.95) for children. It's open mid-May to mid-August, Monday to Friday from 7am to 7pm, Saturday and Sunday 11am to 5pm. Take tram no. 2 from the National Theater.

BEACHES   Avoid the polluted inner-harbor area. The nearest and most popular beach is at **Hovedøya,** which is also the site of a 12th-century Cistercian monastery erected by English monks. Swimming is from a rocky shore. From Oslo's central station, local trains run frequently throughout the day to Sandvika. Also try **Drøbak,** 38km (24 miles) south of Oslo (take bus no. 541).

Oslovian beach devotees say **Gressholmen** and **Langøyene,** a 15-minute ride from Vippetangen, have the finest beaches in the vicinity. Nudism is practiced at beaches on the south side of Langøyene.

The closest clean beaches are those west of the Bygdøy peninsula, including **Huk** (where there's nude bathing) and **Paradisbukta.** Bygdøy can be reached by bus no. 30 from the National Theater. There are also beaches at **Langåra,** 16km (10 miles) west of Oslo. Take the local train to Sandvika and make ferry connections from there.

You can reach a number of beaches on the east side of the fjord by taking bus no. 75B from Jernbanetorget in East Oslo. Buses leave about every hour on weekends. It's a 12-minute ride to **Ulvøya,** the closest beach and one of the best and safest for children. Nudists prefer **Standskogen.**

GYMS   Male and female weight lifters call **Harald's Gym,** Hausmannsgate 6 (*©* **22-20-34-96**), the most professional gym in Oslo. Many champion bodybuilders have trained here, and its facilities are the most comprehensive in Norway. Nonmembers pay 70NOK ($9.30) for a day pass. It's open Monday to Friday from 10am to 9pm, Saturday and Sunday noon to 6m.

JOGGING   Marka, the forest that surrounds Oslo, has hundreds of trails. The easiest and most accessible are at Frogner Park. You can also jog or hike the trails along the Aker River, a scenic route. A great adventure is to take the Sognasvann train to the end of the line, where you can jog along the fast-flowing Sognasvann stream. **Norske Turistforening,** Storgata 28 (*©* **22-82-28-00**), sells maps outlining jogging trails around the capital, and the staff can give you advice about routes.

SKATING   Oslo is home to numerous skating rinks. **Grünerhallen,** Seildduksgate 30 (*©* **22-35-55-52**), admits the public for pleasure skating. For a 2-hour session, the price is 20NOK ($2.65) for adults, 5NOK (65¢ for children. Skate rentals cost 10NOK to 20NOK ($1.35–$2.65). Grünerhallen is open October to March; days and hours are erratic because it's used primarily for hockey, so call in advance. Other skating rinks include **Narvisen,** Spikersuppa, near Karl Johans Gate (*©* **22-33-30-33**), open October to March.

SKIING   A 15-minute tram or bus ride from central Oslo to Holmenkollen will take you to Oslo's winter wonderland, **Marka,** a 2,579km (1,612-mile) ski-track network. Many ski schools and instructors are available in the winter. You can even take a sleigh ride. Other activities include dogsled rides, snowshoe trekking, and Marka forest safaris. There are 14 slalom slopes to choose from, along with ski jumps in all shapes and sizes, including the famous one at

Holmenkollen. For information and updates on ski conditions, you can call Skiforeningen, Kongeveien 5 (② **22-92-32-00**). The tourist office can give you details about the venues for many of these activities.

TENNIS The municipal courts at **Frogner Park** are usually fully booked for the season by the locals, but ask at the kiosk about cancellations.

Njårdhallen, Sørkedalsceien 106 (② **22-14-67-74**), offers indoor tennis Monday to Thursday from 7am to 10pm, Friday to Sunday 7am to 8pm. Book your court well in advance. During nice weather, you might prefer outdoor tennis at **Njårds Tennis,** Jenns Messveien 1 (② **22-14-67-74**), a cluster of courts that are generally open whenever weather and daylight permit.

9 Shopping

THE SHOPPING SCENE

Oslo has many **traffic-free streets** for strollers and shoppers. The heart of this district is the **Stortorvet,** where more than two dozen shops sell everything from handicrafts to enameled silver jewelry. At the marketplace on Strøget, you can stop for a glass of beer at an open-air restaurant in fair weather. Many stores are clustered along **Karl Johans Gate** and the streets branching off it.

BEST BUYS Look for bargains on sportswear, silver and enamelware, traditional handicrafts, pewter, glass by Hadeland Glassverk (founded in 1762), teak furniture, and stainless steel.

SHIPPING GOODS & RECOVERING VAT Norway imposes a 19.4% value-added tax (VAT), but there are ways to avoid paying it. See "Taxes" in "Fast Facts: Norway," in chapter 2. Special tax-free exports are possible; many stores will mail goods home to you, which makes paying and recovering tax unnecessary.

SHOPPING HOURS Most stores are open Monday to Friday from 9am to 5pm, Saturday 9am to 3pm. Department stores and shopping malls keep different hours—in general, Monday to Friday 9am to 8pm, Saturday 9am to 6pm. Many shops stay open late on Thursday and on the first Saturday of the month, which is called *super lørdag* ("super Saturday"). During the holiday season, stores are open on Sunday.

SHOPPING MALLS

Mall shopping is a firmly entrenched tradition in Oslo thanks to the uncertain weather. When it rains or snows, discerning shoppers have several malls from which to choose.

Our favorite is **Paléet,** Karl Johans Gate 37-43, set on Oslo's most central and most opulent shopping street. The weatherproof complex consists of 45 different shops and boutiques, all of them relatively upscale and flooded with light from skylights. You can purchase candles, incense, sweaters, art, housewares, cosmetics—you name it. Thirteen different restaurants, including burger and beer joints and one serving Indian food, refuel weary shoppers. You can also stop to admire a bronze statue of skating great (and former movie star) Sonja Henie.

Oslo City, Stenersgate 1, opposite the Central Station, is the biggest shopping center in Norway—loaded with shops and restaurants.

Also near the Central Station, **Galleri Oslo,** at Vaterland, has been called Europe's longest indoor shopping street. Businesses are open daily until midnight, including Sunday. A walkway connects Galleri Oslo to the Central Station.

Aker Brygge is a unique shopping venue by the Oslofjord. It carries a wide variety of merchandise, and the complex also includes restaurants, theaters, cinemas, and cafes.

SHOPPING A TO Z
ANTIQUES

Blomqvist Kunsthandel   Built as an auction house by its original owners in 1870, this place is full of history and style. Its two large rooms have glass ceilings creating tons of natural light. Inside you'll find either one of their six annual auctions or one of their many Norwegian art exhibitions. In 1918 a gallery show released the full collection of an artist by the name of Edvard Munch. His prints and canvasses can still be seen here during one of the temporary exhibitions. While this venue acts as an auction house, items up for bid include antiquity ranging from fine jewelry and paintings to furniture and sculpture. Tordenskolds gate 5. ✆ 22-70-87-70. T-banen: Nationaltheatret.

Far & Sonn Brukt Antikkmarked   This huge secondhand and antique emporium sells just about anything for the home. Within its large open space you'll find mainly 18th- to 19th-century furniture, including rocking chairs, dressers, lamps, fine china, and antique bed frames. The array of merchandise sold ranges from state-of-the-art electronics to rare out-of-print books. 3 Sanner Gate. ✆ 22-35-05-36. Tram: 1, 4, or 9.

ARTS & CRAFTS

Baerum Verk   For a unique adventure, head outside of town to a restored iron works site dating from 1610. Here you'll find more than 65 different shops selling handicrafts and other items, including jewelry and woolens, plus exhibitions and six restaurants. If time remains, visit the iron works museum on site and see a smelting production dating from the 17th century. Verksgata 15, Baerum Verk. ✆ 67-13-00-18. Bus: 143 or 153.

Den Norske Husfliden   Near the marketplace and the cathedral, Husfliden is the display and retail center for the Norwegian Association of Home Arts and Crafts, founded in 1891. Today it's almost eight times larger than any of its competitors, offering an unparalleled opportunity to see the finest Norwegian design in ceramics, glassware, clothing, furniture, and woodworking. It also carries souvenirs, gifts, textiles, rugs, knotted Rya rugs, embroidery, and wrought iron. Goods are shipped all over the world. Møllergata 4. ✆ 22-42-10-75. T-banen: Stortinget.

Norway Designs   This is the only store in Norway that came into being as the result of a crafts exhibit. Shortly before it was established in 1957, an exposition of Norwegian crafts went to Chicago and New York, and it attracted a lot of attention. The upscale merchandise here—crystal, pewter, jewelry, and knitwear—emerged from the innovative designs of that exposition. The store's distinguished owner, Mr. Westlund, refuses to display or sell what he refers to as "touristic junk." Stortingsgaten 28. ✆ 23-11-45-10. Tram: 2, 8, or 9.

BOOKS

ARK Qvist   This light, airy, and welcoming bookshop specializes in English and Norwegian titles. There is a large focus on fiction from both countries as well as extensive biography, history, and true crime sections. Its convenient location places it just next door to the American Embassy. Drammensvn 16. ✆ 22-54-26-00. T-banen: Nationaltheatret.

Bjorn Ringstrøms Antikvariat   One of the largest bookstores in Oslo houses a wide selection of Norwegian and Norwegian-American authors. They are also deeply rooted in books pertaining to Norwegian history and politics. A wide range of collectibles can also be found, ranging from antique books and color plates, to records and maps. This century-old structure lies directly across the street from the Museum of Applied Art. Ullevalsvn 1. 🕐 **22-20-78-05.** T-banen: Stortinget.

Damms Antiqvariat   This is the oldest antiquarian bookstore in all of Norway, in business since 1843. This warm and friendly place is full of history and intrigue, offering a wonderful selection of fiction and travel books. Although they focus mainly on Norwegian titles, you may come across a first edition of a Hemingway or Steinbeck novel. Among some of the more rare treasures, you'll find a page from the *Catholicon,* the first book ever printed with a nonreligious subject matter. Tollburgate 25. 🕐 **22-41-04-02.** T-banen: Nationaltheatret.

Tanum Karl Johan   This fine bookstore in the center of town is the largest and most comprehensive in Oslo. It offers a vast selection, including many English titles. Karl Johans Gate 37-41. 🕐 **22-41-11-00.** T-banen: Stortinget.

CHINA & CERAMICS

Abelson   Just behind the Royal Palace, and in business since the 1960s, this store sells a wide array of items from whimsical ceramic sculpture and figurines to classic wood home furnishings. Wine glasses, plates, bowls, and fine linens are also a draw. Cozy, and with a great sense of style, this is a wonderful place to begin your shopping day. Skovvn 27. 🕐 **22-55-55-94.** T-banen: Nationaltheatret.

Gastronaut   This small and intimate space sells an array of its own exclusive china, glass, and cutlery. The china collections from Spain are simple but elegant, and a bit pricey, but worth it if you're serious about your table settings. Spanish olive oils, spices, and specialty foods can also be found here. Bygdøy Alle 56. 🕐 **22-44-60-90.** Bus: 30, 31, or 32.

DELI (FOR YOUR PICNIC)

A Taste of Norway   This place is the most famous deli in Oslo. Quality not quantity is their self-described motto, and they do live up to their words. You'll find anything you need to create the perfect outdoor meal. Cured and smoked meats from all over Europe hang on its walls along with homemade jams and jellies on their shelves, a wide array of sharp and mild cheeses, and as they claim, the best smoked salmon in the world. A specialty of the house is *Fenalnlaar,* cured and seasoned sheep's meat. The only beverage is beer, which is supplied by a local brewery. Tordenskiolds gate 7. 🕐 **22-42-34-57.** T-banen: Nationaltheatret.

DEPARTMENT STORES

Glasmagasinet   Claiming that smaller boutiques tend to charge more, locals usually head for this big department store, which specializes in unusual home and kitchen accessories. It's the largest outlet in Norway for the Hadelands Glassverk (Glassworks); there's also a coffee shop and a restaurant. Stortorvet 9. 🕐 **22-42-53-05.** T-banen: Stortinget. Bus: 7, 8, 11, 37, or 92.

Steen & Strøm   The largest department store in Norway, Steen & Strøm specializes in Nordic items. Look for hand-knit sweaters and caps, hand-painted wooden dishes reflecting traditional Norwegian art, and pewter dinner plates made from old molds. There's a souvenir shop on the ground floor. Kongensgate 23. 🕐 **22-00-40-00.** T-banen: Stortinget.

FASHION
For Everyone

H&M   This large worldwide chain of stores is very well known for selling high-quality goods at reasonable prices. They carry everything from children's apparel to trendy and fashionable clothing for men and women. Also on the menu are accessories, including a large selection of handbags and belts. Stemers gate 1 (Oslo City Shopping Center). ℂ **23-15-99-00**. T-banen: Jermbanetorget.

Skandinavisk Hoyfjellutstyr   This massive store has a great selection of all things outdoor. You'll find almost everything to suit your needs for a skiing or climbing adventure. Clothing items include tons of Gore-Tex jackets, fleece, thermal wear, and hiking boots. Knives, flashlights, goggles, sleeping bags, and all sorts of gadgets are also for sale. Bogstadsvn 1. ℂ **23-33-43-80**. T-banen: Majorstuen.

For Men

Peak Performance   This store is definitely the number one choice for the outdoorsman who seeks the most stylish in performance clothing. The styles and colors seem limitless: jackets, shirts, accessories, whatever. Their variety of Gore-Tex and fleece items is also a draw. Bogstadsvn 13. ℂ **22-96-00-91**. T-banen: Majorstuen.

For Women

MA   Heavy on Norwegian designers, this fashion boutique also offers some of the best in Italian, Australian, and Belgian designs. Shoes and other accessories are plentiful too. Prices range from "obscene" to reasonable. Hegdehaugsvn 27. ℂ **22-60-72-90**. Tram: 15.

Oleana   This shop carries the award-winning designs of Solveig Hisdahl. Clothing items are made mainly of wool and silk and include elegant knitwear, skirts, cardigans, and shawls. Other items feature jewelry and silk scarves from some of the top Norwegian designers. Stortingsgaten 8. ℂ **22-33-31-63**. T-banen: Nationaltheatret.

Ove Harder Finseth   This unique clothing store stars the painstaking and laborious productions of designer Ove Finseth. Each one-of-a-kind dress or gown is full of color (no black or gray), intricately detailed and wonderfully ornate. The client list is quite impressive. Even the princess of Norway had her wedding gown designed here. Custom-made jewelry, bags, and hats are also sold. Pilius Plass 3. ℂ **22-37-76-20**. T-banen: Girneanetorgen.

Soul   From Milan to Paris this store keeps on top of the ever-changing fashion industry. The selection will meet all of your high-fashion needs, from bags by Prada and shoes by D&G. Even Beatle Paul McCartney's daughter, Stella, is here with her new hot-selling clothing label Chloe. Vognhallene, Karenlyst Alle 18. ℂ **22-55-00-13**. T-banen: Skoyen.

FOLK COSTUMES

Heimen Husflid   This leading purveyor of modern and traditional Norwegian handicrafts and apparel carries antique and reproduction folk costumes. More than three dozen different *bunads* (styles) include different regions of Norway, both north and south. Hand-knit sweaters in traditional Norwegian patterns are a special item, as are pewter and brass goods. It's about a block from Karl Johans Gate. Rosenkrantzgate 8. ℂ **22-41-40-50**. T-banen: Stortinget. Tram: 7, 8, or 11.

FURNITURE

Rom for Ide   This is one of those stores that never seems to follow trends but always ends up looking trendy. This furniture outlet, hidden away from the city's shopping streets, specializes in modern yet classic designs. The contemporary and sleek look is the product of Norway's best and brightest new designers.

Aside from furniture, Norwegian arts and crafts are also interesting. Jacob Aalls gate 54. ✆ **22-59-81-17**. T-banen: Majorstuen.

Tannum   The furniture sold here is contemporary and stylish. Going on its 60th year in business, the outlet pushes the envelope when presenting the latest in modern furnishings. Tons of glass-and-steel accents on clean and good-looking pieces are imported from Italy, Germany, Sweden, Denmark, Holland—basically everywhere but Norway. Stortings gate 28. ✆ **22-83-42-95**. T-banen: Nationaltheatret.

JEWELRY, ENAMELWARE, PEWTER & SILVER

David-Andersen   This outstanding jeweler, established more than a century ago, sells enameled demitasse spoons and sterling silver bracelets with enamel. They're available in many stunning colors, such as turquoise and dark blue. Multicolored butterfly pins are also popular in gold-plated sterling silver with enamel. David-Andersen's collection of Saga silver was inspired by Norwegian folklore and Viking designs, combined with the pristine beauty of today's design. The store also offers an exquisite collection of pewter items. Karl Johans Gate 20. ✆ **22-41-69-55**. T-banen: Stortinget.

Esaias Solberg   Opened in 1849, this is the largest and oldest venue for antique and second-hand gold and silver in Oslo. Brands of watches sold here include Rolex and Patek Phillipe as well as countless others. They also sell diamond-studded gold and silver necklaces, brooches, and earrings. Outside of jewelry, they also offer some wonderful antique coffee sets, trays, and goblets. The owner of this place has a simple motto, "Antique jewelry is no more expensive than modern jewelry, and any secondhand jewelry sells at half of what it originally cost." Kirkeresten. ✆ **22-86-24-80**. T-banen: Jernbanetorget.

Heyerdahl   Between the City Hall and Karl Johans Gate, this store offers an intriguing selection of silver and gold Viking jewelry. There are also articles in pewter and other materials, including Viking vessels, drinking horns, and cheese slicers. It has an array of trolls, as well as one of Oslo's largest collections of gold and silver jewelry. Roald Amundsens Gate. ✆ **22-41-59-18**. T-banen: Nationaltheatret.

MUSIC

Benni's   Located just a 5-minute walk south from the Royal Palace in the city center, this chain music store is known throughout Norway for having the largest selection of hip-hop, R&B, and funk in the country. Hard rock and the Top-40 can also be found here. The owner prides himself on having an array of up-and-coming international acts. Aker Brygge. ✆ **22-83-70-83**. T-banen: Nationaltheatret.

Los Lobos   Straight out of 1950s Hawaii, this independent music store caters to all genres and styles of music outside of the mainstream. Aside from music ranging from blues to techno, you'll find cigarette cases, Hawaiian and bowling shirts, tons of denim, belt buckles, snakeskin boots, and much more. Don't expect to find the Top-40 here; this place is for the more alternative music listener. Thorvald Meyers gate 30. ✆ **22-38-24-40**. Tram: 11 or 12 (to Olaf Ryes).

Norsk Musikforlag   This centrally located store's selection of CDs, records, and tapes is the best in Oslo. Karl Johans Gate 39A. ✆ **22-17-34-70**. T-banen: Stortinget.

PERFUME

Gimle Speiz   This large and welcoming perfumery is filled with the best in perfume and skin-care items. All employees are trained make-up artists who provide applications and skin-care consultations. They also carry an array of clothing and accessories that are sold exclusively at their store. Under the same ownership, and only 50m (165 ft.) away, is **Gimle Parfymeri,** Bygdøy Alle 39 (② **22-44-61-42**), a tiny and traditional perfumery that deals only in high-end and quite pricey scents. Bygdøy Allé 51B. ② **23-27-11-05**. T-banen: Majorstuen.

SOUVENIRS & GIFTS

William Schmidt   Established in 1853, William Schmidt is a leading purveyor of unique souvenirs. It carries pewter items (from Viking ships to beer goblets), Norwegian dolls in national costumes, woodcarvings—the troll collection is the best in Oslo—and sealskin items, such as moccasins and handbags. The shop specializes in hand-knit cardigans, pullovers, gloves, and caps, and a selection of sweaters made from mothproof, 100% Norwegian wool. Karl Johans Gate 41. ② **22-42-02-88**. T-banen: Stortinget.

SWEATERS

Oslo Sweater Shop   Some 5,000 handcrafted sweaters are in stock here, close to the Royal Palace. Try them on before you buy. In theory, at least, you can tell the origin of a Norwegian sweater by its pattern and design, but with the increase in machine-made sweaters and the increased sophistication of Norwegian knitwear, the distinctions are increasingly blurred. Here, as in virtually every other sweater shop in Oslo, only about 10% of the sweaters are handmade—the remainder are high quality and first rate, but most likely crafted on an electric knitting machine. Sweaters start at around 990NOK ($132), rising to a maximum of 3,000NOK ($399). Other items include necklaces, pewterware, souvenirs, and Norway-inspired trinkets. At the Clarion Hotel Royal Christiania, Biskop Gunnerus Gate 3. ② **22-42-42-25**. Bus: 30, 31, or 41.

10 Oslo After Dark

Oslo has a bustling nightlife. Midnight is not the curfew hour. The city boasts more than 100 night cafes, clubs, and restaurants, 35 of which stay open until 4am.

Autumn and winter are the seasons for cabaret, theater, and concerts. There are four cabarets and nine theater stages. Oslo is also a favorite destination of international performing artists in classical, pop, rock, and jazz music.

For movie lovers, Oslo has a lot to offer. The city has one of the most extensive selections in Europe, with 30 screens and five large film complexes. Films are shown in their original languages, with subtitles.

THE ENTERTAINMENT SCENE

The best way to find out what's happening is to pick up a copy of *What's On in Oslo,* detailing concerts and theaters and other useful information.

Oslo doesn't have agents who specialize in discount tickets, but it does have an exceptional number of free events. *What's On in Oslo* lists free happenings as well as the latest exhibits at art galleries, delightful destinations for the early part of an evening.

Tickets to the theater, ballet, and opera are sold at box offices and at **Billettsentralen,** Karl Johans Gate 35 (② **81-53-31-33**). Tickets to most sporting and cultural events in Oslo can be purchased by computer at any post office in the city. The same postal clerk who sells you stamps can also sell you a voucher for a ticket to the ballet, the theater, or a hockey game.

The world-famous **Oslo Philharmonic** performs regularly under the leadership of Mariss Janson. There are no Oslo performances between June 20 and the middle of August.

If you visit Oslo in the winter season, you might be able to see its thriving opera and ballet company, **Den Norske Opera.** Plays given at the **Nationaltheatret** (where Ibsen is regularly featured) are in Norwegian. Those who know Ibsen in their own language sometimes enjoy hearing the original version of his plays.

THE PERFORMING ARTS
CLASSICAL MUSIC

Oslo Konserthus   Two blocks from the National Theater, this is the home of the widely acclaimed Oslo Philharmonic. Performances are given autumn to spring, on Thursday and Friday. Guest companies from around the world often appear on other nights. The hall is closed from June 20 until mid-August, except for occasional performances by folkloric groups. The box office is open Monday through Friday 10am to 5pm, and Saturday 11am to 2pm. Munkedamsveien 14. © 23-11-31-11. Tickets 200NOK–700NOK ($27–$93). T-banen: Stortinget.

THEATER

Nationaltheatret (National Theater)   This theater at the upper end of the Students' Grove opens in August, so it may be of interest to off-season drama lovers who want to hear original versions of Ibsen and Bjørnson. Avant-garde productions go up at the **Amfiscenen,** in the same building. There are no performances in July and August. Guest companies often perform plays in English. The box office is open Monday through Friday 8:30am to 7:30pm, and Saturday 11am to 6pm. Johanne Dybwads Plass 1. © 81-50-08-11. Tickets 150NOK–220NOK ($20–$29) adults, 85NOK–170NOK ($11–$23) students and seniors. T-banen: Nationaltheatret. Tram: 12, 13, or 19.

OPERA & DANCE

Den Norske Opera (Norwegian National Opera)   The Norwegian opera and ballet troupes make up Den Norske Opera. The 1931 building, originally a movie theater, was dedicated to the Norwegian National Opera in 1959. It's also the leading venue for ballet—the companies alternate performances. About 20 different operas and operettas are staged every year. There are no performances from mid-June to August. Unlike those for some European opera companies, tickets are generally available to nonsubscribers; seats can be reserved in advance and paid for with a credit card. The box office is open Monday through Saturday 10am to 6pm (to 7:30pm on performance nights). Storgaten 23. © 23-31-50-00. Tickets 170NOK–320NOK ($23–$43), except for galas. Bus: 56, 62, or 66.

SUMMER CULTURAL ENTERTAINMENT

Det Norske Folkloreshowet (Norwegian Folklore Show) performs from July to early September at the Oslo Konserthus, Munkedamsveien 15 (© 23-11-31-11 for reservations). The 1-hour performances are on Monday and Thursday at 8:30pm. Tickets cost 160NOK ($21) for adults, 90NOK to 110NOK ($12–$15) for children (T-banen: Stortinget).

The ensemble at the **Norwegian Folk Museum,** on Bygdøy, often presents folk-dance performances at the open-air theater in the summer. See *What's On in Oslo* for details. Most shows are given on Sunday afternoon. Admission to the museum includes admission to the dance performance. Take the ferry from Pier 3 near the Rådhuset.

SPECIAL & FREE EVENTS

Oslo has many free events, including summer jazz concerts at the National Theater. In front of the theater, along the Students' Grove, you'll see street entertainers, including singers, clowns, musicians, and jugglers.

Concerts are presented in the chapel of **Akershus Castle & Fortress,** Akershus Command, on Sunday at 2pm. During the summer, promenade music, parades, drill marches, exhibits, and theatrical performances are also presented on the castle grounds.

In August the **Chamber Music Festival** at Akershus Castle & Fortress presents concerts by Norwegian and foreign musicians.

The **Oslo Jazz Festival,** also in August, includes not only old-time jazz, but also classical concerts, opera, and ballet performances.

FILMS

American and British films are shown in English, with Norwegian subtitles. Tickets are sold for specific performances only. Many theaters have showings nightly at 5pm, 7pm, and 9pm, but really big films are usually shown only once in an evening, generally at 7:30pm.

Two of the city's biggest theaters are the **Colosseum,** on Freitjoj Nansens vei 6 (T-banen: Majorstua), and **Filmteatret,** Stortingsgaten 16 (T-banen: Nationaltheatret). Most tickets cost 90NOK ($12) for adults, half-price for children; at Monday and Thursday matinees the cost is 65NOK ($8.65) for adults, 45NOK ($6) for children. For information about all films presented in Oslo call © **82-03-00-01.**

THE CLUB & MUSIC SCENE
DANCE CLUBS & DISCOS

Smuget   This is the most talked-about nightlife emporium in Oslo, with long lines, especially on weekends. It's behind the Grand Hotel in a 19th-century building that was a district post office. There's an active dance floor with disco music, and a stage where live bands (sometimes two a night on weekends) perform. The clientele includes artists, writers, rock stars, and a cross section of the capital's night owls. The complex is open every night except Sunday. A restaurant serves Thai, Chinese, Norwegian, Italian, and American food from 8pm to 3am; live music plays from 11pm to 3am; and there's disco music from 10pm till very late. Half-liters of beer cost 39NOK ($5.20); main courses run 80NOK to 175NOK ($11–$23). Rosenkrantzgate 22. © **22-42-52-62.** Cover 60NOK–70NOK ($8–$9.30). T-banen: Stortinget.

NIGHTCLUBS

Bristol Night Spot   The entrance to this cellar nightclub is visible from the sidewalk near the Bristol Hotel's main entrance. With an intimately lit restaurant, a dance floor (the band starts playing at 8pm), and a cellar tavern, this has become one of the most popular places in Oslo for older singles—mostly confirmed heterosexuals around age 40 and up. The underlit, shadowy, and very crowded cellar bar attracts aggressive and fast-moving types. You may get the feeling that many of the patrons are recently divorced, about-to-be-divorced, or frequently divorced and looking for better days. Don't even think that this is a place for young hipsters. Conservative dress is suggested.

Main dishes include poached salmon with butter-cream sauce, chateaubriand with béarnaise sauce, filet of veal Oscar with asparagus, and mixed grill. Cocktails include a Norwegian bomb called *Fjellbekk* (mountain stream), made with aquavit, vodka, lime juice, and Sprite. Meals begin at 250NOK ($33), drinks at

65NOK ($8.65). It's open Monday to Saturday 9pm to 3am. Reservations are recommended. In the Bristol Hotel, Kristian IV's Gate 7. © **22-82-60-30.** Cover 100NOK ($13). T-banen: Stortinget.

Bryggeporten Bar & Nattklubb   This place is Alter Brygge's biggest nightclub. You'll find a huge bar and dance floor downstairs, and another dance floor and some lounging couches upstairs. The music selection depends on the night. Thursday offers live pop and soft rock acts; Wednesday is Latin night with salsa and merengue; and on Friday and Saturday DJs spin everything from hip-hop to techno. This is a comfortable place to unwind and have fun. It's open Wednesday through Saturday from 6pm to 3am. You must be at least 25 years old to enter. Stranden 1. © **22-87-72-00.** Fri–Sat cover 100NOK ($13). T-banen: Nationaltheatret.

Dockside Cafe og Bar   With its prime location right on the pier and its stylish interior, this place is a draw for an older and sophisticated crowd. People come here to either relax and enjoy a sporting event on one of the bar's giant-screen televisions or to see some of the best live musical acts in the city of Oslo. Saturday night offers live jazz and Tuesday evening is devoted to some of the best new up-and-coming talent in Norway. Something special takes place here on every other Monday night when students from Oslo's Opera University are recruited to perform. It's open daily from 2pm to 2am. Bryggetorget 10. © **22-83-80-58.** T-banen: Aker Brygge.

The Dubliner   This cozy and rustic bar is one of the first Irish pubs in Oslo. Housed in a building dating from 1666 the Dubliner holds true to its traditional Irish ancestry once you're inside. The crowd here does vary in age but consists mostly of Oslo's Irish and English communities. It offers a typical pub-grub type of menu and plenty of Irish beers on tap. On Friday and Saturday nights traditional and contemporary Irish music can always be heard. On Tuesdays they hold "jam sessions" where local musicians can bring their instruments and play at being rock stars for the night. Open daily from noon to 2:30am. Radhusgata 28. © **22-33-70-05.** Fri–Sat cover 60NOK ($8). T-banen: Stortinget.

Headline   Amid the bustling bars and nightlife of Rosenkrantz' gate, Headline doesn't disappoint with its mellow, candlelit atmosphere and giant bar. The variety of music is a draw with the DJ playing everything from salsa to hard rock. The owner, Mette Iversen, was a participant on the TV show *Robinson Expeditions,* the Norwegian equivalent of the U.S. show *Survivor.* So don't be surprised if you spot the occasional TV star. Open Monday to Saturday 6pm to 3:30am. Rosenkrantz Gate 16. © **22-41-02-02.** Fri–Sat cover 50NOK ($6.65). T-banen: Nationaltheatret.

Restauranthuset Scotsman   The huge, chaotic Scotsman offers several floors of entertainment. For a la carte dining, with an emphasis on beef, head to the cellar restaurant. For nightly live music, and a colorful clientele, check out the English-style pub on the first floor. If dancing is your thing, you'll want to stop in the second-floor disco. For the gambler, the third floor features pool tables and off-track horse betting. The fourth floor is strictly for private parties. The fifth and sixth floors have a fully equipped fitness center to help you burn off your trip to the cellar. And, finally, the Scotman's seventh floor has six neatly kept double rooms (350NOK/$47 per night) if you can't make your way home. Open daily noon to 3am. Karl Johans gate 17. © **22-47-44-77.** T-banen: Nationaltheatret.

JAZZ & ROCK

Blå   This is the leading jazz club in Oslo. Dark and industrial with lots of wrought iron and mellow lighting, this place books some of the best jazz acts in the world. The crowd is a mix of young and old, dressed in casual but sophisticated attire. The weeknights focus strictly on jazz with the weekend providing more of a disco atmosphere, recruiting DJs from all over the world to spin the best in techno and house. Open Monday to Thursday and Sunday 8pm to 1am, and Friday and Saturday 8pm to 3:30am. Brennerivn 9C. (C) **22-20-91-81.** Cover 50NOK–120NOK ($6.65–$16). T-banen: Jernbanetorget.

Herr Nilsen   This is a conventional pub on most evenings, with recorded jazz. On Wednesday at 9pm and Saturday at 4pm and 11pm, live jazz is played to an appreciative audience. Expect everything from progressive jazz to Dixieland or blues. The rest of the time, entrance is free. Beer, depending on the time of the evening, costs 36NOK to 49NOK ($4.80–$6.50). It's open Monday to Saturday 10am to 3am, Sunday noon to 3am. C. J. Hambros Plass 5. (C) **22-33-54-05.** Wed and Sat cover 75NOK–100NOK ($10–$13). T-banen: Stortinget.

Mono   If you're looking for a relatively underfinanced punk-rock nightclub with beer-stained walls and a decor that could withstand, undisturbed, an invasion from a foreign army, this is it. It's a haven for the alternative, boozy, and occasionally alienated youth culture of Oslo. There's recorded music virtually all the time, a changing roster of live bands (many of them from the U.S.) appearing every Sunday to Thursday beginning around 10:30pm, and recorded house and garage-style dance music every Friday and Saturday. Whenever there's live music, the cover varies from 30NOK to 60NOK ($4–$8); otherwise, it's free. It's open Monday to Saturday from 3pm to 3:30am. Pløensgate 4. (C) **22-41-41-66.** T-banen: Stortinget.

Rockefeller Music Hall   With a capacity of 1,200 patrons, this concert hall and club is one of the largest establishments of its kind in Oslo. It's one floor above street level in a 1910 building, formerly a public bath. Live concerts feature everything from reggae to rock to jazz. When no concert is scheduled, films are shown on a wide screen. Simple foods, such as pasta and sandwiches, are available in the cafe. Most of the crowd is in the 18-to-37 age bracket. It's usually open Sunday to Thursday 8pm to 2:30am, Friday and Saturday 9pm to 3:30am. Show time is about an hour after the doors open. Torggata 16. (C) **22-20-32-32.** Tickets 100NOK–700NOK ($13–$93), depending on act. T-banen: Stortinget.

THE BAR SCENE
PUBS & BARS

Bar 1   For a connoisseur of brandy, this small cognac-and-cigar bar is the ultimate. You'll find close to 300 different varieties of cognac, plus a selection of the finest whiskeys. Accompany your libation with one of their wide selection of Cuban and Dominican cigars. As you could imagine, you'll find a subdued yet sophisticated crowd here. It's open daily 4pm to 3:30am. Holmensgate 3. (C) **22-83-00-02.** Tram: 22.

Beach Club   This place embodies a classic American diner with Norwegian flair. Its large booths and tables are welcoming—and the burgers, great. There is a bar but not much of a social scene, with mostly businessmen having drinks. Mellow, loungy music plays every night. It's open Tuesday to Saturday 11am to midnight, Sunday to Monday noon to 2pm. Aker Brygge. (C) **22-83-83-82.** T-banen: Nationaltheatret.

Beerpalace   As you might guess, beer is the main draw at this English-style pub. The atmosphere is intimate and cozy with exposed brick walls and couches in the upstairs lounge. A dartboard and pool table provide excitement and entertainment on the first floor. Softly played rock 'n' roll completes the mood. It's open Monday to Thursday 1pm to 1:30am, Friday 1pm to 3am, and Saturday noon to 3am. Holmensgate 3. ℭ **22-83-71-55.** Tram: 10 or 12.

Bibliotekbaren (Library Bar)   In a lobby that evokes the Edwardian era, this is a perfect spot for people-watching. Sheltered behind racks of leather-bound books, which you can remove and read, you'll feel like you're in a well-furnished private club. There's live piano music at lunchtime, when you can order from a selection of open-faced sandwiches for 40NOK to 80NOK ($5.30–$11). Specialty cocktails have such coy names as "Take Me Home" and "Norwegian Kiss." It's open daily from 10am to 11:30pm; alcohol service starts at 1pm. A beer will cost you 52NOK ($6.90); mixed drinks begin at 80NOK ($11). In the Bristol Hotel, Kristian IV's Gate 7. ℭ **22-82-60-22.** T-banen: Stortinget.

Buddha Bar   Everyone clamors to get into this bar and nightclub. Often, even on weeknights, long lines of hipsters form outside the place. The incense-scented interior contains rooms dotted with iconic statues of Buddha—fat-bellied Chinese versions and ascetic-looking ones from Burma and Thailand—all staring benignly over a pan-European, gay/straight crowd. Celebrity sightings here include Bruce Springsteen and various members of the Rolling Stones. There's a dining area (Restaurant Fogo) shoved into a side room, where set menus cost from 400NOK to 650NOK ($53–$86). But most people come here to drink, meet other like-minded extroverts, and perhaps to dance. The minimum age for entrance, unless you're very, very cool and attractive, is 28. It's open Tuesday to Sunday 7pm till 3am, but the heat doesn't really begin to rise till around 10:30pm. Klingenberggata 4. ℭ **22-82-86-50.** Cover 70NOK ($9.30), sometimes waived, depending on business and the mood of the security staff. Bus: 30, 31, 32, 45, or 8.

C-In   Emerging as one of the hottest nightclubs in Oslo, this joint draws huge crowds. The attractive young patrons are always dressed to impress and on the prowl. The club's typical lounge style includes leather couches, dim lighting, and an ultralong bar. Thursdays attract students who bob their heads to the latest pop and R&B, while weekends draw older, more sophisticated patrons who dance to pounding techno. It's open Tuesday to Monday 6pm to 3am. Karl Johans Gate 6B. ℭ **22-41-00-14.** Cover 50NOK ($6.65). T-banen: Sentralstasjon.

Etoile Bar   This elegant bar with a Far Eastern motif is attached to Norway's most famous hotel, the Grand. You might see members of Parliament from across the street. The "Star Bar" has views of historic Oslo. Out-of-town businesspeople mingle at night with a young spirited Oslo crowd. To reach the bar, you take a special elevator to the right of the hotel entrance. Beers cost 48NOK ($6.40), stronger drinks from 60NOK ($8). The bar is open Monday to Saturday 7am to 12:30am. In the Grand Hotel, Karl Johans Gate 31. ℭ **23-21-20-00.** T-banen: Stortinget.

Fridtjof's Pub   This Norwegian pub offers a cozy retreat for a late-night drink. It consists of a ground floor with deep red walls, comfortable sofas, and some tables and chairs. The second floor has much of the same, providing an unobstructed view of the crowd below. Both floors have interesting photos of polar expeditions, mainly because it's named after Fridtjof Nansen, the first Norwegian to explore successfully the North Pole. On Sunday local musicians are recruited to play the in-house piano. In summer the party usually moves outside where you can enjoy views of the harbor and city hall, which lies directly across the street. It's open daily noon to 1am. Fridjof Nansen's Plass 7. ℭ **22-33-40-88.** T-banen: Nationaltheatret.

John's Bar   This unflashy, unglamorous pub enjoys a powerful cachet among the hip denizens of Oslo's night. In the case of decor, less is more. When it comes to patrons, you can expect just about anyone or anything: Frostbitten fishermen exhausted from hauling in herring from the North Sea, or perhaps a group of grisly bikers in town for some binge drinking. It's open Wednesday to Sunday 10pm to 3am. Universitetsgata 26. ✆ **22-42-44-20**. Tram: 5, 6, or 7.

Limelight   Steeped in the atmosphere of the theater, this fashionable bar next door to the Oslo Nye Teater is a favorite rendezvous for drinks before or after a show. It's open daily 6pm to midnight. Beer and mixed drinks cost 65NOK ($8.65) and up. In the Grand Hotel, Karl Johans Gate 31. ✆ **23-21-20-36**. T-banen: Stortinget.

Lipp   Consistently this restaurant/bar has been one of the hottest spots in Oslo since its opening in 1991. It offers three levels of food and drink with mellow house grooves echoing throughout. The clientele here is the "see and be seen" type, so try and look your best. The menu, a French and Italian fusion, never seems to disappoint. It's open daily 4pm to 2am. Olav V's Gate 2. ✆ **22-82-40-60**. T-banen: Nationaltheatret.

Oro Bar   This glamorous tapas bar, associated with the restaurant Oro, evokes the stylish and hip locales of warmer climates. An intensely fashionable crowd—in intensely expensive clothing—drops in for meals and people-watching. You can eat or just have a drink. A heaping platter of assorted tapas is 250NOK ($33). It's open Monday to Saturday 6pm till 2am. Tordenskioldsgate 6A (entrance on Kjeld Stubs Gate). ✆ **23-01-02-40**. T-banen: Stortinget.

Oslo Mikrobryggeriet   This small, English-style pub attracts a mixed, 30-something crowd. Aside from some cognac and whiskey, offerings include six in-house beers, the most popular being "Oslo Pils." With its cozy and warm atmosphere, and good music, this brewery is sure to please. It's open Wednesday to Friday 3pm to 3am, Saturday noon to 3am, and Sunday 3pm to 1am. Bogstadvn 6. ✆ **22-56-97-76**. T-banen: Majotsstuem.

Rederiet   On the top floor of the Radisson SAS Plaza Hotel, this bar is known as the most glamorous in Oslo. And at 100m (328 ft.) above the ground, it's also the tallest bar in Europe. In the ultra-modern interior, surrounded by a glass ceiling and walls, you'll find Oslo's young, professional elite. The view and people-watching are worth the trip. It's open Monday to Thursday 4pm to 1am, Friday and Saturday 4pm to 2am, and Sunday 5pm to 1am. Sonja Henie Plass 3. ✆ **22-05-80-00**. T-banen: Jernbanetorget.

Sir Winston Pub & Pianobar   In the style of a traditional English pub, this place has a cozy, friendly atmosphere with comfortable couches and laid-back, lounge music. You'll find anyone here from slick businessmen sipping martinis to neighborhood college kids putting back a few pints while watching the game. Books and pictures of Sir Winston crowd the wall. An open fireplace provides warmth on cold Norwegian nights. It's open Sunday to Thursday noon to 2am, and Friday and Saturday 11am to 3am. Karl Johans Gate 10. ✆ **22-41-14-41**. T-banen: Jernbanetorget.

Summit 21   On the 21st floor of the Radisson SAS Scandinavia Hotel, this bar competes with Rederiet when it comes to the best crowd and the best views in town. However, it's mainly known for serving Oslo's best strawberry daiquiris and for its view of the city from the men's room window. Frequented by businesspeople, and almost everyone else between the ages of 23 and 60, the lively bar is preferred to the Rederiet by many out-of-towners. It's open Monday to

Thursday 4pm to 1am, Friday and Saturday 4pm to 2:30am. Holbergsgate 30. © **23-29-30-00.** T-banen: Nationaltheatret.

CAFES

Café-Bar Memphis   This is a hip, industrial-looking bar with a fondness for such U.S.-derived kitsch as Elvis memorabilia and late, late drunken nights that feature Jack Daniels and beer. There's a limited roster of menu items (seafood pastas, scrambled eggs with ham or bacon and toast), but most of the clients come for cocktails, priced at 69NOK to 72NOK ($9.20–$9.60) and meeting with friends and acquaintances. It's open Monday to Thursday 11am to 1am and Friday and Saturday 11am to 3am. Thorvald Meyersgate 63. © **22-04-12-75.** Tram: 11, 12, 30.

Café Fiasco   Although the owners established this cafe to cater to commuters, the business goes way beyond just serving a fast glass of beer to travelers waiting for their trains. It's oddly located on a sloping, pedestrian ramp that interconnects the bus and railway stations, with views of the surrounding skyscrapers. Inside, you'll find a welcome jolt of humanity and a sense of multiculturalism. Reggae, soca, and hip-hop music blare over a sometimes-scruffily dressed crowd that's far from bourgeois. Coffee, depending on what's in it, costs from 13NOK to 68NOK ($1.75–$9.05); cocktails begin at 72NOK ($9.60). Late at night, long after the commuter trade has ended, the place and surrounding pedestrian passageways become an aggressive singles scene. It's open Monday to Friday 8am to 8pm, Saturday 11am to 3am, and Sunday noon to 2am. Schweigaardsgate 4. © **22-17-66-50.** T-banen: Jernbanetorget.

Café Onkel Donalds   Of the many bars and pubs that flourish after dark in Oslo, this is the most artfully designed (in this case by well-known Norwegian architect Petter Abrahamsen in 2001). Its soaring interior spaces evoke the entranceway to a postmodern opera house, and a network of short staircases will take you from the surging energy of the glossy-looking main bar to a series of more intimate mezzanines. The house special cocktail is an Onkel Donald, a head-spinner combining vodka, peach liqueur, cranberry juice, and sour mash. Lots of dialogues and romances have credited this bar as their catalyst. It's open daily 11am to 3am. Universitesgata 26. © **22-42-44-20.** Tram: 5, 6, or 7.

Clodion Art Cafe   It's like a circus here. The walls are splashed with tons of bright colors and art from local artists. During the day this hip, fun cafe offers a light lunch menu, and is pet-friendly. In the evening there's a happening social scene with all sorts of people barging through the doors. Open daily 10am to 1am. Bygdøy Alle 63. © **22-44-97-26.** T-banen: Majorstuen.

Lorry   This busy, suds-drenched cafe was established 120 years ago as a working-class bar. Since then, the surrounding neighborhood (virtually across the street from the park that flanks the Royal Palace) has zoomed upward in prestige and price. Now, the cafe's low-slung, wood-sided building is tucked among villas. There's an outdoor terrace for warm-weather dining, but the heart and soul of the place is its Victorian, black-stained interior. Offerings include 130 kinds of beer, 11 of which are on tap. From 5 to 10:30pm, the menu consists of a short list of platters of the day, priced at 100NOK to 150NOK ($13–$20) each, and from around 10:30pm to closing, all everybody seems to do here is drink. It's open Monday to Saturday 11am to 3am, and Sunday noon to 1am. Parkveien 12. © **22-69-69-04.** Tram: 11, 12.

GAY & LESBIAN BARS

This city of 500,000 has two gay bars. Pick up a copy of *Blick* for 30NOK ($4) available at most newsstands within the central city. Otherwise call Gay/Lesbian Visitor Information (☏ **22-11-05-09**), Monday to Friday 9am to 4pm.

London Pub   This is the most consistent and reliable gay pub in Oslo, with a relatively mature crowd of unpretentious gay men, and—to a much lesser extent—women. Set within the cellar of a building a few steps from the prestigious Bristol Hotel, it contains a battered-looking, beer hall–style trio of underground rooms with two bar areas and a pool table. At its best—during busy periods, usually late in the week—this place can be fun, convivial, and genuinely welcoming to newcomers from faraway places. At its worst, it can be glum and depressing. Whether you like it or not, this is a mainstay of gay life in Oslo. It's open Monday to Friday 6pm to 4am, Saturday and Sunday 3pm to 4am. C. J. Hambros Plass 5 (entrance on Rosenkrantzgate). ☏ **22-70-87-00.** T-banen: Stortinget.

Soho   This place rivals the London Pub, which tends to attract a more mature clientele, as the preeminent gay (both male and female) venue in Oslo. It's accessible via a covered passageway that leads from the street. Your experience here will vary hugely depending on when you arrive. The venue can either be animated or morbidly comatose, but if open, be sure to check out the upper or lower floors (there's a total of four bars on four floors), which open or close according to need. Open Wednesday and Thursday 5pm to 3am, Friday and Sunday 3pm to 3am, Saturday noon to 3am. Kirkegaten 34. ☏ **22-42-19-00.** Fri–Sat cover 70NOK ($9.30), additional 200NOK ($27) for drag shows some Fri and Sat at 10pm and midnight. Bus 8, 30, 31, 32, or 45.

6

Side Trips from Oslo

Stretching for 100km (62 miles), Oslofjord is Oslo's link to the open sea. Touring the fjord's western and eastern banks is richly rewarding. Of all the towns to visit, the most interesting are **Halden** and **Fredrikstad** on the eastern bank, and **Tønsberg** on the western bank.

The eastern shore also has many beaches with fine sands frequented by Oslovians in summer, especially July. Even then, however, the waters may be too cold for you if you come from hotter climes than Norway. The western side of the fjord was the site of several Viking settlements, and some of their remains or ruins can be seen today.

1 Moss & the Isle of Jeløy

55km (34 miles) S of Oslo

Moss was a port for the Vikings as they set out on their raids. Today it is a major transportation hub for the eastern Oslofjord area, receiving ferry traffic heading north from Denmark. Except for dining or staying at its major historic hotel, there is little reason for a prolonged stopover at this bustling commercial port and industrial area. But if you're exploring the east bank of Oslofjord, chances are you'll pass through the town.

Moss is the provincial capital of Østfjord, a land of forests, pastoral farmland, and industrial towns. Industry in Moss ranges from glass blowing to shipbuilding. Its craftspeople have been known since the Middle Ages. In 1814 a treaty was signed here uniting Sweden with Norway.

The town spills over onto the Jeløy Peninsula, which has a beach frequented in summer by many Oslovians.

From Moss you can take a ferry across Oslofjord to the town of Horten (see section 5, "Horten & Åsgårdstrand," later in this chapter) on the west bank.

ESSENTIALS

GETTING THERE Moss is serviced by eight trains per day from Oslo (trip time: 50 min.). Call ℂ **81-50-08-88** in Oslo for rail information. **Nor-Way Bussekspress** (ℂ **81-54-44-44**) runs buses from Oslo to Moss. Buses depart from Jernbanetorget in Oslo. From Oslo, motorists can head south following the signs to E6.

Ferries leave from Frederikshavn in the north of Jutland, Denmark, at the rate of one per day, the trip by sea to Moss taking 11 hours. If you're in Moss and want to see some of the attractions on Oslofjord's west bank, you can take a ferry over to Horten. Ferries leave on the hour daily from 6am to 1pm, the trip across the fjord taking half an hour.

VISITOR INFORMATION The **Moss Turistkontor,** Fleischersgate 17 (ℂ **69-25-32-95**), is open Monday to Friday 9am to 5pm.

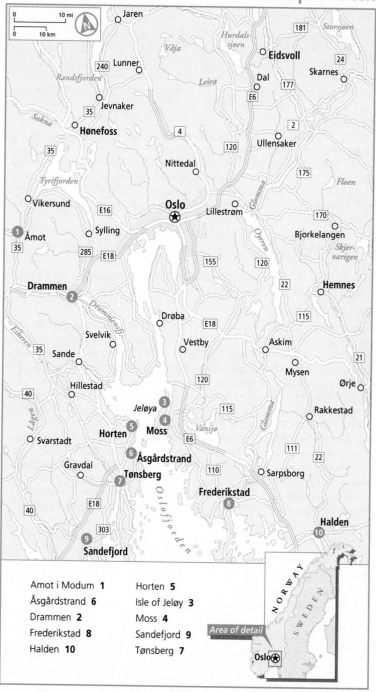

Amot i Modum **1**

Åsgårdstrand **6**

Drammen **2**

Frederikstad **8**

Halden **10**

Horten **5**

Isle of Jeløy **3**

Moss **4**

Sandefjord **9**

Tønsberg **7**

Area of detail

SEEING THE SIGHTS

On the island of Jeløy, a 5km (3-mile) drive from the center of Moss, stands **Galleri F15,** Alby Gård (© **69-27-10-33**), which is an art and handicrafts center installed on an old homestead. Today it is used for displaying regional handicrafts and exhibitions of photography. It's a minor sight, to be sure, but of some interest if you're in the area. Open June to August Tuesday to Sunday 11am to 7pm; September to May Tuesday to Sunday 11am to 5pm. Admission is 40NOK ($5.30) or free for children 15 and under.

If you're driving around the area, consider a summer visit to the little town of **Son,** lying 10km (6 miles) to the north. It's an old fishing village that once lured a great deal of painters and authors who turned it into an artists' colony. Today Son has some fame among Oslovians as a summer resort, and it's particularly busy in July when locals flock here for sailing and swimming.

WHERE TO STAY & DINE

Hotel Refsnes Gods ★★★   Some insiders cite this as the most elegant and chic hotel in the greater environs of Oslo.. It originated with a soaring and fanciful pair of symmetrical towers in 1767 as the pleasure pavilion of the area's richest landowner. (Unheated for winter use at the time, it was solely conceived as a warm-weather entertainment venue for himself and his well-connected friends.) Eventually, a modern wing containing bedrooms and lots of modern facilities were added. Today the place is the largest and most stately looking building on the mainly residential island of Jeløy.

Some aspects of this hotel evoke a sophisticated museum, partly because of the five original drawings by Edvard Munch that hang in the public rooms, and partly because each of the bedrooms displays original artworks by an individual artist, usually Scandinavian. Expect a wide array of room styles, ranging from small to spacious, from cozy and old-fashioned to modern, each with colors evoked by the paintings they contain. Bathrooms are newly installed and well maintained, each with tub and shower.

Virtually everyone who stays here opts for a meal within the hotel's well-known restaurant. In the tasteful circumstances that reflect the Norwegian bourgeoisie at its best, you'll enjoy fixed-price meals, ranging from 295NOK ($39) for two courses up to 650NOK ($86) for six courses. (King Oscar, an early-20th-century king of Norway, was one of this place's earliest and most prestigious guests.) Menu items, based on European/Continental models, change with the season. If you don't speak Norwegian, the menu will be translated for you by the polite staff. Ingredients include the freshest varieties of oysters, shellfish, lobster, venison, poultry, beef, and game. Dishes may include a cream of truffle soup; braised filets of sushi-quality tuna marinated in a mushroom-enriched *coulis* of herbs; and filets of venison served in a port-enriched lingonberry sauce. There are two lunch services every day, usually at 11am and again at 1pm; and a more loosely scheduled evening service that runs Monday to Saturday from 5 to 10pm; and Sunday from 3 to 10pm. Advance restaurant reservations are recommended.

Godset 5, Island of Jeløy, N-1502 Moss. ℂ **69-27-83-00.** Fax 69-27-83-01. www.refnesgods.no. 61 units. Mon–Thurs 1,420NOK–1,570NOK ($189–$209) double, 2,500NOK ($333) suite; Fri–Sun and daily June 21–Aug 15, 1,190NOK–1,340NOK ($158–$178) double, 2,200NOK ($293) suite. AE, DC, MC, V. From Moss, drive 3.75km (2 miles) west of town, following the signs to Jeløy. **Amenities:** Restaurant; bar; heated (year-round) outdoor pool; golf course; exercise room; sauna; concierge; babysitting; laundry service; dry cleaning; beach; boating. *In room:* TV, minibar, hair dryer.

2 Fredrikstad: Norway's Oldest Fortified Town ⭐

96km (60 miles) S of Oslo, 34km (20 miles) S of Moss

Lying at the mouth of Glomma River, Fredrikstad is Norway's oldest fortified town. Visitors come here mainly to see the Old Town (Gamlebyen), one of the best preserved in Eastern Norway.

King Fredrik II founded the town as a trading post between the mainland of Europe and western Scandinavia. Its characteristic landmarks are the 1880 cathedral and its delicate, silver arch Glomma Bridge, which stretches 824m (2,703 ft.) from end to end and rises 40m (131 ft.) over the water.

ESSENTIALS

GETTING THERE   Trains from Oslo's Central Station depart for Fredrikstad about every 2 hours. The trip takes about 1 hour from central Oslo. Call ℂ **81-50-08-88** for rail information.

There is frequent bus service daily from Oslo to Fredrikstad, the trip taking 1½ hours. Take Highway E6 south from Oslo heading toward Moss. Continue past Moss until you reach the junction at Route 110, and follow the signs south to Fredrikstad.

VISITOR INFORMATION   The **Fredrikstad Turistkontor** is on Turistsenteret, Østre Brohode, Gamle Fredrikstad (ℂ **69-30-46-00**). It's open June to September, Monday to Friday from 9am to 6pm, Saturday 10am to 4pm, and Sunday noon to 4pm; October to May, Monday to Friday 9am to 4pm.

SPECIAL EVENTS   During the second week of every July, the **Glomma Festival,** named for the town's river, takes place in Fredrikstad. Many Oslovians drive south to attend this 1-week program of events, highlighted by musical performances. Ritual "duels" are staged, along with sailing ship exhibitions and regattas.

GETTING AROUND   Across the river on the west is a modern industrial section; although a bridge links the areas, the best way to reach the Old Town is by ferry, which costs 6NOK (80¢). The departure point is about 4 blocks from the Fredrikstad railroad station at Strandpromenaden. Follow the crowd out the main door of the station, turn left, and continue down to the bank of the river. You can also travel between the two areas by bus (no. 360 or 362), although most pedestrians prefer the ferry. The ferry operates Monday to Friday from 5:30am to 11pm, Saturday 7am to 1am, and Sunday 9:30am to 11pm.

To call a **taxi,** dial ℂ **69-36-26-00.** If the weather is fair, we recommend renting a **bicycle.** They're available at the tourist office (see above), which requires your driving license or a credit card number as a deposit.

SEEING THE SIGHTS

Fredrikstad was founded in 1567 as a marketplace at the mouth of the River Glomma. **Gamlebyen** (the Old Town) became a fortress in 1663 and continued in that role until 1903, boasting some 200 guns in its heyday. It still serves as a

---

Finds   **Insegran: Famous in Norse Sagas**

If you like to read Norse sagas like we do, visit the ruins of the 13th-century fortress, **Insegran,** on an island directly west of Gamlebyen. This once-mighty fortress stood as a fortification against advancing Swedish armies in the mid-1600s. Various exhibits are mounted here in summer; recent topics included sailing. Insegran is only 400m (1,312 ft.) west of the old town but there is no ferry link. You have to drive south on Route 108 until you see the signposted turnoff.

---

military camp, and is the best-preserved fortress town in Scandinavia today. The moats and embankments make for an evocative walk, recalling the days when Sweden was viewed as an enemy and not a friendly country across the nearby border.

The main guardroom and the old prison contain part of the **Fredrikstad Museum,** Gamleslaveri (© **69-30-68-75**). At the southwestern end of Gamble-byen is a section of the museum in a former guardhouse from 1731. Inside is a model of the old town and a collection of artifacts, both civilian and military, collected by city fathers over a span of 300 years. It's open May to September, Tuesday to Friday and Sunday from noon to 5pm, Saturday 11am to 5pm; closed October to April. Admission is 30NOK ($4) for adults, 10NOK ($1.35) for children.

The cathedral of Fredrikstad, **Fredrikstad Domskirke,** Ferjestedsveien (© **69-30-02-80**), is open Tuesday to Friday from 11am to 3pm, charging no admission. It was constructed in 1860 in a flamboyant Gothic Revival style. Its most notable feature is its stained-glass windows by Emanuel Vigeland, the younger and lesser-known brother of Norway's most famous sculptor, Gustav Vigeland. The church was also decorated by other leading Norwegian artists. The Domkirke lies on the western bank of the Glomma opening onto a small park.

Outside the gates of the Old Town stands what remains of **Kongsten Festning,** the fortress of Frederikstad, which was constructed on Gallows Hill and used by the townspeople as an execution site for criminals. When the Swedes took over the site in 1677, they fortified the stronghold with 20 cannons, underground chambers, passages, and a strong arsenal. Today, you can scramble among the embankments, walls, stockades, and turrets, and try to imagine the fortress as it was. An unkempt, lonely spot today, it is always open, charging no admission. To reach it, walk 15 minutes beyond the Gamlebyen drawbridge, turning off Tornesveien at the Fredrikstad Motell & Camping.

SHOPPING

Since Fredrikstad's heyday as a trading port and merchant base, the Old Town has attracted craftspeople and artisans, many of whom create their wares in historic houses and barns. Many of these glassblowers, ceramic artists, and silversmiths sell their products at local shops. One of the best emporiums is **Plus,** Kirkegatan 28 (© **69-32-06-78**). It's open Monday to Friday from 10am to 4:30pm, Saturday 10am to 2pm, Sunday 1 to 3pm.

Glashytte   This rustic shop acts as a retail store and glass-blowing studio whose merchandise is sold all over the country. They specialize in everything glass with items for sale such as wine glasses and carafes, plates, bowls, and paperweights. You can specify what you need and watch your creation come to life through the skilled hands of local craftspeople. Objects are clear glass or in a wide array of colors. It's open Monday through Saturday from 10am to 4pm. Torsnesvn 1. © **69-32-28-12.** Bus: 541.

WHERE TO STAY

Hotel City   Situated in the town center in close proximity to the rail station, this stylish and modern hotel offers comfortable accommodations. All rooms are furnished with good taste and comfort in mind. Each unit is well maintained and equipped with well-kept bathrooms containing shower units. The fifth floor is known as the "safari floor." Not only is this the one floor where smoking is permitted, but each room is done in a jungle theme with wicker-accented furnishings, tiger-print carpeting, and wall art depicting jungle landscapes and wildlife. The hotel also has two good restaurants, one serving an a la carte international menu the other with lighter, pizza-and-burger fare.

Nygard 44-46, N-1600 Fredrikstad. © **69-31-77-50.** Fax 69-31-65-83. www.hotelcity.no. 102 units. Sept–May 1,295NOK ($172) double; June–Aug 950NOK ($126) double. Rates include breakfast. MC, V. Parking 100NOK ($13). Bus: 31. **Amenities:** 2 restaurants; bar; nightclub; exercise room; sauna; limited room service; laundry service; dry cleaning. *In room:* TV, minibar, hair dryer.

Victoria Hotel   Established in 1883, this Art Nouveau structure is the town's oldest hotel. Since its creation many renovations have led up to the welcoming and cozy hotel you'll find today. Each guest room is well furnished and comfortable. All units contain neatly kept bathrooms with shower units. The restaurant is known for its reasonably priced international cuisine. From the hotel there is a wonderful view of the cathedral grounds.

Turngaten 3, N-1600 Fredrikstad. © **69-38-58-00.** Fax 69-38-58-01. www.victoriafredrikstad.no. 65 units. Sept–May 1,245NOK ($166) double; June–Aug 950NOK ($126) double. Rates include breakfast. AE, DC, MC, V. Free parking. Bus: 31. **Amenities:** Restaurant; bar. *In room:* TV, hair dryer.

WHERE TO DINE

Balaklava Guestgiveri ★ NORWEGIAN   For tradition and atmosphere, this restaurant has no competition in the Old Town. It was built in 1803 as the home of the village priest in a style known in North America as "carpenter Gothic." Today simple but flavorful meals are served in the cellar, near a massive fireplace. There's access to an outdoor courtyard. The well-prepared fare includes baked salmon with dill sauce, filet of sole with lemon-butter sauce, fish-and-clam casserole with herbs, and an assortment of fresh game dishes.

Faergeportgate 78. © **69-32-30-40.** Reservations recommended. 3-course menu 495NOK ($66); 4-course menu 565NOK ($75); 5-course menu 625NOK ($83). AE, DC, MC, V. Daily noon–10:30pm.

Engelsviken Brygge ★ *Finds* SEAFOOD   Set at the edge of the crescent-shaped bay that's dominated by the fishing hamlet of Engelsviken, whose population almost never exceeds 400 hardy souls, this is a hideaway restaurant that's sought out for its atmosphere by diners from as far away as Oslo. It originated a century ago as a simple fisherman's cottage, but in the mid-1990s, its owners added big windows overlooking the sea, enlarged its premises to include a modern kitchen, slapped on some coats of bright red paint, and started serving fish dishes that have become legendary. One good example is the creamy fish soup that's loaded with chunks of fish and shellfish; you can order this excellent dish as a starter or main course. Other offerings include barbecued scampi with pasta shells and salad; a risotto-inspired shrimp and oyster rice; a "symphony" platter loaded high with filet of salmon, catfish, and sea devil; and grilled, poached, or fried versions of most of the fresh fish swimming offshore. For anyone not particularly interested in seafood, there's also a juicy version of fried beefsteak studded with chunks of garlic and served with a creamy peppercorn sauce.

Engelsvikveien 6, in the hamlet of Engelsviken, 15km (9½ miles) NW of Fredrikstad. ✆ 69-35-18-40. Reservations recommended. Main courses 145NOK–235NOK ($19–$31). AE, DC, MC, V. Mon–Sat 5–9pm; Sun 5–8pm. From Fredrikstad, follow the signs to Oslo for 4.75km (3 miles). Then turn left onto the road signposted "Engelsviken."

Majorstuen (Kids) INTERNATIONAL   In an 18th-century house at the edge of the Old Town, this restaurant has a large dining room, a pub, and a warm-weather outdoor terrace. The food is unpretentious but plentiful. Among the most popular dishes are pizzas, fillet of beef served with vegetables and salad, Wiener schnitzel, fish platters, and marinated whale steak in black peppercorn sauce. Majorstuen is the only restaurant in the region that offers whale steak year-round.

Vollportgatan 73. ✆ 69-32-15-55. Main courses 110NOK–245NOK ($15–$33); pizzas (for 1–4 people) 149NOK–189NOK ($20–$25). AE, DC, MC, V. Sun–Thurs noon–10pm; Fri–Sat 11am–10pm.

FREDRIKSTAD AFTER DARK

Mets Rock Café   Named after the New York baseball team, this cafe keeps its American theme with Creole and American food items and a large selection of beer imported from the U.S. Inside you'll find exposed brick walls, dark brown tables, lounging couches, and a hip, young crowd between the ages of 20 to 35. The bar has an impressive selection of cognacs and whiskies and a dance floor that is kept active by the sounds of a DJ. When weather permits, outdoor seating is provided for an al fresco meal. It's open Wednesday to Saturday from 3pm to 2am. Dampskipsbrygga 12. ✆ 69-31-78-99.

Sir Winston's House   Downstairs you'll find an English-style pub with a traditional decor where businesspeople and locals alike can be found sharing a pint at the bar. The second floor is home to a large disco where up to 300 people can dance to the DJ's selection of Top-40 hits. Tables and chairs are also available for a sit-down meal from their Continental menu. It's open daily from 1pm to 3am. Storgata 17. ✆ 69-31-80-80.

SIDE TRIPS FROM FREDRIKSTAD

Because of its meager accommodations, Fredrikstad is most often visited on a day trip from Oslo. However, if you'd like to stay at one of the few hotels in Fredrikstad (see above), you can enjoy a day or two exploring some intriguing nearby sights. The Norwegians and Swedes know of these attractions outlined below, although foreign visitors are rare.

The most concentrated collection of archaeological monuments in Norway lies along Route 110 between Fredrikstad and Sarpsborg to the east. Norwegians have dubbed the highway *Oldtidsveien* or **"Old Times Way"** . Along this old sunken road between the two towns, many ancient stone works and rock paintings have been found. As you drive along, you can stop and visit these signposted sights.

The most idyllic way to tour the Oldtidsveien is by bike if the weather is fair. If it's not, you really shouldn't make this trip.

In the hamlet of **Solberg** is a trio of panels with nearly 100 carved figures, thought to be 3,000 years old. At another stopover, in the village of **Gunnarstorp,** you can see several; standing stones dating from the Iron Age as well as a Bronze Age burial ground. Other ancient attractions are found at the village of **Begby,** which has some depictions of ancient people, including boats and wild animals. At **Hornes** are some rock paintings that depict nearly two dozen ancient boats with oarsmen.

Bridge by Leonardo da Vinci

In Tuscany, Leonardo da Vinci drew the plans for a bridge in 1502. It was never built in his day. However, in 2001 Da Vinci's stunningly modern pedestrian bridge has opened in Norway, of all places.

The 99m (330 ft.) laminated timber bridge links Norway with its eastern neighbor, Sweden, at the town of Aas, a 26km (16-mile) drive south of Oslo. Many Oslovians who have no real intention of going to Sweden drive down to walk across this remarkable piece of Renaissance engineering.

Of course, Da Vinci didn't envision a laminated bridge. He had a 216m (720 ft.) stone span in mind to cross the Golden Horn inlet at the mouth of the Bosporus between Peta and Istanbul. Sultan Bejazet II, at that time a patron of Da Vinci, feared that it was impractical to build such a bridge. The plan died until the original Da Vinci drawings were uncovered among some documents in the late 1950s.

Although the new bridge is only a scaled-down version of what Da Vinci originally designed, it's nonetheless a stunning bit of engineering, standing 8m (27 ft.) high at its pinnacle.

The weight of the relatively light bridge is supported on a trio of arches that join the pathway in the center. They fan out to footholds supporting a base 41m (135 ft.) apart. The bridge is only 23 inches thick in the middle, although the arches curve out to 1.5m (5½ ft.) at their base. Modern engineers claim that Da Vinci understood the principle of distributing the force of the arch by making wide footholds long before bridge makers learned this technique.

At the hamlet of **Hunn** you'll come upon the largest archaeological site in Norway, with some 4,000-year-old remains of Stone Age civilization along with some Viking grave mounds and stone circles, even signs of ancient cultivation methods. The path you take from the main road to the grave mounds was dug out some 2,000 years ago. You can also go to a nearby hill to look at the remains of meager ruins of the Ravneberget fortification, with walls dating from the 4th century A.D.

Along this road you can also visit some attractions not so old. Midway between Fredrikstad and Sarpsborg, you can visit the **Roald Amundsen Centre** at Hvidsten (© **69-34-83-26**), the birthplace in 1872 of Amundsen, who in 1911 was the first explorer to reach the South Pole. A monument is dedicated to him, and the house is filled with memorabilia of his exploits. You'll approach Hvidsten 7km (4¾ miles) east of Fredrikstad along Route 110. The center is open May to August, Friday to Sunday from 10am to 3pm. Admission is 30NOK ($4) for adults, 10NOK ($1.35) for children.

If you end your exploration in Sarpsborg, at a point 14km (8½ miles) east of Fredrikstad, you can visit the **Borgarsyssel Museum,** Kirkegata (© **69-15-50-11**), which is open June to August Tuesday to Saturday 10am to 5pm and Sunday noon to 5pm. This county museum of the province of Østfold is an open-air museum filled with some 30 period structures moved here from various parts of southern Norway. Many cultural artifacts are exhibited, and you can also walk through an herbal garden. Kids enjoy the petting zoo. On site are the ruins of King Øystein's St. Nikolaus Church, built in 1115 but torched by the advancing Swedish army in 1567.

En route back to Fredrikstad you can stop off at the **Storedal Cultural Centre,** at Storedal (© **69-16-92-67**), 8km (5 miles) east of Fredrikstad. This was the birthplace of King Magnus in 1117. He became king of Norway at the age of 13. But 5 years later he was blinded and since then called King Magnus "the Blind." Centuries later the owner of a farm on this site, Erlking Stordahl, was also blind, and decided to erect a center honoring the medieval teenage king. The center is dedicated not only to blind people, but also to those suffering from disabilities. On site is a beautiful botanical garden that you can visit. Two artists, Arne Nordheim and Arnold Haukeland, designed an Ode to the Light "sound sculpture," which translates the fluctuations of natural light into music. The center is signposted from Route 110. It's open from June to August daily 10am to 5pm, charging no admission.

3 Halden: The Burning City

30km (18 miles) S of Fredrikstad, 144km (90 miles) S of Oslo, 2km (1¼ miles) W of Swedish border

Historically, Halden was a frontier outpost heavily fortified to fend off attacks by the Swedes. It was—and still is—known for Fredriksten fortress, where Norwegian patriots successfully held off Sweden's frequent attacks from the east. In fact, Swedish King Karl XII was killed in 1718 when he led an attack on this venerable fortress.

Regional fighters made a bold decision in 1659. To drive out the attacking Swedes, they set fire to their own town. The Swedes retreated, although the fortress withstood the siege and the town fire. Attacked by the Swedes again in 1716, the townspeople of Halden once again torched their city to halt the Swedish advance into Norway. These incidents, along with numerous fires set by Mother Nature, gave the town its nickname: "The Burning City."

Today a prosperous little border town, Halden has the dubious distinction of being the site of the country's oldest nuclear power station. In 1959 nuclear energy was introduced here to fuel regional wood-based industries.

With its population of around 27,000 people, Halden lies at the end of Iddefjord in the far southeasterly corner of Østfold. Halden is bisected by the Tista River and hemmed in by forested hills. It makes an idyllic stopover for those touring the eastern bank of the Oslofjord. If you have time for only one town, make it Fredrikstad. If you can fit two towns into your travel plans, include Halden in your itinerary.

ESSENTIALS

GETTING THERE **By Rail** Halden is a stopover on the main rail links between Oslo and Gothenburg, Sweden, that country's second city on its western coast. Depending on the time of day, trains depart Oslo once every hour or once every two hours. The trip takes 1¾ hours, a one-way ticket costing 175NOK ($23). Call © **81-50-08-88** for rail schedules. The train is quicker and much more recommendable than the bus.

By Bus Nor-Way Bussekspress (© **81-54-44-44**) in Oslo runs buses every 3 hours during the day to the town of Svindsen. Once in Svindsen, you must take a local bus for the final journey south to Halden.

The Mysterious Death of King Karl XII

You can see a monument within Fredriksten Fortress, marking the spot where Swedish King Karl XII was shot during a 1718 siege. Many Norwegian guides tell you that it wasn't their countrymen who killed the king, but one of his own men. A warmongering monarch, Karl had exhausted his troops and tested their loyalty on the battlefield. Many soldiers were tired of him and his endless battles. It has never been proven where the fatal bullet was fired. Swedes maintain that a soldier within the fortress killed Karl. There is strong speculation, however, that he was assassinated by a Swedish soldier eager to return to home and hearth.

By Car Motorists from Oslo can follow E6 south to reach Halden. Driving time is about 1½ hours.

By Ferry From the middle of May until the middle of August, you can enjoy a day's adventure by taking a ferry, MS *Sagasund* (© **90-99-81-00**), departing from Halden and sailing over to Strömstad on the west coast of Sweden. Strömstad used to belong to Norway until 1658. Today it's a colorful seaside resort and an embarkation point for the remote Kloster Islands, Sweden's most westerly isles where cars are prohibited. The warming waters of the Gulf Stream give these islands luxuriant vegetation. The ferry runs on Wednesday, Friday, and Saturday; a return fare to Halden costs 160NOK ($21).

VISITOR INFORMATION A summer only (June 1 to mid-Aug) tourist office at the harbor is open daily from 8am to 8pm. There is also a regular tourist office at Tollboden, Storegata (© **69-19-09-80**), at the bus terminal in the center of town, which is open June to August from 9am to 4:30pm Monday to Friday. From September to May, it's open Monday to Friday from 9am to 3:30pm.

SEEING THE SIGHTS

The most idyllic place to be on a July afternoon when the sun is shining is **Busterudpark** at Busterudgaten in the center of town. This century-old park serves as a reminder of how life used to be in town, complete with a bandstand from 1879. In summer a military band often gives concerts here. The sculptor, Dyre Vaa, erected a monument in the park in 1939 to honor F. A. Reissiger and Oscar Borg for their efforts to promote music in Halden.

Fredriksten Festning (Fredriksten Fortress) ✪ The crowning citadel of Halden, dominating a forested hill, the fort of Fredriksten is still in use by the Norwegian army so all of the complex cannot be visited. The king, Frederick III, ordered that the stronghold be built in 1661 to protect the Danish-Norwegian kingdom against sieges from Sweden, which had already unsuccessfully attacked Oslo and Copenhagen.

The king called in engineers from The Netherlands to build what he hoped—successfully so—would become an impregnable fortress. It took 10 years for these Dutchmen to create this citadel of labyrinthine passages and thick perimeter walls that withstand cannonballs. The gates were heavily fortified, as were the bastions.

> **Tips** **Keep Your Eye on Your Kid**
>
> One thing prevents this fortress from being truly kid-friendly: The tower-
> ing bastions are not fenced in and can be dangerous. If you visit with your
> children, make sure to watch over them carefully.

The Dutch designed the complex of buildings in the shape of a star at the
highest point in the sprawling town. The fortress was constructed on two ridges,
the northern walls stretching from Dronningens Bastion in the west to Prince
Christian Bastion in the east. The southern line of fortifications goes from Prins
Georgs Bastion to the main Overkongen Bastion at the highest point on the hill.

To reach the fortress you can take a steep footpath beginning at Peder Colbjørnsens Gate going up to the principal gatehouse. You can easily spend 2 hours
here, although most visitors absorb it in less than an hour.

In a former prison in the eastern curtain wall, you'll find the **War History
Museum.** Exhibits depict the history of battle in Halden from the 1600s to the
Nazi takeover of Norway in 1940. Another museum, **Byen Brenner** ("the town
is on fire"), explores the history behind the town's unfortunate nickname, "The
Burning City."

An **apothecary** has been installed in the former Commandant's Residence,
which dates from 1754. Modern exhibits trace the history of pharmacology from
early folk remedies that used bird claws to 20th-century advances in medicine.

Bakery and **brewery** exhibits—other surprises—are found within the complex. The bakery could turn out bread for some 5,000 men, and the brewery
could produce 3,000 liters of beer a day.

There is no more idyllic place for lunch in Halden than at the fort's own
Fredriksten Kro, a mellow old pub with outdoor seating in fair weather. You
can order both food and drink here during the day.

Peder Colbjørnsens Gate. ① 69-09-09-80. Admission 40NOK ($5.30) adults, 10NOK ($1.35) children.
Guided tours 45NOK ($6) adults, 20NOK ($2.65) children. May 18–Aug 20 daily 10am–5pm.

Rød Manor ⭐ *Finds* This is one of the most impressive and best-preserved
manor houses in southeastern Norway. The exact age of the historic core of this
building is unknown, although the east wing was added in 1733. Today, much
of the place looks as it did in 1750, when the Tank and Ankers families resided
here. Still elegant, it has lovely interiors filled with objets d'art, hunting trophies,
and one of the largest private collections of weapons in Scandinavia. You can
only see the house by guided tour. On your own, you can stroll the beautiful
English-style gardens with their towering deciduous trees or walk a pathway bor-
dered by hazelnut trees. The symmetrical, baroque–style walkways evoke the
gracious living of a grander era (assuming you were rich). The location is signposted 1.5km (1 mile) west of the town center.

Rød Herregård. ① 69-18-54-11. Admission 40NOK ($5.30) adults, 10NOK ($1.35) children. June 25 to mid-
Aug Tues–Sun 1 and 2pm (additional Sun tour at 3pm). May 20–June 24 and mid-Aug to Sept Sun noon, 1pm,
and 2pm.

WHERE TO STAY

Grand Hotel This centrally located hotel is in a structure originally built in
1898. Its rustic charm is part of its appeal. The rooms are simple and clean with
modern furnishings and well-kept bathrooms with shower units. Dinner is not

served here but there are many restaurants within walking distance. The hotel is just across from the rail station.

Jernbanetorget 1, N-1776 Halden. © **69-18-72-00.** Fax 69-18-79-59. 32 units. Mon–Thurs 860NOK ($114) double; Fri–Sun 690NOK ($92) double. AE, MC, V. **Amenities:** Breakfast room; bar; lounge. *In room:* TV, minibar.

Park Hotel ⚡ This is the more comfortable and up-to-date of Halden's two hotels, with a location about .75km (½ mile) from the town center, in a pleasant garden. Originally built in the 1970s, with about half of the rooms lying within a new wing added in 2000, it's a four-story weatherproof building that offers more amenities, and more diversions, than its only other competitor. There is an exceptionally helpful and well-informed staff. Each of the rooms has wooden floors, a tiled bathroom with shower-tub combinations, and color schemes of soft blues, grays, and beiges.

Marcus Thranes Gate 30, N-1776 Halden. © **69-21-15-00.** Fax 69-21-15-01. www.park-hotel.no. 64 units. Mon–Thurs 1,260NOK ($168) double; Fri–Sun 890NOK ($118) double; daily 1,390NOK ($185) suite. Rates include breakfast. AE, DC, MC, V. Free parking. **Amenities:** Restaurant; bar; exercise room; sauna; babysitting; laundry service; dry cleaning; garden. *In room:* TV, minibar.

WHERE TO DINE

Dickens INTERNATIONAL In winter diners retreat into a 17th-century cellar to enjoy well-prepared and affordable meals. In summer an outdoor table is preferred on a barge floating in the harbor. You won't find grand cuisine here but those dependable favorites often consumed by Norwegians with a mug of beer: a Dickens burger with bacon, nachos with jalapeños, or a chicken salad with crispy bacon. Visitors predominate in the summer months, with regulars returning when the wind blows cold.

Storgata 9. © **69-18-35-33.** Reservations recommended Sat–Sun. Main courses 69NOK–100NOK ($9.20–$13) at lunch, 100NOK–200NOK ($13–$27) at dinner. AE, DC, MC, V. Mon–Thurs 11am–10pm; Fri–Sat 11am–11pm; Sun 1–9pm. Closed Christmas.

Pub Royal NORWEGIAN/INTERNATIONAL Near the waterfront, this English pub and restaurant is a favorite rendezvous point for the locals. They come here for the brew, of course, but also for rib-sticking fare like pizzas made from scratch, juicy hamburgers, a well-flavored beef platter with onions and sautéed mushrooms, along with standard pasta and chicken dishes. The decor? You'll think you've been transplanted to Manchester, England.

Olav V's Gate. © **69-18-00-80.** Main courses 164NOK–235NOK ($22–$31). AE, DC, MC, V. Mon–Sat 11am–midnight; Sun 3–11pm.

HALDEN AFTER DARK

Hannestadgården Halden is so sleepy at night that some Norwegian guides recommend that you overnight elsewhere. But it's not that bad, at least at this night spot, a combined restaurant, dance club, night club, and piano bar all rolled into one. The nightclub, decorated with red furniture and black walls, attracts a young crowd. The bartender specializes in daiquiris, with strawberry being a favorite. The local brew is called Borg. Rock 'n' roll is played nightly in the disco area, and live concerts take place in the piano bar. It's open Monday to Thursday from 3pm to midnight, Friday and Saturday 3pm to 3am. Tollbugata 5. © **69-19-77-81.** Cover 60NOK ($8) after 11pm.

Siste Reis Pub Next to the Grand Hotel building, this is a small, cozy, and friendly Irish-style pub decorated with pictures of local musicians along with classic advertising posters. Close to the train depot, the pub offers many different brews on tap, from Irish Guinness to Danish Tuborg, and especially the local favorite, Borg. Most of the patrons, ranging in age from 18 to 40, come here to talk but also to listen to Irish folk music on the weekdays. On Friday and Saturday recorded rock and roll is the music of the night. Only snacks are served along with the brew. Open Monday to Thursday 6pm to 1am, Friday 6pm to 3am, Saturday 11am to 3am, and Sunday 1pm to 1am. Jernbanetorget 1. (© **69-17-53-07.**

4 Drammen: River City

40km (25 miles) SW of Oslo

This industrial city, timber town, and major port—set in a lovely valley—is virtually the bedroom community for many Oslovians. The fast-flowing Drammen River runs through the city, giving it the title "River City." The city, with a population of 50,000, lies on both banks of the river and was once divided into two parts, Stromsø and Bragernes. These towns were fortified and united in 1811 to form one town. Historically Drammen was the harbor for exporting silver from the Kongsberg Mines, but today it is known as the chief port for receiving foreign cars shipped into Norway. In days gone by, its riverbanks were covered with sawmills, and logs were rafted down the river, stretching for a distance of 45km (28 miles). A few decades ago the Drammen River was known as "one large sewer." But the waters have been cleaned up in recent years, and locals even swim here in summer. Instead of that, you might prefer to take one of the footpaths along the riverbanks, stopping off in a sunny "green lung" area for a picnic. Both cyclists and walkers enjoy these riverbanks. The river itself flows into Drammen Fjord, stretching for 25km (15½ miles).

The port of Drammen figures hugely in Viking lore. Nearly a thousand years ago the Vikings arrived at the port in their warships laden with plunder from foreign raids. Dating from 1070, the *Sagas of Snorre* relate how these Vikings departed and returned along the Oslofjord to "Drofn," as the port of Drammen was once called.

ESSENTIALS

GETTING THERE   From the central station in Oslo, a train leaves every half hour for Drammen, taking 35 minutes and costing 65NOK ($8.65) for a one-way ticket. Buses cost the same and leave with the same frequency, taking the same time. For more information, call (© **81-50-08-88.** Motorists can take E18 to the southwest of Oslo directly into the center of Drammen.

VISITOR INFORMATION   The **Drammen Turistinformasjon,** Bragernes Torg 6 (© **32-80-62-10**), dispenses information about the Drammen itself and the immediate vicinity, including a number of attractions on the western banks of Oslofjord. The office is open Monday to Friday 8am to 3pm.

SPECIAL EVENTS   Water-loving Oslovians head south every summer for the annual **River Festival** in this riverside city. Events feature open-air concerts, dragon boat races, raft-racing, open-air concerts—in total some 100 different events. This festival takes place during a weekend in August; dates change every year. Check with the visitor center (see above) for more details.

SEEING THE SIGHTS

The highlight of the town is the **Spiraltoppen (Spiralen Tunnel)** ✯ stretching for 1,650m (5,413 ft.) to the summit of Bragernes at 200m (656 ft.), which offers a panoramic view of Drammen and the Oslofjord. The tunnel is known as the "spirals of Dramen," because it winds in six huge spirals to the summit. The spirals were created, beginning in 1953, when the people of Drammen stopped quarrying for building stone and began to tunnel for it instead. This not only preserved the beauty of their natural landscape, but also created a scenic wonder. The town people continued this method of conservation until 1961. You can drive here or else take bus no. 41, which makes three trips daily, leaving from the central square, Bragernes Torg, in Drammen. Buses depart at 10:15am, noon, and 2:30pm. The trip takes 15 minutes and costs 18NOK ($2.40).

In summer you can go **hiking** along several footpaths along Spiraltoppen, following a trail that stretches for 2km (1¼ miles). In winter, Spiraltoppen is the launch pad for dozens of **cross-country** and **downhill-skiing trails,** the same trails once followed by the Vikings.

Bragernes Torg, the central market square of Drammen, is the center of local life in Drammen. The square is the largest in Scandinavia and is lined with many antique buildings from 1866 and beyond, including the old **Stock Exchange.** As a sign of the times, there is now a McDonald's on the ground floor of the old exchange (Rådhus, Engenes 1). Also standing on the main square are other historic buildings, including the old town hall, the former jail, and the courthouse, all of whose exteriors can be seen by walking around the square. The old fire station on the square is now a bank.

In summer you can listen to outdoor concerts here and watch other forms of street entertainment, while sitting and enjoying the sun by St. Hallvard's Fountain, honoring a local saint. A market, selling flowers, plants, and produce harvested in the nearby countryside, also takes place on the square in summer.

The most interesting building on the square is **Bragernes Church,** Kirkegata (© **32-83-27-53**), erected in 1871 in the Gothic Revival style. Its well-known altarpiece, the *Resurrection* by Adolph Tidemand, has been copied in some 70 churches all over the country. Admission is free; it's open Tuesday from 1 to 2pm and 6 to 8pm, Wednesday to Friday from 1 to 2pm. There is an organ concert presented every Saturday from 1 to 2pm.

The five-part **Drammens Museum** ⚐ (© **32-83-89-48**) is the chief cultural highlight of the city. It's centered at Gamle Kirkeplass 7, and is open Tuesday to Sunday from noon to 4pm. For 35NOK ($4.65) for adults and 20NOK ($2.65) for children, you are admitted to all the attractions.

At the **main headquarters** at the address above, the museum's art collection is displayed—a rich exhibition of Norwegian paintings from 1800 to the present day. Its best-known painting is *Champagne Girl* by Hans Heyerdahl. The satellite branches of the museum include a manor house at **Marienlyst,** Konnerudgata 7, dating from 1770. This patrician villa is filled with exhibitions. **Austad Manor,** Styrmoesvei 33, is another majestic building with Renaissance paintings and a rich 19th-century interior. An **open-air museum,** displaying 3 centuries of building traditions from the Buskerud district, lies only 300m (984 ft.) from Spiraltoppen (see above). More than 25 antique buildings have been moved to this site. Yet another manor house, **Gulskogen,** Nedre Eikervei 72, contains many beautiful rooms. This patrician residence from 1804 is also surrounded by a park.

OUTDOOR PURSUITS

The "River City" is one of the best open-air cities of Norway and has won prizes for its array of outdoor pursuits, which range from fjord boating to hiking in the nearby hills and forests. The tourist office distributes maps outlining local hikes and nature trails.

For a day cruise, we recommend taking the MS *Dramman* (© **32-83-50-45**) along Oslofjord and the river. The vessel holds up to 70 passengers. Boat trips take place from April to October, costing 2,300NOK ($306) per person.

Moments **Hiking the Fjord Country**

In summer you'll want to leave Drammen for some hikes into the Oslofjord country. You are likely to be joined by some of the athletic locals who, after a long, cold winter, want to enjoy the countryside. The tourist office distributes hiking maps of the area. Our favorite trail goes to the **Kjøsterudjuvet Gorge** ⭐, lying 1km (¾ mile) north of Drammen. Other scenic trails take you to the **Bragernesåsen** forests and to the **Spiralen Tunnel** (see above).

Salmon and trout are caught in the Oslofjord and river, especially in Helle-fossen. From mid-May until the end of August, fishing is very popular in the area. For more information, including information about obtaining a license, call **Drammens Sportfiskere** at ☎ **32-88-66-73.**

Tuesday and Saturday in Drammen attracts fans to the **Drammen Racecourse,** Buskerudvn 200 (☎ **32-21-87-00**), one of the country's 10 permanent betting courses.

In summer, swimming is the big activity at both indoor and outdoor pools. **Sentralbadet** (☎ **32-83-65-86**) is open from mid-August to May, boasting a 25m (82 ft.) indoor pool with a solarium, Nautilus fitness center, a water slide, and a Jacuzzi. Another pool complex with similar facilities is **Marienlystbadet** (☎ **32-83-314-05**), open from late May to mid-August with both indoor and outdoor pools, plus a heated kiddies pool.

In winter, the area around Drammen offers 100km (62 miles) of ski trails, including 45km (28 miles) of tracks lit at night. The tourist office keeps information about all these activities.

SHOPPING

It's almost one-stop shopping in the center of Drammen, as the leading department store, **Steen,** Strom Magasinet, Nedre Storgate 6 (☎ **32-21-39-90**), offers dozens of different specialty departments and dining venues.

Many Oslovians drive out to the **Buskerud Storscenter** (☎ **32-23-15-45**), a mall lying 8km (5 miles) from the heart of Drammen. To reach the mall, take Route 135 out of Oslo, following the signposts to Hokksund. Once at this mammoth mall, you'll find nearly 100 stores and various restaurants. Prices are cheaper than in the heart of Oslo because the rents are much less expensive.

WHERE TO STAY

First Hotel Ambassadeur ⭐⭐ *Kids*   Drammen's finest hotel—built in the 19th century—is better than ever following a massive renovation in 2002. The location is next to the train station, a 5-minute walk from the town's center. The hotel attracts mostly business travelers, but visitors to the Oslofjord stay here too. About 40% of the bathrooms contain tubs and showers, the rest have showers. Decorations are tasteful, and the accommodations are brightened by pastels. Some rooms have pullout sofas, attracting the family trade. On site, the Waldorf is a first-class restaurant serving classic Norwegian specialties such as locally caught salmon and international dishes.

Strømsø Torg 7, N-3044 Drammen. ☎ **31-01-21-00.** Fax 31-01-21-11. www.first-hotels.no. 230 units. 753NOK–1,253NOK ($100–$167) double; 1,598NOK ($213) suite. AE, DC, MC, V. **Amenities:** Restaurant; bar; fitness center; sauna; laundry service; dry cleaning. *In room:* A/C, TV, minibar, hair dryer.

Rica Park   A member of a popular Norwegian chain, this place is decent and fairly standard. Rooms are midsize and have a tasteful, yet bland, decor. All the bedrooms have average-size bathrooms, 27 of which come with tub and shower, the rest have showers. The hotel's drinking and entertainment facilities draw a range of patrons from Drammen youth to the post-30 crowd. There is both formal and informal dining, and you can patronize the facilities even if you don't stay here.

Gamble Kirkelplass 3, N-3019 Drammen. ✆ **32-26-36-00.** Fax 32-26-37-77. www.rica.no. 106 units. 895NOK–1,325NOK ($119–$176) double; 1,500NOK ($200) suite. **Amenities:** 2 restaurants; 2 bars; nightclub; laundry service; dry cleaning. *In room:* TV, minibar, hair dryer (some units), safe.

WHERE TO DINE

Skutebrygga   ✮ FRENCH/NORWEGIAN/ITALIAN   This restaurant's nautical decor—marine artifacts and antique maps and paintings of the coastline—creates a romantic backdrop for the superb cuisine. This traditional Drammen eatery lies along the riverbank, off the main square of town. In summer tables are placed in the courtyard. On cold nights, the fireplace is blazing. The menu includes lutefisk, a traditional Norwegian dish made with specially treated cod. You can also try *pennekgott,* a tender rack of lamb, which is smoked and then steamed. Many dishes are inspired by French or Italian cuisine. The English-speaking staff is polite and friendly.

Nedre Strandgate 2. ✆ **32-83-33-30.** Reservations required. Main courses 175NOK–280NOK ($23–$37). AE, DC, MC, V. Mon–Sat 11am–11pm; Sun noon–9pm.

Teatercafeen   ✮ NORWEGIAN/CONTINENTAL   This restaurant is the best and most sophisticated in town. A mixed clientele, ranging from business people to theater patrons, dine here. An on-site cafe is divided into two separate dining and drinking areas, one smoking, the other nonsmoking. It is filled with comfortable sofas for lounging. The large dining area has picture windows and is also divided into smoking and nonsmoking areas. Menu items are made from fresh, quality ingredients and served in generous portions. A featured appetizer is the excellent smoked Norwegian salmon. You can proceed from that to a savory duck breast in a traditional orange sauce. For a real regional specialty, opt for filet of reindeer in a Madeira sauce with fresh vegetables. Featured nightly is a large selection of well-prepared fish dishes, mainly delectable versions of trout and salmon. There is no finer dessert than the crème brûlée.

Øvre Storgate 17. ✆ **32-21-78-21.** Reservations required. Main courses 100NOK–289NOK ($13–$38). DC, MC, V. Sun–Thurs 4–11pm; Fri–Sat 4pm–3am.

DRAMMEN AFTER DARK

Special events (check locally) are staged at the landmark **Drammens Teater og Kulturhjus,** Øvre Storgate 12 (✆ **32-21-31-00**). Originally constructed in 1870, the theater burned down in 1993 and was rebuilt 3 years later.

The town's hot spot is **Riggen Pub,** Amtmann Blomsgate 4 (✆ **32-83-67-00**), which draws patrons ages 20 to 70. Aass Brewery, one of the oldest breweries in Norway, owns this stone structure. Naturally, the only beer served is Aass beer. Patrons flock here because it offers the best beer around and features live entertainment on Wednesday, Friday, and weekends, ranging from the blues to rock 'n' roll. Hours are Sunday to Thursday from 10am to 1am, Friday and Saturday 10am to 3am. A cover charge of 40NOK ($5.30) is imposed only on Friday and Saturday nights.

Value **One Price for "The Works"**

An all-inclusive ticket for Amot i Modum costs 120NOK ($16) for adults or 100NOK ($13) for seniors, students, and children 15 and over. You can also pay individual admissions (see below) to the various attractions.

DAY TRIP TO AMOT I MODUM ★★

One of the greatest day trips from Oslo is to the small village of Amot, formerly known for its cobalt mines and today a virtual pint-size Disneyland of attractions for the whole family. Amot i Modum lies 70km (42 miles) southwest of Oslo and a 30-minute drive north of Drammen along Route 35.

You can also go by frequent Netbuss Express Service (no. 100 or no. 101) from Drammen. In an hour the bus will deliver you to Amot, a one-way trip costing 60NOK ($8). Once in Amot, the attractions still lie 4km (2½ miles) to the northwest. You can either walk the distance if the day is fair, or take bus no. 105, costing 22NOK ($2.95) one-way.

Royal Blafarvevaerk   The Royal Blafarvevaerk was funded by King Christian VII in 1773. From the mines here, he wanted to extract cobalt, which was eagerly sought by the porcelain and glass industries. Today, the site of the old mines is one of the 10 most visited museums in Norway—a complex of several buildings with a glassworks, exhibitions, a children's farm, a restaurant, and various museums

At the heart of the museum is the glassworks, where exhibitions are staged every summer. There is also a permanent exhibition here entitled "From Cobalt Ore to Blue Pigment." On site is also a Children's Farm along with a cafe, Bodtker Café (Old Copper Inn), where you can order lunch.

In one building, the Wheel House, an exhibition tells the history of the mines. You can buy the makings of a picnic at Bodtker Café, to be enjoyed in the spacious park, which has tables and benches opening onto the Simoa River. There is a bathing spot near the river where you can go for a refreshing dip, plus a small playground nearby. Fishing is free.

You can visit on your own or with a guided tour (in English) for 25NOK ($3.35) per person.

Amot i Modum. © **32-78-67-00.** Admission 60NOK ($8) adults, 40NOK ($5.30) seniors and students, free for children under 15. June 21–Aug 17 daily 10am–6pm; May 24–June 20 and Aug 18–Sept 28 Tues–Sun 10am–5pm.

Nyfossum   The main building at Nyfossum, an old estate, was constructed in the Empire style in the 1820s. You can visit the restored interior, complete with antiques, and wander the surrounding gardens with their rose bushes, carp ponds, and herb beds. Exhibits of old farm equipment are displayed in the on-site barn. From the Royal Blafarvevaerk glassworks, it's a 25-minute walk to Nyfossum.

Amot i Modum. © **32-78-67-00.** Admission 40NOK ($5.30) adults, 30NOK ($4) students and seniors, free for children under 15. June 21–Aug 17 daily 11am–6pm; May 24–June 20 and Aug 18–Sept 28 Tues–Sun 11am–5pm.

Haugfoss ★   Haugfoss is the site of the highest waterfall in Eastern Norway. Many guests prefer to make their first stop here the Thranestua in Blaafarvevaerkets, a coffee house with a pastry shop. After buying a drink and a piece of cake, you can head to the terrace to enjoy the dramatic waterfall. You'll also find a century-old general store and shops selling baskets, fine jewelry made from minerals, and wrought iron. The waterfall can be reached by going up a hill that is signposted from the center of the museum complex. From the glassworks, it's a 5-minute walk to Haugfoss.

Amot i Modum. © **32-78-67-00.** Free admission. June 21–Aug 17 daily 11am–6pm; May 24–June 20 and Aug 18–Sept 28 Tues–Sun 11am–5pm.

Cobalt Mines ⭐   Wearing a special helmet and jacket, you can walk down the arched galleries or tunnels into the mammoth quarries of yesterday. The mines, which have been shored up and made safe, are on several levels. After miners extracted ore from one level, they dug another. The tour ends at the center of the mine, where massive rock walls rise on each side. Small museums at the site display the tools and work methods used by miners 2 centuries ago. The drive here from the glassworks takes about 25 minutes.

Amot i Modum. © **32-78-67-00.** Admission 50NOK ($6.65) adults, 40NOK ($5.30) students and seniors, free for children under 15. June 21–Aug 17 daily 11am–6pm; May 24–June 20 and Aug 18–Sept 28 Tues–Sun 11am–5pm. 8km (5 miles) from the glassworks in Amot i Modum along Malmveien.

Theodor Kittelsen Museum ⭐ (Finds   This museum, near the cobalt mines, possesses the country's largest collection of the haunting, evocative, and mysterious works of this acclaimed national artist. His paintings of the Norwegian landscape, and of trolls and folktales, have made him popular with adults and children. No artist is better at depicting *nøkker* (water sprites) and *nisser* (gnomes) than Kittelsen. In addition to paintings, his oeuvre includes carved furniture, watercolors, and various drawings. On display are some of the illustrations from the much-loved collections of children's books of the team of Asbjørnsen and Moe.

Amot i Modum. © **32-78-67-00.** Admission 40NOK ($5.30) adults, 30NOK ($4) seniors and students, free for children under 15. June 21–Aug 17 daily 11am–6pm; May 24–June 20 and Aug 18–Sept 28 Tues–Sun 11am–5pm.

5 Horten & Åsgårdstrand

Horten: 35km (17 miles) S of Drammen; Åsgårdstrand: 10km (6 miles) S of Horten

Most visitors come to this small port and naval base to catch a car ferry across the Oslofjord to Moss. (The ferry leaves hourly; the trip takes 30 min.) If you have a morning or afternoon to spare, we recommend that you check out the attractions of Horten along with neighboring Åsgårdstrand, a coastal town that's a popular summer bathing spot for Oslovians.

ESSENTIALS

GETTING THERE   A suburban train from the National Theater in Oslo and a train from Oslo's Central Station run frequently through the day to Horten. For information and schedules, call © **81-50-08-88.** Motorists can reach Horten by following E18 south from Oslo via Drammen.

VISITOR INFORMATION   For information about Horten and the surrounding area, go to the **Horten Tourist Office,** Tollbugate 1A (© **33-03-17-08**), which is open in July daily 9am to 8pm. The rest of the year, hours are Monday to Friday 9am to 4pm.

SEEING THE SIGHTS

Horten Bil Museum   The history of the automobile is showcased here, with three dozen automobiles and other vehicles from the turn of the 20th century until the 1970s. The vintage cars are especially intriguing, although more modern car aficionados will stop to admire the sleek Porsches. Cars and motorcycles are displayed chronologically and according to themes.

Sollistrandvn 12. ℭ **33-02-08-68.** Admission 35NOK ($4.65). Mid-June to mid-Sept Sun noon–3pm.

Marinemuseet (Royal Norwegian Navy Museum)   Since Horten was once a major base for the Norwegian Royal Navy, it's only appropriate that its major attraction is this naval museum, located in a munitions depot constructed in the 1850s. The museum is especially rich in marine artifacts of the Danish and Norwegian navies, some of which date from the 1500s. These include ships' bells, figureheads, and one-person submarines, among other displays. On exhibit outside the museum is the world's first torpedo boat, developed in Norway in 1853.

Karl Johns Vern. ℭ **33-03-33-97.** Free admission. May–Sept daily noon–4pm; Oct–Apr Sun noon–4pm.

Norsk museum for fotografi-Preus fotomuseum ⋆ *Finds*   In this unlikely location, you'll find the national museum of photography in Norway, and the world's largest library devoted to books on photography. The exhibitions contain both Norwegian and international photographs. The museum's intriguing collection of **photographs** ⋆ was assembled privately by Leif Preus at this large former naval warehouse. You can see the works of such internationally acclaimed photographers as Tom Sandberg and August Sander. For shutterbugs, the nearly 5,000 cameras are worth the visit, including one that dates from 1840. In one part of the museum, a century-old photographer's studio has been re-created.

Nedre vei 6, Karljohansvern. ℭ **33-03-16-30.** Admission 35NOK ($4.65) adults, 25NOK ($3.35) seniors, 20NOK ($2.65) children. Tues–Sun noon–4pm.

WHERE TO STAY

Hotel Horten Brygge   Positioned close to the waterfront, this hotel opened in 1995 and has been doing a thriving business ever since. It's modern, well maintained and operated, but a bit sterile. Nonetheless, its small to midsize bedrooms are comfortable and decorated in warm tones. Each comes with a small bathroom with shower. The on-site restaurant is more for convenience than grand food.

Strandpromenaden 2, N-3187 Horten. ℭ **33-02-04-20.** Fax 33-02-04-21. www.hortel-horten-brygge.com. 23 units. 700NOK–850NOK ($93–$113) double. Rates include continental breakfast. AE, DC, MC, V. Parking 62NOK ($8.25). **Amenities:** Restaurant; bar; laundry service; dry cleaning. *In room:* TV, minibar, coffeemaker, hair dryer, iron/ironing board.

Norlandia Grand Ocean Hotel ⋆   This is Horten's leading hotel, its oldest part dating from the turn of the 20th century, the other section from the 1980s. Try for a room in the newer wing, as accommodations are more comfortable here. The bedrooms for the most part are midsize, often coming with a small sofa. The most desirable units open onto the fjord, and a few accommodations also contain minibars. The light-colored decor may take the curse off many a gray day. All units contain small bathrooms with showers. The staff will help you organize boating and fishing trips.

Jernanegata 1, N-3187 Horten. ℭ **33-04-17-22.** Fax 33-04-45-07. www.norlandia.no. 105 units. 905NOK–1,205NOK ($120–$160) double; 1,200NOK–1,350NOK ($160–$180) suite. Rates include continental breakfast. AE, DC, MC, V. Closed Dec 22–Jan 5 and 1 or 2 weeks at Easter. **Amenities:** Weekday restaurant; bar; sauna; laundry service; dry cleaning. *In room:* TV.

WHERE TO DINE

During your explorations, drop into the town's main coffee shop, **Kafferiet,** Falsensgate 11 (ℭ **33-03-96-99**), run by a charming couple, Kristoffer Sandven and his wife, Thea. It's a great place for a cup of coffee, and a bite of one of Thea's delectable cakes or at least one of her cookies (bet you can't eat just one). It's open Monday to Wednesday and Friday to Saturday from 10am to 5pm, Thursday 10am to 8pm, and Sunday 11am to 5pm.

Bagatelle Restaurant & Bar NORWEGIAN/CHINESE/SUSHI   Opening in the late '80s, this place quickly became a popular drinking and dining venue, attracting a young, professional set with its good food and drink. In the main dining area, bankers and merchants (usually in ties) enjoy the classic Norwegian dishes, sometimes sampling sushi and Asian dishes too. Our party of friends preferred the Chinese dishes, especially the chicken with cashews, the beef with a savory black pepper sauce, and the sweet-and-sour prawns from the Oslofjord. The Norwegian dishes, which depend on what's available and good at the market, are prepared from classic recipes.

Storg. 45. ℂ **33-04-16-01.** Reservations recommended. Main courses 100NOK–200NOK ($13–$27). MC, V. Daily 1pm–midnight.

Fishland Restaurant ★ SEAFOOD/CONTINENTAL   With its original maritime decorations, Fishland is sheltered in an old fishermen's wharf building. This is an appropriate backdrop for the excellent, fresh fish served here. The wooden building seats 60 diners in cooler weather, but the number can swell to 200 in summer with outdoor seating. The creamy Norwegian clam chowder, including white fish, shrimp, and vegetables, is the best we've tasted along the fjord. The mixed fish platter will give you a sampling of excellent clams, prawns, shrimp, salmon, monkfish, and filet of cod. Not in a mood for fish? The chef prepares a number of meat and poultry dishes, including his specialty, roast breast of duck with a cherry cognac sauce. Finish your repast with the chef's crème brûlée.

Tollbugate 1C. ℂ **33-04-88-10.** Reservations recommended. Main courses 180NOK–260NOK ($24–$35). AE, DC, DISC, MC, V. May–Sept 1 daily noon–2am; Sept 2–Dec and Feb–Apr daily noon–2pm and 5–10pm. Closed Jan.

Sebastian INTERNATIONAL/NORWEGIAN   Set near the center of most of the nightlife in the area, this is a reliable choice for well-prepared food with quality ingredients. The dining is semiformal with white tablecloths and romantic candlelight. Small paintings decorate the brick walls, and there is a pleasant and relaxed atmosphere, with soothing music playing in the background. Fresh flavors and decisive seasoning are reflected in such dishes as the filet of reindeer, the pepper steak with a cognac sauce, and a Norwegian specialty, *leyfish* (dried trout). We launched our meal with the succulent garlic-dressed snails, finishing with hot chocolate cake that was creamy, moist, and a delight.

Storg. 29. ℂ **33-07-16-00.** Reservations recommended. Main courses 149NOK–230NOK ($20–$31). AE, DC, MC, V. Mon–Thurs 4–10pm; Fri–Sat 4–11pm; Sun 2–10pm. Closed Dec 23–Jan 15.

HORTEN AFTER DARK

Pavilion, Storgata 29 (ℂ **33-07-16-02**), is a glass building with a large outdoor terrace, holding up to 400 patrons on a good night in summer. You must be 25 years of age to enter, and the revelers flock here to dance and have a good time. It's a semiformal place, with most of the men in shirts and ties. There is no cover charge, although you'll pay 73NOK ($9.70) for a drink. The music is the latest recorded version from America or the Continent. Open daily 11am to 2am.

Lace, Storgata 29 (ℂ **33-07-16-02**), right next door to Pavillion, offers two dance floors. Lace is much more informal, and attracts the serious party crowd. Most of the patrons range in age from 18 to 30. They have very good DJs and a dramatic lighting system. The cover is 75NOK ($10) and the club is only open Friday to Saturday from 10pm to 2am.

A SIDE TRIP FROM HORTEN: ÅSGÅRDSTRAND

In one lazy afternoon you can explore the little coastal town of Åsgårdstrand on the doorway of Horten. The town achieved fame in the 17th century when shipping and sailing companies were based here. In time it was discovered by artists, including Edvard Munch, Scandinavia's most famous painter. He found inspiration along the coast for some of his best-known works.

Today you can still visit Lykkehuset (Munch's Little House), at Edvard Munch Gate 25 (© 33-08-53-72), a summer house and studio where Munch spent seven summers. Today it's been turned into a museum of Munch memorabilia. When Munch died in 1944, the house remained as it was—basically a primitive fisherman's cabin that the artist had purchased in 1897. It was here that he painted his masterful *Girls on the Bridge, Dance of Life,* and *Melancholy.* Called "the handsomest man in Norway" at the time, the artist is said to have taken advantage of his good looks to romance the local girls during his summer sojourns here. The house is open June to August Tuesday to Sunday 11am to 5pm, and May and September on Saturday and Sunday from 11am to 7pm. Admission is 40NOK ($5.30).

WHERE TO STAY

Åsgårdstrand Hotell   We like this hotel because it lies near the harbor and its rooms open onto scenic seascapes. This stone-and-wood hotel was constructed in 1931, on the site of an earlier hotel. This well-run businessperson's hotel has bedrooms in different sizes. All of them are comfortably furnished in a modern style and well maintained. Each has an immaculately kept private bathroom, half of them with tubs, the rest with showers. The standard on-site restaurant is mainly for the convenience of guests. Nonguests are better off dining at one of the other recommended hotels or restaurants in Horton, which is nearby.

Havnegata 6, N-3167 Åsgårdstrand. © 33-08-10-40. Fax 33-08-10-77. www.asgardstrand-hotell.no. 73 units. 895NOK–1,195NOK ($119–$159) double; 1,800NOK ($239) suite. AE, DC, MC, V. Closed Dec 20–Jan 3. **Amenities:** Restaurant; bar; sauna; laundry service; dry cleaning. *In room:* TV, minibar, hair dryer.

6 Tønsberg: The First Settlement ⊛

102km (64 miles) S of Oslo

Bordering the western bank of the Oslofjord, Tønsberg is Norway's oldest town. And just how old is it? No one is certain. But documentation—including the *Saga of Harald Hårfagre* by Snorre Sturluson—puts the date in 871, when King Harald Fairhair united parts of the country, and the Viking town became a royal coronation site

The Viking ships *Gokstad* and *Oseberg,* on display in Oslo's Bygdøy peninsula, were discovered at a site near Tønsberg. King Olav of Vestfold and King Sigrød of Trøndelag, both killed in battle, have their tombs at Haugar.

In the Middle Ages, Tønsberg became a major Hanseatic trading post for eastern Norway, with links to Rostock along the Baltic. In the 1600s it was known as a major port in eastern Norway, worthy of Bergen in the west.

By the mid-1800s, Tønsberg was a port for whalers in the Arctic and Antarctic Seas, rivaling Sandefjord (see below). It was also the headquarters of Svend Foyn, known as the "father of Norwegian sealing and whaling."

Tønsberg consists of a historic area, filled with old clapboard-sided houses, and a commercial center with a marketplace. The 104-sq.-km (40-sq.-mile) town has some 32,000 residents.

Svend Foyn, who invented modern whaling and seal hunting, was born here.

ESSENTIALS

GETTING THERE   By Train   Trains depart for Tønsberg from Oslo's main railway station (℃ **81-50-08-88**) at intervals of between 60 and 90 minutes from 6am to 11:30pm every day, requiring a travel time of about 90 minutes and a fare of 160NOK ($21) each way. The railway station is in the town center. For information and schedules, call ℃ **33-35-02-00** or visit www.nsb.no.

By Bus   There is no NOR bus service from Oslo.

By Car   Take Route 18 south from Oslo via Drammen.

VISITOR INFORMATION   Tønsberg **Tourist Information** is at Nedre Langgate 36B, N-3100 Tønsberg (℃ **33-35-02-00**). It's open in July daily 10am to 5:30pm; and from August to June, Monday to Friday 8:30am to 4pm. A little tourist kiosk on the island of Tjøme provides information in July, daily from 11am to 5pm.

SEEING THE SIGHTS

We recommend a ride on the historic ship **MS *Kysten I*** (℃ **33-31-25-89**), which was constructed in Trondheim back in 1909. One of the oldest steamships in Norway, the MS *Kysten I* cruises in summer through the skerries south of Tønsberg. Trips last 3½ hours and cost 120NOK ($16) for adults or 10NOK ($1.35) for seniors and children. Departures are from Honnørbryggen, the jetty lying to the north of the tourist office. When the weather's fair, cruises depart at noon daily.

Slottsfjellet, a huge hill fortress near the train station, is touted as "the Acropolis of Norway." It has only some meager ruins, and most people visit for the view from the 1888 lookout tower, **Slottsfjelltårnet** (℃ **33-31-18-72**), rising 17m (56 ft.). It's open May 18 to June 23, Monday to Friday from 10am to 3pm; June 24 to August 18, daily from 11am to 6pm; August 19 to September 15, Saturday and Sunday from noon to 5pm; September 16 to 29, Saturday and Sunday from noon to 3pm. Admission is 20NOK ($2.65) for adults, 10NOK ($1.35) for children.

Nordbyen is the old, scenic part of town, with well-preserved houses. **Haugar** cemetery, at Møllebakken, is in the center of town. It contains the Viking graves of King Harald's sons, Olav and Sigrød.

Sem Church, Hageveien 32 (℃ **33-36-93-99**), the oldest church in Vestfold, was built of stone in the Romanesque style around 1100. It's open Tuesday to Friday from 9am to 2pm; but inquire at the vestry if it's not open during these hours. Admission is free.

Another attraction is **Fjerdingen,** a street of charming restored houses near the mountain farmstead. Tønsberg was also a Hanseatic town during the Middle Ages, and some houses have been redone in typical Hanseatic style—wooden buildings constructed along the wharfs as warehouses to receive goods from fellow Hanseatic League members.

Haugar Vestfold Kunstmuseum ✦   Tønsberg's art museum lies in the center of town in a building from 1918. (Nearby are two Viking grave sites, said to hold the bodies of Olaf and Sigrød, sons of the king, Hårald Hårfagre.) The collection consists of some 130 pieces of art. One wing of the museum is devoted to the paintings of Odd Nerdrum, an internationally famous figurative painter known as "the Rembrandt of Norway." Some of his best-known works include *Man Imitating Cloud, Woman with Doorknob,* and *Hermaphrodite.*

Gråbrødragate 17. © 33-30-76-70. Admission 40NOK ($5.30). June–Aug Mon–Sat 11am–5pm, Sat–Sun noon–5pm; Sept–May Tues–Fri 11am–4pm, Sat–Sun noon–5pm.

Vestfold Fylkesmuseum Lying at the foot of Slottsfjellet, this museum contains many Viking and whaling treasures. One of the chief sights is the skeleton of a blue whale, the largest mammal the world has ever known, sometimes weighing 150 tons. There's also a Viking ship, the *Klastad* from Tjolling, built about A.D. 800.

In the rural section of the museum, visit the **Vestfold Farm,** which includes a 1600 house from Hynne, a timbered barn from Bøen, and a storehouse from Fadum (with the characteristic apron, or platform). The Heierstadloft (about 1350) is the oldest preserved timbered building in Vestfold, and there's a smithy with a charcoal shed, a grain-drying house, and a mountain farmstead.

You can have lunch here at a real mountain farmstead. A typical meal includes *rømmergrøt* (porridge made with sour cream) and other farm foods. The area is perfect for a picnic.

Frammannsveien 30. © 33-31-29-19. Admission 30NOK ($4) adults, 20NOK ($2.65) children. Mid-May to mid-Sept Mon–Sat 10am–5pm, Sun and holidays noon–5pm; closed mid-Sept to mid-May.

WHERE TO STAY

Best Western Grand Hotel ⭐ This is a first-class hotel with an elaborate exterior, a reminder of the hotel's pretensions when it was constructed in 1931. In 1992 the hotel underwent major modifications and improvements. Lying in the center of town, directly south of Hauger, this well-run and inviting hotel caters to an equal mixture of business clients and travelers. Rooms are comfortably contemporary, each with a midsize bathroom with shower (eight also contain bathtubs). A pullout sofa is available for a third guest in a room. Suites come with Jacuzzis. On site, you'll find both a casual restaurant and more formal dining.

Øvre Langgate 65–67, N-3100 Tønsberg. © 33-35-35-00. Fax 33-35-35-01. www.bestwestern.com. 70 units. 850NOK–1,090NOK ($113–$145) double; 1,110NOK–1,310NOK ($148–$174) suite. Rates include continental breakfast. AE, DC, MC, V. Closed Dec 20–Jan 3. **Amenities:** 2 restaurants; bar; limited room service; laundry service; dry cleaning. *In room:* TV, minibar, hair dryer.

Hotel Maritim Last renovated in 2000, this 1955 hotel offers a lot of modern comfort at an affordable price, a 10-minute walk east of the rail station on the main pedestrian street. Located on a square, beside the ruins of the Church of St. Olav, the hotel occupies a five-story building with the reception area on

---

⌒*Moments* Going to the End of the World

In just a half-hour drive you can leave Tønsberg and travel to a marvelously panoramic spot the locals called **Verdens Ende** ⭐, or "World's End." It lies at the southernmost tip of Tjøme, the southernmost island among the low-lying islands and skerries jutting out into the Oslofjord where it empties into the sea. If you don't have a car, take bus 101 from Tønsberg; the ride takes 45 minutes and costs 40NOK ($5.30) one-way. Once here, you'll see a 17th-century "fire basket lighthouse." Actually, the original is gone and this is a copy from 1932.

the third floor. Each room is well furnished and has a color scheme that rivals the spring flowers of Norway. Some of the rooms are quite large. Each comes with a small bathroom with shower. A good restaurant, Fregatten, is on the ground floor. The staff can arrange boat trips or bikes for guests. This hotel is owned and operated by one of Norway's seamen's associations.

Storgaten 17, N-3126 Tønsberg. ℂ 33-31-71-00. Fax 33-31-72-52. www.hotellmaritim.no. 34 units. 850NOK–950NOK ($113–$126) double; 1,100NOK–1,300NOK ($146–$173) suite. Rates include continental breakfast. AE, DC, MC, V. Closed Dec 22–Jan 5 and 4 days at Easter. **Amenities:** Restaurant; bar; laundry service; dry cleaning. *In room:* TV, minibar, hair dryer.

Quality Hotel Tønsberg   This is one of the best hotels in the area. Opening in 2002, the five-story structure is the latest hotel to grace the cityscape of Tønsberg. Its bedrooms are large and most of them open onto views of the fjord. All of them are decorated in pastels and most have carpeting. Two dozen without carpeting are set aside for those suffering from allergies. Each bedroom comes with an immaculately kept private bathroom with shower. Typical Norwegian food is served at the on-site restaurant.

Ollebukta 3, N-3126 Tønsberg. ℂ 800/228-5151 or 33-00-41-00. Fax 33-00-41-01. www.choicehotels.com. 239 units. 850NOK–1,590NOK ($113–$211) double; 1,850NOK–2,590NOK ($246–$344) suite. Children under 5 stay free. Rates include continental breakfast. AE, DC, MC, V. **Amenities:** Restaurant; bar; pool; fitness center; sauna; laundry service; dry cleaning. *In room:* TV, minibar, hair dryer, safe.

WHERE TO DINE

Brygga CONTINENTAL/NORWEGIAN   This is a rustic-looking restaurant with an outdoor terrace opening onto a harbor view. The Norwegian-style decor includes light gray tones and light-colored woods; the walls hung with paintings by a local artist. During the week, Brygga feels like a pub, especially when soccer matches are shown on a big TV screen. The chefs try to please most palates, offering everything from the town's best pizzas to dishes Mrs. Claus serves to Santa—notably filet of reindeer and moose. We prefer their shellfish dishes, recently enjoying their seafood salad studded with shrimp among other delectable items. If you like meat, the chefs will prepare you an excellent beefsteak with béarnaise sauce and a salad.

Nedre Langgate 35. ℂ 33-31-12-70. Reservations recommended. Main courses 150NOK–250NOK ($20–$33). AE, DC, DISC, MC, V. Daily 11:30am–3am.

Himmel & Hav NORWEGIAN/INTERNATIONAL   This minimalist-style cafe, decorated in bright colors, draws the discerning palates of Tønsberg. Some of the specialties would never make the menu of a Greenpeace luncheon: whale steak, for example, or even reindeer. Their whale specialty is called "Free Willy." The filet of reindeer is flavored with fresh thyme and aquavit and served in a savory red wine sauce. Their surf and turf is filet of beef, sautéed with bacon and served with scampi in a Madagascar pepper sauce. This year the filet of halibut won us over. During the day music plays in the Café del Mar.

Brygge. ℂ 33-00-49-80. Reservations required. Main courses 70NOK–180NOK ($9.30–$24) at lunch, 210NOK–290NOK ($28–$39) at dinner. AE, DC, MC, V. Mon–Thurs 11am–11pm; Fri–Sun 11am–3:30am.

Santorini Hanverkeren GREEK/NORWEGIAN   In an 1890 clapboard-sided house, this establishment lures with a tastefully decorated dining room and a summer cafe. The atmosphere is cozy and romantic, lying in the center of town but only 200m (656 ft.) from the sea. It's a relaxed atmosphere, drawing both businesspeople and local families. The chefs are adept at using shrimp, giving it the Greek touch as an appetizer with feta cheese and fresh tomatoes. For a main course, the calamari was a satisfying choice with pan-fried potatoes and a dip. Prime ingredients go into such dishes as filet of beef in a cognac cream sauce or else a pepper sauce and the roast lamb in the chef's special secret sauce. The dessert specialty is a lavish dish of ice cream flambéed with cognac. On Friday and Saturday nights, Greek music rules the joint after 9pm.

Mollergate 6. ℂ **33-31-23-88.** Reservations recommended. Main courses 140NOK–220NOK ($19–$29). MC, V. Tues–Thurs 3–11pm; Fri–Sat 3pm–2am; Sun 2–10pm. July–Aug opens at 11am. Closed Dec 23–Jan 3.

7 Sandefjord

125km (78 miles) S of Oslo; 24km (15 miles) S of Tønsberg

In the Middle Ages, this was one of the most famous stamping grounds of the Vikings. Its natural harbor along a 9.75km (6-mile) fjord made it the whaling capital of the world at one time. A monument remains at the harbor to the once prosperous whaling industry, which made Sandefjord the richest city in Norway. Today, it has built up the third largest merchant fleet in Norway.

Sandefjord attracts summer visitors seeking fun on its 115 islands, its archipelago, and its many beaches. Locals call the town "Bathing City" (*Badebyen* in Norwegian). Yachties from Oslo also fill up the harbor in summer after having sailed through the skerries.

On a summer day we always like to stroll along its waterfront, enjoying the fresh salt air and the beautiful parks and gardens. You'll see a magnificent compound of buildings constructed in 1899 in the dragon motif so popular in Norway. The baths were closed in 1940 at the beginning of the Nazi occupation and the site today is the civic center.

ESSENTIALS

GETTING THERE   The country's second busiest international airport is **Sandefjord Airport Torp** (ℂ **33-42-70-00**). Some budget airlines such as Good Jet and Ryanair use this smaller airport rather than the one in Oslo. In addition to its air link, there is a daily **ferry connection** to Ströstad, Sweden, taking 2½ hours. For schedules and information, call **Scandi Line,** Tollbugata 5 (ℂ **33-46-08-00**).

From Oslo there are several **express trains** reaching Sandefjord in 2 hours. For information and schedules, call ℂ **81-50-08-88.** Frequent **buses** also run between Oslo and Sandefjord daily, and there are also good bus connections between Tønsberg and Sandefjord.

VISITOR INFORMATION   The **Sandefjord Tourist Information Office** is at Torvet (ℂ **33-46-05-90**). In summer it's open Monday to Friday 9am to 6pm, Saturday 10am to 4pm, and Sunday noon to 4pm. Off-season it's open only Monday to Friday 8:30am to 4pm.

SEEING THE SIGHTS

Lying off Storgata, **Commander Christensen's Whaling Museum,** Museumsgaten 39 (ℂ **33-48-46-50**), has a life-size replica of a mighty **blue whale** ★, its tongue alone weighing 3½ tons. The museum records the controversial whaling industry that nearly drove this mammoth sea beast to extinction. In the heyday of whaling, as you learn, Sandefjord sent out vast "floating factories" to process the whale meat and its byproducts. Admission is 25NOK ($3.35) for adults, 10NOK ($1.35) for ages 7 to 17, and free 6 and under. From May to August, it's open daily 11am to 5pm; September daily 11am to 4pm, off-season Monday to Saturday 11am to 3pm and Sunday noon to 4pm.

The other museum of note is also nautical and is open only by appointment (check at the whaling museum, above). **Sandefjords Sjøfartsmuseum (Sandefjord Maritime Museum)** documents Sandefjord's centuries-old link to the sea, on which the town once depended for its survival. Especially intriguing are the sailing ships of the 1800s. The admission is the same as for the whaling museum. However, all participants must hire a guide, costing 400NOK ($53) for everybody. The cost can be shared.

OUTDOOR PURSUITS

After all this maritime history, you too can head for the water if the day is fair. The best beach, **Langeby,** lies 7km (4¼ miles) from the center, and buses from Sandefjord go there hourly. If you don't like Langeby, you'll find dozens of other beaches along the 146km (90-mile) coastline.

The area is a popular site for scuba divers. The best outfitter is **Neptun Dykkersenter,** Kilgaten (℃ **33-46-14-90**), which will rent all the equipment needed to qualified divers.

WHERE TO STAY

Comfort Home Hotel Atlantic ★ *(Kids)*   Built on the site of an older structure, this hotel respected its 1914 origins in its new design. The tasteful interior takes the whaling theme as its motif. Bedrooms have sleek modern styling, and each comes with a private bathroom with shower (six units also have a tub). Suites have their own fireplaces and Jacuzzis, and three rooms are equipped for persons with disabilities. Children under 4 stay free, and children 4 to 16 pay half price if staying in their parent's room. The on-site restaurant serves a light supper in the evening that is free to guests; visitors pay 90NOK ($12).

Jernbanealleen 3, N-3200 Sandefjord. ℃ **33-42-80-00.** Fax 33-42-81-00. www.choicehotels.com. 111 units. 980NOK–1,300NOK ($130–$173) double; 1,465NOK–1,795NOK ($195–$239) suite. Rates include continental breakfast. AE, DC, MC, V. **Amenities:** Restaurant; sauna; laundry service; dry cleaning. *In room:* TV, minibar, hair dryer.

Hotel Kong Carl   This is an old favorite. Near the town center and marketplace, this white clapboard-sided house dates from 1690 and has been an inn since 1721. But it's refurbished frequently, the last major one in 2002. The hotel's cathedral-ceilinged annex is used extensively as a conference center. The bedrooms are simply but comfortably furnished, and come in a wide range of sizes. Most of the accommodations are partially furnished with antiques. All the rooms have midsize private bathrooms, all with shower (five also contain a tub). Lunch and dinner in a regional restaurant, costing 100NOK ($13), is served Monday to Saturday; you can also enjoy a beer on the summer terrace.

Torvgaten 9, N-3201 Sandefjord. ℃ **33-46-31-17.** Fax 33-46-31-19. www.KongCarl.no. 29 units. 850NOK–1,250NOK ($113–$166) double. Children under 5 stay free. Rates include continental breakfast. AE, DC, MC, V. Closed Dec 20–Jan 2 and 1 week at Easter. **Amenities:** Restaurant; limited room service; laundry service; dry cleaning. *In room:* TV.

Rica Park Hotel ★   This is the most stylish, comfortable, and prestigious hotel in the region. Although a chain, this hotel offers personal service. It's idyllically located overlooking the harbor and a city meadow. Each bedroom is furnished with rich fabrics, thick carpeting, and comfortable furnishings. Dark wood pieces stand in contrast to the pastel-colored walls. Originally built in 1958, the entire hotel was refurbished in 2002. Bathrooms are completely up to date and well equipped, with three-fourths of them having a tub as well as a shower. Many locals attend the hotel's gourmet restaurant, Park Garden, for special occasions. Even if you're not a guest, consider dropping in for entertainment. During the summer live shows are staged here with local bands, international artists, and Norwegian cabaret acts.

Strand Promenaden 9, N-3201 Sandefjord. ℂ **33-44-74-00**. Fax 33-44-75-00. www.rica.no. 240 units. 980NOK–1,400NOK ($130–$186) double; 2,000NOK ($266) suite. AE, DC, MC, V. **Amenities:** 2 restaurants; bar; nightclub; saltwater pool; fitness center; sauna; babysitting; laundry service; dry cleaning. *In room:* A/C, TV, minibar, hair dryer, safe.

WHERE TO DINE

Solvold's ★★★ FRENCH/ASIAN FUSION   This is one of the best restaurants along Oslofjord. The chef, Odd Ivar Solvold, has won three national culinary championships, and he certainly deserves his prices and acclaim. For this new building, the chef chose Sven Lund as his architect, the same man who also designs for the king of Norway.

The dining is quite formal, and the wine cellar is on the same floor as the dining area. Foodies celebrate Solvold for his seafood, and he secures the finest catches. His lemon-baked turbot with a carrot and coriander cream is a prize-winning dish indeed, as is his pan-fried seawater crayfish with a crayfish emulsion. Savor his filet of tuna, or else opt for a meat course, none better than the rack of venison in a tangerine sauce. For dessert, we were recently enthralled by his caramelized hazelnut and pistachio custard. Attached to Solvold's is Smak, a less formal restaurant, featuring international dishes such as carpaccio, paella, and sushi.

Thor Dalsgate 9. ℂ **33-46-27-41**. Reservations required. Main courses 225NOK–285NOK ($30–$38). AE, DC, MC, V. Tues–Sat 6pm–1am.

Café 4u.no SANDWICHES   This Internet cafe is one of the most popular places in town for young people. It can also be a light luncheon stopover as you check up on your e-mail, a service that costs 25NOK ($3.35) per half-hour, or 40NOK ($5.30) per hour. A selection of freshly made soups, sandwiches, cakes, along with beer and wine, is available. It's becoming quite a hangout for the area, and background music plays constantly.

Torvet 5. ℂ **33-42-94-98**. Sandwiches 40NOK–55NOK ($5.30–$7.30); coffee from 15NOK ($2). No credit cards. Mon–Fri 8am–6pm; Sat 10am–4pm; Sun noon–5pm.

7

Lillehammer & the Peer Gynt Road

Lying to the east of the western fjord district, eastern central Norway is the virtual playground of Scandinavia, embracing the greatest national parks, the fabled ski resort at Lillehammer, and some of the nation's most panoramic scenery. At times it may seem remote and distant but much of it is within an easy 1- or 2-hour drive to the immediate south of Oslo.

This chapter will guide you on a journey to some of Norway's highest mountain peaks, which are a hiker's paradise in summer and an outdoor ski area in winter.

In addition to its many resorts, this section of Norway is also filled with hidden gems such as the town of Røros, a former copper-mining site that is now preserved as a UNESCO World Heritage Site.

Who knows? When touring the area, you might even meet up with the rare musk ox. But keep your distance and admire him from afar. If threatened, the shaggy creature can come charging at the rate of 60km (37 miles) an hour.

1 Hamar: Gateway to Lake Mjøsa

134km (83 miles) N of Oslo; 58km (36 miles) SE of Lillehammer

Located on the large and scenic Lake Mjøsa, Hamar is the capital of Hedmark County and a bit of a rival of Lillehammer for the winter sports enthusiast. It makes a good stopover en route from Oslo to Lillehammer, but also has many attractions in its own right if you'd like to base yourself here and drive up to the more crowded Lillehammer.

In the Middle Ages, Hamar was the seat of a bishopric, and some ecclesiastical ruins remain from those glory days. Hamar was also the home of Kirsten Flagstad, one of the world's most famous operatic sopranos back in the days when "soprano" suggested something other than a hit TV show.

Hamar's Viking ship–shaped ice-skating hall was the site of skating events during the 1994 Winter Olympics.

ESSENTIALS

GETTING THERE Frequent trains run between Oslo and Hamar, costing 180NOK ($24) one-way and taking 1¼ hours. Nor-Way Bussekspress runs daily from Oslo. Motorists take the E north from Oslo until they see the signposted turnoff for Hamar.

VISITOR INFORMATION The local tourist office is at Torggata 1 (© 62-52-12-17), open May 15 to August 30 daily from 8am to 5pm. In off-season, it is open Monday to Friday 8am to 4pm.

Moments **Sailing on Norway's Oldest Paddle Steamer**

The best way to travel to Hamar is aboard the world's oldest paddle steamer, *Skibladner* (© **62-62-70-85**), which calls not only at Hamar but also at Eidsvoll and Lillehammer, among other points. The ship was built in 1854 and is still in good shape, stretching 50m (165 ft.) long and measuring 5m (17 ft.) wide. It has a cruising speed of 12 knots, and sails from the middle of May to September. On board is a luxurious 70-seat restaurant that's fully licensed and serves regional specialties. The most popular route is between Hamar and Lillehammer, taking 4 hours and costing 220NOK ($29) per person one-way. Ask about jazz evenings aboard the steamer; a night's entertainment goes for 400NOK ($53), including food.

SEEING THE SIGHTS

Hamar Olympiahall This modern sports arena hosted events during the 1994 Winter Olympics. It is built in the shape of a Viking ship, lying within walking distance of the town center. Today it is the site of numerous sports events, performances, and exhibitions, and can hold some 10,000 spectators. It's been called a "sports cathedral without equal." Visits are possible when events aren't being staged.

Åkersvikaveien. © **62-51-75-00.** Admission 20NOK ($2.65); ice-skating late July to mid-Aug 70NOK ($9.30). June 1 to mid-Aug Mon–Fri 8am-6pm, Sat–Sun 10am–6pm.

Hedmark Kunstnersenter (Hedmark Artists' Center) This restored center of art offers changing exhibitions featuring regional artists, mainly painters and sculptors. Check with the tourist office to see what's currently showing. The center is beautifully situated by Lake Mjøsa, west of town, which makes for a pleasant walk along the lake.

Parkgate 21. © **62-54-22-60.** Free admission. Mon–Fri 9am–3pm; Sat noon–3pm; Sun noon–6pm.

Hedmarksmuseet & Domkirkeodden West (1.5km/1 mile) of the town center, the ruins of the nearly 1,000-year-old Hamar Cathedral jut out into Lake Mjøsa. The sight can be reached by a scenic walk, or you can take bus 6 leaving from the Hamar Library, costing 20NOK ($2.65) one-way. These ruins are evocative and call attention to Hamar's once-important role in Norway's ecclesiastical world. The church was constructed of locally quarried limestone, with Romanesque architecture, although later additions were Gothic.

The ruins are protected by a steel-and-glass cover provided in 1998. This protective umbrella is the largest glass construction in Europe, fanning out for 2,600m (8,530 ft.). Today the ruins are used for concerts and plays in summer. Adjoining is an archaeological museum displaying artifacts found in the area, and also an open-air folk museum featuring 18th- and 19th-century houses. In an organic garden you can see nearly 400 different types of herbs.

Strandveien 100. © **62-54-27-00.** Admission 65NOK ($8.65) adults, 30NOK ($4) children, 160NOK ($21) family ticket. May 18–June 15 daily 10am–4pm; June 16–Aug 18 daily 10am–6pm; Aug 19–Sept 8 daily 10am–4:30pm.

Kirsten Flagstad Museum If you've never heard the music of Norway's greatest opera diva, Kirsten Flagstad (1895–1962), it's worth it to come here and listen to her operatic recording in a special room. This museum of Flagstad memorabilia lies 46m (50 yards) from the marketplace and a 10-minute walk

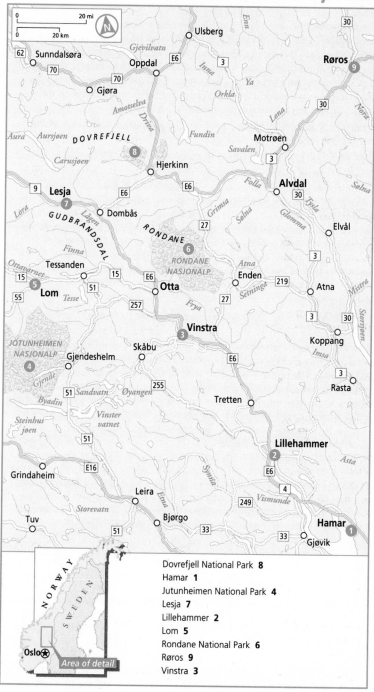

0 | 20 mi
0 | 20 km

Sunndalsøra 62 70

Gjøra 70

Oppdal E6

Ulsberg

Gjevilvatn
Enn
Inna
Ya
Orkla

Røros 9

30

30

Nora

Amotselva

Drina

Aura
Aursjøen DOVREFJELL 8

Carusjøen

Hjerkinn

Fundin

Motrøen

Savalen
3

Alvdal 30

Elvål

Follა
Tjela
Sølna

9 Lesja 7

Dombås

E6

E6

GUDBRANDSDAL
Lågen
Lora

Grimsa

RONDANE

27

Sølna

Glomma

3

Finna
Tessanden

Ottavarnet
15

15

15

E6

Otta

RONDANE
NASJONALP. 6

Atna

Enden 219

Atna

Mistra

55 Lom 5

51

Tesse

257

Frya
Setninga
27

3

30

Storsjøen

Vinstra 3

Koppang

JOTUNHEIMEN
NASJONALP. 4

Gjendeshelm

Gjende

Skåbu

E6

Imsa

Byadin

51

Sandvatn

Øyangen 255

Tretten

3

Rasta

Steinhus-
sjøen

Vinster-
vatnet

51

Lillehammer 2

Asta

Grindaheim

E16

Symna

E6

4

Tuv

Storevatn

Leira

Etna

Bjørgo

51

33

249

Vismunde

33

Hamar 1

Gjøvik

NORWAY
SWEDEN

Oslo

Area of detail

from the rail station. On the ground floor you can purchase records, books about the star, and souvenirs. A special costume room is of particular interest because the Metropolitan Opera contributed some of the gowns that Kirsten wore in her most famous performances. Memorabilia and photographs, including the star's private albums, letters, contracts, and magazine and newspaper publicity round out the exhibit. The collection of recordings here is the largest Flagstad trove in the world, covering her entire career from her first recordings in 1914 to her last memorable recordings in San Francisco.

Kirkegate 11. ✆ **62-53-32-77.** Admission 50NOK ($6.65) adults, 30NOK ($4) children. June 24–Aug 20 Wed–Sun 11am–4pm. Closed Aug 21–June 23.

NSB Jernbanemuseet (National Railway Museum)   This museum, established in 1896 on the shores of Lake Mjøsa, collects and displays bits of Norwegian rail history dating from its beginnings in the 1850s. Vehicles include models from 1861 to 1950, among them three royal coaches and several steam locomotives weighing up to 150 tons. There is a museum park with several station buildings, railway tracks, and other exhibits, as well as a "dining car" serving snacks and refreshments. A small train travels along the grounds of the amusement park.

Strandveien 132. ✆ **62-51-31-60.** Admission 40NOK ($5.30) adults, 30NOK ($4) children. May 29–June and Aug–Sept 18 daily 10am–4pm; July daily 10am–6pm. Closed Sept 19–May 28. Take bus no. 1 from the railway station or walk 30 min. from the town center going north along the shore of Lake Mjøsa.

WHERE TO STAY

First Hotel Victoria   Set between the edge of the lake and the town's main pedestrian shopping street, this hotel originated in the 1850s as a small inn, and grew over the years into the seven-story, modern-looking, gray-sided chain hotel you'll see today. Parts of it are rather grand, especially some of the paneled, big-windowed public rooms whose deep sofas evoke a well-upholstered room in a private home or social club. Three of the rooms sport a frilly decor that the staff defines as "feminine-looking." The remainder are soothing, contemporary, monochromatic, and favored by (usually male) business travelers from other parts of Scandinavia. Most of the bathrooms have tile shower-bath combinations; about half have only showers.

The hotel restaurant, large, contemporary, attractively formal, and outfitted with large windows, is open daily for lunch and dinner.

Strandgata 21, N-2317 Hamar. ✆ **62-02-55-00.** Fax 62-53-32-23. www.first-hotel-victoria.no. 115 units. Mon–Thurs 1,253NOK ($167) double, 1,700NOK ($226) suite; Fri–Sun and mid-June to mid-Aug daily 853NOK ($113) double, 1,500NOK ($200) suite. Rates include breakfast. AE, DC, MC, V. **Amenities:** Restaurant; bar; limited room service; babysitting; laundry service; dry cleaning. *In room:* TV, minibar.

Quality Hotel Astoria ✦   Originally built in the early 1970s in the commercial center of town, this hotel was radically renovated in the late 1990s into a clean, well-managed, middle-bracket enclave of efficiency and warmth. Because of its recent renovations, it promotes itself as "the newest hotel in town." All rooms have a writing table, comfortable, contemporary-looking furniture, and a monochromatic color scheme, depending on the floor it's on, of pale yellow, green, or soft red. Each of the tile-sheathed bathrooms has at least a shower, and about half have shower-tub combinations. The in-house restaurant, the Pepperk-vaerna Mat & Vinhus, is separately recommended in "Where to Dine," below.

Torggata 23, N-2317 Hamar. ✆ **62-70-70-00.** Fax 62-70-70-01. http://choicehotels.no/html/no266799.jsp. 78 units. Mon–Thurs 980NOK–1,350NOK ($130–$180) double; Fri–Sun and June 20–Aug 20 daily 820NOK–920NOK ($109–$122) double. Rates include breakfast. AE, DC, MC, V. Nearby parking 60NOK ($8). **Amenities:** Restaurant; cocktail bar; the "Dirty Nelly" pub; nightclub; disco; babysitting; laundry service; dry cleaning. *In room:* TV, minibar, iron/ironing board.

The Voice of the Century

Kirsten Flagstad (1895–1962), who has a museum of memorabilia dedicated to her in Hamar, remains one of the all-time legends of opera. Interpreting the operas of Henry Purcell or Richard Wagner, among other composers, Flagstad had no equal in her day. At the age of 40, she was planning to retire but was invited to perform at New York's Metropolitan Opera on February 2, 1935. The rest is history. Her performance was broadcast across Canada and the United States, and it created a sensation, music critics labeling her "The Voice of the Century." Her Brunhild in San Francisco ensured her lasting fame in America. Along with Lauritz Melchior, Flagstad is credited with keeping the Metropolitan Opera alive in New York during its difficult days of the Depression on the eve of World War II.

Her popularity waned when she returned to Nazi-occupied Norway to be with her husband, Henry Johansen. It was a naive decision that would harm her incredible popularity in the United States for the rest of her life. During the war, she never sang for the Germans. But her husband, Johansen, in ill health, was arrested by the Norwegians at the end of the war and labeled a war profiteer, even though he'd aided the Allied resistance. He died a year later.

On Flagstad's return to postwar America, a political campaign, labeled in the press as one of "extreme vituperation," was waged against her. Demonstrations marred each one of her performances in New York and San Francisco. Nevertheless, her devoted fans still clung to her. At age 54, when most divas are in retirement, Flagstad continued to perform with the San Francisco Opera, scoring some of her greatest successes with *Tristan und Isolde* and *die Walküre*. During the tragic years of the war, her voice had "darkened" and lost some of its brilliant upper register. But all of her concerts were still sold out by die-hard fans.

Fortunately, her recorded voice remains to win new generations of fans among opera lovers. Many music critics now hail her as "the Diva of the 20th century." Flagstad's recorded voice has become "immortal," glowing with richness, power, and an expressiveness that is not only beautiful but also intensely dramatic.

WHERE TO DINE

Bykjeller'n NORWEGIAN/INTERNATIONAL   This is the largest and most imaginative dining, drinking, and disco venue in Hamar. It was built in 1849 as an inn, and the high-ceilinged interior was transformed into its present incarnation in the 1970s. Many visitors never get beyond the street-level pub, whose thick beams and rustic artifacts make up the setting for foaming mugs of beer, and pub items that include salads, pizzas, sandwiches, and meal-sized platters of fish, steak, pasta, and game. In summer, a beer garden sprawls out into what used to be a stable yard in back. Relatively elaborate dining is available in the stone-vaulted cellar, which was originally conceived as a coal cellar, and which today is artfully illuminated with a mixture of candles and electric lights. Menu items vary with the seasons, but are likely to include lutefisk (especially at

Christmas); sausages and meatballs; pork spare ribs in barbecue sauce; smoked, dried, and thin-sliced mutton; tenderloin steaks; and venison with port wine sauce. There's a disco on the top floor of the restaurant, floored with massive oaken planks and ringed with a wraparound mezzanine that's favored by voyeurs who gaze down at the dancers and the flirts who try to engage them in conversation. The disco is open Friday and Saturday nights from 10pm to 3am. There's a cover charge of 90NOK ($12) that's imposed only on Saturday (not on Fri). Entrance to the disco is free for anyone who dines in the cellar.

Torggata 82. © **62-54-31-00.** Reservations recommended Fri–Sat. Main courses 67NOK–150NOK ($8.90–$20) at lunch, 180NOK–250NOK ($24–$33) at dinner. AE, DC, MC, V. Street-level pub daily 11am–10:30pm. Dinner in cellar-level restaurant daily 6–10:30pm. Disco Fri–Sat 10pm–3am.

Mrs. Sippy's Biffhuset STEAKS/AMERICAN   The most popular steak-house in town lies a short walk from the railway station, within a large and cozy room paneled with dark wood, ringed with leather-upholstered booths, and illuminated with candles and hanging Tiffany-imitation lamps. The menu includes the kind of two-fisted comfort food that tastes fantastic on long dark nights in this cold climate—including some of the items you might have expected in an American steakhouse on Super Bowl Sunday. Examples include New York–style buffalo chicken wings with hot sauce and garlic dip; cream of shellfish soup that's celebrated as some of the best in town; carpaccio of beef tenderloin with arugula and fresh-shaved Parmesan; and an excellent version of New Orleans–style blackened sirloin served with coleslaw and baked potatoes. There's also a fine version of Norwegian catfish with bacon. The house-style dessert that most diners, according to the staff, can't seem to resist is the raspberry cheesecake drizzled with chocolate sauce.

Torggata 3. © **62-53-52-00.** Reservations recommended. Main courses 169NOK–329NOK ($22–$44). AE, DC, MC, V. Sun–Thurs 4–10pm; Fri–Sat 4–11pm.

Pepperkvaerna Mat & Vinhus NORWEGIAN/INTERNATIONAL   The "peppercorn" is the most popular, among locals, of the hotel restaurants of Hamar. Part of its allure derives from the cozy, wine house/tavern decor (paneling, candlelight, and rustic artifacts), and part of it derives from savory preparations of such local ingredients as elk, beefsteak, venison, chicken, and veal. The menu changes with the season, but on the night of our last visit, the best specialties included breast of duck with a honey-flavored blackberry sauce; grilled steak with a brandy, mushroom, and cream sauce; and grilled filets of catfish with coriander and lime. Desserts might include a moist slice of unbelievably fattening chocolate cake.

In the Quality Hotel Astoria, Torggata 23. © **62-70-70-00.** Reservations recommended Fri–Sat. Main courses 95NOK–250NOK ($13–$33). AE, DC, MC, V. Mon–Sat 4–11pm.

HAMAR AFTER DARK

For the largest drinking and dining venue in town, refer to Bykjeller'n under "Where to Dine," above.

The well-attended **Irishman Pub,** Strandgata 31 (© **62-52-33-92**), draws a lively crowd, usually in the 30- to 50-year-old bracket, to its 1930s-era precincts. The decor? Pictures of famous Irishmen line the walls. Recorded music plays in the background except on Friday when live music is heard. On our last visit, the singers owed massive inspiration to both The Beatles and Bob Dylan. Of course, Guinness and Irish whiskeys rule the night. Open Monday 4 to 11pm, Tuesday to Thursday 4pm to 12:30am, Friday and Saturday noon to 2am, and Sunday noon to 11pm.

At the **Nattklubben Munken,** Torgata 23 (© 62-70-70-00), a lively mixture of locals in the 20-to-35 age group come together for drinks and good times. The DJs are alternated frequently, and the latest recorded music of the western world is heard. There's a midsize dance floor that can get very crowded on drunken Friday and Saturday nights. A cover of 80NOK ($11) is imposed, and hours are Thursday to Saturday from 10pm to 2:30am.

2 Lillehammer of Olympic Glory ★★

169km (105 miles) N of Oslo; 363km (226 miles) S of Trondheim

Surrounded by mountains, Lillehammer is one of Europe's favorite resorts. The town, at the head (northern end) of Lake Mjøsa, became internationally famous when it hosted the 1994 Winter Olympics. Today, the sports sites and infrastructure benefit greatly from the two-billion-kroner investment that the government put into Lillehammer to make it worthy of the games. Skiers in winter can take advantage of many of these improvements.

Even with all its upgrades, Lillehammer's appeal still lags far behind the popularity of such chic alpine resorts as St. Moritz in Switzerland or St. Anton in Austria. Sadly, "Winter City," as Lillehammer is called, doesn't get much of that famous alpine sunshine.

However, even if you're not considering it for a ski holiday, Lillehammer is an attractive venue for summer vacationers, as it has a number of attractions and a broad appeal for families.

With a population of 23,000, Lillehammer is surrounded by forests, farms, and small settlements. Its main pedestrian street, **Storgata** ★, is known for its well-preserved wooden buildings.

At the southern end of the Gudbrandsdal valley, Lillehammer was founded as a trading post back in 1827. Over the years, Lillehammer has attracted many artists, such as Jakob Weidemann, who were drawn to its beautiful landscapes and special Nordic light. The most famous artist who lived here was Sigrid Undset, who won the Nobel Prize for literature.

ESSENTIALS

GETTING THERE **By Train** From Oslo, express trains take about 2 hours and 20 minutes, and local trains about 3 hours. Depending on the time of year, there are five to eight trains per day. Call © 81-50-08-88 for information.

By Bus Bus trips between Oslo and Lillehammer take about 2½ hours, and depart two or three times a day.

By Car Head north from Oslo along E6.

VISITOR INFORMATION The Lillehammer Tourist Office is adjacent to the railway station at Torget 2 (© 61-28-98-00). From mid-June to mid-August it is open Monday to Saturday 9am to 7pm. Off-season hours are Monday to Friday 9am to 4pm.

Value **Free Biking Around Lillehammer**

You can borrow city bikes for free, but you must post a 100NOK ($13) deposit. Bikes are parked at Servicetorget at Sigrid Undsets Plass and at the Lillehammer tourist office.

SEEING THE SIGHTS

During the peak summer season, usually June 20 to August 20, the tourist bureau schedules several excursions. These include trips to the **Maihaugen Open-Air Museum (Sandvig Collections)** and voyages on **Lake Mjøsa** aboard the *White Swan of Lake Mjøsa,* an 1850s paddle steamer. See "Sailing on Norway's Oldest Paddle Steamer," earlier in this chapter, for more details. Ask the tourist office (see "Visitor Information," above) for a list of activities.

Hunderfossen Familiepark (Hunderfossen Family Park) *Kids*   Here you'll find an interesting presentation of the most popular Norwegian fairy tales, more than 50 activities for children and adults, and lots of space to roam around. There are a merry-go-round and Ferris wheel, as well as carnival booths, a cafeteria, and a swimming pool. A 12m (40 ft.) troll at the gate welcomes visitors. The park is 12km (7½ miles) north of Lillehammer on E6.

Fåberg. © **61-27-72-22.** Admission 210NOK ($28) adults, 120NOK ($16) seniors, 175NOK ($23) children 3–14, free for children under 3. May–Sept daily 10am–8pm. Closed Oct–Apr. Bus: Hunderfossen from Lillehammer.

Lillehammer Kunstmuseum (Art Museum)   This museum, in the center of town, displays one of Norway's largest collections of national art. The pieces date from the 1830s to the present. Some of Norway's major artists are represented, including Axel Revold, Erik Werenskjold, and Christian Krogh. The many international visitors seek out works by Edvard Munch, the most famous artist in Scandinavia. The collection includes four paintings by Munch, including *Portrait of Ida Roede.* This gallery also possesses one of the biggest collections of paintings from the so-called Norwegian Romantic period. Opened in the winter of 1992, it was one of the major cultural venues during the 1994 Olympics.

Stortorget. © **61-05-44-60.** Admission 60NOK ($8) adults, 50NOK ($6.65) students and seniors, free for children under 16. June 17–Sept 2 Mon–Wed 11am–4pm, Thurs–Sun 11am–5pm; Sept 3–June 16 Tues–Sun 11am–4pm.

Maihaugen Open-Air Museum (Sandvig Collections) ★★   Many Norwegian towns have open-air museums featuring old buildings that have been moved to the site. This is the best of them. This museum consists of 180 buildings, from manor houses to the cottage of the poorest yeoman worker. There are more than 40,000 exhibits. The houses reassembled here and furnished in 17th- to 18th-century style came from all over the Gudbrandsdal (Gudbrands Valley). Of particular interest is the Garmo Stave Church, built in 1200. You can visit 37 old workshops, displaying activities ranging from gunsmithing to wood engraving. A large exhibit covers Norwegian history from 10,000 B.C. to the present. The city's concert hall is also at the museum. Two cafeterias serve Norwegian food. The museum lies about 10 minutes on foot from the town center or a 20-minute walk from the train station. Head up Jernbanegata, turn right onto Anders Sandvigs Gate, and then go left up Maihaugvegen following the signposts.

Maihaugveien 1. © **61-28-89-00.** Admission 120NOK ($16) adults, 55NOK ($7.30) children 7–15, free for children under 7. June–Aug daily 9am–6pm; May and Sept daily 10am–5pm; Oct–Apr (indoor museum only) Tues–Sun 11am–4pm. Bus: Rte. 007.

Norsk Kjøretøy-Historisk Museum (Museum of Norwegian Vehicle History)   Norway's only vehicle museum illustrates the development of transportation from the first sledges and wagons to the car of today. The most interesting, and perhaps sad, exhibitions are the cars left over from Norway's attempt to build up an automobile manufacturing industry. Norway produced the strange "Troll Car," a kissing cousin of Sweden's Saab. The last ones were made in the 1950s and are viewed as collectors' vehicles today. The museum is east of the town center; from the bus stop, head out on Elvegata.

Lilletorget 7. ⓒ 61-25-61-65. Admission 40NOK ($5.30) adults, 20NOK ($2.65) children 7–14, free for children under 7. June 15–Aug 20 daily 10am–6pm; Aug 21–June 14 Mon–Fri 11am–3pm, Sat–Sun 11am–4pm.

OLYMPIC SITES

The **Lillehammer Olympic Park** ✦✦ was the site of the 1994 games and is today one of the major centers for sports in Norway. In **Håkons Hall** there are facilities for fitness training, squash, badminton, football, handball, volleyball, and other pursuits.

Also in the hall is **Norges Olympiske Museum (Norwegian Olympic Museum),** Olympiaparken (ⓒ **61-25-21-00**), the only such museum in Scandinavia, with exhibitions not only about Lillehammer's role as host of the games in 1994, but also featuring exhibits on the entire history of the Olympics up to the present day. In all, there are some 6,000 individual exhibits, as well as movies of the games. Admission is 60NOK ($8) for adults and 30NOK ($4) for children. Open May 19 to August 31 daily from 10am to 6pm. Off-season open Tuesday to Sunday 11am to 4pm.

Lysgårdsbakkene, the ski jump tower (ⓒ **61-25-21-00**), is open daily from mid-June to mid-August 9am to 8pm, charging 15NOK ($2) for admission. You can take a chairlift to the top of the big ski jump for a **panoramic view** ✦✦ of Olympic Park and surrounding area. The chair lift costs 30NOK ($4) for adults and 25NOK ($3.35) for children.

In the upper part of the park, the **Birkebeineren Nordic Center** (ⓒ **61-26-47-00**) has areas for cross-country skiing, plus a ski lodge and a cafeteria. The **Kanthaugen Freestyle Facility** (ⓒ **61-05-42-00**) is one of the most compact facilities of its type in the world, with hills for aerials, moguls, and "ballet." Skiing instruction is offered on the ballet hill.

The **Olympic bobsled Run** (contact Lillehammer's Olympic Park; ⓒ **61-05-42-00**), is not in the park but at Hunderfossen, 15km (9¼ miles) north of the town. This is northern Europe's only artificially refrigerated bobsled and luge track. The track is 1,365m (4,478 ft.) long, and the height difference from start to finish is 114m (374 ft.). The track has 16 curves. From October to March visitors can try bobsledding or "bobrafting." The bobraft is a rubber bob that looks like a giant bathtub. Even in the warmer months from April to September you can still try the bobsled on wheels, which takes 4 passengers per trip at a speed of 100km (62 miles). Rates for the bobraft facility (winter only), bobsled run (winter only), wheeled bobraft (summer only) are the same: 160NOK ($21) per person.

OUTDOOR ACTIVITIES

Hafjell Alpine Center (ⓒ **61-27-47-00**), the main venue for Olympic alpine competitions in 1994, is about 20km (12 miles) from the center of Lillehammer. It has seven lifts and 20km (12 miles) of alpine slopes. The location is 15km (9¼ miles) north of town. A "ski bus," costing 28NOK ($3.70) one-way and taking 20 minutes, runs here from the center of Lillehammer about six times per day. Lillehammer is also the starting point for 402km (250 miles) of prepared cross-country tracks, 5.75km (3 miles) of which are illuminated. The ski center has three lifts and 3.25km (2 miles) of alpine slopes.

Lillehammer gears up in December for its winter sports season. In addition to the ski center, there's an admission-free **skating rink.** It's open in the winter Monday to Friday from 11am to 9pm, Sunday 11am to 5pm. In the winter, you'll also discover festivals, folklore nights, and ski races.

SKIING Lillehammer has a 94m (307-ft.) slope for professionals and a smaller jump for the less experienced. The lifts take skiers 457m (1,500 ft.) above sea level up the slalom slope, and more than 402km (250 miles) of marked skiing trails are packed by machines. The Lillehammer Ski School offers daily classes, and several cross-country tours are held weekly. Ask at the tourist office (see "Visitor Information," above) for details.

SHOPPING

In the center of Lillehammer, **T.J. Strand Lillehammer Glassmagasin,** Storgata 76 (② **61-25-02-03**), sells a number of fine handmade glass and porcelain decorative objects, among other offerings. A respected name in Norwegian handcrafts, **Husfliden,** Storgata 47 (② **61-26-70-70**), presents a vast array of Norwegian products, ideal as gifts or souvenirs. The location is near Sigrid Undsets Plass. One of Norway's oldest established jewelers, in business since 1868, is **Gullsmed Frisenberg,** Storgata 74 (② **61-25-03-36**), now run by the fourth generation of the founding family. Merchandise includes some of the best jewelry selections from Scandinavia's leading designers.

Sport og Fritid, Kirkegata 55 (② **61-25-76-87**), opposite the Lillehammer Art Museum, offers a huge selection of winter and summer attire. Whatever you need in the realm of sports gear you are likely to find here. **Belsvik Match,** Storgata 72 (② **61-25-47-09**), is Lillehammer's oldest and biggest clothing outlet. Merchandise comes in a wide range of price categories. Most visitors prefer to come here for the traditional Norwegian knitwear.

WHERE TO STAY
EXPENSIVE

First Hotel Breiseth ✦ A winning choice, within an easy walk of Olympiapark, this government-rated three-star hotel is also close to the bus and train terminals. A classic building from the 19th century, its location is more convenient than panoramic. Remodeling has been very successful. However, traditional touches remain, as evidenced by the turn-of-the-20th-century public rooms with artwork on the walls and marble pillars holding up ceilings. We always gravitate in winter to the blazing fireplace in the parlor. Guest rooms are small to midsize, but are completely fresh and tastefully furnished with many wooden pieces, along with tiled bathrooms with shower. The suites have both bathtub and shower. One wing caters specifically to those with allergies. The on-site restaurant, Thorvald's Bar & Spiseri, is one of the best hotel dining rooms in Lillehammer.

1–5 Jernbanegaten 1, N-2609 Lillehammer. ② **61-24-77-77.** Fax 61-26-95-05. www.breiseth.com. 89 units. Sun–Thurs 1,253NOK ($167) double, 1,553NOK ($207) suite; Fri–Sat 1,053NOK ($140) double, 1,303NOK ($173) suite. Rates include buffet breakfast. AE, DC, MC, V. **Amenities:** Restaurant; bar; brasserie; sauna; laundry service. In room: TV, minibar, hair dryer.

Molla Hotel ✦✦ This is one of the most modern and desirable hotels in this vast area, rising 11 floors from its location in the town center. It was constructed in 1992 to host visitors to the 1994 Winter Olympics. The hotel is the second tallest building in town, and the site of one of Lillehammer's most sought-after restaurants, which is recommended separately. Bedrooms come in pleasing pastels and are tastefully and comfortably furnished. Rooms are not as luxurious as you might wish for, but contain such grace notes as pine furnishings, quilted bedspreads, and regional art. The bathrooms are rather small, containing only showers. The location is the most romantic in town, a converted mill dating from 1863 set by a rushing stream and waterfall. Another winning feature is the panoramic rooftop bar.

Elvegaten 12, N-2609 Lillehammer. © **61-26-92-94.** Fax 61-26-92-95. www.molla.ol.no. 58 units. 1,095NOK ($146) double. AE, DC, MC, V. **Amenities:** Restaurant; 2 bars; fitness center; sauna; 24-hr. room service; laundry service. *In room:* TV, minibar, hair dryer.

Radisson SAS Lillehammer Hotel ★★ *(Kids*   Set at the halfway point between the open-air museum at Milahaugen and the Olympic Park, this is the best hotel in Lillehammer, opening onto a 3.5-hectare (8½-acre) park. A bit of a climb from the center, it is the most traditional hotel in Lillehammer, having known a previous life as the Lillehammer Hotel. In its latest reincarnation, it is better than ever, a smoothly running and efficient operation with the best facilities in town. A small midrise, it greets you with a fountain at the entrance, a nice touch that sets the tone for the interior. Paintings, paneling, artifacts, and carpeting add to the style of the hotel. Bedrooms are well organized and exhibit the epitome of comfort and taste, with bright fabrics and homelike touches throughout, along with well-groomed bathrooms featuring tubs or showers. The drinking and dining facilities are top rate.

Turisthotelveien 7, N-2609 Lillehammer. [tel **61-28-60-00.** Fax 61-25-73-33. www.lillehammerhotel.no. 250 units. 1,430NOK ($190) double. AE, DC, MC, V. **Amenities:** Restaurant; 3 bars; indoor heated pool; outdoor heated pool; sauna; children's programs; limited room service. *In room:* TV, minibar, hair dryer.

Rica Victoria Hotel ★   Established in 1872, this is an old, traditional choice for vacationers, but it's kept up with the times. The biggest changes occurred in 1963 and 1976 when new wings were added. The complex consists of an older concrete building along with a more modern, six-floor structure. The interior is more gracious than the exterior, with heavy beams, brown-leather sofas, and brass chandeliers, in addition to paintings. Guests gather near the fireplace in the lounge when it's cold outside. Some of the facilities are used by nonguests and locals, including a pub-style steakhouse, a terrace cafe, and a disco. We prefer the bedrooms in the original house to the more sterile newer units. All the rooms are comfortable, featuring small bathrooms with a tub or shower.

Storgata 84B, N-2615 Lillehammer. © **61-25-00-49.** Fax 61-25-24-74. www.rica.no. 118 units. June 14–Aug 14 1,220NOK ($162) double; Aug 15–June 13 1,240NOK ($165) double. Rates include breakfast. AE, DC, MC, V. **Amenities:** 2 restaurants; bar; terrace cafe; disco; limited room service; laundry service. *In room:* TV, minibar, hair dryer.

Rustad Hotel log Fjellsture ★ *(Finds*   You can settle into the wilderness at this favorite spot 18km (11 miles) north of Lillehammer. The log-and-timber chalet is on the edge of a lake, with a dock for swimming and for boats. The property is surrounded by private grounds with views of the water or the mountains. Hiking trails are available in many directions, and there are some 300km (186 miles) of well-prepared cross-country tracks in winter. The staff can arrange swimming, canoe and boat trips, fishing, and a winter ski school. Skis can be rented on site. The bedrooms are small to midsize, each comfortably furnished, containing small bathrooms with showers.

Sjusjøen, N-2612 Lillehammer. © **62-36-34-08.** Fax 62-36-35-74. 46 units. June–Aug 920NOK ($122) double; Sept–May 1,080NOK ($144) double. Rates include breakfast and dinner. AE, DC, MC, V. Free parking. **Amenities:** Restaurant; bar; sauna. *In room:* TV.

INEXPENSIVE

Gjestehuset Ersgård *(Value*   A pleasant family hotel, this inn was created from a 1570 farmstead on the outskirts of town. Ersgård sits atop a mountain overlooking Lillehammer with views of Lake Mjøsa. If you have a car, this choice makes for an ideal stay. The bedrooms are furnished with birch pieces in old-fashioned Norwegian designs. Some of the bedrooms have small bathrooms with showers; occupants of other rooms will find the corridor bathrooms adequate. The generous Norwegian buffet breakfast is reason enough to stay here, featuring everything from herring to goat cheese. Bus service is available twice a day. The hotel lies 1.5km (1 mile) from the town center at Olympic Park; follow the signs to Nordseter if you're driving.

Nordseterveien 201, N-2618 Lillehammer. © 61-25-06-84. Fax 61-25-31-09. www.ersgaard.no. 30 units, 20 with bathroom. 550NOK ($73) double without bathroom; 550NOK–790NOK ($73–$105) double with bathroom. DC, MC, V. Free parking. Closed Dec 23–28. **Amenities:** Breakfast lounge. *In room:* No phone.

WHERE TO DINE
EXPENSIVE
Blåmann Restaurant und Bar MEXICAN/NORWEGIAN Quesadillas with beef and reindeer may seem like an odd juxtaposition of culinary traditions, but this long-standing favorite more or less succeeds in its offerings (although we've had far better quesadillas than those served here). Housed in an old-fashioned building, it offers views of the river on one side of the restaurant. In summer, there is outdoor seating in a "hang" over the Mesna River. A delicious hunter's soup is made with mushrooms, reindeer, and spices, and served with sour cream. You can, of course, order filet of reindeer. Our favorite dish is the mountain trout served in a sour cream sauce with cucumber salad and potatoes. Some of the more exotic main dishes include breast of ostrich. You can also order succulent Norwegian lamb. In summer, no dessert tops the "Berry Trip," a mixed berry medley with homemade ice cream.

Lilletorvet 1. © 61-26-22-03. Reservations recommended. Main courses 190NOK–300NOK ($25–$40). AE, DC, MC, V. Mon–Sat noon–11pm; Sun 1–11pm.

Bryggerikjellern NORWEGIAN This 1814 brewery, a 7-minute walk east of the train station, was transformed in 1969 into a pub/restaurant, offering beer, steaks, and tasty main dishes. It's done a roaring business ever since, and is especially popular in winter with skiers. In fact, when the weather's bad, and no one can ski or climb in the hills, this is one of the most popular watering holes in town. The Norwegian fare is rather typical, and salads are the only appetizers. They'll feed you well in generous portions. Most dishes are priced at the lower end of the price scale.

　Disco Brenneriet (The Distillery) is linked to the restaurant. It's open Wednesday to Saturday from 11pm to 3am. On Friday there's a 60NOK ($8) cover, going up to 70NOK ($9.30) on Saturday.

Elvagata 19. © 61-27-06-60. Main courses 158NOK–398NOK ($21–$53). AE, DC, MC, V. Mon–Sat 6–11pm; Sun 3–10pm.

Paa Bordet Restaurant ✪ NORWEGIAN/INTERNATIONAL This restaurant is housed in a timbered, rustic building dating from 1880. It's long been known locally for its excellent cuisine prepared with quality ingredients. On our most recent visit, we were delighted with the marinated wild salmon and enjoyed a zesty beet root salad as well. Full-flavored dishes include crispy breast of duck with fresh cabbage, baked apple, and an orange sauce, or roasted filet of elk served with creamed Brussels sprouts. All the dishes our party sampled were made with consummate skill, including the pan-fried skate with lobster sauce and fresh green beans. For desserts, you are likely to take delight in a white chocolate confection with a raspberry sorbet.

Bryggerigata 70. © 61-25-30-00. Reservations recommended. Main courses 195NOK–285NOK ($26–$38). AE, DC, MC, V. Mon–Sat 6–10:30pm. Closed July.

Victoriastuen Restaurant ⭐ NORWEGIAN/INTERNATIONAL   Located in a recommended hotel (p. 171), this lobby-level restaurant offers some of Lillehammer's finest dining year after year, with its windows opening onto the town center. The restaurant is nostalgically outfitted in what Norwegians refer to as "farmer's colors"—that is, strong blues and reds with an antiquelike patina. The location is only a 3-minute walk north of the rail station, so it's a convenient address. The kitchen provides quality cuisine, using regional produce whenever possible. Our mountain trout, fried and served in a sour cream sauce, was a delight, as was the fresh catfish in a butter sauce with a cucumber salad. *Frikadeller* (meatballs) are a filling and tasty pleasure, or you may prefer a succulent chateaubriand if you have a more demanding palate and a full wallet.

Charging less, Victorianhjørnet (Victorian Corner) one floor above, is a pub, pizzeria, and steakhouse. It provides good food in far less formal surroundings.

In the Rica Victoria Hotel, Storgate 84B. ℂ **61-25-00-49.** Reservations recommended. Main courses 195NOK–390NOK ($26–$52). AE, DC, MC, V. Daily 11am–2pm and 3–11pm.

MODERATE

Egon Restaurant ⭐⭐ NORWEGIAN/INTERNATIONAL   Housed in an old grinding mill from 1863, this cozy restaurant offers the most atmospheric dining in Lillehammer. Its fame and desirability were assured during the '94 Olympics when First Lady Hillary Clinton selected it as her preferred dining venue during the games. Its windows overlook the river, and there is outdoor seating in summer. The restored mill is decorated with antiques from the days of the original business here.

The menu is large and varied, and food preparation is first rate, with choice ingredients selected by the chef. They concoct a delectable grilled salmon, and they're also good at grilling a steak to perfection. Should you want a fancier main course, we'd recommend the rack of Norwegian lamb aromatically scented with fresh rosemary or the breast of duckling in a tangy orange sauce. You can sit in cozy nooks and intimate booths, admiring the interior as you enjoy excellent food.

In the Molla Hotel, Elvegata 12. ℂ **61-26-92-94.** Reservations required. Main courses 150NOK–200NOK ($20–$27). AE, DC, MC, V. Daily 11am–10:30pm.

INEXPENSIVE

Svare & Berg NORWEGIAN/MEXICAN   A popular bar with a fireplace for evening drinkers, this is also a first-rate restaurant in a traditional setting. It's cozy and casual, and the food is good. The two most popular—justifiably so—main courses are the filet of reindeer and the sautéed salmon served with a white wine sauce. For a change of pace, you can go south of the border to Mexico and order fajitas with beef or chicken. The crepes with berries "from the woods," served with ice cream, is a summer delight.

In the same building is **Nikkers,** a bar/restaurant sharing the same kitchen. It has a lighter menu and offers live music on Friday and Saturday nights. It's open Monday to Saturday 11am to 2am and Sunday 1pm to midnight.

Storgata 83. ℂ **61-24-74-30.** Reservations recommended. Main courses 98NOK–275NOK ($13–$37). AE, DC, MC, V. Mon–Thurs 4pm–midnight; Fri–Sat 4pm–2am; Sun 4–9pm.

Vertshuset Solveig ⭐ NORWEGIAN/INTERNATIONAL   This traditional restaurant is housed in a timbered farmhouse from 1835 that is one of the oldest in Lillehammer. In the middle of the town, it often attracts as many as 150 hungry diners at one time and it manages to feed them all well. The place is informal, with a rustic interior. Reasonable prices and good food await you here, presented in an old-fashioned ambience with such artifacts as hanging brass pots. Appetizers rarely appear on the menu, but the main courses are so big and filling that you'll hardly miss them. The menu doesn't change much except for the day's special, and you can count on sautéed trout or pike served with fresh vegetables. Reindeer comes in a "meat cake" with the chef's special sauce. Different cakes are made fresh daily, and they're usually moist and a delight to the palate.

Storgata 68B. ✆ 61-26-27-87. Reservations recommended. Main courses 100NOK–160NOK ($13–$21); day's special plate with dessert 85NOK ($11). MC, V. Mon–Wed 10am–7pm; Thurs–Sat 10am–9pm; Sun 10am–6pm.

LILLEHAMMER AFTER DARK

Felix Pub & Scene   A pub since 1984, this major venue for the alternative rock scene is housed in a historic building from 1832. Visited by musicians, students, and others, it often stages live concerts on the ground floor of its two floors. Patrons range in age from 18 to 30, and they listen to recorded music—rock, punk rock, whatever—when there are no live bands. Another potent lure for young people is that the pub offers the cheapest pints in Lillehammer. Open daily from 10:30am to 2am. Storgata 31. ✆ 61-25-01-02. Cover 50NOK–100NOK ($6.65–$13) for live music concerts.

Marcello Nightclub   This is the major nightclub for the district, holding at capacity anywhere from 250 to 300 patrons on its dance floor, ranging in age from 30 to 45. The dancers move to recorded music ranging from pop to country. Only beer and wine are sold, and the doorman assured us, "It's easy to get in unless you're too drunk." Open Friday and Saturday 11pm to 3am. Storgata 86. ✆ 61-26-90-90. Cover 60NOK ($8) Fri, 70NOK ($9.30) Sat.

Rocka Bla   This is a music bar with a variety of entertainment. Mostly recorded music, such as rock 'n' roll, is featured, but stand-up comics or live bands (occasionally) entertain. Many patrons watch sports on TV. The relaxed atmosphere attracts those in their 20s and early 30s. This is one of the most popular places in town, with lines forming on weekends. Open Wednesday to Saturday 10pm to 2am. Lilletorget 1. ✆ 61-26-22-03.

Toppen Bar   This bar offers incredible panoramic views, with vistas of Lillehammer, the Olympic areas, and Lake Mjøsa. It's called "Lillehammer's highest watering hole," located on top of the Molla Hotel. Open Monday to Saturday 8pm to 2am. Elvegata 12. ✆ 61-26-92-94.

Tut-Ankh-Amon   With a name like that, this dance club's Egyptian decor comes as no surprise. With dining facilities for up to 250 Cleopatras and their Marc Antonys, this is one of the biggest and most popular nightclubs in the area. A live orchestra plays, but there is often recorded music as well, entertaining patrons in their 20s and 30s. There is often a long line waiting to get in, especially on Saturday night. Open Thursday to Saturday 11pm to 3am. Lilletorget 1. ✆ 61-26-22-03.

3 Vinstra: The Peer Gynt Road

220km (136 miles) NW of Oslo; 61km (38 miles) NW of Lillehammer

The Peer Gynt Road ★★★ between Lillehammer and the little town of Vinstra, takes you right into the heart of Peer Gynt country. Henrik Ibsen came this way when he was researching his masterpiece *Peer Gynt*, published in 1867 and later set to music by Edvard Grieg. Ibsen based his tale in part on the exploits of one Per (spelled with only one *e*) Gynt Haga, a real-life Norwegian folk hero noted for such exploits as riding on the backs of reindeer at breakneck speed.

As you drive through the Gudbrandsdal (Gudbrands Valley), you can travel the same route that bewitched the original hero, and outside Vinstra you can visit a monument to Per Gynt Haga, the Peer Gynt prototype, in the cemetery adjoining the Sødorp Church, 1.5km (1 mile) south of town. The road passes two large resorts, **Skeikampen/Gausdal** and **Golå/Wadahl,** before rejoining E6 at Vinstra.

The Peer Gynt country is an unspoiled mountain region with altitudes varying from 769m to 1,499m (2,526 ft.–4,920 ft.). This is one of Norway's oldest and best-known sports districts. The skiing center at Fefor was opened in 1904, and it was here that the adventurous Capt. Robert Falcon Scott tested the equipment for his expedition to the South Pole.

The region is also a lure to summer travelers, as the Peer Gynt Road passes mountains, farmsteads, fish-filled lakes, wild game, and alpine flowers.

ESSENTIALS

GETTING THERE   By Train   Following more or less the same route as the buses, but taking a bit less time, trains travel from Oslo's Central Station to Gardermoen to Lillehammer to Vinstra, taking about 3¼ hours, and charging around 430NOK ($57) each way. That price includes the fee for reserving a seat, which in light of the many weekenders who go to Peer Gynt country from Oslo, is a good idea. For railway information throughout Norway, call ℂ **81-50-08-88.**

By Bus   Buses depart from Oslo's central bus station, which is immediately adjacent to the town's railway station. They make a stop at the bus station at Gardermoen Airport, then continue on to Lillehammer and then on to Vinstra. There are between three and four of these per day, each maintained by the Norway Express Bus Service. One-way fares for the 3½-hour bus trip are 290NOK ($39) per person. Call ℂ **82-02-13-00** for reservations and information, although it's hard to get through. Otherwise, call the Vinstra tourist office for schedules or click on the region's website (www.peergynt.no) for a limited schedule.

By Car   From Lillehammer, continue northwest along E6 into Vinstra.

By Taxi   Note that once a passenger arrives in Vinstra, either at the bus or the railway station (they're actually the same spot), they'll usually have to migrate by taxi to their hotel. Most hotels are in isolated spots up in the mountains. A taxi fare from Vinstra to Gola, for example, costs around 325NOK ($43) and carries up to four passengers if they don't have too much luggage, and two to three persons if they do have a lot of luggage. Usually a hotel will send a van down to meet its passengers as part of the cost of their hotel package.

VISITOR INFORMATION   The best source of information about touring in the area is found at the **Vinstra Turist og Messekontor,** N-2640 Vinstra (ℂ **61-29-47-70**), open June to August Monday to Friday 8:30am to 5pm; September to May Monday to Friday 8:30am to 4pm.

OUTDOOR ACTIVITIES

The **Peer Gynt Ski Area** ★★★ is ideal for those who'd like to combine cross-country skiing with alpine skiing. All the facilities in the Ski Region are within easy reach of all the hotels in the area. A ski bus links the resorts of Espedalen, Fefor, and Gålå. In all, there are 28km (17 miles) with slopes, 8 lifts, 1 chair lift, and 24 slopes. In the entire area there are 460km (285 miles) of well-prepared trails and 170km (105 miles) of stick marked trails in beautiful surroundings.

Skiers rate the Peer Gynt Trail as Norway's best cross-country skiing area, and floodlit trails in Espedalen and in Gålå make it possible to ski even after dinner.

To ski the area, you can purchase a one-day Troll Pass at the Vinstra office, costing 240NOK ($32) for adults and 195NOK ($26) for children. The pass entitles you to all the lifts in the area.

You can pick up maps and other data at the tourist center at Vinstra (see above).

In summer, **Norske Bygdeopplevelser** (© 61-28-99-70) offers cycling trips and mountain hikes through the Peer Gynt land.

SEEING THE SIGHTS

Bjørnsterne Bjørnson, the author of the national anthem of Norway, lived at an old farmstead, **Aulestad,** in Gausdal, 18km (11 miles) northwest of Lillehammer, from 1875 until his death in 1910. Bjørnson purchased the farm with his wife, Karoline. He won the Nobel Prize for literature in 1903. In 1934, the house was opened as a national museum and today it is filled with Bjørnson memorabilia. It is signposted near the hamlet of Follebu. Aulestad (© **61-22-41-10**) is open in late May and September daily 11am to 2:30pm; June and August daily 10am to 3:30pm, and July daily 10am to 5:30pm. Admission is 50NOK ($6.65).

WHERE TO STAY & DINE

Most people travel the Peer Gynt Road as an excursion from Lillehammer. But if you'd like to stay around for a few days, here are several recommended accommodations. These recommendations are scattered throughout the area at various hamlets and resorts.

Dalseter Hoyfjellshotell _Value_ This hotel, built in 1963 but considerably modernized since, is set on a hillside overlooking forests and mountains. The views are panoramic. Next to some of the best cross-country skiing tracks in the area, it has a homelike, friendly atmosphere. The bedrooms are outfitted in a cozy, comfortable Norwegian regional style, with lots of heat during the Arctic winters. Some of the tidy little bathrooms have a tub-shower combination; others have only a shower. In winter, evening dance music contributes to a festive ski lodge atmosphere. Meals are served in a warm, inviting modern room, and are well prepared.

Gudbrandsdalen, N-2658 Espedal. © **61-29-99-10**. Fax 61-29-99-41. www.dalseter.no. 90 units. 635NOK–735NOK ($84–$98) double. Children under 5 stay free. AE, DC, MC, V. Closed May–June and Oct–Dec 21. **Amenities:** Restaurant; bar; heated indoor pool; 2 saunas. _In room:_ TV.

Fefor Høifjellshotell ★ _Kids_ The core of this hotel dates from 1891, when it was a modestly sized plank-sided mountain inn, sheltering summer hikers and winter skiers from a location beside the Fefor Innsjø (Fefor Lake), 13km (8 miles) east of Vinstra. Today, greatly expanded by a series of modern wings that contain the accommodations, it's an upper-middle-bracket refuge with one of the most charming old central hotel cores in the region. Designed in the Norwegian nationalist style, and the site of the reception area, the bar, and restaurant, it features red Nordic dragons on the roof of its oldest wing, blazing fireplaces, and heavy iron chandeliers. Bedrooms are cozy, wood-trimmed, and contemporary, with views over the lake and the mountains. Each tile and stone-trimmed bathroom boasts a shower-tub combination. Access to the ski lifts requires a 12-minute hike across flat ground from the hotel, but because of the coziness and charm of the place, none of the sport-minded clientele seems to

Bjørnstjerne Bjørnson: Yes, We Love This Land

Ranking along with author Henrik Ibsen, 1903 Nobel prize winner for literature Bjørnstjerne Bjørnson (1832–1910) has left part of his world behind at this old farmstead at Aulestad (see listing above), which the public today can visit in Gaudsal. The author is a towering figure in the history of Norway, having achieved fame as a poet, dramatist, novelist, journalist, editor, public speaker, and theater director.

His immortality was ensured when his poem "Ja, vi elsker dette landet" ("Yes, We Love This Land") was selected as the Norwegian national anthem.

The son of a pastor, Bjørnson grew up in a farming community, later the setting for several of his novels. In 1857–59, he became Ibsen's successor as artistic director of the Bergen Theatre, where he married the actress Karoline Reimers in 1858.

Later, from 1866 to 1871, he was director of the Christiania Theatre in Oslo. While in self-imposed exile between 1860 and 1863, he wrote some of his most enduring works. Some of his best-remembered works today are *The Heritage of the Kurts*, written in 1884 and *In God's Way*, written in 1889.

Later in life he became an ardent Socialist, working for peace and international understanding. Although he enjoyed worldwide fame in his life, and his plays helped to bring "social realism" to Europe, his international reputation today pales when compared to his sometimes friend and always rival, Ibsen.

mind. On the grounds of this hotel are 20 wood-sided, bare-boned cabins, each with cooking facilities, available for 6 to 12 people each year-round. If you enjoy rustic, outdoorsy surroundings, these just might be the perfect accommodations for you. Depending on their size and amenities, they cost 450NOK to 600NOK ($60–$80) per night, without meals or services of any kind.

N-2640 Vinstra. © **61-29-00-99** or 61-29-17-60. www.fefor.com. 120 units. Mon–Thurs 840NOK–950NOK ($112–$126) per person double; Fri–Sun 1,600NOK–1,800NOK ($213–$239) per person double. Rates include half-board. AE, DC, MC, V. Closed Oct–Nov Mon–Thurs and all of May. **Amenities:** Restaurant; bar; indoor pool; outdoor pool; 2 saunas; squash hall; skating rink; boating facilities; children's programs. *In room:* TV.

Gålå Høgfjellshotell ★ *Kids*   There's more of a sense of the 19th-century Norwegian nationalist style, scattered over various areas of this hotel, than there is in most of the other hotels with which it competes. That derives from its origins around 1870 as a high-altitude sanatorium for tuberculosis patients, and its transformation, around 1900, into a hotel. Another part of its allure is its location—within a short walk of the ski lifts, and easily accessible directly from the slopes on skis. Accommodations are nostalgically furnished in a rustic, old-fashioned style, and much about this place evokes a skier's and hiker's boutique hotel. Bathrooms are tiled and accented with stone, and each has a shower-tub combination. Despite its relatively intimate size, the hotel functions as a manager and rental agent for about 130 self-catering cabins, suitable for between 6 and 10 occupants, scattered throughout the nearby district. Each has a kitchen, and amenities that range from bare-boned to relatively plush. They're favored by families and extended groups of friends traveling together. Depending on the season and their size, without meals or services, they cost 4,200NOK to 30,000NOK ($559–$3,990) per week.

N-2646 Gålå. ℭ **61-29-81-09.** Fax 61-29-85-40. 42 units. Winter (with half-board included) Mon–Thurs 780NOK–950NOK ($104–$126) per person double, Fri–Sun 890NOK–1,095NOK ($118–$146) per person double; summer (with breakfast included) 550NOK–620NOK ($73–$82) per person double. AE, DC, MC, V. **Amenities:** Restaurant; bar; indoor pool; cross-country skiing; easy-access downhill ski slopes; children's programs; laundry service; dry cleaning. *In room:* TV.

Golden Tulip Rainbow Skeikampen Hoifjellshotell ★ *Kids*   One of the few hotels remaining open all year, this establishment is one of the finest places to lodge in the ski region. It offers attractive public rooms filled with antique and modern furniture and acres of woodland grounds. The snug and cozy bedrooms, decorated in "Nordic light" pastels, are distributed in such a way that most of them open onto scenic views. Ten of them have bathrooms with bathtubs, the rest have showers. Sports lovers will find a ski lift adjacent to a smaller rope tow for beginners and a ski school with child-care facilities. The hotel is right at the timberline, and both forested and rocky paths are well marked for climbers. On the premises is a Spanish-inspired bodega, with the best wine stock in the region. Wine-tasting parties and semiformal dinners are held here at least three times a week. The hotel lies 38km (23 miles) from the rail station at Tretten, and arrangements can be made to have a car pick you up.

N-2652 Svingvoll. ℭ **61-28-50-00.** Fax 61-28-50-01. www.rainbow-hotels.no. 113 units. 995NOK–1,145NOK ($132–$152) double. Children under 5 stay free. Rates include half-board. AE, DC, MC, V. **Amenities:** Restaurant; bar; heated indoor pool; sauna; day-care facilities. *In room:* TV, hair dryer.

Rainbow Gausdal Høifjellshotell ★   Lying 8km (5 miles) northwest from the town of Svingvoll, this is one of the most traditional lodges in the area. Its original core is from 1876 but was burned to the ground by the Nazis. The oldest wing that survived is from 1921. Other wings were added in 1956, 1984, and the mid-90s, creating a cohesive, well-operated unit. The hotel lies in the center of a small but popular mountain resort of Gausdal, 16km (10 miles) west of Tretten, the nearest railroad station. If you notify them, the owners will send a car to pick you up. Bedrooms are comfortably and tastefully furnished, offering views of the mountains. Each comes with a shower and bathtub. Kilometers of hiking or ski trails surround the hotel, and provisions can be made for downhill or cross-country skiing in winter, horseback riding or hill climbing in summer. There is immediate access to ski lifts, a sports center with a ski school, and ski-rental facilities. On winter nights, a local band plays here and 6 nights a week, year-round, a dance orchestra plays. Even if you're passing through just for the day, you might want to stop in to partake of the hotel's smorgasbord.

Skeikampen, N-2652 Svingvoll. ℭ **61-05-51-50.** Fax 61-05-51-51. www.gausdal.com/hotell. 126 units. Mid-Sept to mid-May (with full board included) Mon–Thurs 1,490NOK ($198) double, Fri–Sun 1,690NOK–2,390NOK ($225–$318) double; mid-May to mid-Sept (with half-board included) 1,190NOK ($158) double. AE, DC, MC, V. Closed 2 weeks in early May and most of Nov. **Amenities:** Restaurant; bar; disco; 18-hole golf course; 3 indoor lighted tennis courts. *In room:* TV.

Wadahl Høifjellshotel ★★   This is one of the more luxurious of the several hotels positioned on the ski slopes around Lillehammer, with an isolated hillside location that allows residents to ski from the hotel's front door to the ski lifts, and then ski back to the hotel from the upper reaches of the surrounding slopes. Cozy and rustic, with a sports-conscious clientele that often drives from as far away as Oslo for weekend getaways, it was originally established in 1900 as a survival station for the high mountains around it. It was transformed into a

resort hotel in 1930, and has been enlarged several times since then, most recently in 1999. Rooms are comfortably furnished and modern looking, each with an immaculately kept bathroom with tub and shower. Midwinter and mid-summer are equally desirable high seasons here, and unlike most other urban hotels in Norway, weekend visits are more, rather than less, expensive, than weekdays. Patrons enjoy the tasty dinners. The hotel lies 17km (10 miles) south-west of Vinstra, site of the nearest rail station, and 14km (8 miles) northwest of Harpefoss.

N-2646 Gålå. © 61-29-83-00. Fax 61-29-75-01. www.wadahl.no. 96 units. Mon–Thurs 650NOK–800NOK ($86–$106) double; Fri–Sun 2,000NOK–2,550NOK ($266–$339) double. AE, DC, MC, V. Closed Nov–Dec Mon–Thurs and May Mon–Thurs. **Amenities:** Restaurant; bar; large outdoor pool; indoor pool; indoor and outdoor lighted tennis courts; sauna; horseback-riding facilities; activity center for access to hiking, hill climb-ing, and cross-country skiing. *In room:* TV, minibar.

4 Lom ⋆ & Jutunheimen National Park ⋆⋆⋆

62km (38 miles) NW of Otta; 180km (112 miles) NW of Lillehammer

Continuing northwest from our last stopover at Vinstra, we turn off the E6 onto Route 15 heading west into Lom, which lies in the center of the Jutunheimen National Park. In one of the most colorful settings of any rustic little village in Norway, Lom straddles the Prestfossen Waterfall and the Bøvra River. A village of great and traditional charm, Lom has retained much of its log-cabin archi-tecture and boasts a stave church from 1170.

Some 905km (562 miles) of its municipal border is covered by glaciers and mountains, the most important and dramatic of which are **Gittertind** at 2,452m (8,044 ft.) and **Baldhøpiggen** at 2,469m (8,100 ft.).

Most of Jutunheimen National Park, one of the greatest parks in Norway, lies in Lom municipality. Lom can also be your gateway to the fjord country, as two of the grandest fjords in Norway, Geiranger and Sognefjord (see chapter 11), are a short drive to the west.

ESSENTIALS

GETTING THERE   Nor-Way Bussekspress buses from Oslo pass through Lom at the rate of three per day, costing 420NOK ($56) one-way and taking 6½ hours. From Lillehammer or Vinstra, continue northwest along E6 until the junction with Route 15, at which point you head west into Lom.

VISITOR INFORMATION   For information about the area, including hiking, head for the **Jutunheimen Reiseliv** (© 61-21-29-90), in the Norsk Fjellmuseum (see below). You can purchase a Fellesbillet costing 80NOK ($11), granting you access to the stave church, the Presthaugen Bygdemuseum, and the Norsk Fjellmuseum (see below). You can also purchase hiking maps here, which are necessary if you plan to tour Jutunheimen Nasjonalpark.

SEEING THE SIGHTS

In the center of Lom, **Stavkyrke** (© 97-07-53-97), dates from 1170 but was enlarged in 1635 when it was restyled in a cruciform shape. In 1667 two naves were added. The church is admired for its early-18th-century paintings and Jakob Saeterdalen's pulpit and chancel from 1793. Charging 30NOK ($4) for adults, free for children, it is open mid-June to mid-August daily from 9am to 9pm.

An even more impressive sight is the **Fossheim Steinsenter** ⋆, with Europe's biggest and most varied exhibition of rare and stunningly beautiful rocks, along with gems, minerals, and fossils, plus jewelry on sale. Part of the museum is devoted to exotic geological specimens gathered from all over the world. The owners take pride in the national stone of Norway, thulite, which was first discovered in Lom in 1820 and is now quarried. Manganese gives thulite its reddish color. Admission free, the center is open from mid-June to mid-August Monday to Saturday 9am to 8pm, Sunday 9am to 7pm. In off-season, it is open Monday to Friday 10am to 3pm.

Norsk Fjellmuseum in Lom (© **61-21-16-00**) is the visitor center for Jutunheimen National Park (see below). The center has a dual role as a museum filled with intriguing exhibits about mountaineering, and an information center for hikers in the park. Exhibits relate both the culture of the mountain people and the park's natural history. A 10-minute mountain slide show is also presented. Admission is 60NOK ($8) adults, 30NOK ($4) children. It is open mid-June to mid-August Monday to Friday 9am to 9pm, Saturday and Sunday 10am to 5pm. In off-season it is open Monday to Friday 9am to 4pm and Saturday and Sunday 10am to 5pm.

JUTUNHEIMEN NASJONAL PARK: "HOME OF THE GIANTS"

This is Norway's greatest national park, dominated by the **towering peaks** ★★ of **Galdhopiggen** and **Glittertind**. It is a land of glaciers, mountains, lakes, and waterfalls. It has more than 60 glaciers and is crisscrossed by valleys that split it up into ridges and high plateaus.

A heavily frequented tourist area since 1813, it has become one of the best developed wilderness tour areas in the north of Europe, with its "linkage" of hotels, tourist huts, and private cabins lying along well-marked trails.

It attracts both the neophyte and the more advanced mountain hiker along with the glacier and rock climbers who descend upon the park in summer.

The beauty of the park, especially its wildflowers in spring, have inspired some of Norway's most famous composers and writers, including Edvard Grieg and Henrik Ibsen.

Although its wild reindeer have departed, flocks of tame reindeer are kept on farmsteads by farmers in Vågå or Lom. Fishermen come to the park to catch red char or mountain trout.

First-timers like to take the high and panoramic **Sognefjellet** ★★, a road linking Lom with Lustrafjorden. Built in 1939 by unemployed youth, this is the best access to the northern tier of the park. The road peaks at 1,434m (4,704 ft.), making it the highest mountain road in the north of Europe. In fact, the elevation is so high that the snow doesn't melt until early July. It can even snow here during the hottest period of the summer.

In all, the park encompasses 3,900 sq. km (6,276 sq. miles), with an amazing number of towering peaks, some 200 of which rise to 1,900m (6,233 ft.). Norway's highest waterfall, **Vettisfossen** ★★, is also found in the park, with its 275m (902-ft.) drop. The waterfall lies a short walk from the Vetti Lodge on the western frontier of the park.

The most popular hike in Norway is along the **Besseggen Ridge** ★★ towering over Lake Gjende. The trail links the mountain lodges of Memurubu and Gjendesheim. One of the most famous lakes in Norway, Gjende appears in the writings of Henrik Ibsen. The author had his Peer Gynt tumble from the ridge into the lake on the back of a speeding reindeer. The lake is 18km (11 miles) long and 146m (479 ft.) deep. Its emerald-green waters are fed by glaciers. In summer, you can rent boats along the lakefront.

Again, obtain complete and detailed maps from the tourist office before setting out into the park, and know that the weather can change at a moment's

Impressions

"It [Besseggen Ridge] cuts along with an edge like a scythe for miles and miles . . . and scars and glaciers sheer down the precipice to the glassy lakes, 1,600 feet below on either side."

—Henrik Ibsen

notice. You can also arrange with the tourist office to hire a guide, which is highly recommended.

WHERE TO STAY

Elveseter Hotell ★★ *Finds*   This is the kind of hotel complex where visitors sometimes regret not spending more than just 1 night. In its role as a hotel, it accepted its first overnight guest in 1870, while it simultaneously functioned as a farmstead whose workers and overseers were completely snowbound for at least 6 months of the year. What you'll see today is a compound of 19 Tolkien-esque buildings, many antique, all of them plank-sided, and some of them with sod roofs. They nestle, in isolated dignity, beside a river on a valley floor that's flanked on both sides by some of the most jagged and constantly snow-covered mountains in Norway. Two of the buildings boast foundations from 1579 and 1640, respectively. Others are newer structures fancifully trimmed in the Norwegian nationalist style, with Viking-inspired motifs that include dragon-prowed ships and frequent references to ancient Norse mythology.

The very existence of this hotel derives from the life work of Åmund Elveseter, an alert 92-year-old patriarch who recently passed the reins of administration to members of his extended family. He's famous throughout Norway for completing and erecting (in 1992) the compound's aesthetic centerpiece: the *Sagasøyla* (Saga column). Rising almost 30m (100 ft.), and capped with bronze statues of Viking lords, it presents a figurative history of Norway from 872 to 1814 in a stately looking format that any city in the world would be thrilled to have as one of its public monuments. Depending on your point of view, the decor of this place is either richly historic—a period piece that revels in the Norwegian national aesthetic—or a slightly dated piece of Scandinavian kitsch. Some of the overnight guests here will be participants in trans-Norwegian bus tours who have stopped after a day's transit across the fjords at this isolated spot of scenic beauty and architectural quirks. Others are avid hikers, climbers, and nature enthusiasts, who use the place as a base for midsummer treks into the surrounding valleys. A wide range of outdoor activities are available here, for supplemental fees. Examples include midsummer cross-country skiing on the high altitudes nearby or on glaciers; every imaginable kind of trekking and climbing, and river rafting. Folkloric shows, presented within an on-site theater, occur frequently, usually as entertainment for one of the visiting bus tours. The hotel is completely closed throughout most of the autumn, winter, and spring.

Bøverdalen. ✆ **61-21-20-00.** Fax 61-21-21-01. www.elveseter.no. 125 units. 800NOK ($106) double. Rates include breakfast. Evening buffet in dining room 225NOK ($30) per person. AE, DC, MC, V. Closed mid-Sept to late May. Bøverdalen lies 24km (15 miles) from Lom. From the hamlet of Bøverdalen, drive 3.25km (2 miles) SW, follow the signs to Elveseter. **Amenities:** Buffet-style restaurant; bar; indoor pool; theater for movies and folkloric expositions; sports facilities that include options for hiking, trekking, and rafting. *In room:* No phone.

Fossheim Turisthotell   Cozy, comfortable, and appealingly old-fashioned, this hotel originated in the heart of the hamlet of Lom in 1897, when it gave overnight shelter to people and horses on one of the country's important mail routes. Radically renovated and enlarged in 1950 and again in 1992, it is still accented with stout ceiling beams and a scattering of Norwegian antiques. It's most famous today for its restaurant, which is separately recommended below. Most clients, who overnight in one of the conservatively decorated and cozy bedrooms, each with shower, wouldn't miss a meal in the dining room.

N-2686 Lom. © **61-21-95-00.** Fax 61-21-95-01. www.fossheimhotel.no. 53 units. Summer 1,080NOK ($144) double; winter 980NOK ($130) double. AE, DC, MC, V. **Amenities:** Restaurant; bar; laundry service; dry cleaning. *In room:* No phone.

Turtagro   One of the most isolated hotels in Norway occupies a forested, mountainside site 9.5km (6 miles) northeast of the hamlet of Fortun and 59km (37 miles) northeast of the village of Sogndal. It originated in 1887, when it functioned as an emergency station for mountaineers and trekkers in the surrounding hills and mountains. In 2000, the hotel's antique core, site of its restaurant, was partially destroyed in a fire, and when it was rebuilt about a year later, an architecturally daring, asymmetrical annex was added a few steps away to house the conventional double rooms. What you'll see today is a trio of red-painted, wood-sided buildings, one of which is exclusively devoted to the housing of the hardworking staff. The more comfortable lodgings are within the artfully minimalist conventional bedrooms, each of which has wood paneling and a no-frills decor that goes well with the sometimes-savage climate outside. The hotel is the centerpiece for a network of up to 22 different hiking trails. Those that are clearly marked don't usually require a guide; those that are not marked shouldn't be attempted by novices on their own. The dining room serves hearty, two-fisted food, flavorful and plentiful, appropriate fuel for the aggressive mountaineering that many of the clients of this place come to do.

N-6877 Fortun. © and fax **57-68-08-00.** www.turtagro.no. 19 units, plus 50 dormitory-style beds in a nearby outbuilding. 2,340NOK ($311) conventional double; 555NOK–750NOK ($74–$100) per person for bed in dormitory-style outbuilding. Rates include full board. AE, DC, MC, V. Closed Nov–Mar. **Amenities:** Restaurant; bar; babysitting; laundry service. *In room:* No phone.

Vågå Hotel *Value*   Country comfortable, big windowed, and well respected, this is the only hotel, and one of the most oft-recommended restaurants, in the hamlet of Vågå, where about half of the county's population of 4,000 people live. Substantial looking and solid, it was originally built in the 1950s, then enlarged and radically reconfigured twice, in the 1960s and again in the 1970s. Its interior is cozy and richly paneled, in ways that make it seem older than it actually is, with local pine. A fireplace, completely sheathed in heat-conductive ceramic tile, throws off a welcome midwinter heat. The comfortably furnished but rather minimalist bedrooms are small to midsize, each with a bathroom with shower. There's a large indoor swimming pool, the kind you can swim laps in. The staff is well versed in the outdoor sporting options of every season that are available within the region. Since the local downhill ski lifts are about 32km (20 miles) away, this hotel attracts less downhill skiers among its clientele, and more cross-country skiers, who have trail options within the surrounding countryside.

N-2680 Vågå. © **61-23-95-50.** Fax 61-23-95-51. www.vagahotel.no. 50 units. 890NOK ($118) double. Rates include breakfast. AE, DC, MC, V. From Lom, drive 32km (20 miles) east, following Rte. 15 and the signs to Otta. **Amenities:** Restaurant; bar; indoor pool. *In room:* No phone.

WHERE TO DINE

Fossheim Restaurant ★★★ NORWEGIAN   Set within the cozy, old-fashioned dining room of a recommended hotel (see above), amid a scattering of 19th-century Danish and Norwegian antiques, this is the most famous and well-recommended restaurant in the region. It owes much of its renown to head chef Kristofer Hoyland, whose imaginative use of local fish and game has been publicized, thanks to local and national newspapers, throughout Norway. Despite frequent modernizations, at least some of the building's original late-19th-century character remains, including lavish use of pinewood paneling and big-windowed views of the mountains and the local stave church. Main courses vary with the seasons, yet are all redolent of the bracing mountain climate of central Norway. The best examples include baked wild salmon served with fresh vegetables and a creamy sauce; whole fried mountain trout served with herbs and a sour cream sauce; award-winning versions of reindeer filet and breast of wild ptarmigan served pinky-rare, each with a creamy game sauce that's enriched with wild mushrooms.

N-2686 Lom. © **61-21-95-00.** Reservations recommended. Fixed-price menus 285NOK–425NOK ($38–$57). AE, DC, MC, V. Daily 1–3pm and 7–10:30pm (until 9pm in winter).

5 Rondane ⚜⚜ & Dovrefjell ⚜ National Parks

Lesja: 159km (99 miles) N of Lom

Rondane and Dovrefjell national parks present you with a landscape carved by the Ice Age. Rondane in particular is impressive, with its barren mountains, narrow canyons, and deep cirques.

Rondane is home to Norway's last herd of wild reindeer. The parks landscapes are varied, with towering mountain peaks, vast expanses of land, waterfalls, and deep valleys cut between the mountains. You can lodge in Rondane—we especially recommend the Brekkeseter mountain farm (see "Where to Stay," below).

ESSENTIALS

GETTING THERE   Two buses a day run from the little town of Otta, lying on the E6 northwest of Lillehammer, and the settlement of Mysusaeter (see below), ending at the Spranghaugen Car Park. This is the start of the most frequented routes through Rondane. The trip takes 45 minutes and costs 25NOK ($3.35) one-way. There is no public transportation to Dovrefjell. Motorists can reach such gateway towns as Lesja or Dombås by taking the E6 northwest of Lillehammer.

VISITOR INFORMATION   For information about both Rondane and Dovrefjell, you can go to the **Nasjonalparksenter,** Sentralplassen, in the town of Dombås (© **61-24-14-44**). Admission is free, and it is open daily from mid-June to mid-August from 9am to 8pm (closes at 5pm off-season). You'll find detailed information about touring either park at this helpful center.

EXPLORING THE NATIONAL PARKS

The little town of Lesja can be your gateway to **Rondane Nasjonalpark,** which lies to its southwest. Henrik Ibsen called Rondane "palace piled upon palace." Created in 1962, the 572-sq.-km (355-sq.-mile) park was the first to open in Norway.

The park is divided into a trio of different mountain areas, all more than 2,011m (6,600 ft.) in elevation. To the east of the Rondane massif rises the peaks of Rondeslotteet at 2,178m (7,145 ft.). To the west are such mountains as Veslesmeden at 2,016m (6,614 ft.), Storsmeden at 1,017m (6,617 ft.), and Sagtinden at 2,018m (6,620 ft.). All these mountains are linked by narrow "saddles." The third group is split by the deep valley of Lungglupdalen and crowned by Midtronden Mountain at 2,114m (6,935 ft.).

One of Norway's great areas for hikers, Rondane has poor soil, and the ground is often covered with lichens instead of more luxuriant flora. The park is peppered with little lakes and rivers, the landscape broken in part by dwarf birch trees.

The area has been inhabited for thousands of years, as ancient Viking burial mounds and centuries-old reindeer traps reveal. More than two dozen types of animals, including reindeer and some 125 species of birds, now populate the park.

Most visitors to the park begin their hikes at the Spranghaugen Car Park, near Mysusaeter, which is reached by bus. From this point, the most popular hike in the park is the 6km (3¾ miles) jaunt to Rondvassbu, followed by a 5-hour return climb to the summit of Storronden at 2,138m (7,014 ft.).

The Sjoa, Europe's best river for rafting, cuts through the park, centered at Heidal with its rushing white waters. The rafting season starts in mid-May and lasts until the end of September. **Sjoa Rafting** in Heidal offers trips through the gorge and other activities in the park. Rafting trips along a 11km (6¾-mile) stretch of the Sjoa run 3½ hours and cost 500NOK to 540NOK ($67–$72). Call ℭ **61-23-61-70** for more information.

The other national park, **Dovrefjell Nasjonalpark,** was enlarged in 2002 to take in more of the surrounding area. The park now includes territory in three counties, making it the largest continuous protected area in Norway. Although still called Dovrefjell, its full name in Norwegian is actually Dovrefjell-Sunndalsfjella National park.

The core of the park was set aside for protection in 1974. The aim was to safeguard the highlands around Snøhetta, which soars to a height of 2,286m (7,500 ft.). Hikers can ascend to Snøhetta in about 6 hours.

The park is home to wolverines, Arctic foxes, and reindeer. It is also the habitat of the rare musk ox. This animal, which can survive at amazingly cold temperatures, also lives in parts of Greenland and Alaska. It can weigh up to 446kg (983 lb.). Obviously its coat is incredibly thick.

In 1931, 10 musk oxen were introduced to Dovrefjell, having been shipped over from Greenland. Since these animals once inhabited Dovrefjell, they were successful in breeding. The herd is estimated to number about 80.

In another section of the park, the Knutshøene rises 1,690m (5,544 ft.), lying to the east of the main route, E6. This section of the park is Europe's most diverse, intact alpine ecosystem.

Before setting out to explore the park, arm yourself with a good map from the visitor center (see above).

One of the best ways to see the park is through an organized tour or with a guide. To arrange for a guide, call **Dovre Eventyr** at ℭ **61-24-01-59.** Among regular tours of the flora and fauna, the outfitter also features musk ox safaris and mountain-climbing courses. In addition, **Dovrefjell Aktivitetsenter** (ℭ **61-24-15-55)** features moose safaris as well, along with family rafting and overnight wilderness camping. Safaris generally cost from 180NOK to 220NOK ($24–$29) per person.

OTHER ATTRACTIONS

In the center of the historic town of Lesja, you can visit **Lesja Bygdatun** (ℭ 61-24-31-53), consisting of a dozen houses moved to this site and revealing how life was lived in tougher days of yore. You can explore farm dwellings, cookhouses, barns, storehouses, and a forgery. Archaeological finds unearthed in the region are also displayed here. An association of farm women bakes and cooks daily at the coffee house and restaurant, serving waffles and other traditional baked goods. On Saturday they serve the famous *rumgraut* (porridge made with

Sigrid Undset Country

Winner of the Nobel Prize for literature in 1928, Sigrid Undset (1882–1949) still enjoys an international audience. She lived and wrote about this area in central Norway, and was known for her novels about Scandinavia in the Middle Ages. Her *Kristin Lavransdatter* became an international bestseller. Her books have been translated into all the major languages of the world. Undset wrote 36 books, and was a great storyteller, probing the labyrinths of the human mind.

Born in Denmark the same year as James Joyce and Virginia Woolf, Undset came to Norway at age 2, where in time she devoured Norse sagas, finding inspiration for her later work.

In 1919 she moved to Lillehammer, after a life in Oslo, the subject of many of her novels. An outspoken critic of Nazi Germany, she fled in April 1940 when the Germans invaded her country. She went to neutral Sweden, not wanting to be taken hostage by the Germans. In the '40s she came to the United States to plead her occupied country's cause. Upon her return to Norway in 1945, she lived for another 4 years, but never wrote another word.

You can recapture some of the atmosphere of Undset's prize-winning trilogy, *Kristin Lavransdatter,* by visiting the **Jørundgard Middelalder Senter** at Sel (© **61-23-37-00**). This medieval farm was re-created in 1995 for the Liv Ullman film of *Kristin Lavransdatter.* The film helped put Undset back on the Norwegian cultural map, especially among young people.

The farm lies in Nord-Sel, 15km (9¼ miles) north of Otta, which is reached along E6. The center consists of 16 buildings and a consecrated stave church. You can join in a guided tour and taste foods of the Middle Ages. The center (© **61-23-37-00**) is open for guided tours, costing 55NOK ($7.30), daily from 10am to 6pm June to mid-September.

sour cream). There is also a craft shop selling embroideries, painted china and glass, wooden bowls, and other items made in Lesja. From June 20 to August 18, it is open daily from 10am to 5pm, charging 30NOK ($4) to enter. Children 14 and under enter free.

WHERE TO STAY & DINE

Bjorligard Hotell   This is the area's most appealing hotel. It evokes a large, contemporary chalet, thanks to exposed planking, weathered siding, and a design that might have been inspired by a mountainside lodge in Switzerland. Redecorated and renovated in 1989, it lies within a 7-minute walk from the village ski lifts. It attracts a sports-oriented and in many cases, rather youthful clientele. Public areas contain paneling, a blazing fireplace, rustic artifacts, and cozy comfortable seating nooks. Bedrooms are contemporary looking, outfitted with pale monochromatic colors and views over the surrounding landscapes. Bathrooms are tiled and modern looking, all with shower-tub combinations.

N-2669 Bjorli. © **61-24-55-23**. Fax 61-24-55-69. 56 units. 990NOK ($132) double. AE, DC, MC, V. Closed May and Nov. Bjorli lies NW of Lesja along E6. **Amenities:** Restaurant; bar. *In room:* TV, coffeemaker.

Brekkeseter ★ *Finds* The origins of this hotel date from 1772, when its central core functioned as a farm for the midsummer production of hay, and the spring and autumn gathering of mosses (used as cattle feed) from the surrounding mountains. Today, set directly atop the tree line (where the forest ends and the rocky uplands begin), the site comprises 25 separate buildings, each an old-fashioned plank-sided testimonial to the building techniques of yesteryear. The largest of these, built in stages between 1772 and 1995, functions as a small-scale, conventional hotel. None of the rooms in this part of the hotel have TVs or phones, but the simple but cozy decor reflects the barren but beautiful landscape outside. Each of the accommodations comes with a small bathroom with shower. If you opt to rent one of the conventional bedrooms, it will come as part of a highly unusual "three-quarter pension" plan, wherein breakfast, a full dinner, and a boxed lunch (which you'll pack yourself from a wide choice of raw ingredients) is included in the rates. If you opt to rent one of the cabins, it will contain a full kitchen, and space for between 2 and 10 occupants. Its price will not include any meals. The hotel's location just outside the boundary of the Rondane National Park assures a plentiful supply of mountain scenery, lots of reindeer grazing nearby, and a splendid sense of isolation, plus easy access to hill climbing, trekking, and cross-country skiing (the hotel rents skis on-site).

N-2673 Høvrigen. *©* **61-23-37-11.** Fax 61-23-43-13. www.brekkeseter.no. 12 units, 17 cabins. 1,360NOK–3,400NOK ($181–$452) double; 680NOK–1,700NOK ($90–$226) cabin (2–10 occupants). Rates for double include three-fourths board; cabin rates do not include meals. AE, MC, V. Closed Easter to mid-June and mid-Oct to Christmas. **Amenities:** Restaurant; availability of trekking guides; babysitting; laundry service. *In room:* No phone.

6 Røros ★★: Norway's Great Mining Town

159km (99 miles) SE of Trondheim; 399km (248 miles) N of Oslo

Tucked away in the mountains of eastern Norway, the old mining town of Røros is now part of UNESCO's World Cultural and Natural Heritage List. It is the most famous and most evocative of Norway's mining towns.

More than three centuries old, it is known for its collection of 80 well-preserved buildings from the 17th and 18th centuries. Many of Norway's old wooden towns have long burned to the ground, but the Old Town of Røros is still so authentic that film companies regularly use the town as an authentic backdrop. One such film was *An-Magrit,* starring Liv Ullmann, the work of Røros's best-known author, Johan Falkberget, who lived in the town until his death in 1967. Some of Astrid Lindgren's *Pippi Longstocking* classics were filmed in Røros as well. It was used as a setting for Siberia in Solzhenitsyn's *A Day in the Life of Ivan Denisovich.*

Røros lies at the northern tier of the Osterdal, a valley to the east of Gudbrandsdalen. It is famous because of its rich copper mines, which were launched in 1644, and ran until going bankrupt in 1977.

ESSENTIALS

GETTING THERE By Plane Røros Airport (*©* **72-41-39-00**) is a 4-minute drive from the center of town. Widerøe Airlines, a partner of SAS, flies to and from Oslo Sunday to Friday.

By Train Røros has rail links with Oslo and Trondheim. Three trains per day arrive Monday through Saturday from Trondheim, taking 2½ hours, and three trains come in from Oslo, taking 5 hours. For train information and schedules, call *©* **81-50-08-88.**

By Bus   Three buses per day connect Trondheim and Røros, Monday through Saturday, taking 3¼ hours.

By Car   From Trondheim, take E6/route 30 south for 2½ hours.

VISITOR INFORMATION   For information, go to the **Røros Reiseliv Turistkontorget,** Peder Hiortsgata 2 (*©* **72-41-11-65**), a block from the train station. From June 25 to August 19, hours are Monday to Saturday 9am to 6pm, Sunday 10am to 4pm. The rest of the year, hours are Monday to Friday 9am to 3:30pm and Saturday 10:30am to 12:30pm.

SEEING THE SIGHTS

The best way to see Røros is to take a guided walk through the Old Town starting at the local tourist office (see above). In summer tours leave several times daily, costing 50NOK ($6.65), but free for children. In the off-season, only Saturday tours are conducted.

In town, you can also visit **Røros Kirke,** Kjerkgata (*©* **72-41-17-42**), which dates from 1650. It was established to cater to the workers in the smelting works. More than a century later, it was substantially rebuilt in the baroque style, seating 1,600 worshippers, amazingly large for a town of this size. It is an eight-sided stone structure with a pulpit sitting over the altarpiece. Admission is 25NOK ($3.35) for adults and free for children, and it is open June 21 to August 15 Monday and Saturday from 10am to 5pm, Sunday 2 to 4pm.

Røros offers several other attractions, including **Røros Museum-Smelthytta,** Mamplassen (*©* **72-40-61-70**), site of the first smelting works in the area, dating from 1646. A model exhibition here illustrates old mining and smelting technology, including ore hoists, waterwheels, horse-drawn winches, and furnaces. One section displays regional costumes from the 1800s. The building is a reconstruction of the original structure, which burned in a fire in 1953. Admission is 60NOK ($8) adults or 30NOK ($4) children. June 12 to August hours are Monday to Saturday 10am to 7pm, Sunday 10am to 4pm (closes at dusk during off-season).

A highlight of a visit to Røros is a side trip to **Olavsgruna** or Olav's Mine, Kojedalen (*©* **72-40-61-70**), lying 9.5km (6 miles) east of Røros. A guided tour will take you through three centuries of mining. The system here consists of two mines, Nyberget and Crown Prince Olav's mine. Nyberget is by far the oldest. The Prince Olav mine was only begun in 1936. The tour on foot takes you 50m (164 ft.) below the surface of the earth and 500m (164 ft.) into the cavern, where miners of yore tolled in miserable conditions. The temperature is about 41°F (5°C) all year. Sound-and-light effects help re-create the mood of the old mines. Mine tours cost 60NOK ($8) for adults and 30NOK ($4) for children. Hours are June 1 to September 1, 6 times daily. In the off-season, tours are conducted only on Saturday. If you're driving, follow the signs along Route 31 to the mines northeast from the center of Røros. Otherwise, a round-trip by taxi will cost 400NOK ($53).

The **Johan Falkberget Museum** honors the area's favorite son. The author (1879–1967) was reared at Trondalen Farm in the Rugel Valley outside Røros. Translated into 20 languages, he became a famous author around the world, his most celebrated book being *An-Magrit,* which was made into a 1969 film starring Liv Ullmann. It tells of a peasant girl who transported copper ore in the Røros mines. Falkberget's early poverty and toil in the mines colored all his works. The trilogies *Christianus Sextus* (1927–35) and *Bread of Night* (1940–59) concern mining life in the 17th and 18th centuries. They emphasize the virtues of hard work and Christian love. A museum of Falkberget memorabilia lies beside Lake Rugelsjø. Admission is 45NOK ($6) for adults, 25NOK ($3.35) for children. Tours are July 1 to August 5 daily at noon, 1pm, and 2pm. From August 6 to 12, tours are daily at noon. Local trains from Røros will take you to Rugeldalen Station, lying 20km (12 miles) north of Røros. You can take a sign-posted track leading up to the museum.

SHOPPING

Silversmiths, woodcarvers, painters, potters, and glassblowers abound in Greater Røros. Of special interest is **Thomasgarden Galleri Kafe,** Kjerkgata 48 (© **72-41-24-70**), which offers some of the most beautiful arts, crafts, pottery, wood sculpture, and metal items in town. Note the player piano from 1929, one of only two in the whole country. Pottery, sculpture, and wall decorations, all of high quality, are sold at **Per Sverre Dahl Keramikk,** Morkstugata 5 (© **72-41-19-89**).

WHERE TO STAY

Bergstadens Hotel   In the center of town near the train station, this hotel was built before World War II but brought up to date during extensive renovations in the '90s. A cozy, well-run choice, it is furnished in a modern Nordic style with light pastels. Half of the bedrooms open onto views of the mountains, and some have balconies. Each comes with a small bathroom with shower (a dozen also contain bathtubs). The staff is helpful in arranging outdoor activities such as horseback riding. One of the bars has live music 2 or 3 days a week. The hotel houses the largest concentration of eating and drinking establishments in town.

Oslovein 2, N-7640 Røros. © 72-40-60-80. Fax 72-40-60-81. 88 units. June–Aug 980NOK ($130) double; Sept–May 1,370NOK ($182) double. Children under 4 stay free. Rates include continental breakfast. AE, DC, MC, V. Free parking. **Amenities:** 2 restaurants; 3 bars; indoor heated pool; sauna; limited room service. *In room:* TV, minibar, hair dryer.

Quality Hotel Røros ⭐   This hotel enjoys good views from its high altitude position over the town, north of the rail station. It was built in the mid-1950s but enlarged and improved many times since its last renovation in 1999. The bedrooms are decorated in light pastels, opening onto a view of the Old Town or the mountains beyond. Furnishings are comfortable and tasteful, each unit coming with a small bathroom with shower (a few contain bathtubs as well). The hotel is used by locals as a sort of dining and dancing center after 9pm.

An-Magrittsvei, N-7361 Røros. © 72-40-80-00. Fax 72-40-80-01. www.choicehotels.com. 167 units. May–Aug 840NOK ($112) double, 1,340NOK ($178) suite; Sept–Apr 1,140NOK–1,445NOK ($152–$192) double, 1,845NOK ($245) suite. Children under 2 stay free. Rates include continental breakfast. AE, DC, MC, V. Free parking. Closed Dec 22–27. **Amenities:** Restaurant; bar; nightclub; sauna; limited room service; laundry service; dry cleaning. *In room:* TV, minibar.

WHERE TO DINE

Vertshuset Røros NORWEGIAN   This establishment offers well-prepared food and comfortable lodgings within one of the oldest and most nostalgically decorated dining and overnight venues in town. Whereas the restaurant directly fronts the street, the hotel is contained within a completely separate, also red-clapboard, building in back, in a central location not far from the village church. Frankly, the place is most famous as a restaurant, with attentive service, lots of early-20th-century decorative objects, and a menu that focuses on fish and game caught, trapped, or shot within the region. Stellar examples include filets of reindeer or elk in juniper berry sauce; grilled trout and salmon caught in local waters, sometimes served *meunière* style, and succulent preparations of lamb.

Beefsteaks are always a good bet, and the selection of wines comes from throughout Europe. The bedrooms, 24 in all, within the separate annex in back, rent for 950NOK to 1,150NOK ($126–$153), double occupancy, with breakfast included. In-room amenities include TV with cable connection and telephone.

Kjerkgata 24, N-7374 Røros. © **72-41-24-11.** Reservations recommended. Main courses 220NOK–260NOK ($29–$35). AE, DC, MC, V. Mon–Sat noon–9:30pm; Sun 1–8pm.

EASY EXCURSIONS

Norway's second largest lake is part of **Femundsmarka Nasjonalpark** ✪ (© **62-45-88-96**), lying to the immediate southwest of Norway bordering Sweden. It became a national park in 1971, and has long been a retreat for falconry. In the park, wild reindeer can be seen grazing at the upper elevations. In summer, nearly three dozen musk oxen call the park home before migrating during the winter months.

From June 10 to August 26, buses go between Røros and Synnervika, a hamlet that is the gateway to the park. Plan for an 8:15am departure. Once at the park, you can take the ferry, MS *Foemund II,* a diesel engine boat that sails from the northern shore of Lake Femunden. The boat sails daily from June 10 to August 25, allowing you to take in the shores of this beautiful lake.

8

Southern Norway

The coastal lands of southern Norway, shaped geographically like a half-moon, are often called Norway's Riviera because of their beaches, bays, and sailing opportunities. Within this area, the Telemark region is known for its lakes and canals, which are used for summer boating and canoeing. From Skien, visitors can explore this water network. Arendal is a charming old town with a harbor near some of the best beaches. Kristiansand S is a link between Norway and the rest of Europe. The Christiansholm Fortress has stood here since 1674, and the town is near Haresanden, a 10km-long (over 6-mile-long) beach.

The southern part of Norway is called Sørlandet, a land of hills, valleys, mountains, rivers, and lakes. The area gets more sunshine than any other place in Norway and northern Europe. Gulf Stream temperatures make bathing possible in summer. This section is the major domestic vacation choice for Norwegians.

Rogaland is the southwestern part of the country, and it has been called "Norway in a nutshell" because of its great variety. Fjords, mountains, green valleys, beaches, old towns and villages, a mild climate, and countless fishing possibilities make this area a prime vacation spot.

The district lives today in the technological future, thanks to its oil industry, but it also harks back to the country's oldest inhabitants. Here, the Viking king Harald Fairhair gathered most of Norway into one kingdom in A.D. 872. The locals say that it was from here that the Vikings sailed to discover America.

Rogaland also consists of the hilly Dalane in the south, the flat Jaeren (farmland), the beautiful Ryfylke, and in the north Karmøy and Haugesund.

1 Kongsberg: Where Silver Was King

84km (52 miles) SW of Oslo; 40km (25 miles) W of Drammen

For more than 2 centuries, Kongsberg was the silver mining town of Norway. It was back in 1623 when two children spotted a big ox butting a cliff with his horns, uncovering a silver vein. Their father hoped to profit from the windfall, but the king heard the news and promptly dispatched his soldiers to force the man to reveal the location of the mother lode.

Suddenly, Kongsberg was overrun. Between the 1623 discovery and 1957, some 1.35 million kilograms of pure "wire" silver filled the king's purse. Even today, though the mines are closed, Kongsberg is still home to the Royal Norwegian Mint, which has been operating in the town since 1686.

Some 4,000 workers are employed today in high-tech companies located here, and instead of silver you'll find industries such as aerospace and car-part production.

The falls of the Lågen River divide the town into two parts. The oldest district, lying west of the river, is the site of the major attractions. The newer part in the east encompasses the visitor information center, the traffic hubs, and the best shops.

Arendal **4**
Dalen **1**
Grimstad **5**
Kongsberg **2**
Kristiansand S **6**
Skien **3**

ESSENTIALS

GETTING THERE   From the Central Station in Oslo, **trains** leave every 2 hours during the day, taking 1½ hours to reach Kongsberg at a cost of 130NOK ($17) for a one-way ticket. For more information, call ☏ **81-50-08-88.** There is also bus service from Oslo aboard **Nettbuss Telemark** (☏ **35-02-60-00**), taking 1½ hours and costing 120NOK ($16) per one-way ticket. Motorists can take the E18 southwest of Oslo to Drammen. From Drammen, continue southwest along Route 11.

VISITOR INFORMATION   Opposite the rail depot, the **Kongsberg Tourist Office,** Storgata 35 (☏ **32-73-50-00**), is open June 25 to mid-August from 9am to 5pm Monday to Friday and from 10am to 5pm Saturday and Sunday. Off-season hours are Monday to Friday from 9am to 4:30pm and 10am to 2pm on Saturday.

GETTING AROUND   You can walk around the Old Town or rent a bike from the tourist office (see "Visitor Information," above) at a cost of 150NOK ($20) per day.

SPECIAL EVENTS   Now beginning its fourth decade, the **Kongsberg International Jazz Festival** in July is attended by some of the most important jazz artists in Europe. The King's Mine and the baroque church are among the choice concert venues for this major musical event. Call ☏ **32-73-31-66** for complete details.

SEEING THE SIGHTS

Kongsberg Kirke ★★, Kirketorget (☏ **32-73-50-00**), the largest baroque church in Norway—and also the most impressive—is found in the old city on the western bank of the Lågen River. Seating a 2,400-member congregation, this 1761 church bears witness to the silver-mining prosperity of Kongsberg. The beautiful interior is made all the more stunning because of three huge, glittering glass chandeliers created at the Nøstetangen Glassworks.

As a curiosity, note that the rococo altar joins the large pulpit, altarpiece, and organ pipes on a single wall. Constructed in the shape of a cross, the church has a tower surmounting one of its transepts. You can still see the royal box, reserved for visits from the king, and the smaller boxes, meant for the top mining officials. Naturally, the church owns many valuable pieces of silver. In olden days, it took six strong men to ring the church's mammoth bell, which was cast in Denmark. Admission is free and guided tours are 30NOK ($4). The church is open mid-May to August 21 Monday through Friday from 10am to 5pm, Saturday from 10am to 1pm, and Sunday 2 to 4pm. Off-season, it's open Tuesday through Friday, from 10am to noon.

You'll find four museums housed in a single converted building that once belonged to the Silver Mining Company at the **Norsk bergverksmuseum** ★, Hyttegata 3 (☏ **32-72-32-00**).

The **Norwegian Mining Museum** traces 3 centuries of silver mining. One 18th-century working model illustrates the entire process of mining and smelting the precious silver ore. The machinery used in the smelting process can still be seen in the basement. Some of the specimens on exhibit are made of pure silver.

Also on site is the **Den Kongelige Mynts Museum,** devoted to the Royal Mint, which was relocated here in 1685. The museum contains a rare collection of coins minted in town. A third museum, the **Kongsberg Arms Factory Museum,** traces the city's industrial history from 1814 onward.

Finally, a fourth museum, **Kongsberg Skimuseum,** honors many local skiers such as Birger Ruud and Petter Hugsted, who went on to Olympic glory and world championships. A historic collection of skis and equipment is on view. The most recent exhibition details the daring exploits of Børge Ousland and Erling Kagge on their ski expeditions to the North and South Poles, where they attracted world attention.

Admission to all museums is 50NOK ($6.65) for adults, 10NOK ($1.35) for children. Hours are from mid-May to August daily 10am to 5pm; September daily noon to 4pm; off-season Sunday to Friday noon to 5pm.

You might also want to explore **Lågdalsmuseet (Lågdal Folk Museum),** Tillischbakken 8–10 (© **32-73-34-68**), a 12-minute stroll southeast from the rail depot. Nearly three dozen antique farmhouses and miners' cottages were moved to this site. This is the most history-rich exhibit of how life used to be lived in the scenic Numedal Valley, which was mainly home to the families of miners and farmers. The 19th-century workshops you'd expect (most open-air museums in Norway have these), but an optics museum and a World War II Resistance Museum come as a surprise. Admission is 40NOK ($5.30) for adults and 10NOK ($1.35) for children. From June 23 to August 15, the museum is open daily from 11am to 5pm. From mid-May to June 22 and August 16 to 31, it is open Saturday and Sunday 11am to 5pm. In the off-season, hours are Monday to Friday 11am to 3:30pm.

The town's big attraction is still the **Kongsberg Sølvgruver** ★★, the old silver mines that put Kongsberg on the map in the first place. To reach these mines, you can take an Expressen Bus from Kongsberg to the hamlet of Saggrenda, taking 10 minutes and costing 40NOK ($5.30). Departures are hourly from Kongsberg. Once at Saggrenda, it is a 15-minute walk to the entrance to the mines, where you can take a guided tour lasting 1 hour and 20 minutes. You can also drive from Kongsberg to Saggrenda, a distance of 8km (5 miles) to the southwest following Route 11.

The tour of the mines begins with a ride on a little train going 2.25km (1½ miles) inside the mountain containing the King's Mine, a journey back into time. The train stops at a depth of 342m (1,122 ft.) below ground. This is the entrance to the King's Mine, which reaches a total depth of 1,070m (3,510 ft.) below the earth. You can still see the *Fahrkunst,* invented by German miners. Dating from 1880, it was the first "elevator" to carry miners up and down. You'll also see the old mining equipment on the tour.

Regardless of the time of year, wear warm clothing before going down into the mines. In July and early August tours are conducted daily at 11am, 12:30pm, 2pm, and 3:30pm. From mid-May to June and in late August, tours run at 11am, 12:30pm, and 2pm. In September, one tour is conducted on Sunday at 2pm. Tours cost 60NOK ($8) for adults or 25NOK ($3.35) for children.

WHERE TO STAY

Quality Hotel Grand ★   In a modern building, this hotel is the finest choice for an overnight in the area. Most of its bedrooms have been recently renovated, and some of them open onto views of a waterfall. Others open onto views of the mountains. Each room is tastefully and comfortably furnished, although accommodations tend to be a bit small. Thirty percent of the units contain bathrooms with tubs and showers, the rest have only showers. The hotel also offers the best drinking, dining, and entertainment facilities in town. Its piano bar is a nightly attraction, and on Friday and Saturday nights from 9pm to 3am there is disco action, costing 80NOK ($11) for nonguests (guests enter free). You also have a choice of light dining in a lounge or more formal Norwegian and international cuisine in the hotel's main restaurant.

Christian August Gate 2, N-3611 Kongsberg. © **32-77-28-00.** Fax 32-73-41-29. www.quality-grand.no. 176 units. 930NOK–1,460NOK ($124–$194) double; 1,480NOK–1,600NOK ($197–$213) suite. Children under 15 stay free in parent's room. Rates include continental breakfast. AE, DC, MC, V. Closed Dec 23–Jan 1. **Amenities:** 2 restaurants; 2 bars; indoor heated pool; sauna; laundry service; dry cleaning. *In room:* TV, minibar, hair dryer, iron/ironing board.

WHERE TO DINE

Gamle Kongsberg Kro NORWEGIAN   This restaurant at Nybrofossen lies next to the waterfall and is not only the most scenically located dining venue in town, but also the spot for the best cuisine. Hearty, regional dishes are served here in generous helpings at affordable prices. In a big white house, the restaurant offers a large dining area, with room for 130 patrons. There are good views of the river and the waterfall from the windows of the restaurant. Food is well prepared, and the recipes are all traditional and familiar. You'll begin with a choice of appetizers such as a shrimp cocktail or a bowl of fish soup, to be followed by main courses dear to the heart of any Norwegian. The chef's specialty is filet of reindeer served in a red wine sauce with baked potato. You can also order beef cooked with bacon and served with a béarnaise sauce. For us, nothing beats the grilled Norwegian salmon, cooked to perfection and served with a white wine sauce. After all that, you might forego the banana split for dessert and opt instead for the wild berries with ice cream.

Thornesvn. 4. © **32-73-16-33.** Reservations recommended. Main courses 188NOK–239NOK ($25–$32). DC, MC, V. Daily 1–10pm. Closed Dec 24–Jan 2.

EASY EXCURSIONS: HEDDAL STAVE CHURCH ✦✦✦

The greatest man-made attraction in Southern Norway, the Heddal Stave Church lies 33km (21 miles) west of Kongsberg, reached by taking Route 11 toward Notodden. This medieval architectural masterpiece is still in use today. Heddal is the largest of the 28 stave churches still remaining in Norway.

The oldest part of the church, the chancel, was built of wood in 1147. About a century later the church was enlarged to its present format. Runic inscriptions reveal that the church was consecrated in 1242 and dedicated to the Virgin Mary. Inside are a beautiful wooden carved chair from 1200, a baptismal font from 1850, and two of the original pillars from the church. The altarpiece is the work of an unknown artist in 1667. The wall painting is from 1668. The church rises 25m (85 ft.) high and is 19m (65 ft.) long.

Dragons and serpents, along with grotesque human heads, are depicted on the portals. An occasional human face can be seen peering out. The church (© **35-02-00-93**) charges 30NOK ($4) for adults; free for children. From June 21 to August 20 it is open 9am to 7pm daily. From May 20 to June 20 and August 21 to September 10 hours are daily 10am to 5pm.

2 Skien: Memories of Henrik Ibsen

138km (86 miles) S of Oslo; 30km (19 miles) W of the Larvik-Frederikshavn (Denmark) ferry connection

Skien is a bustling industrial town and the administrative capital of Telemark country. Long proud of its association with playwright Henrik Ibsen (1828–1906), a native of Skien, it is visited not only for its Ibsen associations, but because it is the principal gateway to Telemark.

Skien is an old town, dating from 1100, although it wasn't until 1358 that it received its royal charter. Fire and floods ravaged Skien over the centuries, destroying the entire town at times. The last disastrous fire occurred in 1886, and a new town had to be created out of the debris. Skien covers an area of 786 sq. km (489 sq. miles), with nearly 32,000 inhabitants.

The main reason most visitors go to Skien today, other than its Ibsen associations, is that it is the gateway to the **Telemark Canal** (p. 197) and the starting point for many trips.

ESSENTIALS

GETTING THERE   Trains run every hour or two from Oslo to Skien, taking 1¾ hours and costing 220NOK ($29) one-way. Call © **81-50-08-88** for schedules. Motorists take the E18 south from Oslo to Larvik until the signposted turnoff (Rte. 36) heading northwest into Skien. You can also fly to the small Sandefjord Airport (© **33-42-70-00**), lying near Skien. Even though it's small, it is the country's second busiest international airport. From the airport, buses run into the center of Skien.

VISITOR INFORMATION   For information, go to the **Skien Tourist Office,** Nedre Hjellegate 18 (© **35-58-19-10**), open June and August Monday to Saturday 10am to 5pm, July daily 10am to 8pm, and September to May Monday to Saturday 9am to 4pm.

SEEING THE SIGHTS

Ibsen left Skien in 1843 when he was 15 years old, returning only briefly as part of an unsuccessful attempt to borrow some money to enter prep school in Oslo. He lived at several addresses in Skien, including a small house in an old neighborhood, Snipetorp 27, near the town center. The house on Snipetorp is one of several in the neighborhood that have been proclaimed protected monuments. Ibsen's former home is now a cultural center and an art gallery.

Bø Sommarland *Kids*   This is the country's largest water park, drawing families from all over Norway during the summer. More than 100 different activities await you here, including a Kid's Waterpark (ideal for small children) and Bøverstranda ("The Beach"), along with water slides, plus Sommarlandelva, a 250m (820 ft.) artificial river. The Flow rider is for those who love skateboarding, "snowboarding," and surfing. Of course, the waves here are artificial, but they are said to be the best of their kind in the world. You can also experience Europe's first (and so far only) roller-coaster flume. Near the entrance is the scenic lake, Steinjønn, where you can borrow a canoe for a ride. The latest attraction is Playworld, one of Europe's largest play castles. There's also a big amusement area, Las Bøgas, with a Ferris wheel, amusement arcade, merry-go-rounds, and lots of games. Entertainment is also presented on stage. The park lies 50km (30 miles) from Skien and 25km (15 miles) from Notodden.

Bø. © **35-95-16-99.** Admission 200NOK ($27). June 8–Aug 18 daily 8am–dusk.

Brekkeparken ✦   This 1780 manor house is the headquarters of the Telemark Museum. Attracting theater buffs from around the world, it allows you to visit Ibsen's reconstructed study and the bedrooms from his Oslo apartment, as well as his "blue salon." In addition, there is a **remarkable collection of folk art from the 1700s and 1800s** ✦, including many authentic pieces such as national costumes, textiles, handcrafts, and woodcarving. As you wander the park in late spring, you can take in the largest **tulip park** ✦✦ in Scandinavia. In addition to the main building, there are some 20 old structures that have been moved here from different districts in Telemark.

Øvregate 41. ℂ **35-52-35-94.** Admission 40NOK ($5.30). Mid-May to Aug daily 10am–6pm.

Venstøp ⭐ Ibsen's childhood home, Venstøp Farm, lies 5km (3 miles) northwest of Skien. The house is furnished with objects actually used by the Ibsen family when they lived here from 1835 to 1843. The building itself dates from the early 19th century, and the dark attic was the inspiration for the playwright's *The Wild Duck.* Two paintings are by Ibsen—he had originally wanted to become an artist, but his wife ("the cat") insisted that he be a playwright. In her words, she "gave" the world a great dramatic talent but spared it a mediocre artist.

Venstøp. ℂ **35-52-35-94.** Admission 40NOK ($5.30). Mid-May to Aug daily 10am–6pm; Sept Sun 10am–6pm.

WHERE TO STAY

Comfort Hotel Bryggeparken This hotel looks much older that it is, because it's constructed in a traditional style close to the harbor and river. In actuality, the five-story brick structure was both built and opened in 2001. Offering the newest and freshest rooms in towns, it is furnished in a contemporary style. Some of the rooms have balconies opening onto water views. All of them are comfortable and tasteful, with small bathrooms, 28 of which contain tubs and showers, the rest contain showers only. From 6 to 9pm nightly, guests can enjoy a light evening meal included in the rate.

Langbryggen 7, N-3724 Skien. ℂ **35-91-21-00.** Fax 35-91-21-01. www.choicehotels.com. 103 units. 1,055NOK–1,275NOK ($140–$170) double; 1,755NOK–1,975NOK ($233–$263) suite. Rates include continental breakfast and light evening meal. AE, DC, MC, V. Closed Dec 20–Jan 2. **Amenities:** Restaurant; bar; sauna. *In room:* TV, minibar, coffeemaker, hair dryer, iron/ironing board.

Golden Tulip Rainbow Hoyers Hotell ⭐ In a structure dating from 1850, this much renovated and improved hotel is one of the leading accommodations choices in town. It's long been a traditional favorite, standing in the center of gardens stretching to the water. It lies a 3-minute taxi ride from the rail station. Its bedrooms, each comfortably and attractively furnished, are among the best in town. All the accommodations come with small bathrooms with showers. The drinking and dining facilities here are some of the finest in Skien.

Kongensgate 6, N-3701 Skien. ℂ **35-90-58-00.** Fax 35-90-58-05. www.rainbow-hotels.no. 75 units. 910NOK–1,400NOK ($121–$186) double; 2,250NOK ($299) suite. Rates include continental breakfast. AE, DC, MC, V. Free parking. Closed Dec 22–Jan 2. **Amenities:** Restaurant; bar; 24-hr. room service. *In room:* TV, minibar, coffeemaker, hair dryer.

Rica Ibsen Hotel ⭐⭐ This well-rated hotel stands near the Brekkepark, where Ibsen is said to have received much of his early inspiration. A stylish hotel, it was designed and built in 1979 of red brick and panes of insulated glass, and is considered the best hotel in town. It boasts a high-ceilinged interior with many trees, whose combined effect is to create the impression of a vast greenhouse burgeoning with seasonal flowers and plants. Each midsize bedroom is well furnished and maintained, and decorated in a contemporary style which is kept up to date. Only 15 units contain bathrooms with tub and shower, the rest come with shower. The staff is helpful in making arrangements for excursions, including trips to the Telemark Canal.

Kongensgate 33, N-3701 Skien. ℂ **35-90-47-00.** Fax 35-90-47-01. www.rica.no. 119 units. June 10–Aug 10 860NOK ($114) double; otherwise 1,330NOK ($177) double; 1,450NOK–1,950NOK ($193–$259) year-round suite. Rates include continental breakfast. AE, DC, MC, V. Closed Dec 22–Jan 2. **Amenities:** Restaurant; bar; indoor heated pool; sauna; limited room service; laundry service; dry cleaning. *In room:* TV.

WHERE TO DINE

Boden Spiseri ⭐ NORWEGIAN/INTERNATIONAL   Even though it was established in 1987, this restaurant has quickly become the town's most charmingly old-fashioned restaurant. A 10-minute walk south of the rail station, it's housed in a clapboard-sided building originally erected as a harbor-front warehouse in the 1870s. It is the oldest building in town. The chefs are busily preparing first-class food with quality ingredients to match the impressive surroundings.

Launch your repast with the likes of shrimp salad with bacon or perhaps a slice of melon with delectable Parma ham. The main courses include a familiar array of typically Norwegian fare such as grilled filet of reindeer served with creamy potatoes and fresh vegetables, and filet of lamb in a port wine sauce. A recommended fish course is the grilled dogfish with white wine sauce, fried potatoes, and fresh vegetables.

Langbryggene 5. ☎ 35-52-61-70. Reservations required. Main courses 200NOK–300NOK ($27–$40). AE, DC, MC, V. Sun–Thurs 6pm–1:30am; Fri–Sat 6pm–2:30am.

Restaurant Couenar _Value_ NORWEGIAN   This is a good choice for moderately priced food served at the oldest and most traditional hotel in town, the Golden Tulip Rainbow Hoyers Hotell (p. 196), which lies almost 1km (about ½ mile) south of the railroad station. During the day many locals drop in for a feast of _smørebrød_—open-faced sandwiches. The kitchen also turns out more substantial and rib-sticking fare. On our last visit, we were enticed by the appetizer of smoked trout, served with a creamy apple and celery salad. The main courses are well prepared and concentrate on Norway's field and steam. Try the filet of reindeer steak with mushrooms and steamed vegetables or the filet of river trout stuffed with shrimp and crayfish. For something more exotic, sample the halibut shipped over from Greenland and served with a mustard and dill sauce. The dessert specialty is vanilla ice cream with raisins, marinated ginger, and a dash of rum.

Kongensgate 6. ☎ 35-90-58-00. Reservations recommended. Main courses 190NOK–230NOK ($25–$31). AE, DC, MC, V. Mon–Sat 4–10pm.

Susannah's Restaurant ⭐ _Finds_ NORWEGIAN   A lively spot for dining, this restaurant is filled with the same bounty of trees and flowers that adorns the greenhouse lobby of the Rica Ibsen Hotel (p. 196), which houses the restaurant. Located in the center of Skien almost half a kilometer (about ¼ mile) from the train station, it's a big-windowed restaurant used by local residents as a dining venue for special occasions. Chefs take infinite pains to turn out flavorful dishes based whenever possible on local products. Fresh fish and Norwegian lamb and beef are their forte. Our party recently enjoyed pan-fried beef Susannah with wild mushrooms, streamed broccoli, and boiled potatoes in a well-flavored mushroom gravy. Desserts, made fresh daily, are quite luscious.

Kongensgate 33. ☎ 35-90-47-00. Reservations recommended. Main courses 186NOK–228NOK ($25–$30). AE, DC, MC, V. Mon–Sat 11am–11pm.

EASY EXCURSIONS: THE TELEMARK CANAL ⭐⭐

Skien is the gateway to the Telemark Canal, which was completed in 1892 and called "the eighth wonder of the world." Five hundred men labored for 5 years on this canal, blasting their way through mountains. Today it contains a total of 28 lock chambers, and the route runs from Skien in the east to the ancient Norwegian town of Dalen in the west. The canal affords a sailing route of 105km (65 miles) with an elevation difference of 72m (236 ft.).

At the turn of the 20th century the canal became known as the "fast route" between eastern and western Norway. Nostalgic canal boats, the MS *Victoria,* the MS *Henrik Ibsen,* and the MS *Telemarken* will take you from Skien to Dalen, a 10-hour trip on this historic waterway, costing 600NOK ($80) round-trip.

For more information and bookings, contact **Telemarkreister,** Handelstorget (② **35-90-00-30**), in Skien.

WHERE TO STAY & DINE IN DALEN

Dalen Hotel ⚹⚹   Set at the terminus of the Telemark Canal, with dragon heads and Viking-inspired gingerbread dripping from its eaves, this historic hotel has some similarities to Norway's medieval stave churches. This hotel is often cited as a fine example of the Norwegian nationalist style. Built in 1894 during the birth of modern tourism, it was a lodging for prominent guests interested in seeing the natural beauty of a region that had just opened thanks to the completion of the Telemark Canal. It has welcomed King Leopold II of Belgium; the king of Siam; and at least two of Norway's late 19th- and 20th-century kings. Today, thanks to almost 20 years of ongoing renovations, its ocher-and-brown, mostly wood-built premises still evokes the fantasy and whimsy of the late Victorian age. It is graced with symmetrical towers, soaring turrets, wide verandas, high ceilings, and bright colors. Don't expect a trend-conscious group of clients here, or a sense that you're in a place that's on the cutting edge of glamour. Instead, you may get the feeling that you're in a rather reverentially preserved national monument that's in an ongoing state of renovation, and infused with an enormous sense of national pride. Rooms come in various shapes and sizes, decidedly old-fashioned but well maintained, each attached to a private bathroom with tub and shower.

N-3880 Dalen I Telemark. ② **35-07-70-00.** Fax 35-07-70-11. www.dalenhotel.no. 38 units. 900NOK–1,200NOK ($120–$160) double. Rates include breakfast. AE, DC, MC, V. Closed Nov–May. **Amenities:** Restaurant; bar; easy access to fishing, hill climbing, and trekking; laundry service. *In room:* TV.

3 Arendal & Merdøy Island

239km (149 miles) SW of Oslo; 69km (43 miles) E of Kristiansand S

The administrative center of the Aust-Agder district, this southern port city was once known as "the Venice of Scandinavia" because of its canals. But following a disastrous fire, these canals were turned into wide streets. The city's sheltered harbor is one of the most colorful along the coast.

For the best look at old Arendal, visit **Tyholmen** in the center, with its handsomely preserved 18th-century wooden houses. The 1992 winner of the Europa Nostra prize for restoration, the district is home today to many artists and craftspeople who have moved in and taken over the old houses. In summer, the harbor, **Pollen,** is filled with boats and people, as this is one of the most popular centers for domestic tourism in Norway. Many Norwegians come here to take boat trips among the neighboring rocks, and they also traverse the delta of the Nid River.

In addition to Ibsen, the region's second-most-famous son was Knut Hamsunm, called the "Balzac of Norway." He won the Nobel Prize in 1918. His novels give a vivid portrait of 19th-century Norwegian values, and his works are still very popular in Germany, almost more so than they are in Norway.

ESSENTIALS

GETTING THERE   By Train   Four trains a day arrive from Oslo, requiring a change of trains at Nelaug. Trip time, including the transfer, is 4½ hours. For schedules and information, call ② **81-50-08-88.**

By Bus   Nor-way Bussekspress buses travel between Oslo and Arendal, taking 1¾ hours and costing 100NOK ($13) for one-way passage.

By Car   From Skien (see above), our last stopover, E18 continues south into Arendal.

VISITOR INFORMATION   For helpful advice about Arendal and the surrounding area, go to the **Arendal Turistkontor,** Langbrygga 5 (© **37-00-55-44**), open mid-June to mid-August Monday to Saturday 9am to 7pm and Sunday noon to 7pm. Otherwise, hours are Monday to Friday 9am to 4pm.

SEEING THE SIGHTS

Arendal Rådhus   The Rådhus, or Town Hall, in the center of town, still houses the administrative offices of the city. It's better known as the second-largest timber building in Norway and the country's single tallest timber structure. Built in 1815, the building has some 300 antique portraits, most of them painted in the 19th century, the largest such collection in Norway.

Rådhusgata 19. © **37-01-30-00.** Free admission. Mon–Fri 9am–3pm.

Aust-Agder Museum ⭐ *(Finds*   This is an unusual museum, a result of the fact that the town's sailors were asked to bring home items from their global sailing that might interest the folks back home. These seafarers succeeded admirably, and the museum opened in 1932. In addition to finds from around the world, the museum also showcases the folk art of the region and is filled with memorabilia of the history of the town, mainly artifacts from its seafaring heyday. The museum lies about 1.5km (1 mile) north of the center; to reach it, follow the signs in the direction of Oslo.

Parkveien 16. © **37-07-35-00.** Admission 20NOK ($2.65) adults, 10NOK ($1.35) children. June 25–Aug 13 Mon–Fri 9am–5pm, Sun noon–5pm. Aug 14–June 24 Mon–Fri 9am–3pm, Sun noon–3pm.

WHERE TO STAY

Clarion Tyholmen Hotel ⭐   Enjoying panoramic views of one of Norway's loveliest harbors, this hotel is the most interesting in town and one of the best bets in the area for an overnight stopover. Architecturally, it was inspired by the 1800s, the heyday of the sailing vessels that put Arendal on the map. The decor of each bedroom reflects the history of a different ship constructed in Norway, and each unit is named for a particular vessel. All the accommodations are decorated in soothing pastels, with modern furnishings and come with midsize bathrooms with tub-and-shower combinations. The hotel's outdoor restaurant is one of the most popular in the area during the summer. The dining facilities here are so excellent that you may want to patronize the hotel for food and drink even if you're not a guest. See below for dining recommendations here. The location is a 2-minute walk south of the bus station.

Teaterplassen 2, N-4800 Arendal. © **37-02-68-00.** Fax 37-02-68-01. www.clarion.no. 60 units. Mid-June to mid-Aug 850NOK ($113) double; off-season Mon–Fri 1,525NOK ($203) double, Sat–Sun 930NOK ($124) double. AE, DC, MC, V. **Amenities:** 2 restaurants; bar; sauna; limited room service; laundry service; dry cleaning. *In room:* A/C, TV, minibar, hair dryer.

Scandic Hotel   Despite frequent renovations, and a foundation that may have supported many buildings before this one, much of what you'll see when you look at this pleasant hotel dates from the late 1960s. Only three of its five floors contain bedrooms; the remaining two floors are entirely devoted to conference and convention facilities, making it the frequent host for corporate conventions from throughout Norway. Bedrooms were all renovated in 2001, and come in monochromatic tones of pale blue, pale green, and earth tones. Each of the tiled bathrooms has its own shower, and a few (only 10) have bathtubs as well. The hotel's steakhouse, Botanica, is separately recommended.

Fiergangen 1, N-4800 Arendal. ✆ 37-05-21-50. Fax 37-05-21-51. www.scandic-hotels.com. 84 units. Mon–Thurs 1,075NOK ($143) double; Fri–Sun and daily from mid-June to mid-Aug 980NOK ($130) double. AE, DC, MC, V. **Amenities:** Restaurant; bar; nightclub; lobby bar with pianist; business center; laundry service; dry cleaning. *In room:* TV, minibar.

WHERE TO DINE

Botanica STEAKHOUSE   This is Arendal's most popular steakhouse. Set on the street level of the Scandic Hotel (recommended above), it boasts a mustard-colored and brown decor, lots of exposed paneling, a pleasant staff, and a warm and cozy setting. Typical but good menu items include T-bone, tenderloin, and pepper steaks, and about every other cut of beef you can imagine. There's also a limited array of fish dishes, especially trout, catfish, and salmon, prepared either with butter and white wine sauce, blackened, or any other way you prefer.

In the Scandic Hotel, Fiergangen 1. ✆ 37-05-21-50. Reservations recommended. Main courses 100NOK–130NOK ($13–$17) at lunch, 200NOK–220NOK ($27–$29) at dinner. AE, DC, MC, V. Mon–Fri 10am–10:30pm; Sat 10am–11pm; Sun 3–10pm.

Ruffan STEAKS/NORWEGIAN   For people with hearty appetites, this is the most favored dining spot in town. However, its food, although good, is not the best in town. The on-site Tre Seil (see below) is better. But the ingredients are market-fresh and deftly handled by a well-trained kitchen staff. Ruffan is a cozy cellar kind of place with nautical decor, housed within Arendal's best hotel, the Clarion Tyholmen Hotel (p. 199). Sometimes the chefs get a little fancy, offering an appetizer such as a West Indian–inspired dish of minced shrimp and chile pepper toasted with grilled avocado and served with soy sauce. They also offer truly excellent stuffed baked potatoes and such standard but well-prepared dishes as lamb chops and perfectly roasted chicken. But most guests prefer their specialty, which is grilled steak. Tender cuts are used, and the steaks are charbroiled to your specifications and served with mashed potatoes in an herb-butter sauce.

In the Clarion Tyholmen Hotel, Teaterplassen 2. ✆ 37-02-68-00. Main courses 210NOK–265NOK ($28–$35). AE, DC, MC, V. Daily 6–11pm.

Tre Seil ✪ NORWEGIAN   "Three Sails," also located in the Clarion Tyholmen Hotel (p. 199), is the most prestigious restaurant in town. With its nautical decor, it offers big windows looking out over the moored yachts and boats bobbing in the harbor. You'll enjoy excellent cuisine and formal service. The upper-crust clientele frequently orders the steak—the best in the area. For a recommended main course, we'd suggest the herb-marinated filet of lamb with squash, onions, and peppers in a creamy game sauce. You might also try the salmon with a sour-cream sauce and Norwegian crabs. We are especially fond of the chef's large prawns gratinée with garlic, herbs, and butter. For a real "taste of Norway," opt for the grilled filet of reindeer saddle or the perfectly grilled filet of salmon caught in Norwegian fjords.

In the Clarion Tyholmen Hotel, Teaterplassen 2. ✆ 37-02-68-00. Reservations recommended. Main courses 175NOK–275NOK ($23–$37); 4-course fixed-price menu 430NOK ($57). AE, DC, MC, V. Mon–Sat 6–11pm; Sun 1–6pm.

EASY EXCURSIONS

In the bay of Arendal, **Merdøy Island** ✪ is like a time capsule. It's virtually intact architecturally from its days as a prosperous 19th-century town. Its clapboard-sided houses still have their allure today.

There are no restaurants, only a small cafe, and a lovely bathing beach.

The **Merdøgaård Museum** (© 37-07-35-00) on the island is run by the Aust-Agder Museum (see below). The museum is the perfectly preserved early-19th-century house of a long-departed sea captain, with the furnishings intact. A guardian lives on the premises to show you around. It's open from June 25 to August 12, daily noon to 4:30pm. Admission is 20NOK ($2.65) adults, 10NOK ($1.35) children.

To reach the island, take a ferry departing for Pollen at Arendal's harbor front. Departures are three or four times daily, and the boat makes stops at two or three other islands before reaching Merdøy. The ferry costs 25NOK ($3.35) each way, and the trip takes 20 minutes. For schedules and more information, call © 37-02-64-23.

Lying 20km (12½ miles) west of the center of Arendal is Grimstad, site of the **Grimstad Bymuseum-Ibsenhuset,** Henrik Ibsen Gate 14 (© 37-04-46-53), in the center of town. Henrik Ibsen worked in this town at a pharmacy while pursuing the pharmacist's daughter. Ibsen wrote his first play, *Catalina,* here. The Grimstad museum includes the old pharmacy and Ibsen's house. Admission is 40NOK ($5.30) for adults, 15NOK ($2) for children. Open May 1 to September 15 Monday to Saturday 11am to 5pm, Sunday 1 to 5pm.

4 Kristiansand S: The Summer City ⊛

526km (327 miles) SE of Bergen; 342km (213 miles) SW of Oslo

Visitors heading to Bergen and the fjord country often arrive in Norway at Kristiansand S (not to be confused with Kristiansund N in the north). The biggest city and an important port of Sørtlandet (the south coast), Kristiansand S has been called "the pearl of the Norwegian Riviera."

Founded by King Christian in 1641, Kristiansand S is a busy port and industrial center, yet it has many charming old streets and antique houses clustered cozily together. Water surrounds the city.

Kristiansand S is the largest town in the south and Norway's largest ferry port. **Kvadraturen,** "the quadrant," is known for its right-angled street plan that was influenced by the Renaissance period's strict adherence to form. **Markens** is the town's pedestrian precinct and meeting place.

The fifth largest city in Norway, with some 75,000 inhabitants, Kristiansand is called *Sommerbyen* or "the Summer City."

ESSENTIALS

GETTING THERE   By Plane   Kristiansand Airport lies at Kjevik, 16km (10 miles) east of the city center. Braathens (© 81-52-00-00) flies from Oslo to Kristiansand. An airport bus runs between Kjevik and the heart of Kristiansand.

By Train   Anywhere from three to six trains link Oslo and Kristiansand daily, taking 4½ hours, a one-way ticket costing 450NOK ($60).

By Bus   Nor-Way Bussekspress buses travel down from Oslo in 5½ hours, a one-way ticket costing 390NOK ($52). Buses run two to four times daily.

By Ferry   International ferries link Kristiansand to Hirtshals in the northern reaches of Denmark's Jutland peninsula. Ferries run three to four times daily, depending on the time of year, the sea voyage taking 4 hours. **Color Line** (© 22-94-44-00) operates these ferries. This is the shortest ferry link between Norway and Denmark. Depending on the time of year, fares can range from

170NOK to 395NOK ($23–$53). The highest fares are charged on weekends from mid-June to mid-August.

By Car From our last stopover at Arendal, the E18 continues southwest in Kristiansand.

VISITOR INFORMATION For help, go to **Destinasjon Sørlandet,** Vestre Strandgate 2 (© **38-12-13-14**), which also distributes bus, train, and ferry schedules. Open June 18 to August 19 Monday to Friday 8:30am to 6pm, Saturday 10am to 6pm, and Sunday noon to 6pm. Otherwise, hours are Monday to Friday 8:30am to 3:30pm.

GETTING AROUND Municipal buses go through the center taking you from point to point at a ticket cost of 15NOK ($2) per ride.

SEEING THE SIGHTS

Agder naturmuseum og botaniske hage The present exhibitions, which opened in 1990, show part of the natural history of south Norway. Colorful minerals are on display, and the museum includes a botanical garden with Norway's largest collection of cacti. As part of the package you can visit Gimle Estate, a 19th-century manor house filled with elegant, antique-heavy interiors, with a historic rose garden planted in 1850. From the center of town, motorists can take the E18 east, crossing a bridge. After the bridge, turn right and follow the signs. Bus no. 22 also runs there.

Gimleveien 23. © **38-09-23-88**. Admission to museum 30NOK ($4) adults, 10NOK ($1.35) children; admission to house and garden 45NOK ($6) adults, 15NOK ($2) children. June 20–Aug 20 Tues–Fri 10am–6pm, Sat–Mon noon–6pm; Aug 21–June 19 Tues–Fri 10am–6pm, Sat–Mon closed.

Christiansholm Festning A landmark along the Strandepromenaden, this fortress dates from 1674. The installation was ordered by King Christian IV of Denmark. The job of the defenders was to protect the Skagerrak Straits from invasion, not only from pirates but also from the roving Swedes. The threat of invasion never came, except once during the Napoleonic Wars of 1807. The walls are 5m (16 ft.) thick, and the fortress was created both by the labor of the local citizenry as well as heavy taxes. The Nazis took over the fortress during their occupation during World War II.

Festningsgata. © **38-07-51-50**. Free admission. May 15–Sept 15 daily 9am–9pm.

Kristiansand Domkirke The cathedral of Kristiansand is the largest church in Norway, with seating for 1,800 worshippers. It was constructed in the neo-Gothic style in 1884. Summer concerts are presented here, especially at the weeklong International Church Music Festival in mid-May, with organ, chamber, and gospel music on tap. You can climb the tower for 20NOK ($2.65) for a **panoramic view** ⭐ of the area.

Kirkegata. © **38-02-11-88**. Free admission. June–Aug daily 9am–2pm.

Kristiansand Dyrepark ⭐ *Kids* Formerly the Kristiansand Zoo, this is today the major family attraction in the south of Norway. It is signposted off E18 at a point 9km (5½ miles) east of the center. "It's our Disneyland," the town mayor told us. It's no Disneyland, but it does provide summer amusements for the area.

The highlight is Nordisk Vilmark, a simulated wilderness area where you can walk on boardwalks over the habitats of wolverines, lynx, wolves, and moose. The zoo itself contains many exotic specimens, including some Arctic species, and animals roam in large enclosures. The park covers an area of 60 hectares

---

Moments Walking the Streets of the Old Town

The best-preserved district of the city is **Posebyen** ✹ along the river in the northeastern part of town. It survived a disastrous fire in 1892 that swept over Kristiansand. The streets are filled with the original one- and two-story houses that accommodated workers in the 19th century. You'll see cozy windows, main entrances with stairs, iron fences, benches, and flowers. The kitchens and bedrooms were built in the rear, with separate doorways leading to little gardens. The most interesting parts of the area lie between Festningsgaten and Elvegata and between Rådhusgaten and Tordenskjoldsgate. The best time to visit is on a Saturday mid-June to August when a market is held with street stalls and all kinds of produce for sale.

(150 acres). Children delight in being taken to Kardemomme by (Cardamom town), based on a well-known children's story by Thorbjørn Egner. Here you can meet the famous characters from the story as they stroll about a "town" suggesting a hamlet in Africa. A pirate ship, a circus, a play land, giraffes, a farm, and other amusements, including a bobsled track and water slide await you.

Signposted along E18. © **38-04-98-00**. Admission, including all activities, 80NOK–200NOK ($11–$27) adults, 65NOK–170NOK ($8.65–$23) children. Highest rates in midsummer. Mid-May to Aug daily 10am–7pm; Sept to mid-May daily 10am–3:30pm. Take the Dyreparkbussen from the center.

Kristiansand Kanonmuseum Lying 8km (5 miles) south of town, the Cannon Museum recalls the dark days of World War II when the occupying Nazi forces were installed here. The museum preserves the German's heavy Vara Battery of cannons, which gave them control over the strategic Skagerrak Straits. The 337-ton cannons could fire at a range of 55km (34 miles). You can visit the big guns and the bunkers where 600 German soldiers and 1,400 laborers lived.

Møvik. © **38-08-50-90**. Admission 50NOK ($6.65) adults, 20NOK ($2.65) children. June 16–Aug 17 daily 11am–6pm; Aug 18–June 15 Mon–Wed 11am–3pm, Thurs–Sun 11am–5pm.

Oddernes Kirke ✹ *(Finds)* One of the oldest and most beautiful parish churches of Norway lies 1.5km (1 mile) east of the town center, reached by bus 22. The nave and choir were built around 1040. The church was dedicated to Saint Olav. Wander the ancient cemetery with its impressive rune stones.

Oddernesvn. © **38-09-01-87**. Free admission. May–Aug Sun–Fri 9am–2pm.

Vest Agder Fylkes-Museum ✹ This is one of the largest open-air museums in Norway, lying 4km (2½ miles) east of town on E18. From all over the Setesdalen region, nearly 50 antique farm and town dwellings were moved to this site. Some are furnished with provincial pieces, illustrating life as it was lived in the 18th and 19th centuries. Traditional costumes of the region are also displayed, along with other artifacts from the past. Folk dancing is staged Wednesday at 5:30pm from mid-June to mid-August. The major building houses thematic exhibitions.

Kongsgård. © **38-09-02-28**. Admission 30NOK ($4) adults, 10NOK ($1.35) children. June 20–Aug 20 Mon–Sat 10am–6pm, Sun noon–6pm; off-season Sun noon–5pm.

NEARBY ATTRACTIONS

The **Setesdalsbanen** in Grovane (© **38-15-64-82**) runs a steam train along 4.75km (3 miles) of narrow gauge track. The locomotive, built in 1894, starts

---

Moments   Heading for the Fish Market

On a lovely evening in summer, stroll down to the Fish Market at Gravane where you can purchase fresh shrimp from one of the vendors and enjoy them on the pier as you people-watch and breathe the fresh air of Norway's all-too-fleeting summer. Small bridges lead to new wooden maritime-inspired structures painted in red and yellow, housing a series of restaurants and shops by the canal. There's no better way to spend an evening in Kristiansand than to spend it here.

---

its run at Grovane, 20km (12 miles) from Kristiansand. It runs for 78km (48 miles) between Kristiansand and Byglandsfjord, providing a vital link between Setesdalen (the Setesdal Valley) and the southern coast. At one time it transported nickel from the mines along with other exports such as timber. In July, departures from Grovane are at 6pm Tuesday to Friday. From June 17 to 30 and from August 1 to September 2, the train also operates on Sunday at 11:30am and 2pm. A round-trip fare is 70NOK ($9.30) for adults, 35NOK ($4.65) for children.

The countryside around Kristiansand is rich with rolling meadows, birch-clad hills, deep valleys, and mountain moors. You'll see panoramic scenery along the E18 going east or west.

You can drive along the E18 to **Mandal,** 42km (28 miles) southwest of Kristiansand (take E18) to Norway's southernmost town. Here you can walk the streets of its historic center, with its old wooden houses, and stroll its long sandy beach, Sjøsanden.

At the southernmost point in Norway is **Lindesnes Fyr** (© **38-26-19-02**), Norway's first lighthouse, dating from 1656. Inside is an exhibition of lighthouse artifacts. Admission is 30NOK ($4) for adults, free for children. Open July and August daily 10am to 9pm; June and September daily 10am to 8pm; May daily 10am to 6pm.

In summer, boat trips are offered to visit the archipelago of offshore skerries (isolated rock islands). Visits are possible to Lillesand to the east and to the island of Brogøy, which lies right off the coast of Kristiansand and offers many scenic strolls and bathing sights. You can sail aboard the MS *Maarten* from Kristiansand daily in summer at 11am. The trip costs 170NOK ($23) for adults or 80NOK ($11) for children. Departures are from the fish quay. The tourist office keeps a list of all the possibilities for boat excursions along the southern coast.

SHOPPING

The largest shopping center in southern Norway lies 12km (7½ miles) east of Kristiansand. **Steen and Strøm Sørlandssenteret** (© **38-04-91-00**) offers 100 stores plus 10 restaurants and cafes, even such centers as a solarium. Closer to the center of town is **SlottsQuartalet,** Tordenskjoldsgate 9 (© **38-02-79-99**), at the top end of the Markens pedestrian street. You'll find various shops and cafes here.

WHERE TO STAY

Clarion Hotel Ernst ★★   The only hotel in town with a doorman, this hotel first opened its doors in 1859. It's been the city's favorite traditional stopover ever since. Even though it's received frequent renovations since then, its owners have taken care to preserve its classic look. Beautifully run and managed, it is preferred by those who shun the more sleekly modern look as exemplified by the Radisson SAS Caledonian Hotel. All the bedrooms come in different sizes with different color schemes, but each one contains a midsize, well-maintained bathroom with tub-and-shower combination. The location is ideal, lying 180m (200 yards) from the central bus terminal, rail station, and ferry dock. It is the only hotel in the area that has a restaurant and bars that rival the drinking and dining facilities at the SAS Caledonian.

Radhusgaten 2, N-4611 Kristiansand S. ⓒ 38-12-86-00. Fax 38-02-03-07. www.ernst.no. 135 units. Summer 1,090NOK ($145) double; off-season Sun–Thurs 1,145NOK ($152) double, Fri–Sat 845NOK ($112) double. AE, DC, MC, V. Parking 90NOK ($12). **Amenities:** Restaurant; 2 bars; nightclub; limited room service; babysitting; laundry service; dry cleaning. *In room:* A/C, TV, minibar, hair dryer.

Quality Hotel Kristiansand ★ *Kids*   This hotel is often called "the children's hotel." Of course, adults can stay here too. The hotel is one of Sørlandet's biggest hotels, lying 11km (6¾ miles) east of the town center. The building is new, and the bedrooms are freshly and comfortably furnished with cheerful pastels and wooden furnishings. Rooms feature private bathrooms with shower/tub combinations. Everything is geared to families with children, including a large playroom, organized kiddie activities, and even a special buffet for youngsters in the dining room. The grounds are also filled with toys.

Sorlandsparken, N-4696 Kristiansand S. ⓒ 38-17-77-77. Fax 38-17-77-80. www.quality-kristiansand.no. 210 units. Summer 1,150NOK ($153) double; winter Mon–Thurs 1,390NOK ($185) double, Sat–Sun 1,150NOK ($153) double. AE, DC, MC, V. Parking 90NOK ($12). **Amenities:** Restaurant; bar; outdoor heated pool; children's center and programs; limited room service; babysitting; laundry service; dry cleaning. *In room:* TV, minibar, hair dryer.

Radisson SAS Caledonian Hotel ★★   Located in the city center, this is the largest hotel in the area. It's also one of the best in the south of Norway. Built in 1968 near the fish market, it remains smart and stylish because of frequent renewals. A stay here is very convenient as the hotel is within walking distance of the train and bus stations as well as the ferry terminal, theaters, cinemas, and the best shopping. The good-sized bedrooms are furnished stylishly with contemporary pieces and adjoin midsize bathrooms with shower-tub combinations. The hotel's restaurant is far superior to a typical hotel dining room, and the drinking facilities, including a pub, disco, and piano bar, are among the best in the city.

Vestre Strandgate 7, N-4601 Kristiansand S. ⓒ 38-11-21-00. Fax 38-02-03-07. www.radisson.no. 205 units. Sun–Thurs 1480NOK ($197) double; Fri–Sat 995NOK ($132) double. AE, DC, MC, V. Parking 90NOK ($12). **Amenities:** Restaurant; 3 bars; limited room service; babysitting; laundry service; dry cleaning. *In room:* A/C, TV, minibar, hair dryer.

Rica Dyreparken Hotel ★ *Kids*   Lying right in one of the most popular holiday parks in Norway, this hotel, which opened in April 2000, was architecturally inspired by Noah's Ark. Lying at the entrance to Dyrepark, the hotel delights children of all ages. All the public lounges and bedrooms have motifs relating to the animal kingdom. You might stay in a monkey room or a horse room. It's Jungle Jim time in many of the bedrooms, with paw prints on the walls. You might sit in a chair of tiger stripes, or be assigned an African safari bed.

The hotel even has its own bridge along the water, as well as a large bar terrace where you can sit out on a summer night enjoying the fresh air. All the bedrooms are equipped with a midsize private bathroom with shower. The in-house restaurant is named—you guessed it—Noah's Ark.

Dyreparken, N-4609 Kristiansand S. ⓒ 38-14-64-00. Fax 38-14-64-01. www.rica.no. 160 units. Summer 1,340NOK ($178) double; off-season 895NOK ($119) double. AE, DC, MC, V. Free parking. **Amenities:** Restaurant; bar; children's center; laundry service; dry cleaning. *In room:* TV.

Villa Frobusdal Hotel ⭐ *Finds* This little discovery, the best B&B in town, lies 300m (984 ft.) northwest of the city center, near the western end of Kirkegata. A family-run hotel, the Villa was converted from a shipowner's private residence constructed in 1917. Everything has been beautifully restored, and the hotel evokes an old house somewhere in England. It's got rustic charm but also comfortable bedrooms, each with a small, shower-only bathroom. The street on which it lies is off the ring road. If you're driving, head north along Festningsgata, following the signs to Evje.

Frobusdalen 2, N-4613 Kristiansand S. ℂ 38-07-05-15. Fax 38-07-01-15. 8 units. Summer 790NOK ($105) double; off-season 690NOK ($92) double. Rates include breakfast. MC, V. Free parking. Closed Dec. *In room:* TV, hair dryer.

WHERE TO DINE

Bakgården NORWEGIAN/INTERNATIONAL The interior of this well-established restaurant is accented with oil-burning lamps, creating a mellow atmosphere. The cuisine is an unending festival celebrating southern Europe, and the chefs frequently add additional flair borrowing recipes from around the world, although dishes are tailored to local palates. Appetizers might include snails in garlic butter, followed by grilled filet of pheasant with grapes or tenderloin steak with mussels. Wild game, beef (sautéed or grilled), and fresh fish round out the menu. The most frequently ordered main dish appears to be Norwegian salmon with fresh dill. In the autumn you can order poached venison with an array of mixed vegetables in a port wine sauce.

Tollbødgate 5. ℂ 38-02-79-55. Reservations required. Main courses 205NOK–298NOK ($27–$40). AE, DC, MC, V. Mon–Sat 6–11pm.

Sjøhuset (Sea House) ⭐ NORWEGIAN Set directly on the harbor front in the center of town, this restaurant is housed in a century-old former salt warehouse whose oxblood-red walls are very distinctive. Inside, you'll see the massive structural beams of the restaurant's original construction and a blazing stone-sided fireplace. In summer, guests prefer the waterfront terrace. Specialties include an assorted platter of fish, including anglerfish and salmon. The fish is poached in white wine and served with a sauce made from Noilly Prat (a famous French Vermouth) along with shrimp, asparagus, and rice. You can also order a dish of salmon, cod, and monkfish with a savory saffron sauce served with perfectly baked potatoes. The meat specialty is chateaubriand with a béarnaise sauce.

Østre Strangate 12A. ℂ 38-02-62-60. Reservations required in summer. Main courses 170NOK–280NOK ($23–$37). AE, DC, MC, V. Mon–Sat 11:30am–11pm.

KRISTIANSAND AFTER DARK

Young people often frequent **Zanzibar,** Dronningens gate 8 (ℂ 38-02-62-44), open throughout the year. Another choice, **Telfords Pub & Tartan Room,** Vestre Strandgate 7 (ℂ 38-11-21-00), is a pub with an authentic Scottish interior and atmosphere. If you'd like to dance all night, try the amusingly named **Dr. Fjeld,** in the Clarion Hotel Ernst, Rådhusgata 2 (ℂ 38-12-86-00). The best piano bar is **Lobbybaren,** Vestre Strandgate 7 (ℂ 38-11-21-00), in the Radisson SAS Caledonian Hotel. In summer **Kick Café,** Dronningens gate 8 (ℂ 38-02-62-44), is the most popular outdoor restaurant and cafe. It's the place to be on a summer night. This is also the site of Zanzibar (see above). Music is played by a DJ all night long at the **CD Night Club,** Vestre Strandgate 7 (ℂ 38-11-21-00), which is also the location of Telfords (see above).

9

Stavanger

With a population of 100,000, Stavanger is the fourth largest city in Norway and the capital of southwestern Norway. Known for its low buildings and wooden houses, the city has been around for 9 centuries.

Stavanger lies in the midst of southwestern Norway in a setting of sandy but very chilly North Sea beaches set against a backdrop of deep blue fjords and towering mountains. The core of the city opens onto one of Norway's most colorful harbors, a delightful medley of the old and the new. You can wander the area's narrow streets for hours, visiting shops, restaurants, cafes, and galleries, as well as a vibrant marketplace.

Lying on Ryfyllkefjord, Stavanger has always been a bustling seaport with a thriving fish-canning industry. Today it's the oil capital of Norway. As a center of wealth and economic clout, it has become one of the most cosmopolitan cities of Scandinavia, yet it also remains a charming seaport amid beautiful surroundings. The old marketplace, where fish and vegetables have been sold since the ninth century, is set against the Domkirke (cathedral; see later in this chapter).

1 Orientation

ARRIVING

BY PLANE Flights land at **Stavanger International Airport** at Sola, 14km (8½ miles) south of the city center. **SAS** (✆ **81-00-33-00**) or **Braathens ASA** (✆ **81-52-00-00**) flies between Oslo, Bergen, and Kristiansand S, and Stavanger. **Widerøe** (✆ **81-00-12-00**) flies from Bergen to Stavanger. These airlines also serve Stavanger from London, Newcastle-upon-Tyne, and Aberdeen, Scotland.

Flybussen (✆ **51-52-26-00**) runs airport buses from Sola to the heart of Stavanger, the trip taking half an hour and costing 45NOK ($6) one-way. A taxi from the airport to the city center goes for 180NOK to 225NOK ($24–$30).

BY TRAIN Direct trains from Oslo require seat reservations and take 8 hours, traveling via Kristiansand S. A one-way fare costs 680NOK ($90). About three trains per day arrive from Oslo in Stavanger, and there is one overnight service. For rail information in Oslo, call ✆ **81-50-08-88.** For more detailed train information in Stavanger, call the Jernbanestasjon, the Stavanger Train Station, at ✆ **51-56-96-10.**

BY BUS There is a daily Nor-Way Bussekspress between Oslo and Stavanger, taking 10½ hours and costing 630NOK ($84) for a one-way ticket. Call ✆ **82-05-33-00** for information and schedules. The same company also offers a bus from Bergen to Stavanger, taking 6 hours and costing 380NOK ($51). There is also service between Kristiansand S and Stavanger, taking 4½ hours and costing 320NOK ($43) one-way.

BY BOAT From Bergen, **Flaggruten** (© **51-86-87-80**) runs an express cata-maran to Stavanger, taking 4½ hours and costing 600NOK ($80) for a one-way trip. **Color Line** (© **81-00-08-11**) sails four ships weekly from Newcastle-upon-Tyne in England to Stavanger. Ferry crossings between Stavanger and Britain take from 17 to 20 hours, costing 400NOK ($53) one-way. There are two to three departures per week.

BY CAR Because of the jagged coastline of western Norway, access by car from Bergen to Stavanger requires a 149km (93-mile) detour, incorporating high-speed motorways and three different ferry crossings. It usually takes 6½ to 7 hours to drive to Stavanger from Bergen. Access in the east from Kristiansand S is much easier. You continue west from Kristiansand S until you reach the end of E18.

ESSENTIALS

VISITOR INFORMATION You can get all sorts of visitor information at **Des-tination Stavanger,** Rosenkildetorget 1 (© **51-85-92-00;** www.destinasjon-stavanger.no). From September to May, it's open Monday to Friday 9am to 4pm, and Saturday 9am to 2pm. From June to August, it's open daily from 9am to 8pm.

CITY LAYOUT Most of Stavanger's attractions lie within an easy walk of the historic harbor. **Vågen Gamle Stavanger,** the old town, is on the western side of Vågen. Ferries to the United Kingdom leave from this point. This historic harbor is now a colorful marina with two sailing ships at anchor and a fish market held daily until 4pm.

Ferries to Haugesund and Bergen depart from the eastern part of town, across a body of water known as **Byfjorden.**

In the center of Stavanger, to the immediate north of the train station, is a large pond called **Breiavann.** Both the bus and train stations lie on the south-ern side of this pond, about a 10-minute walk from the main harbor.

GETTING AROUND Most of the historic central core of Stavanger is walkable, which is about the only way to get around unless you take a taxi. The historic town is filled with narrow streets and pedestrian walkways. If you don't have a rented car, you'll find that local buses fan out to the suburbs, including such neighboring communities as Sola, the site of the airport. Fares start at 12NOK ($1.60). For more information, call © **51-53-96-00.**

If the weather is fair and you'd like to use a bike to get around, you can secure rentals at **Sykkelhuset,** Løkkeveien 33 (© **51-53-99-10**), costing 62NOK ($8.25) per day. If you'd like to do more extensive biking, go to the visitor infor-mation center (see above) and request a *Sykkelkart* or cycling map of the area.

For a **taxi,** call **Norgestaxi Stavanger** at © **08000** or Stavanger Taxicentral at © **51-90-90-90.**

SPECIAL EVENTS Stavanger is called festival city or *festivallryen.* Celebra-tions take place all year. For complete listings at the time of your visit, ask at the visitor information center (see above). Spring's most amusing festival is **MaiJazz,** beginning the second week of May, when internationally known musicians come to Stavanger to perform top-quality jazz. Around mid-June, the **Great Norwegian Humor Festival** takes place, with well-known artists performing. There are revues, street entertainers, and shows for children. The **International Chamber Music Festival** takes place in mid-August, an event that attracts some of the world's most acclaimed classical artists to Stavanger. Some 20 concerts take place within the course of a week. The **Stavanger Wine Festival,** beginning in mid-March and lasting 10 days, celebrates both food and the grape.

FAST FACTS: Stavanger

Banks One of the most central banks for exchanging money is **SpareBank,** Domkirkeplassen (© **51-50-90-00**). You can also exchange money, from June to August, at the visitor information center (see above).

Car Repair Call © **51-53-88-88,** a 24-hour hot line.

Consulates There is no U.S. representative. Brits can go to the **United Kingdom Consulate** at Prinsens Gate 12 (© **51-52-97-13**).

Dental Service There is a dentist open every day to handle emergencies. The name of the dentist is published in the Saturday newspapers. Otherwise call for an appointment at the office of Egil Undem, Kannibakken 6 (© **51-52-84-52**).

Doctor In an emergency, call © **51-53-33-33.** Otherwise, ask your hotel staff to recommend one. All doctors speak English.

Emergencies Call **110** for fire, **112** for police, and **113** for an ambulance.

Laundry If your hotel doesn't have facilities, go to **Renseriet,** Kongsgate 40 (© **51-89-56-53**).

Left Luggage Go to **Byterminalen,** the city terminus Monday to Friday from 8am to 5pm, Saturday 8am to 2:30pm.

Pharmacy Your best bet is **Løveapoteket,** Olav V's gate 11 (© **51-52-06-7**), open daily from 8am to 11pm or 8pm on public holidays.

Post Office The main post office is at Haakon VII's gate 9, open Monday to Wednesday and Friday 8am to 5pm, Thursday 8am to 6pm, and Saturday 9am to 1pm.

2 Where to Stay

Because Stavanger is an oil boomtown and full of business people for most of the year, you'll find expensive hotels and a dearth of good, moderately priced choices. That's the bad news. The good news is that in the summer months and on weekends, the first-class and better-rated hotels slash their prices, and nearly all of them fall into the "moderate" category during peak tourism season.

EXPENSIVE

Clarion Hotel Stavanger ★★ This is Stavanger's second-tallest building and its second-newest hotel. It's a smoothly contemporary blockbuster that's on every corporate list as a well-managed and cooperative hotel closely associated with the city's corporate consciousness. (About 70% of its clients work in the oil or oil services industries.) Set 2½ blocks uphill from the harbor, it lies within a 7-minute walk to every attraction in the old town. It's a tall, elegant, contemporary hotel with 14 stories and a decor that's accented with lots of polished stone, burnished copper, and Nordic birch. Ironically, it's positioned midway between two of its most powerful competitors, the also-recommended Radisson SAS Atlantic and the Radisson SAS Royal Hotels. Pahr Iversen is the locally famous artist who crafted the paintings in the lobby and the tile work in most of the bathrooms, each of which has a shower-tub combination. Once—in an off-handed and not-terribly-scientific contest sponsored by a local newspaper—the beds in this hotel won an award as the most comfortable in town.

Ny Olavskleiv 8, N-4004 Stavanger. © 51-50-25-00. 249 units. Mid-Aug to mid-June Mon–Thurs 1,990NOK ($265) double, 2,100NOK ($279) suite; Fri–Sun year-round and daily from mid-June to mid-Aug 990NOK ($132) double, 2,000NOK ($266) suite. **Amenities:** 2 restaurants; bar; health club with saunas and a view over the town. *In room:* A/C, TV, minibar.

Radisson SAS Atlantic Hotel ⓐ ★ This is the oldest and best known of the SAS-sponsored hotels in Stavanger, and until its height was surpassed around the turn of the millennium by a taller contender in the suburbs, its 13 stories made it the tallest building in town. Everything about it evokes the artfully spare minimalism of the heyday of Scandinavian modern design, thanks to lots of carefully finished hardwood and stone, plus glass and stainless steel. Bedrooms here are well conceived and very comfortable, each with a tiled bathroom and a shower-tub combination, but if you're at all able to afford one of the suites, you'll find them large and supremely comfortable refuges, replete with leather upholsteries, macho-looking hardwoods, and in many cases, big-windowed views over the town.

Olav V's Gate 3, P.O. Box 307, N-4002 Stavanger. © 51-76-10-00. Fax 51-76-10-01. www.radissonsas.com. 354 units. Mon–Thurs 1,595NOK–1,795NOK ($212–$239) double; Fri–Sun and daily from mid-June to mid-Aug 895NOK ($119) double; year-round 2,500NOK–4,500NOK ($333–$599) suite. AE, DC, MC, V. **Amenities:** Restaurant; cafe; reduced rates at a nearby health and exercise club; sauna; laundry service; dry cleaning. *In room:* TV, minibar, hair dryer, iron.

Radisson SAS Royal Hotel ⓐ ★ Built in 1987, and radically renovated in April 2002, this is the smallest, and the most plush, of Stavanger's Radisson SAS hotels. Its rooms rise around an atrium-style lobby that's outfitted with pale oak paneling and pale blue carpets and upholsteries. Bedrooms are outfitted in four different decorative styles, including a warm but minimalist version of Scandinavian modern, a generic Oriental (Pan-Asian) style; a high-tech design, and a style that the hotel refers to as "ecological," featuring lots of handcrafted ceramics and weavings made from non-synthetic materials. All units have shower-tub combinations.

Løkkeveien, P.O. Box 307, N-4002 Stavanger. © 51-76-60-00. Fax 51-76-60-01. www.radissonsas.com. 204 units. Mid-Aug to mid-June Mon–Thurs 1,780NOK ($237) double, Fri–Sun year-round, and daily from mid-June to mid-Aug 995NOK ($132) double; year-round 2,200NOK–3,600NOK ($293–$479) suite. Rates include breakfast. Parking 55NOK ($7.30) per night. AE, DC, MC, V. **Amenities:** Restaurant; bar; indoor pool; entrance to a nearby health and exercise club for 30NOK ($4) fee; sauna. *In room:* TV, minibar.

Skagen Brygge Hotell This is the most architecturally distinctive and perhaps the most visible hotel in town, thanks to its prime harbor-front location in the center of Stavanger's historic core. About 10 of its rooms occupy a 19th-century brick building that's partially concealed on the hotel's back side. But the genuinely dramatic part of this hotel fronts the harbor. As a replacement for warehouses that, throughout the decades, burned to the ground, architects duplicated the look of an interconnected series of steep-gabled, tall and narrow townhouses, modernized with oversize windows and a sense of postmodern flair. Queen Sonia, accompanied by one of her sons, selected this hotel for her lodging in Stavanger in the late 1990s, favoring this hotel (which is all Norwegian owned and not a member of any international chain) above the more international hotels that compete with it on many different price levels. Rooms in the original 19th-century brick core are comfortable, cozy, and warm, with exposed masonry and flowered Laura Ashley fabrics. (Check out the wood-beamed health club within this older section, where brick walls and the mechanism for a 19th-century gear-driven windlass or hoist form part of the decor.) Sunnier,

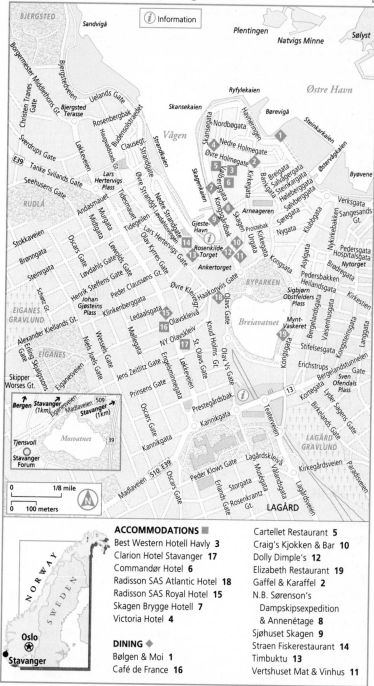

Stavanger Accommodations & Dining

BJERGSTED

Sandvigå

(i) Information

Plentingen

Natvigs Minne

Sølyst

Borgermeister Middelthons Gt.

Bjergstedveien

Christen Tranes Gate

Bjergsted Terasse

Uelands Gate

Rosenbergbak

Budensolstraedet

Skansekaien

Ryfylekaien

Østre Havn

Børevigå

Steinkarkaien

Sverdrups Gate

Haugvaldstads Gt.

Clausegt.

Strandgate

Vågen

Nordbøgata

Havneingen

Skansegata

Østervågkaien

E39

Tanke Svilands Gate

Lars Hertervigs Plass

Øvre Strandgate

Nedre Strandgate

Skagenkaien

Nedre Holmegate

Øvre Holmegate

Valbergata

Kirkegata

Breigata

Banksata

Salvågergata

Steinkargata

Byøvene

Verksgata

Seehusens Gate

Andasmauet

Murgata

Tidemauet

Løvolds Gate

Kondsgårdbak

Skagen

Arneageren

Prostebak

Søregata

Høleberggata

Sølvberggata

Sangesands Gt.

RUDLÅ

Stokkaveien

Brønngata

Steinrgata

Oscars Gate

Midtgata

Lars Hertervigs Gate

Olav Kyrres Gate

Gjeste-Havn

(i)

Rosenkilde Torget

Ankertorget

Nygata

Kirkegata

Urgata

Kongsgata

Klubbgata

Asylgata

Pedersgata

Hospitalsgata

Nytorget

Brødregata

Schartz Gt.

Løvdahls Gate

Henrik Steffens Gate

Peder Claussøns Gt.

Øvre Klevegt.

Haakonviis Gt.

BYPARKEN

Pedersbakken

Heilandsgata

Sigbjørn Obstfelders Plass

Kirkestien

EIGANES GRAVLUND

Johan Gjøsteins Plass

Klinkenberggata

Ledaalsgata

Olavskleiva

Olavs Gate

Breiavatnet

Bergelandsgata

Valsenhusgata

Kongsteingata

Langgata

Alexander Kiellands Gt.

Erling Skjalgssons Gate

EIGANES

Wessels Gate

Niels Juels Gate

Møllegata

NY Olavskleiv

St. Olavs Gate

Knud Holms Gt.

Olav Vs Gate

Mynt-Vaskeret

Stifelsesgata

Erichstrups Gate

Bergelandstunnelen

Skipper Worses Gt.

Eiganesveien

Jens Zeitlitz Gate

Engelsminnegata

Løkkeveien

Prestegårdsbak.

(i)

Teaterveien

Kortegata

Lyder Sagens Gate

Sven Ofendals Plass

Birkelands Gate

Bergen Stavanger (1km)

Madlaveien 509

Stavanger (1km)

Prinsens Gate

Kannikgata

13

LAGÅRD GRAVLUND

Tjensvoll

Mosvatnet

39

Stavanger Forum

Oscars Gate

Kannikgata

Madlaveien 510 E39

Peder Klows Gate

Elands Gate

Storgata

Lagårdskleiva

Muségata

Vålandsgata

Kirkegårdsveien

Paradisveien

Rosenkrantz Gt.

LAGÅRD

0   1/8 mile

0   100 meters

(N)

211

ACCOMMODATIONS ■

Best Western Hotell Havly **3**

Clarion Hotel Stavanger **17**

Commandør Hotel **6**

Radisson SAS Atlantic Hotel **18**

Radisson SAS Royal Hotel **15**

Skagen Brygge Hotell **7**

Victoria Hotel **4**

DINING ◆

Bølgen & Moi **1**

Café de France **16**

Cartellet Restaurant **5**

Craig's Kjokken & Bar **10**

Dolly Dimple's **12**

Elizabeth Restaurant **19**

Gaffel & Karaffel **2**

N.B. Sørenson's
Dampskipsexpedition
& Annenétage **8**

Sjøhuset Skagen **9**

Straen Fiskerestaurant **14**

Timbuktu **13**

Vertshuset Mat & Vinhus **11**

NORWAY

SWEDEN

Oslo

Stavanger

more dramatic, and more panoramic are the big-windowed accommodations in the newer section, some of which might evoke greenhouses if it weren't for their leather-upholstered furniture, hardwood floors, Oriental carpets, and sense of high-tech flair. All accommodations come with immaculate private bathrooms with tub-and-shower combinations. This hotel doesn't have a restaurant of its own, but there are at least 14 eateries and lots of bars within a very short walk.

Skagenkaien 30, N-4004 Stavanger. © 51-85-00-00. Fax 51-85-00-01. www.skagenbryggehotell.no. 110 units. Sun–Thurs 1,450NOK ($193) double, 1,500NOK–2,750NOK ($200–$366) suite; Fri–Sun year-round and daily July 850NOK ($113) double, 1,500NOK–2,750NOK ($200–$366) suite. Rates include breakfast. AE, DC, MC, V. **Amenities:** Entrance to a nearby health and exercise club for 30NOK ($4) fee; exercise area with sauna; laundry service; dry cleaning. *In room:* A/C, TV, minibar, safe.

Victoria Hotel   Inaugurated in 1900 in a building with red-brick-with-stone-trim design that's now carefully preserved as a town landmark, this is the oldest hotel in town. It's set prominently at the edge of the harbor, but in a less-touristed waterfront area used for the mooring of fishing boats and supply ships servicing the North Sea oil platforms. Over the years, the hotel's role in Stavanger has changed: Once its clientele was primarily concerned with the herring and canning industries; now about 85% of its clients are middle-bracket employees within the oil service industries. Expect a thoroughly decent, muted hotel with a helpful staff, and a lobby that's outfitted in a paneled style that you might have expected from a 19th-century hotel in England. Rooms are clean, well maintained, and not overly large, each with conservative traditional furniture and a tiled bathroom with a shower-tub combination. Each has a floor plan that, thanks to the hotel's U-shaped layout and antique shell, is different from each of its neighbors. The in-house bar (the Holmen Bar) and restaurant (Café Leopold) are competent, catering mostly to residents of the hotel. Also onsite is Cartellet Restaurant, which we recommend (p. 214).This is not a hotel where a rock star would be understood or catered to, but if you're a hardworking sales rep for an oil service company, or a leisure traveler with a normal set of expectations, it will work just fine.

Skansekaien 1, N-4001 Stavanger. © 51-86-70-00. Fax 51-86-70-10. www.victoria-hotel.no. 107 units. Mon–Thurs 1,525NOK–1,625NOK ($203–$216) double, 1,995NOK–2,250NOK ($265–$299) suite; Fri–Sun 795NOK–895NOK ($106–$119) double, 1,495NOK–1,995NOK ($199–$265) suite. AE, DC, MC, V. **Amenities:** Restaurant; bar; laundry service; dry cleaning. *In room:* TV, minibar.

INEXPENSIVE

Best Western Hotell Havly *(Value)*   The only member of the Best Western hotel chain in town is positioned on a street that runs parallel to the wharves of the Vågen (harbor), 1 block uphill. Small scale, boxy, and modern, it was built in the 1960s in a low-rise design that doesn't interfere (too much) with the otherwise antique buildings of old Stavanger that rise around it on every side. There's no bar, no restaurant, and very few amenities, but in light of the clean and well-maintained accommodations, and because of the many bars and restaurants that lie within a few blocks, no one seems to care. Don't expect old-fashioned charm or nostalgia, because that isn't what this simple hotel tries to provide. It attracts business travelers from other parts of Scandinavia and there's an aura of brisk, matter-of-fact efficiency permeating a decor that includes smallish, weather-tight windows (without any particularly interesting view) that you might have expected in a Best Western in, say, a cold-climate region of the Pacific Northwest. Despite that, we prefer this hotel's accommodations to those within the comparably priced, and also-recommended Commandør Hotel, which lies within a 2-minute walk. Each room comes with a neat, midsize private bathroom with shower. "Havly," incidentally, translates as "shelter from the ocean."

Valberggate 1, N-4006 Stavanger. ✆ **51-89-67-00.** Fax 51-89-50-25. www.havly-hotell.no. 42 units. Mid-Aug to May Mon–Thurs 1,050NOK ($140) double; Fri–Sun 710NOK ($94) double. June to mid-Aug 610NOK ($81) double. Rates include breakfast. AE, DC, MC, V. **Amenities:** Laundry service; dry cleaning. *In room:* TV.

Commandør Hotel Inexpensive and matter-of-fact, this is a no-nonsense, no-frills hotel located near other hotels that are more, and in some cases, much more, expensive. It was established in the 1970s when five adjoining houses—the oldest of which is 200 years old—were interconnected into one coherent whole, and what had been an outdoor courtyard was covered with a glass sky-light, creating an atrium. Breakfast is served in this three-story hotel, whose rooms are accessible via a labyrinth of meandering hallways and winding stair-cases. Rooms are simple, unadorned, and not overly large. Most have bathrooms with showers; a very limited number have shower-bathtub combinations.

Valberggate 9, N-4006 Stavanger. ✆ **51-89-53-00.** Fax 51-89-53-01. 35 units. Mid-Aug to mid-June Mon–Thurs 995NOK ($132) double; Fri–Sun 650NOK ($86) double; daily between mid-June and mid-Aug 400NOK ($53) double. Rates include breakfast. AE, DC, MC, V. *In room:* A/C, TV.

3 Where to Dine

EXPENSIVE

Bølgen & Moi ★★ CONTINENTAL This restaurant—a member of a high-quality and elite dining chain that now stretches across Norway—lies on the ground floor of the avant-garde premises of Stavanger's oil museum. It maintains a separate entrance, thereby allowing a swarm of diners and drinkers to come and go, regardless of the opening hours of the museum that contains it. Its interior is as spare, angular, metallic, and minimalist as the museum itself. Part of its drama derives from its position, straddling a pier and a rocky headland jutting into Sta-vanger's harbor, seemingly within a stone's throw from the dozens of boats that chug in and out toward oil platforms in the North Sea. In winter, the sometimes-violent seas throw spray across the big windows of the room, which is illuminated mostly by candles. The setting is a foil for cuisine that's more elaborate and cut-ting-edge than what you'll find at many nearby competitors. You know you're going to dine well when you're served such starters as potato soup with sautéed foie gras and white truffle oil, or asparagus with poached quail eggs and a chive-studded hollandaise. The cooking is as freshly inspired as the restaurant's bold surroundings. To see the heights that the chef can reach, order the skate with fresh herbs from the garden and extra-virgin olive oil, or the filet of veal with white asparagus and truffle *jus*. The freshly made desserts are luscious and come in surprising combinations such as a soup of rhubarb with a vanilla crème fraîche, or strawberries with balsamic vinegar and pepper (don't knock it until you've tried it).

In the Norsk Oljemuseum (Norwegian Petroleum Museum), the harbor front, Kjeringholmen. ✆ **51-93-93-51.** Reservations recommended. Sandwiches (lunch only) 75NOK–99NOK ($10–$13); small platters 115NOK–195NOK ($15–$26); main courses 245NOK–315NOK ($33–$42); fixed-price menus 575NOK–1,100NOK ($76–$146). AE, DC, MC, V. Daily 11am–4pm and 6–10pm. Bar till midnight.

Café de France ★ FRENCH Set in a pink-sided building immediately uphill from the SAS Royal Hotel, this restaurant closely adheres to the tenets of classical French cuisine. Elegant, upscale, and richly committed to presenting French food with flair and sensitivity, it's often fully booked with business trav-elers visiting Stavanger to discuss the nuances of their deals. Also expect a roster of the town's prominent and prestigious private citizens, some of whom are already known to Trude, who supervises the dining room, and her husband, Steinar, the hardworking chef. From the kitchens emerge dishes that change with the season but that could conceivably grace some of the grandest tables in France. Some fine examples include two different cuts (they call it "a duo") of lamb arranged on a platter with chanterelles and dauphinois-style potatoes; goose-liver terrine with apple chutney; and lobster with a mango salsa, braised fennel, and fresh artichokes. The cheese board here is particularly esoteric, combining many obscure varieties from the various regions of mainland France.

Eiganesveien 8. © **51-52-86-26.** Reservations recommended. Main courses 325NOK ($43); fixed-price menus 325NOK–795NOK ($43–$106). AE, DC, MC, V. Mon–Sat 6–11pm.

Cartellet Restaurant ✦ CONTINENTAL   Set within the basement of the recommended Victoria Hotel (p. 212), but under completely separate management, this is the most prestigious and expensive restaurant in Stavanger. It's the kind of place where a group of corporate executives could meet, transcend any cross-cultural confusion, and emerge with a huge tab after an altogether safe, well-choreographed business dinner. Don't come here expecting anything cutting edge, either in the realm of cuisine or clientele, as the restaurant is just a wee bit staid, a whole lot conservative, and to some degree, somewhat self-consciously bourgeois. Many locals wouldn't even consider coming here unless their meal was paid for as part of an expense account. The red-brick hotel that contains the restaurant was built at the turn of the 20th century as Stavanger's first hotel. Set immediately adjacent to the harbor, with a separate entrance from that used by hotel guests, it's outfitted in an all-Victorian format that celebrates the grand (and somewhat stuffy) bourgeoisie of the late 19th and early 20th century. Antiques and masses of flowers and candles contrast pleasantly with the russet-colored bricks of its walls. The menu here is reinvented every Tuesday, when the chefs compile their culinary offerings for the next 7 days. ("We virtually re-create ourselves every Tuesday," according to the *maître d'hôtel.*) On our most recent rounds with friends in Stavanger, we were delighted with such enticing dishes as breast of duck roasted in pepper with cured chanterelles and a sweet plum sauce, and roasted redfish with dried tomato, carrot puree, and butter-fried French beans. Two desserts proved to be the most memorable out of all the desserts that we tried in Stavanger: raspberry mousse with almonds and sherbet, and passion fruit cheesecake in a tangy raspberry sauce.

In the Victoria Hotel, Ovre Holmgaten 8. © **51-89-60-22.** Reservations recommended. Main courses 273NOK–315NOK ($36–$42); fixed-price menus 495NOK–815NOK ($66–$108). AE, DC, MC, V. Tues–Sat 6–10:30pm.

Craig's Kjokken & Bar ✦ *Finds* INTERNATIONAL   Oklahoma-born Craig Whitson is a local hit, and he illustrates his down-home style of humor with a dozen dried pigs' heads hanging on the wall. Once you get by that jolt, prepare yourself to "pig out" on some good food. The American sofas with tables can be used for dining, and there is an array of other unusual tables and chairs. The wine list is extensive and excellent, and has won awards. There are more than 600 bottles in the cellar, with such major regions of Europe as Alsace or the Rhone represented along with many Tuscan vintages. A homemade soup of the day hits the spot on a cold day, or try one of the nightly appetizers fashioned from langoustines or fresh scallops. For a main course, a popular dish is a rib and sausage plate with gnocchi, or baked cod cooked in a zesty tomato bouillon. The spring lamb burger is another tasty treat. For dessert, there's nothing finer than the vanilla-laced crème brûlée.

Breitorget. ℂ **51-93-95-90.** Reservations recommended. Main courses 210NOK–270NOK ($28–$36); 5-course fixed-price menu 495NOK ($66). Mon–Sat 6–11pm. Closed Dec 20–Jan 3 and 1 week for Easter.

Elizabeth Restaurant ★★ INTERNATIONAL/SPANISH   One of our favorite restaurants in Stavanger occupies a white clapboard-sided house, originally built in 1860, set directly beside the Breavent (the small pond that's a focal point for Stavanger's town center). Part of the restaurant's charm involves its joint ownership by a partnership of (married) Norwegian and Basque entrepreneurs, Elisabeth Aune and Jesús Gorostiza, whose respective cultures are successfully wed within the walls of this restaurant. The earthier and less formal of the two dining venues is the basement-level bodega, outfitted with ceramic tiles, thick plaster-sheathed walls, and plank-wood tables whose decor evokes an atmospheric tavern in the Pyrenees.

More formal and stylish is the gourmet restaurant upstairs, where a collection of avant-garde art and a sweeping view over the pond adds to the dining allure. Food in the bodega includes bacalao (Iberian-style cod); paella prepared for one or more diners at a time; fish soup, paper-thin slices of Serrano ham, and a highly appealing array of tapas. Upstairs, a roster of more elaborate dishes includes cream of shellfish soup with crabmeat-stuffed ravioli; filet of halibut in orange sauce; scallops with red beets; house-smoked salmon served with an apple and fennel salad; stuffed redfish with tomato vinaigrette; confit of duck with lentils, beans, and a port wine glaze; and filet of lamb with thyme polenta and rosemary sauce.

Notice the wind velocity meter affixed to the uppermost gable of this restaurant. It controls the activity of the water jet in the pond: Whenever the wind blows too hard, as registered by the wind meter, it shuts down the fountain, so that water doesn't blow from the water jet onto passersby who promenade around the lake.

Kongsgate 41. ℂ **51-53-33-00.** Reservations recommended for the formal restaurant, not necessary in the Spanish bodega. In gourmet restaurant, main courses 230NOK–255NOK ($31–$34), fixed-price menus 415NOK–475NOK ($55–$63); in Spanish bodega, servings of tapas 48NOK–175NOK ($6.40–$23), main courses 135NOK–175NOK ($18–$23). AE, DC, MC, V. Mon–Sat 6–11pm (from 5pm for the Bodega).

Gaffel & Karaffel ★ NORWEGIAN/INTERNATIONAL   The "Fork & Carafe" is one of the hippest restaurants in Stavanger. The wooden tables have no tablecloths, the red halls are hung with knives and forks, and there is a popular bar downstairs. The historical building, from 1871, was originally the private home of a fisherman and his family. High-quality ingredients are skillfully handled by a well-trained staff that might tempt you with its garlic-marinated fresh shrimp as an appetizer. For a main course, a pasta specialty is likely to be featured along with such main dish staples—each well prepared—as monkfish with Parma ham and a well-seasoned seafood sauce, or delightful Norwegian lamb with fresh vegetables in a savory sauce. A dessert specialty is *panna cotta,* a pudding of milk and vanilla with fresh fruit.

Øvre Holmegate 20. ℂ **51-86-41-58.** Reservations recommended. Main courses 200NOK–300NOK ($27–$40). AE, DC, MC, V. Daily 6–11pm. Closed Dec 22–Jan 8 and 1 week at Easter.

Straen Fiskerestaurant ★ SEAFOOD   This is one of the best seafood restaurants in Stavanger, its windows opening onto a view of the harbor. It amusingly bills itself as "world famous throughout Norway." The old-fashioned interior is straight from the 1950s with homelike decor and a grandmotherly touch here and there. Begin, perhaps, with the grilled scallops and mushrooms with a tantalizing Jerusalem artichoke puree. You might proceed to the finest item on the menu: Norwegian grilled lobster with a peppery butter. The other main courses maintain a balance between simplicity and elegance, as exemplified by the crab legs with homemade saffron pasta, fresh garlic, and tomato oil, or the poached halibut with pea lentils and a bacon cassoulet with beets—everything served with orange butter. The food is perfectly cooked and appears in generous portions. There is a nightclub upstairs and a sushi restaurant downstairs that's served by the same kitchen.

Nedre Strandgate 15. © **51-84-37-00.** Reservations recommended. Main courses 245NOK–365NOK ($33–$49). AE, DC, MC, V. Mon–Sat 6pm–midnight. Closed Dec 22–Jan 7.

Timbuktu ★ NORWEGIAN/AFRICAN   Hip, stylish, and popular, this restaurant is set beside a cobble-covered square that opens directly onto Stavanger's Vågen (harbor front). Inside, within a decor of pale birch with ebonized trim, there's a busy bar area (open Mon–Sat until between midnight and 1:30am) and somewhat crowded tables. Try the masterly salad of lime- and olive-marinated skate or a platter of very fresh sushi as a main course. Drawing upon the bounty of a rugged land, the chefs will delight you with the catch of the day, such as roasted halibut with pickled fennel in an anise-flavored gravy. You might also savor the roasted lamb with a Madeira-flavored gravy and a side helping of couscous. To wake up your taste buds, opt for the tea-smoked tuna with a jalapeño salsa.

Nedre Standgate 15. © **51-84-37-40.** Reservations recommended. Main courses 215NOK–255NOK ($29–$34). AE, DC, MC, V. Mon–Thurs 6–11pm; Fri–Sat 6–10pm.

MODERATE

N. B. Sørenson's Dampskipsexpedition & Annenétage ★ *Finds* NORWE-GIAN   When the wood-sided warehouse that contains these restaurants was built in 1876, the waters of Stavanger's harbor literally lapped at its foundations, and merchandise could be unloaded directly from ships that could, back then, moor beside it. Today, a road separates its front entrance from the harbor, and the site has been gentrified. The heavy timbers and all-wood interior evoke a rich sense of nostalgia for the 19th-century mercantile days when the strongest odor that was likely to greet you on the premises was that of fish in various states of preservation or decay.

The street-level brasserie (Dampskipsexpedition, or "Steamship Expedition") is by far the more convivial and animated (and cheaper) of the two venues—a warren of varnished pine planks, polished brass, nautical-nostalgic memorabilia, and beer suds. Upstairs, an interconnected series of late-19th-century Victorian parlors is the setting for "Annenétage," a slightly stuffy, much more rigid and pretentious gourmet restaurant whose somewhat uncomfortable decor evokes a strictly conservative great-grandmother's parlor. Menu items served in the street level brasserie include Cajun-spiced filet of pork with a hazelnut-flavored butter sauce; Thai-style chicken; hamburgers "Italiano," with pesto and Parmesan cheese; and a Nordic version of bouillabaisse. Upstairs, food items are fussier and more self-consciously innovative: Examples include crabmeat soup; filet of turbot with cauliflower tempura and a caper sauce; filet of lamb with a sherry sauce; filet of monkfish with saffron-flavored risotto; and a dessert specialty of chocolate marquise with espresso sauce.

Skagen 26. © **51-84-38-20.** Reservations recommended. In street-level brasserie main courses 129NOK–146NOK ($17–$19); in upstairs gourmet restaurant fixed-price menus 598NOK–779NOK ($80–$104). AE, DC, MC, V. Street-level brasserie daily 11am–midnight; upstairs gourmet restaurant Mon–Sat 6–11pm.

Vertshuset Mat & Vinhus ★★ CONTINENTAL One of the old town's most appealing restaurants, this "food and wine house" is set on a street running parallel to the old port, within a simple-looking early-19th-century wooden house. Its interior has been "postmodernized" with a decor that manages to be simultaneously high-tech and woodsy-looking. The staff and the clientele are hip and urbanized and the neat-as-a-pin interior carries just a whiff of old-fashioned nautical memorabilia. Lunches tend to feature *husmanskost* (grand-mother-style) dishes such as Nordic meatballs, filet of reindeer, grilled salmon steaks, and pizzas. Dinners are more elaborate and at least in terms of cuisine, more stylish, with memorable dishes that include salted filets of cod with mashed potatoes and green peas; fried pepper-crusted monkfish; salmon with garlic sauce; or perhaps a "symphony" of different kinds of fish, either fried, steamed, grilled, or broiled. Don't overlook the cozy-looking bar here, the XO Bar, as a possibility for a drink, even if you don't plan on following it up with a meal.

Skagen 10. ℂ **51-89-51-12.** Reservations recommended. Lunch pizzas and platters 109NOK–198NOK ($15–$26); dinner main courses 239NOK–249NOK ($32–$33). AE, DC, MC, V. Mon–Sat noon–11pm; Sun 12:30–10pm. Bar open until midnight or 2am, depending on business.

INEXPENSIVE

Dolly Dimple's PIZZA This is the Stavanger branch of an enormously popular nationwide chain of pizzerias whose Greek-born owner lives in—guess where—Stavanger. It was established in honor of "the world's most beautiful fat girl," in this case, Celesta Geyer, who the owner saw as a sideshow attraction at an American circus in the 1970s. Today, her pen-and-ink likeness (looking even more zaftig and delectable thanks to the many pizzas she has consumed since becoming Norway's official representative to the pizza-loving world at large) is displayed in about 60 locations throughout Norway. Pizzas here are delicious, coming in 25 already-defined versions, in various degrees of spiciness, plus any number of custom-designed others that you can build yourself by indicating to a staff member what you want on it. Regulation standards include, among others, "Los Banditos," made from strips of marinated beef, chicken, Mexican-style tomato salsa, jalapeño peppers, and cheese. More Nordic versions are built with, among others, smoked salmon, crème fraîche, and shrimp.

Kongsgårdsbakken 1. ℂ **51-51-03-30.** Medium pizzas (suitable for 1–2 persons) 110NOK–168NOK ($15–$22); large pizzas (suitable for 2–3 persons) 143NOK–235NOK ($19–$31). AE, DC, MC, V. Sun–Thurs noon–11pm; Fri–Sat noon–midnight.

Sjøhuset Skagen Thanks to a folksy-looking and heavily timbered premises that dates from the mid–19th century, this place is more atmospheric and cozier than the many other pub/restaurants that compete with it nearby. Inside, you'll find a warren of congenially cramped cubicles and mezzanines that hint at its origins as a storage for marine supplies and fish. Frankly, we prefer this place as a drinking-with-snacks venue much more than we do as a restaurant, even though a roster of salads, burgers, and pastas are available, as well as such North Atlantic staples as fish and chips. You can also order a good creamy fish soup made with prawns and mussels or chile-marinated scampi grilled and served on a bed of salad. The place has a lot of charm and historical authenticity. Come here for a drink, at least, especially during clement weather when a wide outdoor terrace provides room for boat- and people-watching.

Skagenkaien 16. ℂ **51-89-51-80.** Main courses 69NOK–109NOK ($9.20–$15). AE, DC, MC, V. Mon–Sat 11:30am–10:30pm; Sun 11:30am–9:30pm.

4 Seeing the Sights

Arkeologisk Museum (Museum of Archaeology) *Kids* The culture and natural history of southwestern Norway for the past 15,000 years is on parade here. Models of prehistoric life attract a lot of attention, as do the changing natural history exhibitions. Educational but fun films are shown. This museum is also the shelter for the public archive of antiquities for Rogaland. It's very family friendly, featuring treasure-hunt games and other activities for kids.

Peder Klowsgate 30A. (C) 51-84-60-00. Admission 20NOK ($2.65). June–Aug Tues–Sun 11am–5pm; Sept–May Tues 11am–8pm, Wed–Sat 11am–3pm, Sun 11am–4pm.

Domkirke (Cathedral) ★★★ This is one of the great churches from the Middle Ages left in Norway and it stands reasonably intact. Constructed over a decade beginning in 1125, the cathedral was dedicated to Saint Swithun. It is said that Bishop Reinald sailed here from Winchester, England, with relics of the saint, to dedicate the cathedral. He carried with him what was said to be the arm of Swithun.

A fire in 1272 swept over the Romanesque structure, destroying most of it. During the church's reconstruction, a Gothic chancel was added. In the new structure, twin square towers and a mammoth porch at the west end were also added. With the coming of the Reformation, the Domkirke lost its precious relics of the saint along with its bells and several altars. A major restoration from 1938 to 1942 was carried out that, for the most part, returned the church to Middle Ages look.

We always time our visit here to coincide with the organ recital at 11:15am Thursday. In such an atmosphere, you'll feel you've gone back 8 centuries.

The length of the Dom is 65m (213 ft.), with the chancel measuring 22m (72 ft.). The original nave is striking in its simplicity but the other parts are more elaborate, including the large round columns and the square capitals. See, in particular, the fine memorial tablets and the **famous pulpit** ★, outstanding examples of baroque art in Norway. The pulpit remains a masterpiece of woodcarving, depicting scenes from the Old Testament. A baldachin honoring the victories of Christ crowns the pulpit. Luxuriantly carved corbels hold up beautiful ribbed vaulting. Some of the capitals are carved with such Norse figures as dragons and griffins.

Haakon VIIs gate. Free admission. May 15–Sept Mon–Tues 11am–6pm, Wed–Sun 1–6pm; Oct to mid-May Wed–Sat 10am–3pm.

Gamle Stavanger ★★★ This is northern Europe's largest and most impressive—and best preserved—settlement of old-fashioned wooden houses. In "Old Stavanger" (its English name) more than 170 buildings from the late 18th century and early 19th century are not only preserved but also fully renovated. The houses were built with money brought back to Stavanger by seafarers who roamed the world. A walk through the narrow streets of Gamle Stavanger is one of the most memorable city experiences in southern Norway. The houses are owned partly by private residents and partly by the city itself.

To reach Old Town, go to the west side of Vågen (the harbor) and climb a steep slope overlooking Strandkaien. Once a district for the working class, the area is now gentrified and rather exclusive, and much attention is focused on these white-washed wooden houses, often with creepers or geraniums growing in flower boxes. The dollhouse homes are often separated by small terraced gardens. In the evening, lampposts from the 1890s light your way through the fog.

Stavanger Attractions

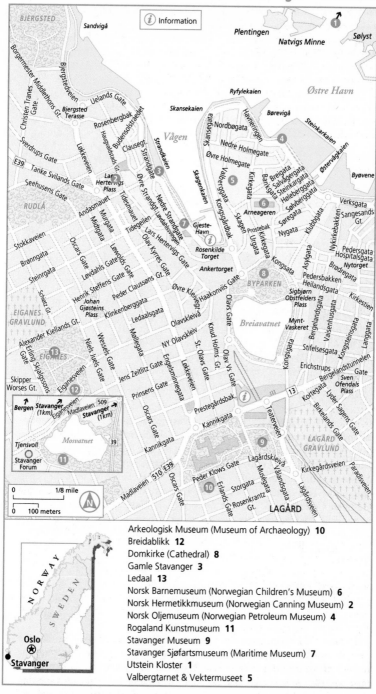

Arkeologisk Museum (Museum of Archaeology) **10**
Breidablikk **12**
Domkirke (Cathedral) **8**
Gamle Stavanger **3**
Ledaal **13**
Norsk Barnemuseum (Norwegian Children's Museum) **6**
Norsk Hermetikkmuseum (Norwegian Canning Museum) **2**
Norsk Oljemuseum (Norwegian Petroleum Museum) **4**
Rogaland Kunstmuseum **11**
Stavanger Museum **9**
Stavanger Sjøfartsmuseum (Maritime Museum) **7**
Utstein Kloster **1**
Valbergtarnet & Vektermuseet **5**

Norsk Barnemuseum (Norwegian Children's Museum) *Kids* This is the greatest playpen in Norway for children ages 5 to 12. In fact, it is one of the best children's museums in all of Europe. Exhibits center around almost anything related to children. You get documentation and exhibitions, of course, but the museum also satisfies a kid's desire to play with toys, the largest collection in the country. Storytelling and performances for children are also staged here.

Sølvberget. ✆ **51-91-23-90**. Admission 65NOK ($8.65). Wed–Fri 1–7pm; Sat noon–5pm; Sun 1–5pm.

Norsk Oljemuseum (Norwegian Petroleum Museum) ★ *Finds* Opened in 1999, this is one of the most unusual museums in Scandinavia, and already a much-photographed landmark in the port. This museum documents how oil was discovered off the coast of Norway in 1969, forever changing the country. The oil industry's celebration of itself, this is a spectacularly dramatic museum, rising as it does directly from the waters of the harbor. It resembles a space-age jumble of tin cans, with hints of an offshore oil platform, and an avant-garde modern combination of stainless steel, granite, and glass. The best parts of the museum are those that convey the huge shock and drama associated with Norway's entrance into the oil industry, which had otherwise been dominated by Arabs and Americans, and Norway's struggle to bone up on the legalities and international agreements.

The museum is not particularly adept at explaining the technicalities of the drilling rituals, and there's something superficial about the science associated with the construction of oil platforms, even though you can wander through a replica of an oil platform that's attached to the main bulk of the museum.

One of the city's finest restaurants, Bølgen & Moi, is within the premises of this museum, which "guards" the entrance to Stavanger's harbor in the way that Sydney's Opera House "guards" the entrance to the harbor to that city.

Kjeringholmen. ✆ **51-93-93-00**. Admission 75NOK ($10). June–Aug daily 10am–7pm; Sept–May Mon–Sat 10am–4pm, Sun 10am–6pm.

Rogaland Kunstmuseum ★ This is Stavanger's museum of fine arts, showing both temporary exhibitions as well as maintaining an impressive treasure trove of art. The museum is open Tuesday to Sunday 11am to 4pm, charging an admission of 50NOK ($6.65). The collection consists of some 2,000 paintings, drawings, and sculptures. Most of these are by Norwegian artists from the beginning of the 19th century to the present. Donated to the museum, the **Halvdan Haftsten Collection** ★ includes some 200 paintings and drawings by eight Norwegian artists between the two world wars. The museum displays the largest and most impressive collection of the **works of Lars Hertervig** ★ (1830–1902), one of the greatest romantic painters of Norwegian landscapes, along with an impressive array of the works of Kitty Kielland. The location 3km (1¾ miles) from the city center is at the northern end of the Old Town close to Mos Lake (Mosvannet), off E18.

Henrik Ibsen Weg 55, Mosvannsparken. ✆ **51-53-09-00**. Admission 50NOK ($6.65) adults; 30NOK ($4) students; free for children under 16. Tues–Sun 11am–4pm. Bus: 30, 31, 70, 99, 130, 143, 150, 152, 156. 170.

Stavanger Museum ★★ This is a five-part museum that you can visit with just one ticket. If you want to see the entire museum, expect to spend the better part of a day scampering from one point to another across the city. At the main museum, you'll be given a map with the location of all the museums.

The main museum is called simply the **Stavanger Museum,** Muségata 16 (✆ **51-84-27-00**), open from mid-June to mid-August daily from 11am to

4pm. From June 1 to June 14 and from August 16 to August 31, it is open Monday to Thursday from 11am to 3pm and Sunday 11am to 4pm. During other months, the museum is open only on Sunday 11am to 4pm. The ticket for all five museums costs 40NOK ($5.30) for adults, 30NOK ($4) for students and seniors, and 10NOK ($1.35) for ages 4 to 6 (3 and under free).

At the main museum at Muségata, you can see a permanent collection of stuffed birds and animals from all over the world. The centuries-old history of Stavanger, dating from the Viking era, is also presented, along with dramatized sound recordings about Stavanger in the 1800s.

The second museum, **Stavanger Sjøfartsmuseum (Maritime Museum)**, Nedre Strandgate 17–19, lies in a converted warehouse dating from 1770. Its permanent exhibition traces the maritime history of Stavanger for the past two centuries, from the days of the herring fleets to the booming oil industry of today.

The facade is a trim and shipshape, clapboard-sided, white-painted building directly on the harbor front. Inside, there's a battered post-and-beam construction showing how artfully timbers were used by 19th-century craftsmen, a sense of the dust, dirt, and economic mayhem of the Industrial Revolution, and the pervasive scent of tar and turpentine. Expect a claustrophobic, dark-toned interior, hundreds of ship models and 19th-century maritime accessories, and a horrendous sense of how hard life was in 19th- and early-20th-century coastal Norway.

You can visit a general store from the turn of the 20th century, a reconstructed merchant's apartment from the early 1900s, a reconstructed shipowner's home, and a sailmaker's loft, along with a memorial room to the philosopher Henrik Steffens. There is also a children's shop on site. This museum is closed in December.

Norsk Hermetikkmuseum (Norwegian Canning Museum), Øvre Strandgate 88A, lies in an old canning factory, with exhibitions tracing the fishing industry, Stavanger's main industry before being replaced by the oil industry, from the 1890s to the 1960s. Some of the machinery is still working, and on the first Sunday of every month the smoking ovens are stoked up. The public can taste newly smoked brisling straight from the ovens. This is the oddest and quirkiest of the museums of Stavanger, and it arouses the most emotion within the Norwegians who visit it. It's also the least polished and the most earthy of the town's museums, and the one that most richly and evocatively portrays the harsh and boring circumstances of factory work during the Industrial Revolution. It's set within a low-slung clapboard building within a neighborhood of increasingly gentrified antique cottages. Inside, about 50 antique machines are displayed, with sepia-toned photographs of how they, along with scores of weary workers, fitted sardines, herring, and bristlings into the galvanized steel tins that were later shipped to homes throughout Europe. Expect an enduring sense of the soot, grime, grease, and fish guts that once permeated this place with odors that stretched for several blocks in all directions. Overall, this museum is one of the most effective and eloquent tributes in Stavanger to the workaday heroism of 19th- and early-20th-century Norway.

The fourth museum, **Ledaal** ⭐, Eiganesveien 45, was built by Gabriel Schanche Kielland, a shipowner and merchant, in the years 1799 to 1803. The mansion is a fine example of the neoclassical style as interpreted in western Norway, with interior furnishings that are mainly rococo, Empire, and Biedermeier. This is the official—but rarely used—residence of the Norwegian royal family during their visits to Stavanger and Røgaland county, of which Stavanger is the capital. It's painted a shade of Pompeiian red and set adjacent to one of Stavanger's most evocative cemeteries. It's separated from a road leading into

(*Moments*   A Bike Ride to the "Three Swords"

On a summer day, we like to get the makings of a picnic and set out to see **Sverd I Fjell,** or the Three Swords monument at Hafrsfjord. This is the spot where King Hårald Fair Hair united Norway into one kingdom in 872. In 1983 Fritz Røed created this monument, and it was unveiled by King Olav. The monument, standing as a symbol of unification, depicts Viking sword sheaths modeled on actual swords found in various parts of the country. The crowns on the tops of the swords represent the Norwegian districts that took part in the epic battle for unification. From the center of Stavanger, bike along Mosvanneet Lake, continuing along Route 510 toward Sola. Allow about half an hour to reach this monument. The area of Møllebukta itself, in which the monument lies, is a popular outdoors spot of great beauty.

Stavanger, about a 15-minute walk uphill from the harbor, by a wall of very large boulders. The look is country-rustic and baronial, and is completely permeated with a sense of genteel 18th-century aristocracy and all-wood construction; closed in December and January.

The fifth museum is **Breidablikk** 🔆, Eiganesveien 40A. Set across the road from Ledaal (see above), it was built by another merchant and shipowner, Lars Berensten, in 1881 and 1882. Both the exterior and interior of the house are preserved in their original condition. It's a teeny weeny bit kitschy, thanks to an exaggerated alpine-*gemütlich* style, a coat of almost too-bright ocher paint (with dark brown trim), and yard upon yard of elaborate gingerbread running along the eaves and verandas. It's Victoriana/Carpenter gone wild, and an amusing sightseeing diversion; closed December and January.

Utstein Kloster 🔆   This is Norway's only preserved medieval abbey. In the ninth century, Utstein was one of the royal residences of Hårald Hårfagre, the Fair Hair, Norway's first monarch. In 1250 it belonged to Magnus Lagabøter (the Lawmender) who as king would draft Norway's first constitution, then the most democratic in the world. Magnus gave Utstein to the canons of an Augustinian order, who constructed their abbey around his fortress at the end of the 1200s. With the coming of the Reformation, Utstein became one of the largest private estates in western Norway. In summer, concerts featuring leading jazz and classical musicians are staged in its chapel.

Mosterøy. 🕐 **51-72-47-05.** Admission 35NOK ($4.65) adults, 10NOK ($1.35) children. May to mid-Sept Tues–Sat 10am–4pm; Sun noon–5pm.

Valbergtarnet & Vektermuseet   Inhabiting a wooden city, the residents of Stavanger lived in constant fear of fire. So from 1850 to 1853, they constructed this historic tower, Valbergtarnet, with a panoramic sweep over Stavanger and its harbor. A guard was stationed here 24 hours a day to be on the lookout for a fire. Today, the site is visited mainly for its **panoramic view** 🔆🔆, one of the most memorable cityscape vistas in southwestern Norway. But a small museum, Vektermuseet, has been installed here as well. The watchman's museum focuses on the guard's duties and the watchman as a symbol of safety.

Valbergjet 2. 🕐 **51-89-55-01.** Admission 20NOK ($2.65). Mon–Fri 10am–4pm; Sat 10am–2pm.

ORGANIZED TOURS Coach tours will take you around to all the scenic highlights of Stavanger, including the sometimes-royal residence and the Three Swords Monument. The tour ends with a visit to Stavanger Cathedral. **Haga Buss** (© 51-67-65-00) conducts 2-hour tours from June to August, with daily departures from the tourist office. The price is 195NOK ($26) for adults and 135NOK ($18) for seniors and children. In summer there are also countless fjord cruises, the most popular of which is a trip to Preikestolen (Pulpit Rock) on the Lysefjord (see below).

5 Shopping

Most shops are open Monday to Wednesday and Friday from 9am to 5pm; Thursday 9am to 7pm, and Saturday 9am to 3pm.

Gjestal Spinneri Motorists and serious shoppers might want to check out this spinning mill, lying 30km (19 miles) southeast of Stavanger in the little village of Oltedal. The spinning mill was established in 1937 and has since become one of Scandinavia's leading producers in the manufacture of hand-knitting yarn and plaids. The mill uses mostly Norwegian lambs wool but also English or New Zealand wool to create ideal, high-quality wool garments. The outlet sells all types of yarn and ready-made sweaters and other woolen products at 30% to 40% below the prices you'll find in most city stores. On site is a cafeteria so you can also make this a luncheon stopover. 4333 Oltedal. © 51-61-22-00.

Helger Myhre Marine Supplies This shop would never be considered a staple on Stavanger's tourist circuit, and many non-Norwegian shoppers might bypass it immediately in favor of a more luxurious venue. But if you've ever sailed a boat, or if you happen to own a boat, or if you merely happen to be fascinated with the thousands of articles you could stockpile *if* you owned a boat, this place is well worth a visit. Nautical hardware (everything you'd need to winch, ratchet, hoist, or belay a sailing craft) is stocked on the street level. Clothing for men, women, and children is upstairs, and a collection of sometimes kitschy-looking "Ahoy, Mate!" souvenirs, many in brass, are scattered around the store. Overall, it provides an insight into the sometimes-obsessive care with which many Norwegians maintain their pleasure craft. Skagenkaien 22. © 51-89-07-20.

Helgi Joensen Sculptural pewter—modern decorative art—reaches its peak in Stavanger at the working studio of this renowned artist who grew up on the coasts of the North Atlantic and found inspiration for his work here. Sculptures are mainly in pewter, and each piece is constructed individually, its texture formed freehand with no casting or molds. One piece of Joensen's sculptural pewter is like an heirloom gift. A visit here is also a chance to explore inside the working studio of a Norwegian artist. Ovre Strand Gate 52. © 51-52-98-99.

Straen Handel This is Stavanger's best all-around gift shop, selling souvenirs and Norwegian memorabilia that's a cut above the plastic stuff you might have seen in other shops. Within a clapboard-sided 18th-century house that's set directly beside Stavanger's harbor, it stockpiles statues, woodcarvings, pewter, and leather wear, as well as sweaters, books, and postcards. More expensive and much more esoteric, it also inventories some highly theatrical copies of medieval Norse helmets, priced at around $600 each—the kind of prop that might best be appreciated by a small-scale opera or theater company somewhere. On the upper floor of this shop, accessible via a stairway that empties into the shop itself, lies the Norwegian Emigration Center. Strandkaien 31. © 51-52-52-02.

Thune Gullsmed & Urmarker This is one of 12 shops in Norway that showcases the beautiful gold work and elegant watches of this leading chain, in addition to diamonds, silver jewelry, cutlery, pewter, and silver tableware. The outlet stocks both its own products, the most original and recommended, as well as international brand names that you can purchase across the world, including Gucci and Armani. Thune was founded in 1857 in Oslo, and has been selling jewelry to several generations of Norwegians. Nygaten 24. © 51-89-07-30.

6 Stavanger After Dark

Broremann Bar This intimate bar holds 60 patrons, mainly between the ages of 30 and 40. The light background music features those oldies but goodies from the likes of Springsteen and Dylan. The bar has large French-style windows, and its brick walls date from 1898. Under high ceilings, pubbers can enjoy the display of local art, which is changed monthly. There is never a cover charge. Skansegate 7. © 51-93-85-10.

Café Akvariet This is the most popular hangout for young people, 18 to 25, in town. There is live music two to five times a week. Patrons go here to meet their friends, and enjoy free Internet access. Beer, wine, and coffee are the drinks of choice, and there is a limited selection of light food. Upstairs is a concert hall where live music is often presented, including rock 'n' roll. Open Monday to Thursday 11am to midnight, Friday 11am to 2am, Saturday 3pm to 2am, and Sunday 6pm to 2am. Student Center, Olavkleiv. © 51-56-44-44.

Café Sting Stavanger is not known for its counterculture or bohemian undercurrents, but the little that exists is most visible here. Set atop the highest hill within the town center, a breathless ten-minute trek from the harbor via a flight of winding concrete steps, it lies adjacent to Valbergstårnet, a mock-medieval stone tower that was originally conceived late in the 19th century as a fire-watch station. The low-slung, white-sided clapboard house that contains the cafe was built in 1850. Inside, you'll find five different rooms, most on the ground floor, and most lined with strikingly modern paintings. By far the greatest business here derives from the establishment's role as a cafe serving pastries, beer, wine, and coffee, usually to liberal-minded members of Stavanger's arts community. Expect a larger-than-usual percentage of gay men and women here, but only on Friday, Saturday, and Sunday nights, when the place takes on more of a lavender luster. The cellar is home to a disco, usually frequented by straights and (to a much lesser extent) gays in their 20s and 30s, that operates Wednesday to Sunday from 11pm to 3am. The cafe is open daily from noon to 1am (Wed–Sat till 3am). Glasses of wine and beer cost 50NOK ($6.65) each; snacks and sandwiches, 69NOK to 209NOK ($9.20–$28), platters such as pastas, burgers, and wok dishes, 92NOK to 129NOK ($12–$17). There is a 75NOK ($10) cover Friday and Saturday nights in the disco. Valbjerget 3. © 51-89-38-68.

Checkpoint Charlie Hard Rock Café Mainly a dance place, this club can hold 200 people on a good night. Drawing a crowd in their 20s, it attracts those who like alternative music and hard rock. Music, often rock 'n' roll, is presented live one to two times a week, at which time a small cover might be imposed. Open daily 8pm to 2am. Nedre Strandgatan 5. © 51-53-22-45.

Chevy's Sports Bar The town's most popular sports bar lies in a cellar, down a flight of battered, beer-stained steps that are accessible from a street that runs parallel and 1 block uphill from the harbor. Inside its windowless interior, you'll find an appealing and deliberately dark room that's reminiscent of the Day-Glo psychedelic decors of the age of Jimi Hendrix. A total of nine TV screens broadcast the same sports event, most often British or Irish rugby, European soccer, or a USA-derived football game. On display are the autographed jerseys of the staff's favorite sports teams. Overall, the crowd here is convivial, extroverted, and accommodating. Open Tuesday to Sunday from 8pm to 2am. Skagen 21. *©* **51-89-52-15.**

The Irishman   This pub, attracting those from their 20s to their 60s, is the expat favorite, drawing a lot of patrons from Ireland, Scotland, and England that are lured by the recorded music they play from those countries—that and the large selection of different whiskies as well as Scotch single malts. Incidentally, they also sell American bourbon. A house band plays live music on Tuesday, Wednesday, and Thursday evenings as well as on Saturday afternoon. Open Monday to Wednesday 5pm to 2am, Thursday and Friday 3pm to 2am, and Saturday and Sunday 1pm to 2am. Holebergatan 9. *©* **51-89-41-81.**

Newsman Pub   This is a sophisticated and earthy British-style pub that its fans have defined as the most literate in Norway. Its decor was inspired by an old-fashioned newspaper office, the kind where lead type might have been supervised by stooped-over men with green eyeshades. You can sit around the woodsy-looking bar, within sightlines of the framed front pages of newspapers from around the English-speaking world, including banner headlines announcing the deaths of Winston Churchill and JFK and the impeachment of Richard Nixon. It's all very adult, and charming in its re-creation of a 1920s-era kind of aesthetic. Rest your pint of beer on any of several old-fashioned lecterns, and perhaps flip through a copy of any of the English-language papers that are displayed, library-style, on rods. There's even an in-house paper, *The Newsman*, that focuses on local politics, personalities, and gossip. The only food items served are snack items such as muffins and sandwiches. Open daily from noon till 2am. Skagen 14. *©* **51-84-38-80.**

Yanks Bar/The New York Nightclub   No other bar in Stavanger represents the city's sometimes raucous oil boom economy as aptly as this one. To Nordic purists, it's a glittery and imperialistic imposition, direct from the U.S., featuring the worst kinds of cultural excess. To lovers of high-volume rock 'n' roll, or to anyone who misses the country-western and rock bars of the United States, it's a gift from Valhalla. Regardless of your point of view, it's the most visible, and whenever there's a concert inside, the loudest, nightspot in town. You'll identify it by the scaled-down, silver-coated copy of the Statue of Liberty prominently positioned near an entrance to a clapboard-sided 19th-century warehouse that directly faces the port. Tip back a beer and a shot or two in the street-level bar (Yanks), where a mixed clientele of hard-drinking, earthy and edgy clients might be visiting from virtually anywhere. And if the amplified electronic music filtering down from upstairs (The New York Nightclub) appeals to you, expect to pay a cover charge. Don't even think of coming here early, since it opens around 10:30pm, and remains open till the first of the morning's fishing trawlers head out of the harbor around 4:30am. Live music is featured upstairs between around midnight and 3am most nights of the week, depending on bookings and whoever's sober enough to actually perform. The cover is 50NOK to 100NOK ($6.65–$13) in The New York Nightclub. Skagenkaien 21. *©* **51-85-95-50.**

Moments Norway's Most Beautiful Fjord ★★★

Poets have been inspired by the 42km (26-mile) **Lysefjord** or "light fjord," many considering it the country's most scenic. The blue waters of the fjord seem to glow even on a gray day. A luminous mist hovers over the fjord. "Time passes at a sedate pace at Lysefjord," or so wrote Olav Pedersen in 1883. "Your thoughts can wander in peace." That statement is still true today. Other writers have claimed that spending time on the majestic fjord allows them to tune in to nature's harmonious symphony. Sunsets here are often a dramatic mauve color tinged with royal purple.

You can take a day trip to the fjord, combining a traditional ferry ride with a new express boat. Of course, weather could be a factor in your decision to go or not to go. For information about schedules and tickets, contact the visitor information center (earlier in this chapter) in Stavanger or call **Rogaland Trafikkselskap** at ① **51-53-96-00.** In summer 3- to 6-hour boat trips are organized to the fjord, which is accessible only by boat. A typical excursion offered by **Fjord Tours** (① **51-53-73-40**) costs 250NOK ($33) for adults, 200NOK ($27) for seniors, and 125NOK ($17) for children 4 to 15.

7 Side Trip from Stavanger

The region surrounding Stavanger, both north and south, is one of the most beautiful in southwestern Norway, with some spectacular natural attractions. Fjord and mountain landscapes come together in a kind of majesty. There are some man-made attractions as well, but Mother Nature wins out over those.

PREIKESTOLEN ★★★ "Pulpit Rock" is a mammoth cube of rock with a vertical drop of 609m (2,000 ft.) over Lysefjord. It can be visited on either a boat or bus trip, or by a car-ferry trip and short drive, taking about 45 minutes from the center of Stavanger. If you want to climb the rock, you can take a boat and bus hiking jaunt. A pathway leads to the top. Jimmy Stewart in the Hitchcock film *Vertigo* would have had a tough time of it here, but if you like panoramic vistas, this rock is for you.

The walk from the car park to Pulpit Rock is 4km (2½ miles), but can take 2 hours each way. The walk has a height difference of 350m (1,148 ft.) and requires both you and your footwear to be in good shape. The last part of the walk passes dizzying drops high above Lysefjord. The weather can change quickly so remember to bring rainwear.

A bus, costing 45NOK ($6) one-way, leaves from the station in Stavanger from early June to early September. The boat is timed to meet ferry departures, which will take you for the final lap of the journey.

You can also sail by the rock on a fjord cruise but it's not as impressive from down below. The *Clipper* sightseeing boat (① **51-89-52-70**) offers daily cruises from Stavanger, ranging in price from 290NOK to 420NOK ($39–$56). **Fjord-Tours** (① **51-53-73-40**) also runs a 1½-hour cruise daily from mid-April to mid-September, costing 190NOK ($25). Tickets for both of these cruises are available from the Stavanger visitor information office (p. 208).

10

Bergen

In western Norway the landscape takes on an awesome beauty, with iridescent glaciers, deep fjords that slash into rugged, snowcapped mountains, roaring waterfalls, and secluded valleys that lie at the end of twisting roads. From Bergen the most beautiful fjords to visit are the Hardangerfjord (best at blossom time, May and early June), to the south; the Sognefjord, Norway's longest fjord, immediately to the north; and the Nordfjord, north of that. A popular excursion on the Nordfjord takes visitors from Loen to Olden along rivers and lakes to the Brixdal Glacier.

On the Hardangerfjord you can stop over at a resort such as Ulvik or Lofthus. From many vantage points, it's possible to see the Folgefonn Glacier, Norway's second-largest ice field. It spans more than 260 sq. km (100 sq. miles). Other stopover suggestions include the summer resorts (and winter ski centers) of Voss and Geilo. For resorts in the fjord district, see chapter 11, "The West Coast Fjord Country."

Bergen, with its many attractions; its good hotels, boarding houses, and restaurants; and its excellent boat, rail, and coach connections, makes the best center in the fjord district. It's an ancient city that looms large in Viking sagas. Until the 14th century, it was the seat of the medieval kingdom of Norway. The Hanseatic merchants established a major trading post that lasted until the 18th century.

Bergen has survived many disasters, including several fires and the explosion of a Nazi ship during World War II. It's a town with important traditions in shipping, banking, and insurance, and its modern industries are expanding rapidly.

1 Orientation

ARRIVING

BY PLANE   Planes to and from larger cities such as Copenhagen and London land at the **Bergen Airport** in Flesland, 19km (12 miles) south of the city. Dozens of direct or nonstop flights go to just about every medium-size city in Norway on such airlines as **SAS** (© **67-59-60-50**) and **Braathens SAFE** (© **55-99-82-50**).

Frequent **airport bus** service connects the airport to the Radisson SAS Royal Hotel, Braathens SAFE's office at the Hotel Norge, and the city bus station. Departures are every 20 minutes Monday to Friday and every 30 minutes Saturday and Sunday. The one-way fare is 60NOK ($8).

BY TRAIN   Day and night trains arrive from Oslo and stations en route. For information, call © **55-96-60-00.** Travel time from Oslo to Bergen is 6 to 8½ hours.

BY BUS   Express buses travel to Bergen from Oslo, Trondheim, Ålesund, and the Nordfjord area. The trip from Oslo takes 11 hours.

The World's Longest Tunnel

Thanks to a tunnel, you can now drive from Oslo to Bergen without having to take a ferry across water. Opening in 2001, the **Laerdal Tunnel** ★★★, stretching for 25km (15 miles) is the longest in the world. It lies on E16, the main road between Bergen and Oslo. The entrance to the tunnel begins at a point 296km (185 miles) northwest of Oslo. Costing $1.1 billion, it is said to be the safest road tunnel on the globe.

Along with high-tech monitoring, fire safety, and air treatment, the tunnel features a trio of large turning caverns (in case you change your mind and want to go back), 16 turning points, and nearly 50 emergency "lay-bys." Some 400 vehicles per hour can go through the tunnel, the ride taking just 20 minutes.

The area up above gets severe weather in winter but all is calm in the tunnel. The high mountain passes at 1,809m (5,935 ft.) are closed in winter. The panoramic, high-mountain road between Aurland and Laerdal, the so-called "Snow Road," is open only in summer.

BY CAR   A toll is charged on all vehicles driven into the city center Monday to Friday from 6am to 10pm. A single ticket costs 10NOK ($1.35); a book of 20 tickets, 90NOK ($12).

The trip from Oslo to Bergen is a mountain drive filled with dramatic scenery. Because mountains split the country, there's no direct road. The southern route, E76, goes through mountain passes until the junction with Route 47; then heads north to Kinsarvik and makes the ferry crossing to E16 leading west to Bergen. The northern route, Highway 7, through the resort of Geilo, heads to the junction with Route 47; then south to Kinsarvik. Take the ferry, and then go west on E16.

Visitors with a lot of time may spend 2 or 3 days driving from Oslo to Bergen. Fjords and snowcapped peaks line the way, and you can photograph waterfalls, fjord villages, and perhaps ancient stave churches.

To reduce driving time, motorists can use a tunnel—11km (almost 7 miles), the longest in northern Europe—that goes between Flåm (see "Flåm: Stopover on Europe's Most Scenic Train Ride," in chapter 11) and Gudvangen. From Gudvangen, follow E16 southwest to Bergen.

VISITOR INFORMATION

The **Bergen Tourist Office,** Bryggen 7 (© **55-32-14-80**), provides information, maps, and brochures about Bergen and the rest of the region. It's open June to August, daily from 8:30am to 10pm; May and September, daily 9am to 8pm; October to April, Monday to Saturday 9am to 4pm. The Bergen Tourist Office can also help you find a place to stay, exchange foreign currency, and cash traveler's checks when banks are closed. You can also buy tickets for city sightseeing or for tours of the fjords.

CITY LAYOUT

Bergen is squeezed between mountain ranges and bounded by water. The center of the city lies between the harbor, **Bryggen** (check out "Seeing the Sights," later in this chapter), the railway station, and the main square, **Torgalmenningen.**

Like Rome, Bergen is said to have grown up around seven hills. For the best overall view, take the funicular to **Fløien.** The northern section of the city is **Sandviken,** which is filled with old warehouses. The area south of central Bergen has recently been developed at an incredible rate.

In the center of Bergen, walk on cobblestone streets as you explore the quayside with its medieval houses and the open-air fish market. The center has colonnaded shops and cafes, and in **Gamle Bergen,** you can step back to the early 19th century.

2 Getting Around

The **Bergen Card** entitles you to free bus transportation and (usually) free museum entrance throughout Bergen, plus discounts on car rentals, parking, and some cultural and leisure activities. It's a good value. Ask for it at the tourist office (see "Visitor Information," above). A 24-hour card costs 165NOK ($22) for adults, 80NOK ($11) for children 3 to 15. A 48-hour card is 245NOK ($33) or 120NOK ($16). Children under 3 generally travel or enter free.

BY BUS

The **Central Bus Station** (Bystasjonen), Strømgaten 8 (© 55-55-90-70), is the terminal for all buses serving the Bergen and Hardanger areas, as well as the airport bus. The station has luggage storage, shops, and a restaurant. City buses are marked with their destination and route number. For **bus information** in the Bergen area, call © 177. A network of yellow-sided city buses serves the city center only. For information, call © 55-59-32-00.

BY TAXI

Taxis are readily available at the airport. To request one, call © 55-99-70-00. A ride from the Bergen Airport to the city center costs 262NOK ($35). Sightseeing by taxi costs about 390NOK ($52) for the first hour and 300NOK ($40) for each additional hour.

BY CAR

PARKING   Visitors can park on most streets in the city center after 5pm. For convenient indoor parking, try the **Bygarasjen Busstation** (© 55-56-88-70), a large garage near the bus and train stations, about a 5-minute walk from the city center. It's open 24 hours a day and charges 15NOK ($2) per hour from 7am to 5pm, 11NOK ($1.45) per hour from 5pm to 7am. You can park for 24 hours for 75NOK ($10).

RENTAL CARS   You might want to rent a car to explore the area for a day or two. **Budget** (© 800/472-3325 in the U.S.) maintains offices at the airport (© 55-22-75-27) and downtown at Lodin Leppsgate 1 (© 55-90-26-15). Its least expensive car is 1,190NOK ($158) per day, which includes the 23% government tax, collision-damage waiver, and unlimited mileage. Rates per day are lower for rentals of a week or more.

Hertz (© 800/654-3001 in the U.S.) has locations at the airport (© 55-22-60-75) and downtown at Nygårdsgate 89 (© 55-96-40-70). For a 2-day rental, its smallest car, a Renault Clio, costs 1,290NOK ($172) per day, including tax, collision-damage waiver, and unlimited mileage.

Avis (© 800/331-2112 in the U.S.) has branches at the airport (© 55-22-76-18) and downtown at Lars Hillesgate 20 (© 55-32-01-30). For a 1-day rental, its smallest car, a Ford Fiesta, costs 1,130NOK ($150) with unlimited mileage. The price includes the 23% tax and the optional collision-damage waiver.

Of course, rates are subject to change. The lowest rates are almost always offered to those who reserve their cars from their home country before they leave.

Remember that Norway imposes severe penalties—including stiff fines and, in some cases, imprisonment—on anyone who drinks and drives.

BY FERRY

You can take a ferry across the harbor Monday to Friday from 7am to 4:15pm; they don't run on Saturday or Sunday. One-way fares are 12NOK ($1.60) for adults, 6NOK (80¢) for children. Ferries arrive and depart from either side of the harbor at Dreggekaien and Munkebryggen. For information, call ℂ 55-32-14-80.

BY COASTAL STEAMER

Bergen is the cruise capital of Norway, home to a flotilla of well-engineered ships that carry passengers, cars, and vast amounts of freight up and down the coast. At least 10 of the boats begin and end their itineraries in Bergen and make about 30 stops en route before landing 5 to 6 days later at Kirkenes, far north of the Arctic Circle, near the Russian border. You can book a berth on any one of these ships for short- or long-haul transits, and do a quick bit of sightseeing while the ship docks in various ports.

Depending on the season and the category of berth you select, a full 11-day round-trip excursion from Bergen to Kirkenes and back costs $895 to $4,000 per person, double occupancy. It's best to book these cruises through the New York City office of the Bergen Line (ℂ **800/323-7436** or 212/319-1300). The line owns some of the ships and acts as a sales agent for the others. If you're already in Norway, talk to any travel agent. You can make arrangements through Bergen-based **Cruise Spesialisten,** Veiten 2B, N-5020 Bergen (ℂ **55-23-07-90**). It has brochures and lots of information concerning the crop of newly built Norwegian cruise ships. They include *Nord Norge* (launched in 1997); *Polarys* (1996); *Nord-kapp* (1996); *Nordlys* (1994); *Richard With* (1993); *Kong Harald* (1993); and the older but stalwart *Narvik* (1982), *Midnatt Sol* (1982), and *Lofoten* (1964).

Other routes head south from Bergen to Stavanger and other ports, and tours go to some of the fjords to the south. For information and reservations, contact the Bergen Line, Cruise Spesialisten (see above), or a local operator. They include **Flaggruten** (ℂ **55-23-87-00**), and **H.S.D.** (ℂ **55-23-87-90**). The firms share offices at P.O. Box 2005, Nordnes, N-5024 Bergen. Faster than many hydrofoils, they go to the inner reaches of the world's longest fjord, the Sognefjord. They stop frequently en route to pick up cargo and passengers, and are worthy vehicles for sightseeing expeditions. Many of them dock at Bergen's inner harbor, near the Stradkaiterminalen.

FAST FACTS: Bergen

Area Code The country code for Norway is **47.** If you're calling from out-side the country, the city code for Bergen is **5.** Inside Norway, no area or city codes are needed. Phone numbers have eight digits.

Banking Bergen has dozens of banks. The most visible is **Den Norske Bank,** Torg Almenning 2 (ℂ **55-21-10-00**). Branches of many of its competitors can be found near the Radisson-SAS Hotel Norge, on Rådstuplass.

Bookstores One of the best, with a wide range of books in English, is **Melvaer Libris,** in the Galleriet, Torgalmenningen 8 (℡ **55-96-28-10**). It's open Monday to Friday from 9am to 8pm, Saturday 9am to 6pm.

Business Hours Most **banks** are open Monday to Friday from 8:15am to 3:30pm, and Thursday until 6pm. Most **businesses** are open Monday to Friday from 9am to 4pm. **Shops** are generally open Monday to Wednesday and Friday from 9am to 4:30pm, Thursday 9am to 7pm (sometimes also on Fri until 7pm), Saturday 9am to 2pm.

Currency Exchange There's a currency exchange at the Bergen Airport. In town, you can exchange money at several banks. When the banks are closed, you can exchange money at the tourist office (see "Visitor Information," above).

Dentists Emergency care only is available at **Bergen Legevakt,** Lars Hillesgate 30 (℡ **55-32-11-20**), 24 hours a day.

Doctors For medical assistance, call **Bergen Legevakt,** Lars Hillesgate 30 (℡ **55-32-11-20**), daily from 4 to 9pm. If it's not an emergency, your hotel can make an appointment with an English-speaking doctor.

Drugstores One convenient pharmacy is **Apoteket Nordstjernen,** at the Central Bus Station (℡ **55-31-68-84**). It's open daily from 8am to midnight.

Embassies & Consulates Most foreign nationals will have to contact their embassies in Oslo if they have a problem; only the **United Kingdom** maintains a consulate in Bergen, at Carl Konowsgate 34–35 (℡ **55-94-47-05**).

Emergencies For the **police,** dial ℡ **112;** to report a **fire,** call ℡ **110;** for an **ambulance,** dial ℡ **113.**

Eyeglass Repair A good optician is **Optiker Svabø,** Strandgaten 18 (℡ **55-31-69-51**).

Hairdressers & Barbers One of the best in town is **Prikken Frisørsalong,** Strandkaien 2B (℡ **55-32-31-51**). It's open Monday to Saturday 9am to 5pm.

Hospitals A medical center, **Accident Clinic,** is open around the clock. It's at Lars Hillesgate 30 (℡ **55-32-11-20**). There is a general hospital, but you can't go directly there; you must go through the Accident Clinic or call **Syke-besøksformidling (Sick Call Help)** at ℡ **55-32-40-60.**

Internet Access Your two best bets are **Accezzo,** next to the Galleriet shopping mall at torgallmenning 8 (℡ **55-30-05-00**), and **CyberHouse Internett Café,** Vetrlidsallmenninggen 13 (℡ **55-36-66-16**).

Laundry Try **Jarlens Vaskoteque,** Lille Øvregate 17 (℡ **55-32-55-04**). It's near the Hotel Victoria in a little alley about 45m (50 yards) northeast of the 17th-century Korskirken church, off Kong Oscars Gate. It's open Monday to Friday from 10am to 8pm, Saturday 9am to 3pm.

Libraries The **Bergen Public Library,** Strømgaten (℡ **55-56-85-60**), is open in July and August on Tuesday, Wednesday, and Friday from 10am to 3pm, Monday and Thursday 9am to 7pm, Saturday 9am to 1pm; the rest of the year, Monday to Friday 10am to 8pm, Saturday 10am to 4:30pm.

Lost Property Various agencies recover lost objects. For assistance, contact the local police station or **Tourist Information** (℡ **55-32-14-80**).

Luggage Storage & Lockers Rental lockers and luggage storage are available at the **Jernbanestasjonen** (railway station), Strømgaten 1, which is open daily from 7am to 11:50pm. The cost is 20NOK ($2.20) per day.

Photographic Needs Go to **Foto Knutsen,** in the Galleriet, Torgalmenningen 8 (℗ **55-31-16-78**). It's open Monday to Friday 8:30am to 8pm, Saturday 9am to 6pm.

Police Call ℗ **112.**

Post Office The main post office is on Småstrandgaten (℗ **55-54-15-00**), 1 block from Torget. It's open Monday to Friday 8am to 6pm, Saturday 9am to 3pm. If you want to receive your mail c/o General Delivery, the address is Poste Restante, N-5002 Bergen. You'll need your passport to pick it up.

Taxes Bergen adds no city taxes to the national value-added tax.

Telephone Public telephones take 1NOK (15¢) coins. Local calls cost 2NOK to 3NOK (25¢–40¢). To call abroad, dial ℗ **00;** to call collect, dial ℗ **115.**

3 Where to Stay

Easily found at Bryggen 7, the **Bergen Tourist Office** (℗ 55-32-14-80) books guests into hotels and secures accommodations in private homes. More than 30 families take in guests during the summer. The booking service costs 15NOK to 30NOK ($2–$4), and prospective guests also pay a deposit that's deducted from the final bill. Double rooms in **private homes** usually cost 360NOK to 400NOK ($48–$53), with no service charge. Breakfast is not served.

The rates quoted for the hotels below include service and tax. Many expensive accommodations lower their rates considerably on weekends and in midsummer. We've mentioned it when these reductions are available, but the situation is fluid, and it's best to check on the spot. All of our recommended accommodations come with private bathrooms unless otherwise indicated.

EXPENSIVE

Clarion Admiral Hotel ⋆   When it was built in 1906, this building was one of the largest warehouses in Bergen, with six sprawling floors peppered with massive trusses and beams. In 1987, it became a comfortable, tastefully appointed hotel, and in 1998, it was enlarged and renovated into the bustling establishment you'll see today. Rooms are a bit smaller than you might hope—with small bathrooms equipped with shower-tub combinations to match—but comfortable, with excellent beds. Many rooms lack water views, but the ones that do open onto flower-bedecked balconies with the best harbor views in town.

Christian Sundts Gate 9, N-5004 Bergen. ℗ **55-23-64-00.** Fax 55-23-64-64. www.admiral.no. 211 units. Mon–Thurs 1,695NOK ($225) double, 1,895NOK–4,000NOK ($252–$532) suite; Fri–Sun 950NOK ($126) double; 1,150NOK–2,550NOK ($153–$339) suite. AE, DC, MC, V. Bus: 2, 4, or 11. **Amenities:** 2 restaurants; bar; limited room service; laundry service; dry cleaning. *In room:* TV, minibar, hair dryer, safe.

First Hotel Marin ⋆⋆   In the heart of Bergen, this first-class hotel is one of Bergen's most modern and streamlined hotels in a brown-brick building lying on a steep hillside. The bedrooms are moderate to spacious in size, and each is handsomely furnished in functional, stylish Nordic modern, with immaculately kept tiled bathrooms equipped with shower-tub combinations. For Bergen, the hotel offers a large number of suites—34 deluxe ones in all—the best of which are a trio of penthouse units with a view so panoramic it encompasses all seven mountains surrounding Bergen. Many accommodations are reserved for non-smokers, and the finest units are in front, overlooking the harbor.

Rosenkrantgaten 8, N-5003 Bergen. ℭ **53-05-15-00**. Fax 53-05-15-01. 131 units. 1,450NOK–1,670NOK ($193–$222) double; 2,210NOK ($294) suite. AE, DC, MC, V. Bus: 1, 5, or 9. **Amenities:** Restaurant; bar; fitness center; sauna; limited room service; laundry service; dry cleaning. *In room:* TV, minibar, hair dryer, safe.

Radisson SAS Hotel Norge 🐦🐦   In the city center, near Torgalmenningen, the Norge has been a Bergen tradition since 1885; it continues to be a favorite of visiting celebrities. The current building opened in 1962 and in 1997 the lobby was upgraded. Rooms are better than ever after a refurbishment, with double-glazed windows, bedside controls, and ample bathrooms with showers and in some cases with bathtubs big enough for two. Ninth-floor units open onto private balconies overlooking the flower-ringed borders of a nearby park. Nonsmoking and wheelchair-accessible rooms are available.

The best service and the best cuisine, both Norwegian and international, are in the Grillen. The American Bar is a piano bar, and Bull's Eye is an English pub. The Night Spot, in the cellar, is a leading nightlife venue.

Nedre Ole Bulls Plass 4, N-5807 Bergen. ℭ **800/333-3333** in the U.S., or 55-57-30-00. Fax 55-57-30-01. www.radissonsas.com. 345 units. 1,845NOK–1,945NOK ($245–$259) double; 2,500NOK–4,000NOK ($333–$532) suite. Rates include breakfast. Children under 18 stay free in parent's room. DC, MC, V. Parking 160NOK ($21); reserve with room. Bus: 2, 3, or 4. **Amenities:** 2 restaurants; bar; heated indoor pool; fitness center; sauna; limited room service; babysitting; laundry service; dry cleaning. *In room:* TV, minibar, hair dryer.

Radisson SAS Royal Hotel 🐦   Opened in 1982, this hotel was built on the fire-ravaged site of old warehouses that had stood here since 1170. It's contemporary, with the finest services and amenities in Bergen. The guest rooms are beautifully maintained, with lithographs and comfortable, upholstered furniture. Newly renovated guest rooms are exceedingly comfortable. Although the bathrooms are small, they have shower-tub combinations and phones. Some rooms are reserved for nonsmokers; some are designed for guests with disabilities.

The hotel has a nightclub, Engelen, and a pub, Madame Felle, named after a lusty matron who ran a sailors' tavern on these premises during the 19th century. The pub's outdoor terrace (Madame Felle's Promenade) does a thriving business in the summer.

Bryggen, N-5835 Bergen. ℭ **800/333-3333** in the U.S., or 55-54-30-00. Fax 55-32-48-08. www.radisson-sas.com. 273 units. May–Sept 1,895NOK ($210) double; Oct–Apr 1,795NOK ($199) double; year-round 2,200NOK–3,500NOK ($244–$389) suite. Rates include breakfast. AE, DC, MC, V. Parking 100NOK ($11). Bus: 1, 5, or 9. **Amenities:** 2 restaurants; 2 bars; heated indoor pool; fitness center; sauna; limited room service; babysitting; laundry service; dry cleaning. *In room:* TV, minibar, hair dryer, safe.

Tips **Saving Money on Your Room**

To save money on hotels, you can purchase a **Bergen Package** that includes not only your room, but also a full breakfast and the Bergen Card (see "Getting Around," above). Depending on the hotel, the cost of the package ranges from 475NOK to 565NOK ($63–$75) per person based on double occupancy. Kids under the age of 16 sleeping in an extra bed in their parents' room are charged 50NOK ($6.65) nightly. The package is available on weekends all year but every day from May 20 to August 31. You can order this package from any travel agency or at the Tourist Information Office in Bergen. For more details, call ℭ **55-55-20-00**.

Bergen Accommodations & Dining

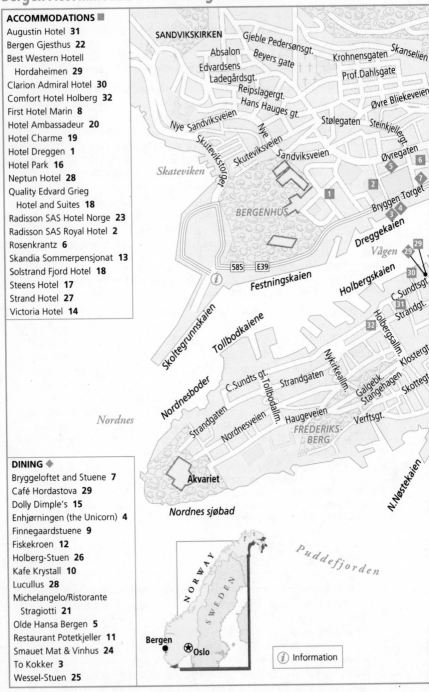

SANDVIKSKIRKEN
Gjeble Pedersønsgt.
Absalon   Beyers gate
Krohnensgaten   Skanselien
Edvardsens
Ladegårdsgt.
Prof.Dahlsgate
Reipslagergt.
Hans Hauges gt.
Øvre Bliekeveien
Nye Sandviksveien
Nye
Skuteviksveien
Stølegaten   Steinkjellergt.
Skuteviksveien
Sandviksveien
Øvregaten
Skateviken
Skuteviksstorget
BERGENHUS
Bryggen Torget
Dreggekaien
Vågen
Festningskaien
Holbergskaien
C.Sundtsgt.
Strandgt.
Holbergsalm.
Tollbodkaiene
Skoltegrunnskaien
Nordnesboder
C.Sundts gt.
Strandgaten
Tollbodalm.
Nykirkealm.
Galgebk.
Stangehagen
Klostergt.
Skottegt.
Nordnes
Strandgaten
Nordnesveien
Haugeveien
FREDERIKS-BERG
Verftsgt.
N.Nøstekaien
Akvariet
Nordnes sjøbad
Puddefjorden

NORWAY
SWEDEN
Bergen
⊛ Oslo

ⓘ Information

MODERATE

Augustin Hotel ⭐ *Finds*   The Augustin has one of the best locations in Bergen—right in the harbor-front shopping district—with front rooms that have terrific harbor views. Constructed in 1909 in the Jugenstil or Art Nouveau style, Augustin has been in the same family for four generations. In 1995 it more than doubled in size by adding a new wing, with new modern rooms (equipped with all the modern trimmings) designed by award-winning Bergen architect Aud Hunskår. More traditional rooms remain in the old section. Bathrooms in both sections have both showers and tubs. The hotel is decorated with lots of art, many pieces from well-known contemporary Norwegian artists. Special accommodations are available for nonsmokers, wheelchair users, and allergy sufferers.

The hotel used to be the site of the Altona, a tavern that had been on this spot since 1600. That nostalgic memory is evoked in the hotel's wine cellar, which is open to the public.

Carl Sundts Gate 24, N-5004 Bergen. ℂ 55-30-40-40. Fax 55-30-40-10. www.augustin.no. 109 units. Mon–Thurs 1,550NOK ($206) double, 1,890NOK ($251) suite; Fri–Sun 800NOK ($106) double, 1,290NOK ($172) suite. AE, DC, MC, V. Bus: 2 or 4. **Amenities:** Restaurant; bar; babysitting; laundry service; dry cleaning. *In room:* A/C, TV, minibar, hair dryer.

Best Western Hotell Hordaheimen   This hotel near the harbor has long been a base for young people from nearby districts. It's operated by the Bondeungdomslaget i Bergen, an association that sponsors cultural and folklore programs. School and civic groups sometimes reserve nearly all the rooms. The hotel was built at the turn of the 19th century and renovated in stages between 1989 and 1995. Lars Kinsarvik, an internationally known designer, created the furniture in the late 19th century. Although Laura Ashley designs are widely featured in the hotel's literature, they are few in number. Some accommodations for nonsmokers are available, and some units are suitable for those with disabilities. The small, simple guest rooms are immaculate, with good beds and tiny bathrooms equipped with shower-tub combinations.

Christian Sundts Gate 18, N-5004 Bergen. ℂ 55-33-50-00. Fax 55-23-49-50. 64 units. May 15–Sept 15 Mon–Thurs 1,450NOK ($193) double, Fri–Sun 850NOK ($113) double; Sept 16–May 14 Mon–Thurs 1,230NOK ($164) double, Fri–Sun 850NOK ($113) double; year-round 1,430NOK–1,550NOK ($190–$206) suite. Rates include breakfast. AE, DC, MC, V. Bus: 1, 5, or 9. **Amenities:** Restaurant; lounge; laundry service; dry cleaning. *In room:* TV, minibar, hair dryer.

Neptun Hotel ⭐ *Finds*   Conservative, unflashy, and distinctly Norwegian, the Neptun was built in 1952, long before many of its more streamlined and trend-conscious competitors. Its eight-story premises attract lots of business, especially from Norwegians riding the *Hurtigruten* (coastal steamers), who consider it a worthwhile and solid choice in the upper-middle bracket. There's loads of unusual art throughout the public areas. Each of the bedrooms has a decorative theme related to its name. For example, rooms named after Ole Bull, Nordahl Grieg, Ludvig Holberg, Salvador Dalí, and Joan Miró have photos or artworks commemorating their namesakes' lives and achievements. When you check in, ask the reception staff for a "business" or a "feminine" room, and a decor that more or less corresponds to those parameters will be assigned to you. Units on the third floor are the most recently renovated (in 2001). About half of the rooms have shower/bathtub combinations; the remainder contain just showers. The hotel's premier restaurant, Lucullus, is one of Bergen's best (see "Where to Dine," below); there's also a likable, bustling brasserie named Pascal Mat & Vin.

Valkendorfsgate 8, N-5012 Bergen. ℂ 55-30-68-00. Fax 55-30-68-50. office@neptun-hotell.no. 124 units. Mon–Thurs 1,660NOK ($221) double, 2,090NOK ($278) suite; Fri–Sun year-round and daily mid-June to mid-Aug 1,170NOK ($156) double, 1,600NOK ($213) suite. AE, DC, MC, V. Bus: 20, 21, or 22. **Amenities:** 2 restaurants; bar; limited room service; babysitting; laundry service; dry cleaning. *In room:* A/C, TV, minibar, hair dryer, trouser press.

Quality Edvard Grieg Hotel and Suites ★ *Finds*   Opened in 1987, this modern, all-suite hotel—Norway's first—lies 19km (12 miles) south of Bergen and 4.75km (3 miles) from the airport. Luxuriously appointed suites are amply sized, with good beds in the rather small sleeping quarters, and a separate lounge. The bathrooms are excellent, with lots of shelf space and shower-tub combinations. Some accommodations for nonsmokers are available, as are units for persons with disabilities. Three suites are wheelchair accessible. Monday to Friday, guests can dine in the intimate and expensive Mozart Restaurant, or can enjoy Norwegian and international food in the H. C. Andersen Restaurant. The lobby bar is cozy, and patrons can also dance at the Amitra nightclub. Free airport transfers are arranged for arriving and departing guests Monday to Friday from 7am to 10pm.

Sandsliåsen 50, N-5049 Sandsli. ✆ **55-98-00-00.** Fax 55-98-01-50. 153 units. Mon–Fri 1,550NOK ($206) suite for 2; Sat–Sun 1,090NOK ($145) suite for 2. Rates include breakfast. AE, DC, MC, V. Free parking. Bus: 30 from the Bergen bus station. **Amenities:** Restaurant; bar; heated indoor pool; fitness center; sauna; limited room service; laundry service; dry cleaning. *In room:* TV, minibar, hair dryer.

Rosenkrantz   This 1921 hotel, near Bryggen in the city center, is a simple, unpretentious choice. The lobby leads to a comfortable dining room and bar. The rooms are pleasantly furnished; the small bathrooms come equipped with shower-tub combinations. Half the rooms are reserved for nonsmokers. Facilities include a TV lounge, a piano bar, a restaurant (Harmoni), and a nightclub (Rubinen) with live music.

Rosenkrantzgate 7, N-5003 Bergen. ✆ **55-30-30-14-00.** Fax 55-31-14-76. rosenkrantz@rainbow-hotels.no. 129 units. 1,520NOK ($202) double. Rates include breakfast. AE, DC, MC, V. Parking 70NOK ($9.30) in adjacent covered garage. Bus: 1, 5, or 9. **Amenities:** Restaurant; bar; piano bar; nightclub; laundry service; dry cleaning. *In room:* TV, minibar, hair dryer.

Victoria Hotel ★ *Value*   One of the oldest hotels in town, Victoria Hotel has a graceful bay-fronted facade. Renovated in 1987, the hotel now operates as one of only two members of the Best Western chain in Bergen. Smaller and more personalized than many equivalently priced hotels in town, and noted for relatively reasonable rates, it's cozy, staffed with concerned employees, and loaded with art—a result of almost 50 years of collecting on the part of the well-traveled owners. Bedrooms are clean and bright, outfitted with contemporary furniture and art. Bathrooms are tiled and modern, each with showers but without bathtubs.

Kong Oscarsgt 29, N-5017 Bergen. ✆ **800/528-1234** in the U.S. or 55-21-23-00. Fax 55-21-23-50. www.victoriahotel.no. 43 units. Mid-May to mid-Sept 1,490NOK ($198) double; mid-Sept to mid-May Mon–Thurs 1,030NOK ($137) double, Fri–Sun 1,490NOK ($198) double. Rates include breakfast. AE, DC, MC, V. Parking 130NOK ($17). Bus: 2 or 4. **Amenities:** Greek restaurant Sokrates (under separate ownership); bar; babysitting; laundry service; dry cleaning. *In room:* A/C, TV, minibar, hair dryer.

INEXPENSIVE

Bergen Gjesthus *Kids*   In the center of Bergen, this five-story building has been a hotel since the 1970s, although it was renovated in 2002. The top floor is reserved for housing for local college students. You're welcomed here without a lot of fuss into bedrooms that come in various sizes. Some of the accommodations used to be small private apartments, so they can generously accommodate four or more people, which makes them a family favorite. Bedrooms have wooden floors, comfortable but simple furnishings, and 13 of the units come with small kitchens. Each accommodation has a small private bathroom with shower.

Vestre torgate 20A, N-5015 Bergen. © **55-31-96-66**. Fax 55-59-90-91. www.hotelbergen.com. 21 units. 690NOK–900NOK ($92–$120) double; 100NOK ($13) per extra person. Rates include continental breakfast. AE, DC, MC, V. Closed Dec 22–Jan 2. Bus: 2, 3, or 4. **Amenities:** Pub; laundry service; dry cleaning. *In room:* TV.

Comfort Hotel Holberg ★ Set near the Nykirk, a 15-minute walk from Bergen's Fish Market, this hotel built around 1995 commemorates the life of the late-18th-century writer and dramatist Holberg, "The Molière of the North," one of the most famous writers in Danish and Norwegian letters. (The writer was born in a since-demolished house on the site of this hotel's parking garage.) The hotel's lobby looks like a testimonial to the author's life, with an informative biography, memorabilia, and photographs of stage productions based on his works. Bedrooms are a modernized, reinterpretation of the Norwegian "farmhouse" style, thanks to wooden floors, rough-textured half-paneling stained in tones of forest green, and big windows, some of them floor-to-ceiling, that swing open directly onto a view of the quiet residential street below. Bathrooms are tiled, about half of them with shower-bathtub combinations, with acute angles that make them seem bigger than they actually are.

Strandgaten 190, Pb 1949 Nordnes, N-5817 Bergen. © **55-30-42-00**. Fax 55-23-18-20. www.choice hotels.no. 140 units. Mon–Thurs 790NOK–1,560NOK ($105–$207) double; Fri–Sun 890NOK ($118) double. Rates include breakfast. AE, DC, MC, V. Parking: 90NOK ($12). **Amenities:** Restaurant; bar; babysitting; laundry service; dry cleaning. *In room:* A/C, TV, minibar.

Hotel Ambassadeur *Value* This cost-conscious, unpretentious hotel was formed from the union in 2002 of two side-by-side competitors, Ambassadeur and the Anker, both built in the 1920s. Everything here is adequate and comfortable, but far from plush. Because the hotel is closer than any other in town to Football Pub (see "Bergen After Dark," later in this chapter), a sometimes raucous sports bar, the guests tend to be out-of-town soccer players in town for matches or locals who have a passionate interest in the game. The bathrooms in each room have showers with floor drains rather than tubs. We prefer rooms on the uppermost (4th) floor beneath the mansard-style roof because of the views over Bergen. Access to these rooms requires climbing an additional flight of stairs above and beyond the floor where the elevator ends.

Vestre Torvgate 9, 5015 Bergen. © **55-90-08-90**. Fax 55-90-05-84. 83 units. Mon–Thurs 900NOK ($120) double; Fri–Sun and daily from mid-June to mid-Aug 800NOK ($106). Rates include breakfast. AE, DC, MC, V. Bus: 1 or 9. **Amenities:** Pub in lobby; much bigger sports pub on ground floor; babysitting; laundry service; dry cleaning. *In room:* TV.

Hotel Charme ★ *Finds* Run by the Ramussen family, this discovery was converted into a B&B in 2001. A pleasant alternative to chain hotels, it offers a personalized welcome. The bedrooms have wooden floors, comfortable, tasteful furnishings, and cushioned chairs, along with private bathrooms with shower. Kids stay free unless they need an extra bed.

Rosenberggate 13, N-5015 Bergen. © **55-23-10-70**. Fax 55-90-72-81. www.hotel-charme.com. 18 units. 690NOK–900NOK ($92–$120) double; 1,300NOK–1,800NOK ($173–$239) suite. Rates include continental breakfast. AE, DC, MC, V. Bus: 2, 3, or 4. **Amenities:** Breakfast lounge; laundry service; dry cleaning. *In room:* TV.

Hotel Dreggen *Kids* Reasonable prices and an accommodating staff make this a family favorite. Located in the heart of Bergen, this hotel is walking distance from the embarkation point for the fjords. Rather dull architecturally from the outside, it improves considerably once you enter the seven-story structure.

Bedrooms are medium in size and have been recently renovated. About one-third of the rooms have private bathrooms with shower-tub combinations.

Sandbrugaten 3, N-5835 Bergen. © **55-31-61-55.** Fax 55-31-54-23. www.hotel-dreggen.no. 31 units (9 with bathroom). 690NOK ($92) double without bathroom, 790NOK ($105) double with bathroom. AE, DC, MC, V. Bus: 2 or 5. **Amenities:** Breakfast room; bar; lounge; 24-hr. room service; laundry service; dry cleaning. *In room:* TV.

Hotel Park ★ This converted 1890 townhouse is in an attractive university area near Grieghall and Nygård Park. The rooms are traditionally furnished, often with antiques. Accommodations vary in size but all have good beds and adequate bathrooms equipped with shower-tub combinations. In the summer, a neighboring building (furnished in the same style) accommodates overflow guests. A delicious Norwegian breakfast is served in the dining room; later in the day sandwiches, small hot dishes, and wine and beer are available there. In the summer, reserve well in advance. The Park is a 10-minute walk from the train and bus stations.

Harald Hårfagresgaten 35 and Allegaten 20, N-5007 Bergen. © **55-54-44-00.** Fax 55-54-44-44. www.parkhotel.no. 33 units. 980NOK ($130) double. Rates include breakfast. AE, DC, MC, V. Parking 50NOK ($6.65). Bus: 11. **Amenities:** Breakfast room; lounge. *In room:* TV, hair dryer.

Skandia Sommerpensjonat This place functions most of the year as dormitory-style housing for students at Bergen's university, but for 2 months in midsummer, it opens its doors to the public. You'll find this inexpensive hostelry, built in 1935, on a central Bergen street surrounded by pubs, bars, and restaurants, a short walk from the Fish Market. It's clean and bare-boned. Students comprise the check-in staff, and services and amenities are about as basic (or nonexistent) as anything we're willing to recommend.

Kong Oscars Gate 22, N-5017 Bergen. © **55-21-00-35.** Fax 55-21-00-36. 40 units (none with private bathroom). 500NOK ($67) double with shared bathroom; 600NOK ($80) double with private kitchenette and shared bathroom. AE, DC, MC, V. Open June 17 to August 13. **Amenities:** Coin-operated laundromat. *In room:* Kitchen, no phone.

Steens Hotel ⟨*Value*⟩ This is a stylish 1890 house that has been successfully converted to receive guests. Owned and operated by the same family since 1950, Steens offers great accommodations at reasonable prices. The bedrooms are moderate in size and comfortable, and the bathrooms, though small, are beautifully maintained. The public rooms have plenty of historic atmosphere, although the bedrooms are modern. The best rooms are in front and open onto a park. Within a short walk are the bus and railway stations, and shops and attractions in the center of town. All doubles have a private bathroom with a shower unit; a few singles are rented without bathroom for 620NOK ($82) per night. Throughout the day coffee and light meals are served.

22 Parkveien, N-5007 Bergen. © and fax **55-31-40-50.** 20 units, 16 with bathroom. 600NOK–920NOK ($80–$122) double. Extra bed 150NOK ($20). Rates include Norwegian breakfast. AE, MC, V. Bus: 1 or 5. **Amenities:** Breakfast room; lounge. *In room:* TV.

Strand Hotel ★ ⟨*Finds*⟩ This hotel was once a decaying hulk with a rowdy clientele. All of that changed after the millennium, when the rooms were radically upgraded and the second-floor bar became a stylish watering hole. A pair of interconnected buildings forms the hotel. Bedrooms are cozy, efficiently decorated, and comfortable, with the added advantage of having views directly over the southern flank of Bergen's famous harbor. Each room has a tiled bathroom in most cases with a shower, but some with a shower-tub combination.

Strandkaien 2-4, N-5013 Bergen. © **55-59-33-00.** Fax 55-59-33-33. 89 units. Late Aug to early June Mon–Thurs 990NOK–1,290NOK ($132–$172) double; mid-June to early Aug all nights and year-round Fri–Sun 920NOK ($122) double. AE, DC, MC, V. **Amenities:** Restaurant; bar; laundry service; dry cleaning. *In room:* TV, minibar, trouser press.

ON THE OUTSKIRTS

Solstrand Fjord Hotel ★★★ *Finds*   This is the most prestigious resort in the region around Bergen. Discerning travelers appreciate its sense of whimsy, isolated location beside the fjord, and history that stretches from 1896. Everything about it evokes the Belle Epoque, including the ocher-colored, gabled exterior dramatically positioned between backyard gardens and the rock-lined coast of the fjord. The setting evokes a romantic getaway to the countryside. Colors used throughout the hotel are rich and jewel-toned. Bedrooms are cheerfully painted, high-ceilinged affairs, with a sophisticated mixture of antique and modern furniture. Each accommodation comes with a luxurious private bathroom with tub and shower. The in-house restaurant serves buffets, priced between 300NOK and 340NOK ($40–$45) per person, every day at lunch and dinner. Advance reservations are recommended for meals that—especially on Sunday between 1 and 3pm—are a magnet for extended families from the surrounding region. The hotel's many amenities include free use of rowboats and putt-putt motorboats as well as access to a nearby 9-hole golf course.

N-5200 Os (24km/15 miles south of Bergen). © **56-57-11-00.** Fax 56-57-11-20. www.solstrand.com. 132 units. Late Aug to early June Mon–Thurs 1,700NOK ($226) double; mid-June to mid-Aug Mon–Thurs and year-round Fri–Sun 1,500NOK ($200) double. AE, DC, MC, V. Rates include breakfast. Closed Dec 22–Jan 3. From Bergen, drive south along the E39, following the signs to Stavanger, turning off at the markers to either Os (the region) or Osøyro (the hamlet that functions as the centerpiece of the Os region). **Amenities:** Restaurant; bar; outdoor pool; exercise room; tennis court; 3 squash courts; saunas; fjord-side beach; watersports program; helicopter landing pad; laundry service; dry cleaning. *In room:* TV, minibar.

4 Where to Dine

VERY EXPENSIVE

Kafe Krystall ★★★ *Finds* CONTINENTAL   Thanks to Jugenstil accessories, the decor of this intimate restaurant evokes Vienna in the era of Sigmund Freud. Billie Holiday music might be playing softly in the cool gray-green parlor. Old-fashioned table settings and the quiet ministrations of a single server (Bergen-born owner Vibeke Bjørvik) create the feeling that you're in a dignified private home. Menu items change every 2 weeks. Our party recently sampled a menu that began delectably with spiced and pan-seared red snapper, accompanied by a shellfish guacamole and mussels sauce, followed by a divine, creamed champagne soup topped with curried, marinated scallops. The rest of the menu consisted of well-balanced flavors, such as the baked sole with fresh tomato and green herbs, served with a fennel and potato purée, and the filet of lamb with caponata. For dessert, our hearts were won over by the vanilla and whiskey *panna cotta* topped with chocolate sauce and a serving of lime-marinated raspberries.

16 Kong Oscarsgate. © **55-32-10-84.** Reservations recommended. Fixed-price menus 475NOK–675NOK ($63–$90). AE, DC, MC, V. Mon–Sat 6–10pm. Bus: 20, 21, 22, 23, 50, 70, 71, 80, and 90.

Lucullus ★★★ CONTINENTAL   This posh, conservative restaurant in the Neptun Hotel is a gourmet citadel. Tasteful art works line the walls of the blue and white room. The starters continue the elegant tone, using high-quality ingredients transformed into flavor-filled combinations such as tuna with sesame on a salad of thinly sliced green beans, or carpaccio with spring vegetables. Such classic main dishes as pan-fried brill with a creamy sauce of foie gras would be welcome at a top-rated Parisian bistro. Our salmon tournedos with capers and a beurre blanc sauce was a celestial offering. The chef is justifiably proud of his tender and flavorful filet of beef Lucullus, the house specialty, although you could also opt for a duo of pheasant with a morel-studded butter sauce or quail with a foie gras risotto. For dessert, it doesn't get much better than white chocolate mousse cake with marinated cherries.

In the Neptun Hotel, Valkendorfsgate 8. ✆ **55-30-68-00.** Reservations recommended. Main courses 305NOK–330NOK ($41–$44). Fixed-price menu 645NOK ($86). AE, DC, MC, V. Mon–Thurs 5–11pm; Fri–Sun 7–11pm. Closed 2 weeks in July. Bus: 20, 21, or 22.

EXPENSIVE

Enhjørningen (The Unicorn) FISH/CONTINENTAL   Part of the charm of this restaurant derives from the not-level floors, the low doorways, and the inconvenient access via narrow staircases to its second-floor dining room. Set within one of the old wooden buildings of the Bryggen complex, adjacent to the harbor, it boasts a history and a name that was recorded as early as 1304. ("The Unicorn" was mentioned in a court trial as the home of a German-born Hanseatic merchant, Herman Skult.) After several fires and the removal of lots of rotted timbers, the inn has been restored to the condition it might have had during the 1700s.

You'll sit in one of several old-fashioned dining rooms set railway-style (end-to-end), and outfitted like an early-19th-century parlor with framed oil paintings, usually landscapes. It's usually mobbed, as the staff struggles to maintain order and a sense of gentility amid swarms of diners, especially in midsummer. The lunchtime buffet focuses on salads and fish; evening meals are more substantial, with choices that include a local and good version of fish soup; savory fresh mussels steamed in white wine with cream, curry, and saffron; cognac-marinated salmon; herb-fried medallions of angler fish with a cream-based pepper sauce; and catfish with bacon and mushroom sauce. The star offering of the restaurant's limited supply of meat dishes is a "no fish Olsen," a bemused way to describe grilled filet of beef with a pepper-flavored cream sauce.

Bryggen. ✆ **55-32-79-19.** Reservations recommended. Main courses 240NOK–275NOK ($32–$37); buffet (lunch only) 175NOK ($23); fixed-price menus 395NOK–520NOK ($53–$69). AE, DC, MC, V. Lunch June–Sept daily noon–4pm; dinner daily 4–11pm. Closed 2 weeks at Christmas. Bus: 5, 21.

Finnegaardstuene ★ (Finds) NORWEGIAN/FRENCH   The foundations of this popular restaurant were laid around 1400, when Hanseatic League merchants used it as a warehouse. Today, some of the woodwork dates from the 1700s, and four small-scale dining rooms create a cozy atmosphere. The chefs have created magic in sleepy Bergen. The menu is well thought out, with carefully prepared dishes. It revolves around Norwegian ingredients, especially fresh fish, and classical French methods of preparation. The menu changes with the season and the inspiration of the chef. It might include platters of crayfish served with filets of French foie gras in a cider and foie gras sauce; lime-marinated turbot with caviar sauce; gratin of monkfish with sea scallops; filets of venison with juniper berry sauce; and breast of duck with lime and fig sauce. Berries from the Norwegian tundra, especially lingonberries and cloudberries, are an appropriate and satisfying dessert.

Rosenkrantzgate 6. ✆ **55-55-03-00.** Reservations recommended. Main courses 285NOK–295NOK ($38–$39); fixed-price menu 635NOK ($84). AE, DC, MC, V. Mon–Sat 4:30–11pm. Closed 1 week at Easter, Dec 22–Jan 8. Bus: 5, 21.

Fiskekroen ★ SEAFOOD/GAME   One of the smallest (36 seats) and most exclusive restaurants in Bergen, this dining room occupies rustically elegant premises in the historic Zacchariasbrygge harbor-front complex. There's a panoramic view of the harbor and a menagerie of stuffed animals. Menu specialties change with the seasons. A fish tank from 1889 reveals some of the night's offerings, including the finest lobster served in Bergen. Chefs also prepare an old-fashioned Bergen fish soup from coalfish, which is delicious, as is the bouillabaisse with three types of Norwegian fish and two types of shellfish. We recently enjoyed a beautifully prepared steamed red snapper with a cauliflower purée, served with a lime pesto and mussel sauce. For a celebratory night, go for the freshly shucked oysters and champagne. If you don't want fish, you might opt for the herb-treated reindeer with creamy mushrooms and bacon. For dessert, fresh strawberries with cream are served in summer, perhaps a crème brûlée with a freshly baked chocolate tart on a cold winter's night.

Zacchariasbrygge 50. ⓒ **55-55-96-46.** Reservations required. Main courses 285NOK–325NOK ($38–$43). AE, DC, MC, V. May–Aug Mon–Sat noon–11pm, Sun 11am–10pm; Sept–Apr Mon–Sat 4–11pm. Bus: 1, 5, or 9.

Restaurant Potetkjeller ★ *Finds*   Set within a few steps of Bergen's Fish Market, this is one of the oldest restaurants in Bergen. Its oldest feature is an antique flagstone floor (the date of construction is unknown) at the base of a cellar whose vaulted ceiling dates from the mid-1400s. (After most of the city's clapboard-sided houses burned to the ground in 1702, the stone-built cellar was used as a dump for the ashes and debris that remained behind. Following restorations in 2000, the cellar is now used for additional seating for the restaurant upstairs. Watch your footing on the floors downstairs, as they're deceptively uneven.) Menu items from the open kitchen are likely to include gazpacho with a shellfish crostini; oven-roasted halibut with saffron and blue mussels, saltwater perch with lentils cooked in red wine; breast of guinea fowl with a foie gras sauce; and a dessert special of baked nectarines with syrup and semifreddo (a combination of mascarpone cheese, brandy, espresso, icing sugar, gluten, grated chocolate, and cream). If you opt for wine to accompany your meal, there will be a different wine for each course, each selected by the evening's chef.

Kong Oscargate 1A. ⓒ **55-32-00-70.** Reservations recommended. Fixed-price menus 405NOK–595NOK ($54–$79) without wine, 695NOK–1,150NOK ($92–$153) with wine. AE, DC, MC, V. Mon–Sat 4–10pm. Bar Mon–Sat 4pm–1am. Bus: 1, 5, 9.

To Kokker ★ FRENCH/NORWEGIAN   To Kokker ("Two Cooks") is a favorite with celebrities, including Britain's Prince Andrew and a bevy of French starlets. Savvy local foodies increasingly gravitate here for the chef's well-considered juxtaposition of flavors and textures. Menu items include such time-tested favorites as lobster soup; whitebait roe with chopped onions, sour cream, and fresh-baked bread; reindeer with lingonberry sauce; and filet of lamb with mustard sauce and *pommes Provençal*. The 1703 building is adjacent to the oldest piers and wharves in Bergen. The dining room, one floor above street level, has scarlet walls, old paintings, and a solid staff that works competently under pressure, albeit without a lot of flair.

Enhjørninggården. ⓒ **55-32-28-16.** Reservations required. Main courses 495NOK–695NOK ($66–$92). AE, DC, MC, V. Mon–Sat 5–10pm. Bus: 1, 5, or 9.

MODERATE

Holberg-Stuen NORWEGIAN   One floor above street level, this restaurant was established in 1927 midway between the harbor front and Ole Bulls Plass. It was named in honor of the 18th-century writer Ludvig Holberg. He divided

(Overrated) A Dining Curiosity of the Middle Ages

Tucked deep inside the cluster of UNESCO-recognized medieval houses of Bryggen stands **Olde Hansa Bergen,** Bryggestredet, Bryggen (🕿 55-31-40-46), a restaurant serving Norwegian cuisine. While dining here, you'll learn how the Hanseatic merchants of Bergen lived more than 400 years ago. But the lesson is a hard one: On your way to your table in this dark, moldy, and somewhat bizarre-looking wooden complex, you're likely to either trip on uneven floorboards or bump your head on crazed, out-of-alignment angles. And, regarding the dining experience, Olde Hansa has made only a few concessions to modern-day aesthetics. Crockery is country-crude and thick, eating utensils weigh like hammers and chisels in your hands, tables and chairs are wobbly and uneven, lighting is dim, and there's a palpable sense that the entire place might not be terribly clean. Worst of all, the service varies from extremely slow to nonexistent and hordes of group tours descend unexpectedly upon a staff that's either hysterically distracted or hopelessly jaded in ways that, indeed, might strike you as medieval. And on especially lackadaisical nights you'll get the distinct feeling that you've entered a national monument that's quaint but utterly bereft of anything approaching efficiency.

The menu here will tell you a lot about the culinary tastes and occasional merriment of Bergen's Hanseatic forebears. Start perhaps with a berry schnapps or a dark honey beer. The "Secret Feasts of the Sea" platter might include salmon eggs, white fish, smoked salmon, kippers, anchovies, and quail eggs along with cheese, herb bread studded with nuts, and smoked salmon. A liver paté comes with onion jam, and wild boar turns up on the menu along with Bergen fish stew flavored with saffron. For dessert, try the rose pudding. Main courses cost from 158NOK to 335NOK ($21–$45), and American Express, Diners Club, MasterCard, and Visa are accepted. Hours are daily from 11am to midnight. Bus: 20, 21, 22, 23, 50, 71, 80, and 90.

his time between Bergen and Copenhagen, and both cities ferociously claim him as part of their cultural heritage. The setting is much like a tavern, with beamed ceilings, an open log fire, and lots of exposed wood. The well-prepared dishes include fish filets in white-wine sauce with prawns, mushrooms, and asparagus; and a variety of meats, some of them grilled. This is a longtime favorite; come here for old-fashioned flavors, not trendy experiments.

Torgalmenningen 6. 🕿 55-31-80-15. Reservations recommended. Main courses 188NOK–200NOK ($25–$27). AE, DC, MC, V. Mon–Sat 11am–11pm; Sun 1–10pm. Bus: 1, 5, or 9.

Smauet Mat & Vinhus ⭐ CONTINENTAL/FRENCH/ITALIAN Tempting smells, and lots of energy, emanate from the open-to-view kitchen of this restaurant in the style of a 19th-century Norwegian farmhouse. Within a decor this authentically Norwegian, you wouldn't expect a cuisine this thoroughly Continental, but that's exactly the combination that you get. Sample the smoked salmon and capers, always an enticing appetizer in Norway. Subtly intermingled flavors emerge in the grilled scallops with a purée of pumpkin.

Other standouts include the monkfish studded with lardoons and served with braised Savoy cabbage; tenderloin of beef enticingly married to tiger prawns; and the cinnamon-scented, pan-fried breast of chicken with pancetta. The location, in a house built in 1870, lies just a few steps from the Ole Bull's Plass.

Vaskerelvsmauet 1. ℂ **55-21-07-10**. Reservations recommended, especially on weekends. Main courses 195NOK–275NOK ($26–$37). AE, DC, MC, V. Sun–Thurs 4–10pm; Fri 4pm–midnight; Sat 5pm–midnight. Closed 1 week at Easter, 10 days between Christmas and New Year's. Bus: 2, 3, or 4.

Wessel-Stuen NORWEGIAN This restaurant (named for the 18th-c. humorist Johan Herman Wessel) has all the trappings of an 18th-century wine cellar. It's decorated in old-tavern style with beamed ceilings, and its adjoining pub is a famous meeting place for locals. Meals are likely to include such dishes as grilled filet of catfish with coriander and lime, grilled tournedos with forest mushroom sauce, and breast of duck with honey-blackberry sauce. The daily steak special is one of the most popular dishes in town. The chefs can be experimental at times, but they're also soundly grounded in the classics.

Engen 14. ℂ **55-55-49-49**. Reservations recommended. Main courses 139NOK–290NOK ($18–$39); fixed-price menu 85NOK–120NOK ($11–$16). AE, DC, MC, V. Mon–Sat 3–11pm; Sun 11:30am–10pm. Bus: 2, 3, or 4.

INEXPENSIVE

Bryggeloftet and Stuene ★ NORWEGIAN The Bryggeloftet and Stuene is the best-established restaurant along the harbor front. At street level, the Stuene has low-beamed ceilings, carved banquettes, and 19th-century murals of old Bergen, along with dozens of clipper-ship models. For a more formal meal, head upstairs to the Bryggeloftet, with its high ceilings and wood paneling. Dinner in either section might include fried *porbeagle* (a form of whitefish) served with shrimp, mussels, and white-wine sauce; roast reindeer with cream sauce; or pepper steak with a salad. Several different preparations of salmon and herring are featured, along with roast pork with Norwegian sour cabbage. This is a quintessential Norwegian place—come here if you're seeking authentic flavors.

Bryggen 11. ℂ **55-31-06-30**. Reservations recommended. Main courses 159NOK–275NOK ($21–$37); lunch smørbrød 85NOK–149NOK ($11–$20). AE, DC, MC, V. Mon–Sat 11am–11:30pm; Sun 1–11:30pm. Bus: 1, 5, or 9.

Café Hordastova NORWEGIAN This elegant cafeteria looks more like a full-service restaurant with its linen tablecloths and upscale cutlery. On the ground floor of Hotel Hordaheimen, this no-nonsense place offers alcohol-free, relatively quick meals. Lunchtime features open-faced sandwiches (*smørbrød*) and simple platters of the day. Dinner offerings are a bit more elaborate, with carved meats, pepper steak, meatballs, and an excellent version of mushroom soup.

In the Hotel Hordaheimen, Christian Sundts Gate 18. ℂ **55-33-51-12**. Reservations not necessary. Lunch main courses 18NOK–105NOK ($2.40–$14); dinner main courses 89NOK–109NOK ($12–$15). AE, DC, MC, V. Mon–Fri 10am–9pm; Sat–Sun 10am–8pm. Bus: 1, 5, or 9.

Dolly Dimple's PIZZA This chain restaurant, which has spread like wildfire across Norway, serves Bergen's most delectable pizzas. Toppings here are savory. The "Salmon Rocket" pizza features sliced smoked salmon, crème fraîche, spring onions, tomato sauce, and cheese, topped with arugula. "Hot Lips" pizza is topped with minced meat, onions, jalapeños, garlic, tomato sauce, and cheese. Salads are made fresh daily, including a Caesar with smoked breast of chicken. Homemade lasagna is featured nightly. Desserts are luscious, including a carrot cake with vanilla ice cream and caramel sauce.

Bergen Storsenter, Stromgaten 8. (C) **55-31-39-39**. Reservations not needed. Medium pizzas (suitable for 1–2 persons) 110NOK–168NOK ($15–$22); large pizzas (suitable for 2–3 persons) 143NOK–235NOK ($19–$31). AE, DC, MC, V. Sun–Thurs noon–11pm; Fri–Sat noon–midnight. Bus: 1, 5, 9.

Michelangelo/Ristorante Stragiotti ⭐ *(Finds)* ITALIAN   This is the best Italian restaurant in Bergen. Michele Stragiotti, an Italian native from Piemonte, owns these side-by-side eateries, a short walk from the Ole Bulls Plass. Michelangelo's is traditional and cozy, with murals of seascapes around the Isle of Capri and a distinct undercurrent of *La Dolce Vita*. Stragiotti's next door is a trimmed-down minimalist testimonial to postmodern Italian simplicity. In either restaurant, expect dishes that include filets of Norwegian beef with your choice of four sauces (mushroom, black peppercorn, tomato, or béarnaise); Norwegian rack of lamb, pastas, fish, and lots of scaloppine choices, including a savory version with Gorgonzola cheese. A *grigliata di pesce*, wherein Italian cooking techniques are applied to very fresh Norwegian fish, is particularly appealing. (Don't confuse Michelangelo/Ristorante Stragiotti with Da Vinci's, another Italian restaurant in town.)

Vestre Torgate 3. (C) **55-90-08-25** (Michelangelo), and **55-90-31-00** (Stragiotti). Reservations recommended on weekends. Pizzas 110NOK–140NOK ($15–$19), main courses 110NOK–249NOK ($15–$33); set-course menu 300NOK ($40). AE, DC, MC, V. Stragiotti daily noon–midnight; Michelangelo daily 3pm–midnight (till 11pm Sun). Bus: 2, 3, or 4.

5 Seeing the Sights

SUGGESTED ITINERARIES

IF YOU HAVE 1 DAY   See the top attractions of Bergen, including the old Hanseatic Bryggen, with its nearby museums. Explore the shops and artisans' workshops along the harbor, and, to end the day, take the funicular to Fløien for a panoramic view.

IF YOU HAVE 2 DAYS   On your first day, follow the suggestions for Day 1. On your second day, head for the Bergen area, which you can reach by public transportation. Visit Troldhaugen, Edvard Grieg's former home. In the afternoon, journey to Ole Bull's Villa, 26km (16 miles) south of Bergen.

IF YOU HAVE 3 DAYS   For your first 2 days, follow the suggestions above. On the third day, take the 12-hour "Norway in a Nutshell" tour (see "Side Trips from Bergen," later in this chapter).

IF YOU HAVE 4 OR 5 DAYS   On the first 3 days, follow the itinerary above. On Day 4, explore the Hardangerfjord and the Folgefonn Glacier by round-trip bus from Bergen (see "Side Trips from Bergen," later in this chapter). On the fifth day, explore the Sognefjord by express steamer, going by bus through Voss, and returning by train to Bergen.

THE TOP ATTRACTIONS

In addition to the sights below, take a stroll around **Bryggen** ⭐⭐⭐. This row of Hanseatic, timbered houses, rebuilt along the waterfront after a disastrous fire in 1702, is what remains of medieval Bergen. The northern half burned to the ground in 1955. Bryggen has been incorporated into UNESCO's World Heritage List as one of the most significant cultural and historical re-creations of a medieval settlement, skillfully blending with the surroundings of modern Bergen. It's a center for arts and crafts, where painters, weavers, and craftspeople have their workshops. Some workshops are open to the public.

Bergen Attractions

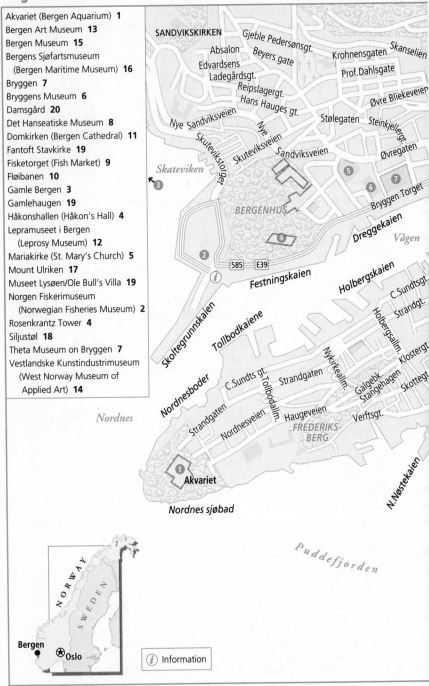

Akvariet (Bergen Aquarium) **1**
Bergen Art Museum **13**
Bergen Museum **15**
Bergens Sjøfartsmuseum
(Bergen Maritime Museum) **16**
Bryggen **7**
Bryggens Museum **6**
Damsgård **20**
Det Hanseatiske Museum **8**
Domkirken (Bergen Cathedral) **11**
Fantoft Stavkirke **19**
Fisketorget (Fish Market) **9**
Fløibanen **10**
Gamle Bergen **3**
Gamlehaugen **19**
Håkonshallen (Håkon's Hall) **4**
Lepramuseet i Bergen
(Leprosy Museum) **12**
Mariakirke (St. Mary's Church) **5**
Mount Ulriken **17**
Museet Lysøen/Ole Bull's Villa **19**
Norgen Fiskerimuseum
(Norwegian Fisheries Museum) **2**
Rosenkrantz Tower **4**
Siljustøl **18**
Theta Museum on Bryggen **7**
Vestlandske Kunstindustrimuseum
(West Norway Museum of
Applied Art) **14**

SANDVIKSKIRKEN
Gjeble Pedersønsgt.
Absalon
Beyers gate
Krohnensgaten Skanselien
Edvardsens
Ladegårdsgt.
Prof.Dahlsgate
Reipslagergt.
Hans Hauges gt.
Øvre Bliekeveien
Nye Sandviksveien
Nye
Skutevikstorget
Skuteviksveien
Sandviksveien
Stølegaten Steinkjellrgt.
Øvregaten
Skateviken
BERGENHUS
Bryggen Torget
Dreggekaien
Vågen
Festningskaien
Holbergskaien
C.Sundtsgt.
Strandgt.
Holbergsalln.
Skoltegrunnskaien
Tollbodkaiene
Nykirkealln.
Galgebk.
Stangehagen Klostergt.
Skottegt.
Nordnesboder
C.Sundts gt.
Tollbodalln.
Strandgaten
Haugeveien
Verftsgt.
Nordnes
Strandgaten
Nordnesveien
FREDERIKS-BERG
Akvariet
N.Nøstekaien
Nordnes sjøbad
Puddefjorden
NORWAY
SWEDEN
Bergen
Oslo

(i) Information

Akvariet (Bergen Aquarium) ★★   A 15-minute walk from the city center, this aquarium contains the most extensive collection of marine fauna in Europe, lying on the outmost reaches of the Nordnes district, with a panoramic view of the entrance to the port of Bergen. The exceptional marine life includes seals, penguins, lobsters, and piranhas. In the outer hall you can get the feel of the fish—dip your hand into the shallow pool of unpolluted water pumped up from a depth of 120m (400 ft.) in the fjord outside. Nine glass tanks, each containing about 62,500 gallons of water, ring the hall. Downstairs, a wide range of marine life in 42 small aquariums demonstrates many colorful forms of sea life and illustrates evolutionary development. A popular attraction is seal and penguin feeding time. In the summer, they eat daily at 11am, 2pm, and 6pm; in the winter, daily at noon and 4pm.

Nordnesbakken 4. ☎ **55-55-71-71.** Admission 80NOK ($11) adults, 50NOK ($6.65) children. May–Sept daily 9am–8pm; Oct–Apr daily 10am–6pm. Bus: 11 from the fish market.

Bergen Art Museum ★★★   Separated into a trio of buildings overlooking Lille Lungegårdsvann Lake, this ever-growing and expanding art museum possesses one of the most impressive collections in Norway.

Bergen Billedgalleri is devoted to both Norwegian and international art extending from the 13th to the 20th centuries. The collection is known for its magnificent **Greek and Russian icons** ★ from the 1300s and its **Dutch paintings** ★ from the 1700s. Seek out, in particular, *Birch in the Storm,* a famous painting by J. C. Dahl, as well as *Vardøhus Fortress* by Peder Balke. When the gallery dips into **modern art,** there is a bit of camp, as in their display of poetry and an exhibition by Yoko Ono as well as Bjørn Carlsen's mixed media piece, "Mother I don't Want to Die in Disneyland." The photography of Tom Sandberg confirms his reputation as one of Scandinavia's greatest photographers.

The impressive Rasmus Meyer Collection features paintings from the 18th century up to 1915. We come here to gaze upon **Edvard Munch's masterpieces** ★★, especially the trio *The Woman in Three Stages, Melancholy,* and *Jealousy.* Some of the best paintings of the **Norwegian Romantics** also hang here, including works by J. C. Dahl, Harriet Backer, and Nikolai Astrup, the latter known for depicting dramatic landscapes in Western Norway. In addition to the art, note the decorated ceiling and wall painting in the **Blumenthal Room** ★ from the 18th century.

Some of the greatest **modern art** ★★ in western Norway is found in the Stenersen Collection. Most of the work, by Norwegian and international artists, is from the 20th century, and includes northern Europe's most extensive collection of **Paul Klee's works** ★★. The masters of modern art are all here: Picasso, Edvard Munch, Joan Miró, Vassily Kandinsky, Max Ernst, and a host of lesser artists.

Rasmus Meyers Allé 3–7 and Lars Hillesgate 10. ☎ **55-56-80-00.** Admission 35NOK ($4.65) to each permanent collection or 35NOK ($4.65) for temporary exhibitions. Combined ticket to all 3 galleries 50NOK ($6.65). Guided tours 20NOK ($2.65). Mid-May to mid-Sept daily 11am–5pm; off-season Tues–Sun 11am–5pm. Bus: 1, 5, or 9.

Bergen Museum ✦ Part of the University of Bergen, this two-in-one museum consists of both a Cultural History Department and a Natural History Department. Founded in 1825, the museum formed the basis for launching the university in 1946 after the defeated Nazis had ended their occupation.

Naturhistorisk Samlinger is filled with displays and exhibitions from the Ice Age, including prehistoric fossils. However, visitors come here mainly to see the **whale collection** ✦ (northern Europe's largest collection), and the exhibits of snakes, Norwegian birds, and crocodiles (displayed in various ways—stuffed, fossilized, preserved in jars). The origins of the creatures in the collection ranges from Greenland to Africa. You can also visit a plant house and a botanical garden.

The Kulturhistork Samlinger features exhibitions and displays on art history, archaeology, and anthropology. For many, this is the most interesting of the museums as it covers everything from Egyptian mummies to "Ibsen in Bergen," which traces the writer's growth as a playwright during the 6 years he spent from 1851 to 1857 with the Norwegian Theater in Bergen. You'll also find the largest collection of **Norwegian church art** ✦ in the country, a display of delicate Viking jewelry, and exhibits devoted to such North American cultures as the Aleut and Inuit.

Cultural History Department, Håkon Sheteligs Plass 10; Natural History Department, Muséplass 3. ℂ **55-58-93-60** for the Natural History Dept. and the Cultural History Dept. Admission for both museums: 30NOK ($4) adults, 15NOK ($2) seniors. Children and students free. May 15–Aug Tues–Sat 10am–3pm, Sun 11am–4pm; off-season Tues–Sat 11am–2pm, Sun 11am–3pm. Bus: 2, 3, or 4.

Bergens Sjøfartsmuseum (Bergen Maritime Museum) In a scenic location in the middle of the campus of the University of Bergen, this museum presents the history of shipping in Western Norway. Exhibits show the importance of the shipping industry to a port city, and displays include models of the Viking ships that terrorized Europe. Also on display are paintings and marine artifacts rescued from the North Sea. Exhibits also deal with Norway's role in World War II during the Nazi occupation.

Hårald Harfagresgate 1. ℂ **55-58-93-60.** Admission 30NOK ($4) adults, 15NOK ($2) seniors, free for children. June–Aug Tues–Sun 10am–5pm. Bus: 2, 3, or 4.

Bryggens Museum This museum displays artifacts unearthed during extensive archaeological excavations of Bryggen from 1955 to 1972. Exhibits include remains of the oldest buildings in Bergen (from the 12th c.) in their original settings. You can also see runic inscriptions and changing exhibits. The museum illustrates the daily and cultural life of Bergen in the Middle Ages.

Bryggen. ℂ **55-58-80-10.** Admission 30NOK ($4) adults, free for children. May–Aug daily 10am–5pm; Sept–Apr, Mon–Fri 11am–3pm, Sat noon–3pm, Sun noon–4pm. Bus: 20, 21, 22, 23, 50, 70, 71, 80, and 90.

Damsgård ✦ *Finds* This rarely visited manor house from 1770 is the finest example of 18th-century rococo timber architecture in western Norway. The roof is of black glazed tiles from The Netherlands, a sign of grand extravagance back then. In 1983, the municipality of Bergen acquired the house and its furnishings. The interior is painted in a "jolly range of baroque colors." After a visit inside, wander through the lavish baroque gardens, with their ponds, Grecian sculpture, and flora.

Laksevåg. ℂ **55-32-51-08.** Admission 30NOK ($4) adults, free for children. May–Aug Tues–Sun 11am–4pm. Bus: 60, 70, or 71. 3km (1¾ miles) west of Bergen on Rte. 582.

Det Hanseatiske Museum ✦ In one of the best-preserved wooden buildings at Bryggen, this museum illustrates Bergen's commercial life on the wharf centuries ago. German merchants, representatives of the Hanseatic League centered in Lübeck, lived in these medieval houses built in long rows up from the harbor. With dried cod, grain, and salt as articles of exchange, fishers from northern Norway met German merchants during the busy summer season. The museum is furnished with authentic articles dating from 1704.

Finnegårdsgaten 1A, Bryggen. ℂ **55-31-41-89.** May–Sept admission 40NOK ($5.30) adults; Oct–Apr, admission 25NOK ($3.35) adults; free for children year-round. June–Aug, daily 9am–5pm; Sept–May, daily 11am–2pm. Bus: 1, 5, or 9.

Domkirken (Bergen Cathedral)   For 9 centuries this has been a place of worship, although it's faced turbulent times. The first stone church was built in the mid-12th century and dedicated to Olav the Holy, patron saint of Norway. By the 13th century the Dom was in the hands of the Franciscan brothers, but the fires that swept Bergen in 1248 and again in 1270 caused massive damage.

Under a grant from King Magnus ("the Lawmender"), the friars reconstructed a beautiful church, which stood here in 1301. Regrettably, the massive Bergen fires of 1463 and again in 1488 swept over the church. With the coming of the Lutheran Reformation, the first Lutheran bishop claimed the old Franciscan church and turned it into the cathedral of Norway's oldest diocese. Unfortunately, two more fires destroyed the cathedral in 1623 and 1640.

The present building dates from its major restoration in the 1880s, which saw the addition of beautiful stained-glass windows with biblical motifs. All that remains from the 13th century are the Gothic choir stalls and the foundations of the towers. Since the Battle of Bergen in 1665, a cannonball has been imbedded in the West Wall.

Kong Oscarsgate and Domkirkegate. ℂ **55-55-20-00.** Free admission. Late May to Aug Mon–Sat 11am–5pm, Sun 10am–1pm; off-season Tues–Fri 11am–2pm, Sat 11am–3pm, Sun 10am–1pm. Bus: 1, 5, or 9.

Fantoft Stavkirke ⭐ (Finds)   This is a rare opportunity to see what a wood-built stave church looked like, even if it's "merely the mock." In the Middle Ages Norway had a total of 750 stave churches, but only 30 are still standing. Architecturally, these churches were unique with their "dragon heads," carved doorways, and "staves" or vertical planks. The original stave church was constructed in Fortun in Sogn in 1150 and moved to Fantoft in 1883 at a point 5km (3 miles) south of Bergen. Regrettably, a self-styled "Satanist" burned it to the ground on June 6, 1992. The present church is an exact duplication of the original. Adjacent to the church is a large cross from 1050. It was moved here from Sola in Rogaland.

Fantoftveien 46, Paradis. ℂ **55-28-07-10.** May 15–Sept 15 daily 10:30am–2pm and 2:30–6pm. Admission 30NOK ($4) adults, 20NOK ($2.65) students, 5NOK (65¢) children. From the bus station in Bergen, take any bus leaving from platforms 19, 20, or 21. Departures every 20 min. for the 10-min. jaunt to the stave church. Get off at Fantoft. From the bus stop, it's a 10-min. walk up the hill.

Fisketorget (Fish Market) ⭐   For our first lunch in Bergen, we always head to this bustling market for freshly opened oysters, a real treat from the sea. Another popular option is freshly boiled shrimp to eat as you take in views of the waterfront. Some vendors also offer a baguette for your lunch—none better than smoked salmon with some mayonnaise and fresh cucumber. The market is a photographer's delight with fishermen in their mackintoshes and Wellington boots and weather-beaten fishmongers (often women) in dirty, long white aprons having their pictures taken as the catch of the day is hauled in.

Bergen Harbour. June–Aug Mon–Fri 7am–5pm, Sat 7am–4pm; Sept–May Mon–Sat 7am–4pm. Bus: 1, 5, or 9.

Fløibanen   A short walk from the fish market is the station where the funicular heads up to Fløien, the most famous of Bergen's seven hills. The view of the city, the neighboring hills, and the harbor from 320m (1,050 ft.) is worth every øre. Once here, you can take one of several paths that provide easy walks through a lovely wooded terrain with views of lakes and mountains in the distance. In summer you can order lunch at a restaurant here, which is open daily, and is also a souvenir shop.

Vetrlidsalm 23A. ✆ **55-33-68-00.** Round-trip 60NOK ($8) adults, 25NOK ($3.35) children. May 25–Aug Mon–Fri 7:30am–midnight, Sat 8am–midnight, Sun 9am–midnight; Sept–May 24 Mon–Thurs 8am–11pm, Fri–Sat 8am–11:30pm, Sun 9am–11pm. Bus: 6.

Gamle Bergen ⭐   This collection of more than 40 wooden houses from the 18th and 19th centuries is set in a park. The Old Town is complete with streets, an open square, and narrow alleyways. Some of the interiors are exceptional, including a merchant's living room in the typical style of the 1870s, with padded sofas, heavy curtains, and potted plants. It might call to mind Ibsen's *Doll's House.*

Elsesro and Sandviken. ✆ **55-39-43-00.** Admission 50NOK ($6.65) adults, 25NOK ($3.35) children and students. Houses mid-May to Aug only, guided tours daily on the hour 10am–5pm. Park and restaurant daily noon–6pm. Bus: 1 or 9 from the city center (every 10 min.).

Gamlehaugen   The king's official Bergen residence was originally occupied in the 19th century by Christian Michelsen, one of the first prime ministers of Norway after it separated from Denmark in 1814. It's open for just a short time each summer. The rambling wood-sided villa lies about 10km (6¼ miles) south of the city, overlooking the Nordåsvannet estuary. Its gardens are open to the public all year. Don't expect the hoopla you might see at Buckingham Palace—the venue is understated, discreet, and (probably for security reasons) aggressively mysterious.

Fjøsanger. ✆ **55-92-51-20.** Admission 10NOK ($1.35) adults, 5NOK (65¢) children. June–Sept 1, Mon–Fri 10am–1pm. Closed Sept 2–May. Bus: Fjøsanger-bound bus from the Central Bus Station.

Håkonshallen (Håkon's Hall)   If you walk along the water from Bryggen, you come upon the Håkonshallen, built between 1247 and 1261. It was damaged in a 1944 fire caused by the explosion of an overloaded Nazi munitions ship, and later restored. (The explosion damaged nearly every building in Bergen, and sent the ship's anchor flying almost to the top of a nearby mountain.) Håkonshallen is the largest and most imposing building remaining of a former royal residence when Bergen was the political center of the 13th-century kingdom of Norway. Guided tours are conducted hourly.

Bergenhus, Bradbenken. ✆ **55-31-60-67.** Admission 20NOK ($2.65) adults, 10NOK ($1.35) children. Mid-May to Aug daily 10am–4pm; Sept to mid-May daily noon–3pm, Thurs until 6pm. Closed various days in May. Bus: 1, 5, or 9.

Lepramuseet i Bergen (Leprosy Museum)   Visiting a former lepers' colony might not be your idea of a hot time, but this complex holds fascination for some visitors. Exhibits focus on the country's contribution to leprosy research, especially the work of Dr. Armauer Hansen, who gave his name to Hansen's disease, the modern name for leprosy. In the Middle Ages, St. Jørgens Hospital here was a hospital for lepers, and many of the oldest buildings date from the beginning of the 1700s. The museum also exhibits the Bergen Collection of the History of Medicine.

Kong Oscarsgate 59. ✆ **55-55-20-00.** Admission 30NOK ($4) adults, 15NOK ($2) children. May 20–Aug daily 11am–3pm. Bus: 1, 5, or 9.

Mariakirke (St. Mary's Church) ★★   The oldest building in Bergen (perhaps dating from the mid–12th c.) is this Romanesque church, one of the most beautiful in Norway. The oldest ornament in the church is the altar. The baroque pulpit, donated by Hanseatic merchants, bears carved figures depicting everything from Chastity to Naked Truth. Church music concerts are given from May through August several nights a week.

Dreggen. ℭ **55-31-59-60.** Admission 10NOK ($1.35) adults; free for children; free to all Sept 10–May 17. May 18–Sept 9 Mon–Fri 11am–4pm; Sept 10–May 17 Tues–Fri noon–1:30pm. Bus: 5, 9, 20, 21, or 22.

Mount Ulriken ★★   For one of the grandest views in western Norway, visit Bergen's highest mountaintop, Ulriken, at 642m (2,106 ft.). The attraction lies at Landaas, 5km (3 miles) southeast from the center of Bergen. The Ulriksbanen (ℭ **55-55-20-00**), the most famous cable car in western Norway, runs up the mountain. A shuttle bus departs for the Ulriksbanen from the Tourist Information Center in Bergen (p. 228) daily from May to September. Off-season departures depend on the weather. Once at the cable-car station, you can walk for 3 hours north along a well-trodden track to the top of the Fløibanen funicular railway, with scenic vistas in all directions.

Landaas. ℭ **55-55-20-00** for the cable car. Return fare 70NOK ($9.30) adults, 35NOK ($4.65) children. Combined cable car and shuttle bus 120NOK ($16) adults; half price children. May–Sept shuttle bus departures every 30 min. 9:15am–10:45pm. Off-season departures depend on the weather. Cable car in summer daily every 7 min. 9am–5pm; off-season daily 10am–5pm.

Norgen Fiskerimuseum (Norwegian Fisheries Museum)   More than you'd ever want to know about fishing—unless you're a fisherman—is presented in this specialized museum that traces the history of the fishing fleet, so vital to the economy of Bergen, through the ages. The nature and management of fisheries is presented in some detail, as are depictions of the sea and its vast, though diminishing, resources. The controversial Norwegian custom of whaling and sealing is also on show, as is the much less controversial fish farming. The processing of fish, such as the vital cod, is revealed along with exportation methods.

Bontelabo 2. ℭ **55-32-12-49.** Admission 20NOK ($2.65) adults, 10NOK ($1.35) students and seniors, free for children. June–Aug daily 10am–6pm; Sat–Sun 11am–6pm. Bus: 1, 5, or 9.

Rosenkrantz Tower   This defense and residential tower was constructed in the 13th century by the governor of Bergenhus (Bergen Castle), Erik Rosenkrantz. Two older structures were incorporated into the tower: King Magnus the Lawmender's keep, from about 1260, and Jørgen Hanssøn's keep, from about 1520. It was rebuilt and enlarged in the 1560s. The panoramic view of the seaport of Bergen is worth the trek here. There are guided tours of the tower and Håkonshallen (see above) about every hour.

Bergenhus, Bradbenken. ℭ **55-31-43-80.** Admission 20NOK ($2.65) adults, 10NOK ($1.35) children. May 15–Aug 31 daily 10am–4pm; Sept 1–May 14 Sun noon–3pm. Bus: 1, 5, or 9.

Siljustøl ★ *(Finds)*   Although most visitors flock to Edvard Grieg's former home at Troldhaugen, Bergen has an important Norwegian composer of its own: Harald Saeverud. Born in Bergen in 1897, the young composer studied first in his hometown before going on to Berlin where he met some of the greatest of the 20th-century German composers. Upon returning to Bergen in 1934, he married wealthy Marie Hvoslef.

The money for constructing his home, Siljustøl, was a wedding gift to the composer and his new bride. The imposing place—set on 70 beautiful hectares (176 acres)—is like a piece of west Norway in miniature. Upon completion in

Grieg: The Chopin of the North

"I am sure my music has the taste of codfish in it," or so wrote Norway's greatest composer, Edvard Grieg, born in Bergen in 1843, the son of a salt-fish merchant. Like Ole Bull (p. 255), Grieg became the towering figure of Norwegian Romanticism.

Shipped off to the Music Conservatory in Leipzig from 1858 to 1862, Grieg fell under the heavy influence of German Romanticism but returned to Oslo (then called Christiania) with a determination to create national music for his homeland, then struggling for a self-identity different from Denmark.

Back home, he fell heavily under the influence of his country's folk music and "fjord melodies." In the year 1868 he finished *Piano Concerto in A Minor,* his first great masterpiece. That work is said to evoke Norway as no other composition had ever done or has done since.

When Grieg met the great Norwegian writer Bjørnstjern Bjørnson, the author realized that he'd found the writer to compose music for his poems. Their most ambitious project was a national opera based on the history of the Norwegian king, Olav Trygvason.

Meeting Henrik Ibsen for the first time in 1866, not in Norway but in Rome, Grieg agreed to compose the music for Ibsen's dramatic poem *Peer Gynt.* After this grand success, Grieg also set music to six poems by Ibsen. In 1888 and 1893 Grieg published *Peer Gynt Suite I* and *II,* which remain popular orchestral pieces to this day. Bjørnson was furious that Grieg had teamed with Ibsen, and the work on their national opera never came to fruition.

In 1874 Grieg returned to Bergen where he created such world-fabled compositions as *Ballad in G minor,* the *Norwegian Dances for Piano,* the *Mountain Thrall,* and *The Holberg Suite.* He'd married Nina Hagerup, the Norwegian soprano, and together they moved into Troldhaugen, their coastal home that today is one of the major sightseeing attractions of Bergen.

It was at Troldhaugen that Grieg created such works as *Piano Sonata for Violin and Piano in C minor,* the *Haugtussa Songs,* the *Norwegian Peasant Dances and Tunes.* His last work was *Four Psalms,* based on a series of Norwegian religious melodies.

In spite of poor health and the loss of one lung, Grieg maintained a grueling schedule of appearances on the continent. But he always came back to Troldhaugen for the summer. Eventually on September 4, 1907, his body couldn't take it anymore. As he prepared to leave for yet another concert, this time in Leeds, England, he collapsed at the Hotel Norge in Bergen and was hospitalized, where he died of what doctors called "chronic exhaustion."

1939, Siljustøl was the largest private home in Norway with 63 rooms. The house is made of wood and natural stone, and has six toilets, although the composer preferred a hole in the floor, the more old-fashioned plumbing of Norway.

During the Nazi occupation, Saeverud wrote a trio of "war-symphonies" and one called "Ballad of Revolt" in honor of the Norwegian resistance to the Nazis. Today that latter composition stands as a symbol for the struggle against dictatorship and occupation.

After the war he composed music for Henrik Ibsen's dramatic poem, *Peer Gynt.* Twelve concert pieces extracted from this work are among the most frequently played orchestral works today.

In 1986 Saeverund became the official composer for the Bergen International Music Festival. He lived in Bergen until his death in 1992 at the age of 95. After being given a state funeral, he was buried at Siljustøl where his grave site is a pilgrimage destination among fans.

Rådal (near Rte. 553 to the airport), 12km (7½ miles) from the center. ✆ 55-92-29-92. Admission 50NOK ($6.65) adults, free for children. June 19–Aug 4 Wed–Fri and Sun 11am–4pm; Aug 5–Nov 3 and Apr 21–June 18 Sun noon–4pm. Bus: 30 from Bergen Bus Station.

Theta Museum on Bryggen ★ *Finds*   This little cell was the seat of clandestine Bergen resistance during the darkest days of the Nazi takeover of the city in World War II. It is also Norway's tiniest museum. The one room operated until 1942 when it was discovered by the Germans who destroyed it. The present room is a reconstruction. The freedom fighters called themselves the "Theta Group," and their aim was to establish contact and communication with the Norwegian government in exile in England. The museum is also the hardest to find in Bergen. Look for a unicorn figurehead on an old Bryggen building. Then walk down the adjoining little alley until you see a sign directing you to the cell on the third floor.

Enhjørningsgarden. ✆ 55-31-53-93. Admission 20NOK ($2.65) adults, 5NOK (65¢) children. Mid-May to mid-Sept Tues, and Sat–Sun 2–4pm. Bus: 1, 5, or 9.

Troldhaugen (Trolls' Hill) ★   This Victorian house, in beautiful rural surroundings, was the summer villa of composer Edvard Grieg. The house still contains his furniture, paintings, and other mementos. His Steinway grand piano is frequently used at concerts given in the house during the annual Bergen festival, and at Troldhaugen's summer concerts. Grieg and his wife, Nina, are buried in a cliff grotto on the estate. At his cottage by the sea, he composed many of his famous works.

Troldhaugveien 65, Hop. ✆ 55-91-17-91. Admission 50NOK ($6.65) adults, free for children. Jan–Apr 20 Mon–Fri 10am–2pm; Apr 21–Sept daily 9am–6pm; Oct–Nov, Mon–Fri 10am–2pm, Sat–Sun 10am–4pm. Closed Dec. Bus: To Hop from the Bergen bus station (Platforms 18–20); exit, turn right, walk about 180m (200 yards), turn left at Hopsvegen, and follow signs (15-min. walk). Hop is about 5km (3 miles) from Bergen.

Vestlandske Kunstindustrimuseum (West Norway Museum of Applied Art)   In the center of Bergen, this unique (for Norway) museum has one of the largest collections of Chinese applied art outside China. Its main attraction is a series of huge marble Buddhist temple sculptures created over a range of centuries. The collection also includes applied art from 1500 to the present day, with special attention paid to the Bergen silversmiths of the 17th and 18th centuries, who were celebrated for their heavy but elaborate baroque designs. Their collection of tankards, for example, is stunning. Most of them are embossed with flora motifs and others are inlaid with silver coins.

Permanenten, Nordahl Bruns Gate 9. ✆ 55-33-66-33. Admission 40NOK ($5.30). May 15–Sept 14, Tues–Sun 11am–4pm; Sept 15–May 14, Tues–Sun noon–4pm. Bus 1, 5, or 9.

IN NEARBY LYSØEN

To reach the island of Lysøen, 26km (16 miles) south of Bergen, drive or take a bus (from Platform 20 at the Bergen bus station, marked FANA-OS-MILDE) to

Ole Bull: Romantic Musician & Patriot

One of the most colorful characters in the history of western Norway was Ole Bull (1810–70), the founder of Norway's national theater and a virtuoso violinist. Leading one of the most remarkable lives of the 19th century, he was not only a celebrated composer, but also a fervent Utopian socialist and an international ambassador of Norwegian culture on his frequent international concerts. He became friends with Liszt, Schumann, Longfellow, Ibsen, and Hans Christian Andersen among other celebrated men of the day. Bull had a great influence on Edvard Grieg, and his best-known piece is "Saeterjentens Sondag" for violin and piano.

Born in Bergen, Ole Bull was immediately recognized as a child prodigy. Amazingly he joined the Bergen Philharmonic Orchestra when he was only 8 years old. One of the great violin virtuosos of all time, a sort of Victorian Mantovani, he won fans in such diverse places as the United States, Cuba, Moscow, and Cairo. He almost single-handedly rekindled an interest in Norwegian folk music both in Norway and abroad. In time, the people of Norway began to regard him as a national symbol.

After his first wife, a French woman, died, Ole Bull married Sara Thorp, of Madison, Wisconsin, and together they built a summer villa at Lysøen in 1872. That villa can be visited today. The strikingly handsome musician let his hyperactive imagination run wild as he created an architectural fantasy he called "Little Alhambra," with its Russian onion dome, pierced-wood Moorish arches, arabesque columns, and elegant trelliswork. It was on Lysøen that he died in 1880, and was given one of the largest attended funerals in Norway. The last of the great Norwegian Romanticists was laid to rest.

Visitors today wander across his "fairy tale" 70-hectare (175-acre) property with its romantic paths studded with gazebos and white shell sand. In the natural native pine forest, Ole Bull added exotic trees and bushes from all over the world that would grow in Bergen's chilly clime.

You can also visit a statue and fountain dedicated to this virtuoso performer on Ole Bulls Plass in the heart of Bergen.

Sørestraumen on Road 553. Take the Ole Bull ferry across the channel from Sørestraumen, Buena Kai. The round-trip fare is 40NOK ($5.30) for adults, 20NOK ($2.65) for children. When the museum and villa are open, ferry schedules coincide with the site's hours, and boats depart for the mainland at hourly intervals. The last boat leaves a few minutes after the museum closes.

Museet Lysøen/Ole Bull's Villa   This villa and concert hall were built in 1872–73 for the world-famous violin virtuoso and Norwegian national hero, Ole Bull. The building, now a national monument, is preserved as it was when the musician died in 1880. The building itself is an architectural fantasy of the 19th century, with a dome, curved staircase, cutwork trim, and gingerbread gables. Bull built 13km (8 miles) of romantic trails that meander around the island. Lysøen. ① 56-30-90-77. Admission 25NOK ($3.35) adults, 10NOK ($1.35) children. Guided tours early May to Sept Mon–Sat noon–4pm, Sun 11am–5pm; closed Oct to early May. Transportation: See "Organized Tours," below.

ORGANIZED TOURS

For information about and tickets to tours, contact **Tourist Information,** Bryggen 7 (© **55-32-14-80**).

The most popular and highly recommended tour of Bergen is the 3-hour city bus tour. It departs daily at 10am and covers the major attractions, including Troldhaugen and "Old Bergen." It operates May to September and costs 250NOK ($33) for adults, 160NOK ($21) for children.

WALKING TOUR	HISTORIC BERGEN

Start:	The Fish Market.
Finish:	West Norwegian Museum of Decorative Arts.
Time:	1 hour.
Best Time:	Any day between 8am and 5pm (when it's not raining, of course).
Worst Time:	When cruise ships anchor.

❶ Fish Market

Around the turn of the 19th century, this broad esplanade at the innermost reaches of Bergen's harbor teemed with fishermen selling their catch, as well as the blood, guts, and carcasses. Today, in a much-sanitized format, it's a venue for crafts, knitwear, carved Siberian and Lappish souvenirs, and to a lesser degree, fish and seafood.

From here, walk west along the Strandkaien, hugging the harbor front on your right-hand side, making a small detour inland at the Strandkaien's end. Within a block, at an angular jog in the avenue known as the Strandgaten, you'll see the solid, partially fortified walls of:

❷ City Wall Gate

This gate was originally built in 1550 as a checkpoint in a once-continuous wall that surrounded Bergen. Today, it stands isolated amid the newer buildings and broad avenues that surround it on all sides. There's a cheap clothing outlet on its ground floor, and an obscure, rarely visited museum (the Buekorps Museum) upstairs.

From here, walk west along Strandgaten, noting the many shops that line the street on either side. Within about 5 minutes, you'll reach one of Bergen's most visible houses of worship:

❸ Nykirken

Noteworthy features of this church are the Danish-inspired, mansard roof from around 1761; the copper-capped baroque spire; and its location overlooking the entrance to Bergen's harbor.

From here, walk steeply uphill for a block along the Nykirkeallmenningen, and turn left onto the narrow confines of the cobble-covered Ytre Markeveien, noting the antique wood-sided houses on either side. Walk 4 short blocks to the Kippersmauet, and then turn left, walking down a steep, cobble-covered alleyway where, at no. 23 and 24 there was a disastrous fire in 2001. (A pair of 14-year-old boys is credited with detecting the fire, and pounding on the doors of neighboring houses, an act that saved the entire wood-built neighborhood from burning to the ground.)

> ☕ **TAKE A BREAK**
> Café Retro, Klosteret 16 (© **55-31-16-16**). Loaded with the kitsch and artful debris of the age of Sputnik, with shelves filled with 1950s-era toasters, fans, and ashtrays (all of which are for sale as art objects in their own right), it sells sandwiches made from "ecological" (organic) breads, priced at 25NOK to 40NOK ($3.35–$5.30) each, coffee, tea, soda, and pastries. It's open daily from 11am to 7pm.

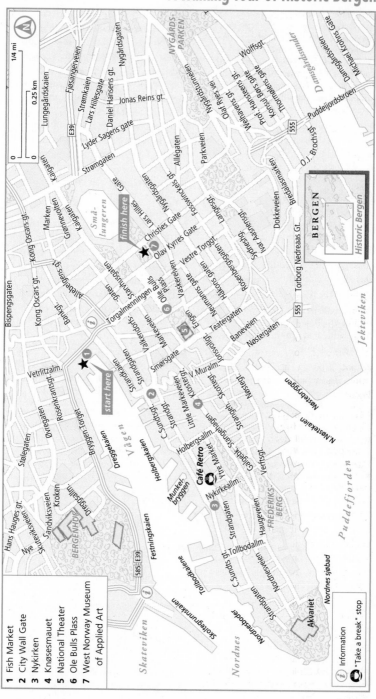

1 Fish Market
2 City Wall Gate
3 Nykirken
4 Knøsesmauet
5 National Theater
6 Ole Bulls Plass
7 West Norway Museum
  of Applied Art

Now, retrace your steps uphill back to the Ytre Markveien, and then turn right onto the big square (Holbergsallmenningen), originally conceived as a firebreak. Cross the wide boulevard (Klosteret), and walk east for 1 short block, turning right (sharply downhill) on the impossibly narrow cobble-covered alleyway identified within a few steps as the:

❹ Knøsesmauet

You'll immediately find yourself hemmed in, somewhat claustrophobically, by the antique wooden houses of a district known as the Klosteret. Composed of compact and, in most cases, impeccably well-maintained wooden houses immediately adjacent to one another. Even today, the risk of fire among the brightly painted historic buildings is a much-feared issue. Especially vulnerable are what local firefighters refer to as "chimney houses"—ones where cement, stucco, or ornamental masonry facades have been added to an otherwise mostly wooden building.

Continue descending the cobble-covered, steeply sloping length of the Knøsesmauet, bypassing brightly painted wooden houses prefaced, in some cases with tiny gardens. Cross over the Skottogaten, and continue walking downhill. Turn left onto the St. Hansestredet. (Sankt Hanse is the patron saint of the summer solstice, often invoked in midsummer with bouquets of midsummer flowers such as the ones that adorn the sides of the houses along this street.) St. Hansestredet, within 2 short blocks, merges with the busy traffic of the Jonsvollsgaten, a wide commercial boulevard. Walk east for about 3 minutes, cross over the Teatergaten, and continue walking east along Engen, the eastward extension of the Jonsvollsgaten. On your left rises the stately looking, Art-Nouveau bulk of the:

❺ National Theater

This arts complex is rich with memories. It was established by violinist Ole Bull, who envisioned it as a showcase for Norwegian-language drama and music. Today, performances of such Broadway-style musicals as *Kiss Me, Kate* alternate with more serious,

mostly Norwegian works. Details to look for inside and out include life-size portrait statues of Bjørneson, author of Norway's national anthem, and Ibsen, who served as the theater's director for 5 years. (The stern and magisterial-looking granite sculpture of Ibsen, completed in 1982, and set into the lawns of the theater's eastern side, was considered so ugly that it remained in storage for many years.) On the theater's tree-shaded western side, just outside the entrance to its lobby, is a flattering likeness, in bronze, of Nordahl Grieg, often referred to as the Norwegian version of Winston Churchill because he warned of the Nazi menace before many of his colleagues in the Norwegian Parliament.

If it's open, walk into the theater's lobby, a survivor of a disastrous fire in 1916, and of a Nazi bomb that fell directly into its lobby in 1944. Completely restored in the late '90s, the lobby has an understated Art-Nouveau style, and portraits of great Norwegians lining its walls.

Now, with your back to the ornamental eastern side of the theater, walk easterly along the:

❻ Ole Bulls Plass

Descend the gradual slope and note the grand commercial buildings that rise on either side. Broad and wide, and flanked with flower beds, restaurants, bars, and shops, it was originally laid out, in an era when virtually everything that flanked it was made of wood, as a firebreak. Today, it's an architectural showcase of Bergen, named after Norway's first musical superstar.

Descend along the Ole Bulls Plass, past a violin-playing statue of the musical star himself. When the street opens onto the broad esplanade known as Olav Kyrres Gate, note on the right-hand side the turn-of-the-19th-century brick facade of the:

❼ West Norway Museum of Applied Art

The statue of a seated male, lost in thought, set into a niche on the museum's facade commemorates the 19th-century painter J. C. Dahl. It was crafted by one of Norway's first widely celebrated woman sculptor, Ambrosia Tønnesen. The abstract sculpture set onto the lawn in front of the museum, composed of a series of rainbow-colored concentric hoops, is in honor of Bergen-born, early-20th-century composer Harald Saeverud.

6 Outdoor Activities

FISHING In the region around Bergen, anyone can fish in the sea without restrictions. If you plan to fish in fresh water (ponds, streams, and most of the best salmon and trout rivers), you'll need a permit. These are sold at any post office. You'll also need the permission of the owner of the land on either side of the stream. Information and fishing permits, which cost 95NOK to 150NOK ($13–$20), are available from **Bergen Sportsfiskere** (Bergen Angling Association), Fosswinckelsgate 37 (✆ **55-32-11-64**). It's open Monday to Friday from 9am to 2pm.

GOLF The **Åstvelt Golf Course** (✆ **55-18-20-77**) has nine holes and is open to nonmembers; call in advance. It's a 15-minute drive north of Bergen on E16. You can also take the Åsane bus from the central station in Bergen. Greens fees range from 200NOK to 250NOK ($27–$33). The newest and best golf course is **Meland Golf Club,** lying 36km (22 miles) north of Bergen at Meland/Frekhaug (✆ **56-17-46-00**). This is an 18-hole, par-73 golf course with a pro shop, lockers, and changing facilities. The setting is on 90 hectares (225 acres) in the midst of forests, lakes, and mountains. Greens fees Monday to Friday are 330NOK ($44), going up to 350NOK ($47) on Saturday and Sunday.

SWIMMING The **Sentralbadet,** Theatersgaten 37 (✆ **55-56-95-70**), has a heated saltwater indoor pool. An open-air pool whose season is limited to the fleeting Nordic summer is at **Nordnes Sjøbad,** Nordnes. For hours, check with the Bergen tourist office. At either pool, adults pay 20NOK ($2.65), children 15NOK ($2).

TENNIS **Paradis Sports Senter,** Highway R1, Paradis (✆ **55-91-26-00**), lies 6.5km (4 miles) south of Bergen. The club has five indoor courts, four squash courts, four badminton courts, a health club and gym, and a solarium. It's open Monday to Friday from 9am to 10pm, Saturday 10am to 6pm, Sunday noon to 6pm.

WALKING Only 10 minutes away from town by the funicular, several roads and footpaths lead to **Mount Fløien,** an unspoiled wood and mountain terrace with lakes and rivers.

The **Bergen Touring Club,** Tverrgaten 4–6 (✆ **55-32-22-30**), arranges walking tours farther afield and supplies information on huts and mountain routes all over Norway. It also provides maps and advice on where to hike. The office is open Monday to Friday 10am to 4pm (until 6pm on Thurs).

7 Shopping

Shoppers who live outside Scandinavia and spend more than 310NOK ($41) in a tax-free tourist shop can receive a refund up to 18.5% of the purchase price when they leave Norway. See "Fast Facts: Norway," in chapter 2, for details.

THE SHOPPING SCENE

Bargain hunters head to the **Marketplace (Torget).** Many local handicrafts from the western fjord district, including rugs and handmade tablecloths, are displayed. This is one of the few places in Norway where bargaining is welcomed. The market keeps no set hours, but is best visited between 8am and noon. Take bus no. 1, 5, or 9.

HOURS   Stores are generally open Monday to Friday from 9am to 6pm (until 8pm Thurs and sometimes Fri), Saturday 9am to 4pm. Shopping centers outside the city are open Monday to Friday from 10am to 8pm, Saturday 9am to 6pm. Some food stores stay open until 8pm Monday to Friday and 6pm on Saturday.

SHOPPING A TO Z
ART GALLERIES

Galleri Fisk   About a decade ago, this space was used for the exhibition and sale of fish. Today, gilled creatures, ice, and seaweed have been replaced with artworks produced by students within Bergen's university system. Hours are erratic, and since it's a basically underfunded venue for struggling newcomers, there's no phone. Big windows let in lots of light. Kong Oscarsgate 46. No phone (check www.khib. no/fisk). Bus: 20, 21, 22.

Hordaland Art Center and Café   An artistic focal point of the historic neighborhood that contains it, this is a publicly funded art gallery that puts on as many as 12 different art exhibitions each year. Originally completed in 1742, it served as a school for the children of the local parish for many years. There's a children's play area, and a cafe on site where sandwiches and platters are available. Schedules are erratic, varying with each exhibition. Klosteret 17, Nordnes. ☏ 55-90-01-40. A 5-min. walk from Torgallmenningan.

DEPARTMENT STORE

Sundt & Co.   Many Bergeners remember this leading department store from childhood shopping expeditions with their parents. The store now faces stiff competition from such newer emporiums as Galleriet (see "Shopping Mall," below). Torgalmenningen. ☏ 55-32-31-00.

FASHION

Berle Bryggen   Set directly on the quays, near the innermost edge of Bergen's historic harbor, this is a large, well-stocked gift and clothing store with an upscale and well-chosen collection of men's and women's sweaters, pewter, troll dolls, and gift items. It's also a repository for the diverse articles of clothing that, when worn collectively, are referred to by the Norwegians as *Bunad,* the Norwegian national costume. Bryggen 5. ☏ 55-31-73-00.

Kløverhuset   Next to the fish market on the harbor, this four-story shopping center has been Bergen's largest fashion store since 1923. Besides carrying the latest in modern design, it also offers bargains, such as moderately priced and attractively designed knit sweaters, gloves, and Lapp jackets. The special gift shop is open only in the summer. Strandgaten 13–15. ☏ 55-31-37-90.

Viking Design   Opposite the Flower Market, this shop has the most unusual knitwear in Bergen—many of its designs have won prizes. In addition to fashion, there is also a selection of quality pewter produced in Bergen, along with a selection of intriguing Norwegian gifts and souvenirs. Items purchased can be shipped abroad. Strandkaien 2A. ☏ 55-31-05-20.

Finds Shopping Tour

Norway has a centuries-old tradition of crafts, which undoubtedly developed to help people pass the time during the cold, dark winters when farm families were more or less housebound for months. Some of the major crafts were woodcarving, weaving, and embroidery, and these skills live on today at many local artist and craft centers. Some of the best areas include Hardanger (around the Hardangerfjord, near Bergen); and Song (just north of the Sognefjord, also near Bergen); and Telemark (the district around Skien, within a day's drive from Oslo). For a true, behind-the-scenes look at Norway, **Five Stars of Scandinavia,** 13104 Thomas Rd., KPN, Gig Harbor, WA 98329 (© **800/722-4126**), will set up a self-drive, self-guided tour for you, factoring in everything they know about local artisans.

HANDICRAFTS

In and around **Bryggen Brukskunst,** the restored Old Town near the wharf, many craftspeople have taken over old houses and ply ancient Norwegian trades. Crafts boutiques often display Bergen souvenirs, many based on designs 300 to 1,500 years old. For example, we purchased a reproduction of a Romanesque-style cruciform pilgrim's badge. Other attractive items are likely to include sheepskin-lined booties and exquisitely styled hand-woven wool dresses.

Prydkunst-Hjertholm The leading outlet for glassware and ceramics purchases much of its merchandise directly from the artisans' studios. The quality goods include glass, ceramics, pewter, wood, and textiles. Gift articles and souvenirs are also available. Olav Kyrres Gate 7. © **55-31-70-27.**

Yin-Yang In the 1960s, we'd have referred to this place as a "New Age head shop." Today, it's a bit more gentrified, focusing on art objects, woodcarvings, and jewelry from India, Indonesia (especially Bali), and sari-like clothing for women. There's also a selection of books telling how to grow marijuana in cold climates such as Norway, leading us to believe that the New Age is alive, well, and thriving here. Teatergatan 16. © **55-32-87-83.** Bus: 2, 3, or 4.

JEWELRY

Juhls' Silver Gallery Next to the SAS Royal Hotel, along the harbor front, Juhls' displays the town's most unusual selection of quality jewelry. The designers take for their inspiration the constantly changing weather of the far north, and, in their words, provide "a cultural oasis in a desert of snow." Bryggen. © **55-32-47-40.**

LEATHER, LATEX & FETISH

X-STREME A visit to this place is sure to alter any preconceived ideas about Norwegian wholesomeness and propriety that you might have. This is one of the few fetish shops in all of Norway. The roster of leather, latex, and metal-accented garments might not be appropriate for your next reunion or school-board meeting, but some items are avant-garde fashion statements in their own right. Jonsvollsgate 5. © **48-21-11-66.** Bus: 11.

QUILTS

Anne Kari's Quilt Shop Winter nights are long and dark in Bergen, and as a means of fighting off the cold and loneliness, many residents divert themselves with quilting and the perfection of quilting patterns. At this cramped and claustrophobic shop near the National Theater, you'll find all manner of quilting supplies, any of which can keep you diverted for days or months at a time. Teatergaten 25. ℭ 55-24-40-40. Bus: 2, 3, or 4.

SHOPPING MALL

Galleriet   This is the most important shopping complex in the Bergen area, with 70 stores offering tax-free shopping. Close to the fish market, it displays a wide array of merchandise and features summer sales and special exhibitions. It has several fast-food establishments, too. Torgalmenningen 8. ℭ 55-30-05-00.

SPORTSWEAR

G-Sport Gågaten   This store has virtually everything you'd need for virtually every sport available within Norway. Inventory changes radically throughout the seasons, with an emphasis on cycling and hiking in summer and downhill and cross-country skiing in winter. There are special high-energy food supplies (1 tablespoon will give you the temporary strength of a gorilla), and high-tech outdoor gear whose high price tag reflects the newest trends in sportswear and rough-weather gear. Strandgaten 59. ℭ 55-23-22-22. Bus: 1, 5, or 9.

WROUGHT IRON

Smijern Kunst   Ironmongering has been practiced in Norway for thousands of years. Here, you'll find fanciful wrought-iron lamps, door hardware, light fixtures, candleholders, and household gift items. Strandgaten 21 ℭ 55-32-71-70. Bus: 1.

8 Bergen After Dark

THE PERFORMING ARTS

Den National Scene   September to June is the season for Norway's oldest theater, founded in the mid–19th century. It stages classical Norwegian and international drama, contemporary plays, and musical drama, as well as visiting productions of opera and ballet. Engen 1. ℭ 55-54-97-10. Tickets 180NOK–280NOK ($24–$37). Bus: 2, 3, or 4.

Grieghallen   The modern Grieg Hall, which opened in 1978, is Bergen's monumental showcase for music, drama, and a host of other cultural events. The stage is large enough for an entire grand opera production, and the main foyer comfortably seats 1,500 guests for lunch or dinner. Snack bars provide drinks and light snacks throughout the performances. The upper floors house the offices of the Philharmonic Orchestra.

The Bergen Symphony Orchestra, founded in 1765, performs here from August to May, often on Thursday at 7:30pm and Saturday at 12:30pm. Its repertoire consists of classical and contemporary music, as well as visiting opera productions. International conductors and soloists perform. Lars Hillesgate 3A. ℭ 55-21-61-50. Tickets 100NOK–350NOK ($13–$47). Closed July. Bus: 2, 3, or 4.

SUMMER CULTURAL ENTERTAINMENT

Bergen Folklore   The Bergen Folklore dancing troupe performs from June to August on Tuesday and Thursday at 9pm. The program, which lasts about an hour, consists of traditional folk dances and music from rural Norway. Tickets are on sale at the tourist office (see "Orientation," earlier in this chapter) and at the door. Bryggens Museum, Bryggen. ℭ 97-52-86-30. Tickets 100NOK ($13) adults, free for children. Bus: 1, 5, or 9.

FILMS

Bergen has two large movie theaters, **Konsertpaleet,** Neumannsgate 3 (© **55-56-90-83**), and **Forum,** in Danmarkplass (© **55-20-62-48**), which show all films in their original versions. The earliest performance is at 11am, the latest at 11pm. Tickets usually cost 85NOK ($11).

THE CLUB & MUSIC SCENE

Café Opera   Built in the 1980s, this is a large stone bar that is both a restaurant and a cafe serving food. After the kitchen closes, it becomes a nightclub on two floors. On Tuesday nights, there is a jam session where musicians entertain or poetry is read. The stage is open to anyone. On other nights DJs mix and blend the music, depending on their individual tastes. The cafe is host to international DJs and bands on most Thursdays, Fridays, and Saturdays. A crowd in their 20s and 30s find this one of the more amusing joints after dark. Engen 18. © **55-23-03-15.** Bus: 2, 3, or 4.

Den Studeslose   Many musicians and artists hang out here at what is called a "culture bar." Live bands perform music—everything from blues to pop—7 nights a week. The nightclub is in the basement of the dance club, Maxime. Under a low ceiling, guests, ranging in age from 30 to 60, hang out and have fun. Open Sunday to Wednesday 10pm to 3am, Thursday to Saturday 10pm to 3:30am. Ole Bulls Plass 3. © **55-30-71-36.** Cover 40NOK ($5.30) Mon–Thurs, 80NOK ($11) Fri–Sat. Free Sun. Bus: 2, 3, or 4.

Engelen   This is one of Bergen's more elegant discos. Wednesday to Friday night, an older, sedate crowd gathers to enjoy the music and ambience. On Saturday, beware—the atmosphere changes drastically with the arrival of noisy, fun-seeking 20-somethings. Light meals are available. Drink prices begin at 74NOK ($9.85), 55NOK ($7.30) for a beer. It's open Wednesday to Saturday from 9pm to 3am. In the Radisson SAS Royal Hotel, Bryggen. © **55-54-30-00.** Cover 60NOK–80NOK ($8–$11), free to hotel guests. Bus: 1, 5, or 9.

Kafe Kippers USF   A favorite rendezvous for artists, this club plays some of the best jazz music in Bergen. Every Friday night they have a live jazz artist performing; otherwise it's the best in "listening jazz." International food is served, around the globe from Norway via American to Malaysia. In winter they hold 80 patrons in snug comfort inside. In summer, the on-site outdoor restaurant, Kaien, becomes the largest in Bergen with 500 seats available, opening on fjord waters. Georgenes Cerft 3. © **55-31-00-60.** Cover 100NOK–150NOK ($13–$20) Fri. Bus: 13.

Madam Felle   Dark, woodsy-looking, and cozy, this is an animated and crowded pub with limited food service and live music that packs the place with 20- and 30-somethings 4 nights a week. On those nights (always Fri and Sat, plus 2 weeknights whose schedule changes frequently), live music plays between 9 and 11pm, with a cover charge that might be free, or which might rise to 150NOK ($20), depending on the season and the mood of the staff. The pub is named after an early-20th-century matriarch who became a noted innkeeper at a spot near here, and something of a legend within Bergen. Bryggen. © **55-54-30-58.** Cover: 150NOK ($20) some Fri–Sat. Bus: 20, 21, 22, 34, 50, 70, 80, and 90.

Maxime   One of Bergen's most reliable drinking venues caters to men and women who are unattached (or trying to be). In a prominent location near the Hotel Norge, it boasts three bar areas. Food is served every day from noon to around 9:30pm, making it a well-known lunchtime spot. The bars are open

Monday to Saturday from 7pm to 1am, Sunday 3pm to 1am. Less popular, but a viable alternative on Saturday night, is the cellar-level disco. It's open Thursday to Saturday 11pm to 2:30am. Regardless of where you drink it, a large beer costs 50NOK ($6.65). Ole Bulls Plass. ✆ 55-30-71-35. Cover 55NOK ($7.30) for the disco. Bus: 2, 3, or 4.

Rick's Café   This is something of a labyrinth, with rooms devoted to the after-dark pursuit of cabaret and comedy (there's a small stage for small-scale acts); some serious drinking (on cold winter's nights, things can get rather sudsy); or a general, friendly pick-up (no doubt encouraged by the bar's potent cocktails). It's open Wednesday to Saturday from 5pm till around 2am, depending on business. Veiten 3. ✆ 55-55-31-31. Bus: 1, 5, or 9. No one under 24 permitted.

Rubinen   Rubinen is one of Bergen's most popular nightclubs, attracting an over-35 crowd of mostly married couples. It plays all kinds of music, including country-western and rock. Drinks cost about 75NOK ($10). It's open Wednesday to Saturday from 10pm to 3am, with live music nightly. Rosenkrantzgate 7. ✆ 55-31-74-70. Cover 80NOK ($11). Bus: 2, 3, or 4.

Zachen Piano Bar   One of the most popular piano bars in western Norway opens onto panoramic views toward the fjord. Built of pine, the bar attracts a diverse crowd, ranging in age from 20 to 50. First-class piano players from throughout Europe are imported here. During five nights of the week, they also stage karaoke. The excellent piano music is heard Wednesday to Sunday. Open Sunday to Thursday noon to 1am, Friday noon to 2am, and Saturday 11am to 2am. Torget 2. ✆ 55-55-96-40. Bus: 1, 5, or 9.

THE BAR SCENE

Altona   This is one of the oldest known bars in Bergen. Some of the stone walls and the wooden ceiling are original, dating from the 1600s. Lying in the basement of the Augustin Hotel, its walls are painted white and the bar is decorated with modern sculptures. Patrons, ranging from 30 to 60 years old, come here to listen to the recorded classical music and to enjoy the elegant drinks, including champagne, cognac, and the best Scotch whiskey. Open Monday to Thursday 6pm to 1:30am and Friday and Saturday 6pm to 2:30am. Strandgaten 81. ✆ 55-30-40-72. Bus: 2 or 4.

Baklommen   This small bar with its old Chesterfield chairs is a quiet and romantic retreat, lying downstairs from the To Kokker restaurant. A more mature crowd, aged 30 to 60, comes here to escape from a lot of the pub row-diness of Bergen. In the heart of the Hanseatic Wharf, this bar plays recorded jazz music in the background. Open Tuesday to Saturday from 6pm to 1am. Enhjørningsgarden. ✆ 55-32-27-47. Bus: 1, 5, or 9.

Bar Ugla   At this brown nightclub, leave your attitude at the door. This battered-looking pub has an active bar at one end and a stage in the middle. When we last dropped in, the highly danceable rock 'n' roll/rockabilly was from a talented band from Romania. Expect an undulating crowd of straights, gays, and everyone else in between. Beer costs around 48NOK ($6.40) per foaming mug. Ugla (the name translates as "the Owl") is open every day from 2 to 7pm for mostly low-key drinking. Then it reopens from 10pm till 3 or 3:30am, depending on the crowd and the mood of the staff. Olav Kyrres Gate 28. ✆ 55-30-63-70. Bus: 1 or 9.

Dr. Livingstone Travellers Café   Every surface bears some kind of tribute to the world's "great" travel experiences at this restaurant and bar. You'll take your pick of three distinct subdivisions, some of whose walls are painted with pithy

Fun Fact **The Brown Scene**

What does a Norwegian mean when he refers to a brown nightclub? It's a raucous, boozy, semisleazy joint where off-duty prostitutes, bikers, harbor-front riffraff, slumming suburbanites, business travelers on short-term leaves from their spouses, and all manner of fringe society get together for a rollicking good time. Don't say you haven't been warned.

quotes from African explorer Dr. Livingstone himself ("Wagon traveling is a prolonged way of picnicking"). A glassed-in area is devoted exclusively to designer coffees, with or without a shot of liqueur. Bar areas are on the upper and lower floors. The entire complex is open for food service Monday and Tuesday from noon to 10pm and Wednesday to Sunday from noon to 11pm. Bar service continues nightly till between 1 and 4am, depending on business. Tapas cost from 39NOK to 59NOK ($5.20–$7.85); burgers, sandwiches, and salads cost 82NOK to 99NOK ($11–$13), and meal-size platters cost 239NOK to 249NOK ($32–$33). Kong Oscarsgate 12. ℂ **55-56-03-12.** Bus: 6.

Dyvekes Vinkjeller   A sense of spookiness permeates this cozy drinking den. In 1849, a famous Norwegian bandit (Gjest Baardsen, the "Robin Hood" of Norway) drank himself to death here. And recently, drinkers have reported sightings of a young serving wench in 17th-century costume who takes drink orders from patrons, and then disappears without bringing the desired quaffs. Come here for glasses of wine, priced from 61NOK to 85NOK ($8.10–$11); glasses of beer; colorful patrons (both living and dead); and a genuine sense of Norwegian history. It's open Sunday to Friday 6pm to 12:30am, Saturday 3pm to 12:30am. Hollendergaten 7. ℂ **55-32-30-60.** Bus: 20, 21, 22.

The English Pub   This is one of the most authentic duplications of a merrie Olde English pub in Norway, with battered paneling, a pool table, much-used dartboards, foaming mugs of beer, and a clientele composed of equal parts local office workers and nearby residents. It's open Monday to Thursday from 7pm to 1am, Friday to Sunday from 3pm till 2am. Ole Bulls Plass. ℂ **55-30-71-39.** Bus: 2, 3, or 4.

Fotballpuben   This is the biggest sports pub in Bergen, a rocking and rolling beer-soaked place with an undeniable affection for football (i.e., soccer), and to a lesser degree, rugby. Feel free to wander through this crowded establishment's labyrinth of inner chambers, whose corners and edges are sometimes upholstered with vinyl padding (installed with a fear of falls from inebriated sports fans?). Screens blow up the action of sports events in progress (or prerecorded) whenever there's a soccer stadium with an intensely contested match. The staff prides itself on serving the cheapest beer in Bergen, priced from 32NOK to 39NOK ($4.25–$5.20) per mug, depending on the time of day. It's open Monday to Thursday from 9am to 1am, Friday and Saturday 9am to 2am, Sunday noon to 1am. Vestre Torggate 9. ℂ **55-36-66-61.** Bus: 1 or 9.

Kontoret (The Office)   The most frequented pub in the city center, the Kontoret is next to the Dickens restaurant and pub. Drinkers can wander freely between the two places, which are connected. In the Kontoret Pub you can order the same food served at Dickens, although most people seem to come here to drink. The local brew is called Hansa; a half-liter of draft beer is 53NOK ($7.05). It's open Sunday to Thursday from 4pm to 1am, Friday and Saturday noon to 3am. In the Hotel Norge, Ole Bulls Plass 8–10. ℂ **55-36-31-33.** Bus: 2, 3, or 4.

Landmark Café   You wouldn't expect such a hip nightclub and pub to be within an art museum, but in the case of this large, high-ceilinged cube of a room on the museum's back side, that's exactly the case. Danceable music emerges from a DJ's station on one side; a bar at another end of the room serves beer and sandwiches, and electronic art in kaleidoscopic color is beamed against yet another. It's open daily from noon to 12:30am, rocking and rolling long after the museum is closed tight like a drum. Windows directly overlook the large, octagonal reflecting pool on the museum's back side. Pastas and salads cost from 48NOK to 67NOK ($6.40–$8.90) each. In the Bergen Art Museum, Rasmus Meyers Allé 3 and 7. ℭ **55-31-77-55.** Bus: 1, 5, 9.

Margarita's Bar & Restaurant   Set a few steps downhill from the lower stage of the Fløibanen cable car, this is Bergen's most animated, popular, and cutting-edge Spanish bodega. Margaritas range in price from 48NOK ($6.40) during happy hour (daily from 5–8pm) to 79NOK ($11), and are based on the fruit of the day, which might include melon, mango, or strawberries. A long list of tapas, priced from 45NOK to 110NOK ($6–$15) per portion, can accompany any of your drinks on the street level, and some clients opt to order two or three different selections for something approximating a full-fledged dinner. If you prefer your Iberian food in more formal settings, there are two separate but rather cramped Spanish restaurants on the upper floor of this place. Both of them are open daily from 5 to 11pm. The street-level bar is open Sunday to Thursday 3pm to 1am, Friday 3pm to 2am, and Saturday 2pm to 2am. Vetrelidsalmenning 15. ℭ **55-96-20-10.** Bus: 6.

Zacchariasbrygge Pub   On the harbor front of Old Bergen, in the same oxblood-colored former warehouse as the restaurant Fiskekroen (see "Where to Dine," earlier in this chapter), this is one of Bergen's most popular, and sometimes noisiest, pubs. Piano music and a live singer accompany copious quantities of flowing suds. A half-pint of lager goes for 72NOK ($9.60), and French and Italian wines by the glass cost about the same. There's additional, quieter seating upstairs. Open Monday to Friday from 11am to 12:30am, Saturday noon to 12:30am, Sunday 1 to 10pm. Zacchariasbrygge 50. ℭ **55-55-96-40.** Bus: 2, 3, or 4.

A GAY CAFE

Café Fincken   This cafe and bar serves refreshments, wine, and beer. It's open Monday to Saturday from noon to 2am, Sunday 3pm to 2am. The clientele is mostly gay and lesbian. There's a new art exhibition every month. Nygårdsgaten 2A. ℭ **55-32-13-16.** Bus: 2, 3, or 4.

9 Side Trips from Bergen

SOGNEFJORD ✸✸✸

Norway's longest and deepest fjord, the **Sognefjord** is a geologic and panoramic marvel. The terrain soars upward from the watery depths of the North Atlantic, and many waterfalls punctuate its edges with spray. The best way to view the fjord involves a full-day jaunt that's possible only between May 18 and September 15. It combines self-guided travel by boat, bus, and rail. Begin by heading to the Bergen harbor front (the Strandkaien), where you'll board a ferry for the 4½-hour ride to the fjord-side hamlet of Gudvangen. A bus carries participants on to the town of Voss (see "Voss," in chapter 11). In Voss, after exploring the town, you can board a train to carry you back to Bergen. Many schedule permutations are possible, but one that's particularly convenient is leaving Bergen at 8:30am and returning at 5:15pm. The combined round-trip fare is 630NOK ($84). Details on this and other explorations by public transport are available from the tourist office (see "Orientation," earlier in this chapter).

NORWAY IN A NUTSHELL ★★★

This 12-hour tour has been cited as the most scenically captivating 1-day tour of Norway. Its breadth and diversity of landscapes encapsulates the majesty of the country's fjords and mountains.

Several different transit options operate throughout the day. The one most aggressively recommended by Bergen's tourist office runs from June to August only. It starts at 8:30am at **Bergen's** railway station. After a 2-hour train ride, you disembark in the mountaintop hamlet of **Myrdal,** where you can sightsee for about 20 minutes. In Myrdal, you board a cog railway for one of the world's most dramatically inclined train rides. The trip down to the village of **Flåm,** a drop of 870m (2,900 ft.), takes an hour and passes roaring streams and seemingly endless waterfalls.

After a 1-hour stopover in Flåm, where you can have lunch or take a brief hike, you board a fjord steamer for a ride along the Sognefjord. You reach the fjord-side town of Gudvangen after a 2-hour ride. After 30 minutes in Gudvangen, you board a bus for the 75-minute ride to Voss. There you spend 30 minutes before boarding a train for the 75-minute ride back to Bergen. Arrival is scheduled for 8:18pm.

Expect only a rushed overview of each town, as there is more scenery than you can digest in a 12-hour day. The round-trip fare, excluding meals, is 630NOK ($84) for adults, 315NOK ($42) for children under 12. There are discounts for holders of Eurailpasses or Scanrail passes. For more information, contact Bergen's **Tourist Office** (© **55-32-14-80**).

11

The West Coast Fjord Country

Western Norway is the heart of the fjord country. Norwegian fjords are narrow arms of the sea, snaking their way inland. It took three million years to form the furrows and fissures that give western Norway its distinctive look. At some points the fjords become so narrow that a boat can hardly wedge between the mountainsides.

Fjords have been of enormous significance to Norwegians through the ages. They served as lifelines to those who settled in the harsh mountain landscape. Instead of building roads to each house and village, they used the easily accessible and navigable fjords. Thus, inland regions and coastal regions were linked together as the fjords enabled commodities to be transported to the old trading stations. Imagine how centuries ago the people used to row across the fjord to visit church on Sunday mornings.

Bergen is the best departure point for trips to the fjords: To the south lies the famous Hardangerfjord and to the north the Sognefjord, cutting 178km (111 miles) inland.

Voss, about 1½ hours from Bergen, is a famous ski resort that is also well situated between both the Hardangerfjord and the Sognefjord.

This chapter starts in the towns around the Hardangerfjord—Lofthus, Kinsarvik, Eidfjord and Ulvik—makes a detour to Voss, and then moves north to the towns around the Sognefjord including Balestrand and Flåm.

GETTING THERE Bergen is the traditional gateway to the fjord country. From Bergen, you have a choice of several options for getting about the district; the most expensive is by private car. Most of the towns and villages have road connections, although you'll have to take several car-ferries to cross the fjords. Boat excursions, many of which leave from Bergen, are the traditional way to see the fjords. In summer, dozens of possibilities await you. Contact the tourist office in Bergen for details (see "Orientation," in chapter 10).

Of the towns recommended in this chapter, Voss, both a winter ski center and a summer mountain resort, has the best rail connections with Oslo and Bergen. But all of the fjord towns and villages are connected by buses that make their way carefully through the mountains and along the fjords, with vistas in all directions. Of course, travel by bus from place to place is time-consuming and often there are only two to five departures a day, depending on business, so you have to plan your connections in advance. Details about bus routes in the fjord district are available at the Central Station in Bergen.

1 Utne: A Trio of Fjords ✸

130km (81 miles) E of Bergen; 45km (28 miles) N of Odda

Utne has a view of the entrances to three fjords: Indre Samla, Granvin, and Eid. Across Utnefjorden, the formidable bulk of Oksen rises from the headland separating the Granvin and the Eid fjords. A great ravine breaches the steep

The West Coast Fjord Country

Hustadvika

Kristiansund **1**

64
Averøya
70
65

Bud

Øygard
Tingvoll

Molde **2**

1

Langfjorden

Sekken

64

9 1

Åndalsnes **3**

Sjøbolt

E751

63

Ålesund **4**

NORWAY
SWEDEN
9

Festoy

650

Ulstelnvik

Sandsøy

Kvamsøy
Gurskøy

1
Volda

655

Eidsdal

West Coast
Fjord Country

⊗ Oslo

Stadlandet

Hellesylt

63

Selje

60

Geiranger **5**
Polifoss

Aursjøen

Måløy

Nordfjord-
eid

Hornindalsvatnet

Stryn **6**

15

Sikkelbreen

15

Bremanger-
landen

Frøysjøen

614

Utfjorden

Kjøs

Loen **7**

60

Olden **8**

Loen-
vatnet

Lundadalsvn.

Frøya

Ålfotbreen

Hovden

615

Byrkjelo

Eimhjellvatnet

1

Jostedalsbreen **9**

Flora

Skorpa

5

Naustdal

Askrova

Swanøy

Skjolden

Jotunheimen

Stavfjorden

Fjærland **10**

55

Lustrafjord

Tyin

Atløy

Størehaug

13

Veitastrondsvn.

53

Afjorden

57

Balestrand **11**

Sogndal

Årdalstangen
E16

Leirvik

1

55

55

Sula

Lavik

Revsnes

Borlaug

Hisarøy
Rutledal

Ytre
Oppedal

Byknesoy

Duesund

13

E16

Flåm **12**

Fosney
Leirvåg

1

Vinje

50
Stolsvatn

Romarheim

Strandvatn

57

Voss **13**

Holsnøy

Veafjorden

Dale

Ulvik **14**

Geilo **19**

Blomøy

Bruravik

Eidfd.
Haugastøl

Toftøy
Askøy

Eidfjord **15**

Store

Bergen

Norheim-
sund

7

Kinsarvik **17**

16

Algerøy

48

Utne **17**

7

Sotre

49
Jondal

18
Lofthus **18**
Vervatnet

Langesjøen

Halhjem
Mundheim

13

Hardanger
Bjørnesfjorden

Bjørnafjorden

Varaldsøy

Ringedalsvn.

Odda

HARDANGERVIDDA
NASJONALPARK

0   20 mi
0   20 km

slope of Oksen. Utnefjorden is almost 3.25km (2 miles) wide opposite Utne and nearly 822m (2,700 ft.) deep in places, making it deeper than any other part of the Hardangerfjord.

Utne is at the northern end of the Folgefonn peninsula, with mountains looming nearby. Two valleys converge on the town, Utnedalen to the east and Fossdalen to the west. The river through Fossdalen forms fine falls as it drops through the woods toward the end of its course, dividing into two branches as it reaches the fjord.

GETTING THERE

In the west, board the **ferry** at Kvanndal; in the east, at Kinsarvik. There are frequent departures. **Train** connections are possible from Voss 38 km (24 miles) to the east, on the main Bergen-Oslo line. **Bus** connections are made via Odda in the south and from Bergen in the west. By **car,** head east from Bergen along the E16. At Kvanndal, board the ferry for Utne.

SEEING THE SIGHTS

Founded in 1911, the **Hardanger Folk Museum** ⊛, lying near the ferry quay at Utne (℃ **53-66-69-00**), exhibits old timber buildings, furnished according to their eras, from several parts of Inner Hardanger. By the fjord are old boathouses and a general store that once stood on the quay side. In the administrative building are local arts and crafts, national costumes, and data on the fruit-growing industry. The famous Hardanger fiddle, so beloved by Ole Bull and Edvard Grieg, came from this area. The museum owns several of these antique fiddles, and you can also visit a fiddle-maker's workshop.

The museum charges 40NOK ($5.30) for adults; free for children. From May to June, it's open Monday to Friday 10am to 3pm, Saturday 10am to 4pm, and Sunday noon to 4pm. In July and August hours are Monday to Saturday 10am to 6pm, Sunday noon to 4pm.

When fjords were the highways of western Norway, Utne was an important junction. The **Utne Hotel** (see below) opened in 1772.

WHERE TO STAY & DINE

Utne Hotel ⋆⋆⋆   Dating from 1722, this is Norway's oldest hotel in continual operation. To settle a war debt, King Christian VII granted Sergeant Børsem permission to operate an inn here, and it's been going strong ever since. Børsem's family ran the hotel until 1995 when new owners took over. Torbjørg Utne (1812–1903)—nicknamed Mother Utne—gave the hotel the romantic character it still possesses today. By the mid–19th century the hotel offered "the best quarters in the country." Today, a foundation owns the well-preserved hotel, which has a distinctive atmosphere and intimate ambience. Only a few minutes' walk from the ferry quay, the antique-filled place offers generous hospitality. The well-maintained bedrooms have the gracious comfort of the 19th century, and all of them come with well-kept bathrooms with tub-and-shower combinations.

The cuisine is one of the major reasons to stay here: It's one of the finest in the fjord country. A complete meal of Norwegian specialties costs 300NOK ($40), and the dining room is open to nonguests. The staff can arrange mountain sightseeing tours as well as boat trips on the fjords.

N-5797 Utne i Hardanger. © **53-66-10-88.** Fax 53-66-10-89. 25 units. 1,150NOK–1,250NOK ($153–$166) double. Children under 12 stay free. Rates include continental breakfast. AE, DC, MC, V. Closed Nov 1–Apr 15. **Amenities:** Restaurant; bar; babysitting. *In room:* A/C, minibar, coffeemaker, iron/ironing board, safe.

2 Lofthus: Center of the Hardangerfjord

379km (236 miles) W of Oslo; 140km (87 miles) E of Bergen

A favorite spot in the Hardanger district is sleepy Lofthus, once the haunt of Edvard Grieg and other artists. On the fjord, the resort is enveloped by snow-capped mountains, farms, and orchards. Hovering in the background is the Folgefonn Glacier.

Lofthus is actually the collective name for several groups of farms—Helleland, Eidnes, Lofthus, Opedal, Århus, and Ullensvang—extending from north to south along the eastern coastal slopes of Sørfjorden, 6km to 8km (4 miles–5 miles) south of Kinsarvik Bay.

The discovery of a runic stone at Pedal, the oldest and largest group of farms established that the area has been peopled since about A.D. 600. Cistercian monks came to Opedal 7 centuries later and pioneered a fruit-growing industry. Their footpaths are still used and many have benefited from the 616 steps, the Monks' Staircase, that makes its way up the steep gradient to the Vidda.

The church and buildings of Ullensvang lie around the mouth of the Opo River. The Gothic stone Ullensvang church was probably built at the end of the 13th century, and the builders may have been Scottish masons. Although the church has irregular hours, it's usually open during the day from May to mid-September. Ullensvang was the name of the ancient farm where the *prestegård* (church farm) stands facing the church. It is now the name of the church, the hamlet, the parish, and the *kommune* (county), and the site of the most famous hotel in the region (see below).

ESSENTIALS

GETTING THERE   Board the ferry at Kvanndal for Kinsarvik where you can make bus connections south to Lofthus. **Train** connections are possible from Voss, 49km (31 miles) to the east, on the main Bergen-Oslo line. **Bus** service takes 1 hour from Odda in the south, 15 minutes from Kinsarvik in the north. From Bergen you can go by express bus/boat in 2½ hours. **Motorists** can take the E16 east from Bergen to Kvanndal, where you can board a car ferry to Kinsarvik. At Kinsarvik, head south on Route 47 to Lofthus.

VISITOR INFORMATION   The summer-only **Lofthus Tourist Information Office** (© **53-66-11-90**) is open daily from June to August noon to 5pm.

SEEING THE SIGHTS

An El Dorado for nature lovers and fjord fanciers, Lofthus, along with Ulvik (see below), is one of the best centers for taking in the glories of **Hardanger-fjord** ★★★. Your hotel can usually arrange boat trips or else you can go to the tourist office (see above) and see what excursions might be available at the time of your visit.

Flowing in a north and easterly direction, the fjord stretches out for 179km (111 miles). Along the western coast of Norway, the fjord is broad and open but when its "fingers" dig inland into several branches, it often becomes very narrow. The banks of the fjord are a delight in spring. You get not only wild flowers but also lots of blossoming fruit trees along its sloping banks.

The **waterfalls** along both banks are stunning, and reason enough to explore the fjord. When the snows melt in the early spring, the waterfalls that rush down the mountains are at their most powerful.

Motorists can drive along the fjord, taking in its vast panorama. From Skånevik, a small ferry port at the head of Skånevikfjord (a branch of the Hardangerfjord), routes 48, 11, 13, and 7 run for 193km (119 miles) all the way to Northelmsund, the main center of the north side of Hardangerfjord. This road also bypasses Lofthus, as well as Odda, the principal settlement along Hardangerfjord.

You will also be able to take in views of **Folgefonna** , Norway's third largest glacier. It stretches for 37km (22 miles). At its widest point, it measures 16km (10 miles).

WHERE TO STAY

Hotel Ullensvang   Built in 1846, and last renovated in 2002, this romantic inn lies on the edge of the Hardangerfjord. It was a retreat of Edvard Grieg. His piano is still kept in a cottage on the grounds. He came here for the first time in 1878 and returned to spend many a summer, finding inspiration for his music such as "Springtime," "The Hoberg Suite," and the "Peer Gynt Suite."

The hotel was greatly expanded in the 1970s and is now a beautifully equipped structure with a garden opening onto the shoreline with views of the Folgefonna glacier. Run by the Utne family for four generations, it offers rooms ranging from standard to deluxe. All are handsomely furnished and come with well-maintained private bathrooms with combinations of tubs and showers. Scandinavian kings, Emperor Wilhelm II, and European nobility have patronized the hotel. Tours of the surrounding area, including the best beauty spots along Hardangerfjord, can be arranged with local guides.

N-5774 Loftus i Hardanger. (C) **53-67-00-00.** Fax 53-67-00-01. www.hotel-ullensvang.no. 157 units. 1,980NOK ($263) double; from 2,850NOK ($379) suite. Rates include breakfast and dinner. AE, DC, MC, V. Closed Dec 22–30. **Amenities:** Restaurant; bar; heated pool; tennis court; squash court; gym; spa; sauna; rowboats for fjord cruises; sailboats; game room; salon; limited room service; laundry service; solarium. *In room:* TV, minibar, hair dryer.

Ullensvang Gjesteheim *(Finds* This is a cozy, homelike guesthouse in the town center, furnished and run with a personal touch. Bedrooms are comfortably furnished, if a bit old-fashioned, and bathrooms in the corridors are shared and most adequate for the job. The dining room serves a Norwegian *koldboard* (cold board) for breakfast, and also dishes up home-cooked Norwegian specialties at lunch and dinner, including such dishes as filet of reindeer. Lunch and dinner menus range from 95NOK to 165NOK ($13–$22) for a main course.

N-5774 Lofthus i Hardanger. (C) **53-66-12-36.** Fax 53-66-15-19. 17 units, none with bathroom. 650NOK ($86) double. Children under 5 stay free in parent's room. Rates include continental breakfast. MC, V. Closed Dec 23–Jan 1. **Amenities:** Restaurant; bar. *In room:* No phone.

WHERE TO DINE

Restaurant Ullensvang *Value* NORWEGIAN Some of the best fjord country dining is found at this old inn (see previous recommendation). Such famous composers or writers as Edvard Grieg and Bjørnstjerne Bjørnson have sung the praise of these viands. The windows of this three-level restaurant open onto dramatic views of the fjord. Guests flock here for the big buffet spread where you'll find at least 65 dishes, everything from jellied salmon to homemade cakes. Many of the dishes have strong regional flavor, as exemplified by the filet of reindeer or the red deer with a rich game sauce laced with herbs. Fish fanciers gravitate to the flounder or catfish with steamed fresh vegetables. In summer expect those delectable cloudberries that are similar to a yellow raspberry. They can be served as a soufflé or else (and we prefer this) just fresh with cream.

Lofthus i Hardanger. © **53-67-00-00.** Reservations required. Buffet 375NOK ($50); main courses 250NOK ($33) a la carte. AE, DC, MC, V. Daily noon–2:30pm and 7–9:30pm. Closed Dec 22–30.

3 Kinsarvik: Holiday on the Kinso River

119 km (74 miles) E of Bergen; 38km (24 miles) S of Voss; 374km (233 miles) W of Oslo

The main village of **Kinsarvik** stands on a glacier-formed ridge at the mouth of the Kinso River, which flows into four magnificent waterfalls as it drops from the plateau to Husedalen on its way to the sea. Since early times, Kinsarvik has been the marketplace for the region.

Kinsarvik was Hardanger's principal timber port in the 17th and early 18th centuries. When the export of timber was transferred to Bergen in 1750, Kinsarvik developed a shipbuilding industry that continued until 1870, when the village became a center for woodcarving. Today one of its principal manufacturers is a pewter factory.

The plot of grass that slopes to a stony beach near the Kinsarvik ferry terminal is **Skiperstod**, site of a boathouse for naval long ships from about 900 until 1350.

ESSENTIALS

GETTING THERE The **Bergen Railroad** running between Bergen and Oslo will take you to the Voss station, the nearest terminal to Kinsarvik. There are 14 arrivals and departures a day. From Voss, you can journey to Kinsarvik by bus. Trip time from Oslo to Voss is 5½ hours. **Bus** service takes 1¼ hours from Odda, 15 minutes from Lofthus. The bus trip from Bergen takes 2½ hours, and 50 minutes from Voss, the nearest rail connection. **Motorists** can take E16 east from Bergen to Kvanndal, and then board a car ferry to Kinsarvik. **Boats** leaving from Kvanndal on the northern coast of the Hardangerfjord take about 45 minutes.

VISITOR INFORMATION **Turist-Informasjonen** (© **53-66-31-12**), in the village center, is open daily as follows: May 1 to June 20 9am to 5pm, June 21 to August 20 9am to 7pm, August 21 to September 1 9am to 5pm. At other times information is available from the **Kinsarvik Library** (© **53-67-15-77**), also in the village center.

SEEING THE SIGHTS

Kinsarvik Church ★ *Finds* Said to have been constructed by Scottish master builders at the end of the 12th century, this is one of the oldest stone churches in Norway. The interior was restored in 1961 to its pre-Reformation condition. It has a 17th-century pulpit painted by Peter Reimers, a painted and carved altarpiece, and medieval frescoes. The church is constructed in a vaguely Roman style, and chalk paintings on the walls show the "weighing of souls" in judgment by Archangel Michael. The admission-free church is open daily from May to September 15 from 10am to 4pm.

Borstova, the building on the fjord side of the green facing the church, was constructed partly from the timbers of St. Olav's Guildhall, the meeting place of the local guild until 1680. It's now a council chamber and social center.

The stone **column** *(minnestein)* on the green commemorates the local men who fought in the wars that led to the end of Norway's union with Denmark in 1814.

The **Tillegg i Tekst (Hardanger Recreation Park)**, in the middle of Kinsarvik, is open daily mid-May to mid-August. It is an ideal place for a picnic on a summer day. You can pick up picnic supplies from the town's only grocery store, SPAR (✆ 53-66-31-77), which is located in the town center, a 2-minute walk from the Best Western Kinsarvik Fjord Hotel (no street address).

Lying 6.5km (4 miles) from Kinsarvik on Route 13 to Odda, a minor road forks left providing an alternative route to Lofthus. A short distance from the fork leads to the entrance to the **Skredhaugen Museum** (✆ 90-17-41-15), a branch of the Hardanger Folk Museum at Utne. A collection of 10 timber houses gathered from the Hardanger area and furnished according to the period can be viewed. There is also an art gallery of regional works on view. The museum is open June 10 to August 20 Monday to Saturday 11am to 4pm, Sunday noon to 4pm. Admission is 35NOK ($4.65), free for children.

Kinsarvik is also an excellent base for exploring all the attractions of the Hardangerfjord area, including the Hardangervidda mountain plateau. You can rent rowing boats and canoes here to explore the fjord. The tourist office (see above) will tell you how to reach the Nykjesøyfossen waterfall, or else the best viewpoint for taking in the panoramic of the better-known Vøringfossen waterfall. Many sights in Lotthus, Utne, Eidfjord, and Ulvik can also be easily explored from a base at Kinsarvik.

WHERE TO STAY & DINE

Best Western Kinsarvik Fjord Hotel ★   Even though a Best Western chain member, this hotel is still family run, offering personal service and warm fjord hospitality. Built in 1952, it was greatly expanded in 1993 and most recently renovated in 2002. Right by the Hardangerfjord, it's rich in historical interest and is a first-class choice for those seeking the experience of combined fjord and mountain landscapes. It's also one of the best-equipped hotels in the area. Bedrooms are completely modern, some with hardwood floors, others with carpets. Each comes with a newly remodeled bathroom with tub-and-shower combination. Nonguests exploring the area during the day can patronize the hotel's fixed-price lunch for 130NOK ($17) or the dinner buffet of regional fjord specialties for 300NOK ($40). There is live music 7 nights a week in summer.

N-5782 Kinsarvik. ✆ **53-66-31-00.** Fax 53-66-33-74. 70 units. 1,150NOK ($153) double; 1,300NOK ($173) suite. Children under 12 stay free. Rates include continental breakfast. AE, DC, MC, V. Closed Jan. **Amenities:** Restaurant; bar; fitness center; sauna; 24-hr. room service; babysitting; laundry service; dry cleaning. *In room:* TV, coffeemaker (some units), hair dryer.

4 Eidfjord: Western Gateway to Hardangervidda

149km (93 miles) E of Bergen; 336km (209 miles) W of Oslo

At the northern tip of the Hardangerfjord lies the Eidfjord district. Approximately 1,000 people live here, supporting themselves with agriculture, tourism, and cottage industries. The area is a paradise for hikers and home to the continent's largest herd of wild reindeer. Mountain trout with sour cream is a regional food specialty.

ESSENTIALS

GETTING THERE   Take the **train** from Bergen to Voss, where a connecting bus will take you the rest of the way. **Buses** for Eidfjord depart three or four times a day from Voss, taking 1¾ hours. Part of the route across the Eidfjord itself requires a 10-minute ferryboat ride from Ulvik. In summer the ferry departs every 10 minutes, and in winter every 40 minutes. From Odda in the south, **motorists** take Route 47 north; from Geilo in the east, go along Route 7 west. The drive takes an hour.

VISITOR INFORMATION The **Eidfjord Tourist Office** (© 53-67-34-00) lies in the town center and is open June to August daily from 9am to 7pm. There are no street names.

SEEING THE SIGHTS

The county contains nearly one-quarter of the **Hardangervidda National Park** ★★, the largest mountain plateau in Europe, rising 1,000m (3,280 ft.) to 1,200m (3,937 ft.) high, and covering an area of 7,500 sq. km (12,070 sq. miles). The park is home to some 20,000 wild reindeer, the herd supplemented in the summer months by horses, goats, and sheep brought here by local farmers to graze. The park is also home to the southernmost habitats of the snowy owl, the Arctic fox, the lynx, and other creatures from the frozen tundra of the north. The park is also the home of a diverse bird population, ranging from ravens to eagles. Hiking trails carved centuries ago by footpaths of early settlers cut through the mountainous area, leading to a series of more than a dozen tourist huts (log cabins). The local tourist office (see above) will provide maps and more information if you want to go hiking.

Before going on a hike, stop in at the **Hardangervidda Naturscenter** (© 53-55-59-00), Øvre Eidfjord, which shows an informative 20-minute movie and offers geological exhibitions of the park. On site is a restaurant that makes a good luncheon stopover, plus a souvenir shop. It's open in June to August daily from 9am to 8pm. From April to May and in September and October hours are daily 10am to 6pm. Admission is 70NOK ($9.30) for adults, 35NOK ($4.65) for children.

Several canyons, including the renowned **Måbø Valley,** lead down from the Hardangervidda plateau to the fjords. Part of the 1,000-year-old road across Norway, traversing the Måbø Valley, has been restored for hardy hikers. At a point 18km (11 miles) southeast of Eidfjord you'll see the dramatic **Voringfoss Waterfall** ★, dropping 145m (475 ft.). It's reached along Route 7.

About 14km (9 miles) from Kinsarvik en route to Eidfjord, off Route 7, is the **Bu Museum,** Ringøy (© 53-66-69-00). It has three old houses containing furniture and domestic and craft equipment. The basement of an old farmhouse is filled with artifacts dating from the Stone Age to modern times. The museum also has a collection of national costumes from the Hardanger area. It's open June 1 to August 10, daily from 11am to 4pm, and by request the rest of the year. Admission is 50NOK ($6.65) for adults, 30NOK ($4) for seniors and students, and free for children under 12.

Back in the center of Eidfjord, the **Eidfjord Kirke** dates from the 14th century. Built of stone, it can be visited with a guide; ask at the tourist office to make arrangements for you.

(**Fun Fact** Sultry, Tropical Norway

Did you know that some half a billion years ago, Norway was situated south of the equator? You can learn more astonishing facts like this at the Hardangervidda Naturscenter in the Eidfjord district.

You can also make an excursion to a small mountain farm at **Kjeåsen Farm** ⊛, lying 6km (3¾ miles) northeast of Eidfjord. This is one of the most panoramic sites in all the fjord country. If you climb to the top of the mountain, allow 3 hours there and back. The climb is extremely difficult and only recommended for those in Olympic competition physical shape. The farm lies 600m (1,968 ft.) above sea level by the Simafjord.

Numerous lakes and rivers offer good trout fishing, and in two rivers, the Eio and the Bjoreio, as well as in Eidfjord Lake, you can fish for salmon. The local tourist office has rowboats and bicycles for rent.

WHERE TO STAY & DINE

Eidfjord Hotel   Right next door to the Eidfjord bus stop, this hotel was originally built in 1974 to house workers from the Tyssedal Power Station nearby. In 1994 it was converted into this comfortable fjord hotel. Bedrooms have wooden floors and solid, comfortable furnishings, with half of the accommodations opening onto views of the fjord. Each unit comes with a small, shower-only bathroom. On site is a well-run dining room serving quite good Norwegian food, with meals starting at 160NOK ($21).

N-5783 Eidfjord. ℂ **53-66-52-64.** Fax 53-166-52-52-12. 28 units. 890NOK ($118) double. Children under 6 stay free in parent's room. Rates include continental breakfast. DC, MC, V. Closed Jan. **Amenities:** Restaurant; bar; sauna; limited room service. *In room:* TV, no phone.

Fossli Hotel ⊛ *(Finds)*   This local landmark dates from 1891 when it was constructed by Konow Lund, a local farmer. For four generations, members of the Garen family have directed the hotel, which was massively renovated in 1990. Today it offers basic but exceedingly comfortable bedrooms, opening onto views of the Måbø Valley. Many of the rooms are decorated with period pieces from the 1930s to the 1950s. Each comes with a small bathroom with shower. Good-tasting and rather classic Norwegian food such as reindeer and freshly caught trout are served, with meals costing from 175NOK ($23). The staff can arrange hunting and fishing trips along Hardangerfjord.

Vøringsfoss, N-5783 Eidfjord. ℂ **53-66-57-77.** Fax 53-66-50-34. 30 units. 920NOK ($122) double. 460NOK ($61) extra person. Rates include continental breakfast. AE, DC, MC, V. Closed Oct–May 19. **Amenities:** Restaurant; bar; limited room service. *In room:* No phone.

Hotell Voringsfoss ⊛   This hotel, completed in 2001, lies by the fjord in Nedre Eidfjord, close to the bus station. Since 1880 visitors to Eidfjord have been staying in an old hotel that stood on this spot. But it was completely torn down and rebuilt, although an old-fashioned decor remains, with a plentiful use of antiques. Some 40 of the rooms open onto views of the fjord. Most of them are carpeted and quite large. The 40 rooms that open onto the fjord also contain complete tub-and-shower bathrooms, the rest equipped with shower. The dinner buffet here at 195NOK ($26) is the best tasting and best value at the resort. There's entertainment at the piano bar Monday to Saturday.

N-5783 Eidfjord. ℂ **53-67-41-00.** Fax 53-67-41-11. 81 units. 790NOK–1,230NOK ($105–$164) double; 1,500NOK–2,000NOK ($200–$266) suite. Children under 16 stay free. Rates include continental breakfast. AE, DC, MC, V. Closed Jan. **Amenities:** Restaurant; bar; laundry service. *In room:* A/C, TV, minibar.

5 Ulvik: Misty Peaks & Fruity Fjord Farms ⊛

149km (93 miles) E of Bergen

Ulvik is a rarity—an unspoiled resort. It lies like a fist at the end of an arm of the Hardangerfjord, and is surrounded in the summer by misty peaks and fruit farms.

The village's 1858 church is attractively decorated in the style of the region. It's open June to August, daily from 9am to 5pm. Concerts are presented here.

ESSENTIALS

GETTING THERE   If you're not driving, you can reach Ulvik by train or bus from Bergen or Oslo. From either city, take a train to Voss, where you can catch a bus for the 40km (25-mile), 45-minute ride to Ulvik. Buses run from Voss daily, five times in the summer, three in the winter. In Ulvik the bus stops in front of the Ulvik church in the town center. There's no formal bus station.

VISITOR INFORMATION   Contact the **Ulvik Tourist Office,** in the town center (© **56-52-63-60**). It's open May 15 to September 15, Monday to Saturday from 8:30am to 5pm, Sunday 1 to 5pm; September 16 to May 14, Monday to Friday 8:30am to 5pm. The office can arrange excursions, from trips on fjord steamers to bus tours of the Osa mountains.

SEEING THE SIGHTS

A number of do-it-yourself excursions begin at Ulvik; see the tourist office for details. They change seasonally and depend on the weather. You can explore the Eidfjord district, which is the northern tip of the Hardangerfjord and a paradise for hikers. It's home to some 1,000 people and the continent's largest herd of wild reindeer. Mountain trout attract anglers to the area.

The Ulvik area offers some of the best walks in the fjord country. These are part of what is known as the **Kulturlandskapsplan** ★, and are divided into four different walks, including the stone-covered grave mounds at Nesheim and Tunheim, the cotter's farm at Ljonakleiv, and a restored country mill in Nordallen in Osa. The tourist office sells a manual, *Heritage Trails of Ulvik,* outlining details on all these walks evoking ancient times. The same office will provide information about organized walks on Tuesday and Thursday in summer along forests road and into the mountains.

SHOPPING

In the center of Ulvik is the summer-only **Husfidsnovae** (no phone), a small craft shop run by locals who spend their long winter nights concocting arts and handicrafts. For most of them, it's only a hobby; for others, a full-time job as a crafter. You'll find woven tablecloths and tapestries, Hardanger embroidery, knitwear, crocheted tablecloths, beadworks for Hardanger folk costumes, ceramics, woodwork, and silver jewelry—all handmade in Ulvik. Hours are irregular, but give it a try to see if it's open.

WHERE TO STAY & DINE

Rica Brakanes Hotel ★   There's a famous view of the Hardangerfjord and the surrounding forest from this well-recommended hotel. It's near the town center, at the edge of the fjord. The original building, from the 1860s, burned during a World War II bombing raid and was reconstructed in 1952. Today all that remains of the original building is one small dining room. The rest of the hotel is airy, sunny, and comfortable. The guest rooms are small but well maintained, with good beds and sparkling-clean bathrooms with shower-tub combinations. In the summer, plane rides over the fjords can be arranged, and windsurfing and boat rentals are available.

N-5730 Ulvik. © **56-52-61-05.** Fax 56-52-64-10. brakanes.hotel@hl.telia.no. 144 units. 1,470NOK ($196) double; 3,000NOK ($399) suite. Rates include breakfast. AE, DC, MC, V. Free parking. **Amenities:** Restaurant; bar; indoor heated pool; 2 tennis courts; fitness center; sauna. *In room:* TV, minibar.

Ulvik Fjord Pensjonat *(Value*   Ulvik Fjord Pensjonat, constructed in two stages, in 1946 and 1977, is one of the finest guesthouses along the Hardangerfjord. The rooms are spacious and pleasantly furnished in regional Norwegian style. Most units contain well-kept bathrooms with shower-tub combinations. You'll be welcomed by the Hammer family, which won the Norwegian Hospitality Prize in 1989. A sauna and solarium are available for guests' use.

N-5730 Ulvik. ✆ **56-52-61-70.** Fax 56-52-61-60. www.ulvikfjordpensjonat.no. 19 units, 17 with bathroom. 620NOK ($82) double without bathroom; 780NOK ($104) double with bathroom. Rates include breakfast. V. Free parking. Closed Oct–Apr. **Amenities:** Restaurant; bar; lounge. *In room:* Hair dryer.

Ulvik Hotel   Updated in 1996, the guest rooms are modern and comfortable, with good beds and well-maintained bathrooms equipped with shower-tub combinations. More than half the units overlook the fjord. A dining room serves excellent Norwegian food; the shrimp and salmon are the most popular items on the menu. The hotel is on the fjord in the town center.

N-5730 Ulvik. ✆ **56-52-62-00.** Fax 56-52-66-41. 57 units. 860NOK–1,150NOK ($114–$153) double. Rates include breakfast. AE, DC, MC, V. Free parking. **Amenities:** Restaurant; bar; lounge. *In room:* TV.

6 Voss: A Winter Playground ★

38km (24 miles) W of Ulvik; 101km (63 miles) E of Bergen

Between two fjords, Voss is a famous year-round resort, also known for its folklore. It was the birthplace of the American football hero Knute Rockne. Maybe the trolls don't strike fear in the hearts of farm children anymore, but revelers dressed as trolls still appear in costumed folklore programs to give visitors a little fun.

Voss is a natural base for exploring the two largest fjords in Norway, the **Sognefjord** to the north and the **Hardangerfjord** to the south. In and around Voss are glaciers, mountains, fjords, waterfalls, orchards, rivers, and lakes.

ESSENTIALS

GETTING THERE   From Ulvik, take Highway 20 to Route 13; then follow Route 13 northwest to Voss. If you're not driving, there's frequent train service from Bergen (travel time is 1¼ hr.) and Oslo (5½ hr.). There are six daily buses from Bergen (1¾ hr.) and one bus a day from Oslo (9 hr.).

VISITOR INFORMATION   The **Voss Information Center** is at Hestavangen 10 (✆ **56-52-08-00**). It's open June to August, Monday to Saturday from 9am to 7pm, Sunday 2 to 7pm; September to May, Monday to Friday 9am to 4pm.

SEEING THE SIGHTS

St. Olav's Cross, Skulegata, is near the Voss Cinema. It's the oldest historic relic in Voss, believed to have been raised when the townspeople adopted Christianity in 1023.

A ride on the **Hangursbanen cable car** (✆ **56-51-12-12**) will be a memorable part of your visit. It offers panoramic views of Voss and its environs. The mountaintop restaurant serves refreshments and meals. The hardy take the cable car up, and then spend the rest of the afternoon strolling down the mountain. A round-trip ride costs 60NOK ($8) for adults, 40NOK ($5.30) for children 8 to 16, free for children under 8. Entrance to the cable car is on a hillside, a 10-minute walk north of the town center. It's open in summer and winter, but closes during the often gray and rainy months of May and September to December.

Finnesloftet   This is one of the oldest timbered houses in Norway, dating from the mid–13th century. It's located about 1.5km (1 mile) west of Voss and is a 15-minute walk west from the train station.

Finne. ✆ **56-51-16-75.** Admission 20NOK ($2.65) adults, 10NOK ($1.35) children. Tues–Sun 11am–4pm. Closed Aug 16–June 14.

Vangskyrkje   This 1277 church with a timbered tower contains a striking Renaissance pulpit, a stone altar and triptych, fine woodcarvings, and a painted ceiling. It's in the center of Voss, a 5-minute walk east from the train station. Call in advance if you would like to reserve an English-speaking guide.

Vangsgata 3. ✆ **56-51-22-78.** Admission 15NOK ($2) adults, free for children under 17. Daily 10am–4pm. Closed Sept–May.

Voss Folkemuseum   Almost a kilometer north of Voss on a hillside overlooking the town, this museum consists of more than a dozen farmhouses and other buildings dating from the 1500s to around 1870. They were not moved here, but were built on this site by two farm families.

Mølster. ✆ **56-51-15-11.** Admission 35NOK ($4.65) adults, free for children. May–Sept daily 10am–5pm; Oct–Apr Mon–Sat 10am–3pm, Sun noon–3pm.

SKIING

Voss continually adds to its facilities, and is definitely in the race to overtake Geilo and Lillehammer as Norway's most popular winter playground. Its chair lifts, ski lifts, and aerial cableway carry passengers up 788m (2,625 ft.).

The town offers what it calls a "ski circus." Beginners take the Hangursbanen cable car; one ski lift (900m/3,000 ft. long) goes from Traastolen to the top of Slettafjell (with a wide choice of downhill runs); the Bavallen lift is for the slalom slopes; and the downhill runs are at Lonehorgi.

Lessons at the **Ski School** (✆ **56-51-00-32** in winter, or 56-51-34-36 in summer), at the end of the cable-car run, are moderately priced. The tourist office and hotels can arrange bookings. All equipment is available for rent.

Children over 7 are allowed on the slopes. A special branch of the Ski School handles these youngsters. Baby-sitting is available for children under 7.

OTHER OUTDOOR PURSUITS

This is Valhalla for fishermen, as there are some 500 lakes and rivers in the greater vicinity of Voss. A local fishing license, costing 50NOK ($6.65), is available at the post office or the tourist office. You can catch trout and char with only local tackle. Fishing guides can be booked through the tourist office.

Mountain hikes are possible in all directions. Ask at the tourist office about how you hook up with the **Bulken Walking Association,** which sponsors "The Voss Trip" from April to October, a 14km (8½ mile) long, marked walking track, costing 15NOK ($2) per person.

Voss also offers the best paragliding in Norway, with flights conducted daily in summer from 11am to 5pm, costing 700NOK ($93) per person. The starting point is the **Voss Adventer Senter** (✆ **56-51-36-30**), in the center of town.

Parasailing, water-skiing, and banana boating are possible at the Vangsvatnet, in front of the Park Hotel Vossevangen. The season is from May to October. Parasailing costs 450NOK ($60), water-skiing 200NOK ($27), and banana boating 700NOK ($93). For information, call **Parasailing Voss** (✆ **56-51-03-21**).

River sports are big, and there is a number of outfitters, mainly the **Voss Rafting Center** (✆ **56-51-00-17**), offering not only rafting, but canyoning and river-boarding as well, at prices beginning at 500NOK ($67) per person. Their base is near the Park Hotel, a 3-minute walk from the rail station. The season goes from May 1 to October 1. Other outfitters include **Voss Ski & Surf** (© **56-51-30-43**), featuring river kayaking for both neophytes and more skilled kayakers, and **Nordic Ventures** (© **56-51-00-17**), offering guided sea kayaking through the Sognefjord, past waterfalls and mountain scenery.

WHERE TO STAY
MODERATE
Fleischers Hotel ★ On the lakefront beside the Voss train station, Fleischers Hotel couldn't be more convenient. The gracious 1889 frame hotel has a modern wing with 30 units, all with private showers, toilets, and terraces overlooking the lake. In the older part of the hotel, the rooms are old-fashioned and more spacious. The restaurant serves an a la carte menu; main courses cost 145NOK to 235NOK ($19–$31). In the summer, a buffet is served for 325NOK ($43).

Evangerveiten 13, N-5700 Voss. © **56-52-05-00.** Fax 56-52-05-01. www.fleischers.no. 90 units. 1,350NOK ($180) double; 1,600NOK ($213) suite. Rates include breakfast. AE, DC, MC, V. Free parking. **Amenities:** Restaurant; bar; lounge; indoor heated pool; sauna; limited room service; babysitting; laundry service; dry cleaning. *In room:* TV, minibar.

Hotel Jarl In this centrally located hotel are comfortably modern singles, doubles, and suites. Guest rooms and bathrooms are a bit small, but the beds are firm. The bathrooms are also a bit cramped but are neatly kept and equipped with shower-tub combinations. Built in 1972, the hotel was enlarged and renovated in 1996. You can take your meals in the pleasant dining room or the intimate bistro and bar.

Voss Sentrum, N-5700 Voss. © **54-51-99-00.** Fax 56-51-37-69. 78 units. 995NOK ($132) double. Rates include breakfast. AE, DC, MC, V. Free parking. **Amenities:** Restaurant; bar; nightclub; indoor heated pool; sauna. *In room:* TV, minibar, safe.

Park Hotel Vossevangen The product of a 1990 merger, this hotel consists of two sections (originally the Park Hotel and the Vossevangen Hotel), joined by a covered passageway. The guest rooms are attractively furnished and contain well-kept bathrooms with shower-tub combinations. The hotel is family-owned and houses the best restaurant in town, the Elysée (see "Where to Dine," below). Facilities include the Café Stationen, the Pentagon Dance Bar, the Stallen Pub, and the Pianissimo Bar. It's in the town center, about 90m (100 yards) from the train station.

Uttrågate, N-5701 Voss. © **56-51-13-22.** Fax 56-51-00-39. 131 units. 1,150NOK–1,590NOK ($153–$211) double. Rates include breakfast. AE, DC, MC, V. Free parking. **Amenities:** Restaurant; bar; lounge; babysitting. *In room:* TV, minibar.

INEXPENSIVE
Kringsjå Pension This pleasant three-story guesthouse is in the center of Voss; some parts were built in the 1930s, others much more recently. The public rooms are spacious and airy, and the guest rooms are simply, comfortably furnished, with good beds but small bathrooms with shower-tub combinations. Breakfast is served daily, and other meals are sometimes available. The hall bathrooms are well maintained and are also equipped with shower-tub combinations.

Strengjarhaujen 6, N-5700 Voss. © **56-51-16-27.** Fax 56-51-63-30. www.kringsja.no. 18 units, 14 with bathroom. 600NOK ($80) double without bathroom; 750NOK ($100) double with bathroom. Rates include breakfast. AE, DC, MC, V. Free parking. **Amenities:** Lounge. *In room:* No phone.

Nøring Pensjonat   The Nøring is a first-class pension built in 1949 near the river, about a 10-minute walk from the town center. It provides clean, functional accommodations, which are small but comfortable, with well-kept bathrooms with shower units. Half of the rooms face the mountains. The boarding house serves good, hearty breakfasts, plus light meals (with beer or wine) at lunch and dinner. The lounge opens onto a terrace.

Uttrågate 41, N-5700 Voss. ℂ 56-51-12-11. Fax 56-51-12-23. 20 units, 9 with bathroom. 600NOK ($80) double without bathroom; 790NOK ($105) double with bathroom. Rates include breakfast. AE, DC, MC, V. Free parking. **Amenities:** Restaurant; bar; lounge. *In room:* No phone.

WHERE TO DINE
MODERATE

Elysée FRENCH/NORWEGIAN   The decor of this prestigious restaurant includes trompe-l'oeil murals based on a modern interpretation of the Parthenon. It features such dishes as baked sea scorpion, filet of lamb marinated in honey, and a daily game dish. Homemade ice cream with berries and vanilla sauce makes a smooth dessert. The food here is satisfying and based on fresh ingredients. You leave feeling you've had an adequate meal, substantial and hearty. There's an extensive wine list.

In the Park Hotel Vossevangen, Uttrågate. ℂ **56-51-13-22.** Reservations recommended. Main courses 185NOK–255NOK ($25–$34); lunch smorgasbord 275NOK ($37); fixed-price dinner 350NOK ($47). AE, DC, MC, V. Sun–Thurs 1–10:30pm; Fri–Sat 1–11pm.

Fleischers Restaurant ⚜ NORWEGIAN   The dining room of this landmark hotel, a few steps from the Voss train station, hasn't been altered since the hotel opened over a century ago. Long the leading restaurant in the Voss area, the Victorian-style Fleischers remains the traditionalists' favorite. Its lunchtime smorgasbord is a lavish array of all-you-can-eat Norwegian delicacies. Specialties include smoked salmon and filet of beef, lamb, pork, and veal. This is authentic cuisine that would have pleased Ibsen—a real "taste of Norway." What you don't get is dash and culinary sophistication.

Evangerveiten 13. ℂ **56-52-05-00.** Reservations recommended. Lunch smorgasbord 195NOK ($26); main courses 160NOK–255NOK ($21–$34); summer buffet 325NOK ($43). AE, DC, MC, V. Mon–Sat 1–10:30pm; Sun 1–9:45pm.

INEXPENSIVE

Vangen Café NORWEGIAN   The least expensive cafeteria-style outlet in Voss is one floor above street level over a small souvenir shop and food market. It's in the center of town, a 5-minute walk south of the train station. Soft drinks and fruit juices are sold, but no alcohol. The *dagens menu* ("today's menu") is the best food value in town.

Vangen Super-Market, Vangsgata. ℂ **56-51-12-05.** Smorgasbord 35NOK–42NOK ($4.65–$5.60); *dagens menu* (daily specials) 85NOK–125NOK ($11–$17). No credit cards. Mon–Fri 10:30am–6pm; Sat 10:30am–4pm; Sun noon–6pm.

VOSS AFTER DARK

Fleischers Top Spot Nightclub   In the cellar of Fleischers Hotel (see "Where to Stay," above) you'll find this well-established nightspot. Dance bands play nightly for an older crowd that's dressed up a bit. Many people come here just to drink—beer costs 53NOK ($7.05). The club is open Monday to Thursday from 9:30pm to 1am, Friday and Saturday until 3am. In Fleischers Hotel, Evangerveiten 13. ℂ **56-52-05-00.** Fri–Sat cover 60NOK ($8); no cover for hotel guests.

7 Balestrand: Center for Sognefjord /★/★

90km (56 miles) N of Voss; 219km (136 miles) NE of Bergen; 204km (126 miles) SW of Fjaerland

Long known for its arts and crafts, Balestrand lies on the northern rim of the Sognefjord, at the junction of the Vetlefjord, the Esefjord, and the Fjaerlandsfjord.

When Esias Tegnèr wrote of the snow-covered mountains and the panoramic Sognefjord in the saga of Fridtjof the Brave, the book sold widely and sent an array of artists to the area in the mid–19th century.

Soon Hans Gude, Hans Dahl, Johannes Flintoe, and other well-known Scandinavian artists were painting the fjord and mountain landscapes. Their art became so popular that regular visitors started to flock to Balestrand to take in the glories of the area for themselves—and so they have continued to this day.

ESSENTIALS

GETTING THERE   From Voss, continue driving north on Route 13 to Vangsnes and board a car ferry for the short crossing northwest to Balestrand. You can also take a train from Bergen or Oslo to Voss or Flåm, and then make bus and ferry connections north to Balestrand. Bus and ferry schedules are available at the Voss tourist office (𝄞 **56-52-08-00**) and the Flåm tourist office (𝄞 **57-63-21-06**). From Bergen there are daily express boats to Balestrand; the trip takes 3½ hours.

VISITOR INFORMATION   The **Tourist Office** (𝄞 57-69-16-17 in winter, or 57-69-12-55 in summer) is in the town center. From June to August, it's open daily from 8:30am to 10pm; May and September, daily 9am to 8pm; October to April, Monday to Saturday 9am to 4pm.

SEEING THE SIGHTS

The staff at the tourist office can help you plan a tour of the area and put you in touch with local craftspeople. Pick up a list of excursions and buy tickets for one of the scheduled 1½-day tours—for example, a taxi plane across the **Jostedal Glacier.**

Kaiser Wilhelm II, a frequent visitor to Balestrand, presented the district with two statues of Old Norse heroes, King Bele and Fridtjof the Bold. They stand in the center of town. Another sight is the English church of **St. Olav,** a tiny wooden building that dates from 1897. The church is closed to the public, but its construction can be admired.

You can explore the area by setting out in nearly any direction on scenic country lanes with little traffic or a wide choice of marked trails and upland farm tracks. The tourist office sells a touring map. There's good sea fishing, as well as lake and river trout fishing. Fishing tackle, rowboats, and bicycles can all be rented in the area.

Back in Balestrand, near the ferry dock, you can visit the **Sognefjord Aquarium** (𝄞 57-69-13-03), with its exhibition of saltwater fish. Especially interesting is the marine life from the world's deepest fjord. The cast of denizens of the deep include Esefjord herring "lip fish," eels, and sharks. The exhibition consists of a number of large and small aquaria, both indoors and out on the jetty. The marine environments have been authentically recreated, including the tidal belt at Munken, the sandy seabed around Staken. A man-made model of Sognefjord shows the currents of the fjord and provides an impression of its depth. There is also an audiovisual presentation. The admission of 25NOK ($3.35) includes an hour of canoeing on the fjord. It's open from mid-April to May and

---

Fun Fact   **A Boot for the Kaiser**

Kaiser Wilhelm II of Germany was on holiday in the village of Balestrand, visiting a friend, when World War I broke out. Norwegian authorities gave the Kaiser an ultimatum to leave their territory by 6pm that very day. Not being a man to have his pleasures cut short, Kaiser Wilhelm took his jolly good time drinking his tea and savoring impressions of the surrounding landscape before heading full steam out the fjord aboard his yacht, minutes before the deadline expired.

---

mid-August to October daily from 10am to 4pm; June to mid-August daily 9:30am to 6pm.

EXCURSIONS ON THE SOGNEFJORD ★★★

The reason most visitors base in Balestrand is to explore the mighty **Sognefjord,** one of the greatest and most impressive—also one of the deepest—in the world, stretching for a total length of 205km (127 miles). It spreads its powerful "fjord fingers" as far as Jostedalsbreen, the country's largest glacier, and to Jotunheimen, Norway's tallest mountain range. Its greatest depth is 1,308m (4,291 ft.). The widest and most dramatic part of the fjord stretches from the coast to Balestrand. After Balestrand the fjord grows much narrower.

If you have a choice, opt for a late spring visit when thousands upon thousands of fruit trees can be seen in full bloom along both banks of the Sognefjord. The entire district is ideal for skiing, sailing, mountain hiking, and other outdoor activities.

The best way to see the fjord is to take a boat from Bergen operated by Fykesbaatane (✆ **55-90-70-70**). Balestrand is a stopover on the Bergen-to-Flåm line, with departures from Bergen leaving once a day, taking 5½ hours and costing 550NOK ($73) per person.

WHERE TO STAY & DINE

Dragsvik Fjord Hotel   Almost a kilometer from Balestrand and 270m (300 yards) from the ferry quay at Dragsvik, this hotel is a bargain. Doubles in the new wing have the most up-to-date plumbing. The units are comfortable, though small. They're well maintained, but bathrooms equipped with shower-tub combinations are tiny. The large dining room offers a panoramic view of the Fjaerlandsfjord. You can rent bicycles, rowboats, and motorboats.

Dragsvik, N-6899 Balestrand. ✆ **57-69-12-93.** Fax 57-69-13-83. www.dragsvik.no. 19 units. Feb–May and Sept–Oct 730NOK ($97) double; June–Aug 785NOK ($104) double. Rates include breakfast. AE, MC, V. Free parking. Closed Nov–Jan. **Amenities:** Restaurant; bar; limited room service. *In room:* Hair dryer.

Kviknes Hotel ★★   Built in 1913 as a summer retreat for Europeans, this hotel was much enlarged in 1970. At its core it's an elaborately detailed building with balconies opening onto the edge of the fjord. All but a few of the guest rooms have fjord views. They vary widely in size and style. The most popular units are those in the original structure, with old-fashioned Norwegian style, flowery fabrics, good beds, and spacious bathrooms with shower-tub combinations. Some of these accommodations are furnished with antiques. The less personal rooms are in the annex, where bland Nordic style prevails. Bathrooms tend to be very small. Many of the accommodations are set aside for nonsmokers, and others are wheelchair accessible. The hotel has a large dining room, several lounges, and a dance club.

An extensive buffet is served every night; lunches are less elaborate, with brasserie-style meals. Sports such as water-skiing, windsurfing, and fjord fishing can be arranged, as can helicopter flights to the Jostedal Glacier.

Balholm, N-6898 Balestrand. © **57-69-42-00.** Fax 57-69-42-01. www.kviknes.no. 210 units. 1,360NOK ($181) double; 1,560NOK ($207) suite. Rates include breakfast. AE, DC, MC, V. Free parking. Closed Oct–Apr. **Amenities:** Restaurant; bar; fitness center; Jacuzzi; sauna; 24-hr. room service; babysitting; laundry service; dry cleaning. *In room:* TV, hair dryer.

8 Flåm: Stopover on Europe's Most Scenic Train Ride ⓐ

96km (60 miles) SE of Balestrand; 165km (103 miles) E of Bergen; 131km (81 miles) E of Voss

Flåm (pronounced "Flawm") lies on the Aurlandsfjord, a tip of the more famous Sognefjord. In the village you can visit the old church (1667), with painted walls done in typical Norwegian country style.

ESSENTIALS

GETTING THERE   By **car** from Balestrand, take Route 55 east along the Sognefjord, crossing the fjord by ferry at Dragsvik and by bridge at Sogndal. At Sogndal, drive east to Kaupanger, where you'll cross the Ardalsfjord by ferry, and head south to Revsnes. In Revsnes, pick up Route 11 heading southeast. Drive east until you connect with a secondary road heading southwest through Kvigno and Aurland. From Aurland, take Route 601 southwest to Flåm. The whole trip takes 2 to 3 hours, depending on weather and road conditions.

The best and most exciting approach to Flåm is aboard the **electric train from Myrdal** ⭐⭐⭐, which connects with trains from Bergen and Oslo. There are no railway lines of the adhesion type anywhere in the world steeper than the Flåm Railway. The gradient is 55/1,000 on almost 80% of the line (i.e., a gradient of 1 in 18). The twisting tunnels that spiral in and out of the mountain are manifestations of the most daring and skillful engineering in Norwegian railway history. The electric train follows a 19km (12-mile) route overlooking an 883m (2,900-ft.) drop, stopping occasionally for passengers to photograph spectacular waterfalls. The trip takes 50 minutes. In winter about four or five trains a day make the run to Flåm. In summer, depending on business, service begins at 7:40am and runs throughout the day. Tickets must be purchased in advance. The one-way fare from Myrdal to Flåm is 125NOK ($17).

Bus travel is less convenient. One **bus** a day Monday to Saturday runs between Aurland and Flåm. The trip takes 30 minutes.

From May to September, two **ferries** per day cross the fjord between Aurland and Flåm. The trip takes 30 minutes.

Flåm can also be reached by high-speed **express boats** from Bergen, Balestrand (see above), and Leikanger. The boats carry passengers only. In Bergen, call **Fylkesbaatane** (© **55-90-70-70**); the one-way trip costs 550NOK ($73).

VISITOR INFORMATION   The **tourist office** (© **57-63-21-06**) is near the railroad station. It's open May to September, daily from 8:30am to 8:30pm.

SEEING THE SIGHTS

Flåm is an excellent starting point for car or boat excursions to other well-known centers on the **Sognefjord,** Europe's longest and deepest fjord. Worth exploring are two of the wildest and most beautiful fingers of the Sognefjord: the Nærøyfjord and the Aurlandfjord. Ask at the tourist office about a summer-only cruise from Flåm to both fjords. From Flåm by boat, you can disembark in Gudvangen or Aurland and continue by bus. Alternatively, you can return to Flåm by train.

There are also a number of easy walks in the Flåm district. A map with detailed information is available from the tourist office.

SHOPPING

One of the biggest gift shops in Norway, attracting mainly train passengers, is **Saga Souvenirs** (✆ 57-63-22-44). Here you'll find all those regional products visitors like to haul away from Norway and take back home. There's an excellent selection of knitwear, along with jewelry and the inevitable trolls.

WHERE TO STAY & DINE

Fretheim Hotel ★★★   A gem of a hotel, this is one of the most charming of all the fjord hotels of western Norway, with a pedigree dating from 1866. A modern annex was added in 2002, although the original and cohesive allure of the place remains. We'd stop over here to patronize the bar, if nothing else, as it opens onto a panoramic vista of the fjord waters. The location is just 50m (164 ft.) from the railway station. Long renowned for its hospitality—even King Harald has dropped in—it continues to maintain its high standards.

The staff is most helpful in planning fjord cruises or else horseback riding in the area. Rooms are decorated in light colors and range from small to midsize; try, if possible, to get an accommodation with a balcony opening onto the fjord. All units contain bathrooms with tub-and-shower combinations. Even if you're a nonguest consider stopping off to patronize their excellent restaurant, with salmon, of course, being the chef's specialty. Price ranges from 85NOK to 185NOK ($11–$25), but the real deal is the 295NOK ($39) buffet dinner. Live music will entertain you in the bar.

N-5743 Flåm. ✆ **57-63-63-00**. Fax 57-63-64-00. www.Fretheim-hotel.no. 138 units. 1,390NOK ($185) double; 3,980NOK ($529) suite. Children under 6 stay free in parent's room. Rates include continental breakfast. AE, DC, MC, V. Closed Oct 1–Apr 25. **Amenities:** Restaurant; bar; limited room service; laundry service; dry cleaning. *In room:* TV, hair dryer, safe.

Heimly Pension *Value*   At the edge of the fjord, this simple lodge was built in the 1950s as a family-run pension. It later housed the clients of a nearby ski school. Designed in the style of an A-frame chalet, it offers a ground-floor lounge, guest rooms with bathrooms equipped with shower units and views over the fjord on the two upper floors, and a separate pub and restaurant in an annex across the road.

N-5743 Flåm. ✆ **57-63-23-00**. Fax 57-63-23-40. www.heimly.no. 26 units. 690NOK–880NOK ($92–$117) double. Rates include breakfast. AE, DC, MC, V. Free parking. Closed Dec 24–Jan 2. **Amenities:** Restaurant; bar. *In room:* No phone.

9 Geilo: Summer & Winter Fun ★

109km (68 miles) SE of Flåm; 239km (149 miles) E of Bergen; 239km (149 miles) W of Oslo

One of Norway's best-known ski resorts is also an attractive summer resort. Geilo lies some 792m (2,600 ft.) above sea level in the Hol mountain district. Although it's not strictly in the fjord country, it's included here because it's a "gateway" there en route from Oslo to Bergen.

The Geilo area boasts 130km (81 miles) of marked cross-country skiing tracks.

ESSENTIALS

GETTING THERE   From Flåm, motorists return to Aurland to connect with Route 50. It runs southeast through the towns of Steine, Storestølen, Hovet, and Hagafoss. In Hagafoss, connect with Route 7 going southwest into Geilo. If you're dependent on public transportation, forget about the meager long-distance bus service and opt for the train connections via Oslo or Bergen. From Oslo, the fare is 385NOK ($51) per person one-way, the trip taking 3½ hours; and from Bergen, 350NOK ($47) one-way, taking 3 hours.

VISITOR INFORMATION   The **Turistinformasjonen** office is at Vesleslåtteveien 13 in the town center (© **32-09-59-00**). It's open June to August, daily from 9am to 9pm; September to May, Monday to Friday 8:30am to 5pm, Saturday 8:30am to 3pm. The town doesn't use street addresses, but everything is easy to find.

OUTDOOR ACTIVITIES

Geilo is both a summer and a winter destination, although its claim to fame is as a skiing resort, the main season lasting from January to March. If you plan on doing a lot of skiing, it's best to purchase the **Vinterlandkoret Ski Pass** at the tourist office. This pass, costing 220NOK ($29) per day or 900NOK ($120) per week, is good for all five ski centers in the area as well as the network of slopes in such nearby resorts as Ål, Uvdal, and Hemesdal.

For such a small resort, Geilo boasts a surprising array of five different ski centers. Our most preferred is **Geilo Skiheiser** (© **32-09-59-20**), with 24km (15 miles) of slopes, many as good as those in the Swiss Alps, plus 130km (81 miles) of cross-country trails along with 18 lifts and a "ski-board" tunnel.

The favorite area for families is **Vestlia** (© **32-09-55-10**), west of Ustedalsfjord. Other ski centers are found at **Havsdalsenternet** (© **32-09-17-77**), which Norwegian young people have adopted as their favorite; **Sloatta** (© **32-09-02-02**), with its wide range of alpine and cross-country trails (though not as good as those of Geilo Skiheiser above); and, finally, **Halstensgård** (© **32-09-10-20**), which we suggest you skip unless you're here for a long time and want to ski every trail.

In all, Geilo, Norway's most popular winter resort, offers 18 lifts and 33 runs. All the ski centers are linked by a free shuttle bus service. Cross-country skiers will find a total of 220km (137 miles) of marked trails through forests, hills and moors to **Hardangervidda,** Europe's largest mountain plateau (see "Eidfjord: Western Gateway to Hardangervidda," earlier in this chapter.)

In summer, mountain tracking is the passion. Some of the greatest hikes in central Norway are open to you, and the Geilo tourist office is most helpful in offering expert guidance and furnishing maps. There is a network of marked routes and pathways established since ancient days. When you get tired of hiking, you can always take up canoeing, cycling, or horseback riding.

Geilo cable cars take you to the top of the resort at 1,060m (3,477 ft.) above sea level. From that vantage point, marked trails split off in many directions.

To go rafting and canoeing, call **Dagali Rafting** (© **32-09-38-20**), which organizes trips in the Dagali and Sjoa areas around Geilo. Depending on the day of the week, trips begin at 250NOK ($33), going up to 700NOK ($93). On your own, you can rent canoes and rowboats at **Geilo Camping,** Geilo Aktiv (© **32-09-47-25**).

For horseback riding, call **Hakkesetstølen** (© **32-09-09-20**). You can ride the happy trails from June to October.

To go biking in the area stop by first at the Geilo tourist office for a cycling map. On your rented bike, you can set out to explore summer roads leading into the surrounding mountains. Bikes can be rented in the center of Geilo at **Intersport Geilo** (© **32-09-09-70**), costing 100NOK to 200NOK ($13–$27) per day.

Fishermen flock here to try their luck in the region's nearly 100 mountain lakes or stretches of river, which can be fished from June to September. A fishing license costing 45NOK ($6) is available at the tourist office, and fishing boat rentals and tackle are available for rent through **Geilo Camping** (© **32-09-07-33**), costing 120NOK ($16) per day.

SEEING THE SIGHTS

The most exciting possibility is to book an organized tour at the tourist office for glacier trekking on **Hardangerjøkulen** at 1,860m (6,102 ft.). These are available Monday, Wednesday and Friday from July 1 to September 15. The tour takes 10 hours and costs 530NOK ($70) per person, including a train ride to and from Finse.

A number of other tours are offered as well: rafting from 650NOK to 750NOK ($86–$100), river boarding (a new high-adrenaline sport involving a white-water trip downstream on a high-impact plastic board-cum-floatation device) from 650NOK to 750NOK ($86–$100), and a 2-hour moose safari for 350NOK ($47). This latter jaunt is offered only on Thursday evening (when the moose can be seen) from July 1 to September 15.

Back in the center of town, but only in July, you can visit **Geilojorget,** a 17th-century farm, which is open daily from 11am to 5pm. Some old houses, 2 or 3 centuries old, have been moved to the site and are open for guided tours. You can see how farmers lived at the time and visit such buildings as a storage house or the cattle barn. Cultural activities are also presented at the time, including folk music shows. On site is a cafe serving old-time dishes. Ever had a sour cream cookie?

WHERE TO STAY
VERY EXPENSIVE

Dr. Holms Hotel ★★★   One of the most famous resort hotels in Norway, this is the finest place to stay in the area. Here, near the railroad station, you get elegance, comfort, and traditional styling. Dr. J. C. Holms opened the hotel in 1909, and there have been many changes since, including the addition of two wings and a swimming complex. The most recent face-lift took place in 1999. Original works of art decorate the hotel. Guest rooms are beautifully furnished in traditional style and offer many luxuries including good beds, and well-kept bathrooms with shower-tub combinations.

N-3580 Geilo. © **32-09-57-00.** Fax 32-09-16-20. www.drholms.com. 127 units. May–Aug 1,015NOK ($135) double; Sept–Apr 1,520NOK ($202) double; year-round 1,790NOK–2,270NOK ($238–$302) suite. Rates include breakfast. Rates may be higher during Christmas and New Year's. AE, DC, MC, V. Free parking. **Amenities:** Restaurant; bar; indoor heated pool; fitness center; sauna; limited room service; babysitting; laundry service; dry cleaning; library. *In room:* TV, minibar.

MODERATE

Bardøla Hoyfjellshotel   In tranquil surroundings over a kilometer east of the train station lies this well-run hotel. Built in the 1930s, it's been expanded and renovated many times. It attracts many guests in summer and winter, partly because it has a higher proportion of suites than any other hotel in the region. Each year the hotel renovates five rooms and five suites. Many of the traditionally styled guest rooms are generous in size. All have ample bathrooms with shower-tub combinations.

N-3580 Geilo. © **32-09-04-00.** Fax 32-09-45-01. www.bardoela.no. 128 units. May–Aug 920NOK ($122) double (rates include breakfast); Sept–Apr 1,280NOK–1,350NOK ($170–$180) double (rates include half-board); year-round 500NOK ($67) supplement for suite. Rates higher during Christmas and New Year's. AE, DC, MC, V. Free parking. **Amenities:** Restaurant; bar; indoor and outdoor pools; 2 outdoor tennis courts; fitness center; sauna; limited room service. *In room:* TV, minibar, hair dryer.

Hotel Vestlia   This isn't a fancy hotel, but it keeps guests coming back. It's almost a kilometer east of the train station, 180m (200 yards) from the ski lifts and cross-country slopes. Built in the 1960s, the hotel was completely renovated in the early 1990s, with all the bathrooms equipped with shower-tub combinations renewed in 1999. The regular guest rooms are furnished in an attractive ski-chalet style with lots of wood; some large family rooms, with four beds, cost the same as regular rooms. About half the accommodations are in comfortable annexes scattered about the grounds. In addition to its obvious allure to skiers, the hotel is a good summer choice—guests can go hiking, boating, or horseback riding. Live dance music is provided almost every evening year-round except Sunday.

N-3580 Geilo. ⓒ **32-09-06-11.** Fax 32-08-72-01. 75 units. May–Aug 1,500NOK ($200) double; Sept–Apr 1,800NOK–2,400NOK ($239–$319) double. Rates include half-board. AE, DC, MC, V. Free parking. **Amenities:** 3 restaurants; bar; indoor heated pool; fitness center; sauna; babysitting; laundry service; dry cleaning. *In room:* TV, minibar.

WHERE TO DINE
Most visitors to Geilo eat in their hotels.

Hallingstuene   ★★★   NORWEGIAN/INTERNATIONAL   Set within a red-painted, antique house near the railway station, this is the most elegant restaurant in Geilo. It's also the most famous, thanks to its chef/owner, Frode Aga, who appears frequently on Norwegian television. You'll dine surrounding by dozens of old-fashioned landscapes in an atmosphere evocative of a mountain cottage in a Norwegian forest. Menu items manage to be simultaneously elegant and rustic, many of them composed from locally available ingredients. Examples include grilled mountain trout; carpaccio of reindeer; and an old-fashioned starter, *rake fiske,* which consists of boiled mountain trout that's marinated (or preserved) for 3 months in a mixture of salt brine and sugar. Main courses include a pungent version of grilled filets of either venison or reindeer, served in a wine-flavored game sauce, with forest mushrooms. Dessert might be boiled and sweetened cloudberries with vanilla ice cream.

Geiloveien 56. ⓒ **32-09-12-50.** Reservations recommended. Main courses 220NOK–280NOK ($29–$37). AE, DC,MC, V. Tues–Sun 5–10pm (until 11pm Sat).

Ro Kro *Value* NORWEGIAN   This cafeteria is one of the most affordable restaurants in town. Daily offerings include salads, sandwiches, pastas, stews, and grills. Unlike many cafeterias in Norway, this one maintains a full bar and a selection of beers.

In the Ro Hotell, Geiloveien. ⓒ **32-09-08-99.** Reservations not accepted. Main courses 60NOK–125NOK ($8–$17). AE, DC, MC, V. Daily 9am to 8 or 10pm, depending on business.

10 Fjaerland: Artists & Mountaineers ★★
62km (37 miles) S of Olden

Without road connections until 1986, Fjaerland lies along the banks of the Fjaerlandsfjord, a scenic branch of the greater Sognefjord. Its population of 300 hearty souls hasn't changed considerably since the Viking age. Many of its most stouthearted citizens emigrated to America at the turn of the 19th century.

The center of the Fjaerland is a section called Mundal, with a church, school, shops, and accommodations. Its population, incidentally, is the most well read in Scandinavia, and its secondhand bookshops are legendary. Book lovers from all over the world come here to peruse its shops, as Fjaerland is called "The Book town of Norway."

The landscape shaped by glaciers through various ice ages over the past three million years and the towering mountains, glacier rivers, and U-shaped valleys have attracted landscape painters from all over the world.

Mountaineers find the terrain some of the most challenging in Norway, as both the Supphelle Glacier and the Bøya Glacier come down to the floor of the valley in Fjaerland. Both of these glaciers are "pups," the term for chunks of ice that fall from a massive glacier, in this case, Jostedalsbreen, the largest on the European continent. The lower Supphelle, at an elevation of 60m (196 ft.) is the lowest lying glacier in southern Norway.

ESSENTIALS

GETTING THERE   From the resort of Balestrand (see earlier) ferries depart from Fjaerland at 8:15am daily. Several buses run daily between Fjaerland and the transportation hub at Sogndal, taking 45 minutes and costing 80NOK ($11) one-way. Daily buses also run to and from Stryn (see below), taking 2 hours and costing 175NOK ($23) one-way. Motorists from Olden can take E39, following the signposts to Skei, a village at the base of Lake Jølster. There the road goes under the glacier for more than 6km (4 miles) for the final lap into Fjaerland. The tunnel on the Skei road is free; however, if you're driving from Sognal expect to pay a toll of 150NOK ($20).

VISITOR INFORMATION   The **Fjaerland Tourist Information Center** (© **57-69-32-33**) lies on the main road in Mundal and is open daily at 9am to 5pm June to August. It also doubles as a bookshop.

SEEING THE SIGHTS

This is great hiking country in summer, as parts of Fjaerland lie within the **Jostedalsbreen Nasjonalpark (Jostedalsbreen National Park)** ★★★, a landscape that ranges from mountains to glaciers, from fjords to low-lying valleys. One of the most frequented and scenic routes at the southern tier of the park lies between Lunde and Fjaerland, crossing Marabreen.

At the head of the fjord lies the **Bøyaøyri Estuary** ★, a protected nature reserve, lying 2km (1¼ miles) north of the village. In the spring and fall migrations, some 90 species of birds can be spotted passing through the area. Some 50 species make their nests at Fjaerland so birdies from all over Scandinavia flock here.

The best trail for the average visitor in good physical condition is from the Supphelle Valley up to the mountain hut Flatbrehytta. The more adventurous go on from this mountain hut to explore the glaciers. The local sports association in Fjaerland has mapped out 10 other trails, ranging from a relatively easy 1-hour walk to more difficult treks of 5 to 6 hours. At visitor information you can pick up a map, *Turkart Fjaerland*, for 60NOK ($8), outlining all these walks in great detail.

It's possible to drive within 500m (1,640 ft.) of the Supphelle Glacier. You can stroll over and touch the ice. During a period in summer from the first of July to August 10, you can take guided glacier trips on Supphelle, starting from the car park at the northeast of the Norsk Bremuseum (see below), 4km (2½ miles) off Route 5. Trips leave Monday to Saturday at 9am. The jaunt includes a hike up the Kvanneholtnipa Mountain at 1,640m (5,380 ft.).

In town you can visit the **Norsk Bremuseum (Norwegian Glacier Museum;** © **57-69-32-88)**, which is open June to August daily from 9am to 7pm. In April and May and again in September and October, it's open daily 10am to 4pm. Admission is 75NOK ($10) for adults or 35NOK ($4.65) for children, with a family ticket going for 160NOK ($21). This is very much a hands-on museum. Exhibits inform you about how fjords are formed, and there is a multiscreen audiovisual show on the Jostedal Glacier. You can perform your own experiments with thousand-year-old glacier ice. You can also see a mammoth tusk from the largest mammal ever to live in Norway; it's some 30,000 years old. Exhibits also tell the story of Ötzi, "the man from the ice," whose 5,000-year-old body was found in a glacier in the European Alps in 1991.

You can also visit **Astruptunet** ★, lying across the southern shore of Lake Jølster and reached from the center of Fjaerland after a 10-minute drive. Celebrated for his landscapes, Nicolai Astrup (1880–1928) was one of the country's best known and most reproduced artists. You can visit the studio where he died and wander about a colony of little sod-roofed buildings. Some of his artwork is on view. Guides bring Astrup alive again with their colorful anecdotes. On site is a cafe serving sour cream porridge, waffles, and coffee. The location is at Sandal i Jolster (© **57-72-67-82**), and admission is 50NOK ($6.65) adults or 25NOK ($3.35) for children. It's open daily from May 23 to the end of September from 11am to 4pm.

SHOPPING

Norway's book town offers some 20,000 books for sale in a dozen or so second-hand shops, which remain open from mid-May to the beginning of September from 10am to 6pm daily. Most of the titles are in Norwegian, but they are many English-language books, including some rare ones. Contact **Den norske bokbyen** at © **57-69-22-10** for more information.

WHERE TO STAY & DINE

Hotel Mundal ★★ Beloved of landscape painters and glacier hikers for decades, this hotel dates from 1891 and has been operated by the same family ever since. A bit quirky, with its wooden scrollwork, peaked roofs, cavernous dining room, and round tower, it would be the choice of the Adams family were they traveling the fjord country. In the center of Fjaerland, it lies 3km (1¾ miles) from the glacier museum. Although old fashioned, it has kept abreast of the times with constant improvements. The helpful staff will offer bikes or rowing boats, and assist you in your mountain- and glacier-climbing plans.

Bedrooms come in a range of sizes and styles, but all are comfortably and traditionally furnished, with private bathrooms equipped with tub and shower. Even if you're passing through for the day, consider a traditional Norwegian meal of regional specialties. Lunch costs from 85NOK ($11), with a lavish four-course dinner going for 370NOK ($49).

N-6848 Fjaerland. © **57-69-31-01.** Fax 57-69-31-79. www.fjordinfo.no/mundal/contact.html. 35 units. 925NOK–1,035NOK ($123–$138) double; 1,215NOK ($162) suite. DC, MC, V. Closed mid-Sept to mid-May. **Amenities:** Restaurant; cafe; bar; lounge; laundry service; library. *In room:* TV.

11 Loen/Olden/Stryn & the Jostedal Glacier

50km (30 miles) S of Hellesylt

This cluster of little towns and resorts, within easy reach of each other, virtually form one community and are used as the base for trips to the Jostedalsbreen National Park.

The largest settlement, with a population of only 1,500, is **Stryn,** the capital of the upper Nordfjord district.

Olden is one of the best centers for excursions to the Briksdals Glacier. Its population is 800. Even smaller is **Loen,** with only 400 residents. Loen lies at the mouth of the panoramic Lodalen valley and is used by many as the gateway into the national park. The village itself is touristy and of little interest but it makes a good refueling stop for some of the most dramatic excursions in Norway.

ESSENTIALS

GETTING THERE Stryn is your gateway to the area, as it is linked by public transportation to major cities in Norway. Nor-Way Bussekspress travels west from Oslo at the rate of three times daily, taking 8½ hours and costing 525NOK ($70) one-way. There are also three to five buses daily from Bergen, taking 6 hours and costing 380NOK ($51) one-way. The buses also stop at Olden and Loen.

Motorists leaving Geiranger (see below) can continue south to Stryn, taking the ferry across the Geirangerfjord to the town of Hellesylt, the trip taking less than about an hour. From Hellesylt, take Route 60 into Stryn. Once at Stryn, you can drive immediately to the east to Loen or south to Olden. Distances are short—for example, Loan lies only 10km (6¼ miles) from Stryn.

VISITOR INFORMATION The **Stryn & Nordfjord Reisemål** (© 57-87-40-40) is most helpful, dispensing information about touring the entire area, including hiking trips into the national park. It offers a free booklet, *Guide for Stryn,* outlining trips and cycling routes, and it also rents mountain bikes at the rate of 50NOK ($6.65) per day. In July it's open daily from 8:30am to 8pm; in June and August daily 8am to 6pm, and in September to May Saturday and Sunday 9am to 4pm.

There is also **Olden Tourist Information** (© 57-87-31-26) in the center of the village, open June 10 to August 15 from 10am to 6pm daily.

SEEING THE SIGHTS

In addition to the wonders of Norway's largest glacier, Jostedal, the little towns and villages of Olden, Loen, and Styrn are also good bases for trips on the **Nordfjord** ★★★, which is the only fjord to rival the scenic wonders of Sognefjord. The panoramic Nordfjord, with its deep blue waters, penetrates inland from the coast for 100km (62 miles) before it abruptly halts at the glacier itself. If you have a car, you can **drive the length of the north bank** ★★ along Route 15 almost to the head of the fjord at Loen. This is one of the grand motor trips of the fjord country. In the distance are snow-capped mountain peaks, and along the way are many grazing pastures, fjord farms, and rock-strewn promontories.

JOSTEDALSBREEN NATIONAL PARK ★★★

Jostedalsbreen is an ice plateau, spreading across 487 sq. km (783 sq. miles) dominating the inner Nordfjord district and stretching out in the direction of Sognefjord and the majestic Jotunheimen mountains. Sprawling northeast from Route 5 to Route 15, it plunges a total of two dozen "arms" into the neighboring valleys.

In certain parts, the mammoth ice mountain is 400m (1,312 ft.) thick, reaching up to 1,950m (6,397 ft.) above sea level. Wildlife includes reed deer, elk, brown bear, and smaller creatures such as hares and elusive squirrels.

For years until the advent of modern engineering, the glacier formed an almost impenetrable barrier between the east and west of Norway.

Beginning in 1991, Norway placed the glacier under the protection of the Jostedalsbreen Nasjonalpark (Jostedalsbreen National Park). For general information about the park and touring it, get in touch with **Statens Natur-oppsyn** at ℂ **57-87-72-00** in Oppstryn.

Before setting out, visit the **Jostesdalsbreen Nasjonalparksenter** at Oppstryn (ℂ **57-87-72-00**), lying 15km (9¼ miles) east of the town of Stryn. Exhibits tell you everything you ever wanted to know about glaciers—and a lot more. You're treated to a panoramic history of the glacier from "attacks" by meteorites to avalanches. We found a highlight to be wandering through the "arctic garden" with 325 species of endemic plant life. The center is open May to September daily from 10:30am to 5:30pm, charging 55NOK ($7.30) for adults, 30NOK ($4) for children.

NIGARDSBREEN ★

The Jostedal is particularly noted for its glacial "arms," sometimes called "tongues," which shoot out into valleys, flowing from the plateau glacier. The most famous of these glacial tongues is **Nigardsbreen.** This section is a remnant of the ice sheet that covered Norway 10,000 years ago.

The well-preserved moraine landscape looks much as it did centuries ago, or so scientists believe. Biochemical dating has also found that many moraines date from the "Little Ice Age" that culminated only about 250 years ago. At that time a deterioration in climate make the Jostedal glacier grow, as its tongues surged forward, damaging farms and vegetation in the valley. The Nigard valley and the Nigard glacier are still studied by scientists every year who keep a sort of watch on it.

Nigardsbreen is one of the most popular areas for climbing and walking, a virtual ice blue wonderland of deep crevasses and oddly shaped pinnacles. From May until mid-September, walks are possible. During the other months, weather conditions are too harsh.

At Nigardsbreen you can visit the **Jostedal Breheimsenteret** at Jostedal (ℂ **57-68-32-50**), which is designed in the shape of twin ice peaks divided by a crevasse, nicknamed the "Glacier cathedral." In addition to a film on the glacier, you can see exhibits about the formation and continued movement of this awesome ice block.

The center is open May 20 to June 20 and August 22 to September daily from 10am to 5pm. From June 21 to August 21, hours are daily from 9am to 7pm. Admission is 50NOK ($6.65) for adults, 20NOK ($2.65) for children.

In Jostedal you can hook up with **Jostedalen Breførarlag** (ℂ **57-68-31-11**) for guided glacier walks, including a short trip across the Nigardsvatnet and a hike along the glacier arm. Tours take 1½ hours, costing 100NOK ($13). Two-hour walks on ice are also possible in summer, leaving at 11:30am daily, costing 225NOK ($30) per person. From June 22 to August 10, there is an additional afternoon departure leaving at 2:30pm.

BRIKSDALSBREEN (THE BRIKSDAL GLACIER) ★★

One of the most dramatic natural sights of Norway, this glacier is reached from the large village of Olden by taking a signposted panoramic road for 24km (14 miles). The route winds its way to the double glacial "arms" of the Briksdals-breen and Brenndalsbreen ice masses. The Briksdals glacier is not only the most accessible but also the most stunning. Nearby residents grew alarmed in the 1990s when it advanced by 300m (984 ft.), but it now seems to be retreating.

The water flowing from the glacier forms a trio of lakes in the valley, which have a dramatic emerald-green color. For a part of the jaunt up the glacier, you can take a two-wheeled cart pulled by a *stolkjerre,* one of those sturdy-footed fjord horses.

Along the way you pass by a thundering waterfall. At the end of the track, hikers may wander deeper into the glacier mass to a height of 1,700m (5,577 ft.), a distance of only 346m (1,194 ft.) above sea level. In summer the glacier can be seen "pupping"—that is, giving birth to smaller chunks of ice that fall from the mother lode.

Rides are available from **Oldedalen Skysslag** (© 57-87-68-05), costing 230NOK ($31) for adults and 115NOK ($15) for children, for the 15-minute jaunt.

The best organized tours are conducted by **Briksdal Breføring** (© 57-87-68-00) at the Briksdalsbre Fjellstove at Briksdalsbre, a small hotel. A 3-hour hike on the ice costs 250NOK ($33). In summer there are five departures a day, beginning at 10am, with the last one setting out at 4pm.

STRYN

Stryn was put on the map by British fishermen coming to catch salmon in its waters back in the 1860s. Since then it has grown and developed into a major tourist center in the fjord district. The **Stryn Sommerskisenter** (Summer Ski Center) lies on the Tystigen branch of the Jostedalsbreen. This area offers the country's best summer skiing, and is a popular setting for photographers capturing beauties skiing in their bikinis. Its longest run stretches 2,100m (6,889 ft.), with a drop of 518m (1,699 ft.). In addition, some 10km (6¼ miles) of cross-country ski tracks are offered. Lift tickets for 1 day cost 250NOK ($33), and ski equipment is available for rent. For more information, call the center at © 92-25-83-33.

The road to the ski center, **Gamble Strynefjellsvegen** ⭐, is one of the most dramatic in central Norway, with hairpin curves. It goes past waterfalls, glacier arms or tongues, and opens onto panoramic vistas at an altitude of 1,139m (3,736 ft.).

OLDEN

This little resort makes a great launch pad for jaunts to the Briksdal glacier (see above). In town you can visit **Singersamlinga** (© 57-87-31-06), which displays the artwork of William Henry Singer of Pittsburg, a famous American millionaire. Singer and his wife, Anna Spencer, spent summers in Olden from 1913 until the late '30s. He was fond of painting landscapes of western Norway. The house can be visited by appointment by calling © **57-87-31-06.** The cost is 20NOK ($2.65) for adults, or 10NOK ($1.35) for children.

LOEN

A small fjord farming hamlet, this is a summer resort with many outdoor pursuits. It is also the site of some of the best accommodations in the area.

From Loen you can take one of the most scenic trips in the area to the beautiful **Kjenndal Glacier** ⭐ lying 17km (11 miles) along a glacial lake, the Lovatnet. This is the least visited of the glaciers, and is less crowded in summer.

You can take a boat, the *Kjenndal,* going up Lovatnet from Sande and costing 150NOK ($20) per person, including a return bus from the Kjenndalstova Kafe (© **94-53-83-85**), a cafe-restaurant with some of the most panoramic views of the area. The cafe is close to the Kjenndal Glacier with cascading waterfalls as a backdrop as you enjoy your freshly caught trout. The cafe is closed from October to April.

From the cafe it's a 2km (1¼-mile) hike to the glacier's face. Boats depart from Sande June to August, leaving daily at 10:30am.

You can drive up, but the toll road above Lovatnet narrows to a single track. The toll is 30NOK ($4).

WHERE TO STAY & DINE

Alexandra 🌟🌟 The most luxurious hotel in the area, the Alexandra dates from 1884 and has been run by the Grov family since it first opened. It was last renovated in 1998, its modernization done at the sacrifice of some of its old-fashioned charm. The hotel is also the best equipped in the area, making it the only real resort hotel. All the bedrooms are different in size, but all come with new furnishings. Each unit is equipped with a well-maintained bathroom with shower and tub (a few have shower only). The location makes a good base for touring the attractions of the Nordfjord and the national park, including the Briksdal Glacier. It's also a fine choice for dining for nonguests, serving a lavish buffet dinner costing 375NOK ($50) per person.

N-6789 Loen. ⓒ 57-87-50-00. Fax 57-87-50-51. www.alexandra.no. 191 units. 1,350NOK–1,740NOK ($180–$231) double; 2,800NOK ($372) suite. Children under 5 stay free. Rates include buffet breakfast. AE, DC, MC, V. Closed Dec 15–27 and Jan 1–25. **Amenities:** Restaurant; 3 bars; pool; fitness center; sauna; 24-hr. room service; babysitting; laundry service; dry cleaning. *In room:* TV, minibar, hair dryer.

Briksdalbre Although primarily a restaurant, it's also a lodge offering you a rare chance to stay near the Briksdal Glacier. The original lodge was constructed in 1890, but it's been rebuilt many times, most recently in 1997. Bedrooms are simply furnished, and have small bathrooms equipped with showers. Expect little in the way of amenities, as most of the staff is engaged in tending to the restaurant. However, they will advise on glacier walking and even arrange a trip in a horse and carriage. The lodge serves some of the best regional cuisine in the area, and is particularly busy at lunchtime. The cuisine is very regional, with many different cod and salmon dishes caught in local waters (ever had deep-fried cod jaws?). Typically you can order filet of reindeer in a well-flavored sauce or else sautéed trout. Dinners range from 100NOK to 180NOK ($13–$24) and are served daily from 8:30 to 9:30pm, with no reservations needed.

N-6792 Briksdalbre. ⓒ 57-87-68-00. Fax 57-87-68-01. www.briksdalsbre.no. 6 units. 700NOK ($93) double. Rates include continental breakfast. AE, DC, MC, V. Closed Nov–Apr. *In room:* No phone.

Loen Pensjonat 🌟 *Finds* Built in 1910, this B&B is family-friendly. It lies on a sheep farm but in summer the owners send the herd to the upper elevations for better grazing in the mountains. The little inn has a large garden with beautiful views of the fjords. The location is only 400m (1,312 ft.) from the center of Loen, in the middle of great hiking and fishing country, with many opportunities for glacier trekking. The carpeted bedrooms are small to medium in size, coming with doubles or twins. Five of the units have a bathroom with shower; occupants of the other rooms share the adequate bathrooms in the corridors.

N-6789 Loen. ⓒ 57-86-76-24. Fax 57-87-76-78. 14 units, 5 with private bathroom. 400NOK ($53) double without bathroom; 500NOK ($67) double with bathroom. Children stay free in parent's room. No credit cards. **Amenities:** Breakfast lounge. *In room:* No phone.

Olden Fjordhotel 🌟 Very close to the Briksdal Glacier, this is a good base for glacier excursions, and a center for such activities as summer skiing, horseback riding, and fishing trips. Built in 1971, the hotel added a modern annex in 1996. It is one of the best-maintained hotels in this fjord and glacier country, with renovations every winter. There are two types of units, either standard or superior. The standard rooms are medium in size and are well furnished, offering good comfort. The superior rooms have more style and are larger, with a sitting area included. These are allergen-free. The superior rooms contain bathrooms with tub and shower, the standard units coming with shower. The hotel is one of the liveliest in the area at night, with live piano music. The on-site restaurant serves one of the best and largest buffet dinners in the area for 325NOK ($43).

N-6788 Olden. ℂ 57-87-04-00. Fax 57-87-04-01. 60 units. 1,200NOK–1,400NOK ($160–$186) double. Children under 3 stay free. Rates include continental breakfast. AE, DC, MC, V. Closed Oct–May. **Amenities:** Restaurant; bar; babysitting. *In room:* TV, coffeemaker (some units), hair dryer.

Visnes Hotel ⭐   Two classical buildings from 1850 and 1896 were blended to form this unique hotel for the area. The building from 1896 was originally a hotel, then a school, and was later used for various other purposes before it was restored and reopened as a hotel unit in 1999. It retains much of the aura of an alpine hotel in Austria, lying a 5-minute walk from the heart of Stryn. Ask for a bedroom with a balcony opening onto a view of the fjord. Many of the rooms maintain a classic style from the 1930s, and all come equipped with tidily kept bathrooms with shower. The on-site restaurant is the best in town, serving a three-course dinner for 295NOK ($39) with both Norwegian and French specialties.

Prestegen 1, N-6781 Stryn. ℂ **57-87-10-87.** Fax 57-87-20-75. www.visnes.no. 15 units. 650NOK–995NOK ($86–$132) double; 1,295NOK ($172) suite. Rates include continental breakfast. AE, DC, MC, V. Closed Sept–May. **Amenities:** Restaurant. *In room:* No phone.

12 Geirangerfjord: Norway's Most Spectacular Fjord ⭐⭐⭐

85km (53 miles) SW of Åndalsnes; 413km (256 miles) NE of Bergen; 455km (282 miles) NW of Oslo

Most Norwegians consider Geirangerfjord, a favorite body of water for cruises, their most majestic. The fjord stretches out for 16km (10 miles) and is 292m (960 ft.) deep. The village of Geiranger, one of the most famous resorts in the fjord country, is set at the very head of this narrow fjord.

Perched on rocky ledges, high above the fjord, are a number of small farmsteads. Waterfalls, such as the celebrated Seven Sisters (Syr Søstre), the Wooer, and the Bridal Veil, send their shimmering veils cascading down the rock face.

Almost daily in summer, large cruising liners anchor in the Geirangerfjord, as they have done since 1869. Occasionally some of the world's best-known vessels are moored here at the same time.

The fjord is so deep that the behemoth *Queen Elizabeth 2* has sailed safely this far inland. Such depth was created by the Ice Age, when mammoth masses of ice widened and deepened existing valleys. When the ice melted, former valleys became fjords. The Geirangerfjord is hemmed in by mountain walls rising to a height of 1,600m (5,249 ft.).

ESSENTIALS

GETTING THERE   Geiranger is linked by regular ferry service to the old Viking port of Hellesylt. The **Møre og Romsdal Fylkesbåtar ferry** ⭐⭐⭐ costs 35NOK ($4.65) per passenger or 110NOK ($15) per day, and is the most magnificent ferry route in all of Norway. Take the ride even if you don't need to get to the other side. Depending on the season, fjord ferries run from May 1 to September 25 at the rate of 4 to even 10 a day, the latter only in the peak season of July. For information and schedules, call ℂ **71-21-95-00.**

From the first of April until the end of September, Hurtigruten **coastal steamers** also sail into Geiranger but only when en route to the North Cape.

The most frequently used public transport is a daily **bus** in summer running from Åndalsnes (see below), taking 3 hours and costing 140NOK ($19). For the visitor wanting wild fjord scenery, the morning bus from Åndalsnes goes on from Geiranger to Langvatn, and on the way back to Geiranger takes a rather thrilling 10km (6¼-mile) jaunt just for visitors. The bus goes up to the summit of Dalsnibba at 1,500m (4,921 ft.), stopping at Flydalsjuvet (see below). The return fare is 100NOK ($13) per person.

By **car,** it's also possible to reach Dalsnibba by toll road, costing 50NOK ($6.65) per vehicle. From Stryn, take routes 15/63 into Geiranger. The mountain road, known as Strynefjellsveien offers gleaming white snow and views of glacier "tongues" well into the summer months. The final stretch to Geiranger is called **Geirangervegen** ★★★ and takes you through 38 bends, offering fantastic mountain and fjord views at every turn. The most dramatic routing is to drive the famous Trollstigvegen from Åndalsnes (see below), a 2-hour scenic drive along Route 63.

VISITOR INFORMATION   In the post office complex adjacent to the quay, the **Geiranger Tourist Office** (© 70-26-30-99), is open only from mid-May to early September. Hours are variable.

SEEING THE FJORD

Called "the most beautiful fjord in the world," **Geirangerfjord** ★★★ invites exploration. The best and least expensive way to see the majesty of the fjord is to take a regular ferry service between the port of Hellesylt (see above) and Geiranger, with sails daily from May to September. An organized tour, however, gives you a greater view, going closer to the banks.

The best jaunts are run by **Geiranger Fjordservice** (© 70-26-30-99), offering 1½-hour sightseeing boat tours at a cost of 75NOK ($10) per person. Bookings can be made at the tourist office. Departures are June to August at the rate of five times daily. From June 25 to the end of July, there is also a tour in the evening.

Geiranger is also blessed with having some of the finest excursions in the fjord country, notably to **Dalsnibba** ★★★, lying 21km (13 miles) to the south. Opened in 1889, this dramatic road goes through a valley hemmed in by tall mountains until it reaches a lookout point at 1,500m (4,921 ft.). There are many panoramic lookout points along the way. You're rewarded with a dramatic view at the top. As one local told us, "This is the lookout point where Satan took Jesus to tempt him with the beauty of the world."

A second great excursion is the **Flydalsjuvet** ★★, lying 4km (2½ miles) south of Geiranger. This gigantic overhanging rock, opening onto the fjord, is the most photographed in Norway, especially by cruise-ship passengers. To reach it, take the sign-posted road to Stryn until you see the turnoff.

SHOPPING

E-Merok Turisthandel (© 70-26-30-14) has been selling gifts and souvenirs to visitors since 1928 from its location in the center of the village overlooking the fjord. Their specialty is Norwegian knitwear, including a fine selection from the prestigious manufacturer, Dale of Norway. They also sell items in silver and gold, along with Norwegian enamel, pewter, and crystal, as well as souvenirs. In summer they remain open daily from 9am to 10pm. **Audhild Vikens Vevstove** (© 70-26-32-12) also has a large selection of gifts and souvenirs as well as clothes, knitted goods, pewter, books, music, and other items.

WHERE TO STAY & DINE

Geiranger Hotel ★★   In the center of the village, its best rooms facing the fjord with scenic balconies, this is the durable favorite. A hotel has stood on this spot since the 1860s but today's facility is completely up to date. Overcrowded with summer visitors, the hotel nonetheless manages to offer personalized service. Last renovated in 1995, the bedrooms are midsize and comfortably carpeted, some painted in the deep greens and blues of the fjord itself. Most units have a tub-and-shower combination, the rest with shower. Nonguests often stop in to patronize the 300-seat Restaurant Skageflå, serving regional specialties. A Norwegian buffet at 275NOK ($37) is a special delight. The staff can arrange for you to rent rowboats to explore the fjord, or else advise on how to obtain a fishing license to fish that same body of water.

N-6216 Geiranger. ℂ **70-26-30-05.** Fax 70-26-31-70. www.geiranger.no. 151 units. 1,150NOK–1,270NOK ($153–$169) double. Children under 4 stay free. Rates include continental breakfast. AE, DC, MC, V. Closed Oct–Apr. **Amenities:** Restaurant; bar; outdoor pool. *In room:* TV.

Grand Fjordhotel   This 1996 inn looks like a Norwegian country lodge with a wooden interior. Its magnet is its sixth-floor restaurant with a panoramic view of fjord waters and some of the world's greatest cruise ships coming and going. The bar/lounge on the sixth floor is the best place to begin or end an evening at Geiranger. Bedrooms are tastefully though rather simply furnished and are midsize and immaculately maintained. The carpeted rooms open onto views of the fjord, and 42 of them have tub and shower, the rest with shower. Many cruiseship passengers are found in the restaurant in summer, enjoying the classical Norwegian buffet of regional specialties at a cost of 250NOK ($33) per person. The staff can arrange boat rentals for tours of the fjord, or book tours on sightseeing vessels.

N-6216 Geiranger. ℂ **70-26-30-90.** Fax 70-26-31-77. www.grandfjordhotel.com. 48 units. 980NOK–1,080NOK ($130–$144) double. Children under 4 stay free. Rates include continental breakfast. MC, V. Closed Oct–Apr. **Amenities:** Restaurant; bar; laundry service. *In room:* TV, hair dryer.

Union Hotel ★★★   An old family hotel dating from 1891, this is one of the area's largest hotels, scenically perched along fjord waters. It's also an all-time favorite. Over the years, it's hosted kings, queens, and kaisers, plus thousands of visitors. The hotel was last renovated in 2001, and it's never looked as good. The bedrooms are beautifully furnished, some with balconies. Try to book into the 50 or so accommodations with views of the fjords; the other units have mountain views. All come with immaculately kept bathrooms with tub-and-shower combinations. The hotel restaurant is the finest in the area, serving a classic Norwegian buffet for 300NOK ($40), although you can dine a la carte as well. The staff can arrange for you to use a rowboat, and cars, owned by the hotel, can be rented by the day for excursions. In summer a live band entertains for dancing.

N-6216 Geiranger. ℂ **70-26-83-00.** Fax 70-26-83-51. www.union-hotel.no. 168 units. 1,230NOK ($164) double; 2,700NOK ($359) suite. Children under 12 stay free. Rates include continental breakfast. AE, DC, MC, V. Closed Dec 15–Feb 1. **Amenities:** Restaurant; bar; pool; sauna; limited room service; babysitting; Turkish bath. *In room:* TV, minibar, hair dryer.

13 Åndalsnes: Launch Pad for Trollstigveien ✪

127km (79 miles) E of Ålesund; 1,058km (658 miles) W of Oslo

Although situated in one of the greatest regions of scenery in Norway, Ådalsnes itself is rather banal. That's because the invading Nazis in 1940 bombed it out of existence. The king and his family used Åndalsnes as their exit route in their dramatic escape from Norway, following the German invasion of their borders. The royals made it, but Åndalsnes was left to pay the price.

The town today is modern, and no one wants to talk about when it was used as a military base for the Nazis.

ESSENTIALS

GETTING THERE   **Trains** run daily from Oslo to Åndalsnes, taking 6 to 8 hours. From June 15 through August 30 daily **buses** link Åndalsnes to Geiranger, taking 3 to 4 hours. Daily buses also run to Ålesund (trip time: 2½ hr.) and to Molde (trip time: 1½ hr.). **Motorists** take E6 northwest from Oslo toward Lillehammer. At Dombås, head west on the E9 to Åndalsnes.

VISITOR INFORMATION   At the train station, the **Åndalsnes og Romsdal Reiselivslag Tourist Office** (② **71-22-16-22**) dispenses information. It's open June to August Monday to Saturday 9am to 7pm, Sunday 1 to 7pm.

SEEING THE SIGHTS

Åndalsnes is the starting point for one of the great motor drives in Norway: the **Trollstigvegen** ☆☆, a 2-hour drive along Route 63 south to Geiranger. The highway climbs to 620m (2,034 ft.) over a distance of 8km (5 miles). The Ørneveien or "Eagle's Road" down to Geiranger was a marvel of Norwegian engineering upon its completion in 1952.

Along the way you'll encounter 11 hairpin turns. The last hairpin curve is called **Ørnsvingen** ☆☆☆ or "Eagle's Bend," offering one of the great views in the fjord country—that of the Geirangerfjord. The dramatic route will take you right in Geiranger. This road for daredevils has a 1:12 gradient. To make matters even more exciting, it's one lane for most of the hair-raising journey.

If you're driving or even on a bus, vehicles stop in front of the thundering **Stigfossen Waterfall** ☆, its waters dropping 180m (590 ft.).

Vegmuseum, Trollstigen (② **71-22-14-65**), is a little museum at the pass, with exhibitions relating the story of how this incredible road came to be. It's open late June to mid-August daily from 11am to 3:30pm, charging an admission of 15NOK ($2).

Another grand highlight of the area is en route to **Dombås** (Rte. 9). Both road and train lines follow the Troll Wall or **Trollveggen** ☆, a major challenge for mountaineers, rising 1,800m (5,905 ft.). A combined Norwegian and English British team "conquered" it in 1965.

The visitors' center (see above) distributes more than a dozen leaflets outlining the best hiking trails through the **Romsdalen Alps,** a string of mountains enveloping Åndalsnes. The most dramatic route is the full-day jaunt that begins 50m (164 ft.) north of Åndalsnes and climbs to the summit of **Nesaksla Mountain** ☆☆, rising 715m (2,345 ft.) over Åndalsnes. At the top you're rewarded with another one of those awesome panoramas. On a clear day you can see down to the Romsdalsfjord. From here the climb continues to the summit of **Høgnosa** at 991m (3,251 ft.) and on to Åkesfjellet at 1,215m (3,986 ft.).

The **Romsdalsfjord** ☆ is one of the most scenic in western Norway, cutting a deep gash into the earth and extending west of Åndalsnes. The tourist office can arrange 4-hour fishing tours of the fjord at a cost of 250NOK ($33) per person. A local license can be obtained.

WHERE TO STAY & DINE

Grand Hotel Bellevue ☆   The original Grand that stood here dated from 1870. But in 1940 the Nazis firebombed it during their invasion of Norway.

Don't miss the display of photographs in the lobby documenting the hotel's poignant history. It was completely rebuilt in 1954 and last renovated in 2000. It is your best base for exploring the fjord and mountain country around Åndalsnes. The bedrooms range from midsize to spacious, and the suites open onto balconies with views of the mountains and the fjord waters. Most of the well-maintained bathrooms have showers; a few are equipped with both tub and shower. The staff can arrange sightseeing, golf, and fishing for salmon in a nearby river or for cod in the ocean. The on-site restaurant is the best choice for dining in Åndalsnes even if you're not a guest. The fresh salmon is a delight, and meals cost from 100NOK to 130NOK ($13–$17).

Andalgata 5, N-6301 Åndalsnes. (?) 71-22-75-00. Fax 71-22-60-68. 84 units. 495NOK–795NOK ($66–$106) double; 1,095NOK ($146) suite. AE, DC, MC, V. **Amenities:** Restaurant; bar. *In room:* TV, minibar.

Rauma Hotel *Value*   Rising from the debris of the war-damaged town around it, this hotel was originally constructed in 1946. Its four floors were renovated in 1989. The bedrooms are traditionally furnished and comfortable, some of them quite large. They open onto a view of the rooms and come equipped with a small bathroom with shower. This is not an exciting choice, but it is durable and serviceable and provides good value. There's an unpretentious cafe restaurant on site serving sandwiches during the day, with dinners costing from 62NOK to 140NOK ($8.25–$19).

Vollan 16, N-6300 Åndalsnes. (?) 71-22-12-13. Fax 71-22-63-13. 15 units. 850NOK ($113) double. Rates include continental breakfast. AE, DC, MC, V. **Amenities:** Restaurant; bar; laundry service; dry cleaning. *In room:* TV, minibar.

14 Ålesund: The Great Fishing Harbor ★★

127km (79 miles) W of Åndalsnes; 131km (82 miles)—plus 2 ferry rides—SW of Kristiansund N; 59km (37 miles)—plus 1 ferry ride—SW of Molde

Ålesund is at the top of the fjord country, spread over three islands in an archipelago, with the snowcapped Sunnmøre Alps in the background. The islanders once earned their living from fishing.

After a fire destroyed the town in 1904, Ålesund was rebuilt in the style of the times, Art Nouveau. Towers, turrets, and medieval romantic facades are pure Art Nouveau, and the Ålesund version includes elements from Nordic mythology. The newly created town in our view is even more beautiful than Bergen. It lies on a fishhook-shaped peninsula in the sea.

ESSENTIALS

GETTING THERE By Plane The easiest way to reach Ålesund is to fly from such cities as Oslo, Trondheim, and especially Bergen, arriving at the Ålesund/Vigra airport. There are also daily flights from Bodø, Kristiansand S, Røros, Stavanger, and Tromsø. Flights are on SAS (© 70-10-49-00) or Braathens (© 70-11-49-00). The airport is a 20-minute ride north of Ålesund on the island of Vigra. Until 1987, reaching the town center from the airport required a ferryboat transit whose services were sometimes cut off during storms. Since then, a 14½km (9-mile) network of bridges and tunnels connects Ålesund with four inhabited offshore islands.

By Train Go to Åndalsnes and then take a bus from the rail station to Ålesund. A daily train arrives from Oslo.

By Bus More tourist buses run June 15 to end of August. Good connections are possible from Åndalsnes, the nearest rail terminal. There are one to three buses daily from Åndalsnes, taking 2½ hours and costing 165NOK ($22) one-way. One bus a day also arrives from Bergen, taking 11 hours. One or two buses a day arrive from Trondheim, taking 7½ hours.

By Coastal Steamer   The coastal steamer departs Bergen daily at 10pm and arrives at Ålesund at noon the following day.

By Car   Take the A69 west from Åndalsnes all the way to Ålesund. A car ferry operates between Åndalsnes and Ålesund.

VISITOR INFORMATION   The **Ålesund Reiselivslag,** Rådhuset (© **70-15-76-00**), provides tourist information June to August, Monday through Friday from 8:30am to 7pm, on Saturday from 9am to 3pm, and on Sunday from noon to 5pm; the rest of the year, Monday through Friday from 8:30am to 4pm.

SEEING THE SIGHTS

There are many sights in Ålesund, most works of nature. The mountain guardian of the area is **Aksla** at 182m (600 ft.), a scenic sanctuary with a terrace restaurant, offering a view of fjord landscape, ancient Viking islands, and the Sunnmøre mountains. From the center you take 418 steps up to Aksla to the lookout point, **Kniven** (the knife). To reach the ascent point, go along Lihauggata reached from the pedestrian shopping street, Kongensgata, which is one of the best streets for viewing the Art Nouveau–style architecture. Motorists can also reach Aksla by road by taking Røysegata east of the core, following the signposts for Fjellstua.

In the harbor nestles the flat island of **Giske,** believed to have been the birthplace of Rollo, 10th-century founder of the Duchy of Normandy and father of William the Conqueror. Giske is the site of a 12th-century marble church, many stretches of white sandy beaches, and the Makkevika bird sanctuary.

Until recently, the only access to many of the surrounding areas was by ferryboat, whose services were sometimes cut off during stormy weather. In 1987, a 14.5km (9-mile) network of tunnels was built connecting Ålesund to four nearby islands, including Giske, the island of **Vigra** (site of the city's airport), and the inhabited islands of **Ellingsøy** and **Valderøy.**

If you have time for only one island, we suggest you make it Giske, which was the historic seat of the Arnungane, a famous Viking family whose feudal control lasted from 990 to 1582.

At Giske you can visit the 12th-century **Giske Kirke,** a marble Romanesque church ([tel **70-18-80-00**) that was restored in 1756. Admission is 15NOK ($2), and hours are from June 1 to August 20 Monday to Saturday from 10am to 5pm and on Sunday from 1 to 7pm. Bus 64 runs from the center of Ålesund, taking half an hour and costing 40NOK ($5.30) one-way.

Several tours that begin in Ålesund are designed for bird-watchers. The most popular and best of these head to the island of **Runde** ★★, 67km (42 miles) southwest of town. This is Norway's southernmost bird rock, where on jagged cliffs half a million sea birds, representing nearly 250 species, breed each year. They are protected from humans by strict government regulations and from natural enemies by the forbidding terrain.

You can see colonies of these birds beginning in May. They stick around until late in July before flying out. The migrating puffins are worth the trek alone, but you'll also see the razor-billed auk, guillemots, auks, storm petrels, kittiwakes, gannets, and other sea birds.

The best tour is a 2½-hour boat ride leaving May to August daily from Runde Quay at 11am, 1pm, and 4pm. The cost is 100NOK ($13) per person; call ✆ **70-08-59-16** to make a reservation.

For more information, contact the summer-only **Runde Reiselivslag** (✆ **70-01-37-90**), which keeps irregular hours.

You can take a bus and catamaran tour from the Ålesund's Skateflukaien Quay, taking 2½ hours and costing 150NOK ($20) one-way. Departures are from mid-June to mid-September. You leave Ålesund on a catamaran, going to the neighboring island of Hareid where you then board a bus for Fosnavåg, which will take you into Runde for the boat tours (see above). You can go back to Ålesund by bus, the last one out at 5pm.

Ålesund Museum 🐦 *Finds*   The development of hunting and fishing methods, shipbuilding, and life in Ålesund before and after the big fire of 1904 are the subjects of this museum off Korsegata near the harbor. The museum's focal points include a large-scale model of Ålesund and one of the most famous boats of the Norwegian fjords, the *Brudeegget*. Originally built in 1904 in the difficult-to-capsize shape of an egg, it became the prototype of thousands of covered rescue boats. Its sturdy design has helped save hundreds of lives after mishaps during stormy weather in the Norwegian seas. Especially interesting are exhibits of the dreaded German occupation from 1940 to 1945.

Rasmus Rønnebergs gate 16. ✆ 70-12-31-70. Admission 30NOK ($4) adults, 10NOK ($1.35) children. June 15–Aug 15 Mon–Fri 11am–4pm, Sat–Sun noon–3pm; off-season Mon–Fri 11am–4pm, closed Sat–Sun.

Atlanterhavsparken ★ *Kids*   This is one of Scandinavia's finest aquariums. Lying along the oceanfront at Tueneset, 3km (1¾ miles) west of Ålesund, it is in fact one of the largest aquariums in Europe. In addition to its tanks of marine life, it offers hiking trails, a cafeteria, bathing sites, and even outstanding diving venues. The sea park was constructed into coastal surroundings and seems at one with the ocean. Kids are always delighted to see divers feeding the fish by hand in the Atlantic Ocean tank. This underwater scene takes place at the 1pm feeding.

Tueneset. ✆ 70-10-70-60. Admission 85NOK ($11) adults, 55NOK ($7.30) children. June 15–Aug 15 Sun–Fri 10am–7pm, Sat 10am–5pm; Aug 16–June 14 Tues–Sat 11am–4pm, Sun noon–5pm. Take bus 18.

Sunnmore Museum & Borgundkaupangen ★★ *Kids*   The site of this settlement was the most important ecclesiastical center between Bergen and Trondheim from the end of the Viking period (around 1000) to 1500. The open-air museum contains some 50 original buildings dating from the late Middle Ages to around 1900. Outbuildings include a sawmill, a boat-builder's shed, a fishermen's inn, and a small 1743 boarding school. The boat halls feature 30 special boats—one of Norway's largest collections of fishing boats as well as an exact replica of the *Fjørtoft* boat from the Viking era. The Museum Quay is home to the *Heland*, a fishing boat built in 1937 and a "Shetland Bus" dating from World War II. The *Borgundknarren* is an exact replica of a Viking trading vessel from 1000. A replica of the *Kvalsund* (8th c.) drops anchor at the quay in summer. The main building focuses on the cultural history of Sunnmøre, with a cafe and a handicrafts shop. The Medieval Museum was built over the excavated remains of 12th-century buildings. The exhibit depicts daily life in a market town back then.

Borgundgavlen. ✆ 70-17-40-00. Admission 50NOK ($6.65) adults, 15NOK ($2) children. Mar 1–June 3 Mon–Tues and Fri 11am–3pm, Sun noon–4pm; June 4–23 Mon–Fri 11am–4pm, Sun noon–4pm; June 24–Aug 31 Mon–Sat 11am–5pm, Sun noon–5pm; Sept Mon–Fri 11am–3pm; Oct–Dec Mon–Tues and Fri 11am–3pm, Sun noon–4pm. Lies 4km (2½ miles) east of town center by bus 13, 14, 18, or 24.

WHERE TO STAY
EXPENSIVE

Comfort Hotel Bryggen ⭐ *Finds*   The steeply gabled, six-story hotel was originally constructed in 1906 as a fish-processing factory. Renovated in 2003, it is today a tasteful, well-run hotel, among the best in the area. The hotel contains a library with a working fireplace and a glassed-in display of the tools used by the workmen who constructed the original building. The interior decor incorporates the thick walls and massive beams of the original structure into an otherwise modern design. The bedrooms are contemporary and tastefully furnished, half of them opening onto views of the water. Each unit comes with a small bathroom with shower. The place is completely unpretentious and homelike.

Apotekergata 1-3, N-6004 Ålesund. ℭ 70-12-64-00. Fax 70-12-11-80. www.comforthotel.com. 85 units. June 24–Aug 11 995NOK ($132) double; otherwise 1,000NOK–1,560NOK ($133–$207) double; year-round 1,850NOK–1,950NOK ($246–$259) suite. Children under 12 stay free in parent's room. Rates include breakfast and dinner. AE, DC, MC, V. **Amenities:** Restaurant; bar; sauna; laundry service; dry cleaning. *In room:* TV, minibar, hair dryer.

Quality Scandinavia Hotel ⭐   Set on a gently sloping street in the town's historic core, this hotel was originally built in 1905 after the great fire destroyed its predecessor. Today it's one of the most authentic Art Nouveau buildings in Ålesund. Renovated in 2002, it offers midsize and tastefully furnished bedrooms with either antiques or reproductions. Bathrooms are freshly restored and immaculately kept, 30 of them coming with tub and shower, the rest with shower. The staff is especially helpful in arranging boat rides on the fjords or bird-watching at Runde. The on-site restaurant serves mainly Italian food.

Lovenvoldgata, N-6002 Ålesund. ℭ 70-15-78-00. Fax 70-15-78-01. www.choicehotels.com. 65 units. 790NOK–1,100NOK ($105–$146) double; 1,800NOK–2,100NOK ($239–$279) suite. Children under 5 stay free. Rates include breakfast. AE, DC, MC, V. Closed Dec 20–Jan 6. **Amenities:** Restaurant; bar; pub (with live music on weekends); limited room service; laundry service; dry cleaning. *In room:* TV, minibar, hair dryer.

Radisson SAS ⭐⭐   This sleek, modern hotel rises five floors and attracts business clients or else summer vacationers. Its major feature is its restaurant opening onto panoramic views of the surrounding islands. It's run by a top-notch staff that will help you arrange sightseeing or fishing trips. Some of the rooms also open onto views of the neighboring islands and the fjord waters. Bedrooms are either carpeted or else offer wooden floors. Each unit is tastefully furnished and all the units except suites are doubles. About 40 of the rooms on the third floor come with bathtubs, the rest with showers.

Sorenskriver Bullsgate 7, N-6002 Ålesund. ℭ 70-16-00-00. Fax 70-16-00-01. www.radissonsas.com. 131 units. June–Aug 890NOK ($118) double; Sept–May 940NOK–1,440NOK ($125–$192) double; year-round 3,500NOK ($466) suite. Children under 12 stay free in parent's room. Rates include breakfast buffet. AE, DC, MC, V. Parking 60NOK ($8). **Amenities:** Restaurant; bar; limited room service; laundry service; dry cleaning. *In room:* TV, minibar, coffeemaker (some units), hair dryer.

Rainbow Hotel Noreg ⭐   One of the most desirable hotels in Ålesund dates from 1954. Most of what you see today was the result of a complete overhaul in 2002. This conventional-looking hotel lies at the edge of the historic center near the bus station. Bedrooms have modern styling and wooden floors, the most desirable units opening onto views of the harbor. Fifteen of the accommodations come with a small bathroom with tub and shower, the rest with shower. The staff helps you plan sightseeing or fishing trips. On site is a well-run restaurant, specializing in Norwegian dishes, especially fish.

Kongensgate 27, N-6002 Ålesund. ℂ **70-12-29-38.** Fax 70-12-66-60. www.rainbowhotel.no. 110 units. 1,295NOK ($172) double. Children under 11 stay free in parent's room. Rates include continental breakfast. AE, DC, MC, V. Closed Dec 22–Jan 3. **Amenities:** Restaurant; 3 bars; nightclub; limited room service. *In room:* TV, minibar, hair dryer.

MODERATE

Rica Parken ✦ Built in 1981, and last renovated in 2001, this nine-floor hotel has a tasteful modern design throughout. Lying a 5-minute walk north of the bus station, most of its bedrooms open onto scenic views of harbor and mountains. All the rooms are comfortable but a bit bland. Each comes with a small and immaculate private bathroom, half with tub and shower, the rest with shower. There is a little park behind the hotel, and a beautiful walk into the mountains begins right outside the hotel.

Storgata 16, N-6002 Ålesund. ℂ **70-12-50-50.** Fax 70-12-21-64. www.rica.no. 145 units. 999NOK–1,540NOK ($133–$205) double; from 1,800NOK ($239) suite. Rates include continental breakfast. AE, DC, MC, V. Closed Dec 22–27. **Amenities:** Restaurant; bar; sauna; laundry service. *In room:* TV, minibar, hair dryer.

WHERE TO DINE
EXPENSIVE

Brasserie Normandie ✦ FRENCH/INTERNATIONAL/NORWEGIAN This is one of the top restaurants in town. Known for its good food, wine selection, and service, this restaurant attracts those who appreciate the delicacies of the sea. Authentic regional produce is harmoniously blended with international recipes. Recommended starters are the fish soup, the most savory in town, and the salmon, which has been marinated in gin with fresh herbs and is served with a mustard sauce. The fish platter is the town's finest, loaded with carefully prepared monkfish, catfish, salmon, mussels, scallops, and shrimp. You can also order an herb-flavored roasted filet of lamb, finishing your meal with one of the different pastries made fresh daily. You dine by candlelight with fresh flowers on your table.

Storgata 16, in the Rica Parken Hotel. ℂ **70-12-50-50.** Reservations required. Main courses 268NOK–279NOK ($36–$37). AE, DC, MC, V. Mon–Sat 6–11pm. Closed Dec 22–27.

Hammer og Kanari ✦ *Finds* NORWEGIAN/SEAFOOD Opening in 2000, this restaurant quickly became known as one of the finest in Ålesund. Its seafood is among the freshest in this part of the fjord district. The restaurant lies on Ålesund's pedestrian street with a panoramic view over the harbor. The service is excellent, as is the cuisine. The walls are decorated with paintings from the north or else photographs of old Ålesund. Our recently sampled fried scallops with lemon dressing made a perfect appetizer. Later our party was delighted with a series of fish dishes, including cod with bell peppers, pesto, and potatoes and a sweet and tender butter-fried monkfish. For the rare odd meat fancier, there is an array of such dishes as filet of pork in a sherry sauce with fresh vegetables.

Kongens gate 19. ℂ **70-12-80-08.** Reservations recommended. Main courses 235NOK–260NOK ($31–$35). AE, DC, MC, V. Mon–Sat 6–11pm.

Orient Bar & Restaurant ✦ *Finds* SUSHI/JAPANESE/CHINESE This is the only sushi restaurant in the fjord district. In a white building, with stylish furnishings, the restaurant comes as a real surprise. Its dishes are full of flavor and served in harmonious combinations. Our tuna and king crab salad set the tone for an array of dishes that were imaginative and carefully crafted. For a main course, you'll have a choice of the latest catch, no doubt crayfish, king prawns, Norwegian salmon, monkfish, mussels, and scallops. You can also order sukiyaki with fresh vegetables. The Orient special for two is a savory assortment that features everything from satay lamb to grilled steak and cod balls. The locals delight in the deep-fried banana ice cream.

Kongens gate 30. ✆ **70-10-71-71.** Main courses 140NOK–270NOK ($19–$36). AE, DC, MC, V. Mon–Thurs 10am–11pm; Fri–Sat 10am–midnight; Sun 1–11pm.

Sjøbua Fiskerestaurant ★★ SEAFOOD   The rustic walls of this former 1904 warehouse were retained in this restaurant, where parts of its foundation piers are sunk into the harbor. You can select a lobster from the holding tank near the entrance and retire to the maritime-style bar for a drink. In the coldest months, a blazing fireplace may greet you. If you arrive in summer, you might prefer a seat in the Flottman's Bar next door, under the same management. The chefs here are in top form as proven by their tangy fish platter with three differ-ent types of whitefish, salmon, mussels, and shrimp. The pan-fried monkfish is especially recommendable, coming with a curry cream sauce. Lobster selected from the tank can be steamed or served grilled with a shellfish sauce.

Brunholmgate 1. ✆ **70-12-71-00.** Reservations recommended. Main courses 260NOK–285NOK ($35–$38). AE, DC, MC, V. Mon–Sat 2–11pm.

MODERATE

Restaurant Fjellstua (Value) NORWEGIAN   The food at this cafeteria-style restaurant is good, but the view is the reason to come here. This mountaintop restaurant opens onto one of the most panoramic vistas in the fjord country. You can drive to the restaurant's mountaintop location via a complicated system of roads or climb the 418 rock-hewn steps from a parking lot below.

The chef specializes in fish, including *bacalao* (cod), monkfish, and freshly caught fjord salmon. At lunch you might want to settle for sandwiches and burgers. At night, if you don't want fish, tender beef emerges perfectly cooked from the charcoal grill. Other savory meat choices include well-flavored lamb cutlets and pork schnitzels.

Aksla Mountain. ✆ **70-10-74-00.** Reservations recommended. Main courses 150NOK–300NOK ($20–$40). AE, DC, MC, V. Daily 11am–8pm. Closed Nov–Mar 15.

Restaurant Gullix ★ (Kids) INTERNATIONAL   This place near the Town Hall has the ambience of a charming Iberian *tasca* (tavern). It's a casual, relaxed atmosphere, and local families are in heavy attendance, along with summer visi-tors from anywhere. The chef specializes in paella, a traditional Valencian rice dish. The other appetizing offerings include some of the town's best fish soup, for a starter, followed by tender and well-flavored sirloin with fresh vegetables and potatoes, or fried catfish in a white wine sauce studded with mussels. The restaurant opens onto views of the harbor.

Radstugata 5B. ✆ **70-12-05-48.** Reservations recommended. Main courses 150NOK–240NOK ($20–$32). AE, DC, MC, V. Daily 2–11pm.

ÅLESUND AFTER DARK

Hos Naboen Pub   This small, traditional pub playing recorded music is one of the most popular in town, attracting patrons ranging in age from 20 to 60. It's a friendly, convivial place with the hardcore regulars showing up in winter, giving way to summer visitors from abroad. Typical pub grub is served. Open Monday to Thursday 9:45am to 1am, Friday and Saturday 9:45am to 2am.

In the Rainbow Hotel Noreg, Kongensgate 27. ✆ **70-12-29-38.**

0 nightclub   This fairly new nightclub is the most popular in town, with an upstairs bar area and a downstairs bar with a dance floor. It draws the young people of Ålesund, nightly, ranging in age from 21 to 35. These patrons dance to recorded music, and the DJ changes every month. Open Friday and Saturday 9pm to 2:30am. In the Rainbow Hotel Noreg, Kongensgata 27. (℗ 70-12-29-38. Sat cover 50NOK–100NOK ($6.65–$13).

15 Molde: City of Roses

59km (37 miles) N of Ålesund; 50km (31 miles) NW of Åndalsnes

Norway's "town of jazz and roses" is famed for its view of 87 white-capped Romsdal Alps. When the Nazis attacked Norway during World War II, Molde briefly became, in effect, the country's capital, since the king and the gold reserves were here. King Haakon VII hid in a forest outside the town until he and his son, the future King Olav V, could board a boat for England. Three hundred houses were destroyed during the German bombings in 1940.

The name of Molde, from the Molde farm that occupied much of the area, has appeared in records since the Middle Ages. It was officially recognized as a trading place in 1614, and King Christian IV signed a royal decree declaring that Molde was a trading city in 1742. This modern, pleasant town of 18,000 citizens celebrated its 250th anniversary in 1992.

Molde occupies one of the most scenic locations in the northern fjord country, lying between the Romsdal mountains and one of Norway's most dramatic coastlines. On the Romsdalfjord, in the More og Romsdal district, Molde is an ideal starting point for excursions along the coast and into the surrounding untamed area.

ESSENTIALS

GETTING THERE   By Plane   Arø Airport (℗ 71-21-47-10), bordering the coast, lies 4km (2½ miles) east of the heart of Molde. **Breethens** (℗ 71-21-97-00) offers three to five flights daily to and from Oslo. Once here, bus 252 goes from the airport into the center, taking 10 minutes and costing 25NOK ($3.35).

By Train   You can go from Oslo as far as Åndalsnes (see earlier) by train. From there, you must take a connecting bus to Molde. Call ℗ 71-22-48-78 for schedules.

By Bus   Buses run between Ålesund and Molde daily taking 2 hours and costing 120NOK ($16) one-way. There is a ferry crossing at Vestnes. Call ℗ 71-58-78-00 for schedules.

By Car   Driving should take about 1½ hours from Åndalsnes or Ålesund, 3 hours from Dombås, or 4 hours from Trondheim. From Trondheim, take the E6 south to Dombås and then connect with the E69 west. From Ålesund, take the E69 east. From Molde, board the ferry to Vikebukt and then go east on the E69.

By Ferry   Coming from either Ålesund or Åndalsnes, board the frequent car ferries at Vikebukt or at Vestnes for the crossing north to Molde. In July only, at the height of the tourist season, there is an express ferry *Fjørtoft*, between Ålesund and Molde, taking 2½ hours and costing 170NOK ($23) one-way. It sails twice daily Monday to Friday at that time.

By Coastal Steamer   The coastal steamer *Hurtigruten* visits Molde on its way between Bergen and Hammerfest (both directions).

VISITOR INFORMATION   The **Molde Travel Association,** Storgata 1 (© **71-25-71-33**), will provide tourist information and assist in arranging excursions. Open June 15 to August 15 Monday to Friday 9am to 6pm, Saturday 9am to 4pm, and Sunday 10am to 3pm. In the off-season, it's open Monday to Friday 8:30am to 3:30pm.

SPECIAL EVENTS   The preeminent event on the Molde calendar is its international **Jazz Festival** sponsored around the middle of July and attended by some 60,000 fans. The major open-air concerts are held near the Romsdalsmuseet, although many indoor venues are used as well, including the Idrettenshus or Sports Hall. For more information, contact the **Molde International Jazz Festival,** Box 271, N-6401 (© **71-21-60-00;** www.moldejazz.no). Tickets, costing from 100NOK to 275NOK ($13–$37) for seats, are available through **BilletService** at © **81-53-31-33.**

SEEING THE SIGHTS

The view of the 87 peaks of the **Romsdal Alps** ★★★ is worth the trip to Molde. The most scenic and most dramatic peaks are the **Romsdalshorn** at 1,559m (5,115 ft.) and the **Troll Tinder** at 1,905m (6,250 ft.). You can also see the island-studded Romsdalfjord. The best vantage point for all of this wonder is the **Belvedere Varden,** rising 396m (1,300 ft.) over Molde. Visitors can take a taxi up and ask the driver to wait for 20 minutes or so while you absorb the view. An alternative way for the more athletic is to walk up a marked trail from the center. Allow about an hour of huffing and puffing to reach the top.

Molde Domkirke   In the heart of town near Torget, Molde Cathedral, created by architect Finn Bryn in 1957, is the largest postwar cathedral in Norway and the third church to rise on this site. The old altarpiece, *Resurrection,* by Axel Ender is from the church that the Nazis bombed in April 1940 when they learned that the king was escaping from Molde. As the bombs were falling, a local patriot ripped out the painting with a knife and managed to save it from the Nazi fire.

Kirkebaken 2. © **71-11-14-60.** Free admission. Daily 10am–3:30pm.

Rådhuset (Town Hall)   This 1966 Town Hall, near Torget, is a well-conceived municipal building of concrete and glass. *The Rose Maiden* fountain celebrates Molde as the "town of roses." Marble floors and stone walls blend harmoniously, and domes and skylights capture the northern lights. The roof terrace has a garden with 2,000 roses.

Rådhusplassen. © **71-11-10-00.** Free admission. Mon–Fri 8am–4:30pm.

Finds Memories of the Literati

Today, the famous **Moldegård** house, Fannestrandveien 40, lying 1km (½ mile) east of Molde, is privately owned and can only be viewed from the outside. It was the main house of the original Molde farm, built in 1710 by Hans Nobel. Bjørnstjern Bjørnson, who wrote Norway's national anthem, among other poems, often visited here, taking his last trip to Moldegård in 1907. The cottage's more famous association is with Henrik Ibsen who lived here in 1885 and used this beautiful rococo building for the setting of one of his best-known plays, *Rosmersholm.*

Romsdalmuseet (Romsdal Museum) ★★ *Kids*   A 10-minute walk, northwest of the center, is this open-air museum with some 40 buildings, all moved to the site. Buildings range from a 16th-century *aarestue* (log cabin) to a medieval-style chapel. Walk down Bygata, the main street, taking in a composite church constructed from remnants of wooden stave churches that had to be razed. Children in regional costumes perform folk dances.

Romsdal Park. ✆ **71-20-24-60.** Admission 40NOK ($5.30) adults, 30NOK ($4) children. Mid-June to mid-Aug daily 11am–6pm; mid-Aug to mid-June daily 11am–3pm.

NEARBY ATTRACTIONS

Part of the previously explored Romsdal Museum, the **Fiskerimuseet** (Fisheries Museum; ✆ **93-42-54-06**) lies on the island of Hjertøya. Its collection consists of more than two dozen buildings moved here from the western coast of Romsdal, including dwellings, boathouses, a mechanic's workshop, and other maritime buildings. There is a number of authentic old fishing boats and gear, and you can see how the Norwegian coastal fishermen, sealers, and whalers lived in olden times. A water taxi leaves from the marketplace, Torget, in the center of Molde during the museum's open hours. The round-trip fare is 40NOK ($5.30) for adults and 30NOK ($4) for children. Trip time is 10 minutes. The Fisheries Museum keeps the same hours as the Romsdal Museum (see above); your ticket to the major museum also entitles you to visit this attraction as well.

Another attraction, **Trollkirka (Troll's Church)** ★, near Eide, is a natural wonder with seven underground caves and grottoes. There's also a 14m (45-ft.) waterfall. Going through these grottoes, with their subterranean streams, is a mystical experience. To reach the gateway to the cave, you have to walk up from the signposted main road, a distance of 2.5km (1½ miles). Allow about 1 hour to make the trip, and wear sturdy shoes. Bus 241 goes to the site two to seven times per day. The area is an open site and can be explored at any time.

To wander back into the past, you can visit **Vey Stone Church** dating from the 11th century on **Vey Island.** The little village of Kaupangen on the island was the center of Romsdal until the 14th century, and has a rich Viking past. If you'd like to visit, make your request through the Molde tourist office, which will give you a key to the church. You're taken here by a boatman for a cost of 60NOK ($8) per person; although each boat must have at least four people.

Finally, motorists, armed with a map and directions from the tourist office, can drive 2 hours up Langfjorden and along the lake Eikesdalsvatneet, to the waterfalls at **Mardalsfossen** ★★. At one time this was the highest waterfall in the world, a two-level cascade dropping 655m (2,149 ft.). Its greatest single drop is 297m (975 ft.). Mardalsfossen only flows between mid-June and mid-August. (How did Mardalsfossen lose its status among the top waterfalls of the world? Its power was extinguished by a hydroelectric project in the 1970s that was constructed in spite of massive protests by Norwegian environmentalists who at one time formed a human chain to prevent the project. They obviously did not succeed.)

WHERE TO STAY
EXPENSIVE

Quality Hotel Alexandra Molde ★★   This is the town's choicest hotel address, named for Princess Alexandra of Wales, who checked in here in the 1880s. After being destroyed and reconfigured over the years, it consists of three different structures from the '50s, '70s, and '80s, all facing a common grassy area. This is the major venue for guest artists appearing in July at the jazz festival. The hotel stands on the main street of town, overlooking the public gardens and the nearby fjord. The comfortable bedrooms are furnished in a sleek modern style. A few of the bathrooms come with tub and shower, but most of the units contain only a shower. The hotel is one of the best equipped in town, and its restaurant (Vartshusaet; see review below) and bar are popular with locals and visitors.

Storgata 1-7, N-6401 Molde. ℰ **71-20-37-50.** Fax 71-20-37-87. www.choicehotels.com. 163 units. June–Aug 940NOK ($125) double; Sept–May 1,360NOK ($181) double; year-round from 1,495NOK ($199) suite. Children under 12 stay free in parent's room. Rates include breakfast. AE, DC, MC, V. Parking 50NOK ($6.65). Closed Dec 15–Jan 3. **Amenities:** 2 restaurants; bar; indoor pool; gym; sauna; babysitting; laundry service; dry cleaning. *In room:* TV, minibar, hair dryer.

Rica Seilet Hotel Molde ★★ This is the newest, and we think best, hotel in town, rising 15 floors. Built in 2002 in a style that resembles a boat, it offers midsize to large rooms, some carpeted, others with wood floors. Most of the accommodations open onto views of the fjord, and some of the suites have a balcony. About 30 of the rooms have showers and tubs, the rest with showers. This is a well-run "ship," and its on-site facilities, such as an excellent restaurant, make it a good bet.

Gideonvegen 2, N-6412 Molde. ℰ **71-11-40-00.** Fax 71-11-40-01. www.rica.no. 169 units. 850NOK–1,295NOK ($113–$172) double; 2,000NOK–3,500NOK ($266–$466) suite. Rates include breakfast. AE, DC, MC, V. Free parking. **Amenities:** Restaurant; Sky Bar; fitness center; sauna; limited room service; laundry service; dry cleaning. *In room:* TV, minibar, hair dryer.

MODERATE

Comfort Hotel Nobel Originally built in 1920, this is one of the few buildings—and the only hotel in Molde—that was not destroyed by Nazi bombs in the '40s. Although the reception area retains some of its antique accessories, the hotel has been modernized and enlarged. Today it offers some of the best and the most up-to-date accommodations in Molde in the moderate price range. A few of the better rooms have views of the sea; these are booked first, of course. Each comes with a well-maintained private bathroom with shower (six have tub and shower). The staff can arrange trips to the museums or to the mountains. Under separate management, Amalie, a restaurant, is on the same site; see below.

Amtmann Kroghsgaten 5, N-6413 Molde. ℰ **71-25-15-55.** Fax 71-21-59-54. www.choicehotels.com. 49 units. June 15–Aug 15 750NOK ($100) double; Aug 16–June 14 1,050NOK ($140) double. Children under 12 stay free in parent's room. Rates include continental breakfast. AE, DC, MC, V. Closed Dec 22–Jan 3. *In room:* TV, minibar.

Rica Holdl Motel Dating from the late 1940s, this building was converted into a hotel in 1998, and right away became one of the town's most desirable, upholding the traditions of this leading Norwegian chain. Opening onto harbor views, with the mountains in the backdrop, the hotel sets high standards. Guests are comfortably housed in carpeted, midsize rooms with a choice of twins or a "honeymoon bed." Nearly all the small, tiled bathrooms come with shower (two with tub and shower). In lieu of any on-site hotel amenities, breakfast is served in your room.

Storgata 8, N-6400 Molde. ℰ **71-20-35-00.** Fax 71-20-35-01. www.rica.no. 88 units. 850NOK–1,295NOK ($113–$172) double; 990NOK–1,295NOK ($132–$172) suite. Children under 4 stay free. Rates include continental breakfast. AE, DC, MC, V. Free parking. *In room:* TV, minibar, hair dryer.

INEXPENSIVE

Hotel Molde In the commercial center near Torget, the market square, this hotel first opened its doors in 1910. Regrettably, the Nazis bombed it in World War II. Today, following renovations in 2001, it's one of the more up-to-date choices in town. Painted as gray as a Norwegian November afternoon, it is a privately owned and family-run establishment. Rooms are merely functional but well kept and comfortably furnished with wooden floors and small bathrooms (with shower). The on-site restaurant, The Red, is a more popular venue than the hotel itself (see below).

Storgata 19, N-6413 Molde. © **71-21-58-88.** Fax 71-21-58-90. 36 units. May 1–Sept 3 550NOK–790NOK ($73–$105) double; Sept 4–Apr 790NOK–980NOK ($105–$130). Children under 3 stay free. Rates include continental breakfast. AE, DC, MC. Free parking. **Amenities:** Restaurant; bar; laundry service; dry cleaning. *In room:* TV, minibar.

WHERE TO DINE

Amalie ♠ SEAFOOD/NORWEGIAN We always like to drop in here on a rainy day, using it as a shelter from the storm. That it serves some of the best food in town is another compelling reason to visit. It's a cozy ambience—rustic, but with a classic elegance—and the walls contain original art from some well-known Norwegian as well as international artists. Its seafood is fresh, all of it caught off the western coast of Norway. For an appetizer, sample a standard fish soup or one made from shellfish, or maybe fresh mussels in white wine sauce. For an entree, try the "fish symphony," which lured us by its melody: two pieces of whitefish, the best of the catch of the day, with crayfish and lobster sauce. The pepper steak was also tender, juicy, and well flavored, as was the lamb filet flavored with mustard and served with a cheese gratinée.

Amtmann Kroghsgaten 5. © **71-21-30-50.** Reservations recommended. Main courses 150NOK–265NOK ($20–$35). AE, DC, MC, V. July daily 4–11pm; Aug–June Tues–Sat 4–11pm. Closed Jan.

Lubbenes ♠♠ NORWEGIAN This 1860s alpinelike chalet, 2km (1¼ miles) from the town center, is one of the best restaurants. Its chefs put a modern spin on classical Norwegian food. You get generous portions of regional specialties. Waiters dash about serving perfectly executed dishes such as sautéed filet of reindeer in a velvety smooth cream sauce or fried catfish in another savory sauce. The chefs also prepare beef in a tangy onion sauce. For a starter, we recommend the lobster soup, the town's finest, or the fish soup of the day. Scampi flavored with sautéed onions is another good appetizer.

Sanestrandsvn 117. © **71-21-12-86.** Reservations recommended. Main courses 180NOK–250NOK ($24–$33). AE, DC, MC, V. Daily 4–9pm. Closed Jan.

The Red INTERNATIONAL On the street level of the Hotel Molde (see above), this restaurant serves a medley of food that has won it many admirers locally and from abroad. Many fjord dwellers like to come here for a change of pace from the usual offerings in the area. The chefs roam the world for inspiration, stopping off, perhaps, at Louisiana before heading on to Mexico. You might be served quesadillas with chicken or Cajun-blackened catfish. We've delighted in their seafood pasta and their barbecued scampi.

In the Hotel Molde, Storgata 19. © **71-21-58-88.** Reservations recommended. Main courses 100NOK–200NOK ($13–$27). AE, DC, MC, V. Daily 11am–10pm.

Vartshusaet This well-patronized restaurant, located in the Quality Hotel Alexandra Molde (see above), a short walk from Town Hall, has known various incarnations. It's currently decked out in Norwegian-tavern style with antiques and massive ceiling timbers. This is the busiest restaurant in town if you visit at the time of the jazz festival. If you've traveled Norway the menu is all too familiar, but fine regional products are used even if the recipes are pretty much the same as many other establishments. The inevitable fish soup appears on the menu, and it's good tasting and generous in proportion. For spicier fare, ask for the garlic shrimp as an appetizer. The marinated house salmon is the chef's specialty, and it's invariably good and fresh. That other favorite, cod, is prepared poached, fried, or baked with different sauces. Meat fanciers opt for the filet of reindeer with fresh vegetables.

In the Quality Hotel Alexandra Molde, Storgata 1-7. © **71-20-37-50.** Reservations recommended. Main courses 150NOK–200NOK ($20–$27). AE, DC, MC, V. Daily noon–11pm.

16 Kristiansund N & the Historic Grip Isles

68km (42 miles) N of Molde; 1,059km (658 miles) NW of Oslo; 652km (405 miles) N of Bergen

Almost entirely destroyed by World War II, the coastal town of Kristiansund N is spread over three islands and has been rebuilt into a modern city. Today it's the main service base for oil activities on the mid-Norwegian continental shelf. The Draugen and Åsgård oil fields lie off its coast.

With a population of 17,000 citizens, Kristiansund makes a good stopover for those who have made it all the way to the fjord country's northern outposts.

The city itself looks dull and modern, although the setting is panoramic. Its harbor is one of the finest along the western coast of Norway.

Since the 18th century, Kristiansund is often written with an "N," so visitors won't confuse it with the largest city along the southern coast of Norway—Kristiansand S.

In its early days, cod fishing was the mainstay of its industry. A drying process took place on shore, producing *klippfish* or dried cod, which kept many a homeowner in food for the winter.

ESSENTIALS

GETTING THERE **By Plane** Kvernberget Airport (© **71-68-30-10**) lies close to the town center, a 15- to 20-minute drive east. Three arrivals a day wing in from each of Norway's biggest cities: Oslo and Bergen. The bus trip from the airport to the center takes 15 minutes, and the bus will stop at individual hotels. For flight information about **Braathens,** the city's largest carrier, call © **81-52-00-00.**

By Train The nearest railway stations are in Oppdal and Åndalsnes, with bus connections meeting the trains.

By Bus There are daily bus connections to Trondheim, Molde, Oppdal, and Åndalsnes. Call © **71-58-78-50** for schedules.

By Car From Molde, E39 follows Moldefjord before veering inland. At a point 58km (36 miles) later, you come to a mammoth suspension bridge, stretching for 623m (2,044 ft.). This span links mainland Norway with the islet of Bergsøya, requiring a 60NOK ($8) toll. The islet is the launch pad for the undersea Freifjord, a tunnel stretching out for 5km (3 miles) and requiring a toll of 75NOK ($10). This is the start of Route 70 into Kristiansund, which lies a distance of 25km (15½ miles) to the west.

By Coastal Steamer In addition to cruise ships and trawlers, at least two coastal steamers arrive at Kristiansund every day on their way from Bergen to the North Cape or from the North Cape southward to Bergen. Identified in Norwegian as *hurtigruten,* they carry the passengers and the bulk of the supplies that keep the town alive.

VISITOR INFORMATION For information about the area, head to **Kristiansund Reiselivslag,** Kongens Plass 1 (© **71-58-54-54**). Open mid-June to mid-August Monday to Friday 9am to 7pm, Saturday and Sunday 11am to 4pm. Otherwise, Monday to Friday 8:30am to 3:30pm.

SPECIAL EVENTS   **Opera Week** thrives during the dark days of February, usually the first 2 weeks of the month. Concerts are held in the Festiviteten Culture Center, Kong Olav's Gate 1, the same building as the tourist office.

SEEING THE SIGHTS

One of Kristiansund's most frequently photographed buildings is the fan-shaped **Kirkelandet Kirke,** Langveien (© 71-67-49-77). Built in 1964 with interior walls that slope steeply inward toward the choir, it's still a trend-setting design in the use of reinforced concrete for nontraditional religious architecture. Open June through September daily from 10am to 7pm; October through May daily 10am to 2pm.

Kristiansund's only museum contains five different branches scattered in various locations throughout the town. its headquarters is the **Nordmøre Museum** ✵, Knudtzondalen (© 71-67-15-78), on the edge of town near the Atlanten Stadium. Its exhibits show how people have survived in central Norway for 9,000 years, and stresses the importance of cod as the most sought-after product in the North Sea before the discovery of oil. The grounds surrounding the museum contain a handful of antique farm buildings imported from other parts of the region. This branch of the museum is open year-round: Tuesday through Friday from 10am to 2pm, on Saturday from noon to 6pm, and on Sunday from noon to 3pm. Admission costs 20NOK ($2.65) for adults and 10NOK ($1.35) for children. The bus stop for all but a handful of city buses lies nearby (the stop's name is "Idrettshall Svømmehall").

The remaining branches of the museum are in the center of town, within a short walk from one another, along the town's harbor front. They include the **Woldbrygga** section, which is set in a turn-of-the-19th-century cooperage whose exhibits are devoted to the once-flourishing crafts of barrel- and rope-making. Nearby is the **Milnbrygga,** an 18th-century warehouse containing statistics, memorabilia, and artifacts of the town's *klippfish* (cod) industry. Also within a short walk is the **Hjelkrembrygga,** another antique warehouse (from 1835) originally built for the storage of cod and devoted today to a social history of 19th-century working conditions with unusual collections of antique photographs of a departed way of life. Each of these museums is open daily June 16 to August 17 Monday to Saturday noon to 6pm and Sunday 1 to 4pm. The cost for visits to each of them is 20NOK ($2.65) for adults and 10NOK ($1.35) for children.

The final branch of the museum is an outdoor shipyard founded in 1867, the **Mellomvaerftet,** whose antique forge and harbor-front setting contain a curious mixture of antique and modern boat-building equipment. Visitors are welcome to wander about whenever they want (within reason) winter and summer, to observe the restoration of a changing collection of modern and antique boats. Entrance to the boatyard is free, although you may want to hire one of the yard workers as a guide for a tour priced at around 20NOK ($2.65) per person.

NEARBY ATTRACTIONS

Often likened to Scotland's St. Kilda, **Grip** ✵✵, 14.5km (9 miles) offshore from Kristiansund, is one of the most fascinating of Norway's isolated islands. Until the 1970s it was the only one that was permanently occupied. Site of a lighthouse and thousands of sea birds, it's mostly occupied by summer residents and, if legends are true, the ghosts of sailors whose ships washed ashore during storms. From mid-May until late August, a ferryboat leaves for Grip from Kristiansund's harbor twice a day, costing 150NOK ($20) for adults, 75NOK ($10) for children, round-trip. Because accommodations on the island are very limited, you'll want to take a morning ferryboat ride (about 30 min. long) from Kristiansund to Grip, explore the island for 2 or 3 hours, and return the same day to Kristiansund. There's a simple cafe-style restaurant near the ferryboat landing to help you pass the time as you wait for your return.

You can also visit the sparsely inhabited offshore island of **Smøla** by taking a ferry from Kristiansund's harbor. There's an intermediate stop on Edøy, site of a stone church dating from 1250. The ferry departs throughout the year two to four times a day, depending on the day of the week and the season. Passage costs 80NOK ($11) each way for adults, half price for children. If you want to take a car to Smøla, you'll have to make a detour from Kristiansund, drive several kilometers out of your way, and take two car ferries for a combined toll of around 127NOK ($17).

WHERE TO STAY

Quality Hotel Grand ✦   Originally built in 1890 as the grandest hotel in the region, this place has seen many changes over the years. But it's still a good choice, particularly after a wholesale renovation in 2002. Bedrooms are comfortable and tastefully furnished. Bathrooms are small but adequate, each with a shower. The hotel lies a 5-minute walk south of the bus station.

Bernstorffstredet 1, N-6509 Kristiansund N. ✆ **71-57-13-00.** Fax 71-57-13-01. www.choicehotels.com. 109 units. June 20–Aug 17 840NOK ($112) double; otherwise 945NOK–1,410NOK ($126–$188) double; year-round 1,600NOK ($213) suite. Children under 5 stay free in parent's room. Rates include continental breakfast. AE, DC, MC, V. Parking 62NOK ($8.25). **Amenities:** Restaurant; bar; limited room service; laundry service; dry cleaning. *In room:* TV, minibar, hair dryer.

Rica Hotel Kristiansund ✦   Centrally located by the quay in this oil town, this first-class hotel attracts mainly business people for most of the year, filling up with summer visitors as the coastal steamer passes by. Built in 1987, the building rises 10 floors and is crowned by a Sky Bar, offering panoramic views in all directions. It's the liveliest hotel in town, with a nightclub going Friday and Saturday from 10pm to 3am. Once or twice a week there is live music in the pub. Bedrooms are comfortably and tastefully furnished in a modern design, and have recently been redecorated. About half of them open onto a view of the harbor. The small bathrooms come with tub and shower.

Storgata 41, N-6500 Kristiansund N. ✆ **71-67-64-11.** Fax 71-67-79-12. www.rica.no. 102 units. Mon–Thurs 1,440NOK ($192) double, 1,700NOK ($226) business double; Fri–Sun 950NOK ($126) double, 1,210NOK ($161) business double. Children under 3 stay free in parent's room. Rates include continental breakfast. AE, DC, MC, V. Free parking. **Amenities:** Restaurant; bar; fitness center; sauna; limited room service; babysitting; laundry service; dry cleaning. *In room:* TV, minibar, coffeemaker (business units), hair dryer.

Tulip Inn Rainbow Kristiansund   A first-class hotel, this establishment opens onto views of the mountains. Attracting both leisure travelers and businesspeople, it has been accommodating overnight guests since 1985, and housing them with considerable comfort from its position right across the street from the harbor. The bedrooms, many of which open onto views of the sea, are furnished in a modern Scandinavian style that's also cozy. The bathrooms are small but neatly maintained, each with a tub and shower. The on-site restaurant is known for its fresh fish.

Storgata 17, N-6509 Kristiansund N. ✆ **71-57-03-00.** Fax 71-57-03-10. www.rainbow-hotels.no. 49 units. 1,145NOK ($152) double. Children under 5 stay free in parent's room. Rates include breakfast. AE, DC, MC, V. Free parking. **Amenities:** Restaurant; bar/nightclub; laundry service; dry cleaning. *In room:* TV, minibar, hair dryer.

WHERE TO DINE

Consulen NORWEGIAN/FRENCH   One of the most popular restaurants in town, Consulen is housed on the lobby level of this previously recommended hotel south of the bus station. The decor includes comfortable banquettes and lots of wood trim. Menu items change daily and are most satisfying. You might begin with melon with Norwegian ham or else an appetizer of grilled scampi with curry sauce. There is a studied simplicity to the cooking—nothing fancy, each dish properly prepared. Try the grilled salmon in a creamy fish sauce with fresh vegetables or the filet of reindeer with bacon and mountain berries. They also do a good filet of pork with grilled scampi. For dessert, they are known for their homemade ice cream.

In the First Grand Hotel, Bernstoffstredet 1. *C* **71-57-13-00**. Reservations recommended. Main courses 130NOK–300NOK ($17–$40). AE, DC, MC, V. Mon–Sat 4:30–10:30pm. Closed 1 week at Christmas, 1 week at Easter.

Smia Fiskerestautrant ★★ SEAFOOD/NORWEGIAN   Installed in a former blacksmith's shop, this place serves great seafood in a picturesque setting. The atmosphere of exposed bricks, antique furniture, and a burning fireplace are in keeping with the style of this 1787 house. The fish soup is the best in town. You might also select a starter such as king crab salad or scallops and prawns. For a main course, the grilled monkfish with vegetables and a white wine sauce is a star, although you may want to try one of the dried cod dishes, for which the town became famous. You can finish off with a caramel pudding or perhaps ice cream with whisky.

Fosnagate 30B. *C* **71-67-11-70**. Reservations recommended. Main courses 110NOK–215NOK ($15–$29). AE, DC, MC, V. Mon–Fri 4–11pm; Sat 2–11pm; Sun 2–9pm.

KRISTIANSUND N AFTER DARK

Most of the action is found at the **Tulip Inn Rainbow Bar** (*C* **71-57-03-00**) in the Tulip Inn Rainbow Kristiansund (see review above). In a cozy setting with leather chairs, this is an informal place to gather for drinks. Every Wednesday is karaoke night, and sometimes a live band is brought in on Friday and Saturday nights. It's open Monday to Saturday 8pm to 1:30am. There's often a 40NOK ($5.30) cover on Friday and Saturday nights if there is live entertainment.

Trondheim

Founded by the Viking king Olaf I Tryggvason in the 10th century, Trondheim is Norway's third-largest city and was until the early 1200s the country's capital. Scenic and pleasant, it's a bustling university center, with expansive avenues created after a fire razed most of the town in 1681. The city lies on the south bay of the Trondheim Fjord, at the mouth of the Nidelven River.

Noted for its timbered architecture, Trondheim retains much of its medieval past, notably the Gothic-style Nidaros Cathedral. Pilgrims came from all over Europe to worship at the shrine of Olaf, who was buried in the cathedral and canonized in 1031.

The city's fortunes declined during the Reformation. Under the Nazi occupation Trondheim became the base of German naval forces in northern Norway, with U-boats lurking deep in its fjord.

Today Trondheim is a progressive city with a rich cultural life. Its town center is compact and best explored on foot. Most of the historic core of Trondheim lies on a small triangular island surrounded by water but linked via bridges.

Tronkheim lies some 684km (425 miles) north of Bergen, and 552km (343 miles) northwest of Oslo.

1 Orientation

ESSENTIALS

ARRIVAL

BY PLANE   Flights to Trondheim land at **Vaernes Airport** (© 74-84-30-00), lying 32km (21 miles) east of the city center. Most visitors fly here from either Bergen or Oslo. There are also daily connections to and from Copenhagen. Service is provided by **SAS** (© 74-80-41-00) and by **Braathens ASA** (© 74-84-32-00).

Once you arrive at the airport you can take an airport bus, **Flybussen** (© 73-82-25-00), costing 55NOK ($7.30) for a one-way trip into the center. The trip takes 40 minutes, ending at the rail depot. From the center of Trondheim, buses leave on Erling Skakkes gate daily from 5am to 9pm. Departures Monday to Friday are every 15 minutes, with curtailed departures on Saturday and Sunday. You can also take a taxi from the airport to the center, costing around 500NOK ($67) per person.

BY TRAIN   Two trains a day arrive from Stockholm (trip time: 12 hr.) and three trains per day arrive from Oslo (trip time: 7 hr.) into **Trondheim Sentralstasjon.** A typical fare—say, from Oslo to Trondheim—costs 650NOK ($86) one-way. Trondheim also has links to Bodø if you're heading for the Arctic Circle. This latter trip takes 10 hours, costing 750NOK ($100) one-way. For rail information, call © 81-50-08-88.

BY BUS   Buses from various parts of Norway arrive at the **Rutebilstasjon,** or city bus terminal, adjoining Trondheim Sentralstasjon, where the trains pull in. Trondheim lies at the crossroads of bus travel in Norway, as it is a transportation hub between southern Norway, including Oslo and Bergen, and northern Norway, including the city of Bodø. The most frequented bus route is from Oslo, taking 9½ hours and costing 600NOK ($80) one-way. The more difficult route from Bergen takes more than 14 hours, costing 750NOK ($100) one-way. For information about long-distance buses, contact **Norway Buss Ekspress** (© 81-54-44-44).

BY BOAT   The **Hurtigruten coastal steamer** (© 77-64-82-00) stops in Trondheim. In addition, **Fosen Teraffikklag Kystekspressen boats** (© 72-57-20-20) travel between Kristiansund N and Trondheim, taking 3½ hours and costing 410NOK ($55). Departures are at Pirterminalen Quay in Trondheim.

BY CAR   From Oslo, motorists can take the express highway E6 north, going via Lillehammer all the way into Trondheim.

VISITOR INFORMATION
Contact the **Trondheim Tourist Office,** Munkegaten 19 (© 73-80-76-60; www.trondheim.com), near the marketplace. The staff can also make hotel reservations or arrange for rooms in a private home. Double rooms in private homes cost from 350NOK ($47); the service fee is 20NOK ($2.65), which is deducted at checkout time. The tourist office is open September 4 to May 14 Monday to Friday 8:30am to 4pm; May 15 to June 4 and August 21 to September 3 Monday to Friday 8:30am to 6pm, Saturday and Sunday 10am to 4pm; June 5 to June 25 and August 7 to August 20 Monday to Friday 8:30am to 8pm, and Saturday and Sunday 10am to 6pm; and June 26 to August 6 Monday to Friday 8:30am to 10pm and Saturday and Sunday 10am to 8pm.

GETTING AROUND
You can travel all over Trondheim and to outlying areas on city buses operated by **Trondheim Trafikkselskap (TT),** Dronningens Gate (© 73-50-28-70). Tickets for **single rides** are sold on buses for 22NOK ($2.95) for adults, 11NOK ($1.45) for children 4 to 16; children under 4 travel free. If you don't have exact change, you'll get a credit slip from the driver, which can be redeemed at the TT office or on a later trip. A **day card** for 24 hours of unlimited rides costs 55NOK ($7.30) per person.

For a local **taxi,** TrønderTaxi maintains 24-hour service (© 73-90-90-73). The biggest taxi rank is found at Torvet, the market square, and also at the central rail station. For local bus information serving the Greater Trondheim area, call © 73-50-28-70.

Amazingly, a fleet of some 200 green bikes is available free at racks scattered around the city. To secure one, insert a 20NOK ($2.65) coin. When you're through with the bike, bring it back and your coin will be returned. Naturally, you should lock the bike again. The whole system will make you want to write an ode to the joys of living in a civilized country.

CITY LAYOUT
From the Trondheim train station simply walk south across the bridge to the triangular-shaped island forming the city's central core. The center is called **Midtbyen.** In Norse sagas it was referred to as Nidarneset or the Nidar headland. The best way to explore this area is on foot, and you can easily walk to all the major attractions, including Nidaros Cathedral and the Archbishop's Palace.

The very center of Trondheim is the **Torvet,** or market square. A major street, **Kongens Gate,** splits the island into two parts. The **Fish Market,** reached from Torvet by walking north along Munkegate, lies to the north.

At Nidareid by the narrow isthmus between the river and the fjord lies ancient **Skansen.** The remnants of the old city fortifications toward the west can still be seen. Today this area is a green park with a panoramic view of the fjord.

The **Bakklandet** district is the most easily accessible from the rest of Trondheim via the "Old Town Bridge," an early-20th-century iron structure that is the most-often-photographed bridge in Trondheim. Noted for its slightly out-of-kilter antique wooden houses built for low-income canning factory workers and fishermen, the area used to stink of rotting fish, and in the 1910s and 1920s, it came very close to being demolished. But after the demise of the town's fishing industry and the end of the town's canning factories, a greater emphasis was placed on preserving the site as a historical record of days gone by. Today, its most famous cafe is the **Café Gåsa (Café Goose),** its celebrated restaurant is **Bryggen,** and its most famous pub is the **Den Gode Nabo ("The Good Neighbor") Pub.** The neighborhood also holds a number of students' pubs, one of which is the **Kaktus** (see later in this chapter). The neighborhood is quite small—40 buildings or so—and easily toured on foot.

 FAST FACTS: **Trondheim**

Automobile Association Driving in the wilds of central Norway in the vast open stretches around Trondheim might be hazardous if the weather turns bad. For directions or information about road conditions or even reroutings, call **Norwegian Automobile Association** at ℰ **73-95-73-95.**

Consulates There is no U.S. consulate. The consulate for Great Britain is at Beddingen 8 (ℰ **73-60-02-00**).

Dentists If you need emergency assistance, call ℰ **73-50-55-00.**

Emergencies For a fire, dial ℰ **110,** for the police ℰ **112,** and for an ambulance ℰ **113.**

Hospitals For nonemergencies, your hotel can put you into contact with an English-speaking doctor. For a medical emergency, call ℰ **73-52-25-00.**

Internet Access Go to the Trondheim Public Library, Peter Egges Plass 1 (ℰ **72-54-75-00**). From July 1 to August 12, it is open Monday, Tuesday, Thursday, and Friday 9am to 4pm, Wednesday 9am to 7pm, Saturday 10am to 3pm. At other times, hours are Monday to Thursday 9am to 7pm, Friday 9am to 4pm, Saturday 10am to 3pm, and Sunday noon to 4pm. The service is free through 2003.

Laundry If you don't use the services your hotel provides, you can go to **Elefanten Vaskeri,** Mellomveien 20 (ℰ **73-51-29-89**), which is open Monday to Friday 10am to 6pm and Saturday 11am to 4pm. It's the northernmost laundromat in Norway.

Parking Garages The major garages are **Bakke P-hus,** Nedre Bakklandet 60 (ℰ **72-54-64-97**), and **Midtbyen P-hus,** Sandgata 28 (ℰ **73-51-51-80**).

Pharmacies The most central pharmacy is **Apotek Svanen,** Kongens Gate 14B, at Torvet (ℰ **73-99-03-70**), the market square. Hours are Monday to Friday 8:30am to 5pm, Saturday 9am to 3pm.

Police The police station is at Kongens Gate 87 (📞 **73-89-90-90**).

Post Office The main post office is at Dronningens Gate 10 (📞 **73-95-84-00**), open Monday to Friday 8am to 5pm, Saturday 9am to 2pm.

Telephone Avoid expensive phone surcharges at your hotel by making your calls at **Telecommunications,** at Kongens Gate 8 (📞 **73-54-30-11**).

2 Where to Stay

Many hotels offer special summer prices from mid-June to the end of August. The rest of the year, hotels offer weekend discounts if you stay two nights.

EXPENSIVE

Britannia Hotel ⭐ The grande dame of Trondheim hotels, built in 1897, this white-stucco structure is graced with a majestic slate-covered dome and tower reminiscent of the grand Victorian monuments of England. Conservative, stable, and dependable, but lacking a cutting-edge sense of glamour, the Britannia offers a physical plant that, frankly, would be more appealing if some badly conceived modernizations hadn't been made in the 1960s. The ornate Palm Garden (see "Where to Dine," later in this chapter), with its Art Nouveau winter garden, fountain, and piano, captures the grand spirit. The renovated guest rooms have wooden floors. The most tranquil units front the courtyard, but are also the smallest rooms. Most accommodations are medium size with excellent beds and tiled bathrooms with shower-tub combinations.

Dronningens Gate 5, N-7001 Trondheim. 📞 **73-53-53-53.** Fax 73-51-29-00. www.britannia.no. 247 units. Mon–Thurs 1,500NOK–1,850NOK ($200–$246) double; Fri–Sun 950NOK ($126) double; year-round from 3,200NOK ($426) suite. Rates include breakfast. AE, DC, MC, V. Parking 186NOK ($25). Bus: 2, 5, 6, 7, or 9. **Amenities:** 3 restaurants; 3 bars; fitness center; sauna; limited room service; babysitting; laundry service; dry cleaning. *In room:* TV, minibar, hair dryer.

Clarion Grand Olav Hotel ⭐⭐ This six-story hotel is the most stylish in Trondheim. It was designed in 1989 by the architect of the nearby Radisson SAS Royal Garden Hotel, a close competitor. The hotel (which became the Clarion Grand in 1998) is adjacent to a building complex that includes elegant boutiques and Trondheim's largest concert hall. Its modern interior is plush and imaginative; guest rooms are decorated in one of 27 different styles. Rooms have good beds and ample bathrooms, with shower-tub combinations and state-of-the-art plumbing.

Kjøpmannsgaten 48, N-7010 Trondheim. 📞 **73-80-80-80.** Fax 73-80-80-81. www.grandolav.no. 106 units. 1,130NOK–1,900NOK ($150–$253) double; 3,000NOK–6,000NOK ($399–$798) suite. Rates include breakfast. AE, DC, MC, V. Parking 150NOK ($20). Bus: 54. **Amenities:** Restaurant; bar; limited room service; laundry service; dry cleaning. *In room:* A/C, TV, minibar, hair dryer.

Radisson SAS Royal Garden Hotel ⭐⭐ This is the most architecturally dramatic and innovative hotel in Trondheim. Originally built in 1984 to replace a row of waterfront warehouses that had burned down in a fire, it rises on stilts—a glowing, glass-sided jewel-box—abruptly above the Nid River, so close to the water that you can catch salmon from your balcony if you're so inclined. Inside is an intriguing array of angled glass skylights, stone floors, soaring atriums, and plants. As a reaffirmation of the hotel's importance, during the May 2002 royal wedding of Norway's Princess Martha-Louise, members of the royal

Trondheim Accommodations & Dining

ACCOMMODATIONS ■

Best Western Chesterfield Hotel **19**
Britannia Hotel **13**
Clarion Grand Olav Hotel **22**
Comfort Hotel Bakeriet **21**
Gildevangen Hotell **18**
Hotel Fru Scholler **3**
Lilletorget **16**
Radisson SAS Royal Garden
   Hotel **23**
Scandic Hotel Prinsen **6**
Scandic Hotel Residence **4**
Trondheim Hotell **5**
Viking Hotel **14**

DINING ◆

Akropolis **20**
Bølgen & Moi Trondheim **17**
Bryggen **10**
Café-Conditorei E. Erichsen **12**
Café Gåsa (Café Goose) **9**
Egon Tårnet **11**
Fru Inger **1**
Grenaderen **7**
Havfruen (Mermaid) **24**
Jonathan's **13**
Kvilhaugen Gärd
   (Rest Hill Farm) **11**
Odin's **14**
Palm Garden **13**
Prins Olavs Grill **23**
Restaurant Egon **15**
Sushi Bar **2**
Tavern På Sverresborg **8**

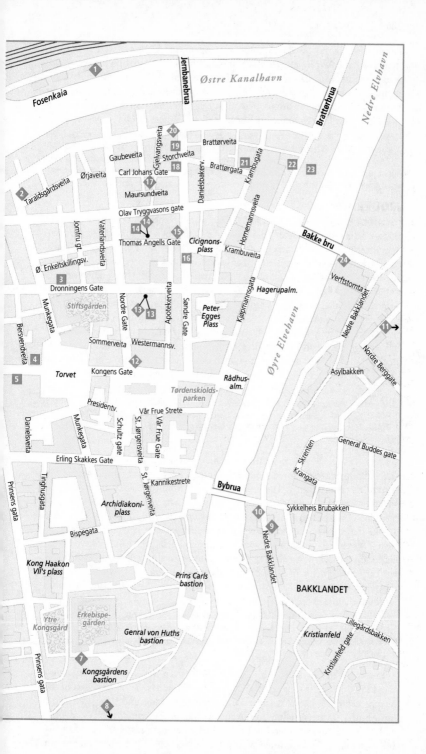

Fosenkaia

Jernbanebrua

Østre Kanalhavn

Brattørbrua

Nedre Elvhavn

Gaubeveita

Gjelvangsveita

Storchveita

Brattørveita

Krambugata

Ørjaveita

Carl Johans Gate

Brattørgata

Taraldsgårdsveita

Maursundveita

Danielsbakerv.

Hornemannsveita

Jomfru gt.

Vaterlandsveita

Olav Tryggvasons gate

Thomas Angells Gate

Cicignons-
plass

Krambuveita

Bakke bru

Verftstomta

Ø. Enkeltskillingsv.

Dronningens Gate

Kjøpmannsgata

Hagerupalm.

Nedre Bakklandet

Nordre Berggate

Munkegata

Stiftsgården

Nordre Gate

Apotekerveita

Søndre Gate

Peter
Egges
Plass

Øyre Elvehavn

Bersvendveita

Sommerveita

Westermannsv.

Kongens Gate

Rådhus-
alm.

Asylbakken

Torvet

Tørdenskiolds-
parken

General Buddes gate

Danielsveita

Presidentv.

Vår Frue Strete

Skrenten

Munkegata

Schultz gate

St. Jørgensveita

Vår Frue Gate

Krangata

Erling Skakkes Gate

Tinghusgata

St. Jørgenveita

Kannikestrete

Bybrua

Sykkelheis Brubakken

Prinsens gata

Archidiakoni-
plass

Nedre Bakklandet

BAKKLANDET

Bispegata

Kong Haakon
VII's plass

Prins Carls
bastion

Lillegårdsbakken

Ytre
Kongsgård

Erkebispe-
gården

Genral von Huths
bastion

Kristianfeld

Prinsens gata

Kongsgårdens
bastion

Kristianfeld gate

families of Belgium, Sweden, Luxembourg, Spain, and Denmark were all housed here in what could have been a security- and protocol-related nightmare—and it all went off with barely a hitch. Rooms are comfortable and tastefully contemporary, outfitted in pale tones of gray, earth tones, and/or blue. About half have shower-tub combinations. The most elegant of the hotel's restaurants, the Prins Olavs Grill, is recommended separately in "Where to Dine," below.

Kjøpmannsgaten 73, N-7010 Trondheim. © **73-80-32-21.** Fax 73-80-32-50. www.radissonsas.com. 298 units. Mon–Thurs 1,640NOK ($218) double, from 2,500NOK ($333) suite; Fri–Sun and daily mid-June to Aug 995NOK ($132) double, 1,110NOK ($148) suite. AE, DC, MC, V. Bus: 1, 4. **Amenities:** 2 restaurants; panoramic bar with pianist; nightclub with live jazz and blues; indoor pool; health club and exercise center; sauna; concierge; boutiques; limited room service; babysitting; laundry service; dry cleaning; solarium. *In room:* TV, minibar.

MODERATE

Comfort Hotel Bakeriet ★ *(finds)* One of my favorite hotels in Trondheim occupies the mock-fortified, solid-looking premises of what functioned between 1863 and 1963 as the largest bakery in Norway. Today some aspects of the place might remind you of a museum, thanks to a number of displays that showcase the ovens, cooling racks, and paraphernalia associated with the building during its early days. Some of these displays, including elaborate costumes worn by some of the bakery employees around the turn of the century, even decorate the upstairs hallways that lead to the large and very comfortable bedrooms. Many of these have carefully finished half-paneling and easy chairs and settees, and each has a large tiled bathroom with a shower-tub combination. There's even an underground railway, once used to transport raw materials for the bread and its ovens, that stretches from here to a point in Trondheim near the cathedral.

Brattørgata 2, N-7010 Trondheim. © **73-99-10-00.** Fax 73-99-10-01. 109 units. Mon–Thurs 1,570NOK ($209) double; year-round Fri–Sun and mid-June to mid-Aug daily 1,045NOK ($139) double; year-round 1,750NOK ($233) suite. Rates include breakfast and Mon–Thurs a light evening supper. AE, DC, MC, V. Bus: 1, 4. **Amenities:** Breakfast room and lounge; sauna; babysitting; laundry service; dry cleaning; Turkish bath. *In room:* TV, minibar.

Hotel Fru Scholler ★ *(finds)* In the center of town, close to the marketplace, this building was handsomely converted from a structure that stood here at the turn of the 20th century. The foundations date from the 17th century, but the building has seen many changes over the years. Impressively modernized, it is now one of the better small hotels in the historic core.

The staff is one of the most helpful we encountered in Trondheim, arranging tickets for concerts in summer and booking sightseeing excursions for you. The bedrooms for the most part are large; each unit is well furnished, and the floors are carpeted. Twelve of the accommodations are equipped with a tub-and-shower combination; the rest contain showers only. And, for such a prime location, the prices are most affordable.

Dronningens Gate 26, N-7011 Trondheim. © **73-87-08-00.** Fax 73-87-08-01. www.euronet.no/ kulturhotell/hotell_fru_scholler.htm. 853NOK–1,175NOK ($113–$156) double. Rates include continental breakfast. AE, DC, MC, V. Closed Dec 20–Jan 2. Bus: 1, 4. **Amenities:** Cafe/bar; laundry services; dry cleaning. *In room:* TV, minibar, hair dryer, iron/ironing board.

Scandic Hotel Prinsen This six-story hotel from the early 1960s was renovated in 2000 and is today one of the city's better hotels. Set in the heart of the historic center, the hotel is a blend of harmonious colors and solid, substantial furnishings. It caters mainly to business clients in the winter but is a favorite with visitors in the summer. Most of the bedrooms are midsize and comfortably and tastefully furnished, often with wooden Norwegian provincial pieces, but some can be rather small. If you need more space, request a larger room when reserving. Most of the small bathrooms have shower units, although some come with tub and shower. Many of the bedrooms also open onto a view of the fjord waters. On site is the oldest pub in Trondheim, **Kieglekroa.** Even nonguests come here to sample the locally famous steak (called the "Fairytale Steak") served in the on-site Pinocchio restaurant.

Kongens Gate 30, N-7417 Trondheim. ✆ **73-80-70-00.** Fax 73-80-70-10. 81 units. 796NOK–1,350NOK ($106–$180) double. Children under 12 stay free. Rates include continental breakfast. AE, DC, MC, V. Bus: 1, 4. **Amenities:** Restaurant; bar; pub; coffee shop; limited room service; laundry service; dry cleaning. *In room:* TV, minibar, hair dryer.

Scandic Hotel Residence   On the market square opposite the Royal Palace, the Hotel Residence, built in 1915 in Jugend (Art Nouveau) style, has recently been renovated. Accommodations are tastefully decorated, and the units in front open onto the marketplace. The generously sized guest rooms have triple-glazed windows and good beds. The big marble bathrooms offer great shelf space, shower-tub combinations, and, in some cases, bidets. Much of the hotel's ground floor is given over to the **Café Amsterdam,** a trio of rustically decorated rooms reminiscent of a Dutch tavern, with an area for drinking and separate areas for well-prepared platters and snacks.

Munkegaten 26, N-7011 Trondheim. ✆ **800/528-1234** in the U.S., or 73-52-83-80. Fax 73-52-64-60. residence@scandic-hotels.com. 66 units. Sun–Thurs 1,450NOK ($193) double; Fri–Sat 996NOK ($132) double. Rates include breakfast. AE, DC, MC, V. Parking 50NOK ($6.65). Bus: 2, 5, 6, 7, or 9. **Amenities:** Restaurant; bar; laundry service; dry cleaning. *In room:* TV, minibar, hair dryer.

Viking Hotel   Built in the early 1990s and set behind a modern, angular facade that might remind you of a somewhat foreboding office building, this middle-bracket hotel has rooms that are comfortable, cozy, and even a tad plush. Accommodations are outfitted in monochromatic tones of blue, green, or soft yellow, each with hardwood floors, a decor that's vaguely inspired by the Victorian age of England, and each with a meticulously tiled bathroom that's more up to date and appealing than that of any other hotel in its price category in Trondheim. All have showers but no bathtubs. Of its 35 units, only a dozen are specifically configured as doubles, the rest being single rooms favored by European business travelers during corporate excursions to Trondheim. Overall, it's an excellent and reasonably priced choice that's conveniently located in the town's commercial core. Its unpretentious tavern-style restaurant (Odin's) serves excellent food, which is separately recommended in "Where to Dine," below.

Thomas Engells Gate 12B. N-7011 Trondheim. ✆ **73-51-21-33.** Fax 73-51-43-14. www.vikinghotel.no. 35 units. Mon–Thurs 1,095NOK ($146) double; Fri–Sun and mid-June to mid-Aug daily 700NOK–800NOK ($93–$106) double. AE, DC, MC, V. Bus: 1, 4. **Amenities:** Restaurant; bar; babysitting; laundry service; dry cleaning. *In room:* TV.

INEXPENSIVE

Best Western Chesterfield Hotel ✮ *Finds*   This small, cozy, centrally located, English-inspired hotel has a lobby that doubles as a pub and, to further push the Anglophile theme, a collection of leather-upholstered Chesterfield sofas. Built in 1947, it originally functioned as a doctor's office and an office building, but in 1992, it was transformed into the charming, seven-story hotel you see today. Only breakfast is served, but in winter, a light evening meal is included, buffet-style, as part of the price. Bedrooms are medium size, high ceilinged, and very pleasant, with a sense of old-fashioned styling, full-grained wooden furniture, and modern-looking tile-covered bathrooms, each with showers but not tubs.

Søndregate 26, N-7010 Trondheim. © **800/528-1234** in the U.S., or 73-50-37-50. Fax 73-50-37-55. hotel@online.no. 43 units. Mon–Thurs 1,025NOK ($136) double; Fri–Sun and mid-June to mid-Aug daily 775NOK ($103). AE, DC, MC, V. Bus: 1, 4. **Amenities:** Pub-style lobby bar; sauna; laundry service; dry cleaning; solarium. *In room:* TV, minibar.

Gildevangen Hotell ★ *Value*   One of Trondheim's most architecturally distinctive antique hotels, the Gildevangen sits behind a dramatic-looking facade of massive, carefully chiseled stone blocks. Originally built in 1910 as an office building and transformed into a hotel in 1930, it offers clean, uncomplicated, and quiet bedrooms, each of which has a floor plan that's a bit different from that of its neighbors. Only breakfast is served here, but from Monday to Thursday a light evening meal is included in the overnight price. Most of the bedrooms have tiled bathrooms with shower stalls, and in some rare instances a shower-bathtub combination. Each has big windows, generous dimensions, and high ceilings.

Søndre Gate 22B, N-7010 Trondheim. © **73-87-01-30.** Fax 73-52-38-98. www.rainbow-hotels.no. 110 units. Mon–Thurs 1,245NOK ($166) double; Fri–Sun 850NOK ($113) double, if you present a ScanPass hotel pass, available for a 1-time fee of 90NOK ($12). AE, DC, MC, V. Bus: 1, 4. **Amenities:** Concierge; babysitting; laundry service; dry cleaning. *In room:* A/C, TV, minibar.

Lilletorget *Value*   Situated in a public office building, this hotel lies close to the attractions at the historic center. An experienced staff runs an immaculately kept and tastefully furnished place. Bedrooms are done in a classical style and are quite cozy with cushioned furniture and small bathrooms; most have carpeted floors. The doubles have tub-and-shower combinations; the singles come with showers. The hotel was recently renovated, and it's especially welcoming to families.

Cicignons Plass, N-7011 Trondheim. © **73-80-63-00.** Fax 73-53-21-43. www.lilletorget.no. 44 units. 740NOK–1,050NOK ($98–$140) double. Children under 10 stay free. Rates include continental breakfast. AE, DC, MC, V. Closed Dec 20–Jan 2. Bus: 1, 4. *In room:* TV, minibar, hair dryer.

Trondheim Hotell   This hotel near the market square offers medium-size guest rooms with upholstered classic bentwood furniture. Many have an extra foldaway bed. Some rooms are suitable for persons with disabilities, and others are reserved for nonsmokers. The beds are good, and the bathrooms, though small, are equipped with shower-tub combinations. Constructed in 1913, the hotel was renovated and expanded in 1990. If you're up for a swinging evening out, the nearby Monte Cristo Disco admits hotel guests free.

Kongens Gate 15, N-7013 Trondheim. © **73-50-50-50.** Fax 73-51-60-58. www.rainbow-hotels.no. 131 units. 1,245NOK ($166) double. Rates include breakfast. AE, DC, MC, V. Parking 113NOK ($15). Bus from airport stops here. **Amenities:** Restaurant; bar; lounge; laundry service. *In room:* TV, minibar, hair dryer.

3 Where to Dine

Try the local specialty *vafler medøst* (**waffle and cheese**), sold at most cafeterias and restaurants.

EXPENSIVE

Bølgen & Moi Trondheim ★ CONTINENTAL   This is the northernmost branch of a marketing group of six Norwegian restaurants, each supervised by a partnership of what is quickly becoming Norway's most visible pair of trend-setting restaurateurs. It's so fashionable that the Norwegian Princess Martha-Louise and her fiancé selected it as the site of a prewedding dinner party for 100 of their friends in May 2002. If you opt to dine here, be alert to the different options available inside. There's a bar and brasserie on the street level, and a smaller, more exclusive and more expensive restaurant upstairs. Both areas are lined with unusual modern art, and thanks to the angular steel-and-glass modernism, the decor has often been likened to that of an airport waiting lounge. Those unfortunate comparisons quickly fade, however, when the food is served. Trondheim's freshest oysters are served here, with a choice of fresh lemon or a savory vinaigrette. We recently discovered another delightful appetizer: poached sea trout with tsatziki (cucumber-yogurt sauce) and a creamy dollop of cauliflower. The chefs proceed to tantalize you with the likes of breast of duck with a thyme-flavored pancake filled with red cabbage, or else the "French Connection": a choice cut of entrecôte served with a perfectly made béarnaise sauce with french fries. You'll think you've been miraculously delivered to a Left Bank bistro in Paris.

Carl Johansgate 5. ⓒ **73-56-89-00.** Reservations recommended. Restaurant main courses 220NOK–260NOK ($29–$35); fixed-price menus 395NOK–650NOK ($53–$86); 8-course surprise menu with wine 1,000NOK ($133). Brasserie set-course lunch 290NOK–490NOK ($39–$65); main courses 75NOK–175NOK ($10–$23). AE, DC, MC, V. Brasserie Mon–Sat 11am–10pm; restaurant Tues–Sat 6–9:30pm. Bus: 1, 4.

Bryggen ★★ NORWEGIAN/FRENCH One of the most atmospheric restaurants in Trondheim is in a 1749 warehouse with a heavily trussed brick interior. It's on the verdant banks of the Nidelven River, a few steps from the town's oldest bridge, the Gamle Bybro, and just a 10-minute walk from the town center. Inside, a baronial collection of supremely comfortable furniture evokes the chateau life. The menu varies with the season. It might include fish-and-shellfish soup, medallions of reindeer in juniper-berry cream sauce, or poached fresh fish of the day. You'll find the staff devoted, professional, and justifiably proud of the intriguing cuisine, which is likely to feature such unusual dishes as fresh asparagus with quail eggs and a mousseline sauce, or halibut in an oyster and sherry sauce. The members of our party recently were delighted with such dishes as fresh Norwegian lamb with spinach and a mustard-flavored thyme sauce, and the filet of veal with glazed sweetbreads and a foie gras sauce. There's an extensive wine list and an impressive selection of cognac and cigars.

Øvre Bakklandet 66. ⓒ **73-52-02-30.** Reservations recommended. Main courses 240NOK–290NOK ($32–$39); 3-course fixed-price menu 475NOK ($63); 5-course fixed-price dinner 650NOK ($86). AE, DC, MC, V. Mon–Sat 6pm–midnight. Bus: 1, 5, or 9.

Fru Inger ★ SEAFOOD This is one of the two or three most important and most popular seafood restaurants in Trondheim. It's not as chic, cutting-edge, and sophisticated as the also-recommended Havfruen (see below), but it serves an intelligent, imaginative cuisine at somewhat less expensive prices. Named after a 1950s-era cargo ship (*Fru Inger,* or "Miss Inger") now based in Mexico, it's housed in a glass-sided pavilion that overlooks the old and new fishing vessels moored beside a canal, a short walk from the railway station. Inside, a navy-blue color scheme, varnished mahogany, and pin lighting work to enhance the nautical decor. Our most recently sampled starter was lime- and chile-marinated scallops served on a salad bed of fresh tomato and sweet peppers. Drawn from the cold, deep waters of Norway, shark is delectably served with smoked salmon, a skewer of fresh vegetables, and risotto. The salt-baked filet of cod came with a savory basil sauce. If you're here on a summer day, opt for the rhubarb soup with cinnamon ice cream.

Fosenkaia. ⓒ **73-51-60-71.** Reservations recommended. Main courses 99NOK–299NOK ($13–$40) at lunch, 185NOK–299NOK ($25–$40) at dinner; fixed-price menus 325NOK–373NOK ($43–$50). AE, DC, MC, V. May–Sept Mon–Sat noon–midnight, Sun noon–8pm; Oct–Apr daily 5pm–midnight. Bus: 1, 4.

Grenaderen ★ *Finds* NORWEGIAN   The setting of this place is a much-gentrified update of what was built more than a century ago as a blacksmith shop. Today, amid flickering candles and a collection of 19th-century wood- and metal-working artifacts, you get a sense of rustic, old-fashioned Norway, much spiffed up from the dingy smoke-filled days when the place would have been a lot less appealing. Menu items include some of the time-tested workhorses of the Norwegian culinary repertoire, including gin-marinated smoked salmon; cream of fish and shellfish soup; small-scale platters of fish roe, served with very fresh bread and Norwegian butter; a traditional air-dried fish specialty, lutefisk, that's notoriously difficult to make and in this case served with bacon; several kinds of grilled beefsteaks, some accompanied with grilled shrimp; barbecued pork ribs; and a dessert specialty, wild berry parfait with whiskey sauce.

Kongsgårdsgata 1. ℂ **73-51-66-80.** Reservations recommended. Main courses 200NOK–290NOK ($27–$39). AE, DC, MC, V. Mon–Sat noon–10pm; Sun 2–9pm. Closed Sept–May Mon. Bus: 2, 5, 6, 7, or 9.

Jonathan's ★ NORWEGIAN/FRENCH   One of the best hotel restaurants in town, Jonathan's is designed in the manner of a Mediterranean wine cellar, with antiques, a big, open fireplace, and waiters colorfully dressed as troubadours. The beautifully prepared food relies on high-quality ingredients. Dinner might include canapés of shrimp, smoked salmon, and local caviar, followed by grilled salmon garnished with shellfish and fresh vegetables, or a grilled steak—perhaps a veal schnitzel.

In the Brittania Hotel, Dronningens Gate 5. ℂ **73-53-53-53.** Reservations required. Main courses 210NOK–245NOK ($28–$33). AE, DC, MC, V. Daily 5–11pm. Bus: 2, 5, 6, 7, or 9.

Palm Garden ★★ NORWEGIAN/INTERNATIONAL   This is the most elegant restaurant in Trondheim, evocative of the Belle Epoque era. Illuminated with a Victorian-era skylight, it is ringed with exotic-looking columns inspired by the Corinthian/Moorish look. There is some of the atmosphere of the ambulatory of a medieval cloister. True to its namesake, the restaurant is filled with palms. Lunch is formatted as a sandwich-and-salad buffet, attracting many of the town's leading business clients. Dinner is grandly elaborate, with an array of top-quality dishes prepared with the finest of ingredients. Standards remain high here—the classic cuisine never seems to bog down on repeated visits over the years. The service is also the most grandly formal in town.

Begin, perhaps, with a marinated wild salmon in a fennel bouillon with apple salsa, or else a delightful creamed curry mussel soup (the little ravioli in the soup are stuffed with mussels). For real Norwegian flavor, opt for the top side of stag, with fresh mushrooms, creamed vegetables, and—just the right touch—red whortleberry chutney. This year we also enjoyed the loin filets of veal stuffed with Parma ham and fresh sage, served with pickled tomatoes, mashed Fondant potatoes, and artichokes. For dessert, try a specialty rarely found outside Scandinavia: warm cloudberries from the Arctic tundra, served in this case with hazelnut ice cream.

In the Britannia Hotel, Dronningens Gate 5. ℂ **73-53-53-53.** Reservations required. Lunch sandwich and salad buffet 150NOK–200NOK ($20–$27); dinner main courses 235NOK–280NOK ($31–$37). AE, DC, MC, V. Daily 11am–3pm and 7–11pm. Bus: 2, 5, 6, 7, or 9.

Prins Olavs Grill ★ CONTINENTAL   Set on the lobby level of the also-recommended hotel (see earlier), this restaurant is named after a once-majestic sailing ship, the *Alexandra,* which was commissioned early in the 20th century by the British Navy. It was purchased (and renamed the *Prins Olav*) by the

Norwegian navy in the 1930s, and then sunk by the Nazi air force in 1940. Today, some of the ship's gilded architectural fretworks and embellishments, as well as a photographic history of the vessel, decorate the walls of a room that's noteworthy for its sense of comfort and well-being. Dishes that emerge from the busy, open-to-view kitchen, include such appetizing starters as a crayfish tortellini swimming in a zesty tomato bouillon or a monkfish kabob with crème fraîche set off tantalizingly with a taste of mint. Some of the recipes are satisfyingly familiar, including the pan-fried steak of salmon in an herb oil, or the oven-baked turbot dressed up with an orange fennel salad and shellfish sauce. The chefs reach out to the globe for inspiration when they take a tuna fish, smoke it with chile peppers and serve it with baked sweet potato, sour banana salsa, and a lime beurre blanc. If you opt for a meat course, you can hardly do better than the leg of pheasant fricassee with Jerusalem artichokes, everything coming with a lemon confit. Trondheimers take delight in the chef's grilled filet of beef and tongue with creamy summer cabbage, soya gravy, and a deep-fried chile pasta. For dessert, nothing beats the chocolate cake with Irish coffee accompanied with strawberry "slush" and mocha caramel.

In the Radisson SAS Royal Garden Hotel, Kjøpmannsgaten 73. (℃ **73-80-32-21.** Reservations recommended. Main courses 250NOK–265NOK ($33–$35); fixed-price menus 465NOK–560NOK ($62–$74). AE, DC, MC, V. Mon–Sat 5–11pm. Closed July. Bus: 1, 4.

MODERATE

Havfruen (Mermaid) ★★ SEAFOOD   Set amid a cluster of some of the oldest warehouses in town, along the Nidelven River, this is the most important fish restaurant in Trondheim, and the most atmospheric. Built around 1800 on the site of a much older warehouse, it's studded with old beams and trusses and lots of authentic antique charm. Meals are prepared in the open-to-view kitchen and served by a staff with impeccable manners and technique. Consider a drink in the cozy bar downstairs, where the modern look of a bubbling aquarium offsets an otherwise vintage setting of enormous warmth, coziness, and charm. The staff seems to enjoy evaluating and offering advice about the daily harvest of fish. The menu changes each season, based on local fish migration patterns. You might begin enticingly enough with the steamed mussels in white wine or the smoked trout served with a sauce made of mussels, oysters, and mushrooms. The creamy fish chowder is the town's best. For a main course, you are likely to be won over by the poached Arctic char served with chorizo and an herb orange sauce or the grilled tuna with a vegetable roulade and a tomato beurre blanc.

Kjøpmannsgaten 7. (℃ **73-87-40-70.** Reservations required. Main courses 235NOK–285NOK ($31–$38). AE, DC, MC, V. Mon–Fri 5pm–midnight; Sat 6pm–midnight. Closed Dec 21–Jan 6. Bus: 2, 5, 6, 7, or 9.

Kvilhaugen Gärd (Rest Hill Farm) ★ *(Finds* NORWEGIAN   Surrounded by the trees and lawns of a prosperous residential suburb, about 4km (2½ miles) east of Trondheim's commercial core, this charming and historic restaurant, convention center, and pub is contained in what used to be the barn of an important manor from the early 19th century. The focal point of the compound is a white-painted wooden manor house, whose battered interior is opened only for large groups and corporate conventions. The most convivial part of the compound today, however, is the red-sided barn *(fjøset)*, originally built around 1820, which still retains signs indicating to diners and drinkers which area of the interior used to be reserved for cows, sheep, and pigs. Be careful not to bump your head against the massive antique ceiling beams as you enjoy either midafternoon snacks or full meals that might include melon with Parma ham; creamy fish soup; chicken salad; baked trout, Arctic char, turbot, or salmon; and roasted filets of beef or reindeer. The food is good, wholesome, regional fare, made with well-chosen ingredients and cooked with local flavor. In midsummer, large areas of the lawn outside are transformed into a genteel version of a beer garden, but the rest of the year, the dining stays inside the warm, woodsy, barn-like structure adjacent to the amiably rundown manor house.

Blussuvollsbakken 40. ℂ **73-52-08-70.** Reservations recommended for meals, not necessary for tea, coffee, or snacks. Snacks 55NOK–105NOK ($7.30–$14); main courses 165NOK–240NOK ($22–$32). AE, DC, MC, V. Tues–Thurs 4pm–midnight; Fri–Sat 4pm–1am; Sun 2–9pm. Bus: 63.

Odin's *Value* NORWEGIAN   Set on the street level of the also-recommended hotel, this is a cozy, woodsy tavern whose street-facing doors and windows are virtually removed in summer for maximum exposure to fresh air and late-lasting daylight. Be warned in advance that you'll be expected to give your food and drink order at the bar counter. Drinks are usually carried from the bar back to table by the diner; platters of food that take a bit of time to prepare will be cheer-fully carried to the table by a staff member. Dishes are savory, generously por-tioned, and filling and may include hamburger platters; filet steaks with pepper sauce; a "symphony of fish" composed of assembled filets, with sauces, from local waters; and lighter fare such as pastas, salads, and pita bread with salad.

In the Viking Hotel, Thomas Engells gate 12B. ℂ **73-51-21-33.** Main courses 98NOK–180NOK ($13–$24). AE, DC, MC, V. Daily 10am–10pm. Bar Sun–Thurs until midnight; Fri–Sat until 2am. Bus: 1, 4.

Sushi Bar JAPANESE   This is one of only two sushi restaurants in Trond-heim, and of the two, this is the one we prefer. Set on the town's main street, the "Champs-Elysées" of the town, it's outfitted in cheerful tones of orange, soft red, yellow and white, with large oil paintings and a big glass display of raw fish, behind which a team of experts filet, roll, and prepare wooden and ceramic trays of artfully simple raw fish, many of which come ultrafresh from local waters. The best value is a sushi main course platter, consisting of 10 pieces of sushi and six pieces of *makki* (fish filet rolled, with rice, into a roulade). Priced at 196NOK ($26), it sells for less than what you'd have paid if you had assembled and paid for each of its components individually.

Munkegaten 39. ℂ **73-52-10-20.** Main courses 135NOK–198NOK ($18–$26); fixed-price dinner with wine 275NOK ($37). AE, DC, MC, V. Mon–Thurs 3–10:30pm; Fri–Sun 3–11:30pm. Bus: 2, 5, 6, 7, or 9.

INEXPENSIVE

Akropolis GREEK   This is the best of the two or three Greek restaurants in Trondheim, and at least some of its business comes from Norwegians who remember their long-ago holidays in Greece with nostalgia. It's set inside the cel-lar of a white-fronted masonry building across the river from the railway station. It has two dining rooms, each outfitted (in blue and white with lots of panel-ing), like a Greek tavern somewhere in the Peloponnesus. All the Greek favorites appear on the menu and are admirably prepared, including moussaka, curried shrimp, a meal-size portion of Greek salad, various kabobs, roasted lamb aro-matically flavored with herbs, and, our favorite, pork souvlakia. All of these dishes might be preceded with a tantalizing assortment of mezes (small, bite-size dishes intended as starters).

Fjordgata 19. ℂ **73-51-67-51.** Reservations recommended. Main courses 138NOK–185NOK ($18–$25); fixed-price menu (served daily 3–6pm only) 98NOK ($13). AE, DC, MC, V. Daily 3–10:30pm (Fri–Sat until mid-night). Bus: 1, 4.

Egon Tårnet AMERICAN In the early 1980s, the skyline about 4km (2½ miles) east of Trondheim was altered with the addition of a soaring television transmittal tower, at the top of which an elegant and exclusive restaurant served glamorous, high-ticket meals. About a decade later, the owners downsized the gourmet aspects of the restaurant, refocusing the high-altitude dining venue into a family-friendly burger, pizza, and steak joint with a menu that's equivalent to what you might find in an American Denny's or IHOP. The result incorporates all the engineering marvels of the original upscale restaurant (a revolving deck that takes about an hour for a full circle, and big-windowed views that sweep out for kilometers in all directions) with a burger-and-fries menu that's much more affordable than the setting and the circumstances would suggest. Expect a menu that features club sandwiches and BLTs, about a dozen kinds of pizza, stuffed baked potatoes, meal-size salads, Tex-Mex tacos and fajitas, blackened chicken, ribs, and grilled steaks. An elevator will carry you, without charge, from the parking lot to the restaurant's upper levels.

Otto Nielsensveien 4. 🕐 **73-87-35-00.** Reservations recommended Fri–Sat nights. Pizzas, burgers, salads, and platters 85NOK–209NOK ($11–$28). AE, DC, MC, V. Mon–Thurs 11am–11pm; Fri–Sat 11am–11:30pm; Sun noon–10pm. Bus: 20 or 60.

Restaurant Egon AMERICAN Nothing about this place even pretends to be gourmet or even upscale. It's set in the center of town in an early-20th-century stone building that was originally built as a bank. Within a labyrinth of dark, woodsy-looking pub areas and dining rooms, the restaurant serves the Norwegian equivalent of American-style diner food. There's a beery kind of sudsiness to the place, an appropriate foil for the pizzas that emerge from the open-to-view brick-lined ovens. In summer, the venue spills out onto the terrace outside. This is a member of the same chain, incidentally, as the also-recommended Egon Tårnet, a short distance outside of town.

Thomas Angellsgate 8 (entrance on Søndregate). 🕐 **73-51-79-75.** Pizzas, burgers, salads, and platters 85NOK–209NOK ($11–$28). AE, DC, MC, V. Sun–Thurs 11am–midnight; Fri–Sat 11am–1am. Bus: 1, 4.

Tavern På Sverresborg ⭐ *Finds* NORWEGIAN No restaurant in town offers more authentic Norwegian cuisine than this historic eatery, 4.75km (3 miles) south of Trondheim's commercial center. Built as a private merchant's house in 1739 and later transformed into a clapboard-sided tavern, it's one of the few wooden buildings of its age in this area. Cramped and cozy, it's the town's most vivid reminder of the past, with wide-plank flooring and antique rustic accessories. The most desirable and oft-requested table is directly in front of a fireplace in a side room, and as such it's usually reserved in advance. There's an emphasis on 18th- and 19th-century recipes. Try *blandet spekemat*, served with flatbrød; it consists of thinly sliced smoked ham, diced meat, slices of salami, smoked mutton, and garnishes of lettuce and tomato. For a real taste of Norway, opt for the creamy fish soup or the Norwegian-style meatballs (the size of Ping-Pong balls), and most definitely the pancakes and platters of herring. In summer rhubarb soup is a specialty.

Sverresborg Allé, at Trøndelag Folk Museum. 🕐 **73-87-80-70.** Reservations recommended. Snack-style main dishes 80NOK ($11); main courses 60NOK–130NOK ($8–$17). MC, V. Mon–Fri 4–10pm; Sat 2–10pm; Sun 2–9pm. Bus: 8 or 9.

THE LEADING CAFES

Café-Conditorei E. Erichsen PASTRIES/LIGHT FARE Set beside Trondheim's busiest all-pedestrian street, this is a cafe and pastry shop that many local residents remember with fondness from their childhoods. In the 1850s, well-heeled travelers from England, in Trondheim for salmon fishing, made the place into something approaching a private club, and throughout the post–World War II era, it was transformed into an occasional hotbed of political discussion. Today, much mellowed by time, it features tables that extend from its beaux-arts interior out onto the sidewalk during clement weather. Every evening after around 6pm, the cozy and somewhat sedate venue of coffee, tea, and pastries is transformed into a more hip, adult, and permissive venue of a liquor bar. The consistently most famous client here, a regular, is celebrity artist Håkon Bleken, a huge name in Norway's world of contemporary painting and portraitist for members of the royal families of Norway and Sweden. Don't expect the culinary variety and sophistication of a bona-fide restaurant—instead, what you'll get is cheerful and amiable service, several kinds of coffee and tea, and pastries, burgers, quiches, pastas, and salads.

Nordre Gate 8. (©) **73-87-45-50.** Salads, sandwiches, pastas, quiches, and burgers 59NOK–108NOK ($7.85–$14). AE, DC, MC, V. Mon 9am–midnight; Tues–Thurs 9am–1am; Fri 9am–2am; Sat 9:30am–2am. Bus: 1, 4.

Café Gåsa (Café Goose) NORWEGIAN   This is Trondheim's most famous cafe, a counterculture monument and an ecologically conscious destination for liberal Norwegians visiting from other parts of the country. It occupies a simple brownish-red antique house whose exterior is draped with flowering vines, and whose interior is covered with rustic bric-a-brac that might have been gathered from farms and attics throughout the region. There's a glassed-in sun porch, a sense of a makeshift decor that you might expect to see on a commune in Vermont, and a rustic, slightly battered countertop area where you order and pay for the food that a duo of chefs haul out from a claustrophobic, steamy, and open-to-view kitchen. Menu items include sandwiches, salads, stuffed baked potatoes, chicken with rice and chile, and grilled moose with lingonberry sauce. Some of the most sophisticated food is served from 3 to 9pm, when an upscale restaurant next door (Bryggen) sends over a platter of the day (usually fish) that's sold for the reasonable price of 89NOK ($12).

Øvre Bakklandet 58. (©) **73-51-36-58.** Sandwiches, salads, snacks, and platters 65NOK–89NOK ($8.65–$12). AE, MC, V. Daily noon–1pm. Food service daily noon–9pm. Bus: 1, 5, or 9.

4 Seeing the Sights

Erkebispegården (Archbishop's Palace) ★★   Lying close to the cathedral precincts, this is the oldest secular building in Scandinavia, having been started in the second part of the 1100s. Until the Reformation came in 1537 and the ruling archbishop got the boot, this palace was the home of every reigning ecclesiastical authority in Trondheim. Once the archbishops were gone, it became the official address for the Danish governors, and was later taken over by the Norwegian military. Today it's one of the best-preserved buildings of its type in Europe. On site is the **Archbishop's Palace Museum,** featuring original sculptures from **Nidaros Cathedral** (see below) along with archaeological discoveries from the palace site. You can see, for example, the coin workshop just as archaeologists discovered it.

The Lavetthuset section of the museum features temporary art exhibitions, and the palace also has its own medieval chapel, which was consecrated in 1997.

Kongsgårdsgata. (©) **73-53-91-60.** Admission 35NOK ($4.65) adults, 20NOK ($2.65) children. May 1–June 19 Mon–Fri 11am–3:30pm, Sat 11am–3pm, Sun noon–4:30pm; June 20–Aug 20 Mon–Fri 10am–5pm, Sat 10am–3pm, Sun noon–5pm; Aug 21–Sept 14 Mon–Fri 11am–3:30pm, Sat 11am–3pm, Sun noon–4:30pm; Sept 15–Apr Mon–Sat 11am–3pm, Sun noon–4pm. Bus: 2, 5, 6, 7, or 9.

Moments **An Escapist's Retreat**

The **Ringve Botaniske Hage** (Ringve Botanical Gardens) lie on Lade Allé 58 (© **73-59-22-96**) and form part of the University of Trondheim's Museum of Natural History and Archaeology. This is one of the finest places to be on a summer day in Norway. You can wander through a historic and Renaissance-styled herb garden, enjoying the trees of the northern hemisphere. The entire park is laid out in the English garden style. Head for the nearest bench—and the day is yours. The admission-free park is open all day.

Kristiansen Festnung   Located about 2km (1¼ miles) east of the center of town, this is a stone-sided, thick-walled vestige of the military power of whatever army happened to be occupying Trondheim during the 17th and 18th centuries. It was built by the Danes between 1681 and 1682 as a defense against the Swedes during the reign of Christian IV, and it alone is credited with repelling the attacks of the Swedish army in 1718, and thereby saving Trondheim from "foreign" occupation. It was built according to the most advanced military wisdom of its day, in a nine-sided design that might have been influenced by the French military architect, Vauban. Between 1816 and 1901, it functioned as the headquarters of Trondheim's fire-fighting brigades. Under the Nazi occupation, the fort was used as a place of execution for members of the Norwegian Resistance; a plaque has been erected in their memory. On warm days, expect to see sunbathers and families with children playing on the verdant lawns that have replaced the muddy, pounded-earth floor of the historical fort. From its ramparts, you'll see what some locals define as the best **panorama** ★★ in town, encompassing fjords, towers, and the rest of Trondheim.

Rosenborg. No phone. Free admission. Daily 24 hr. Bus: 63.

Nidaros Cathedral ★★★   Dating from the 11th century, this cathedral is the most important, most historic, and most impressive ecclesiastical building in Scandinavia. It's located in the town center, near the Rådhus. The burial place of the medieval Norwegian kings, it was also the site of the coronation of Haakon VII in 1905, an event that marked the beginning of modern Norway.

Construction actually began on the cathedral in 1070, and some of its oldest parts still remain, mainly from the middle of the 1100s. Following the battle of Stiklestad, King Olaf Haraldson was entombed under the high altar. In time, Olaf became Saint Olaf, and his remains were encased in a gem-studded shrine.

The cathedral has weathered several unfortunate events. It's been a victim of several fires that swept over Trondheim. The church was reconstructed each time in its original Gothic style. (The section around the transept, however, is Romanesque.) During the Reformation, the cathedral was looted of precious relics. By 1585, Nidaros had been reduced to the status of a parish church. Around 1869 major reconstruction work was begun to return the gray sandstone building to its former glory.

The west facade is particularly impressive, with its carved figures of royalty and saints. It's especially appealing after dark, when the facade is floodlit (the lights usually stay on every evening till midnight—it's worth a stroll even if you have to make a detour to do it). The interior is a maze of mammoth pillars and

Trondheim Attractions

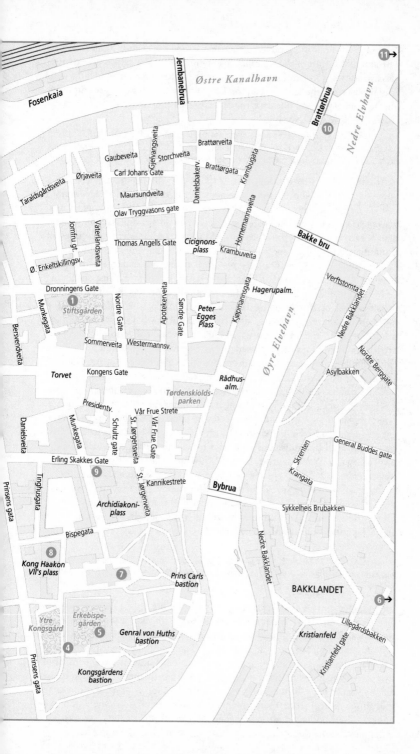

Østre Kanalhavn

Fosenkaia

Jernbanebrua

Brattørbrua

11 →

Nedre Elvhavn

10

Brattørveita

Gaubeveita
Storchveita
Gjelvangsveita

Carl Johans Gate

Ørjaveita

Brattørgata

Brattørveita

Danielsbakerv.

Krambugata

Taraldsgårdsveita

Maursundveita

Olav Tryggvasons gate

Hornemannsveita

Bakke bru

Jomfru gt.

Vaterlandsveita

Thomas Angells Gate

Cicignons-
plass

Krambuveita

Ø. Enkeltskillingsv.

Verftstomta

Dronningens Gate

1

Stiftsgården

Nordre Gate

Apotekerveita

Søndre Gate

Peter
Egges
Plass

Kjøpmannsgata

Hagerupalm.

Nedre Bakklandet

Nordre Bergsgate

Munkegata

Bersvendveita

Sommerveita

Westermannsv.

Øyre Elvehavn

Asylbakken

Torvet

Kongens Gate

Tørdenskiolds-
parken

Rådhus-
alm.

Danielsveita

Presidentv.

Vår Frue Strete

Schultz gate

St. Jørgensveita

Vår Frue Gate

Skerpten

General Buddes gate

Krangata

Erling Skakkes Gate

9

Tinghusgata

Kannikestrete

Bybrua

Sykkelheis Brubakken

St. Jørgenveita

Prinsens gata

Archidiakoni-
plass

Bispegata

Nedre Bakklandet

BAKKLANDET

6 →

8

Kong Haakon
VII's plass

7

Prins Carls
bastion

Ytre
Kongsgård

Erkebispe-
gården

5

Genral von Huths
bastion

Lillegårdsbakken

Kristianfeld

Kristianfeld gate

4

Prinsens gata

Kongsgårdens
bastion

columns with beautifully carved arches that divide the chancel from the nave. The grandest feature is the stunning **rose window** ★. The cathedral's **stained-glass windows** ★, when caught in the proper light, are reason enough to visit. Gustav Vigeland, the famous sculptor, carved the **gargoyles and grotesques** ★ for the head tower and northern transept. A small museum inside displays the **crown jewels** ★★ of Norway.

Bispegaten 5. ☎ 73-53-91-60. Admission to cathedral and museum 35NOK ($4.65) adults, 20NOK ($2.65) children. Cathedral and museum May 1–June 19 and Aug 20–Sept 14 Mon–Sat 9am–3pm, Sun 1–4pm; June 20–Aug 19 Mon–Sat 9am–6pm, Sun 1–4pm; Sept 15–Apr Mon–Sat noon–4pm, Sun 1–3pm. Bus: 2, 5, 6, 7, or 9.

Nordenfjeldske Kunstindustrimuseum ★★ This is the single greatest museum of central Norway, and it also holds one of the most eclectic collections in the country. Dating from 1893, the museum is devoted to applied arts, placing special focus on the changing trends in world art, especially in modern design and handcrafts. You'll see both historical and modern collections of furniture, textiles, silver, and a lot more, along with temporary exhibitions.

Displayed on the lower floor, the historical exhibitions span the period from 1500 to 1990, specializing in furnishings from northern Europe, including Germany and England. The **Arts and Crafts collection** focuses on the creative breakthroughs of British craftsman and designer William Morris and his followers at the end of the 1800s and is rich in metal craft, avant-garde ceramics, printed textiles, and metal craft. The **Art Nouveau collection** is heavy on French art; most of it was purchased at the 1900 World Exhibition in Paris. An entire salon on the lower floor is devoted to the contributions in Art Nouveau architecture by architect and designer Henri Van de Velde, a citizen of Belgium.

The **Contemporary Collection** concentrates on objects created in the postwar era—not only in Europe but from as far away as Australia or even America. Scandinavian design gets the most focus, of course, and there is an interior entirely designed by Finn Juhl, the Danish architect, in 1952. Of special interest are 200 **wall hangings and tapestries by Hannah Ryggen** ★, clustered in one gallery. This Swedish artist, born in 1894, married Hans Ryggen, the Norwegian painter, and lived outside Trondheim until her death in 1970.

Other collections include a **Costume Exhibition,** with garments dating from the 17th century. The era of the 1920s and 1930s is most heavily represented. Other exhibitions are devoted to some **300 pieces of jewelry** in modern design and a **Japanese collection** showcasing that country's creativity in metalwork, lacquer, textiles, and pottery.

Munkegaten 3–7. ☎ 73-80-89-50. Admission 40NOK ($5.30) adults, 20NOK ($2.65) children, students, seniors. June 1–Aug 20 Mon–Sat 10am–5pm, Sun noon–5pm; off-season Tues–Sat 10am–3pm (Thurs until 5pm), Sun noon–4pm. Bus: 1, 4.

Ringve Museum ★★ Visited only on guided tours, this is the only Norwegian museum specializing in musical instruments from all over the world. Set on the Ringve Estate on the Lade Peninsula, the building originated in the 1740s as a prosperous manor house and farmstead. The mansion was the birthplace of Admiral Tordenskiold, the Norwegian sea hero. The museum today consists of two parts—the museum in the manor house and a permanent exhibition in the estate's former barn. In the barn you can hear the special sound of Norwegian folk music instruments; there's even a hands-on exhibition where you can discover the budding musician in yourself. At specified times, concerts are given on carefully preserved antique instruments, including an impressive collection of spinets, harpsichords, clavichords, pianofortes, and string and wind

Fun Fact **The First European to Discover America**

Trondheimers have no doubt who first discovered America—or, put more politically correct, the first European to discover an already inhabited continent. Here is the official line as taught in local schools: "Leiv Eiriksson sailed to Nidaros in the year A.D. 999. The visit to Olaf Tryggvason's new royal farm must have been a success. Leiv Eiriksson became the king's man and stayed as a guest all winter. Spring came and he was a changed man. He had been baptized as a Christian. He launched his mighty boats at Skipakrok and sailed over the ocean to Greenland and further, far, far to the west. Leiv Eiriksson made the discovery of a lifetime—America."

To honor Leiv Eiriksson, there is an emigrant monument, **Leiv Eiriksson Statue** at Pirsenheret, Brattøra (bus to Pirterminalen). It was a gift from Americans of Scandinavian heritage to honor Trondheim's own millennium celebration in 1997. The statue was erected and dedicated to emigrants who left Norway to seek a new life in America. The monument is an exact copy of the original, which stands in Seattle.

instruments. Also on the premises is an old *kro* (inn) that serves waffles, light refreshments, and coffee.

Lade Allé 60 (3.25km/2 miles east from the center of town at Ringve Manor). (℃ 73-92-24-11. Admission 70NOK ($9.30) adults, 25NOK ($3.35) children, 40NOK ($5.30) students, 140NOK ($19) family. Guided tours May 20–June daily at 11am, noon, 12:30pm, and 2:30pm; July–Aug 10 daily at 11am, 12:30pm, and 4:30pm; Aug 11–31 daily at 11am and 2:30pm; Sept daily at 11am and 3pm; Oct–May 19 Sun at 11am and 4pm. Bus: 3 or 4.

Rustkammeret/Hjemmefrontmuseet   One of Norway's oldest museums, this is a combined army museum and a "Home Front Museum," both connected with the Archbishop's Palace (see above). In the army museum, the history of the military is traced from the days of the Vikings. Of more recent vintage, the Home Front Museum presents the drama of central Norway during the Nazi occupation in World War II.

Kongsgårdsgata. (℃ 73-99-52-83. Free admission. June–Aug Mon–Fri 9am–3pm, Sat–Sun 11am–4pm; Mar–May and Sept–Oct Sat–Sun 11am–4pm. Closed Nov–Feb. Bus: 2, 5, 6, 7, or 9.

Stiftsgården   This buttercup-yellow royal palace near the marketplace was built as a private home by a rich merchant's widow in the 1770s, when Trondheim began to regain its prosperity. It's the largest wooden building in northern Europe, with 144 rooms encompassing approximately 1,080 sq. m (12,000 sq. ft.). The exterior walls were notched together, log-cabin style, then sheathed with wooden exterior panels. The unpretentious furnishings represent an amalgam of design styles.

Munkegaten 23. (℃ 73-84-28-80. Admission 50NOK ($6.65) adults, 25NOK ($3.35) children, 100NOK ($13) family. Guided tours every hour on the hour. Mon–Sat 10am–5pm; Sun noon–5pm. Closed Sept to late June. Bus: 2, 5, 6, 7, or 9.

Sverresborg Trøndelag Folk Museum ★★   One of Norway's major folk-culture museums, this complex is filled with farmhouses, cottages, churches, and town buildings, representing aspects of everyday life in the region over the past 3 centuries. Standing 5km (3 miles) west of the center, the complex is composed of 60 historic, laboriously dismantled and reassembled buildings, all made from wood and stone, including the first all-brick building in Trondheim (ca. 1780). Among the compound's most interesting buildings are the 200-year-old barns, many with sod roofs, many painted red, and most built of weathered natural wood. There's a cafe on the premises, but if you want a good meal, we recommend that you head next door to the celebrated restaurant **Tavern På Sverresborg** (see "Where to Dine," earlier in this chapter), which serves traditional Norwegian dishes. The proudest possession here is Norway's northernmost stave church. The museum is surrounded by a nature park with animals.

On the grounds of the folk museum, within an antique building hauled in from some other part of the province, is an all-separate museum, the **Sverresborg Ski Museum.** Entrance to the ski museum is included in the price of admission to the Folk Museum, and hours are the same, too. Tracing the history of skiing in Norway, it contains antique skis from the 1600s to today, some carved in patterns inspired by the Vikings, and some with fur or sealskin cladding, which prevented them from sliding backwards during cross-country skiing.

Sverresborg Allé. ✆ **73-89-01-00.** Admission 75NOK ($10) adults, 25NOK ($3.35) children. June–Aug daily 11am–6pm; off-season Tues–Sat 11am–3pm, Sun noon–4pm. Bus: 8 or 9.

Trondheim Kunstmuseum A relatively undiscovered museum, this art gallery is imbued with a big collection of Norwegian art from around the early 19th century and going up to the millennium. There is also a fairly good treasure trove of Danish art as well, along with a limited selection of international artists. The most intriguing part of the museum is a hall of lithographs by Edvard Munch, Scandinavia's most famous artist.

Bispegt. 7B. ✆ **73-53-81-80.** Admission 40NOK ($5.30) adults, 20NOK ($2.65) children, students, and seniors. June–Aug daily 10am–7pm; off-season Tues–Sun 11am–5pm. Bus: 4.

Trondhjems Sjøfartsmuseum (Maritime Museum) An old penitentiary from 1725 has been turned into a Norwegian maritime showcase. Exhibits include models of sailing ships, marine instruments, and figureheads. You'll discover such exhibitions as the harpoon gun from the whaler *Star I,* and objects dug up from the frigate *The Pearl,* which sank off Norwegian waters in 1781.

Fjordgata 6A. ✆ **73-89-01-00.** Admission 25NOK ($3.35) adults, 15NOK ($2) children, students, and seniors. June–Aug daily 10am–4pm. Bus: 4.

Tyholttårnet This 120m (400-ft.) concrete tower, built in 1985 to relay radio signals along the coast, is the tallest structure in central Norway. The tower, 5km (3 miles) east of Trondheim, offers a sweeping view over the entire area, and has a revolving restaurant, Egon Tårnet, near the top (see "Where to Dine," earlier in this chapter). You can go to the viewing gallery even if you don't patronize the restaurant; admission to the tower is free for diners.

Otto Nielsens Vei 4, Blussuvoll. ✆ **73-87-35-00.** Free admission. Mon–Sat 11am–11:30pm, Sun and holidays noon–10pm. Bus: 20 or 60 (ask the driver to tell you when to get off).

Vitenskapsmuseet (Museum of Natural History and Archaeology) The collections and exhibits at this university museum cover natural history, archaeology, and the social history of central Norway from prehistoric times to the Middle Ages. Special features include a diorama display of birds, archaeological displays, collections of church art, and a small ethnographic exhibit. One exhibit shows the most important habitats of central Norway and central

Finds   Zealots, "Perverts" & the Ax Man

Munkeholmen (Monk's Island), is a small, grim, and inhospitable island a short distance offshore from Trondheim's core. In summer, daily ferries depart from a point at the northern terminus of Munkegata at hourly intervals between 10am and 7pm for the 30-minute jaunt offshore for picnicking, bird-watching, and beach excursions on the island. Round-trip passage costs 45NOK ($6) for adults, 25NOK ($3.35) for children under 15. Bookings can be made at the **Lilletorget Hotel,** Cicgnons Plass (Littletorget; ☎ 73-52-05-24). You can buy picnic ingredients at the Ravnkloa fish market, a few steps from the landing piers.

But there's more to this sparse island than fun, games, and picnicking sites. For hundreds of years, beginning in 1658, the island functioned as a prison and an execution site, with a prominent hangman's scaffold, instruments of torture, and wooden blocks where ax men would lop off the heads of wretches condemned as criminals, "perverts," or enemies of the church or state. Before that, in the 11th century, the island was developed by Benedictine monks into one of the first two Christian monasteries in Scandinavia, housing zealots who shivered away the winters as winds and snows howled down the edges of the fjord. You can take a guided tour of the island's **historic fortress** for 25NOK ($3.35) for adults or 15NOK ($2) for children. If you haven't brought picnic fixings, a cafe and snack bar are built into the much-restored fortifications

Today Monk's Island is moderately popular as a destination for beachgoers, historians, and bird-watchers, even though the beach is small, gravelly, and relatively narrow, and the island is very small. Some locals even insist the place is haunted. What you may come away with—at least in our opinion—is a pervasive sense of melancholy and a profound new appreciation for the hardships and severity of life in medieval Norway. Most first-timers to Munkeholmen return to Trondheim and head immediately for the nearest bar for food, drink, and a replenishment of whatever good cheer they might have lost during their excursion.

Incidentally, **Munkegata,** the broad boulevard known ironically (facetiously?) as the "Champs-Elysées of Trondheim," was named after the medieval monks who lived here and who made frequent, sometimes daily, processionals between the landing pier at the avenue's base and Trondheim's cathedral, a 20-minute walk to the south.

Scandinavia. The exhibit also reveals how people have used and exploited nature through history.

At the Norwegian University of Science and Technology, Erling Skakkes Gate 47. ☎ 73-59-21-45. Admission 25NOK ($3.35) adults, 10NOK ($1.35) children. May–Aug Mon–Fri 9am–4pm, Sat–Sun 11am–4pm; Sept–Apr Tues–Fri 9am–2pm, Sat–Sun noon–4pm. Bus: 63.

ORGANIZED TOURS

At the Tourist Information Office (see earlier), you can purchase tickets for guided tours of the city, lasting 2 hours and taking in the highlights. Departure is from Torvet or Market Square daily at noon from May 27 to August 25. Adults pay 160NOK ($21), with children under 16 charged 75NOK ($10).

The tourist office also sells a 1½-hour sea tour, going along the canal harbor and up the River Nidelven and out to the fjord. From June 23 to August 18, it leaves Tuesday to Sunday at 2pm, costing 100NOK ($13) for adults and 50NOK ($6.65) for ages 3 to 14. From July 3 to August 4, there is an additional departure at 4pm, and from August 21 to September 8, there are tours on Wednesday, Friday, and Sunday at 2pm.

The tourist office will also book you on an evening boat tour, lasting 1½ hours, departing at 6:30pm from Ravnkloa from June 30 to August 4, costing 100NOK ($13) for adults or 50NOK ($6.65) for ages 3 to 14.

WALKING TOUR   TRONDHEIM'S HISTORIC CENTER

Start:	Torvet at the junction of Munkegata and Kongens gate.
Finish:	Torvet.
Time:	2½ hours.
Best Time:	Mornings after 8:30am when the Fiskenhallen is at its most active.
Worst Time:	Any time in midwinter after 4pm when it's dark, or one of the typical rain soggy days of Trondheim.

Begin your tour at the:

① Torvet

Trondheim's most prominent traffic circle, at the edge of which is the Tourist Office, and in the middle of which rises the **Trondheim Torg**, a soaring granite column. At its top stands a statue of the world's most handsome Viking—in this case, an idealized portrait of Olaf Trygvasson, founder (in A.D. 997) of Trondheim. Markings on the pavement, tracking the seasonal direction of the sun, define the column on which he stands as the world's largest sundial.

From here, walk north along the Munkegata (the "Champs-Elysées of Trondheim"), whose exceptional width was conceived as a fire-break during the rebuilding of Trondheim after a fire destroyed many of the city's wooden buildings in 1681. On your right-hand side, within a 2-minute walk, is the wood-sided, rustic-looking exterior of Trondheim's most prestigious home, the low-slung 18th-century premises of the:

② Kongen Lige/Stiftsgården (Royal Residence)

Built in 1778 as the home of the (then-Danish) king, and with 140 rooms that cover almost 4,000 sq. m (13,123 sq. ft.) of floor space, it's the largest secular all-wooden building in northern Europe. Positioned (at least in the opinion of modern-day security guards) alarmingly close to the street, it's the home of the Norwegian monarch and his/her associates whenever they're in Trondheim on official business. If you're interested in visiting its interior as part of the occasional 30-minute tours conducted only in midsummer, know in advance that its entrance is on the back side, near the building's functional and rather unimaginative garden.

Continue walking north along the Munkegata to the:

③ Ravnkloa Fiskehalle

This glass-sided, very clean, and modern locale offers some of the most interesting food sales in Trondheim. The venue is a good place for a snack. Opt for a bagful of fresh peeled (or unpeeled) shrimp, or perhaps a salmon sandwich at this cornucopia of fresh seafood. For more details on this place refer to the box (see "Beauty from the Sea—On Ice," below).

A Walking Tour of Historic Trondheim

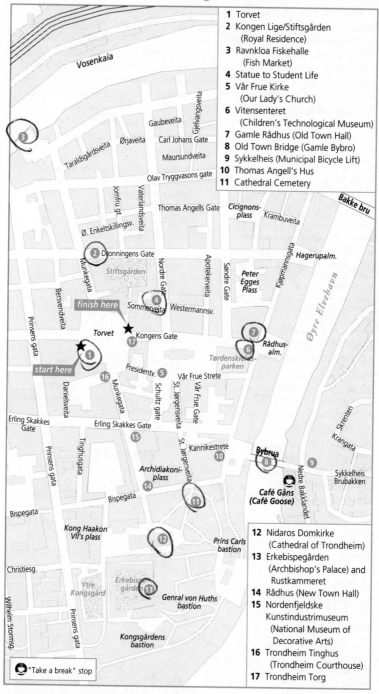

1 Torvet
2 Kongen Lige/Stiftsgården
  (Royal Residence)
3 Ravnkloa Fiskehalle
  (Fish Market)
4 Statue to Student Life
5 Vår Frue Kirke
  (Our Lady's Church)
6 Vitensenteret
  (Children's Technological Museum)
7 Gamle Rådhus (Old Town Hall)
8 Old Town Bridge (Gamle Bybro)
9 Sykkelheis (Municipal Bicycle Lift)
10 Thomas Angell's Hus
11 Cathedral Cemetery

12 Nidaros Domkirke
   (Cathedral of Trondheim)
13 Erkebispegården
   (Archbishop's Palace) and
   Rustkammeret
14 Rådhus (New Town Hall)
15 Nordenfjeldske
   Kunstindustrimuseum
   (National Museum of
   Decorative Arts)
16 Trondheim Tinghus
   (Trondheim Courthouse)
17 Trondheim Torg

Vosenkaia

Gaubeveita
Gjelvangsveita
Ørjaveita Carl Johans Gate
Taraldsgårdsveita
Maursundveita
Olav Tryggvasons gate

Jomfru gt.
Vaterlandsveita

Thomas Angells Gate Cicignons-plass Krambuveita
Ø. Enkeltskillingsv.

Bakke bru

Munkegata
Nordre Gate
Apotekerveita
Søndre Gate
Kjøpmannsgata
Hagerupalm.

2 Dronningens Gate
Stiftsgården
Peter Egges Plass

Bersvendveita
finish here
Sommerveita 4 Westermannsv.
Prinsens gata

Torvet Kongens Gate
17
1
start here
16
Presidentv. 5 Vår Frue Strete
Tørdenskiolds-parken

7 Rådhus-alm.
6

Øyre Elvehavn

Danielsveita
Munkegata
Schultz gate
St. Jørgensveita
Vår Frue Gate

Erling Skakkes Gate
Erling Skakkes Gate
15
Kannikestrete
10

Skrenten
Krangata

Bybrua
8
Nedre Bakklandet

9
Sykkelheis
Brubakken

Tinghusgata
Prinsens gata

St. Jørgensveita

Archidiakoni-plass
14

Café Gåns
(Café Goose)

Bispegata
Bispegata

11

Kong Haakon
VII's plass

12
Prins Carls
bastion

Christiesg.

Ytre
Kongsgård

Erkebispe-gården
13
Genral von Huths
bastion

Wilhelm Stormsg.
Prinsens gata

Kongsgårdens
bastion

"Take a break" stop

337

Adjacent to the fish market is the ferryboat pier for the boats that travel to Munkeholmen (Monk's Island), a short distance offshore.

Fronting the piers is a contemporary-looking statue, erected in 1990 by artist Nils Aas, and dedicated to *Den Siste Viking* (The Last Viking). Its somber caricature was inspired by a novel *(Den Siste Viking)* by Johan Bøjer, a former resident of Trondheim who honored the brave and tough fishermen of Norway for their bravery and fortitude.

From here, walk east along the Fjordgata, then right (south) onto the all-pedestrian Nordre Gate, whose edges are lined with Trondheim's densest collection of shops. Within a few blocks, rising from the center of the street, you'll see an exuberant testimonial to young love, the:

④ Statue to Student Life

This is a life-size, male-female depiction of young people swept away in a frenzy of love, dancing ecstatically on a pile of granite books.

Continue walking south on Nordre Gate to the smaller of the town's two medieval churches:

⑤ Vår Frue Kirke (Our Lady's Church)

Built in 1150 and enlarged in 1686 and again in 1739, this bulky, boxy, and dignified church (and its bell tower, tacked onto the existing structure in 1739) is almost as wide as the nave of the church itself. Regrettably, there were once 17 medieval churches in Trondheim. Now only two (this church and the cathedral, visited later as part of this walking tour) remain. Consider yourself lucky if you happen to arrive during its rare, regularly scheduled opening hours (Wed only 11am–2pm).

From here, turn left onto Kongens Gate and walk east for about a block to Kongens Gate 1. Here, at the corner of the Kjøpmannsgate, behind an impressive-looking 19th-century red brick facade, is the:

⑥ Vitensenteret (Children's Technological Museum)

Originally designed in 1833 as the Trondheim branch of the Bank of Norway, it was rebuilt in 1900 into the late-Victorian design you see today. Most visitors come here as part of school groups from the surrounding region, and unless you have small children in tow, we recommend you move on to other venues.

Directly across Kongens Gate, behind a Hanseatic-inspired façade that's adorned with an eight-pointed star-shaped window and the city's seal, is the:

⑦ Gamle Rådhus (Old Town Hall)

Originally built in the 1700s, this is now mostly a decorative monument, since most of Trondheim's day-to-day administrative duties are handled by a contemporary-looking new Town Hall positioned close to the cathedral and noted later as part of this walking tour.

Now, turn right onto Kjøpmannsgate. In a short distance, on your left-hand side, you'll see a row of the oldest warehouses in town, each individual building painted in a cheerful palette of colors. A short distance later, on your left, you'll arrive at the wood planks and iron girders of the:

⑧ Old Town Bridge (Gamle Bybro)

Originally built of wood in 1861 as a replacement for an all-wood predecessor in 1685, this is the most evocative, beloved, and frequently photographed bridge in Trondheim. Locals refer to it as the "Bridge of Happiness" and claim that your dreams will come true if you wish for them fervently as you walk across it. As you're articulating your dreams, note the neo-Gothic mass, atop the ridge on the distant horizon to your right, of the headquarters of Trondheim's University. Also look to your left from the bridge, noticing the dozens of carefully preserved 18th- and 19th-century warehouses rising on pilings above the river—proof of how extensive the maritime economy of Trondheim once was.

Continue walking straight across the cobble-covered intersection (Øvre Bakklandet on one side and Nedre Bakklandet on the other) after you cross the bridge, and walk uphill along the street identified as Sykkelheis. Within 27m (30 yards), on the right-hand side, you'll see the civic government's contribution to fresh air and exercise, the:

9 Sykkelheis (Municipal Bicycle Lift)

Designed to assist bike riders in their ascent of the steep hill, this mechanized conveyor belt (most of which is concealed underground beneath a metal-edged groove in the pavement) hauls bicycles, with their riders, up a steeply inclined stretch of a scenic bike path. The cost for 15 minutes of continuous operation is 100NOK ($13), which you can pay by inserting coins into the machine's coin slot. Frankly, most individual riders either walk their bikes or cycle in low gear up the relatively short hill, but as a conversation piece, the Sykkelheis is worth a look.

From the Sykkelheis, retrace your steps downhill, and turn left onto Øvre Bakklandet. Within a few steps, behind the vine-covered brown-plank facade of one of the first buildings on your right, you'll find an appropriate place to:

TAKE A BREAK
Café Gåsa (Café Goose), Øvre Bakklandet 58 (② 73-51-36-58), Trondheim's most famous cafe, where you dine on such delicacies as grilled moose with lingonberry sauce. For more on the cafe, see "Where to Dine," earlier in this chapter.

Now, retrace your steps back across the Old Town Bridge. When you reach the other side, turn left onto Kjøpmannsgata and walk for about a minute. When you reach a clearing in the bank of trees on your left (the side toward the river) look in the far distance to a point across the river on the crest of a stony ridge, for a view of Trondheim's once-strategic 18th-century military stronghold, Kristiansen Festnung, which is separately described in "Seeing the Sights," earlier in

this chapter. During clement weather, a Norwegian flag proudly flies from its summit. When Kjøpmansgate intersects with Bispegate, turn right and look on the Bispegate's right-hand side for a view of Trondheim's most elaborate baroque building, the:

10 Thomas Angell's Hus

Originally built in 1770, and extensively restored according to its original design in 1903, this was conceived as a retirement home for indigent widows. Later, its venue was expanded to allow widows to cohabit with well-recommended widowers outside the bounds of traditional marriages—a liberal 19th-century trend of which many Trondheimers seem appropriately proud. There's a pleasant garden in the building's interior courtyard, but hours of visitation are erratic, and the doors are very likely to be locked at the time of your visit.

Continue walking west along the Bispegate, detouring into the intensely evocative:

11 Cathedral Cemetery

Cemetery walks aren't for everyone, but this one is spiritually evocative and appropriately eerie. For centuries, grave sites here were reserved only for the town's more prominent citizens, and consequently, many of the grave markers are carefully planned sculptures in their own right. Note the location of this cemetery on your visit in the daylight hours; you may want to make a return visit, perhaps late at night and—preferably—when it's raining and the wind is howling.

Its majestic trees and undulating walkways lead to the cemetery's centerpiece, the:

12 Nidaros Domkirke (Cathedral of Trondheim)

We think this is the single most amazing, stunning, and majestic building in Norway. Spend some quality time here and plan on a return sometime before you leave Trondheim for a second view of the cathedral's amazing back side (we define it as the most spectacular bas-relief in Europe). Plan

Moments Beauty from the Sea—On Ice

Some Norwegians believe that genuine beauty can be found in the fruits of the sea, and even if you don't agree, you should make a point to visit one of Norway's most appealing indoor fish markets, **Ravnkloa Fiskehalle** ⭐ (℃ 73-52-55-21). Set at the northern terminus of the Munkegata, adjacent to the ferry piers servicing Munkholmen Island, this is a glass-and-steel structure of impeccable cleanliness—with the kind of hard-surface interior that gets hosed down frequently as a means of taking away some of the fishiness. Inside, a series of independent vendors sell meat on one side and stunning-looking fish, laid out in ordered rows on beds of ice, on the other. The variety and freshness of the scenario is memorable, and even if you're not—as a traveler—prepared to actually cook your purchases, you still might be tempted by the salmon sandwiches, fish salads, and small platters designed as take-out food—perhaps the raw ingredients for a picnic on Munkholmen Island or elsewhere. Idea: Consider buying a half-kilo of shrimp per person, along with fresh bread, butter, and mayonnaise (sold here in tubes that you squeeze like toothpaste). Purchase a glass of beer from the on-site beer tap, commandeer one of the indoor or outdoor tables, and dine like Neptune himself. Platters, which include such fare as pan-fried turbot with risotto, or warm fish cakes with salad, cost 50NOK to 70NOK ($6.65–$9.30) each; sandwiches cost 35NOK ($4.65), and stuffed crab backs goes for 49NOK ($6.50). The complex is open Monday to Friday from 10am to 6pm, Saturday from 10am to 4pm.

your second visit after dark, when much of cathedral's exterior is illuminated nightly until around midnight. For more on this cathedral, see "Seeing the Sights," earlier in this chapter.

Through a medieval gatehouse that's accessible from the cathedral's back side, wander into the vast and interesting courtyard that was created by the juxtaposition of two rambling buildings:

⓭ The Erkebispegården (Archbishop's Palace) and the Rustkammeret (Hjemmefrontmuseet)

The architecture on this square takes you back to the dim, often unrecorded past of Norway in the Middle Ages. Erkebispegården is the oldest secular building in Scandinavia; work started on the structure in the second half of the 12th century. Rustkammeret, or

the army museum, is one of the oldest structures in Norway.

From here, return to the cathedral's front side, and walk briskly north along the Munkgata. The first building you'll see on the Munkegate's right-hand side (on the eastern corner of the Bispegata), is Trondheim's:

⓮ Rådhus (New Town Hall)

This is not to be confused with the Gamle Rådhus, visited earlier on this tour. This modern, fortresslike brick building is where most of the day-to-day administrative functions of city government are carried out, and it's not open to the public for casual visits.

Continue walking north along the Munkgata. At the corner of the Erling Skakkes Gate, on the street's eastern flank, you'll see Trondheim's homage to the contemporary decorative arts of Norway, the:

⑮ Nordenfjeldske Kunstin-dustrimuseum (National Museum of Decorative Arts)

Here exhibits celebrate Norway's contribution to the tenets of modern decor and designs in glass, wood, textiles, and metal.

Continue your northward progression along the Munkegata, admiring the occasional piece of public sculpture along its path. Our favorite is the life-size representation, in bronze, of a group of grazing deer. About a block farther along the same street, at Munkegata 20, behind a bas-relief sculpture from the 1940s, is the:

⑯ Trondheim Tinghus (Trondheim Courthouse)

The courthouse facade bears a post–World War II frieze with symbols and personalities important to the history of Trondheim. Its interior is not open for casual visits.

From here, a bit to the north, is the Torvet, site of the:

⑰ Trondheim Torg

The soaring granite column is straddled on top by the handsome Viking. You're now back at the point where you started this walking tour.

5 Activities Indoors & Out

In summer the people of Trondheim take to their great outdoors. Summer is short, and they aim to make the best of it.

FISHING Fishing aficionados throughout Norway have heard about the waters below the Leirfossen Dam, 8.75km (5½ miles) south of Trondheim's center. When it was built, no provisions were made—much to the rage of ecologists—for the migration of salmon to spawning grounds upriver. Consequently, the waters at the dam's base have traditionally been teeming with a rich variety of marine life, especially salmon. The largest salmon ever caught at the dam's base weighed 31.8 kilograms (70 lb.)—an awe-inspiring record. In addition, the River Nidelva is one of the best salmon and trout rivers in Norway. For more information about fishing licenses, contact **TOFA** (Trondheim og Omland Jakt- og Fiskeadministrasjon), Leirfossvn 76 (© 73-52-78-23), the authority controlling fishing in Trondheim and its surroundings.

GOLF Just a 5-minute drive from the Trondheim Airport at Vaernes, **Stjørdal Golfklubb** (© 74-84-01-50) is the only 18-hole golf course between Rena in the south and Narvik in the north. For Norway, its season is long, lasting from May until the end of October. Another of the city's golf courses, **Trondheim Golfklubb,** lies at Sommerseter in Bymarka. This 9-hole course opens onto panoramic views of the city. The Midnight Golf Tournament takes place here in June. For play time, call © 73-53-18-85.

HIKING The greenbelt on the outskirts of Trondheim is called **Bymarka,** and locals use the woodland as a giant park. It offers 60km (40 miles) of gravel paths, plus 80km (50 miles) of ordinary paths. In winter skiers find 80km (150 miles) of tracks including six that are floodlit. In summer the Lodestien (The Lode Trial) stretches for 14km (9 miles), going along the Lode Peninsula and opening onto panoramic views of Trondheimsfjord. A shorter and equally scenic trail, the Nidelvstien, runs along the banks of the Nidelva River, going from Tempe to the waterfalls at Leirfossene.

SKIING On the eastern flank of the Vassfjellet mountains, the **Vassfjellet Skisenter** (ski center) lies in a sheltered position with good snow conditions. The area begins 8km (5 miles) south of the city limits, and offers six tow lifts, including one for kids, plus 10 runs in all. The area boasts 4km (2½ miles) of

> ## Moments　A Midsummer Night's Dream: Warm-Weather Ski-Jumping in Trondheim
>
> An offbeat adventure that might appeal to those with a high-adrenaline thirst for cathartic and voyeuristic danger involves the brave athletes who stay well rehearsed in ski-jump techniques throughout the summer. The **Granåsen Ski Jump** in Trondheim (about 8km/5 miles south of the center), along with the slightly older and Olympic-famous ski jump in Lillehammer, are the only ski jumps in the world that prepare for summer by lining their downhill slopes with high-impact, very slippery plastic. The result is a bizarre, even surreal sport—warm-weather ski-jumping—that's televised throughout Norway, drawing fans from around the region. The schedule for these events is highly fluid (after all, they're rehearsals, not competitions), and seem to crop up at erratic moments that sometimes (but not always) correspond to the arrival of cruise ships near the town's harbor. If you want to attend such an event, ask the tourist office for information on when the next rehearsals will be conducted. Entrance is free.

the largest illuminated slopes in Norway. Ski buses run to the area. For more information, call ✆ **72-83-02-00.**

SWIMMING **Pirbadet & the 3-T Fitness Center,** Havnegate 12 (✆ **73-83-18-00**), lies in one of the most exciting buildings in Trondheim. Perched beside the sea and the town's commercial piers and separated from the rest of the city by the sprawling bulk of the railway station, this futuristic-looking, mostly glass free-form structure houses one of the best-equipped gyms in Norway (the 3-T Fitness center) and Pirbadet, a collection of pools, water slides, Jacuzzis, and wave-making machines that's among the most up to date of any indoor pool in the world. It's municipally funded, and clients tend to be office workers early in the morning, school swim classes at midday, and recreational swimmers later in the day. On weekends, several thousand recreational swimmers cram into its sun-filtered interior. Entrance to the Pirbadet pool complex costs between 75NOK ($10) and 100NOK ($13) for adults, depending on what time of day they arrive; and entrance to the 3-T fitness center is 100NOK ($13).

TENNIS Trondheim has several courts, both indoor and outdoor. For reservations at a court close to your hotel, call **Trondhjems Tennisklubb** (mobile) at ✆ **93-63-55-01.**

6 Shopping

Annes Keramik Founded in 1797, this outlet is your best bet for ceramics based on 2-centuries-old Trøndelag-styled designs, mainly in green, yellow, and blue. A number of intriguing household wares are also sold at this small store. Open Monday, Wednesday, and Friday 9:30am to 5pm; Thursday 9:30am to 7pm, and Saturday 9:30am to 4pm. Kongesgt 27. ✆ **73-52-53-82.**

Arne Ronning This is the finest outlet for Norwegian knitwear, outfitting the whole family in sweaters and cardigans that can last for a generation or so. It also offers the largest selection of menswear in Trondheim. Open Monday, Wednesday,

and Friday 9am to 5pm, Thursday 9am to 7pm, and Saturday 9am to 4pm.
Nordregt 10. ✆ **73-53-13-30.**

Galleriet, Trondheim Berukunstforening At the Byrhaven Shopping
Center, this is a small store on the ground floor of the mall. But it's choice, with
an intriguing selection of glasswork, pottery, silver, jewelry, women's clothing,
textiles, ceramics, and more. It's a showcase for applied arts from the Trøndelag
district. Open Monday to Friday 10am to 8pm, Saturday 9am to 6pm. Olav Tryg-
gvasonsgt 26. ✆ **73-53-51-10.**

Gift Shop at Sverresborg Trøndelag Folk Museum The gift shop in the
museum's reception building stocks some of the most genuinely charming handmade objects in Trondheim, including hand-woven tablecloths and generally
endearing hand-knit children's clothing. Open from June to August daily 11am
to 6pm; off-season Tuesday to Saturday from 11am to 3pm, Sunday noon to
4pm. Sverrsborg Allé. ✆ **73-89-01-00.**

Mattis Lilleberg Since 1878 this outlet has been dazzling Trondheimers and
keeping them warm with their knitwear. Sweaters come in many different styles,
and you can also purchase wool jackets and hats, along with clothing for
women, bags, gloves, and leather items. Open Monday, Wednesday, Friday 9am
to 5pm, Thursday 9am to 7pm, Saturday 9am to 3pm. Munkegt 58. ✆ **73-52-32-60.**

Modern Art Gallery This is the city's largest art gallery. Local artists, including some of the best in the area, are represented at this store along with international artists. It carries paintings, watercolors (most often central Norway
landscapes), prints, lithographs, and some sculptures. Open Monday, Wednesday, and Friday 9:30am to 5pm, Thursday 9:30am to 7pm, and Saturday
9:30am to 4pm. Olav Tryggvasonsgat 33. ✆ **73-87-36-80.**

7 Trondheim After Dark

If you're here in late July, at the time of the **St. Olaf Festival,** Dronningensgt 1B
(✆ **73-92-94-70**), you can enjoy organ concerts, outdoor concerts, and even
opera at the Nidaros Cathedral. The internationally acclaimed **Trondheim Symphony Orchestra,** Olavskvartalet, Kjøpmannsgt 46 (✆ **73-99-40-50**), presents
concerts weekly with some of Europe's most outstanding conductors and soloists.

    Monte Cristo, located in the Trondheim Hotell (see "Where to Stay," earlier
in this chapter), has a disco.

Bar 3B Sweaty, shadowy, and candlelit, this is the most extreme of the town's
counterculture bars, loaded with clients in their 20s, 30s, and 40s who sometimes
proclaim proudly how much they resist hanging out at more mainstream, "bourgeois" bars. Within an environment sheathed in colors of blue and black and the
occasional mirror, expect a clientele of bikers, tattoo freaks, students, and the rou-
tinely disgruntled. Two bars lie on two different floors of this place, and if you
manage to strike up some dialogues (and have a drink or two), you might actually have a lot of fun. It's open Monday to Saturday from 2pm to 2:30am or
3:30am, depending on business, and Sunday from 8pm to 2:30am. Brattørgate 3B.
✆ **75-51-15-50.**

Dalí Minimalist, hip, artsy, and accented in many places with flickering candles,
this smoke-filled, offbeat bar and cafe has a somewhat cynical clientele that tries
(and sometimes succeeds) to emulate the cynical absurdities of Salvador Dalí himself. There's recorded, highly danceable music that plays every Friday and Saturday
from 11pm till closing, at which time there's a cover charge of 30NOK to 50NOK

($4–$6.65), depending on the mood of the door staff. The place is open Monday to Thursday from 3pm to 1am; Friday from 3pm to 3:30am, and Saturday from noon to 3:30am. Tapas cost from 29NOK to 65NOK ($3.85–$8.65). Chess players and hipsters are welcome, and anything to do with the colors selected by Princess Martha-Louise for the royal wedding in Trondheim in May 2002 (soft pink and mint green) are expressly forbidden. Here, at least, it's better to stick to basic blacks and neutral monochromes. Brattørgate 7. ℂ 73-87-14-40.

Den Gode Nabo ("The Good Neighbor") Pub   This is our favorite pub in Trondheim. It occupies the cellar of the same 250-year-old warehouse that houses Bryggen, a prestigious and expensive restaurant that's separately recommended in "Where to Dine," above. You enter a low-ceilinged labyrinth of rough-hewn timbers and planking, eventually choosing a seat from any of dozens of slightly claustrophobic banquettes, being careful not to hit your head on the timber-built trusses as part of the process. Before you get too comfortable, however, we advise that you continue walking as deep into the innards of this place as possible, for access to the woodsy-looking bar area, where up to nine kinds of beer on tap cost from 48NOK to 70NOK ($6.40–$9.30) per mug. During clement weather, the seating options expand outside onto a wooden platform floating on pontoons in the swift-flowing river Nid, a romantic and soothing refuge from which you get a water-level view of the way Trondheim's antique warehouses were built on pilings sunk deep into the riverbed. It's so atmospheric that it's been the setting for some widely distributed TV broadcasts. *Hint:* Consider timing your visit for between 4 and 6pm, when Bryggen will send down an elaborate *dagensmeny* (platter of the day) that's priced at around 70NOK ($9.30)—a lot less than what it would have cost upstairs. After that, between 6 and 9pm, food from the short list of "pub food" isn't quite the bargain that it is for the early birds, but it will always including steaming bowls of the pub's well-known fish soup. Priced at 70NOK ($9.30) per portion, it might be either red (tomato-based) or white (cream-based), depending on the mood of the chef on the day of your arrival. You can be a good neighbor at this place every day between 4pm and 1am. Øvre Bakklandet 66. ℂ 73-87-42-40.

Kaktus   This is one of Trondheim's counterculture bars—the kind of place where bourgeois airs are either ridiculed or simply not tolerated, where the clients tend to be students in their early 20s, and where many of the patrons seem to have known one another throughout the duration of their university careers. Music by Billie Holiday might be playing softly, avant-garde photographs are for sale, and the staff may or may not be acting weird almost as a matter of defiant public policy. We especially admired the bulky and thick-topped wooden tables, which were crafted in India. Open Monday to Saturday 11am to 1am; Sunday 11am to 11pm. Nedre Bakkland 6. ℂ 73-51-43-03.

Kontoret   This is a hip, charming, and popular bar for sophisticated adults, with a brasserie that's attached. Newcomers are made to feel welcome, and the decor is many notches above that of some of its nearby competitors. Minimalist, warm, elegant, and unpretentious, it's outfitted in tones of terra-cotta and stainless steel, with modern paintings and the kind of soft, indirect lighting that makes everyone look a bit more relaxed and charming than they might naturally be. Its bartender won an award in the early 1990s for a drink that's still showcased here, a Barroom Rose. Priced at 72NOK ($9.60), it's made with dark rum, banana liqueur, strawberry syrup, and egg yolks. There's bar food served here, some of it rather elegant (cream of salmon soup, confit of duck with soy sauce),

Burgers, Bangers & a Soccer Fetish

Your choice of sports bars in athletic-conscious Trondheim will eventually say a lot about your politics and your cultural background. And in a town where discussions about sports can gobble up large portions of a long winter night, which of the town's two major sports bars to hang out in can be important indeed.

The more Anglophilic of the two is the **Kings Cross Pub & Shakespeare Restaurant,** Sondre Gate 7 (✆ **73-87-83-80**). Battered, woodsy, and named after the subway station in one of London's earthier districts (Kings Cross), it welcomes as many as 600 screaming fans, some of them imported for specific televised matches from as far away as Denmark. Stenciled onto the walls and ceilings are some of Will Shakespeare's pithier verses, adding food for thought to a menu of sandwiches, salads, and pub grub whose portions are recommended for appetites that are 1) peckish, 2) quite hungry, 3) starving, or 4) "I'm a pig." Beers and cocktails are imaginative and varied, and the place can be a lot of fun. Hours are Monday to Thursday 11:30am to 2am, Friday 11:30am to 2:30am; Saturday 10:30am to 2:30am; Sunday 1pm to 1am.

In friendly competition is **Harvey's,** Nordre Gate 23 (✆ **73-53-60-56**), which is bigger, glossier, more technologically sophisticated, and much more tuned to North American, as opposed to European, tastes in sports, drinks, and food. A total of seven TV screens play up to a maximum of two separate sporting events simultaneously. The food is better, too—more closely akin to the juicy-steaks-with-all-the-fixings kind of cuisine you'd expect in the slaughterhouse district of Chicago. Platters cost from 59NOK to 159NOK ($7.85–$21), and despite the high-tech emphasis on state-of-the-art broadcasting, there's something cozy and retro about this place. It's pure, reheated Americana with enough sporting and down-home memorabilia to add a soothing note of kitsch. Open Monday to Wednesday from 4pm to midnight, Thursday and Friday 4pm to 2am, Saturday noon to 2am, and Sunday 4pm to 1am.

with platters priced at 74NOK to 115NOK ($9.85–$15); more substantial food is served in the brasserie. Opening hours of the bar are Monday to Thursday 11am to 1am; Friday and Saturday 11am to 2am. Nordre gate 24. ✆ **73-60-06-40.**

News Café & Nightclub   Set at the edge of Trondheim's busiest shopping street, this popular bar and cafe has become the darling of the 20- and 30-ish crowd of hipsters. A painted mural behind the busy bar area successfully combines elements from the skylines of Chicago, New York, and Dallas into a fictional American city, a kind of mecca that many of the clients here would like to live in, or at least visit for a while. There's a disco upstairs, open only Friday and Saturday nights. Otherwise, people come here to read the papers (they're stocked here—that's why they call it the News Café) and drink concoctions like the Diablo. Priced at 74NOK ($9.85), the Diablo is made from lemon-flavored rum, peach schnapps, cranberry juice, and whiskey sour mix. Frozen cappuccinos and milkshakes (both alcohol-laced and virgin) and espresso are available too. A limited bar menu includes stuffed baked potatoes, salads, cheese toasts, sandwiches, fish and chips, nachos, and desserts. Snacks and platters cost 50NOK to 139NOK ($6.65–$18). The place is open daily from 11am to 3am (till 3:30am on Fri–Sat). Nordre Gate 11. © **73-80-23-90.** Fri–Sat cover in disco 50NOK–80NOK ($6.65–$11).

8 Side Trips from Trondheim

Unlike Oslo or Bergen, Trondheim isn't surrounded by a lot of "must-see" satellite attractions. But all true Norwegians, or Norwegian-Americans, head for Stiklestad.

STIKLESTAD   Lying 90km (56 miles) northeast of Trondheim, Stiklestad is the most famous historic site in Norway. It was the site of an epic battle on July 29, 1030, between the forces of King Olaf Tryggvason and a better-equipped army of Viking chieftains. The battle marked the twilight of the Viking era and the inauguration of the Middle Ages, a transition that would greatly change the face of Norway.

Although Olaf lost the battle and was killed, in death he triumphed. Word of his death spread, and in time he was viewed as a martyr to Christianity. His followers made him a saint, and as the years went by Saint Olaf became the very symbol of Norway itself. In the wake of his martyrdom, Christianity quickly spread across the land, and monasteries sprouted up all over the country. As his fame and popularity grew, Olaf's grave site at Nidaros Cathedral in Trondheim became the goal of nationwide pilgrimages. In time, his death would lead to the unification of Norway under one king.

Every year on the anniversary of his death, a pageant is staged at the open-air theater in Stiklestad, using 350 actors and drawing thousands in the audience. Launched in 1992, the **Stiklestad Nasjonale Kulturhus** (© **74-04-42-00**) is like a virtual theme park, with exhibitions of the famous battle, plus a folk museum and a church from the 12th century. Some of the artifacts on display here were actually relics of the battle, which were discovered by archaeologists.

The open-air **Stiklestad Museum** is a living tableau of regional village life from the 17th century. In summer there are demonstrations of farm life. On site is a carpenter's cottage, a water mill, and an old-fashioned sauna, 18th-century style.

Stiklestad Kirke ✦ is a Romanesque church from 1150. It was built over a former wooden church on the exact spot where it is believed that King Olaf was felled in battle. In 1500 the nave of the little church was extended, and some 9 centuries later a series of 16th-century frescoes that had been used to decorate the walls of the nave were uncovered. At one time a stone that was said to have been the rock on which Olaf leaned before he died was on display here. In medieval times, it was said that the stone had miraculous healing powers, but in time it disappeared, never to resurface. A soapstone baptismal font from the 12th century is the only artifact remaining from ancient times. A series of paintings in the chancel, commissioned for the 900th anniversary of the battle, relate the events of that fateful day.

The center can be visited from June to mid-August daily from 9am to 8pm. In the off-season, hours are Monday to Friday 9am to 4pm and Saturday and Sunday 11am to 5pm. In summer, admission is 80NOK ($11) adults, 40NOK ($5.30) children. In the off-season the price is reduced to 60NOK ($8) for adults, or 30NOK ($4) for children. On site is a restaurant with a museum cafe.

There is no train station at Stiklestad. The nearest depot is at Verdal, lying 6km (3¾ miles) away. The train from Trondheim to Verdal takes 1¾ hours, costing 145NOK ($19). At Verdal you can take any bus; all go within 2km (1¼ miles) of the site, costing 22NOK ($2.95); the trip takes only 15 minutes. Motorists from Trondheim can reach the center by taking the E6 northeast.

Tromsø

Tromsø, the gateway to the Arctic, is a North Sea boomtown, a trade and financial center. The surrounding snow-topped mountain peaks reach 1,800m (6,000 ft.), and mountain plateaus have good fishing lakes and birch forests.

With 50,000 inhabitants, Tromsø is the administrative center of the county of Troms, a trade center and the site of one of Norway's four universities. It serves as the capital of northern Norway, and it's the country's fourth largest finance center.

Lying 400km (250 miles) north of the Arctic Circle, Tromsø gets the Midnight Sun from May 14 to July 30—but not one ray comes through from November 25 to January 21. The climate has a heat record of 86°F (30°C) and a low of –4°F (–20°C).

The title of "Paris of the North" is a bit much, but Tromsø surprised even 19th-century visitors with its sophistication. Apparently, they had expected polar bears to be roaming the streets. A church was established here as early as the 1200s, and Tromsø was a thriving community in the Middle Ages.

Its city charter wasn't granted until as late as 1794, however. This trading station and fishing port attracted seamen who trafficked in polar bears, seals, and Arctic foxes. Many famous explorers, such as Roald Amundsen, set off from Tromsø on their famous expeditions to the Arctic ice cap.

The city limits of Tromsø, the largest municipality in Norway, extend for 2,558 sq. km (987 sq. miles), though most of the area is hardly built up. Home to some 60,000 residents, 13,000 of whom are students at the world's northernmost university, Tromsø is about the same size as Luxembourg.

1 Orientation

ARRIVING

1,744km (1,084 miles) N of Oslo; 566km (352 miles) N of Bodø

BY PLANE Flights from Oslo, Bergen, and Trondheim arrive at Langnes Airport, 13km (8 miles) west of the center of Tromsø. Flights from Oslo take 1 hour, 40 minutes; flights from Bergen 3 hours, 10 minutes. Tromsø also has air links with Trondheim in central Norway and such far northern outposts as Alta, Hammerfest, Honningsvåg, and Kirkeness. Tromsø is served by such carriers as **SAS** (© 81-00-33-00), **Widerøe** (© 81-00-12-00), and **Braathens** (© 81-52-00-00). For general information, call the Tromsø Airport at © 77-64-84-00.

BY TRAIN There is no rail link. The nearest connection is via Narvik (see chapter 14). From Narvik, you'll have to go the rest of the way overland by bus (see below).

BY BUS **Nor-way Bussekspress** (© 82-02-13-00) runs two daily express buses to Tromsø from Narvik (see chapter 14) taking 5 hours and costing 310NOK ($41) each way. In summer, **Tromsbuss** (© 77-67-75-00) maintains a bus (they call it the Tromsø-Nordkapp Ekspressen Bus) that links Tromsø with the North Cape, a trip that takes 13 hours and costs 645NOK ($86) each way.

BY CAR Take E6 from Oslo all the way north.

BY COASTAL STEAMER *Hurtigrute* (coastal steamer; ② **77-64-81-00**) connections link Tromsø with the cities of Narvik and Bodø. There is also a daily year-round service of coastal express liners from Bergen to Tromsø. Twice daily in the summer months, **Tromsø Fylkes Dampskibsseskap** (② **77-64-81-00**) offers express ferries linking Harstad and Tromsø; the trip takes 2½ hours and costs 410NOK ($55).

VISITOR INFORMATION

For information about Tromsø and the surrounding area, call the **Tromsø tourist office**—also known as "Destination Tromsø"—at Storgata 61-63 (② **77-61-00-00**), open June to mid-August Monday to Friday 8:30am to 6pm and on Saturday and Sunday from 10am to 5pm. Off-season hours are Monday to Friday 8:30am to 4pm.

Outdoor activities, of course, depend on the season in Tromsø. Everything focuses on the weather. The tourist office keeps a list of current activities and outfitters at the time of your visit. In summer the area around Tromsø and the mountains beyond feature more than 100km (62 miles) of hiking trails that can be reached by funicular. For more details, such as guided mountain tours or even "glacier walking," call **Svensbury Tursenter** (② **77-71-22-25**). There is even a ski center in Tromsø, but with the long, dark days of winter the trails have to be floodlit. Perhaps the sunny Alps would be more enticing.

CITY LAYOUT

The center of Tromsø lies on the eastern shore of the island of **Tromsøya.** It is divided by hills from the western shore and the airport at Langnes. A bridge and tunnel link the mainland of Norway to the island of Tromsøya. Coastal steamers pull into the piers at the foot of Kirkegata right in the town center.

The heart of town is small enough to make walking around it relatively easy. Running in a north/south axis, the main street is **Storgata.** At the center of this street is **Stortorget,** the main square of town opening onto the harbor. Stortorget is the site of a daily open-air market selling flowers and crafts. The most bustling and busiest part of town lies south of Storgata reaching the harbor. Some major streets include **Strandgata, Skippergata,** and **Skansegata.** This area is filled with shops, restaurants, bars, and cafes.

For attractions outside the center, there are buses to take you there.

GETTING AROUND

If you arrive at the airport, **Flybuss** (② **77-67-02-33**) will take you into the center in about 15 minutes, costing 35NOK ($4.65) for a one-way fare. A city bus also makes the run for 20NOK ($2.65), and you can take a taxi for around 80NOK ($11).

Local buses branch out from the center to serve Greater Tromsø. A one-way ride costs 20NOK ($2.65). If you plan to use the buses a lot, you can purchase a 24-hour pass for 55NOK ($7.30) at the tourist office.

The major taxi stand is at Strandveien 30 (② **77-60-30-00**), outside of Øldhallen.

In summer, consider cycling around. Bikes are rented at **Sportshuset,** Storgata 87 (② **77-66-11-00**).

FAST FACTS

The main **post office** is at Strandgata 41 (© **77-62-40-00**). If you patronize the **Amtmandens Datter Pub,** Grønnegata 81 (© **77-68-49-06**), you can have Internet access for free. The pub, named for the 1830s novel by Camille Collett, is open June to August Sunday to Thursday 3pm to 1:30am, Friday 3pm to 3am, Saturday noon to 3am. In off-season months, hours are Monday to Saturday noon to 3am, Sunday 3pm to 3am. To pick up a detailed map of North Norway, or an English-language book, head for **Centrum Libris,** Sjøgata 31-33 (© **77-68-35-40**).

2 Where to Stay

EXPENSIVE

Clarion Hotel Bryggen ★   Built in 2001, this is the newest large-scale hotel in Tromsø, with a harbor-front position that's only a few steps from two of its competitors (the Comfort Home Hotel With and the Rica Ishavshotel). The hotel has a contemporary-style lobby, wide upstairs hallways, and big-windowed bedrooms that are comfortably laid out, usually with a writing table. Bathrooms are tiled, brightly lit, and very modern. Most of them only have showers, but about 40 of them have shower-tub combinations. One of our favorite spots here is the outdoor hot tub on the rooftop terrace near the hotel's sauna. As icy rain falls, hot-tubbers soak up the heat while admiring panoramas over the frigid waters of Tromsø's harbor. There's a restaurant, the Astro, on the lobby level, open daily for lunch and dinner.

Sjøgate 19-21, N-9291 Tromsø. © **77-78-11-00**. Fax 77-78-11-01. www.choicehotels.no. 121 units. Mon–Thurs 1,590NOK ($211) double; Fri–Sat 1,030NOK ($137) double; daily 1,719NOK–2,900NOK ($229–$386) suite. AE, DC, MC, V. **Amenities:** Restaurant; bar; rooftop sauna with outdoor hot tub. *In room:* TV, minibar.

Radisson SAS Hotel Tromsø ★★   Built in 1965, and reigning today as the grande dame hotel of Tromsø, this is the oldest and best established of the town's large-scale hotels, and with 10 stories and almost 200 rooms, it's the largest in northern Norway. Rooms are a bit smaller and the design is less dramatic and cutting-edge than at such competitors as the Rica Ishavshotel, but this boxy-looking staple has a larger array of food and beverage facilities and amenities than any of its competitors. Also, much to the frustration of the other hotel managers, it's the best signposted hotel in town. (Local building codes, just after this hotel was completed, severely restricted the signage that newer hotels were allowed to display.) Bedrooms are cozy, well furnished with a contemporary "Scandinavian modern" decor, each with a tiled, shower-tub combination. Its dance bar (Charlie's), its most upscale restaurant (Grillen), and the most famous of its bars (Rorbua) are all separately recommended within other sections of this chapter.

Sjøgata 7, N-9259 Tromsø. © **77-75-90-16**. 195 units. Mon–Thurs 1,285NOK ($171) double; Fri–Sun year-round and mid-June to mid-Aug daily 950NOK–1,095NOK ($126–$146) double; year-round 2,200NOK–3,000NOK ($293–$399) suite. Rates include breakfast. AE, DC, MC, V. **Amenities:** 3 restaurants; 2 bars; health club/sauna in big, well-furnished area on top floor; babysitting; laundry service; dry cleaning. *In room:* TV, minibar, trouser press.

Rica Ishavshotel ★★★   Built in 1995, this is the most dramatic looking hotel in the region; a conversation piece that resembles a metallic-looking space-age yacht. It's also the town's most dramatic site, at the edge of the harbor, a few steps from the busiest quay in town. The lobby is cozy and warm, with a postmodern edge. Lots of business travelers stay here; because of that, about half of

Tromsø Accommodations & Dining

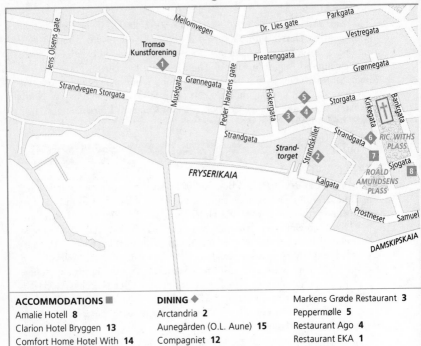

ACCOMMODATIONS ■

Amalie Hotell **8**
Clarion Hotel Bryggen **13**
Comfort Home Hotel With **14**
Comfort Hotel Saga **7**
Radisson SAS Hotel Tromsø **9**
Rica Ishavshotel **10**

DINING ◆

Arctandria **2**
Aunegården (O.L. Aune) **15**
Compagniet **12**
Emma's Drømmekjøkken
  (Emma's Dream Kitchen) **6**
Grillen **9**

Markens Grøde Restaurant **3**
Peppermølle **5**
Restaurant Ago **4**
Restaurant EKA **1**
Steakers **11**
Store Norske Fiskekompani **16**
Vertshuset Skarven A.S. **2**

the rooms are designated as singles. Whether they're single or double, all rooms have a subdued decor, with tiled bathrooms, shower-tub combinations, and Nordic modern furniture. The main lobby features live piano music every evening from 7:30pm until midnight. The more panoramic of the hotel's two bars is the Skipsbroen, set on the hotel's uppermost floor.

Fr. Langes Gate 2, N-9008 Tromsø. ℂ **77-66-64-00**. Fax 77-66-64-44. www.rica.no. 180 units. Mon–Thurs 1,615NOK ($215) double, 1,735NOK–3,995NOK ($231–$531) suite; Fri–Sun and mid-June to mid-Aug daily 1,095NOK ($146) double, 1,245NOK–3,995NOK ($166–$531) suite. AE, DC, MC, V. **Amenities:** Restaurant; 2 bars; exercise room; sauna; concierge; babysitting; laundry service; dry cleaning. *In room:* TV, minibar.

MODERATE

Comfort Home Hotel With   Built in a six-story format in 1989, and named after Richard With, a 19th-century sea captain who contributed to the development of Tromsø and the far north of Norway, this hotel is cozy, warm, and comfortable. Set behind a modern, twin-gabled facade immediately adjacent to the waterfront, it offers rooms with hardwood floors; a woodsy, well-upholstered decor, sometimes with leather chairs; big, weather-tight windows; and tiled bathrooms, each with a shower-tub combination.

Sjøgata 35-37, N-9001 Tromsø. ℂ **77-68-70-00**. Fax 77-68-96-16. www.with.no. 76 units. Mon–Thurs 1,490NOK ($198) double; Fri–Sun and mid-June to mid-Aug daily 970NOK ($129) double. Rates include breakfast and light evening supper (buffet 6–10pm). AE, DC, MC, V. **Amenities:** Jacuzzi; sauna; library. *In room:* TV, minibar.

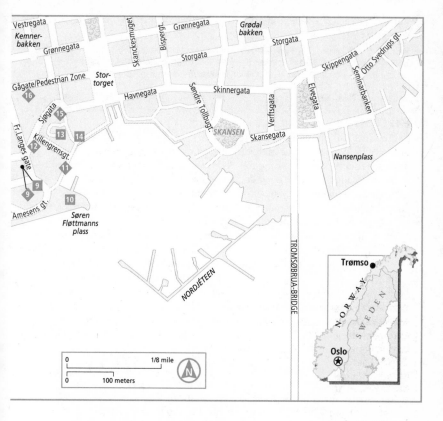

Comfort Hotel Saga Not as architecturally exciting as the Rica Ishavshotel, and not as upscale or as plush as the SAS Radisson, this is a conservative, somewhat boxy and banal-looking hotel that's close to Tromsø's wood-sided cathedral. It was built in 1969, and each of its rooms was renovated between 1995 and 2000, with the most recently renovated rooms positioned on the uppermost (5th) floor. Accommodations are warm and comfortable, each with contemporary, blond-toned wooden furniture, wooden floors, and a bathroom with a shower-tub combination. This hotel has a library devoted exclusively to comic books, many of whose characters are seen only within Scandinavia.

Richard Withs Plass 2, N-9008 Tromsø. (**C**) **77-08-11-80.** Fax 77-68-23-80. 66 units. Mon–Thurs 1,200NOK–1,300NOK ($160–$173) double, 1,500NOK ($200) triple; Fri–Sun and mid-June to mid-Aug daily 835NOK–935NOK ($111–$124) double, 1,135NOK ($151) triple. Rates include breakfast and light evening supper (buffet 6–9:30pm). AE, DC, MC, V. Parking 65NOK ($8.65). **Amenities:** Laundry service; dry cleaning; library. *In room:* TV, alcohol-free minibar, tea/coffeemaker, hair dryer, trouser press.

INEXPENSIVE

Amalie Hotell *Value* Set in a former office building, almost immediately adjacent to the Radisson SAS Hotel, this hotel is known for its cheap rates and simple but well-maintained and comfortable rooms. (It's also known for an outdoor bronze statue of a naked girl who looks perpetually chilly against the rains and snows of midwinter Tromsø.) Bedrooms are simple and cheerful, evoking the dormitory room you might have occupied in college, without frills and with sturdy, utilitarian wooden furniture. Each comes with a small private bathroom with shower.

Sjøgata 5B, N-9008 Tromsø. © **77-66-48-00.** Fax 77-66-48-10. www.amalie-hotell.no. 48 units. Mon–Thurs 925NOK–995NOK ($123–$132) double; Fri–Sun 825–895NOK ($110–$119) double. Rates include breakfast and light evening supper (6:30–9pm). AE, DC, MC, V. **Amenities:** Restaurant. *In room:* TV, minibar.

3 Where to Dine

EXPENSIVE

Arctandria ★★ SEAFOOD   This place is known as the best fish restaurant in a town by locals who often make their living from the sea and have high standards for seafood. It's set on the top floor of a sprawling antique warehouse immediately adjacent to the water, in the commercial heart of town. The somewhat somber, museum-like interior softens during the dinner hour, when flickering candles add a sense of romance. Virtually everything on the menu, with a few exceptions, features fresh fish, except for whale meat, seal meat, and, in the words of the manager, "an occasional reindeer, but only if it's caught while swimming between nearby islands offshore." Starters include mussel soup; a platter containing three different kinds of fish roe; and carpaccio of whale meat. Main courses include grilled stockfish served with roasted mushrooms and bacon, pan-fried cod, filet of Arctic char with hazelnuts, and grilled Arctic shark steak with pepper sauce, cranberries, and grilled mushrooms.

Strandtorget 1. © **77-60-07-20.** Reservations recommended. Main courses 160NOK–250NOK ($21–$33). AE, DC, MC, V. Mon–Sat 5–11pm.

Compagniet ★★ NORWEGIAN   Set within an old-fashioned building, directly across the street from the Comfort Home Hotel With and the Clarion Hotel Bryggen, this restaurant is noted as the most charming in town. That was the opinion of members of Norway's royal family during a trip they made to Tromsø in August 2002. The cuisine is original and consists of only the freshest ingredients, usually local. All dishes are prepared with a finely honed technique, as exemplified by the Arctic sea char flavored with fresh chives and a tantalizing fish roe. From Norwegian meadows comes a tender and flavorful rack of lamb served with a timbale of mushrooms, and from the far north, filet of reindeer in a blueberry sauce. The service is the best in Tromsø, and the wine cellar is wide ranging. On site is a bar and nightclub, open Sunday to Thursday from 6pm to 2am, and Friday and Saturday from 6pm to 4am.

Sjøgata 12. © **77-65-42-22.** Reservations required. Main courses 196NOK–274NOK ($26–$36). AE, DC, MC, V. Mon–Sat 6–11pm.

Emma's Drømmekjøkken (Emma's Dream Kitchen) ★★★ NORWE-GIAN   If there's such a thing as a "culinary personality" in Tromsø, it is Emma (aka Anne Brit), owner of this cozy restaurant across the street from Tromsø's cathedral. Born on a faraway Norwegian island near the Lofotens, she specializes in the cuisine of the far north of Norway. The restaurant contains only 30 seats, so reservations are important. We were so enthralled with the appetizers that we hardly made it to the main course—Arctic scallops and scampi fried in a chile and garlic oil, a ceviche of trout and halibut with a Japanese wasabi cream, or cream of oyster soup that was delectable. We suggest the fish as a main course, such as the poached filet of trout with Thai lemon grass, tomato concassé, white wine sauce, and smoked salmon. For a meat dish, we'd also recommend a grilled filet of veal with raisin sauce and fresh morels. For dessert, Emma will enchant you with her orange cheesecake with nuts and a papaya sauce or her blueberry granite with a white chocolate mousse. Before dinner you can descend into the wine cellar, site of an impressive inventory of bottles. If you order champagne, it will be dramatically uncorked by a saber-wielding somme-lier who chops off the neck of the bottle rather than uncork it. Emma, with relief, claims there's never been a shattered bottle.

Kirkegata 8. (© 77-63-77-30. Reservations required. Main courses 245NOK–295NOK ($33–$39); fixed-price menus 595NOK–699NOK ($79–$93). AE, DC, MC, V. Mon–Sat 6–10:30pm. Closed 1 week at Christmas.

Grillen ☆ NORWEGIAN This is the most upscale of the three recom-mended restaurants within the town's hotels. The interior evokes a baroque din-ing room in one of western Norway's 18th-century mansions, thanks to wide plank floors, dignified and traditional-looking furniture, dark colors, and enough space between tables to allow a sense of intimacy and—if you need it—secrecy. The charming staff members serve food that celebrates the culinary tra-ditions and raw ingredients (shellfish, reindeer, and cold-water fish) of Norway's far northern tier. Examples of the cuisine include six different preparations of mussels, including a version with curry. For a true taste of Norway, enjoy such palate-pleasing dishes as poached salt cod with an onion and tomato sauté, or else pan-fried filet of reindeer with a carrot and celery purée spiced with a juniper-berry sauce. For dessert, we opted for the delicious lime cheesecake with a coulis of berries. Immediately adjacent to this restaurant is a bar (Charly's), where diners can dance to a live orchestra.

In the Radisson SAS Hotel Tromsø, Sjøgata 7. (© 77-75-90-16. Reservations recommended. Fixed-price menus 11:30am–5pm 125NOK ($17), 5–11pm 325NOK ($43); main courses 178NOK–295NOK ($24–$39). AE, DC, MC, V. Mon–Sat 11:30am–11pm.

Markens Grøde Restaurant ☆☆ *Finds* CONTINENTAL/NORWEGIAN This small, upscale, and relatively famous (in these parts) restaurant has the aura of a private parlor in an old-fashioned home. Menu items emerge from an open kitchen, whose odors waft appealingly out into the dining room. The best exam-ples include willow grouse served with mushrooms and cloudberry sauce; rock ptarmigan with a black currant sauce and herb-baked potatoes; and a "symphony" of fish comprised of monkfish, trout, and catfish, all of them steamed and served with a tarragon sauce. Especially interesting is the game platter that contains filet of reindeer, breast of grouse, and filet of venison, all covered with bacon-flavored Madeira sauce and braised wild mushrooms. Desserts, the most creative in Tromsø, include a saffron and lemon mousse with mascarpone cream, served with chile peppers, baked pineapple, and fresh apricots. Don't confuse this stylish restaurant with the adjacent suds-and-sandwich pub of the same name.

Storgata 30. (© 77-68-25-50. Reservations required. Main courses 258NOK–306NOK ($34–$41); fixed-price menus 399NOK–559NOK ($53–$74). AE, DC, MC, V. Tues–Sat 5:30–11pm; Sun 5:30–10pm.

Peppermølle ☆ INTERNATIONAL One of Tromsø's genuinely warm and appealing restaurants is "the Peppermill," which is set one floor above the street level of a modern building along the town's main shopping thoroughfare. It was established in 1972, and since then, has attracted clients who have included Roald Amundsen, who ate his last meal here before one of his explorations of the Antarctic. There are a total of three separate dining rooms, including the "green room," and "the middle room." But the most interesting of the lot is the "Amundsen Room," which is lined with photos of Norway's Polar explorers, many of whom used Tromsø as their base of operations before heading to points much farther north. Menu items are savory and well prepared, and include a

---

Moments **Aurora Borealis: The Northern Lights**

The northern lights are one of nature's most spectacular and mysterious phenomena. In the right conditions, they can be seen in the night sky north of the Arctic Circle in winter. The most practical place to view them in Norway is Tromsø. If seeing these lights is one of your goals, plan to be in Tromsø for at least 3 days in order to increase your odds of getting the right atmospheric conditions. Anytime in the period from November to March is good, but the end of December with its 24 hours of darkness is best.

---

tartare of smoked salmon; broiled tenderloin with a tarragon-flavored mustard sauce; tenderloins stuffed with crayfish and served with crayfish sauce; and filet of monkfish fried with mushrooms, shrimp, and crème fraîche.

Storgata 54. © **77-68-62-60.** Reservations recommended. Main courses 226NOK–275NOK ($30–$37). AE, DC, MC, V. Mon–Thurs 4–11pm; Fri–Sat 3–11pm; Sun 3–10pm.

Store Norske Fiskekompani ★ SEAFOOD A visible monument on Tromsø's dining scene, this place is on the town's main shopping street. The decor looks older than it is. Menu options, for starters, include extremely fresh seafood, such as a tartare of salmon and scallops flavored with coriander and truffle oil, cream of lobster soup with pistachio oil and scallops, or salted redfish with sour cream and onions. Main courses include grilled whale steak with anchovy sauce and rösti-style potatoes; fried filet of sea char with spinach, fennel, and almonds; and a seafood bouillabaisse made only with fish that thrive in the Arctic waters offshore, served (incongruously) with a garlic-laced aioli inspired by the cuisine of Provence.

Storgata 73. © **77-68-76-00.** Reservations recommended. 196NOK–265NOK ($26–$35). AE, DC, MC, V. Mid-May to Sept daily 5–11pm. Closed Oct to mid-May.

MODERATE

Restaurant Ago NORWEGIAN Clean, and about as neat as any restaurant we've seen in Norway, this relatively new establishment maintains a busy pub and cocktail bar on its street level and a comfortable upstairs dining room. Lunches focus on salads; bowls of shrimp; fried scampi with red onions; steamed mussels; and lasagna. Dinners are more elaborate, and include platters of wild game; coconut soup; a creamy version of salmon-with-shellfish soup; and grilled halibut with sherry-glazed shallots.

Storgata 57. © **77-64-79-80.** Reservations recommended for dinner, not necessary at lunch. Main courses 74NOK–115NOK ($9.85–$15) at lunch, 168NOK–257NOK ($22–$34) at dinner. AE, DC, MC, V. Mon–Sat 11:30am–3pm and 3:30–11pm.

Steakers **Kids** STEAKS This warm, darkly lit steakhouse, the most popular in town, is adjacent to the wharves where the coastal steamers dock, midway between the Rica and Clarion hotels. From its big windows, by candlelight, you can watch the arrivals and departures of the fishing and cargo ships. Simple, grilled beefsteaks come in sizes that range from petite (150g/5 oz.) to boneless tenderloins that weigh in at a knockout 400 grams (14 oz). More elaborate meat dishes are stuffed, basted, or marinated, and might include a "Chicago gangster" (tenderloin marinated with garlic-flavored butter); a rack of barbecued ribs; and steaks marinated in—among other things—tequila and chile peppers. There's also a limited array of fish, including catfish Provençal, burgers for kids, and a salad bar. Dessert might include cheesecake drenched with a coulis of fresh raspberries.

Fr. Langesgt. 19. © **77-61-33-30.** Reservations recommended. Main courses 154NOK–234NOK ($20–$31). AE, DC, MC, V. Mon–Fri 3–11pm; Sat–Sun 2–10pm.

INEXPENSIVE

Aunegården (O. L. Aune) *Value* NORWEGIAN   Named after a 19th-century butcher shop (O. L. Aune) that stood here for many years, this restaurant is a culinary icon in a city loaded with worthy competitors. The setting includes a Victorian-era tearoom near its entrance, and a darker, less prim series of dining rooms lined with slabs of volcanic rock in back. It's busy throughout the day in roles that include a tearoom and "light lunch" restaurant, with more substantial and serious-sounding dinner specialties in the evening. Lunch items include tuna sandwiches on baguettes, salads, pastas, club sandwiches, and a Nordic version of bouillabaisse; dinner items include whale steak marinated in pesto, marinated scampi, and catfish fried in curry.

Sjøgata 29. © **77-65-12-34.** Reservations recommended. Main courses 82NOK–129NOK ($11–$17) at lunch, 178NOK–225NOK ($24–$30) at dinner. AE, DC, MC, V. Mon–Thurs 10:30am–midnight; Fri–Sat 10:30am–12:30am; Sun 1–10:30pm.

Restaurant EKA INTERNATIONAL   You'll find this simple restaurant in the cellar of Tromsø's Fine Arts Museum. Don't expect comfort, since everything about this place suggests the museum's need to transform a cold anteroom into a profit-generating food emporium. Thankfully, there's a culinary flair to the menu, which may include cassoulet of snails, omelets with salads, salade niçoise, and wok-fried vegetables with salsa and oregano.

In the cellar of the Tromsø Kunstforening (Fine Arts Museum), Muségata 2. © **93-22-72-23.** Reservations not accepted. 1-course lunch with coffee 40NOK ($5.30); main courses 48NOK–82NOK ($6.40–$11). No credit cards. Mon–Fri 11am–4pm; Sat–Sun noon–5pm.

Vertshuset Skarven A.S. *Value* NORWEGIAN   This cafeteria is the cheapest of a trio of restaurants within a 19th-century warehouse adjacent to the waterfront. In the large and high-ceilinged room you'll be surrounded by lots of nautical memorabilia, antique farm implements, hanging models of 19th-century clipper ships, and an unusual collection of stuffed birds. Food items include hearty stews, baked filet of fish, pork cutlets, soups and sandwiches—the kind of hearty fare that might be served in the homes of many of the town's older residents. Overall, this is a cheap and highly atmospheric place for a drink, snack, or meal.

Strandtorget 1. © **77-60-07-20.** Reservations not accepted. Sandwiches 34NOK–75NOK ($4.50–$10); platters 79NOK–85NOK ($11). AE, DC, MC, V. Sun–Thurs 11:30am–12:30am; Fri–Sat 11:30am–1am.

4 Seeing the Sights

There's a small-scale cable car, the **Fjellheisen,** that hauls sightseers in orange-and-red gondolas from a spot near the Arctic Cathedral in Tromsdal, uphill to a small, not-very-exciting cafe and restaurant (**Fjellstua Restaurant**), 420m (1,380 ft.) above sea level. Your vertiginous trip is rewarded with a **panoramic view** ★★ from the restaurant that extends out over the surrounding countryside. The cable car operates only from June to September at 30-minute intervals every day between 10am and midnight. Round-trip passage costs 70NOK

Tromsø Attractions

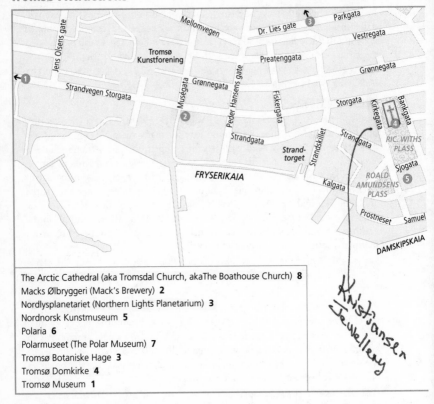

The Arctic Cathedral (aka Tromsdal Church, akaThe Boathouse Church) **8**
Macks Ølbryggeri (Mack's Brewery) **2**
Nordlysplanetariet (Northern Lights Planetarium) **3**
Nordnorsk Kunstmuseum **5**
Polaria **6**
Polarmuseet (The Polar Museum) **7**
Tromsø Botaniske Hage **3**
Tromsø Domkirke **4**
Tromsø Museum **1**

($9.30) for adults, 30NOK ($4) for children 6 to 16, free for children under 6. Round-trip transport of a bicycle (some bike and hiking trails originate near the cable car's upper station) costs 30NOK ($4). A family round-trip ticket (two adults and an unlimited number of their children) costs 170NOK ($23).

Full meals in the Fjellstua Restaurant cost around 200NOK ($27) each, and include reindeer, dried cod, and fish. Although the tourist office tries to promote this as a big-deal kind of excursion, it's actually kind of tame. The cable car is a bit of a weak-lemonade replay of something the Swiss and Austrians do in ways that are flashier and higher.

The Arctic Cathedral (aka Tromsdal Church, aka The Boathouse Church) ★★ North Norway's most distinctive-looking and controversial church rose from a location across the harbor from downtown Tromsø in 1965, requiring a transit of the town's longest bridge, completed in 1960, to reach it. Since then, its simple A-frame design has evolved into one of the town's most visible symbols, and—thanks to the late-night concerts conducted here for cruise-ship passengers between May and September—one of the most frequently visited sights in the area. Its theme, thanks to huge stained-glass windows set into the triangular-shaped front of the church, is a celebration of the light that filters through a grid-work of thin glass strips, the effect of which has been described as mystical, especially during the brief moments of daylight that

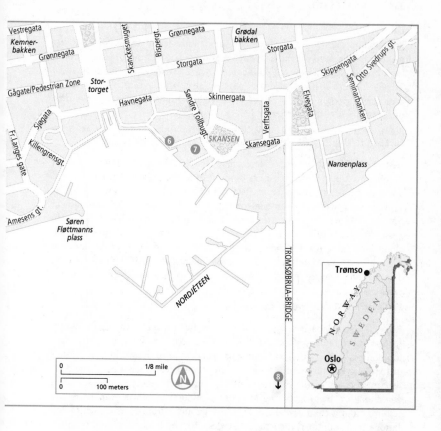

creep up to this far northern outpost during the middle of winter. Consistent with Norway's long established custom of hanging replicas of sailing ships within Norwegian churches as a good luck charm for the vessels' occupants, the shape of the organ at the back of the church resembles the sails of a ship. Other references to the Arctic's climate and culture abound: The crystal chandeliers evoke icicles; and the predominant color of the huge stained-glass windows is a rich and variegated tone of Arctic blue. Incidentally, when the pope paid an official visit to this remote place on June 11, 1989, it drew a relatively small crowd of around 2,000 people.

Tromsdal. ℂ **77-75-35-00.** Free admission during worship services; otherwise 20NOK ($2.65) adults, 15NOK ($2) children 7–15, free for children under 7; admission to concerts 60NOK ($8), no discounts available for children or students. Mid-Apr to May daily 3–6pm; June to mid-Aug daily 10am–8pm; mid-Aug to Sept daily 3–6pm. Otherwise the church is closed except for Sun worship services. Concert times coincide with the arrival of cruise ships, but they're usually scheduled for around 10pm every night between mid-May to mid-Aug.

Macks Ølbryggeri (Mack's Brewery)   This is one of the northernmost microbreweries in the world. Launched in 1877, it's been going strong ever since. The brewery currently turns out nearly two dozen brews, including Haakon and Macks Pilsner. Tours are conducted of the brewery, and you're given a beer stein as a souvenir. You can also sample the brew at the on-site Ølhallen Pub.

Storgata 5. ℂ **77-62-45-80.** Tours Mon–Fri 100NOK ($13), Sat 200NOK ($27). Oct–May Mon–Thurs 9am–5pm; Fri 9am–6pm; Sat 9am–3pm; June–Sept Mon–Fri 9am–6pm, Sat 9am–3pm. Closed Sun.

Nordlysplanetariet (Northern Lights Planetarium) ⭐ Here you can enjoy the northern lights, the midnight sun, and the starry sky, in Norway's first planetarium open to the public, which is also the northernmost planetarium in the world. Experience the city in the film *Arctic Light* and the multimedia show *Tromsø, Tromsø*, or travel into space with the space-shuttle film. This attraction is especially recommended to those who arrive in Tromsø too late to view some of the wonders of the northern sky.

Hansine Hansensv. 17, Breivika. ℂ **77-67-60-00**. Admission 50NOK ($6.65). Shows in English June to late Aug Mon–Fri 1:30pm and 4:30pm; late Aug to May schedule varies; call for information.

Nordnorsk Kunstmuseum In its new quarters, the Art Museum of North Norway traces art and applied art from 1838 to the present day, with special attention paid to Northern Norwegian artists. It features non-Norwegian artists as well, along with sculpture and photography. Anything by Edvard Munch, Scandinavia's greatest artist, attracts the most attention, even if it's a lesser work. Lesser-known artists such as Christian Krohg and Axel Revold are displayed, along with the romantic peasant scenes of Adolph Tidemand and the beautiful rugged Norwegian landscape paintings of Johan Dahl and Thomas Fearnley. The National Gallery in Oslo frequently sends up major works for temporary exhibitions.

Sjøgata 1. ℂ **77-68-00-90**. Free admission. Mon–Sat 11am–5pm.

Polaria ⭐ Polaria is a Disney-esque scientific homage to the ecologies, climates, and technological potentialities of the Arctic. Inaugurated in 1998 in a location beside the waterfront, immediately adjacent to the world headquarters of the Polar Institution of Norway (a deeply respected subdivision of the Norwegian Ministry of the Environment), it's one of the most frequently visited attractions in town, attracting as many as 80,000 visitors a year. Its design resulted from a contest wherein 45 noted architects from North America and Europe each submitted their respective designs. The result as viewed from the town evokes a weather-tight factory, industrial looking in wood, glass and stainless steel that looks like it could survive the harshest Arctic winter. Viewed from any of the boats out on the harbor, its stainless steel surfaces resemble a jagged ice floe pressed into fragile but irregular vertical alignments.

The self-defined goal of this attraction involves "awakening a respect in everyone that enters for the Arctic environments," and the dioramas and tableaux—some with artificially induced snow flurries behind thick sheets of Plexiglas, will leave you with a deeper understanding of the complex and delicate ecosystems of the Arctic. There's an IMAX-size movie theater where an 18-minute film, shot mostly on the Norwegian/Russian island of Svalbard, celebrates the beauty and biodiversity of the Arctic. There's an aquarium holding what might be the ugliest fish anywhere, some of them close enough to reach out and touch. (The halibut, we're told, are among the most vicious. Watch out—they bite, and only touch the exhibits where that's signposted as one of your options.) Where the signs indicate, you can reach out and touch some of the species—a favorite of families with children, but an act that always leaves us feeling a bit queasy.

There's an interactive section where you can push various buttons that activate exhibits showing the effects of environmental pollution, plus a 7-minute retrospective demonstrating how the gas and oil reserves under the Arctic tundra result from millions of years of geology. There's an indoor pool for the care, shelter, and feeding of Arctic seals, with regular feedings and seal gymnastics. And in the lobby, there's a genuinely wonderful gift shop—one of the most

interesting in town—selling souvenirs and some remarkably
items, including hand-painted lacquered boxes hauled in from a
frontiers with Russia.

Hjarmar Johansens gata. ✆ **77-75-01-00.** Admission 75NOK ($10) adults, 55NOK ($7.30, students, 40NOK ($5.30) children 3–16. Mid-May to mid-Aug daily 10am–7pm; mid-Aug to mid-May daily noon–5pm.

Polarmuseet (The Polar Museum) ★ Not to be confused with Polaria, a
space-age celebration of the Arctic's ecosystems (described separately above), the
Polar Museum showcases the bravery and ingenuity of the 19th- and early-
20th-century fishermen, hunters, whalers, trappers, and explorers who made the
Arctic their home. The museum is set into an interconnected wood-sided complex of red-painted buildings adjacent to Tromsø's harbor. A bronze statue of
explorer Roald Amundsen is positioned directly in front of the museum. Inside,
in an antique warehouse whose stout timbers illustrate the construction techniques of the 19th century, you'll find gruesome photographs and dioramas
showing how genuinely rough life in the frozen north could be, even as late as
the 1960s. On display are antique versions of the hempen ropes, sealskins,
sledges, and survival equipment that kept the fishing, hunting, and whaling
industries alive. Regrettably, all captions associated with the exhibitions are in
Norwegian, but if you ask, a staff member will give you abbreviated pamphlets
in English that superficially describe each of the exhibits.

Søndre Tollbugatell. ✆ **77-68-43-73.** Admission 40NOK ($5.30) adults, 30NOK ($4) students and children 6–18, free for children 5 and under; 80NOK ($11) family ticket, granting entrance to 2 adults plus any number of children under 16. July–Aug daily 10am–7pm; off-season daily 11am–3pm.

Tromsø Botaniske Hage ★ (Finds) This is the world's northernmost botanical
garden. Arctic tundra and alpine landscapes converge here. The setting is beautiful, with slopes, a stream, a pond, and terraces. Many of the plants are from the
Arctic and Antarctic, as well as various alpine locations. You've seen better botanical gardens, we are certain, but not one growing rare specimens this far north.

Breivika. Free admission. May–Sept daily 24 hr.

Tromsø Domkirke One of Norway's largest wooden churches, this is a barn-
like, yellow, "carpenter Gothic" monument in the heart of town that's difficult
to heat in winter. It is the world's northernmost Protestant cathedral, lying
182m (200 yards) from the harbor. Consecrated in 1861, it was the creation of
architects D. J. Evjen and Heinrich Grosch. Seating 750 persons, the cathedral
shows some classical and Swiss influences. The altarpiece, painted by Christian
Brun, is a copy of one within Bragernes church in Drammen. Built by Claus
Jensen in 1863, the organ was one of his largest works. In 1944, the church was
at the center of history when it was used by evacuees during the Nazi-enforced
evacuation of Finnmark and Northern Troms. In 1994, the church was restored
and returned to its original colors.

Storgata 25. ✆ **77-66-25-80.** Free admission. Tues–Sat 10am–6pm; Sun 10am–2pm.

Tromsø Museum ★ Built in the 1960s, and associated with the University of
Tromsø, this museum sprawls over three floors and addresses various aspects of
natural science (including loads of information on the ecology, botany, geology, and
zoology of Norway's far north). There are also exhibits about the Sami people and
some very interesting exhibits about the cultural history of Norway's far North.

Our favorite exhibit contains Norwegian church art crafted between the
Middle Ages and the 17th century—at least the little bits of it that remain, since
so much of it was burnt during the Norwegian Reformation. The church art

works that are on display in the museum escaped destruction during the Reformation because they were kept in church basements and outbuildings, considered less valuable than the works that were actually on display in churches and was. Many of the pieces on exhibition here are "carpenter Baroque" altarpieces and large-scale crucifixes either made in private workshops in Tromsø, or bought and shipped up north from faraway Bergen by German Hanseatic traders.

Note that the gift shop in the lobby here is especially interesting, with accurate copies of Viking jewelry that's a lot better than what's sold in some of the town's tourist shops. Many of the exhibitions are kid friendly, especially a life-size dinosaur that kids can enter and explore.

Lars Thoringsvei 10. ℂ **77-64-50-00**. Admission 30NOK ($4) adults, 15NOK ($2) students and children 7–18, free for children under 7. Mid-Sept to mid-may Mon–Fri 9am–3:30pm, Sat–Sun 11am–5pm; mid-May to mid-June and mid-Aug to mid-Sept daily 9am–6pm; mid-June to mid-Aug daily 9am–8pm.

5 Shopping

Bianco Footwear   This shop is Tromsø's exclusive distributor for the footwear of the most hip and cutting-edge shoe manufacturer in Scandinavia, Denmark-based Bianco Footwear. When a bevy of blonde and buxom female beauties failed to promote consumer interest in the company's line of footwear, Bianco's art department opted for an all-male lineup of cross-dressing (and not particularly pretty) models, sassily sporting Bianco's women's line of shoes and clothing. Today, on oversize posters prominently displayed both inside and outside the shop, you'll be exposed to the most controversial ad campaign in recent Scandinavian history. Be reassured that if you happen to be male and not into cross-dressing, the company markets conventional men's clothing and shoes as well. The store owners call their campaign "extreme art based on solid commercial profits." The Norwegian marketplace seems to agree. Strandgate 26. ℂ **77-65-61-90**.

Hekle-Kroken   Early in their childhoods, many residents of Norway's far north learn different ways to while away the long winter nights. Many of them turn to arts and crafts. If you're interesting in seeing what's available in terms of quilting, embroidery supplies, and knitting patterns, head for this grandmotherly-looking repository of all the ingredients you'll need to engage in some of the most popular hobbies in the region. The setting is a plank-sided antique building in the heart of town. Skippergate 6. ℂ **77-68-17-87**.

Husfliden   As we mentioned above, in the review of Hekle-Kroken, winter nights in Tromsø are long, dark, and very cold, and many locals labor, from within their well-heated and weather-tight homes, at arts and crafts. If you're a knitter, a quilter, an embroiderer, or a leatherworker, this shop stocks your raw materials. There's also a small inventory of handmade sweaters knitted by people loosely affiliated with the store. The staff here tends to be elderly, kindhearted, grandmotherly aficionados of the arts and crafts scene. Sjøgata 4. ℂ **77-68-56-30**.

Intersport Sports Huset   This is the biggest sporting goods store in town, with subdivisions that focus on the equipment you'll need for every conceivable sport, in any season, that's practiced in this severe Arctic climate. Scattered over two separate floors of a showroom in the heart of town, the store stocks bicycles, hiking equipment, white-water rafting and kayaking equipment, all manner of skis, and a state-of-the-art collection of boots, backpacks, and severe-weather clothing. Frankly, the staff isn't always too well trained here, and some don't seem to have a clue as to what it is they're actually selling, but if you're motivated to figure out the inventories on your own, there are many worthwhile options. Storgata 39. ⑦ **77-66-11-00.**

Krant Kunstgalleri   Established in 1908 as a window-making shop, this place has evolved into a combination gift shop, framing gallery, and art gallery. The third- and fourth-generation owners spend a lot of their energies showcasing the paintings of about 70 Norwegian artists, many of them residents of the country's far north, and all of them clustered within the same sales and marketing union. You can pick up some unusual examples of handmade glass, postcards, and posters. If you decide to invest in an original painting, etching, or lithograph, prices range from 25NOK to 40,000NOK ($3.35–$5,320) depending on the artwork's size and the reputation of the artist. Strandgata 30. ⑦ **77-61-52-60.**

6 Tromsø After Dark

Blå Rock Café   You'll be greeted at the entrance to this battered but congenial pub with a sign that screams ROCK AND ROLL RULES, and if you opt to abide by that premise, you might find yourself having a perfectly marvelous, albeit a bit grungy, time. The setting is a blue-sided wooden house at the end of the town's main shopping street (Storget). The staff is friendly, the youthful clientele looks like it was just assigned *Catcher in the Rye* as a reading assignment, and the pub's visual and musical references invariably revolve around punk cultural icons from Britain and the U.S. They stock about 50 kinds of beer here, most if it priced at around 48NOK ($6.40) for a foaming half-liter mugful. It's open Monday to Thursday 11:30am to 2am, Friday and Saturday from 11:30am to 3am, and Sunday 1pm to 2am. Strandveien 14. ⑦ **77-61-00-20.** Cover 30NOK ($4).

Charly's   This is a crowded, convivial singles bar that attracts a usually horny crowd of adult women and men from Tromsø and the surrounding region. Interconnected through a wide doorway with the also-recommended Grillen Restaurant, it's the kind of bar where—according to the hotel's public relations staff—it's almost impossible not to get lucky if that's what you set out to do. There's no cover charge. Throughout the night, a combination of recorded and live dance music, sometimes from a small dance orchestra, provide the tunes. It's open Wednesday to Saturday from 8pm till between 1 and 3am, depending on business. In the cellar of the Radisson SAS Hotel Tromsø, Sjøgata 7. ⑦ **77-75-90-16.**

Driv Café (Studenthuset $ Kulturscenen Driv A/S)   For virtually any activity in Tromsø that's aimed at, organized by, or attended by university students, this antique wood-sided warehouse, set directly adjacent to the harbor in the heart of town, will be involved in some way. It was originally built in 1902 as a warehouse for fish, and today, its thick interior beams and aged planking evoke an age when hardworking, hard-drinking fishermen, hunters, trappers, and whalers made their sometimes precarious living from the sea. Today's there's a simple cafe filling up the seaward side of the place, and a bigger and more battered-looking bar area where bulletin boards list virtually every cultural activity available within the region. The cafe is open Monday to Thursday from noon till 2am, and Friday and Saturday from noon to 3:30am. Some kind of concert is scheduled every Wednesday and Thursday night beginning around 9:30pm, and every Friday and Saturday the place becomes a disco and pickup bar between 10pm and 2am. Entrance fees to concerts range from 30NOK to 60NOK ($4–$8), depending on the artist, and admission to the disco costs 20NOK ($2.65). Søndre Tollbodgate 3B. ⑦ **77-60-07-76.**

Le Mirage   The leather sofas at this cutting-edge bar are deep, plush, and comfortable, and the walls are painted in a conversation-inducing shade of scarlet. It exists as a hipster bar, with a striking-looking postmodern decor that's in deliberate contrast to the more rustic pubs that surround it on all sides. The 20-something clientele is hip enough to remain completely unfazed at the way this bar, somewhat confusingly, seems to have been repeatedly designated, often in newspaper articles in many different languages throughout Europe, as a gay bar. If you ask one of the barmaids about it, she'll politely maintain that the place is predominately straight, and we'd tend to agree. But despite that, we still suspect that this, more than any other bar, is the most gay-tolerant and accommodating in town. It's open Monday to Thursday noon to 2am, Friday and Saturday noon to 3:30am, and Sunday 2pm to 2am. There is no cover charge. Storgata 42. © 77-68-52-34.

Markens Grøde Vin- og kaffebar (Markens Grøde Wine and Coffee Bar)   During daytime hours, there's a hush about this place that might remind you of a public library, thanks to (Norwegian-language) newspapers and magazines, and a kind of stoic silence that's encouraged by the not-very-attentive staff, some of whom might be hung over from their carousing the night before. After dark, however, the place heats up into a convivial and animated pub, where clients drink, snack on sandwiches and light platters, and talk. Farm implements hang from the ceiling, and paneling lines the walls. At least in our opinion, this is as laissez-faire and indulgent a watering hole as you're likely to find in Tromsø. Beer costs 39NOK ($5.20) per mugful, wine costs from 269NOK ($36) per bottle, toasts and sandwiches cost from 57 to 67NOK ($7.60–$8.90), and platters cost from 89 to 109NOK ($12–$15). Don't confuse this place with the more expensive and more upscale Markens Grøde restaurant, which is separately recommended in "Where to Dine." There is no cover charge. Storgata 30. © 77-68-25-50.

Rorbua Pub   This is Norway's most famous pub thanks to the fact that one of Norway's most popular weekly TV talk shows, *Du skal høre mye,* whose name roughly translates as "You've Heard a Lot" is broadcast from here. The show attracts a million viewers every Wednesday night. Despite the fact that the hotel that contains the pub was built in 1965, the thick timbers and rough-textured planking evokes a fisherman's cottage *(rorbua)* from the late 19th century. If you happen to be in town during one of the filmings (usually at 7pm on either Mon or Thurs), you can prereserve, through the hotel, free tickets in advance. Otherwise, there's live music in the pub every Wednesday to Sunday beginning around 8:30pm. There is no cover charge. In the cellar of the Radisson SAS Hotel Tromsø, Sjøgata 7. © 77-75-90-16.

14

The Route to the North Cape

Northern Norway.

The name itself can give you a chill, conjuring up thoughts of polar bears, the summer midnight sun and arctic winters of total darkness. It is an eerie and fascinating land of deep fjords, snow-capped mountains, vast open plains, dramatic island formations, and even fertile farmland (although the growing season is short).

Northern Norway is the land of the *Sami* or *Lapps,* where you come face to face with nature under the foreboding sky of **Finnmark,** the name of the region. Rushing rivers and lakes are teeming with fish, and many tiny, weather-beaten fishing hamlets depend almost entirely on the sea for their livelihood.

For most visitors, the ultimate goal is the North Cape, or "the end of the world," as the ancient Vikings called it.

Traveling in North Norway and meeting the *Nordlendinger* (northerners) is an adventure in travel.

However it may not be as cold as you think. Because of the warming influences of the Gulf Stream, Finnmark has the longest ice-free coast in the Arctic region. Finnmark shares the same latitudes as Siberia, Greenland, and Alaska.

Of course, flying is the fastest way of to get here, but you can also drive toward the Arctic Circle from such cities as Bergen on one of Europe's most scenic drives. Don't, however, underestimate driving times. Allow at least 3 days to reach the Arctic Circle from Bergen or 5 days to the North Cape.

1 Mo i Rana: Arctic Circle City

450km (280 miles) N of Trondheim

It's not pretty, but "Mo on the Ranafjord" is your gateway to the Arctic Circle, which crosses its municipal boundaries from east to west. With a population of some 25,000 people, it is the third largest city in the north of Norway. It is also the gateway to one of the largest wildernesses in Europe.

The buildings are ugly boxes for the most part, but welcoming havens on a cold and windy day. Its rapid population growth in recent years is because of the steel and iron industry.

Use Mor i Rana only as a refueling stop. You don't visit it for its grand architecture, but for the magnificent setting that it occupies, with adventure travel possible in all directions.

ESSENTIALS
GETTING THERE   The quickest way is to fly in on a daily flight from Trondheim, arriving at the Røssvoll airport, lying 14km (8½ miles) from the center. **Widerøe Airlines** (© 81-00-12-00) flies here. You can also arrive by train at the **Mo i Rana Train Station** (© 75-15-01-77). Two or three trains arrive daily from Trondheim, costing 600NOK ($80) one-way and taking just under 7 hours. Bus

Coastal Steamer: The Way to Go

Coastal steamers ★★ are elegantly appointed ships that travel along the Norwegian coast from Bergen to Kirkenes, carrying passengers and cargo to 34 ports. A total of 11 ships make the journey year-round. Along the route, the ships sail through Norway's more obscure fjords, revealing breathtaking scenery and numerous opportunities for adventure. At points along the way, passengers have the opportunity to take sightseeing trips to the surrounding mountains and glaciers, and excursions on smaller vessels.

The chief cruise operator is the **Norwegian Coastal Voyage/Bergen Line,** 405 Park Ave., New York, NY 10022 (✆ **800/323-7436** or 212/319-1300). Various packages are available. Tours may be booked heading north from Bergen, south from Kirkenes, or round-trip. The 7-day one-way northbound journey costs $551 to $4,113 per person, including meals and taxes. The 12-day round-trip voyage from Bergen to Kirkenes and back to Bergen is $818 to $6,134 per person. For information on these and other trips, including air-cruise packages from the United States, contact the Bergen Line.

service takes longer, is inconvenient, and saves you neither time nor money, so it's not recommended. Motorists can take the E6 north from Trondheim.

VISITOR INFORMATION   Near the Sørlandsveien roundabout, **Polarsirkelen Reiseliv,** Ole Tobias Olsensgate 3 (✆ 75-13-92-00), offers information about the area and is one of the most helpful tourist bureaus in Norway. From mid-June to early August it is open Monday to Friday 9am to 8pm, Saturday 9am to 4pm, Sunday 1 to 7pm. In off-season it's open Monday to Friday 10am to 3pm.

SEEING THE SIGHTS
Within the town itself are some minor attractions, but if your time is severely limited, it would be better spent taking a tour of the wilderness.

The **Rana Museum of Natural History,** Moholmen 15 (✆ 75-14-61-80), reveals the flora and fauna of the Arctic Circle, with a number of "touch-me-if-you-want" exhibits of particular appeal to families with young kids. The fascinating geology and ecology of this Arctic wilderness comes alive here. Admission is 10NOK ($1.35). Open mid-June to mid-August 9am to 3pm and 7 to 10pm Monday to Friday. In the off-season open Monday to Friday 9am to 3pm.

Rana Museum of Cultural History, Fridtjof Nansensgate 22 (✆ 75-14-61-70), recaptures the life and living conditions of the people who settled in this harsh section of Norway. Exhibits trace the history of Mo through the 20th century, focusing on the old farming communities nearby. Of particular interest are artifacts of the Sami (Lapp) culture. The center is also the venue for frequent concerts and temporary art exhibitions. Admission is 15NOK ($2). Open Monday to Friday 10am to 3pm and 7 to 9pm. It is also open in summer on Saturday from noon to 3pm.

North of Mo (30km/19 miles) lies the grandest natural attraction in this part of Norway, the **Svartisen Glacier** ★★★ (means "black ice" in Norwegian).

Alta **7**
Bodø **2**
Hammerfest **8**
Honningsvåg **9**
Karasjok **6**
Lofoten Islands **4**
Mo i Rana **1**
Narvik **3**
Nordkapp (North Cape) **10**
Vesterålen Islands **5**

ARCTIC OCEAN

Nordkapp ⑩   Berlevåg
Honningsvåg ⑨   Vardø
Hammerfest ⑧   ○Lebesby   Vadsø
   Laksélv   Kirkenes
Alta ⑦   E6   Utsjoki
⑤ Tromsø   Karasjok ⑥ *Inarijärvi*   RUSSIA

Norwegian Sea   Lenvik○
LOFOTEN ISLANDS
④ Hadsel   Narvik ③   ○Enontekiö   FINLAND
Svolvær○   Kiruna   Kittilä
Skutvik○   ○Vittangi
Bodø ② E6   SWEDEN   Pelkosenniemi
Fauske   ○Gällivare
Jokkmokk
ARCTIC CIRCLE   Övertorneá
Mo i Rana ①
   Sorsele   Luleå   0   100 mi
   0   100 km

Svartisen is second in size in the country only to the Jostedal Glacier. The ice plateau is 1,005m (3,330 ft.) above sea level, covering 370 sq. km (229 sq. miles) of high mountains and narrow fjords.

Svartisen (more accurately known as Engen Glacier) consists of two main glaciers, the Østisen (East Glacier) and Vestisen (West Glacier). One arm of the West Glacier is the lowest lying glacier on the European mainland. The glacial arm continues all the way down to Engenbrevannet Lake. It continues to grow, advancing 40m (131 ft.) a year. Motorists driving along Route 17 by Holandsfjorden can see many arms of the glacier stretching down between mountain peaks.

The Vestisen icecap is the most interesting part to visit if your time is limited. The **Engen Skyssbåt** (② **94-86-55-16**) operates two ferries running across Holandsfjorden, taking 15 minutes and costing 40NOK ($5.30). From June to August, the ferries run 12 times daily Monday to Friday from 7:30am to 8pm, and 10 times on Saturday and Sunday 10am to 8pm. Ferries depart from the Holand and Brasetvik quays.

You can also drive to the glacier by going north from Mo on the E6 for 12km (7½ miles), following the signs to the glacier for 23km (14 miles). At the end of the line, you'll find Svartisbåten boats (② **75-16-23-79**) crossing the lake and coming within 2.5km (1½ miles) of the Østerdal arm of the glacier. From the disembarkation point, it's still a 3km (2-mile) hike up to Austerdalsvatnet lake and the glacier.

Near the ferry landing is the **Svartisen Turistsenter** (© **75-75-00-11**), opening May to September daily from 9am to 5pm. Here you can book a guided walk across the glacier for 200NOK ($27) per hour, plus the cost of any equipment you'll need.

The glacier is part of the **Saltfjellet-Svartisen Nasjonalpark** ★★★, stretching over a landmass of 2,015 sq. km (1,307 sq. miles). The park takes in the ice field of Svartisen, along with various moorlands that reach as far east as the Swedish border.

Information can be obtained from the tourist office in Mo i Rana about hiking trails in the park. The trails can be approached from Route 77, which heads east off the E6 to the Swedish frontier.

Norway's best known "show cave," **Gronligrøtta** ★ (© **75-13-25-86**) lies in the hamlet of Grønli, 26km (16 miles) northwest of Mo. The only cave with electric lights in Scandinavia will illuminate your way as you take the half-hour tour into the cave with its underground river. As a curiosity you can see a mammoth granite block ripped off by a glacier and dumped into the cave by the sheer force of the onrushing waters. Visits cost 70NOK ($9.30) for adults, 35NOK ($4.65) for children. The cave can be toured hourly and daily from mid-June to mid-August from 10am to 7pm.

EN ROUTE TO BODØ

North of Mo i Rana (80km/50 miles) toward the Arctic Circle, you'll come to the **Polarsirkelsenteret**, on E6. It offers a multiscreen show depicting the highlights of Norway. Many people send cards and letters from here with a special postmark from the Arctic Circle. There's also a cafeteria and gift shop on the grounds. The center is at N-8242 Polarsirkelen (© **75-12-96-96**). It's open in May and June, daily from 9am to 6pm; July to September, daily 8am to 10pm. Admission is 50NOK ($6.65).

Continue north to Fauske, and then follow Route 80 west along the Skjerstadfjord. Depending on weather conditions, you should reach Bodø in under an hour.

WHERE TO STAY

Comfort Hotel Ole Tobias ★ *Finds*   Built in 1993, this is the smallest, the newest, and the coziest hotel in town. The hotel was named after Ole Tobias (1827–1912) a local priest, inventor, and visionary whose well-publicized treks (on foot) between Trondheim and Bodø led to the construction of a railway for the transport of fish from the Arctic waters of the north to canning factories and consumers of the south. Reproductions of many of Ole Tobias' photographs hang, framed, throughout the hotel. If you come here, expect an aura that's akin to a well-mannered but extroverted private club. Its social headquarters is within the hotel basement, site of a cozy bar and restaurant. Here, you'll find a wide-screen TV, a light evening buffet (available nightly from 7–9pm) that's included in the price of a room, and willingness on the part of many of the clients to dialogue over drinks. Decor of the bedrooms includes a use of deep-toned "farmer romantic" colors; thick pine furniture, and turn-of-the-20th-century nostalgia, including representations of trains woven into the carpets. Each of the rooms has a bathroom with tiled surfaces. About half of them have a shower, and the others contain a shower-tub combination.

Thora Meyersgate 2, N-8602 Mo i Rana. © **75-15-77-77**. Fax 75-15-77-78. www.ole-tobias.no. 30 units. Mon–Thurs 870NOK–1,200NOK ($116–$160) double; Fri–Sun and June to mid-Aug daily 770NOK–870NOK ($102–$116) double. AE, DC, MC, V. **Amenities:** Restaurant; bar; sauna; limited room service. *In room:* TV, iron/ironing board.

Golden Tulip Rainbow Hotel Holmen   Originally built in 1949, reconstructed in the late 1960s, and radically renovated in the late 1980s, this is a boxy-looking but comfortable hotel, attracting business travelers and enjoying a reputation as the most stable and most central hotel in town. Rising three stories above a barren-looking neighborhood of waterfront commercial and efficiently weather-tight buildings, it opens into a bland but soothing decor of contemporary furniture. One of the best parts about this place is its staff, a well-informed group of English, Norwegian, and Lappish-speaking locals who work hard to convey the most interesting aspects of Mo i Rana. Each room has a pale-toned color scheme, wood-grained paneling, and a tile-sheathed bathroom. About half of the rooms have shower-tub combinations, the others only showers. The in-house restaurant serves Norwegian and international food.

Thomas Von Westensgt. 2, N-8624 Mo i Rana. (C) **75-15-14-44.** Fax 75-15-18-70. www.rainbow-hotels.no. 44 units. Mon–Thurs 740NOK–1,290NOK ($98–$172) double; Fri–Sun and mid-June to mid-Aug daily 740NOK–790NOK ($98–$105) double. AE, DC, MC, V. **Amenities:** Restaurant; pub; lobby bar; laundry service; dry cleaning. *In room:* TV, minibar.

WHERE TO DINE

Babette's Gjestebud   GREEK/TURKISH/MEDITERRANEAN   Babette's is a cozy, candlelit tavern, with lots of exposed wood, and warmth that's particularly welcome in this frigid climate. It was named after the Danish film *(Babette's Feast)* in which closed and bitter psyches were released and healed through good food, good wine, and love. The chef focuses on grilled meats and fresh salads, some of them garnished with feta cheese and Mediterranean herbs. Don't expect a particular allegiance to the cuisines of either Greece or Turkey, since what is served is a simplified blend of them both. Expect a medley of grilled meats, salads garnished with ham slices and/or shrimp; pastas that include a savory version with curried chicken, and body-warming starters such as French onion soup with your choice of either garlic-butter or herb-butter bread.

Ranheimgt. 2. (C) **75-15-44-33.** Reservations recommended. Main courses 135NOK–200NOK ($18–$27). AE, DC, MC, V. Daily 11am–midnight.

Caesar's   ITALIAN/NORWEGIAN   The best-recommended "Continental" restaurant in Mo i Rana is on the street level of a solid, modern-looking building near the railway station. The walls in the terra-cotta and ocher-colored dining room are adorned with paintings of the Italian landscape and copies of works by Michelangelo. Caesar's serves the best Italian food, and some of the best Norwegian food, in town. Your meal might begin with a platter of fried asparagus with garlic-flavored snails; deep-fried calamari or a shrimp cocktail; and a pungent form of pasta flavored with scampi and blue cheese. Main courses include Norwegian catfish with a cream-enhanced tomato sauce; medallions of veal with a bacon-flavored mushroom sauce; and—for something genuinely Norwegian—fried reindeer with lingonberry sauce.

Jan Banegaten 12. (C) **75-13-04-00.** Reservations recommended. Main courses 149NOK–300NOK ($20–$40). AE, DC, MC, V. Mon–Sat 11am–midnight; Sun 2–10pm.

MO I RANA AFTER DARK

Ramona, Fridtjof Nansensgata 28 ((C) **75-13-40-00**), is the only genuinely viable nightclub and dance club in town. Because of the lack of competitors, and a floor space that sprawls over an area that's bigger than the ground floors of many of the region's department stores, it promotes itself as the largest nightclub in north Norway. The space, set within an ugly commercial building in the heart of town, is subdivided by banquettes and arrangements of seating areas, into three "regions," painted in tones of pink or yellow. There are bars scattered strategically throughout, and a clientele whose age and priorities change according to whichever night of the week you happen to arrive. According to popular hipster wisdom, Thursday nights attract the student crowd, with a lot of 18-year-olds wearing various forms of punk-inspired clothing. Saturday is for an older, recently divorced-and-somewhat-embittered-but-still-hoping-for-an-active-dating-and-sex-life crowd over 30. Friday is the let-down-your-guard and be-sure-not-to-drive-your-own-car-home-because-you've-been-drinking crowd. The place is open every Tuesday to Saturday from 10pm to 3am, charging an entrance fee of 60NOK ($8) per person.

2 Bodø: Gateway to the North ⟨★⟩

479km (466 miles) N of Trondheim; 1,430km (889 miles) N of Bergen; 1,305km (811 miles) N of Oslo

This seaport, the terminus of the Nordland railway, lies just north of the Arctic Circle. Visitors flock to Bodø, the capital of Nordland, for a glimpse of the midnight sun, which shines brightly from June 1 to July 13. But don't expect a clear view of it—many nights are rainy or hazy. From December 19 to January 9, Bodø gets no sunlight at all.

Bodø is Nordland's largest city, with some 40,000 inhabitants living at the northern entrance to Salt Fjord.

Although burned to the ground by the retreating Nazis at the end of World War II, the city dates back to 1816 when it was founded by merchants from Trondheim seeking a northern trading post. In time it became one of the leading fishing centers of Norway, specializing in the drying of cod. It has also become known for its ship repair yards.

Bodø faces an archipelago rich in bird life. No other town in the world boasts such a large concentration of sea eagles.

From Bodø you can take excursions in many directions to glaciers and bird islands; perhaps the most important are to the Lofoten Islands (see later in this chapter).

ESSENTIALS

GETTING THERE If you're not driving or traveling by coastal steamer, you can reach Bodø from major cities throughout Norway, usually with connections through either Trondheim or Oslo, on **SAS** (✆ **75-54-47-00**). The airport lies just over a kilometer southwest of the city center, and is accessed by a bus (it's marked CENTRUMS BUSSEN) that departs at 20-minute intervals every Monday to Friday. Passengers arriving on a Saturday or Sunday hire one of the many taxis waiting at the arrivals gate. Bodø is at the end of the Nordland rail line.

Two **trains** a day leave Trondheim for Bodø. The trip takes 10 hours, 20 minutes.

For **bus** information, contact **Saltens Bilruter** in Bodø (✆ **75-54-80-20**). Fauske is a transportation hub along the E6 highway to the north and Route 80 west to Bodø. From Fauske there are two buses a day to Bodø. The trip takes an hour and 10 minutes. If you take the train from Stockholm to Narvik (north of Bodø), you can make bus connections to Fauske and Bodø, a total trip of 5 hours.

Motorists can continue north from Mo i Rana, our last stopover, until they come to the junction with Route 80 heading west to Bodø.

VISITOR INFORMATION   The **tourist office, Destination Bodø,** is at Sjøgaten 3 (© **75-54-80-00**), in the town center. It's open mid-June to mid-August, daily from 9am to 8:30pm; mid-August to mid-June, Monday to Friday 9am to 4pm.

SEEING THE SIGHTS

Bodin Kirke   This intriguing onion-domed church can be visited along with a trip to the Norwegian Aviation Museum (see below). It lies about 1km (½ mile) southeast of the museum. Dating from 1240, the church has seen many changes over the years. Many 17th- and 18th-century baroque adornments were made to jazz up what had been a severe interior.

Gamle Riksvei 68. © **75-54-80-00**. Free admission. June–Aug Mon–Fri 10am–2:30pm. Closed Sept–May. Bus: 23 from the station.

Bodø Domkirke   Completed in 1956, this is the most notable building constructed since German bombers leveled Bodø on May 27, 1940. It features tufted rugs depicting ecclesiastical themes, wall hangings, and a stained-glass window that captures the northern lights. A memorial outside honors those killed in the war with the inscription NO ONE MENTIONED, NO ONE FORGOTTEN. There's also an outstanding spire that stands separate from the main building.

Torv Gate 12. © **75-52-17-50**. Free admission. May–Sept daily 9am–2:30pm. Closed Oct–Apr.

Nordlandmuseet (Nordland Museum)   In the town center, the main building of this museum is one of the oldest structures in Bodø. Here you'll find, among other exhibits, artifacts recalling the saga of local fishermen and artifacts from the Lapp culture. There's also a "dry" aquarium, along with silver treasure dating from the Viking era.

Prinsengate 116. © **75-52-16-40**. Admission 30NOK ($4) adults, 15NOK ($2) children under 15. Mon–Fri 9am–3pm; Sat 10am–3pm; Sun noon–3pm.

Norsk Luftfartsmuseum (Norwegian Aviation Museum)   This museum takes you on an exciting "flight" of Norway's civil and military aviation history. The museum is constructed in the shape of an airplane propeller. You're allowed to have a close encounter with large and small aircraft such as the Spitfire, JU52, and U2. Hands-on demonstration reveals to you the dynamics of flight. In addition to the exhibition of aircraft, the museum shows a collection of photographs about the largest predators in the Nordic countries, including lynx, bears, wolves, and the wolverine. Humans are also included in the list of predators. The museum was built at the same site as a German airfield in World War II.

The museum lies 2km (1¼ miles) Olav V gata. © **75-50-78-50**. Admission 70NOK ($9.30) adults, 50NOK ($6.65) children. June–Aug Mon–Fri and Sun 10am–7pm, Sat 10am–5pm; Sept–May Mon–Fri 10am–4pm, Sat–Sun 11am–5pm. Bus: 23.

ON THE OUTSKIRTS

Blodveimuseet ★ *Finds*   On the southeastern outskirts of the city, a distance of 5km (3 miles), you can visit this "Blood Road Museum." The museum re-creates those horrible POW days during 1942 to 1945 when the Nazis held an iron grip on northern Norway before burning it to the ground during their infamous retreat. Thousands of European prisoners of war labored to build a system of road and railroads in the area, and, of course, many lost their lives. In Saltdal alone there were 15 to 18 different prisoner-of-war camps, with nearly 10,000 Russian, Serbian, and Polish prisoners held captive.

The "Road of Blood" extended for 2km (1¼ miles) from Saltnes to Saksenvik from the center of Rognan. People still walk this horrible road today, noting the blood cross a prisoner painted on a rock face.

At Saltnes, about 1km (½ mile) east of Rognan, the Blood Road Museum contains a collection of original rural buildings, the oldest dating from 1750. The original German barracks are here as well, revealing the harsh life of the prisoners. The museum was opened in 1995 as part of Norway's 50th anniversary of its liberation from the Nazis.

Bygetunet, Saltnes, outside Rognan. © 75-68-22-90. Admission 50NOK ($6.65). June 20–Aug 20 Mon–Fri 9:30am–4pm, Sat 1–4pm, Sun 1–6pm; closed rest of year.

ACTIVE SPORTS

If you'd like to go horseback riding under the midnight sun, **Bodø Hestecenter,** Soloya Gård (© 75-51-41-48), about 14km (9 miles) southwest of Bodø, rents horses. Buses go there Monday to Friday morning and evening and Saturday morning. For more information, ask at the Bodø Tourist Office. The cost is 100NOK ($13) for a 45-minute ride.

At the visitor's center (see above) you can pick up maps detailing the best hiking in the area, especially in the **Bodømarka** (Bodø forest) with its 35km (22 miles) of marked trails. For detailed touring, including overnighting in the forest, contact **Bodø og Omegn Turist-forening,** the Bodø Mountain Touring Association (© 75-52-48-90), which operates a dozen cabins in the forest.

Svømmehallen, Sivert Nielsens Gate 63 (© 75-55-75-20), is Bodø's largest and busiest indoor swimming pool. It's open September to May, Tuesday to Friday from 10am to 8pm, Saturday and Sunday 10am to 3pm; June to August, Monday, Wednesday, and Friday 10am to 2pm, Tuesday and Thursday 3 to 8pm (closed Sat–Sun). Admission is 40NOK ($5.30) for adults, 20NOK ($2.65) for children under 18.

A popular man-made attraction, **Saltstraumen Opplevelsesenter,** or adventure center, lies at Saltstraumen, route 17 (© 75-56-06-55), and is fun for the whole family. The center gives an in-depth preview through exhibits and artifacts tracing the history of the area and its people from the Ice Age to the coming of the Vikings. An on-site aquarium includes a pond for seals and fish found in regional waters. Admission is 60NOK ($8). From May to mid-June, it's open daily from 11am to 6pm; mid-June to late June and from mid-August to late August, open daily from 10am to 7pm; July to mid-August, open daily 9am to 8pm; September, open Saturday and Sunday only 11am to 6pm.

EXPLORING A SPECTACULAR LANDSCAPE

THE MAELSTROM From Bodø, you can take a bus to the mighty maelstrom, the **Saltstraumen Eddy** ⚓, 33km (20 miles) south of the city. The variation between high- and low-tide levels pushes immense volumes of water through narrow fjords, creating huge whirlpools known as "kettles." When the eddies and the surrounding land vibrate, they produce an odd yelling sound. Saltstraumen is nearly 3.25km (2 miles) long and only about 167m (500 ft.) wide, with billions of gallons of water pressing through at speeds of about 10 knots. It's best to go in the morning when it's most dramatic. Buses from Bodø run five times a day Monday to Saturday, twice on Sunday. The cost is 56NOK ($7.45) for adults round-trip, half-price for children. A round-trip taxi excursion costs 500NOK ($67) for two passengers.

VISITING A GLACIER One of Norway's major tourist attractions, **Svartisen Glacier** ⚓⚓⚓ was previewed under Mo i Rana (see earlier), but can also be visited from Bodø. About 161km (100 miles) from Bodø, the glacier can be reached by car, although a boat crossing over the Svartisenfjord is more exciting. Tours to the glacier on the Helgeland Express, a combination bus-and-ferry excursion, are offered from Bodø several times in the summer (usually every 2nd Sat July–Aug). The cost is 390NOK ($52) for adults, 200NOK ($27) for children under 16. The tours leave Bodø at 1pm and return around 8pm. You can go ashore to examine the Engaglacier and see the nearby visitor center (© 75-75-00-11). The local tourist office, or the local tour operator **Nordtrafikk** (© 75-72-12-00), can provide more information and make reservations. Depending on ice conditions, the visitor center may be able to arrange boat transportation across a narrow but icy channel so you can have a closer look at the ice floe.

WHERE TO STAY

The **Bodø Tourist Office** (see above) can help you book a room in a hotel.

EXPENSIVE

Radisson SAS Royal Hotel ★★   By far the finest hotel in the area, this glistening structure is an inviting oasis. A complete renovation of the exterior, the public rooms, and all of the guest rooms was completed in 2000. The good-sized guest rooms are furnished in sleek contemporary style and decorated in a number of motifs, including Japanese, Nordic, Chinese, and British. Rooms have medium-size bathrooms equipped with shower-tub combinations. The Royal is located on the main street at the harbor front.

Storgaten 2, N-8000 Bodø. © 800/333-3333 in the U.S., or 75-52-41-00. Fax 75-52-74-93. 190 units. June–Aug 855NOK ($114) double, 1,440NOK ($192) suite; Sept–May 1,500NOK ($200) double, 2,250NOK ($299) suite. Rates include breakfast. AE, DC, MC, V. Free parking. **Amenities:** 2 restaurants; 2 bars; lounge; fitness center; sauna; babysitting; laundry service; dry cleaning. *In room:* TV, minibar, hair dryer.

Rica Hotel ★   Located at the harbor and offering a view of Vestfjorden, this is one of Bodø's best hotels, built in 1986 and enlarged in 1990. Most of the somberly furnished rooms have large writing desks. Only moderate in size, rooms are comfortable and well maintained, with good beds and small bathrooms equipped with shower-tub combinations. The hotel has two popular restaurants (see "Where to Dine," below).

Sjøgata 23, N-8001 Bodø. © 75-54-70-00. Fax 75-54-70-55. hotel@diplomat-hotel.no. 103 units. Mid-June to Aug 5 790NOK ($105) double; Aug 6 to mid-June 1,440NOK ($192) double; year-round 1,440NOK ($192) suite. Rates include breakfast. AE, DC, MC, V. Free parking. **Amenities:** 2 restaurants; bar; fitness center; sauna; limited room service; laundry service; dry cleaning. *In room:* TV, minibar, hair dryer.

MODERATE

Bodø Hotell *Value*   Opened in 1987, this hotel, located in the town center about 2½ blocks from the harbor, is known for its good value. The rooms are modern and while the bathrooms are small, they are clean and equipped with shower units. The hotel also offers rooms for nonsmokers and persons with disabilities.

Professor Schyttesgate 5, N-8001 Bodø. © 75-52-69-00. Fax 75-52-57-78. www.bodohotell.no. 31 units. Fri–Sat and June 20–Aug 15 daily 600NOK ($80) double; Sun–Thurs 850NOK ($113) double; year-round 750NOK–1,000NOK ($100–$133) suite. Rates include breakfast. AE, DC, MC, V. Free parking. Closed Dec 20–Jan 3. **Amenities:** Bar; lounge; laundry service; dry cleaning. *In room:* TV, hair dryer.

Golden Tulip Rainbow Nordlys Hotel   The newest hotel in town rises six floors overlooking Bodø's harbor. Inside there is a collection of valuable contemporary art—some of which is for sale. The guest rooms are contemporary have color schemes of yellow with wooden floors, original artwork on the walls, and contemporary styling, plus a tiled bathroom with a tub-shower combination. Groups like this hotel, and the staff is genuinely kind to individual travelers as well. Egon, the hotel's restaurant, specializes in robust American and Norwegian fare.

Moloveien 14, N8001 Bodø. ℂ 75-53-19-00. Fax 75-53-19-99. www.rainbow-hotels.no. 150 units. Mon–Thurs 850NOK–1,415NOK ($113–$188) double; Fri–Sun 850NOK ($113) double. AE, DC, MC, V. **Amenities:** Restaurant; small gym; babysitting. *In room:* TV, minibar.

INEXPENSIVE

Norrøna   The Norrøna is run by the nearby Radisson SAS Royal Hotel, which uses it primarily as a bed-and-breakfast. Its prime location, in the center of Bodø is one of its chief advantages. The simply furnished guest rooms, though small and plain, are comfortable. Each unit contains a well-kept bathroom with a shower-tub combination. Guests enjoy the same privileges as patrons of the more expensive Radisson SAS Royal Hotel. The hotel operates a British-style pub called Piccadilly.

Storgaten 4, N-8000 Bodø. ℂ 75-52-41-18. Fax 75-52-33-88. 99 units. 600NOK–750NOK ($80–$100) double. Rates include breakfast. AE, DC, MC, V. No parking. **Amenities:** Bar; lounge; sauna; laundry service; dry cleaning. *In room:* TV.

WHERE TO DINE

China Garden CANTONESE   This well-managed restaurant, run by emigrants from Hong Kong, is one of the only Asian restaurants in town. It serves sophisticated, flavorful Chinese food. Two favorite dishes are sweet-and-sour prawns and sweet-and-sour pork served with black beans and garlic. Although it doesn't rank with Oslo's better Chinese restaurants, China Garden is a welcome change of pace this far north.

Storgata 60. ℂ 75-52-71-25. Reservations recommended. Main courses 92NOK–139NOK ($12–$18). AE, MC, V. Sun–Thurs 2–10:45pm; Fri–Sat 2pm–midnight.

Holmer ✿ NORTH NORDIC/CONTINENTAL   Bodø's most recommended restaurant opened in December 2001 and is named after the town's first mayor—a 19th-century patriarch who did much to establish Bodø as an important settlement in the Norwegian far north. The outside is a conventional-looking red brick structure. The inside was designed from architectural remnants that were salvaged from a century-old farmhouse once located in the area. Within this cozy venue you can enjoy the most thoughtfully prepared and sophisticated cuisine in town. The best examples include grilled scallops served with coconut cream sauce and baked tomatoes; a cream-based version of soup made completely with local fish and shellfish; duck breast with an herb-based creamy risotto and a purée of celery; and filet of venison with a "wilderness" sauce that's made by boiling the venison bones into a thick reduction that's flavored with wild herbs and berries. The crème brûlée, or perhaps a parfait made from fresh Arctic berries, make worthy desserts.

Dronningensgate 26. ℂ 75-52-50-50. Reservations recommended. Main courses 190NOK–245NOK ($25–$33). AE, DC, MC, V. Mon–Fri 6–11pm; Sat 5–11pm.

Rica Hotel Restaurants NORWEGIAN/INTERNATIONAL   Although the Rica is best known for its well-maintained accommodations, it also runs two restaurants (the Spisestuen and Blix) that serve some of the best food in town. Usually the Spisestuen serves lunch and the Blix dinner, but the arrangement changes depending on the number of bus tours and cruise ships expected.

Wherever the meal is served, you're likely to be joined by local residents. Entree choices include lasagna, steak, filet of reindeer, fish soup, and fresh local fish. You don't get palate-tantalizing excitement here, but the solid, reliable fare uses some of the freshest ingredients available this far north.

In the Rica Hotel, Sjøgata 23. (*C*) **75-54-70-00.** Main courses 209NOK–230NOK ($28–$31); daily lunch plates 130NOK ($17); lunch buffet 200NOK ($27). AE, DC, MC, V. Daily 7–11pm.

BODØ AFTER DARK

The largest nightclub in Bodø is the **Rock Café und Nightclub,** Tollbugata 13B ((*C*) **75-50-46-33**), which can hold up to 550 patrons, mostly in their 20s and 30s. Live bands perform twice a month. The DJs here are some of the best in the north of Norway. Open Friday and Saturday 9am to 3am, charging a cover of 50NOK ($6.65).

Opened in 1991, **Bonsak Piano Bar,** Sjøgata 17 ((*C*) **75-52-29-90**), is housed in a modern building—like everything else in town—and it attracts a wide range of patrons, ages 25 to 50. There is always live piano music, and on the second floor there is a disco playing Europe's Top 40. The cover charge of 50NOK ($6.65) is only levied on Friday and Saturday nights. Open Monday to Thursday 8pm to 2:30am, Friday and Saturday 8pm to 3:30am, and Sunday 8pm to 1am.

Finally, **Nordloenningen,** Storgata 16 ((*C*) **75-52-06-00**), is a laid-back cellar pub often featuring live music, such as blues, country, or rock. They also serve pub grub ranging from burgers to omelets. The paintings on the walls are done by local artists. The patrons range in age from 20 to 50. A cover charge is imposed only on Friday and Saturday nights, ranging from 60NOK to 80NOK ($8–$11). Open Monday to Thursday 1pm to 1:30am, Friday and Saturday 1pm to 2:30am, and Sunday 2pm to 1:30am.

3 Narvik: World War II Battleground

301km (187 miles) NE of Bodø; 1,647km (1,022 miles) NE of Bergen; 1,479km (919 miles) N of Oslo

This ice-free seaport on the Ofotfjord is in Nordland *fylke* (country), 403km (250 miles) north of the Arctic Circle. Narvik, founded in 1903 when the Ofoten (not to be confused with "Lofoten") railway line was completed, boasts Europe's most modern shipping harbor for iron ore. It's the northernmost electrified railway line in the world. It covers a magnificent scenic route, through precipitous mountain terrain and tunnels, over ridges, and across tall stone embankments.

Only 11km (6½ miles) from Narvik, Straumsnes station is the last permanent habitation as you go east. The last Norwegian station, Bjørnfjell, is well above the timberline and about 3 hours from Kiruna, Sweden, some 140km (87 miles) north of the Arctic Circle. You can catch a train at Kiruna to Stockholm. A road connects Kiruna and Narvik.

Narvik looms large in the history books on World War II. On a tragic day in April 9, 1940, 10 Nazi destroyers entered Narvik waters to sink two Norwegian battleships. On April 10, a series of five British destroyers arrived to take the German boats on in combat. The battle at sea resulted in the sinking of two destroyers on each side.

On April 12, the British sent planes to attack the Germans. Allied forces were successful in reclaiming Narvik by late May. However, it was to be only a momentary victory. In early June, the Nazis came back to decimate Narvik. The port of Narvik became a graveyard not only of men but also of ships from Germany, Britain, Norway, France, and The Netherlands. On June 8, Narvik surrendered to the invading Nazis, who stayed here until the Allies chased them out on May 8, 1945.

The rebuilt Narvik is an eyesore, but is surrounded by panoramic woodlands, fjords, and mountains.

ESSENTIALS

GETTING THERE From the Lofoten Islands, take the ferry to Skutvik. Take Route 81 northeast to the junction with E6, and then take E6 north to Bognes. Cross the Tysfjord by ferry. Continue north on E6 to Narvik.

The **train** from Stockholm to Narvik takes 21 to 24 hours. There are also two buses a day from Fauske/Bodø (5 hr.).

VISITOR INFORMATION The **Narvik Tourist Office** is at Konensgate 66 (© 76-94-33-09). It's open daily from 9am to 4pm.

SEEING THE SIGHTS

To get a good look at Narvik, take the **Gondolbanen cable car** (© 76-96-04-94), whose departure point is located directly behind the Norlandia Narvik Hotel, a 10-minute walk from the town center. The car operates from March to October, and the round-trip fare is 85NOK ($11) for adults, 50NOK ($6.65) for children 6 to 15 (5 and under free). In just 13 minutes it takes you to an altitude of 640m (2,100 ft.), at the top of Fagernesfjell. You can see the impressive panorama of the town and its surroundings. From mid-February to mid-June, and in August and September, the cable operates Monday to Friday from 1 to 9pm and every Saturday and Sunday from 10am to 5pm. From mid-June to the end of July it operates daily from noon to 1am. It is closed otherwise.

The **midnight sun** shines from May 27 to July 19.

Nordland Røde Kors Krigsminnemuseum (War Museum) Near Torghallen in the town center, this is one of the most important sights in Narvik. Most of Narvik was destroyed by the Germans, who occupied it until the end of the Second World War. Following Hitler's attack on Denmark and Norway, a bitter battle for Narvik and its iron ore raged for 2 months. German forces fought troops from France, Poland, and Norway, and a considerable British flotilla at sea. Events of that era are depicted, as well as experiences of the civilian population and foreign POWs.

Kongens gate. © 76-94-44-26. Admission 40NOK ($5.30) adults, 10NOK ($1.35) children. Mar–June 7 daily 11am–3pm; June 8–Aug 20 Mon–Sat 10am–10pm, Sun 11am–5pm; Aug 21–Sept daily 11am–3pm. Closed Oct–Feb.

Ofoten Museum The Ofoten Museum has artifacts tracing the oldest human settlements in the area. They go back to the Stone Age, which is revealed in rock carvings. Other exhibits (including a scraper for animal skins and a flint-and-tinder box) show how the people lived and worked in the area. Most of the display is from the 20th century, beginning with the construction of the rail line.

Administrasjonsveien 3. © 76-96-00-50. Admission 30NOK ($4) adults, 5NOK (65¢) children. July Mon–Fri 11am–3:30pm, Sat–Sun noon–3pm; Aug–June Mon–Fri 10am–4pm.

OUTDOOR ACTIVITIES

The Narvik tourist office (see above) is especially helpful in providing a wealth of information about activities in the great outdoors that surround their city.

The mountainous landscape attracts hikers in summer. Glacier trekking with local guides is popular. For more information contact **NordNorsk Klatreskole** (© 76-94-30-39). Another good source of advice and help is the **North Norwegian School of Mountaineering** (© 76-95-13-53).

One of the great golf courses in North Norway is the **Narvik golfklubb at Skomendalen** (© 76-95-12-01), lying 18km (11 miles) south of Narvik. In a dramatic setting, surrounded by mountain peaks, this is the world's northernmost 18-hole golf course (par 72). A full round of golf costs 300NOK ($40), with club rental going for 100NOK ($13). To reach the course from Narvik, follow the signs to Skjomdal to just before the Skjomen Bridge on E6.

Narvik has a long skiing season, lasting from November until early June. The cable car (refer to "Seeing the Sights," above) will deliver you up some 1,000m (3,280 ft.) where you'll find trail and off-piste skiing. For more information about conditions, call the **Narvik Ski Center** at © 76-96-04-94.

Divers from all over the world are attracted to Narvik waters, scene of a major World War II naval battle. Three German destroyers are still underwater. More than 50 planes, both Nazi and Allied, were also gunned down. **Narvik Dykk & Eventyr** (© 99-51-22-05) can make arrangements for this incredible undersea adventure.

Narvik Arrangement (© 76-96-79-70) offers a diversified sports program including fishing trips on Ofotfjord. The outfitter also arranges Killer Whale Safaris from mid-October to late December. Some 60 whales might be spotted at this time. In addition excursions with a dog sled can also be arranged, using thoroughbred Siberian huskies.

WHERE TO STAY

These hotels are located among the few buildings in Narvik that survived World War II.

MODERATE

Grand Royal ★   The Grand Royal hotel is the largest and best equipped in Narvik. It opens onto the main street in the town center, between the train station and the harbor. Built in the 1920s, it has seen many enlargements since. It's called the Grand Royal because the late King Olav was a frequent visitor and his portraits adorn some of the public rooms. The comfortable, good-size rooms are tastefully and traditionally furnished. The well-equipped, medium-size bathrooms with shower-tub combinations are the best in town. The finest restaurant in town is also here (see "Where to Dine," below). The recently redecorated lobby bar is one of the best cocktail bars in northern Norway.

Kongensgate 64, N-8501 Narvik. © 76-97-70-00. Fax 76-97-70-07. 119 units. 1,000NOK–1,390NOK ($133–$185) double; 1,600NOK ($213) suite. Rates include breakfast. AE, DC, MC, V. Free parking. Bus: 14, 15, 16, or 17. **Amenities:** 2 restaurants; 2 bars; sauna; babysitting; laundry service; dry cleaning. *In room:* TV, minibar, hair dryer, safe.

INEXPENSIVE

Nordst Jernen Hotel   In the town center, south of the bus station, the Nordst Jernen has long been known as one of the best hotel values in the area. Guest rooms are decorated in pastels to offset the winter gloom. Rooms vary in size, but all are comfortable and well maintained. Bathrooms are small but equipped with shower-tub combinations.

Kongensgate 26, N-8500 Narvik. © 76-94-41-20. Fax 76-94-75-06. 24 units. 750NOK ($100) double. Rates include breakfast. DC, MC, V. Free parking. Bus: 14 or 16. **Amenities:** Restaurant; lounge. *In room:* TV, hair dryer, safe.

WHERE TO DINE

Pub und Kro INTERNATIONAL   Less expensive and less formal than the Grand Royal's main dining room (see below), this cozy restaurant is one of the most popular venues for dining and drinking in town. The menu offers an array of fresh foodstuff with zesty flavors and spices—providing a change of pace from reindeer. For a main course, try the marinated steak prepared in a Tex-Mex style or traditionally with mushrooms or a béarnaise sauce. The pizza and a creamy pasta carbonara are also good choices.

Kongensgate 64. ⓒ 76-97-70-77. Reservations recommended. Main courses 125NOK–200NOK ($17–$27). AE, DC, MC, V. Mon–Thurs 11am–12:30pm; Fri–Sat 11am–1:30pm; Sun noon–1am.

Royal Blue ⚜ NORWEGIAN   The best restaurant in the region is decorated, appropriately, in strong royal blues. It's the preferred choice of visiting dignitaries, including the king. Service is polite and the food delectable. Specialties include sauna-smoked ham with asparagus, cured salmon with crème fraîche, reindeer curry with Brussels sprouts and apricots, and large beefsteaks. Royal Blue is located on the lobby level of the Grand Royal (see "Where to Stay," above). The menu changes seasonally.

In the Grand Royal Hotel, Kongensgate 64. ⓒ 76-97-70-00. Reservations recommended. Main courses 200NOK–350NOK ($27–$47). AE, DC, MC, V. Daily 11am–11pm. Bus: 14, 15, 16, or 17.

NARVIK AFTER DARK

Popular with skiers in winter, the **Norlandia Narvik Hotel Pub,** Skistuaveien 8 (ⓒ 76-96-48-00), attracts drinkers and partiers ages 18 to 30. The top dance music of the '40s is often played, as dancers gyrate on the wooden floor encased by wood paneling and stone walls. Open Monday to Friday 7:30pm to 1:30am and Saturday and Sunday 7:30pm to 2:30am.

A student hangout, **Malmen,** Kongensgate 44 (ⓒ 76-94-20-00), is a dance club with a nautical decor. The music is varied, often alternative or hip-hop. Friday and Saturday nights are devoted to disco when a 50NOK ($6.65) cover charge is levied. Open Sunday to Thursday 8pm to 1am and Friday and Saturday 8pm to 3am.

Resepten, Industriveien 5 (ⓒ 76-94-26-38), is a 50-seat cozy bar whose walls are adorned with artwork from Norwegian artists. Light background music is played most nights, giving way to rock on the weekends. Some of the beers on tap come from Newcastle-upon-Tyne. Most patrons here range in age from 30 to 50. Open Monday to Thursday 8pm to 1am, Friday and Saturday 8pm to 3am.

4 The Lofoten Islands: The Soul of Norway ⚜⚜⚜

Svolvaer (southernmost point of the Lofoten): 280km (174 miles) N of Bodø; 1,425km (886 miles) NE of Bergen; 1,250km (777 miles) N of Oslo

The island kingdom of Lofoten, one of the most beautiful regions of Norway, lies 197km (123 miles) north of the Arctic Circle. Its population of 35,000 spreads over large and small islands. Many visitors come just to fish, but the area offers abundant bird life and flora. The midnight sun shines from May 25 to July 7.

The Lofoten Islands stretch from Vågan in the east to Røst and Skomvaer in the southwest. The steep Lofoten mountain peaks—often called the Lofotwall—shelter farmland and deep fjords from the elements.

The major islands are Austvågøy, Gimsøy, Vestvågøy, Flakstadøy, Moskenesøy, Vaerøy, and Røst. The southernmost part of Norway's largest island, Hinnøy, is also in Lofoten. Vestfjorden separates the major islands from the mainland of Norway.

The Gulf Stream contributes to the seasonal Lofoten fishing, Lofotfisket. Beyond Lofoten, and especially in the Vestfjord, Arctic Sea cod spawn; huge harvesting operations are carried out between January and April.

The first inhabitants of the Lofoten Islands were nomads who hunted and fished, but excavations show that agriculture existed here at least 4,000 years ago. The Vikings pursued farming, fishing, and trading; examples of Viking housing sites can be seen on Vestbågøya, where more than 1,000 burial mounds have been found.

From the 14th century on, the people of Lofoten had to pay taxes to Bergen. This was the beginning of an economic dominance lasting for 6 centuries—first executed by the German Hansa tradesmen, and then by their Norwegian heirs.

Harsh treatment of local residents by the Nazis during the Second World War played a major part in the creation of the famous Norwegian resistance movement. Allied forces that landed here to harass the German iron-ore boats sailing from Narvik withdrew in June 1940. They evacuated as many Lofoten residents as they could to Scotland for the duration of the war.

Today the Lofotens have modern towns with shops, hotels, restaurants, and public transportation.

In addition to hotels, guesthouses, and campsites, the Lofoten Islands offer lodging in old traditional fishing cottages known as *rorbuer*. The larger (often two stories), usually more modern version is a *sjøhus* (sea house). The traditional *rorbu* was built on the edge of the water, often on piles, with room for 10 bunks, a kitchen, and an entrance hall used as a work and storage room. Many rorbuer today are still simple and unpretentious, but some have electricity, a wood stove, a kitchenette with a sink, and running water. Others have been outfitted with separate bedrooms, private showers, and toilets. **Backroads** (© **800/462-2848**) is the best and most convenient booking agent or try Destination Lofoten (see below).

ESSENTIALS

Svolvær is the largest town on the archipelago's largest island. It is your best center for exploring the archipelago, as it is linked to the other chain members by both ferry and express boats.

GETTING THERE   From Bodø, drive east on Route 80 to Fauske. Take E6 north to Ulvsvåg, and head southwest on Route 81 toward the town of Skutvik. From Skutvik, take the 2-hour ferry to Svolvær. For ferry information and reservations, contact **Ofotens og Vesterålens Dampskibsselskab A/S,** Box 375, N-8451 Stokmarknes (© **76-96-76-00**).

You can fly to Svolvær on **Widerøe Airline,** which has seven flights a day from Bodø. For information, call © **75-51-35-00** in Bodø, or **81-00-12-00** for reservations.

You can also travel the Lofotens by using a combination of rail, bus, and ferry. Many visitors take a train to Bodø, and then transfer to a bus that crosses from Bodø to Svolvær on a ferry. Most bus departures from Bodø are timed to coincide with the arrival of trains from Oslo, Bergen, and other points. Buses also take passengers from elsewhere in Norway to Ulvsvåg, then on to Skutvik, where you can board a ferry to Svolvær. For information on train-bus-ferry connections, contact **Destination Bodø Office** (© **75-54-80-00**).

The coastal steamer calls at Stamsund and Svolvær. The steamer departs from Bodø at 3pm daily.

VISITOR INFORMATION   Contact **Destination Lofoten,** Box 210, N-8301 Svolvær (© **76-07-30-00**), near the ferry docks in a big red building. It's open July to mid-August, daily from 9am to 9:30pm; mid-June to June 30 and mid-August to August 31, daily 9am to 8pm; September to mid-June, Monday to Friday 8am to 4pm.

GETTING AROUND At the tourist office at Svolvær you can pick up a free pamphlet, "Lofoten Info-Guide," with information about all ferries and buses throughout the archipelago. All inhabited islands are linked by ferry, and buses service the four major islands, including Svolvær. Motorists can drive the E10 from Svolvaer to the outer rim of Lofoten, a distance of 130km (80 miles). One of the great drives in the north of Norway, this will immediately bring you into a close encounter with life as lived by the Lofoten island people.

SVOLVAER

This bustling modern port town, the preferred base for exploring the Lofoten, lies on the island of Austvagøy, the northernmost in the archipelago. Here you will find the best hotels and restaurants. Most of the Lofoten cultural attractions are within an easy reach if you decide to base in Svolvaer.

On the eastern coast of Austvagøy, Svolvaer lacks the charm of the other fishing communities, but nothing tops it as a refueling stop. Even if the port is a bit dull, its surroundings of craggy backdrops and sheltered bays is most scenic.

SEEING THE SIGHTS

Lofoten Krigsminnemuseum, Fiskergata 12 (© **76-07-00-49**), is the finest museum in the north devoted to the tragic World War II era. There is a stunning collection of 1940s photographs, some of which document the 1941 commando raid on the islands. Also on display is a collection of military uniforms. Admission is 40NOK ($5.30) for adults or 15NOK ($2) for children. Open mid-May to mid-August daily from 11am to 4pm.

Daredevils are lured to Svolvaer in an attempt to conquer the most daring (and dangerous) climb in the Lofoten. They surmount the **Svolvaergeita** (Svolvaeur goat), at 40m (131 ft.). This stone column is perched on a hill behind the port, and is known for its two pinnacles, which locals have labeled the horn or the horns of a goat. There's a 1.5m (5 ft.) jump between the two "horns." In no way do we recommend that you attempt this, even if an Olympic athlete. If you're a tamer soul, you'll be content to admire the scenery.

Better for your physical well-being is to take the ferry ride to the islet of **Skrova,** which makes for one of the best strolls in the area. From Svolvaer ferries leave from the port taking only half an hour to reach Skrova, costing 25NOK ($3.35) per person. If it's a sunny day, you can stroll around taking in panoramic seascapes.

One of the most dramatic boat rides in the Lofotens is the short trip into the impossibly narrow **Trollfjord** ⭐, stretching for 2km (1¼ miles). This is part of the channel that separates the Lofoten island of Austvagøy from the Vesterålen island of Hinnøya. Coastal steamers can barely navigate this narrow passage, without scraping the rock walls on either side. Trollfjord is the most easternmost in Lofoten, and was the scene of the famous "Battle of the Trollfjord," as related by Johan Bojer in this novel *The Last Viking.* The artist Gunnar Berg (1863–93) was there at the time, and recorded the dramatic event on canvas. His painting is on view at the Svolvaer Town Hall. Ask at the tourist office (see above) about linking up with a boat tour of Trollfjord. Departures are from June 10 to August 20, costing 300NOK ($40) per person.

SHOPPING

The purchase of art in the Lofoten is not an idea that immediately grabs most consumers. But artists have long been drawn to the archipelago because of the particular quality of its northern lights. The leading gallery is **Nordnorsk**

Kunstnersentrum (© 76-07-00-22) on the island of Svinøya, lying 1km (½ mile) from the center of Svolvaer. This North Norwegian Artist's Center is run by the artists themselves, offering a wide range of paintings, plus handicrafts, posters, and other items. From June 11 to August 15 it is open daily 10am to 6pm. Off-season hours are Tuesday to Sunday 11am to 3pm. Entrance to the permanent museum collection costs 30NOK ($4) for adults and 20NOK ($2.65) for students and senior citizens. Free for children under 15.

WHERE TO STAY

Anker Brygge ★★ On a tiny island in the middle of Svolvaer harbor, this is one of the most atmospheric choices in the area. The quay-side structure dates from 1880 when it was a fish-landing station with its own "saltery" and barrel factory. After a major restoration, it was converted into an inn. Guests can stay in individual cottages that are rustically adorned with timbers but also have all the modern conveniences. These are called *rorbu* cabin suites. Each rorbu cabin is distinctively furnished; you may feel as if you're staying at some remote lodge in the wilds of a far northern frontier post. Rorbu suites lie on the quay side or along the shore, with views of the harbor and the Lofoten mountains. All come with small bathrooms with shower.

Lamholmen, N-8300 Svolvaer. © **76-06-64-80.** Fax 76-06-64-70. www.anker-brygge.no. 270 units. 1,000NOK–2,500NOK ($133–$333) cottage. Rates include continental breakfast. AE, DC, MC, V. **Amenities:** Restaurant (closed Jan–Feb); bar; sauna; laundry service; dry cleaning. *In room:* TV.

Norlandia Royal Hotel At the crossroads of town, this newly renovated hotel is one of the finest choices in town. It was constructed in 1974 in a five-story format. The bedrooms are midsize and attractively furnished in a modern mode, each opening onto views of the distant mountains and the nearby sea. Some floors contain carpeted rooms, the rest offering wooden floors. All of the units are equipped with small but efficiently organized private bathrooms with tub-and-shower combination. The on-site restaurant is one of the best hotel dining rooms at the port, and on Wednesday, Friday, and Saturday nights from 10pm to 3:30am there is disco dancing.

Sivert Nilsensgata 21, N-8311 Svolvaer. © **76-07-12-00.** Fax 76-07-08-50. www.norlandia.no. 48 units. 800NOK–1,095NOK ($106–$146) double; 1,500NOK ($200) suite. Rates include continental breakfast. AE, DC, MC, V. **Amenities:** Restaurant; bar; limited room service; babysitting; laundry service; dry cleaning. *In room:* TV, minibar, hair dryer.

Rainbow Vestfjord Hotel This building was a former warehouse that stored marine supplies and fish. After extensive remodeling in the late 1980s, it reopened as this well-managed hotel. The guest rooms are functional but comfortable, many of them overlooking the sea. The bathrooms are tiny, with shower-tub combinations. Facilities include a lobby bar and a pleasant restaurant that specializes in fish and steaks. It serves sustaining fare—nothing remarkable.

Box 386, N-8301 Svolvær. © **76-07-08-70.** Fax 76-07-08-54. 63 units. Sun–Thurs and June–Aug 1 daily 1,295NOK ($172) double; Aug 2–May Fri–Sat 700NOK ($93) double; year-round 1,495NOK ($199) suite. Rates include breakfast. AE, DC, MC, V. Free parking. **Amenities:** Restaurant; bar; limited room service; laundry service; dry cleaning. *In room:* TV, minibar, hair dryer.

Rica Hotel Svolvaer ★ This is one of the most luxurious choices on the island. Right next to the water, it was opened in 1995, and is renovated and kept in tiptop shape every year. The bedrooms are in separate rorbu cabins built of wood. These open onto your private harbor-view terrace. Some guests fish right from their own quarters from these decks. Each is comfortably furnished, containing immaculate private bathrooms with shower. Norwegian specialties, mainly fish, are served in the first-class restaurant on site. The restaurant is constructed in the shape of a boat, opening onto panoramic vistas of the ocean.

Lamholmen, N-8301 Svolvaer. ℂ **76-07-22-22.** Fax 76-07-20-01. www.rica.no. 147 units. 945NOK–1,290NOK ($126–$172) double. Rates include continental breakfast. AE, DC, MC, V. Closed Oct–Feb 20. **Amenities:** Restaurant; bar; limited room service; dry cleaning. *In room:* TV.

Royal Hotel Lofoten   About half the well-furnished rooms at this 1975 hotel overlook the sea. It's in the town center, near the express steamer quay. The look is rather functional, but maintenance is good. The bathrooms, though cramped, are sparkling clean and equipped with shower-tub combinations. On the premises are a bar and a lively disco. Restaurant Lofoten specializes in fish and steak.

Sivert Nelsen Gate, N-8300 Svolvær. ℂ **76-07-12-00.** Fax 76-07-08-50. 48 units. 1,095NOK ($146) double; 1,400NOK ($186) suite. Rates include breakfast. AE, DC, MC, V. Free parking. **Amenities:** Restaurant; bar; lounge. *In room:* TV, minibar.

Svinøya Rorbuer ★★ *Finds*   Nothing is as authentic to the Lofoten experience as staying in one of these cottages across a bridge on the island of Svinøya, site of Svolvaer's first settlement. You're welcome at the reception area, which is a virtual museum of the Lofoten. The reception was once the general store for the community and was the first shop ever to open in Svinøya. Then you are shown to one of the historic, restored cabins. The main building is from 1820, and some of the cabins are from the 19th century, others modern but constructed in the old style. All of these fishermen's cabins are furnished to a high standard, and each is equipped with a small bathroom with shower. Extra amenities include a well-equipped kitchen. The inn contains the town's best restaurant (see below).

Gunnar bergs vei 2, N-8300 Svolvaer. ℂ **76-06-99-30.** Fax 76-07-48-98. www.svinoya.no. 30 cabins. 1,200NOK–2,400NOK ($160–$319) double. Rates include continental breakfast. AE, DC, MC, V. **Amenities:** Restaurant; bar; Jacuzzi; laundry service; dry cleaning. *In room:* Kitchen, no phone.

WHERE TO DINE

Børson Spiseri ✦ SEAFOOD   The town's best restaurant is housed in the previously recommended Svinøya rorbuer across a bridge on the island of Svinøya. We'd come here for the atmosphere alone, but fortunately the food is first rate. The restaurant has been installed in an old quayside building from 1828, a setting for an "Arctic menu" that features some of the freshest fish we've ever consumed in the north. The setting is old-fashioned with antiques from 2 centuries ago along with maritime artifacts such as fishing equipment and old boats. What chef can top their deep-fried cod tongue served as an appetizer with sour cream and a salad? The traditional dried cod for which the Lofoten is famous is served with bacon and potatoes. One excellent dish is rockfish in a white wine sauce with potatoes and fresh vegetables. The roasted Lofoten lamb filet comes with creamy potatoes. In summer you can opt for fresh fruit for dessert, or else crème brûlée the rest of the time.

Gunnar Bergs vei 2. ℂ **76-06-99-30.** Reservations recommended. Main courses 180NOK–250NOK ($24–$33). AE, DC, MC. Daily 4–11pm. Closed Mon in winter and also Jan.

KABELVÅG

Much more romantically situated than Svolvaer is the port of Kabelvåg, lying 5km (3 miles) to the south. The port of wooden buildings encircles the shore of a narrow inlet. In its heyday it was the major village in the Viking era, a position it maintained until the early years of the 20th century. The first rorbuer or fishermen's cottages were erected here in 1120.

If the weather is sunny, many visitors prefer to walk here from Svolvaer. Otherwise, buses run from Svolvaer taking 15 minutes and costing 18NOK ($2.40) for a one-way fare.

SEEING THE SIGHTS

For 110NOK ($15) you can purchase (at any of the sites) a combination ticket, granting admission to the Lofoten Museum, the Lofoten Aquarium, and the Galleri Espolin.

Lofoten Museum, Storvagan (© 76-07-82-23), was constructed over the site of the first town built in the polar world. The regional museum depicts past life in the Lofoten, and excavations continue at the site of an old trading post. On the museum grounds you can visit a boathouse with antique boats, rorbu cabins from the 18th and 19th centuries, and cultural artifacts dating from prehistoric and medieval times. Admission is 45NOK ($6) or adults, 15NOK ($2) for children. Open June 1 to 14 and August 16 to 31 daily 9am to 6pm. From June 15 to August 15 open daily 10am to 10pm. In May and September open Monday to Friday 9am to 3pm.

Close by and opening onto the sea, **Lofoten Aquarium,** Storvågan (© 76-07-86-65), offers nearly two dozen aquariums of various sizes filled with fish and other marine animals, including mammals, from the Arctic world. Of special interest are the seal and otter ponds. There is also a salmon farm exhibit, and much attention is given the "noble" cod, which has sustained life in these parts for centuries. Admission is 70NOK ($9.30) for adults, 25NOK ($3.35) for children ages 5 to 15, and free for children 4 and under. Hours are January to May 1 Monday to Friday 9am to 3pm; May 2 to 31, Monday to Friday 9am to 3pm and Saturday and Sunday 11am to 3pm; June 1 to August 31 daily 9am to 6pm; September to December Monday to Friday 9am to 3pm. The distinctive, contemporary **Galleri Espolin,** Storvågan (© 76-07-84-05), is devoted to the works of pictorial artist Kaare Espolin Johnson (1907–94), one of Norway's best-known artists. Espolin was drawn to the archipelago and was fascinated by its life and that if its fishermen. Amazingly, this almost lyrical artist was practically blind for most of his life. He painted not only the fishermen but also their wives, their boats, and the drama they faced at sea. From June 11 to August 8 it is open daily 10am to 9pm (closing earlier off-season). Admission is 40NOK ($5.30) for adults, 15NOK ($2) for children.

On the eastern approach to town, along E10, stands **Vågan Kirke** (© 76-07-82-90), a church from 1898 that is the second largest wooden church in Norway, with a seating capacity of 1,200. It was constructed to house the seasonal population of fishermen who came mostly for the winter catches, swelling the population of little Kabelvåg. Admission is 15NOK ($2), but the church keeps no regular hours (usually open during the day in summer).

WHERE TO STAY

Kabelvåg Hotell   In the center of the little port, this hotel is a 1995 reconstruction of the original Art Deco villa that once stood here. It is also the site of the best restaurant in town (see below). Rising only three floors, it looks like an antique wooden structure on its exterior, but inside it is modern and completely up to date. The small to midsize bedrooms are rather simply but comfortably furnished, opening onto views of the ocean and mountains. Each unit comes with a small and immaculately kept bathroom with tub and shower.

Kong Øysteinsgate 4, N-8310 Kabelvåg. (℃ **76-07-88-00.** Fax 76-07-80-03. 28 units. 1,300NOK ($173) double. Children under 8 stay free in parent's room. Rates include breakfast and dinner. AE, DC, MC, V. Closed Oct 1–May 15. **Amenities:** Restaurant; bar; laundry service; dry cleaning. *In room:* TV, hair dryer.

Nyvagar Rorbuhotell (★ *Finds* This contemporary rorbu cabin resort offers architecture based on those rustic cabins inhabited by fishermen who came in winter to harvest the cod. But the contemporary living is far more comfortable and elegant than those men of the sea used to endure. The location is convenient, lying only a 3-minute stroll from the museums just previewed. This hotel offers one of the most helpful staffs in the area, each of whom is skilled at ranging such adventures as deep-sea rafting or "eagle safaris," as well as fishing boat jaunts. Each of the well-furnished cabins contains two bedrooms, along with small bathrooms with shower. Expect wood furnishings and wood walls. About half of the units open onto views of the harbor. Even if not a guest, you might visit its quayside pub with outdoor table service in summer. In the main building, the Lorchstua Restaurant serves an array of regional dishes of the north.

Storvagan 22, N-8310 Kabelvåg. (℃ **76-06-97-00.** Fax 76-06-97-01. www.dvgl.no. 30 units. 1,360NOK ($181) cabin. Rates include continental breakfast. AE, DC, MC, V. Closed Sept–Apr. **Amenities:** Restaurant; bar; sauna; laundry service; dry cleaning. *In room:* TV.

WHERE TO DINE

Krambua SEAFOOD/NORWEGIAN In the rebuilt Art Deco villa, the previously recommended Kabelvåg Hotell, this restaurant is the best at the port. It has a mellow atmosphere, decorated with old books, antiques, and animal skin furnishings. You feel you're in the far north if you dine here, especially when you're served whale carpaccio.

Since many politically conscious readers will object to eating whale meat, an endangered species, you can settle for the smoked salmon instead. Main courses include the island mainstay, cod, served here after a "soft" baking in the oven. It comes with a white wine sauce and butter-boiled vegetables. Meat-eaters might prefer the filet of reindeer with sautéed potatoes. In summer, wild berries from these Arctic climes adorn the menu or your plate.

Kong Øysteinsgate 4. (℃ **76-07-88-00.** Reservations recommended. Main courses 160NOK–200NOK ($21–$27). AE, DC, MC, V. Mon–Sat 11am–11pm; Sun 2–8pm. Closed Oct 1–May 15.

HENNINGSVAER (★

The nickname of "Venice of the North" is a bit much, but that shouldn't obscure the fact that this is the liveliest and most artistic of Lofoten villages. Lying 20km (12½ miles) southwest of Svolvaer, this is the largest fishing village in the Lofoten. Every structure has an exterior of its own, as the village was built without any professional architects. Bus 510 runs here from Svolvaer, taking 35 minutes and costing 40NOK ($5.30) one-way.

SEEING THE SIGHTS

At the **Lofoten Hus Gallery** (★, Hjellskoeret (℃ **76-07-15-73**), you can see Norway's largest collection of its north country painters, dramatically installed in a former fish-canning house. The major focus centers on the paintings of the well-known artist Karl Erik Harr, plus other notable artists who came to the Lofoten at the end of the 19th century. Frank Jenssen presents a 20-minute slide show of Lofoten landscapes and its people, with unique photographs of the white-tailed eagle. Open June 11 to August 12 10am to 9pm (closes earlier in winter). Admission is 60NOK ($8) for adults or 25NOK ($3.35) for children.

WHERE TO STAY

Henningsvaer Bryggehotel ★ This is a white-painted house idyllically placed on the quay by the harbor against a backdrop of mountains. Although the setting is old-fashioned and picture postcardy, the interior design is contemporary and stylish. In all, it's a good choice as your base for exploring the northern Lofoten. Built in 1995, it rises three floors. For decor, it uses pictures of the Lofoten from the 1900s. Bedrooms are midsize and attractively and comfortably furnished, each with a small shower. On site is Bluefish, one of the best restaurants on the island (see below). The staff will help you arrange sea trips, including rafting and fishing.

Hjellskoeret, N-8312 Henningsvaer. ✆ **76-07-47-50.** Fax 76-07-47-30. 31 units. 1,160NOK ($154) double; 3,000NOK ($399) suite. Children under 12 stay free in parent's room. Rates include continental breakfast. AE, DC, MC, V. Closed Oct 1–Mar 1. **Amenities:** Restaurant; bar; sauna; 24-hr. room service; laundry service; dry cleaning. *In room:* TV.

Henningsvaer Rorbuer ★ *Finds* Lying just outside the center of the village, this is an atmospheric choice of rorbu or fishermen's cabins standing at quay side against the backdrop of the "Lofoten Wall" (a string of mountains). You're housed in cabins that simulate a fisherman's cottage from long ago, but can enjoy all the modern amenities. Rooms open onto panoramic views of the Vestfjorden and Mount Vågakallen. These quay-side buildings were converted from old fish-landing warehouses. Its special feature is a quay-side wood-fired sauna and a large wooden bathtub. In addition, the hotel's boat, *Kysten,* will take you for trips around the archipelago, and the staff will also arrange deep-sea fishing trips in summer. You can also rent boats, and ask to be hooked up with a deep-sea rafting trip. Cabins contain two or three bedrooms, a kitchenette, and a bathroom with shower.

Banhammaren 53, N-8312 Henningsvaer. ✆ **76-07-46-00.** Fax 76-07-49-10. www.henningsvar-rorbuer.no. 21 cabins. 1,250NOK ($166) double. MC, V. **Amenities:** Bar; cafeteria; sauna. *In room:* TV, kitchen, phone (some units).

WHERE TO DINE

Bluefish Restaurant NORWEGIAN/SEAFOOD Attached to the previously recommended Henningsvaer Bryggehotel, this is one of the island's best restaurants, often feeding 60 satisfied diners at a time. You sit at wooden tables enjoying views of the sea from the restaurant's windows. Some of the freshest seafood on the island is served here, although environmentalists shun the smoked whale since that animal is an endangered species. Fresh salmon is aromatically baked with herbs and served with fresh vegetables. You can also order that food staple of the Lofoten, cod. It's most often fried and served with a lobster sauce or else a white wine sauce. Boiled halibut is another fine choice, appearing in a creamy butter sauce with cucumber salad and boiled potatoes. The chef does excellent sorbets such as blackberry or strawberry using fresh berries in summer.

In the Henningsvaer Bryggehotel, Hjellskaeret. ✆ **76-07-47-50.** Reservations recommended. Main courses 150NOK–300NOK ($20–$40). AE, DC, MC, V. Mon–Sat 3–10pm; Sun 3–6pm.

Fiskekrogen ★★ NORWEGIAN/SEAFOOD This quay-side restaurant is the town's finest, and chef/owner Otto Asheim is acclaimed in the area. It even enjoys patronage from Queen Sonja, who first discovered it in her backpacking days through the Lofoten and has returned several times since. The chef is skilled at serving fish almost any way you want it. He cooks with robust flavor and intelligent associations of ingredients, using regional produce whenever possible. His fare is based on the season and what's fresh and good at the market. He does wonders with the famed cod of the area, and also serves his own "homemade" caviar. His sautéed salmon or catfish is always tempting. Your best bet might be to order his seafood platter with the best of the goodies of the day.

Dreyersgate 19. (℗ **76-07-46-52**. Reservations needed in summer. Main courses 175NOK–300NOK ($23–$40). AE, DC, MC, V. Daily 4–10pm in summer (irregular winter hours).

VESTVÅGØY

If time remains you can consider a trip to the second major island in the archipelago. Home to some 11,000 people, Vestvågøy is relatively flat.

If you base here, we'd recommend you skip the air and bus transport home of **Leknes** and head inside the **Stramsund** to the immediate east, the best base along the southern coast. You can find accommodations here (see below). Stramsund is the island port where the coastal steamers from Bergen stop.

Buses from Leknes take only 30 minutes to reach Stramsund, costing 30NOK ($4) one-way. Leknes can be reached by bus from Svolvaer, taking 2 hours and costing 95NOK ($13) one-way.

SEEING THE SIGHTS

In the hamlet of Borg, archaeologists have dug out the **biggest Viking Age building** ⋆⋆ ever found. It's been turned into the **Viking Museum of Borg** (℗ 76-08-49-00). The museum has been built up around this impressive full-scale reconstruction of a Viking chieftain's house, measuring 83m (272 ft.) in length. Also on display is the Viking shop *Lofotr*, reconstructed as a replication of the Gokstad ships. The ruins were discovered in 1981 when a farmer was plowing his fields.

The museum setting duplicates the aura of the Iron Age, with light flickering from the hearths or else gleaming from cod liver oil lamps. The smell of tar fills your nostrils. Demonstrations of handicrafts authentic to the Viking era are presented. Artifacts unearthed are on display as well, including gold foil fertility figures, Frankish pottery, and Rhineland glass. Outside you can see some domestic animals such as horses, sheep, and hens that would have been commonplace 1,000 years ago.

Admission is 80NOK ($11) for adults, 65NOK ($8.65) for seniors and students, and 40NOK ($5.30) for children, including a guided tour. From May 20 to September 3 open daily 10am to 7pm; otherwise, only Friday 1 to 3pm. The Svolvaer bus to Leknes passes by the entrance to the museum.

WHERE TO STAY & DINE

Stamsund Lofoten This hotel in the heart of town offers a view of the harbor. The small guest rooms are simply furnished but have good beds, and many have well-kept bathrooms equipped with shower-tub combinations. On the premises are a bar and a restaurant that serves standard Norwegian fare.

N-8340 Stamsund. (℗ **76-08-93-00**. Fax 76-08-97-26. www.stamsund.no. 28 units. 760NOK–994NOK ($101–$132) double. Rates include breakfast. AE, DC, MC, V. Free parking. **Amenities:** Bar; lounge. *In room:* TV, minibar, hair dryer.

Stamsund Rorbuer ⋆ *(Finds* These old fishermen's cabins have been renovated with modern comforts and are the most romantic place to stay on Vestvagøy.

Located at the middle of the harbor in Stamsund these cabins await you with two to six beds each, all equipped with a private bathroom with shower, kitchen, and living room. An old klipfish (dried cod) storehouse, the Skjaerbrygga, has been turned into a good restaurant. There is also a library and lounge with a fireplace. *The Times* in London pronounced this establishment the "world's best youth hostel."

N-8340 Stamsund. (℃) **76-05-46-00.** Fax 76-05-46-01. 27 cabins. 1,070NOK–1,320NOK ($142–$176) double. AE, DC, MC, V. **Amenities:** Cafe; restaurant; pub. *In room:* TV.

FLAKSTADØY

Having visited Austvågøy and Vestvagøy, E10 continues west to the next island of Flakstadøy, with most of the population of 1,600 hearty souls living along the northern tier, around the town of Ramberg (see below), which makes the base for exploring the island.

Flakstadøy is serviced by buses running along the main route via Leknes to the end of the line, the curiously named hamlet of Å. If you're motoring you can take a toll tunnel from Vestvagøy (our last stopover) to Flakstadøy for a cost of 70NOK ($9.30) per vehicle.

SEEING THE SIGHTS

If you're touring the island, head for the secluded village of **Nusfjord** ✦, on the south coast, a setting for some of the island's most dramatic scenery. The beauty and/or the bleakness of this remote village has drawn many artists to the area. The European Conservation List has added this 19th-century fishermen's village to its list of protected sites.

You'll find a colony of fishermen's huts, some still inhabited during the winter season or else rented out to tourists in summer.

Rambereg, the gem of the north coast, opens onto a beautiful white beach facing the Arctic Ocean. Just outside the village you can visit **Flakstad Kirke** at Flakstad (℃ **76-09-33-31**), built of wood in 1780 with its distinctive onion-shaped cupola. The altarpiece is older than the church, and the pulpit was painted by Godtfred Ezechiel, a master painter from Bergen. Charging an admission of 20NOK ($2.65), the church is open in summer daily from 10am to 4pm.

The old fishing hamlet of **Sund** lies west of Ramberg along E10. It's visited mainly by those wishing to see the **Sund Fiskerimuseum,** Sund (℃ **76-09-36-29**), near the bridge leading to the next island of Moskenesøy. A collection of fishing huts here contains all the paraphernalia needed to capture cod. The fisherman's cabin or rorbu is the oldest building in Sund, containing a wide range of domestic utensils, tools, and other artifacts used in fisherman's huts of old. On site is a resident smithy known for his iron sculptures of cormorants. The museum is open June to mid-August daily from 10am to 6pm, charging 35NOK ($4.65) for admission or 20NOK ($2.65) for children. A final attraction is **Glasshytta** at Viken (℃ 76-09-44-42). This is the original Lofoten glassblower's cabin, offering products of high quality and innovative design. It is also the home base of north Norway's first glass blower, Åsvar Tangrand, who designed Lofoten's seven-pronged logo, evoking a longboat. The studio, charging an admission of 20NOK ($2.65) for adults or free for children, is open from mid-June to mid-August daily 9am to 7pm (curtailed hours off-season). You can purchase some virtual heirloom pieces here at rather reasonable prices.

WHERE TO STAY

Nusfjord Rorbuer ✦ *(Finds)*   These historic cabins are secluded and tranquil, offering the most authentic and atmospheric way to stay on the island of

Flakstadøy. Many Norwegian families from the south come here for summer holidays, booking a cabin for a week or more, but you can also stay overnight. Outdoor activities such as fishing, boating, and hiking fill one's agenda during the day. Rowboats come with the price of the room, and the helpful staff will also rent you motorboats if you'd like to fish Lofoten waters. The original fishermen's cabins were built around 1900, but the cabins were last renovated in the late '90s. They are constructed of timbers, and the wooden floors are original, the furnishings a mixture of antique and modern. Each comes with a small bathroom with shower. In summer there is also a restaurant (see below), serving mainly seafood.

N-8380 Ramberg. ✆ **76-09-30-20.** Fax 76-09-33-78. 34 cabins. 590NOK–1,495NOK ($78–$199) double. Rates include continental breakfast. AE, DC, MC, V. Closed Sept–May. **Amenities:** Restaurant; laundry service; dry cleaning. *In room:* Kitchenette, no phone.

WHERE TO DINE

Nusfjord Rorbuer Restaurant SEAFOOD/NORWEGIAN In this previously recommended hotel you can enjoy the finest island dining. The restaurant is a cozy, intimate enclave with a rustic decor. At its peak, it seats only 30 diners to this cabin colony of restored fishermen's cabins. The fish soup is a good choice, followed by the local seafood specialties of the day. As a dining oddity, you might opt to sample the deep-fried cod tongues. Meat-eaters can enjoy grilled beef kabobs and a few other dishes. For dessert? It's an old-fashioned apple pie with vanilla ice cream.

In the Nusfjord Rorbuer, at the quay. ✆ **76-09-30-20.** Main courses 140NOK–180NOK ($19–$24). AE, DC, MC, V. June–Aug noon–3am.

MOSKENESØY ✪

Continuing east on E10, we come to the final road link at the hamlet of Å. This glaciated island extends for 34km (21 miles). Nature has turned this landscape into one of the wildest and most fascinating in Norway. The landscape is said to have been sculpted by glaciers. In Moskenesøy we reach the highest peak in the Western Lofoten at Hermannsdalstind, rising to 1,029m (3,375 ft.).

People live on the eastern side of the island, with its sheltered harbors for the fishing fleet. Even if you're not driving, the island maintains good ferry bus links with Leknes, Stamsund, and Svolvaer. Leknes, for example, lies 55km (34 miles) to the east.

Lofotens og Vesterålens Dampskibsselskab (✆ **76-96-76-00**), runs car ferries between Bodø and Moskenes, taking 3 hours and costing 430NOK ($57) per vehicle and driver.

The village of Moskenes with its ferry terminal is a mere refueling stop. You can stop in for information and guidance at the **Fiskevaersferie Lofoten turistkontoret** (✆ **76-09-15-99**), at the harbor. Hours from mid-June to mid-August are daily from 10am to 7pm. In early June and late August it is open Monday to Friday from 10am to 5pm.

SEEING THE SIGHTS

Directly east of Moskenes lies the village of **Reine** ✪, one of the most scenically located in the Lofoten. Its little timber houses seemed to be sucked up by the panoramic of the seascapes here. Midnight sun cruises often set out from here in summer from late May to mid-July. Tours cost 600NOK ($80) and last 6 hours. Ask about tickets at the Moskenes tourist office (see above).

There are many *rorbuer* colonies here, these fishermen's cottages rented out to summer visitors, many of whom book in for a week or two.

The tranquil setting of Reine's lagoon against a backdrop of mountain pinnacles has appeared on many a postcard. For the ultimate panorama, you can climb up to the summit of **Reinebringen** at 670m (2,198 ft.).

You can also ask at Moskenes about 5-hour tours, costing 500NOK ($67), leaving Reine twice daily Friday to Sunday in summer. They take you to the turbulent **Moskestraumen** ✦✦, the strait that separates Moskenesøy from the offshore island of Vaerøy. First written about by Pytheas 2,000 years ago, these wicked straits also inspired nautical tales by Edgar Allen Poe and Jules Verne. Mariners claim that they are the "world's most dangerous waters," yet they attract marine mammals and thousands of seabirds, which can be observed on these organized boat tours.

Lying 3km (2 miles) from Reine is Sakrisøy, which is called the "Lilliput of Lofoten fishing villages." If you want to overnight on Moskenesøy, this would make the best base. In what used to be a barn filled with sheep and cows, you will find **Dagmars Dukke og Legetøy Museum** (✆ 76-09-21-43), in the center of Sakrisøy. In this "journey back to childhood," a local woman has collected more than 2,500 dolls from all over, including antique teddy bears and some historic toys dating from 1860 and beyond. Open June to August daily from 10am to 8pm, and in May and September Saturday and Sunday noon to 5pm. Admission is 40NOK ($5.30) for adults and 20NOK ($2.65) for children.

You reach the hamlet of Å at the end of E10, and from here the only road to take is back to Svolvaer. The little fishing village of Å is the setting of the **Norsk Fiskevaermuseum** (✆ 76-09-14-88), Lofoten's most intriguing fishing museum founded in 1987. Nothing brings alive the role of a Lofoten fisherman like this museum, which covers a boathouse, Norway's oldest cod-liver oil factory, the homes of fishermen, a rorbu cabin, and a 150-year-old bakery, plus exhibits on coastal farming in the Arctic. You can also visit a smithy who still makes cod liver oil lamps. Admission is 40NOK ($5.30) for adults and 30NOK ($4) or children. Hours are late June to late August daily from 10am to 6pm, or Monday to Friday 10am to 4pm off-season.

Close by is **Norsk torrfiskmuseum** (✆ 76-09-12-11), a museum devoted to stockfish, at which you'll learn more than you might ever want to know about Norway's oldest export commodity. You learn what happens when the cod is hauled in from the sea, going through the production processes including drying, grading, and sorting. Italy is one of the biggest consumers of Norwegian stockfish today. Admission is 35NOK ($4.65) for adults, 25NOK ($3.35) for children. From mid-June to mid-August, it is open daily from 11am to 5pm. In early June it is open Monday to Friday 11am to 4pm.

WHERE TO STAY

Sakrisøy Rorbuer   This collection of old-fashioned fishermen's cottages is the best place to stay on island, as the other overnight possibilities consist of camping, caravan sites, hostels, and restored fishing huts. Opening onto the water, this is a series of genuine ocher-colored cottages that have been comfortably converted for guests. Under stone roofs, the cottages contain modern conveniences such as private bathrooms with showers. The buildings date from the 1880s but have been much altered and improved over the years.

Sakrisøy, N-8390 Reine. ✆ **76-09-21-43.** Fax 76-09-24-88. 11 cabins. 650NOK–1,000NOK ($86–$133) double. V. **Amenities:** Laundry. *In room:* TV, kitchen, no phone.

VAERØY

Remote craggy Vaerøy, along with the even more remote island of Rost, lies to the far southwest of the Lofoten archipelago and is a bird-watcher's paradise. Vaerøy's Mount Mostadfjell is the nesting place for more than one-and-a-half million seabirds, including sea eagles, auks, puffins, guillemots, kittiwakes, cormorants, Arctic terns, eider petrels, gulls, and others that breed from May to August.

Vaerøy's population is only 775 hearty souls who live on an island of Lilliputian fishing villages; white sand beaches open onto Arctic-chilled waters, towering ridges, and seabird rookeries.

Ferries from Bodø (℃ **76-96-76-00**) arrive here in 4½ hours, costing 400NOK ($53) for a one-way passage. There is also a ferry link from Moskenes taking less than 2 hours and costing 160NOK ($21) one-way.

For information about the island, the **Vaerøy tourist office** (℃ **76-09-52-10**) lies 200m (656 ft.) north of the ferry terminal at Sørland, which is the principal settlement on Vaerøy. It is open from mid-June to mid-August Monday to Saturday from 10am to 3pm. Some 90% of the population lives at Sørland.

SEEING THE SIGHTS

The hamlet of Sørland lies to the east and south of the mountainous area on the island. At Nordland there is a large pebble beach, **Mollbakken,** right by the road from Sørland. Several burial sites from the Stone Age and also the Viking Age have been found here.

The mighty bird cliffs can be found on the southwesterly side, facing the ocean. During the summer, trips to these cliffs are organized every day. Contact the office for more information.

It's an eerie hike south along the western coast to the almost uninhabited fishing village of **Mastad.** At one time some 150 inhabitants lived here, catching puffins as a source of income, then curing the meat in salt. An unusual puffin dog, called the Mastad dog, was used to catch these puffins.

The only man-made attraction at Vaerøy is the Vaerøy **Kirke,** a wooden church with an onion-shaped dome at Norland. It was taken apart and moved from the village of Kabelvåg and reassembled at Vaerøy in 1799. This is the oldest church in Lofoten. The altarpiece, from around 1400, is a late medieval English alabaster relief, depicting the Annunciation, the three Magi or wise men, the Resurrection, and the Ascension. The church is usually open to visitors in summer but keeps no regular hours.

WHERE TO STAY

Gamble Prestegård (Old Vicarage) ★ *Finds* Built in 1898, this used to be the residence of a Lutheran priest. The hotel is run and owned by the charming Hege Sørli, who welcomes guests in style. Her rooms have been modernized and are tastefully and comfortably furnished. Five of the units contain a small bathroom with shower; guests in the other accommodations share the adequate public facilities. Sometimes it's possible to arrange to have dinner here. She doesn't keep a sign out, but it's the house to the left of the church.

N-8063 Vaerøy. ℃ **76-09-54-11.** Fax 76-09-54-84. www.prestegaarden.no. 11 units. 580NOK ($77) double without bathroom; 640NOK ($85) double with bathroom. No credit cards. No amenities.

Kornelius Kro Built in 1991, this is a series of cabins furnished to a high standard and offering a real snug nest in this remote part of the world. The cabins are spacious, like a big hotel suite, and are comfortably inviting with small bathrooms with shower. Amazingly this place keeps going even in the midst of the harshest, darkest night of winter. However, in summer it becomes quite festive. It is the only bar in town, which means it's popular. It is also known for its wood-fired seawater hot tub, the scene of the only parties in town. While enjoying the tub you can be served drinks from the bar. In winter the bar, with its blazing fireplace, is the coziest nook in town.

N-8063 Sørland, Vaerøy. © **76-09-52-99.** Fax 76-09-57-99. 5 cabins. 350NOK–1,150NOK ($47–$153) double. MC, V. **Amenities:** Restaurant; bar. *In room:* TV, kitchen, coffeemaker, hair dryer.

WHERE TO DINE

Kornelius Kro Restaurant   This is the only game in town. The 110-seat restaurant, installed in a modern building at the previously recommended hotel (see above), is decorated with antique fish netting and nautical equipment. The lounge bar with its cozy fireplace is the most popular venue in town, both for locals and visitors. You can eat dinner by firelight or candlelight. Everything is very informal here, and the place is always open in summer, but only for groups in winter. You might begin with a shrimp cocktail and then inquire as to what the cook has prepared for dinner that night. Most often it's fresh Norwegian salmon and the invariable cod prepared pretty much as you like it. Beefsteak with vegetables is also served.

Sørland. © **76-09-52-99.** Meals 150NOK–250NOK ($20–$33). MC, V. Summer daily 5–10pm.

5 Alta: City of Northern Lights

809km (503 miles) N of Bodø; 329km (205 miles) N of Tromsø; 1,989km (1,236 miles) N of Oslo

At the dawn of the 21st century, Alta was renamed rather romantically Nordlysbyen Alta or "Northern Lights City Alta." For years, this far northern outpost of 17,000 inhabitants belonged to Finland and was inhabited almost solely by the Sami (Lapps), who until the end of World War II held a famous fair here. Because of fires and the Nazi destruction of the city at the close of the war, almost everything looks new and rather dull. People come here for nature, not for town architecture.

Alta is the administrative capital of Finnmark (as opposed to Finland, two names some visitors confuse). The River Altaelva runs through the town, which has somewhat the appearance of a frontier outpost. In its 19th-century heyday, Alta enjoyed patronage by British lords who came here to fish the Altafjord, known to have the best salmon waters in the world.

In one of the major environmental protests in Scandinavia, the Altadammen was constructed in the '70s, rising 100m (328 ft.). A former salmon-spawning stream was diverted for hydroelectric power.

ESSENTIALS

GETTING THERE   The airport at Alta lies 4km (2½ miles) northeast of the center of Elvebakken. Daily flights from Oslo take 3 hours. Most passengers transfer through Tromsø, which receives the most flights in north Norway. From Tromsø to Alta, there are four daily flights. There are no train lines here, but buses run between Tromsø and Alta, taking 7 hours and costing 350NOK ($47) one-way. There is also an express bus (Express 2000) that makes the journey from Oslo in about 27 hours, costing 1,900NOK ($253) one-way. For schedules and information about this bus, call © **78-44-40-90.** Motorists can continue to follow the express road from the south (E6) north to Alta.

VISITOR INFORMATION   For information about the area, go to the **Destinatino Alta tourist office,** Sorekskriverveien 13 (© **78-45-77-77**), in the middle of Bossekop. From mid-June to mid-August, it is open Monday to Friday 8am to 6pm, Saturday 10am to 4pm, and Sunday noon to 4pm.

SEEING THE SIGHTS

A series of rock carvings at **Hjemmeluft** ⭐⭐⭐, southwest of Alta, date from 2,000 to 5,000 years ago and are the biggest collection of prehistoric rock carvings in the north of Europe. These pictographs, discovered in 1973, and now a UNESCO World Heritage Site, form part of the **Alta Museum** (© 78-45-63-30). It is believed that originally the rock carvings were painted in red ochre. They have been repainted in the same color to make them stand out better. The rock carvings from both the Stone Age and the Iron Age are linked from the museum by a series of 3km (1¾ miles) of boardwalks. The carvings depict hunting scenes, with clear likenesses of moose, bears, and reindeer. One stunning carving shows an ancient boat carrying a crew of 32 hunters.

The museum itself shelters an array of exhibitions, related to Finnmark and its history going back 11,000 years. It is open June to August daily 8am to 9pm; May and September daily 9am to 6pm, and October to April Saturday and Sunday 11am to 4pm. Admission is 70NOK ($9.30) for adults, free for children under 12.

From Alta you can take a riverboat excursion along the Alta River up to the **Sautso-Alta Canyon** ⭐⭐⭐ which, at 400m (1,312 ft.), is the "Grand Canyon" not only of Scandinavia but of northern Europe. Over the protests (still raging) of environmentalists, the canyon has been dammed, but still offers massive scenic beauty.

To hook up with a tour, contact **Alta Riverboat Service** (© 78-43-33-78). From June 5 to September 5, 2½-hour tours to the outer canyon cost 350NOK ($47) for adults or 175NOK ($23) for children under 12. Shorter tours of 1 to 1½ hours go for 250NOK ($33) for adults or 125NOK ($17) for children.

SHOPPING

If you'd like to pick up some regional crafts while in the area, there are some rare and exceptional merchandise for sale at **Manndalen Husflidslag** (© 77-71-62-72), lying at Løkvoll in Manndalen reached along the E6 15km (9 miles) west of Alta. The Sami (Lapps) often make marvelous weavings on their vertical looms, some of which are suitable as wall hangings. You can also purchase such clothing as knitwear. Open Wednesday to Saturday 10am to 3pm.

WHERE TO STAY

Park Hotel Alta Sentrum   Built in 1987, this is a cozy alternative to the more expensive and expansive Rica Hotel Alta nearby. Just off the North Cape Road, it provides a suitable and comfortable overnight before pressing on the next day to the outposts in the north. Furnishings are modern, and the small to midsize bedrooms have wooden floors. Each has an immaculate bathroom, eight with a bathtub and shower, the rest with a shower. The hotel was last renovated and expanded in 1999. Breakfast plus a light meal in the evening are served to guests.

E6, N-9501 Alta. © 78-45-74-00. Fax 78-45-74-01. www.parkhotell.no. 31 units. 995NOK–1,195NOK ($132–$159) double; 1,695NOK ($225) suite. Rates include breakfast and light evening meal. AE, DC, MC, V. **Amenities:** Restaurant; sauna; laundry service; dry cleaning. *In room:* TV, hair dryer.

Quality Vica Hotel (Value)   Built right after World War II, this was a former farmhouse before its conversion to an affordable hotel in 1988. In a town of buildings with no architectural distinction, this timber-built structure has some atmosphere and style. Rooms are decorated in a homelike way and tastefully furnished with warm colors and small bathrooms with shower. Many locals drop in for the traditional North Norway fare, a three-course meal in the evening going for 350NOK ($47).

Fogdebakken 6, N-9500 Alta. © **78-43-42-99.** Fax 78-43-47-11. www.vica.no. 24 units. 895NOK–1,295NOK ($119–$172) double. Rates include continental breakfast. AE, DC, MC, V. Closed Dec 22–Jan 5 and 1 week at Easter. **Amenities:** Restaurant; bar; sauna; 24-hr. room service; babysitting; laundry service; dry cleaning. *In room:* TV, minibar (some units).

Rica Hotel Alta ★ This is the city's finest address. Built in the 1980s, it was last renovated in 1998 into a very contemporary design. In an often gray and gloomy climate, this hotel stands out for its brightness, even using white furnishings to decorate its midsize bedrooms. Half of the units are carpeted, the rest offering wooden floors. Each comes with a small and immaculate private bathroom, all with shower and eight with both tub and shower. The Rica has the most dining, drinking, and entertainment facilities in town. Friday and Saturday nights are especially popular here from 10pm to 3am. Sometimes live bands are brought in.

Løkkeveien 1, N-9150 Alta. © **78-48-27-00.** Fax 78-48-27-77. www.rica.no. 155 units. 865NOK–1,394NOK ($115–$185) double. Children under 15 stay free. Rates include continental breakfast. AE, DC, MC, V. **Amenities:** 2 restaurants; bar; disco; sauna; laundry service; dry cleaning. *In room:* TV, minibar.

WHERE TO DINE

Altastua ★★ NORWEGIAN This is the town's best restaurant, serving all that foodstuff that serious foodies journey to the north of Norway to devour: cloudberries, reindeer, moose, and fresh salmon caught in local waters. In an old-fashioned setting, stuffed animals—all trophies—decorate the walls. In such a woodsy setting, you are not surprised to find such appetizers as wild salmon offered, even smoked reindeer heart. For a main course, salmon appears again, delectably with a saffron sauce. The fried filet of moose is served with either a red wine sauce or else a wild game sauce. You can also order tender filet of Norwegian lamb in a red wine sauce. In summer, only the cloudberries with fresh cream will do for dessert.

Løkkeveien 2. © **78-44-55-54.** Reservations recommended. Main courses 258NOK–265NOK ($35). AE, DC, MC, V. Mon–Sat 5–11pm. Closed Dec 21–Jan 9.

ALTA AFTER DARK

The chief hot spot in town is **Alfa-Omega,** Maredgt 14 (© **78-44-54-00**), attracting a crowd whose average age is from 30 to 40. There is no cover, and the place is definitely inspired by Cuba, with recorded salsa music, pictures of Havana, and Cuban cigars. There are seats for 40, but often 70 to 80 patrons crowd in here for the good times. One section is a very laid-back bar, the other a contemporary cafe. Open Monday to Thursday 8pm to 1am, Friday and Saturday noon to 2am.

6 Karasjok: Capital of the Samis

178km (110 miles) NE of Kautokeino; 18km (11 miles) E of Finnish border

This is the capital of the Samis (Lapplanders), with a population of 2,900 inhabitants. Of these, some 90% are of Sami descent, making Karasjok, along with its neighboring town of Kautokeino, a seat of Sami culture.

Karasjok, whose Sami name translates as "river current," thrives in part on reindeer herding. With its many handicrafts and Sami institutions, Karasjok is both the cultural and social hub of Samiland.

The town forms the best place to learn about these once nomadic people who lived on the roof of Europe. The Sami—traditionally called Lapps—have inhabited these inhospitable lands since ancient times. Sami settlements stretch along the entire Nordic region, including Finland, Sweden, and Norway. Some of the Sami maintain links to their ancient culture, whereas others have been assimilated.

The language of the Lapps belongs to the Finno-Ugric group. A large part of Lapp literature has been published in northern Sami, which is spoken by approximately 75% of Lapps. As with all Arctic societies, oral literature has always played a prominent role. Among Lapps, this oral tradition takes the form of *yoikking,* a type of singing. (Once governments tried to suppress this, but now yoikking is enjoying a renaissance.) One of the classic works of Lapp literature is Johan Turi's *Tale of the Lapps,* first published in 1910.

Handicrafts are important in the Lapp economy. Several craft designers have developed new forms of decorative art, producing a revival in Lapp handicraft tradition.

Many members of the Sami community feel that the term *Lapp* has negative connotations; it's gradually being replaced by the indigenous minority's own name for itself, *sábme,* or other dialect variations. Sami seems to be the most favored English translation of Lapp, and the word is used increasingly.

ESSENTIALS
GETTING THERE   The town is reached by bus, most visitors arriving from Hammerfest, the overland trip taking 4½ hours and costing 285NOK ($38) one-way. Motorists can continue east from Hammerfest along E6.

VISITOR INFORMATION   At the junction of E6 and Route 92, **Karasjok Opplevelser Tourist Office** (© 78-46-69-00) dispenses information for the entire area. It is open June to mid-August Monday to Saturday from 8:30am to 7pm and Sunday 10am to 7pm (closes earlier off-season).

SEEING THE SIGHTS
Sami Park, Porsangerveien (© 78-46-88-00), is a kind of Sami Disneyland. A family favorite, this park showcases Sami culture and also shows you a good time. Its multimedia show, Magic Theatre, will introduce you to the world of the Sami, showing their myths, traditions, and handicrafts. You can visit a local campsite and watch reindeer roping as well. You can also enjoy regional meals here. Naturally, there are gift shops, the most interesting items being handmade silver jewelry. The park charges 90NOK ($12) for adults and 60NOK ($8) for children. From June to mid-August, hours are daily 9am to 7pm; 9am to 4pm daily for the rest of August. In off-season it is open Monday to Friday 9am to 4pm.

Sami vourká dávvirat (Sami Museum) ⊛, Museumsgate 17 (© 78-46-99-50), is an open-air museum devoted to the Sami people, their history, and their culture. There are other Sami exhibitions, but this venue is the only one entitled to be called a national museum of Sami culture. Most intriguing is the exhibition of old dwellings and such artifacts as an old hunting trap for wild reindeer, showing how people earned their living. Of special interest are the examples of regional dress used in these subfreezing conditions. Also on display are works by local artists. Admission is 25NOK ($3.35). From June 5 to August 20 hours are Monday to Friday 9am to 6pm, Saturday and Sunday 10am to 6pm. In the off-season hours are Monday to Friday 9am to 3pm and Saturday and Sunday 10am to 3pm.

Since 2000 the **Sametinget (Sami Parliament),** Sámediggi (© **78-47-40-00**), has had its headquarters at this impressive piece of modern architecture encased in Siberian lark wood. To carry out this far north theme, the interior is also filled with native woods such as pine and birch. Unique among parliament buildings, the assembly hall was constructed in the shape of a *gamma* (Sami tent). Tiny bulbs, evoking the northern lights, illuminate the 35,000-volume Sami library. Admission-free tours are conducted Monday to Friday in summer from 8:30am to 2:30pm.

Samisk Kunstnersenter (Sami Artists Center), Jeagilvármádii 54 (© **75-46-90-02**), is an art gallery devoted to Sami painters, with new exhibitions every month. This is not just about folk art; many Sami painters are as modern as the 21st century. Sami art and handicrafts are also sold here. Admission is free, and it is open Monday to Friday 10am to 3pm and on Sunday from noon to 5pm. In summer it is also open on Saturday from 10am to 3pm.

Finally, **Karasjok Opplevelser** (© **78-46-88-10**) organizes adventures in the area, including everything from visits to a Sami camp to gold-panning and river-boat trips. In winter you can even go reindeer sledding like Santa Claus. If you're coming into the area, call in advance to see what type of adventure might be offered at the time of your visit.

Many visitors come from all over the world to hunt and fish in the area. If you'd like some fishing trips and wilderness adventure tours, the man to call is **Nils Rolf Johnsen,** Svenskebakken 35 (© **78-46-63-02**), who makes arrangements for such outings. He can make arrangements for you to stay in *lavvu* (Sami tents) beside Finnmark's largest lake, Lesjavri, with excellent fishing.

SHOPPING   Most visitors who make it this far north like to come back with some souvenirs, particularly the handmade Sami knives, a craft and tradition going back four generations. The best selection of Sami crafts is available at **Samellandssenteret** (© **78-46-71-55**), a shopping center in town.

WHERE TO STAY

Engholm's Huskyi Lodge *Finds*   Next to the Karasjohka River, lying 6km (3½ miles) outside Karasjok, this is a real frontier outpost, which connects you with local life more than any other lodging in the area. You cannot only rent a cabin but go on summer hikes with the huskies, or, when the weather turns, join in a dog sledding tour. Gold-panning, fishing trips, and wilderness tours are also part of the action here. Accommodations are in cozy log houses, each personalized and comfortable. Some of the cabins have private bathrooms; others must share. Most cabins contain a kitchenette as well. In the *Barta,* a special turf-covered log house, guests gather around the open fire sitting on reindeer furs and enjoying good food and drink. Lunch costs 100NOK ($13), with a dinner going for 200NOK ($27).

N-9730 Karasjok. © **78-46-71-66.** www.engholm.no. 5 cabins. 300NOK ($40) double, plus 100NOK ($13) per person. Rates include continental breakfast. V. **Amenities:** Restaurant; bar. *In room:* TV, no phone.

Rica Hotel Karasjok ✦   This is the best hotel in the area, with its cozy bar and dining facilities, the major social hub and entertainment venue for the district. The two-story wooden building looks like a ski lodge. It was built in 1983 but completely renovated in 2001 to offer contemporary bedrooms, with comfortable furnishings resting on wooden floors. The bedrooms open onto views of the surrounding forests; half of them are equipped with bathrooms with a tub and shower, the rest with just a shower. The staff is most helpful in arranging tours regardless of the season—winter dog sled rides and reindeer races or summer riverboat trips.

Porsangervn 1, N-9730 Karasjok. ℭ 78-46-74-00. Fax 78-46-68-02. www.rica.no. 56 units. 910NOK–1,290NOK ($121–$172) double. Children under 4 stay free. Rates include continental breakfast. AE, DC, MC, V. **Amenities:** 2 restaurants; fitness center; sauna. *In room:* TV.

WHERE TO DINE

Rica Hotel Karasjok Restaurant NORWEGIAN Adjacent to Sami Park, this restaurant is the best in the area. Go here for a real taste of the north country. A ski lodge restaurant, it is built of timbers and decorated with native Sami costumes. For an appetizer, its smoked reindeer heart is even better than your mother made for you. This might be followed with such regional dishes as filet of reindeer in a game sauce with vegetables. If you've had enough reindeer, you can opt for the delectable grilled Arctic char with white wine sauce and vegetables. The gourmet's favorite summer dessert in Sami land is a bowl of fresh cloudberries.

In the Rica Hotel Karasjok, Porsangervn 1. ℭ 78-46-74-00. Reservations recommended. Main courses 200NOK–290NOK ($27–$39). AE, DC, MC, V. Daily 11am–11pm.

KARASJOK AFTER DARK

Once again, the **Rica Hotel Karasjok,** Porsangervn 1 (ℭ **78-46-74-00**), is the scene of the "action," whatever there is. Patrons who come here range in age from 20s to 50s. There's no cover, and music is presented 6 days a week in April and from September to December. In summer, locals are out celebrating daylight and sunshine and tend to avoid bars at that time. Open daily from 11am to 11pm.

7 Hammerfest: World's Northernmost Town

2,314km (1,438 miles) N of Bergen; 144km (90 miles) N of Alta; 2,195km (1,364 miles) N of Oslo

The Hammerfest area stretches from Måsøy, near the North Cape, to Loppa in the south. The wide region includes the rugged coasts along the Arctic Sea. The regional capital, Hammerfest, often serves as a base for exploring the North Cape.

Hammerfest is a major traffic hub, and in the summer there's a wide choice of boat and bus excursions. The tourist office (see below) can tell you what's available.

The city lies 70° 39' 48" north and achieved its town status on July 7, 1789, making it the oldest town in northern Norway. The town was founded because of its natural harbor, something that is equally important today for Hammerfest's economic foundation. Despite its geographical position, Hammerfest has maintained its international connections.

A **Meridianstøtta,** or meridian column, stands on the Fuglenes peninsula, across from the harbor. The monument commemorates the work of scientists from Norway, Sweden, and Russia who conducted surveys at Hammerfest between 1816 and 1852 to establish a meridian arc between Hammerfest and the Danube River at the Black Sea. This led to an accurate calculation of the size and shape of Earth.

Today Hammerfest is a modern town with an open and unique atmosphere, where the town's square and harbor are natural meeting places. Hammerfest is an important communication center in the county of Finnmark, and this makes it an ideal starting point for coastal and other scenic excursions in the county.

ESSENTIALS

GETTING THERE If you don't take the coastal steamer, you can drive, although it's a long trek. From Oslo, take E6 north until you reach the junction with Route 94 west. Hammerfest is at the end of Route 94. During the summer, there are three buses a week from Oslo. Travel time is 29 hours. SAS has daily flights from Oslo and Bergen to Alta, where you can catch a bus to Hammerfest (Apr–Sept only). For bus information, call **Finnmark Fylkesrederi** (© **78-40-70-00**).

VISITOR INFORMATION The **Hammerfest Tourist Office,** Strandgate (© **78-41-21-85**), in the town center, is open daily from 9am to 5pm.

SEEING THE SIGHTS

This is the world's northernmost town of significant size, and a port of call for North Cape coastal steamers. Destroyed during the Second World War by the retreating Nazis, it has long since been rebuilt. Lapps from nearby camps often come into town to shop. Count yourself lucky if they bring their reindeer.

The port is free of ice year-round, and shipping and exporting fish is a major industry. The sun doesn't set from May 12 to August 1—and doesn't rise from November 21 to January 23.

For a panoramic view of the town, take a zigzag walk up the 72m (80-yard) **Salen** "mountain." Atop Salen is a 6m- (20-ft.-) tall square tower, with walls built of gray and blue stones. The old tower was torn down during the war, but restored in 1984.

Why not take time to do as 150,000 others have and join the **Royal and Ancient Polar Bear Society** (© **78-41-31-00**) here? Apply in person while you're in Hammerfest. Membership costs 150NOK ($20) annually, and the money is used to protect endangered Arctic animals through conservation programs. The society's building is filled with stuffed specimens of Arctic animals. There's a small museum devoted to the hunting heyday of Hammerfest, which lasted from 1910 to 1950, when eagles, Arctic foxes, and polar bears were trapped by the English, and then German officers during the war. It's in the basement of the Town Hall, on Rådhusplassen. The center is open only June to August, Monday to Friday from 6am to 6pm.

Gjenreisningsmuseet, Söröygatan (© **78-42-26-40**), opened adjacent to the Rica Hotel in 1998. This small museum commemorates the cold bleak years after World War II, when local residents, deprived of most of their buildings, livelihoods, and creature comforts, heroically rebuilt Finnmark and north Norway in the wake of Nazi devastation. Entrance is 40NOK ($5.30) per person, and it is open June to September, daily 10am to 6pm; off-season, daily 11am to 2pm.

Lying a 5-minute walk from the harbor, **Hammerfest Kirke (Church),** Kirkegate 33 (© **78-42-74-70**), was consecrated in 1961 and is known for its avant-garde architecture. Unusual for a church, this kirke doesn't have an altarpiece. Instead you get a large and detailed stained-glass window that is quite beautiful. The altarpiece is found in a hall lying to the right of the main sanctuary. Local carver Knit Arnesen carved the friezes, depicting the history of Hammerfest. Note the chapel across from the church. Dating from 1933, it is the only structure in Hammerfest to survive the Nazi scorched earth retreat in 1945. Admission is free, and the church is open in summer from Monday to Friday 8am to 3pm, Saturday 11am to 3pm, and Sunday noon to 1pm.

For **magnificent vistas** ✮ of Hammerfest and coastal Norway, climb **Salen Hill** at 86m (282 ft.) by taking a zigzagging footpath from the center. Most visitors reach the top in about 15 minutes. On a clear day, you can see offshore islands as well.

If you arrive at noon, you can order lunch at the on-site **Turistua** (© **78-42-96-00**), Salen, which offers a big Norwegian buffet for 190NOK

($25) per person. Although tourists flock here, the name Turistua doesn't come from that. The place was named for a local woman with the last name of "Turi."

There is also a Sami "turf hut" here, **Mikkelgammen,** which can be booked 2 days in advance if you'd like to have a Lappish meal here. Guests gather around a campfire for a three-course meal called *bidos.* Naturally, reindeer is the main course of choice. You get reindeer soup as well as reindeer meat for your main course, followed by Arctic cloudberries in whipped cream. The cost of the meal is 230NOK ($31) per person, followed by a Sami program called *Joik,* including singing (more like chanting) and stories told of life in the far north.

The tourist office also organizes boat trips in the area for those who want to go deep-sea fishing and bird-watching. Offerings can change from week to week, but these 3-hour outings require a minimum of eight people, costing 280NOK ($37) per person.

WHERE TO STAY

Quality Hammerfest Hotel   This guest house opens onto views of the harbor, standing right on the Rådhusplassen (Town Hall Square). Built in 1964, it received its last big renovation in 1992 and is still shipshape today. Its small to midsize bedrooms are tastefully and comfortably furnished, each with a small bathroom with a shower. If you can afford it, go for a suite here as they not only open onto views of the harbor, but they have more luxurious bathrooms with a tub *and* a shower. The hotel has drinking and dining facilities, making it one of the major social hubs of the town. The staff can arrange such adventures as rides in a snowmobile or on horseback, and can advise about fishing in local waters.

Strandgt. 2-4, N-9600 Hammerfest. ℭ **78-42-96-00.** Fax 78-42-96-60. www.hammerfesthotel.no. 50 units. 935NOK–1,250NOK ($124–$166) double; from 1,575NOK ($209) suite. Rates include buffet breakfast. AE, DC, MC, V. Closed Dec 20–Jan 2. **Amenities:** Restaurant; bar; 2 pubs; sauna; limited room service; solarium. *In room:* TV, minibar, hair dryer, iron/ironing board.

Rica Hotel Hammerfest   This is the largest hotel in town and the preferred place to stay in the area. It's in the town center, opening directly onto the waterfront. Built in the mid-1970s on steeply sloping land, the hotel was completely redecorated in 1989 and has been regularly spruced up since then. The small, modern guest rooms are decorated with Nordic-inspired pastels, but the look is strictly functional. Bathrooms tend to be small and each unit contains a shower-tub combination.

Sørøygata 15, N-9600 Hammerfest. ℭ **78-41-13-33.** Fax 78-41-13-11. 80 units. 960NOK–1,325NOK ($128–$176) double; 1,385NOK ($184) suite. AE, DC, MC, V. Bus: 1 or 2. **Amenities:** Restaurant; bar; fitness center; sauna; babysitting; laundry service; dry cleaning. *In room:* TV, minibar, hair dryer.

WHERE TO DINE

Odd's Mat og Vinhus ★★ NORTHERN NORWEGIAN   Since it opened in 1992, this rustic restaurant has become famous thanks to a survey by a Trondheim radio station that voted it the best restaurant in Norway. It's adjacent to the town's largest pier, overlooking the harbor. Inside, every effort has been made to simulate the wild splendor of Finnmark (northern Norway), with the use of roughly textured wood, stone, and many yards of natural hemp knotted into ropes that form curtains. A kitchen opens to the dining room.

The recipes and ingredients are almost completely derived from northern Norway, with an emphasis on fish and game. You might try filet of carp, partially sun-dried, then boiled and served with mustard sauce and bacon fat; or freshly killed grouse prepared "like beef," with a game-laced cream sauce. To start, try the filet of reindeer, served, raw and chopped, like a tartare, or smoked and thinly sliced, like a carpaccio.

Strandgata 24. ✆ **78-41-37-66.** Reservations recommended. Main courses 210NOK–290NOK ($28–$39). AE, DC, MC, V. Mon–Thurs 1–11pm; Fri 1pm–1am; Sat 6–11pm. Bus: 1, 5, or 9.

Rica Hotel Restaurant NORWEGIAN/INTERNATIONAL   This dining room in the cellar of the Rica Hotel Hammerfest opens onto the harbor front. Specialties include pepper steak, filet of reindeer, and delicious daily specials based on the day's catch from the fjord. Some international selections are also served, including Mexican and Chinese cuisine. The Rica Bar and Disco, also in the cellar of the hotel, is open Monday to Thursday from 5pm to 1am, Friday and Saturday 5pm to 3:30am. Admission is 70NOK ($9.30) on Friday and Saturday night; other nights, it's free. The minimum age is 20, and beer costs 45NOK ($6) per half liter.

In the Rica Hotel Hammerfest, Sørøygata 15. ✆ **78-41-13-33.** Main courses 179NOK–259NOK ($24–$34). AE, DC, MC, V. Daily 11am–11pm. Bus: 1 or 2.

HAMMERFEST AFTER DARK

Your best bet is **Banyean & Hans Highness,** Strandgt. 2–4 (✆ **78-42-96-00**), found in the previously recommended Quality Hammerfest hotel. Banyean is a sailor's pub, whereas Hans Highness is more like a nightclub. In the pub you can order plenty of mugs of beer or other drinks along with burgers and pastas. In the nightclub live music is frequently featured, at which time a cover of 40NOK to 100NOK ($5.30–$13) is imposed. Sometimes the night is devoted to karaoke. Most patrons range in age from 25 to 45. Banyean is open daily from noon to 1am, and Hans Highness is only opened on Friday and Saturday from midnight to 3am. If you'd like a cozy retreat from all this Nordic madness, you can head for a drink in the **hotel bar.**

8 Honningsvåg & the North Cape ★★

130km (81 miles) NE of Hammerfest; 2,444km (1,519 miles) NE of Bergen

The world's northernmost village, the gateway to the North Cape, is a completely modern fishing harbor set in a land of forests, fjord waters, and crashing waterfalls, everything bathed in summer by the eerie light of the midnight sun. Only the chapel withstood the German destruction of 1944. It's some 80km (50 miles) nearer to the North Pole than Hammerfest, on the Alta-Hammerfest bus route.

Honningsvåg is on the southern side of the island of Magerøy, connected to the North Cape by a 35km (22-mile) road.

ESSENTIALS

GETTING THERE   If you don't take the coastal steamer, you can reach Honningsvåg by car. From Oslo (a very long trip—about 30 hr. during the period from June–Sept), take E6 north to the junction with Route 95 north. That route leads to Honningsvåg, with one ferry crossing. SAS flies from Oslo or Bergen to Alta; there you can catch a bus to Hammerfest (Apr–Sept only), where you change to another bus to Honningsvåg. For bus information, call **Finnmark Fylkesrederi** (✆ **78-40-70-00**).

VISITOR INFORMATION   The **Honningsvåg Tourist Office,** in the Nordkapphuset (✆ **78-47-25-99**), can give you information on sightseeing boat trips, museums, walks, and deep-sea fishing. The office is open June to August, Monday to Friday from 8:30am to 8pm, Saturday and Sunday noon to 8pm; September to May, Monday to Friday 8:30am to 4pm.

A SPECIAL EVENT The **North Cape Festival,** held for 1 week in mid-June each year, presents a wide display of local culture. During the festival, participants in the **North Cape March** trek from Honningsvåg to the North Cape and back, a total of around 70km (44 miles).

SEEING THE SIGHTS

Check at the tourist office (see above) about organized tours of the area. In the summer the Fuglesafari boat tours visit the splendid bird colony off the shore on the little island of **Gjesvaerstappan.** All sorts of Arctic seabirds, including kittiwakes, skuas, razorbills, gannets, puffins, and cormorants, can be seen on the cliffs, along with seals. The cost of the tour is 400NOK ($53) for adults or 200NOK ($27) for children.

Nordkapphallen This visitor center has a video presentation and museum exhibits. Downstairs you'll find a super-videograph and a cave with a panoramic window facing the Arctic Ocean. On the way to the cave, you'll see several scenes from the history of the North Cape. A monument commemorates the visit of King Oscar (king of Norway and Sweden) to the Cape in 1873, and another exhibit commemorates the arrival of King Chulalongkorn of Siam (now Thailand) who came for a look at the Cape in 1907; Chulalongkorn was the son of the king in the musical *The King and I.* There's also a monument marking the terminus of the "Midnight Sun Road." Although the admission price is steep, the views from inside are incredible and unforgettable. Call before you visit because opening hours and days are subject to change without notice.

Nordkapp. ℭ **78-47-22-33.** Admission 185NOK ($25) adults, 50NOK ($6.65) children, 350NOK ($47) family. Apr 1–May 17 daily 2–5pm; May 18–June 5 daily noon–1am; June 6–Aug 11 daily 9am–2am; Aug 12–20 daily 9am–1am; Aug 21–Sept daily noon–5pm. Closed Oct–Mar.

Nordkappmuseet This museum displays the cultural history of the North Cape, including fishery artifacts and an exhibit that details the effects of the Second World War on the North Cape. The museum lies at the harbor and town center, a 3-minute walk from the coastal steamer and the North Cape Hotel.

In the Nordkapphuset, Fergeveien 4. ℭ **78-47-28-33.** Admission 25NOK ($3.35) adults, 5NOK (65¢) children 6–16, free for children under 6. June 15–Aug 15 Mon–Sat 11am–8pm, Sun noon–8pm; Aug 16–June 14 Mon–Fri 12:30–4pm.

WHERE TO STAY

Arctic Hotell Nordkapp This well-run, relatively small hotel is a favorite with North Cape aficionados who use it as a base for exploring in the area. The hotel opened in the 1960s and was last renovated in the 1990s. A vision of white and blue, it offers cozy, rather basic bedrooms, each furnished with functional pieces. Included with each unit is a small bathroom with shower. The on-site restaurant is really a self-service cafeteria. The hotel is located in the middle of town and has a view of the harbor.

Storgt. 12, N-9750 Honningsvåg. ℭ **78-47-29-66.** Fax 78-47-30-10. 40 units. Summer 980NOK ($130) double; off-season 850NOK ($113) double. Children under 3 stay free. Rates include continental breakfast. AE, DC, MC, V. Closed Dec 24–Jan 6 and 1 week at Easter. **Amenities:** Restaurant; bar. *In room:* TV.

Honningsvåg Brygge ★ *Finds* This family-run establishment was a fish factory until the 1970s when the owners decided to convert it into a hotel. The conversion was a success, and discerning travelers to the North Cape have been making their way here ever since. The walls, ceiling, and floor are all wood, but the furnishings are contemporary. Bedrooms are small to midsize, each cozy and comfortably furnished, with a small bathroom with a shower. On site is Sjøhuset, the best restaurant in town (see "Where to Dine," below).

Vagen 1A, N-9751 Honningsvåg. ℂ or fax 78-47-64-65. 26 units. 1,150NOK ($153) double; 1,600NOK ($213) suite. Children under 12 stay free. Rates include continental breakfast. AE, DC, MC, V. **Amenities:** Restaurant; bar; limited room service; laundry service; dry cleaning.

Rica Bryggen Hotel Opened in 1989, this hotel is filled with facilities and accommodations that lure members of the fishing industry in summer and international visitors in winter. The two-floor hotel offers midsize bedrooms, most of them with a view of the harbor. Each accommodation is carpeted and comfortably furnished, along with small bathrooms with shower. The on-site restaurant offers standard Norwegian fare.

Vagen, N-9750 Honningsvåg. ℂ 78-47-28-88. Fax 78-47-27-24. www.rica.no. 42 units. 960NOK–1,245NOK ($128–$166) double. Children under 12 stay free. Rates include continental breakfast. AE, DC, MC, V. Closed Dec 21–Jan 2 and 2 weeks at Easter. **Amenities:** Restaurant; bar; sauna. *In room:* TV, minibar, coffeemaker.

Rica Hotel Honningsvåg The world's northernmost hotel is located in the central zone, near the quay. Advance reservations are strongly advised. This five-story, yellow-fronted building was enlarged and considerably upgraded in the 1990s. The guest rooms, which have views of the harbor, are functionally furnished with modern but plain pieces. The rooms and bathrooms are a bit small (each equipped with a shower-tub combination), but the beds are comfortable. In this part of the world, you'll happily settle for a roof over your head. Restaurant Carolina (see "Where to Dine," below) is one of the best in town. The hotel also runs an unpretentious grill and offers disco action on Friday and Saturday nights.

Nordkappgata 2–4, N-9750 Honningsvåg. ℂ 78-47-23-33. Fax 78-47-33-79. 163 units. 960NOK–1,260NOK ($128–$168) double; 1,400NOK–1,800NOK ($186–$239) suite. AE, DC, MC, V. **Amenities:** Restaurant; lounge. *In room:* TV.

WHERE TO DINE

Corner NORWEGIAN Ever had Arctic pizza? This is the place for it, along with an array of other regional dishes. A lot of fishermen as well as international visitors flock here for good, affordable food. The 1960s building and decor isn't all that much, but the chef will feed you well at a reasonable price. There are no appetizers to speak of, but the main courses are generous. Your best bet is the grilled and locally caught salmon, which comes with fresh vegetables and potatoes. You can also order locally caught grilled cod or halibut. Meat-eaters may find the veal schnitzel satisfying. Finish your meal with a slice of apple pie and ice cream. A live band sometimes entertains in the adjoining bar.

Fiskerveien 2A. ℂ 78-47-63-40. Main courses 110NOK–140NOK ($15–$19). AE, DC, MC, V. Sun–Thurs 10am–midnight; Fri–Sat 10am–2am.

Restaurant Carolina NORWEGIAN Located in the cellar of the Rica Hotel Honningsvåg, this place is at its most elegant in the winter, when the tour groups are gone. During the summer, the smorgasbord is in the dining room and a la carte dinners are served in the less formal bistro. The cuisine is competently prepared but never exciting; most of the ingredients are shipped in. In the evening music begins at 8pm, and the place is very popular with locals. It's decorated with old-fashioned photographs of Honningsvåg.

In the Rica Hotel, Nordkappgata 2–4. ℂ 78-47-23-33. Reservations recommended. Main courses 160NOK–225NOK ($21–$30). AE, DC, MC, V. Summer daily 5–11pm.

Sjøhuset ★ NORWEGIAN/SEAFOOD The town's best and most elegant restaurant is decorated with nets and fishing poles along with other nautical

> **Finds** **Europe's Real Northernmost Point**
>
> It comes as a surprise to some visitors that the continent's actual northern-most point is not the North Cape but **Knivskjelodden,** lying 9km (5½ miles) south of the cape. Europe's northernmost point is at 71° 11' 08". You can hike the trial, which is not too difficult if you're in good shape. Wear sturdy boots, of course. Figure on about 5 hours there and back. Once there, you'll have a **panoramic sweep** ✦ of the North Cape Plateau. After you've walked the world's northernmost hiking trail, you can sign your name in the hiking association's minute book at Knivskjelodden.

memorabilia. Windows are built around the dining room so that you can take in the view on the pier, especially of boats bobbing in the harbor. It comes as no surprise that fish soup is the best and most requested appetizer. Three types of fresh fish, depending on the catch of the day, appear on the menu. Most often the catch is salmon, catfish, or halibut. The fish can be grilled to your specifications. For a meat course, the most ordered dish is filet of reindeer. In summer, everyone wants to taste the exotic cloudberries at dessert.

Vagen 1. ⓒ **78-47-36-16.** Reservations recommended. Main courses 170NOK–200NOK ($23–$27). AE, DC, MC, V. Summer daily 2–11pm; off-season Fri–Sat 6–10pm.

A TRIP TO THE NORTH CAPE

The **Nordkapp (North Cape)** symbolizes the "top of Europe." In prehistoric times the North Cape Horn was a Sami place of sacrifice. The North Cape's name used to be Knyskanes, but in 1553 it was named "North Cape" by the Lord Richard Chancellor of England, who was searching for a sea passage to China. The road to the North Cape is open to traffic from May 1 to October 20.

The first tour ships arrived in 1879. They anchored in Hornvika Bay, and the visitors had to climb 280m (307 yards) up to the plateau. After the road from Honningsvåg opened in 1956, the flow of tourists turned into a flood. In summer, buses to the North Cape leave daily from outside the tourist office at Fergeveien 4 at Honningsvåg, stop briefly at the ferry terminal across from the Sifi Sommerhotell, and then continue to the visitors' center at the North Cape. The one-way passage from any point along the route is 60NOK ($8) adults, 30NOK ($4) children. For more information, call **FFR** (ⓒ **78-47-58-50**).

On the road to the Cape is a Lapp encampment. It's a bit contrived, but visitors do have an opportunity to go inside one of the tents, and they come away with an idea of how nomadic Lapps used to live.

HONNINGSVÅG AFTER DARK

The Irish pub, **Bryggerie,** Nordkappgate 1 (ⓒ **78-47-26-00**), attracts a varied crowd of patrons who drink endless mugs of beer or listen to recorded music when not conversing. This is one of the world's northernmost microbreweries and you can sample the homemade brews: Oleanton and Oleanton Christmas. Pizzas and light snacks are available. Open Monday to Thursday 10am to midnight, Friday and Saturday 10am to 2am, and Sunday 6pm to midnight.

The competitor is **Norden Pub,** Larsfjorda 1 (ⓒ **78-47-27-11**), a maritime-styled pub and also the leading soccer pub in town. Patrons range in age from 25 to 50. Music, ranging from regional music to Elvis, is live 1 night a week during the summer. Pizza is the snack of choice here. Open Monday to Thursday 6pm to midnight, Friday and Saturday noon to 2am, and Sunday noon to midnight.

Appendix:
Norway in Depth

Imagine a headless sea horse hanging over Denmark, with an elongated tail curving northward along the Swedish border—beyond the Arctic Circle—the tip of its tail brushing against Russian Lapland. This is the shape of Norway, a land that features porcupine ridges of mountain broken in spots by unladylike fingers—fjords—that gouge into the rocky surfaces of the earth.

Norway is a land of waterfalls and rapids, majestic mountains, majestic glaciers, green islands, crystal lakes, pine and spruce forests, steep-sloped farmsteads, secluded valleys, craggy cliffs, peaceful fjords, and fishing villages.

In the north the coastline is dotted with brightly painted houses, their sparkling colors contrasting with the somber grandeur of fjords and mountains. The northern slice of Norway—Finnmark, or Lapland—is low and hilly, bleak and forlorn, peopled in part by nomadic Lapps with reindeer herds.

Norway is an ancient land of myth and legend, mountains, and nature. It also has a strong folklore tradition. As children, Norwegians grow up on stories of huldres (see box, "A Long-Tailed Seducer") and trolls. Trolls—who can be both good and evil and who come in all shapes and sizes—have become part of the folklore of the country. And in their secret hearts, many Norwegians still believe in them.

Trolls have very long noses—but often only one eye per family. To compensate for this lack of vision, some trolls possess as many as 12 heads. In case a Norwegian farmer should chop off one of the troll's heads, three more will grow back in its place. Mrs. Troll has a bigger nose than her husband. She uses it for everything from stirring porridge to whipping the children. Trolls never come out in sunlight. If they should happen to make a sudden appearance during the day, they burst and are petrified as mountains. That's why Norway has so many mountains, so the legend goes.

And mountains Norway has—and fjords and waterfalls unique in Europe.

Go to Norway for an experience not only with folklore, but also with the great outdoors. Spain and Italy overflow with legendary, treasure-filled cities. Norway has nothing to equal them. England has preserved the crooked old architecture from the days of Samuel Johnson. Norway's wooden villages have burned to the ground for the most part. Many of Norway's towns along the coast—such as Bodø—were destroyed during World War II. But in sheer scenic beauty, Norway is about the greatest thing this side of Valhalla.

Norway is a blend of the ancient and the modern. How curious to see a Lapp grandmother—attired in a brightly colored braided costume, bonnet, and deerhide moccasins with turned-up toes—waiting to board an airplane at the Tromsø airport.

Search long and hard enough, and you might turn up a sod-roofed house, where old Grandfather Per—wearing high trousers—sits in a tub-chair in the corner downing his curds-and-whey. On the other hand, his grandson, clad in swimming trunks, will probably be sunning himself on a rock listening to American music on his transistor radio.

> ### *Fun Fact* A Long-Tailed Seducer
>
> At a cafe in Oslo, the wife of our host picked up a fork, leaned over the table, and tapped her husband on the knuckles, "Keep your eyes off the huldre, darling."
>
> The "huldre" was a tall blonde in pants at least three sizes too small.
>
> In Norwegian folklore, a huldre is supposed to be a most beautiful woman—but she has a cow's tail tucked under her skirt, perhaps tied around her waist. And this bovine appendage is always dropping out at the most inopportune times. For her tail to drop off completely, she has to marry a man in a church.
>
> The huldre makes a clever housewife and is resented—for that and other reasons—by Norwegian women. The Anna, Noram, or Birgit who wants to hang onto her husband is not averse to warning him against accepting an invitation to go home with a huldre for the night. The huldre has the power of stretching that night out for 7 years. At least that's what many an errant Olav has claimed when he finally stumbles back to his older spouse.
>
> (Frankly, the tall blonde singled out probably wasn't a real huldre. It was impossible for her to conceal a caudal appendage under those pants. But that didn't matter. The wife knew her to be a huldre—and that was that.)

1 Norway Today

The long, narrow country stretches some 1,760km (1,100 miles) north to south, but rarely more than 96km (60 miles) east to west. Norway is a land of raw nature. It occupies the western and extreme northern portion of the Scandinavia peninsula, bordering Finland, Sweden, and Russia. In the west, its 21,342km (13,339 miles) of coastline confront the often-turbulent North Atlantic Ocean. For more details about the Norwegian coastline, see the box "Norway Just Grows & Grows," below.

There's plenty of breathing room for everybody. When you factor in the Arctic desolation of the north, Norway averages about 20 people per square mile. Most of the four million inhabitants are concentrated in the swag-bellied south, where the weather is less severe. Even so, the population of Oslo, the capital, is less than half a million. Aside from Oslo, there are no really big cities; the populations of Bergen and Trondheim are 208,000 and 134,000, respectively.

Norway does not want to be a melting pot, and immigration is strictly controlled. The largest minority group is the Lapps (or Sami), who live in the far north; they have broad powers of self-government, including their own parliament. Although many people have emigrated from Norway—about one million to America alone—immigration to Norway from other countries has been limited. About 3.2% of the population originally came from Great Britain, Denmark, and Sweden.

Norway is a constitutional monarchy. Although without political power, Norway's royal family enjoys the subjects' unwavering support. The real power is in the Storting, or parliament. Women play a major role in government. Some 40% of all elected officials are women, and women head several government ministries. Many industries—especially energy—are fully or partially state controlled. Oil from the North Sea is a vital resource; the government has a Ministry of Oil and Energy. The government grants large subsidies to agriculture and fisheries.

As a result of their natural surroundings, Norwegians are among the most athletic people in Europe. Nearly every Norwegian child learns to ski as well as walk. They are also among the best-educated people in the world. Norway's educational standard has risen considerably since World War II, and some 90% of Norwegian young people take a 3-year course in academic or vocational school after completing their compulsory education.

About 90% of the population belongs to the national Lutheran church, of which the king is the titular head. Freedom of worship is guaranteed to all.

Because the economy depends significantly on foreign trade, most business is conducted in English. Norway has two official languages, Riksmal and Landsmal, both of Danish origin. The Lapps, the indigenous people of the north, have their own language.

Cultural activities are important in Norway. The government subsidizes book publishing, guaranteeing sales of 1,000 copies of each book published for distribution to public libraries. Encouraging Norwegian writers helps preserve the language. Movie production, limited by population and language, fares poorly, however. Opera is fairly new to the country, and Norway didn't acquire a professional ballet ensemble until 1948. Folk music, however, has roots going back to Norse times, and is still very much alive. Norway encourages the arts by providing a guaranteed income to active artists whose work has achieved and maintained a high standard over a period of years.

2 The Natural Environment

Norway is one of nature's last great frontiers in Europe—mountains, glaciers, and lakes cover 70% of its land. Less than 4% of its territory, mostly in the south-central area, is arable. Within Norway's Jutunheimen range are the highest mountain peaks in Europe north of the Alps. Norway has about 17,000 glaciers. Along the western coast, some 50,000 islands protect the mainland from some of the worst storms in the North Atlantic.

Fun Fact Norway Just Grows & Grows

Without conquering other nations, it's almost impossible for a country to expand its coastline by 25,600km (16,000 miles), but Norway has done just that without invading its neighbors, as the Vikings did in days of yore. Today, the conqueror is a computer.

Norwegian mapmakers in 2002 announced that new computer programs are able to measure thousands of tiny inlets and islands in Norway, something that was virtually impossible 3 decades ago. The old figures gave Norway a coastline of 56,928km (35,580 miles), of which 21,342km (13,339 miles) were on the mainland, 35,586km (22,241 miles) around islands. The new figures suggest that Norway is actually 3,968km (2,480 miles) longer than previously believed and that the distance around islands is 21,872km (13,670 miles) greater.

"We are still the same," Tore Hegheim, a resident of Tromsø, said over the state radio network, NRK. "Only our country got much bigger."

Fun Fact **A 40% Quota for Women on Boards**

In 2002 the Norwegian government informed public companies that it will now be mandatory that boardrooms consist of 40% women. There are 650 public companies in Norway that must comply with this demand. The European Union is closely studying the proposal. Would other countries ever consider such a requirement? Would America? Stayed tuned.

Norway has a varied and changing climate. The coastal zones in the west and east normally experience cool summers and temperate winters. Inland, summers are warm, and winters cold and dry. In the extreme north, 100 days of snowfall each year isn't uncommon.

The fjords are not only a distinguishing feature of Norway's landscape, but a special attraction to visitors. The fjords were created thousands of years ago when the ocean flowed into glacial valleys. These "fingers" of water cut deep into the landscape. The most intriguing of the fjords, the Sognefjord, is more than 160km (100 miles) long and extremely deep.

Norway's rivers tend to be short and volatile. A smooth flow of water is often "agitated" by waterfalls and patches of white water. Because they're not suited for transportation, rivers are primarily sources of food, principally salmon. The longest river in Scandinavia, the Glomma, runs through southwestern Norway.

Norway's position on the globe has earned it the nickname "Land of the Midnight Sun." In summer, towns in northern Norway, such as Tromsø, experience 24 hours of sunshine, followed by 24 hours of darkness in winter. Even in southern Norway, the summer days are long, and the winter nights may last more than 17 hours.

Thick birch and pine forests cover the mountains; in the lowlands, oak forests abound. Spruce forests cover the southeast and middle regions. The steep mountains in the east are among the tallest in Europe and the site of some of the world's most challenging alpine ski runs. There is excellent hiking in the Vassafaret district around Fløm, where the mountains are rounded, gentle, and dotted with alpine lakes and rivers.

The mountains are also home to ravens, eagles, grouse, and gyrfalcons. They serve as a migratory home to the pure-white snowy owl. Norway's countryside and forests teem with Arctic animals such as reindeer, Arctic fox, wolves, bears, lynx, elk, beavers, and otters. Along the coast are nesting grounds for puffins and cormorants; whales, salmon, and cod frolic in the icy seas offshore. Through Norway's conservation efforts and strict regulations regarding the environment, these animals and fish flourish much as they have in the past.

3 History 101

Norway has been inhabited since the end of the Ice Age. The earliest Scandinavian settlers hunted reindeer and other game in these northern lands. Some 5,000 to 6,000 years ago, the inhabitants turned to agriculture, especially around the Oslofjord. Artifacts show that in the Roman era,

Dateline

- 800–1050 The age of the Vikings, when Norsemen terrorized the coasts of Europe.
- 872 Harald Fairhair conquers many small provinces and reigns as first king.

Norway had associations with areas to the south.

THE AGE OF THE VIKINGS

Prehistory ended during the Viking era, roughly A.D. 800 to 1050. Much of what is known about this era wasn't written down, but has been conveyed through sagas passed by word of mouth or revealed by archaeological finds. Some scholars consider the looting of the Lindisfarne monastery in northern England in 793 the beginning of the "age of the Vikings."

"The Vikings are coming!" became a dreadful cry along the coasts of Europe. The victims expected fire and sword. Scandinavian historians are usually kinder to the Vikings, citing the fact they often went abroad to trade and colonize. From Norway, the Vikings branched out to settle in the Orkney and Shetland Islands (now part of Scotland). They also settled in the Scottish Hebrides and on the Isle of Man. Viking settlements were established on Greenland and Iceland, which had previously been uninhabited. The Norse communities on Greenland eventually died out. The sagas claim that in 1001, Leif Eriksson discovered "wineland of the good," a reference to the American continent.

- 1001 Leif Eriksson discovers America (or so the sagas claim).
- 1030 Christianity is firmly established; Olaf II is declared a saint.
- 1066 The Viking Age ends with the defeat of Harald III in England.
- 1350 The Black Death wipes out much of the population.
- 1397 Margaret becomes queen of Norway, Denmark, and Sweden at the Union of Kalmar.
- 1439 Danish rule is imposed on Norway.
- 1814 Norway breaks from Denmark and adopts a constitution, but comes under Swedish rule.
- 1905 The Norwegian parliament breaks from Sweden and declares independence.
- 1914 Norway declares its neutrality in the First World War.
- 1920 Norway joins the League of Nations, ending its isolation.
- 1940 Nazi troops invade Norway; the king and government flee.
- 1945 Norway regains independence and executes its Nazi puppet ruler, Quisling.
- 1960s Oil boom hits Norway.
- 1986 Labour Party installs first female prime minister, Gro Harlem Brundtland.
- 1989 Center-right coalition regains power.

continues

 Did You Know?

- Norwegians have one of the highest per capita incomes in the world.
- While medieval alchemists were trying to make gold, they discovered *akevitt* (aquavit, or schnapps), the national "firewater" of Norway.
- Norway has the world's largest foreign trade per capita.
- The average population density is only 13 inhabitants per square kilometer (almost ½ sq. mile), compared with 96 for Europe as a whole.
- Norway and Russia share a short land border and have disputed control of a sea area the size of Belgium, Switzerland, and Austria combined.
- Hammerfest is the world's northernmost town.

Many scholars, however, claim that the Vikings' long ships reached America long before Leif Eriksson.

The road to unification of Norway was rough. In 872 Harald Fairhair, after winning a battle near Stavanger, conquered many of the provinces, but other battles for unification took decades. Harald was followed by his son, Eric I—"Bloody Axe," to his enemies. Eric began his reign by assassinating two of his eight brothers, and later killed five other brothers. His one surviving brother, Haakon, succeeded him as king in 954. Haakon tried

- 1990 Brundtland becomes prime minister again.
- 1991 Harald V becomes king.
- 1994 Lillehammer plays host to XVII Olympic Winter Games.
- 1995 Norway wins Eurovision Song Contest, an annual cultural event observed by 600 million viewers.
- 1996 Eurovision Song Contest is held in Oslo; Norway takes second place.
- 1998 Oil prices fall, but Norway plunges ahead with costly engineering projects.
- 2001 U.N. group votes Norway most desirable place to live in the world.

unsuccessfully to convert Norway to Christianity. After he died in the Battle of Fitjar (960), Harald II Graafell, one of Eric's sons, became king of Norway. Cruel and oppressive, he died in battle in 970.

Haakon, son of Sigurd of Lade, became the next king of Norway. He resisted Danish attacks and ruled for about 25 years, but died in a peasant riot in 995. After the Battle of Swold in 1000, Norway was divided between Denmark and the Jarl of Lade.

Olaf II Haraldsson was a Viking until 1015, when he became king of Norway. Although oppressive and often cruel, he continued to spread Christianity. Canute of Denmark invaded Norway in 1028, sending Olaf fleeing to England. Canute's son, Sweyn, ruled Norway from 1028 to 1035. Sweyn was forced out when Olaf II was proclaimed a saint and his son, Magnus I, was made king. Magnus was also king of Denmark, a position he lost when Canute's nephew led a revolt against him and he was killed. Olaf's sainthood firmly established Christianity in Norway.

Harald Sigurdsson (known as Harald III) ruled Norway from 1046 until his death in 1066. His death marks the end of the Viking Age.

THE MIDDLE AGES   Wars with Denmark continued, and civil wars raged from 1130 to 1227. Norwegian towns and the church continued to grow. Under Haakon V in the 13th century, Oslo became the capital of Norway. The Black Death reached Norway in 1350 and wiped out much of the population.

From 1362 to 1364 Norway and Sweden had a joint monarch, Haakon VI (1340–80), son of the Swedish king, Magnus Eriksson. Haakon married Margaret, daughter of the Danish king Valdemar Atterdag. Their son, Olaf, was chosen to be the Danish king upon Valdemar's death in 1375. He inherited the throne of Norway after his father died in 1380, bringing Norway into a union with Denmark. The union lasted until 1814.

UNION WITH DENMARK   When Olaf died at the age of 17, Margaret became regent of Norway, Denmark, and Sweden. She ruled through her nephew, Eric of Pomerania, who had become king of Norway in 1389. He was recognized as a joint ruler at Kalmar. Margaret was actually the power behind the throne until her death, in 1412. Eric of Pomerania tried to rule the three countries, but Sweden and Norway rebelled. Eric fled in 1439 and Christopher III of Bavaria became the ruler, imposing Danish rule.

Impressions

I would not enter Norway again for all the firs in Scandinavia. The blight of temperance has settled on the place.
> —Archer Grant of Stroud, Gloucestershire, 1912

November always seemed to me the Norway of the year.
> —Emily Dickinson, 1864

Norway is a hard country: hard to know, hard to shoot over, and hard— very hard—to fall down on: but hard to forsake and harder to forget.
> —J. A. Lees, *Peaks and Pines, Another Norway Book*, 1899

Denmark led Norway into the Seven Years' War of the North in 1563, and took unfair advantage of its position in trade, in the military, and even in surrendering Norwegian land to Sweden.

During the Napoleonic Wars (1807–14), Denmark and Norway were allied with France, although it created much economic hardship. Famine was widespread. In 1814 Frederik VI of Denmark surrendered to Napoléon's opponents and handed Norway over to Sweden. That officially ended 434 years of Danish rule over Norway.

SECESSION FROM SWEDEN On May 17, 1814, an assembly adopted a constitution and chose Christian Frederik as the Norwegian king. May 17 is celebrated as Norwegian National Day. The Swedes objected and launched a military campaign, eventually subduing Norway. The Swedes accepted the Norwegian constitution, but only within a union of the two kingdoms. Christian Frederik fled.

Soon thereafter, Norway suffered through one of its greatest economic depressions. Norway's parliamentary assembly, the Storting (Stortinget), engaged in repeated conflicts with the Swedish monarchs. Bernadotte ruled over both Norway and Sweden as Charles XIV from 1818 to 1844.

By the 1830s the economy of Norway had improved. The first railway line was laid in 1854. Its merchant fleet grew significantly between 1850 and 1880.

From the 1880s on, the Liberals in the Storting brought much-needed reform to the country. But by the end of the century, the conflict with Sweden was growing as more and more Norwegians demanded independence.

In August 1905 the Storting decided to dissolve the union with Sweden. Sweden agreed to let Norway rule itself. In October 1905 Norway held an election, and the son of Denmark's king was proclaimed king of Norway. He chose the name Haakon VII.

AN INDEPENDENT NORWAY Free at last, Norway enjoyed peace and prosperity until the beginning of World War II. Even though the economy was satisfactory, thousands of Norwegians emigrated to the United States around the turn of the century. In 1914 Norway joined Sweden and Denmark in declaring a policy of neutrality. Despite the declaration, around 2,000 Norwegian seamen lost their lives in the war because of submarine attacks and underwater mines.

In 1920 Norway joined the League of Nations, ending its policy of isolation. At the outbreak of World War II, Norway again declared its neutrality. Nonetheless, Allied forces mined Norway's waters in 1940, and the Nazis attacked on April 9, 1940. Great Britain and France provided some military assistance, but

Norway fell after a 2-month struggle. The government and the royal family fled into exile in England, taking 1,000 ships of the Norwegian merchant fleet. In spite of the resistance movement, Nazis occupied Norway until the end of the war in 1945. Vidkun Quisling, the Norwegian minister of defense in the 1930s, served the Nazis as leader of the puppet government.

Quisling was executed following the Nazi retreat from Norway. On June 7, 1945, the government-in-exile returned from Britain. The retreating Nazis had followed a scorched-earth policy in Finnmark, destroying almost everything of value. In the late 1940s, Norway began to rebuild its shattered economy.

After an abortive attempt to form a Nordic defense alliance, Norway and Denmark joined NATO in 1949. The Communist Party tried to secure recognition in Norway, but failed.

By the 1960s oil prospecting in the North Sea had yielded rich finds, which led to a profound restructuring of Norwegian trade and industry. In 1972 Norway voted not to enter the Common Market, following a bitter political dispute.

Norway had a non-Socialist government from 1981 to 1986. In 1986, Labour Party leader Gro Harlem Brundtland headed a minority government as Norway's first female prime minister. She introduced 7 women into her 18-member cabinet. Soon, however, tumbling oil prices and subsequent unemployment led to a recession. The Labour government lost the 1989 elections. A center-right coalition assumed control of government. In November 1990, Brundtland returned to office as prime minister, this time with 9 women in her 19-member cabinet. In 1991 Olav V died and was succeeded by his son, Harald V.

> ### Impressions
>
> *"People shall be made to understand the greatness of my art; when facing it, they shall learn to remove their hats, as if in a cathedral."*
>
> —Edvard Munch

Today the Norwegian government faces many of the same problems that confront other nations: violent crime, drugs, immigration control, unemployment, acid rain, and pollution. Concern about acid rain and pollution, much of which comes from Great Britain, was so great that riots erupted when Margaret Thatcher visited Norway in 1987.

Although some Conservatives objected, Norway applied for membership in the European Union (EU) in 1993. The country also began to assert itself more on the international scene. Thorvald Stoltenberg, the minister of foreign affairs, was named peace negotiator for ravaged Bosnia-Herzegovina, and in clandestine meetings held outside Oslo helped affect a rapprochement between the PLO and Israel. All these history-making events were eclipsed by the XVII Olympic Winter Games, held in Lillehammer in February 1994. In November 1994, Norwegians rejected a nonbinding referendum on EU membership. Following that, everyone waited for the Norwegian parliament to vote on whether the country would join. The parliament deliberately avoided the issue and did not vote on the matter. The referendum, though nonbinding, remains in force, and Norway is not a member of the EU. But that does not mean the country has no economic links with the rest of Europe. In 1994 Norway reinforced its commitments to membership in the EEAA (European Economic Area Agreement), an association initiated in 1992 to ensure its access to the EU's single market. It includes cooperation in a variety of cultural and economic areas.

A Sifter of Viking Secrets

The world press gave scant attention to the death, in 1997, of Norwegian archaeologist Anne-Stine Ingstad, but she was a pioneer, sifting through the sandy soil above a Newfoundland beach to uncover the remains of a Viking outpost.

She was the wife of Helge Ingstad, whose discovery of the site in 1961 produced the first conclusive evidence that Vikings had made a North American beachhead 500 years before Columbus. Vikings sailed from a colony in Greenland to reach the North American continent (today's Canada). Icelandic sagas had described the voyages in detail, and few scholars doubted that Leif Eriksson and other Vikings had made such voyages and explorations. But until the Ingstads made their startling discoveries, no hard evidence of a Viking presence existed— only a spate of spurious artifacts.

The initial discovery was met with skepticism. But once Anne-Stine Ingstad started to dig, most doubts evaporated. Her husband had used vivid geographic descriptions in Icelandic sagas to find the camp described by Eriksson and others. Once the site was discovered, she carried out excavations over several months. In time, she uncovered the foundations of eight buildings, including a large house almost identical to Eriksson's great hall in Greenland.

In 1964 she unearthed a tiny stone spinning wheel, suggesting that female Vikings had used the camp. In 1980 UNESCO designated the settlement, L'Anse aux Meadows, a World Heritage Site, along with the Pyramids of Egypt and the Grand Canyon.

In 1995 Norway won the Eurovision Song Contest for best songs evocative of a country, repeating its sweep of a decade earlier and ensuring that the event would be held there in 1996. As the host country, Norway captured second place.

By 1998 Norway was having its share of troubles, as oil prices plunged to their lowest levels in a decade. Turmoil in financial markets knocked the krone lower and prompted the central bank to double interest rates to 10%. The popular prime minister Kjell Magne Bondevik, who took over the office in 1997, stunned the country by taking a temporary leave from office. His doctors said he was having a "depressive reaction" to too much work and stress. In late 1998, Bondevik came back to his job—and is now running the country.

Today Norway continues pushing forward with major engineering projects. The country is connecting its sparsely inhabited outcroppings and linking its interior fjord-side villages in an effort to stem the flow of people to larger towns and villages. At Hitra, a largely barren island off the west coast, a new 5.5km (3½-mile) tunnel (the world's deepest and 2nd-longest) has been built at a cost of $41 million. It links mainland Norway to a hamlet with some 4,100 residents. On the North Cape at Norway's Arctic tip, a $140 million bridge and tunnel was constructed to Mager Island, home to only 3,600 people (and more than that many reindeer). An additional $135 million went into the earth in the mountains east of Bergen to link the towns of Aurland (pop. 1,900) and Laerdal (pop. 2,250). Its

24km (15½-mile) tunnel casts the previous world record-holder, the 16km (10-mile) St. Gotthard tunnel in Switzerland, into a distant second place.

A more artistic bridge opened in December of 2001. The designer? None other than Leonardo da Vinci in 1502. The 99m (330-ft.) laminated timber bridge links Norway and Sweden over a highway at the town of Aas, 26km (16 miles) south of Oslo.

In 2001, Norway ranked first (with the U.S. in 6th place) as the best country in the world in which to live. The judge? The United Nations Human Development Report. Australia followed Norway in second place, with both countries moving narrowly ahead of Canada. The annual survey is based on statistical profiles of what people can expect in life beyond economic growth.

The year 2001 also was witness to the marriage of Crown Prince Haakon and Mette-Mari Tjessem Hoiby, a single mom who lived with the royal before marrying him. The couple's marriage raised some astonishment among Norway's more conservative factions, since the father of Hoiby's child is a convicted cocaine supplier, and she had been well known on Oslo's "dance-and-drugs house party scene," as one newspaper commentator put it. Some Norwegians wonder if the modern-minded heir to the throne, Prince Haakon, a direct descendant of Queen Victoria, even plans to maintain the monarchy.

4 Food & Drink

MEALS & DINING CUSTOMS   Most working Norwegians seldom eat lunch, grabbing a quick open-face sandwich, or *smørbrød,* at their offices. But in major towns and cities, lunch is generally served from 1 to 3pm. The *middag,* the main meal of the day, is generally eaten between 4:30 and 6pm. Many restaurants serve this popular *middag* from 1 to 8pm. In late-closing restaurants it's possible to dine much later, until around midnight in Oslo. Long after *middag* time a Norwegian family will have *aftens,* a *smørbrød* supper that will see them through the night.

THE CUISINE   The chief criticism leveled against Norwegian cooking is that it's too bland. The food is always abundant (the Norwegians are known for their 2nd helpings), substantial, and well prepared—but no threat to the French for a Cordon Bleu prize. Today, instead of their own cuisine, Norwegians often turn to the Continent or even Asia, to satisfy their taste buds. Foreign restaurants, especially in such cities as Oslo and Bergen, are all the rage.

Norwegians are proud—and rightly so—of many of their tempting specialties, ranging from boiled cod (considered a delicacy) to reindeer steak smothered in brown gravy and accompanied by tart little lingonberries, which resemble wild cranberries.

Norway relies on fish, both freshwater and saltwater, for much of its food supply. Prepared in countless ways, fish is usually well cooked—and always fresh, a good bet indeed. Try, in particular, the aforementioned boiled cod; it's always—but always—served with boiled potatoes.

In early summer, *kokt laks* (boiled salmon) is a highly rated delicacy. *Kreps* (crayfish) is another big production as it is in Finland, and *ørret* (mountain trout), preferably broiled and served with fresh lemon, is a guaranteed treat. A recommendation for top-notch fare: *fiske-gratin* (fish soufflé), delicately seasoned.

Norwegians love their fatty smoked eel *(roket al),* although many foreigners have a tendency to whip by this one on the smorgasbord table. The national appetizer is brine-cured herring with raw onions.

You may want to try reindeer steak or *faar-i-kaal,* the national dish, a heavily peppered cabbage-and-mutton stew served with boiled potatoes. A fisher's or a farmer's favorite is *lapskus* (hash, to us), prepared with whatever's left over in the kitchen. The North American palate seems to take kindly to *kjøttkaker,* the Norwegian hamburger—often pork patties—served with sautéed onions, brown gravy, and boiled potatoes.

The boiled potato is ubiquitous. Incidentally, the Norwegian prefers it without butter—just a bit of parsley. Nowadays fresh vegetables and crisp salads are a regular feature of the Norwegian diet as well.

Rømmergrøt is a sour-cream porridge covered with melted butter, brown sugar, and cinnamon. If they're in season, try the good-tasting, amber-colored *muiter* (cloudberries). An additional treat, well made in Norway, is a pancake accompanied by lingonberries.

Frokost (breakfast) is often a whopping *koldtbord,* the famous cold board, consisting of herring and goat's milk cheese, and often such fare as salmon and soft-boiled eggs, plus *wienerbrød* (Danish pastry). At this time, most visitors encounter the ever-popular *flatbrød,* paper-thin crisp rye bread. Many visitors may not want to spend the extra kroner for this big spread, but those going on glacier expeditions need this early-morning fortification.

Incidentally, *smörgåsbord* and *smørbrød* are very popular in Norway, although they seem to be served here without the elaborate ritual typical of Denmark and Sweden. Customarily, smorgasbord in Norway is only a prelude to the main meal.

DRINK   Norway has strict laws regarding the sale of alcohol. Beer and wine may be served in hotels and restaurants 7 days a week, but hard liquor can be sold only between 3 and 11:45pm—and never on Sunday. Visitors can buy the precious stuff from the Vinmonopolet, the state liquor-and-wine monopoly (see below). The restriction on hard liquor may be a bonus for budgeters, since Norwegian prices are sky-high, in line with all the Scandinavian countries. *Warning:* Unless visitors ask for a favorite brand of gin or scotch, they may be served a sour-tasting Norwegian home brew.

The Norwegians, like the Danes, are essentially beer drinkers. Low in alcohol content is *pils,* a light lager, but the *lagerøl* is so low in alcoholic content (less than 2.5%) that it's a substitute for water only. The stronger Norwegian beer is the Export, available at higher prices. Two other types of beer are Brigg and Zero.

The other national drink is *akevitt* (sometimes written as aquavit or schnapps). Who would ever think that potatoes and caraway seeds could knock a person under the table? It's that potent, although it's misnamed the "water of life." Norwegians gulp down beer as a chaser. Aquavit (try Linie Akevitt) is sloshed around in oak vats all the way to Australia and back—for added flavor.

The stores of **Vinmonopolet,** the monopoly that sells wines and spirits, are open Monday through Wednesday from 10am to 5pm, on Thursday from 9am to 6pm, and on Friday from 9am to 5pm. The Vinmonopolet is closed on Saturday in all towns except Kirkenes, Bodø, Ålesund, Trondheim, Haugesund, and Arendal. Alcoholic beverages are not sold to anyone under 20 years of age.

Index

See also Accommodations and Restaurant indexes, below.

RESTAURANTS

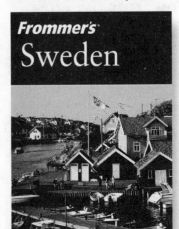

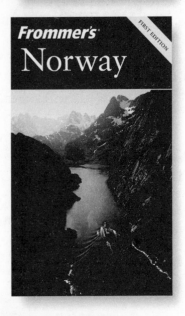

FROMMER'S® COMPLETE TRAVEL GUIDES

Alaska
Alaska Cruises & Ports of Call
Amsterdam
Argentina & Chile
Arizona
Atlanta
Australia
Austria
Bahamas
Barcelona, Madrid & Seville
Beijing
Belgium, Holland & Luxembourg
Bermuda
Boston
Brazil
British Columbia & the Canadian Rockies
Budapest & the Best of Hungary
California
Canada
Cancún, Cozumel & the Yucatán
Cape Cod, Nantucket & Martha's Vineyard
Caribbean
Caribbean Cruises & Ports of Call
Caribbean Ports of Call
Carolinas & Georgia
Chicago
China
Colorado
Costa Rica
Denmark
Denver, Boulder & Colorado Springs
England
Europe
European Cruises & Ports of Call
Florida

France
Germany
Great Britain
Greece
Greek Islands
Hawaii
Hong Kong
Honolulu, Waikiki & Oahu
Ireland
Israel
Italy
Jamaica
Japan
Las Vegas
London
Los Angeles
Maryland & Delaware
Maui
Mexico
Montana & Wyoming
Montréal & Québec City
Munich & the Bavarian Alps
Nashville & Memphis
Nepal
New England
New Mexico
New Orleans
New York City
New Zealand
Northern Italy
Nova Scotia, New Brunswick & Prince Edward Island
Oregon
Paris
Philadelphia & the Amish Country
Portugal
Prague & the Best of the Czech Republic

Provence & the Riviera
Puerto Rico
Rome
San Antonio & Austin
San Diego
San Francisco
Santa Fe, Taos & Albuquerque
Scandinavia
Scotland
Seattle & Portland
Shanghai
Singapore & Malaysia
South Africa
South America
South Florida
South Pacific
Southeast Asia
Spain
Sweden
Switzerland
Texas
Thailand
Tokyo
Toronto
Tuscany & Umbria
USA
Utah
Vancouver & Victoria
Vermont, New Hampshire & Maine
Vienna & the Danube Valley
Virgin Islands
Virginia
Walt Disney World® & Orlando
Washington, D.C.
Washington State

FROMMER'S® DOLLAR-A-DAY GUIDES

Australia from $50 a Day
California from $70 a Day
Caribbean from $70 a Day
England from $75 a Day
Europe from $70 a Day

Florida from $70 a Day
Hawaii from $80 a Day
Ireland from $60 a Day
Italy from $70 a Day
London from $85 a Day

New York from $90 a Day
Paris from $80 a Day
San Francisco from $70 a Day
Washington, D.C. from $80 a Day

FROMMER'S® PORTABLE GUIDES

Acapulco, Ixtapa & Zihuatanejo
Amsterdam
Aruba
Australia's Great Barrier Reef
Bahamas
Berlin
Big Island of Hawaii
Boston
California Wine Country
Cancún
Charleston & Savannah
Chicago
Disneyland®
Dublin
Florence

Frankfurt
Hong Kong
Houston
Las Vegas
London
Los Angeles
Los Cabos & Baja
Maine Coast
Maui
Miami
New Orleans
New York City
Paris
Phoenix & Scottsdale

Portland
Puerto Rico
Puerto Vallarta, Manzanillo & Guadalajara
Rio de Janeiro
San Diego
San Francisco
Seattle
Sydney
Tampa & St. Petersburg
Vancouver
Venice
Virgin Islands
Washington, D.C.

FROMMER'S® NATIONAL PARK GUIDES

Banff & Jasper
Family Vacations in the National Parks
Grand Canyon

National Parks of the American West
Rocky Mountain

Yellowstone & Grand Teton
Yosemite & Sequoia/ Kings Canyon
Zion & Bryce Canyon

FROMMER'S® MEMORABLE WALKS

Chicago	New York	San Francisco
London	Paris	Washington, D.C.

FROMMER'S® GREAT OUTDOOR GUIDES

Arizona & New Mexico	Northern California	Vermont & New Hampshire
New England	Southern New England	

SUZY GERSHMAN'S BORN TO SHOP GUIDES

Born to Shop: France	Born to Shop: Italy	Born to Shop: New York
Born to Shop: Hong Kong, Shanghai & Beijing	Born to Shop: London	Born to Shop: Paris

FROMMER'S® IRREVERENT GUIDES

Amsterdam	Los Angeles	San Francisco
Boston	Manhattan	Seattle & Portland
Chicago	New Orleans	Vancouver
Las Vegas	Paris	Walt Disney World®
London	Rome	Washington, D.C.

FROMMER'S® BEST-LOVED DRIVING TOURS

Britain	Germany	Northern Italy
California	Ireland	Scotland
Florida	Italy	Spain
France	New England	Tuscany & Umbria

HANGING OUT™ GUIDES

Hanging Out in England	Hanging Out in France	Hanging Out in Italy
Hanging Out in Europe	Hanging Out in Ireland	Hanging Out in Spain

THE UNOFFICIAL GUIDES®

Bed & Breakfasts and Country Inns in:	Southwest & South Central Plains	Mid-Atlantic with Kids
California	U.S.A.	Mini Las Vegas
Great Lakes States	Beyond Disney	Mini-Mickey
Mid-Atlantic	Branson, Missouri	New England and New York with Kids
New England	California with Kids	
Northwest	Chicago	New Orleans
Rockies	Cruises	New York City
Southeast	Disneyland®	Paris
Southwest	Florida with Kids	San Francisco
Best RV & Tent Campgrounds in:	Golf Vacations in the Eastern U.S.	Skiing in the West
California & the West	Great Smoky & Blue Ridge Region	Southeast with Kids
Florida & the Southeast	Inside Disney	Walt Disney World®
Great Lakes States	Hawaii	Walt Disney World® for Grown-ups
Mid-Atlantic	Las Vegas	Walt Disney World® with Kids
Northeast	London	Washington, D.C.
Northwest & Central Plains		World's Best Diving Vacations

SPECIAL-INTEREST TITLES

Frommer's Adventure Guide to Australia & New Zealand
Frommer's Adventure Guide to Central America
Frommer's Adventure Guide to India & Pakistan
Frommer's Adventure Guide to South America
Frommer's Adventure Guide to Southeast Asia
Frommer's Adventure Guide to Southern Africa
Frommer's Britain's Best Bed & Breakfasts and Country Inns
Frommer's Caribbean Hideaways
Frommer's Exploring America by RV
Frommer's Fly Safe, Fly Smart
Frommer's France's Best Bed & Breakfasts and Country Inns
Frommer's Gay & Lesbian Europe

Frommer's Italy's Best Bed & Breakfasts and Country Inns
Frommer's New York City with Kids
Frommer's Ottawa with Kids
Frommer's Road Atlas Britain
Frommer's Road Atlas Europe
Frommer's Road Atlas France
Frommer's Toronto with Kids
Frommer's Vancouver with Kids
Frommer's Washington, D.C., with Kids
Israel Past & Present
The New York Times' Guide to Unforgettable Weekends
Places Rated Almanac
Retirement Places Rated

With over 700 airlines, 50,000 hotels, 50 rental car companies and 5,000 cruise and vacation packages, you can create the perfect get-away for you. Choose the car, the room, even the ground you walk on.

Travelocity.com
A Sabre Company
Go Virtually Anywhere.